D1796949

CAUSATION IN LAW AND MEDICINE

Causation in Law and Medicine

Edited by
IAN FRECKELTON
Barrister, Monash University, Australia
DANUTA MENDELSON
Deakin University, Australia

© Ian Freckelton and Danuta Mendelson 2002

Published by
Dartmouth Publishing Company
Ashgate Publishing Limited
Gower House
Croft Road
Aldershot
Hampshire GU11 3HR
England

Ashgate Publishing Company
131 Main Street
Burlington, VT 05401-5600 USA

Ashgate website: http://www.ashgate.com

British Library Cataloguing in Publication Data
Causation in law and medicine
    1. Medical jurisprudence 2. Causation (Criminal law)
    I. Freckelton, Ian R. II. Mendelson, Danuta
    344'.041

Library of Congress Control Number: 2001098002

ISBN 0 7546 2204 5

Printed and bound in Great Britain by MPG Books Ltd, Bodmin, Cornwall

Contents

v

Preface

SIR ZELMAN COWEN

This book is devoted to one of the most profound yet vexing issues in law, namely how to accommodate advances in the medical and scientific understanding of causation within the province of law. It is probably true to say that medical evidence, and inferences drawn from observation, experiments and, nowadays, statistics, allow, or enable, medical science to develop theoretical models and explanations of medical conditions. Modern medical theory and practice accepts that happenings of nature, including medical conditions, are multifactorial, and as such are more likely to be controlled by probability laws than by a single cause. In law, finding the causal connection between a wrongful act and harm is essential to the attribution of legal responsibility. However, as Kirby J observed in *Chappel v Hart* (1998) 195 CLR 232; [1998] HCA 55 [87], both civil law and common law courts

> have searched for principles to provide a "filter to eliminate those consequences of the defendant's conduct for which he [or she] should not be held liable". The search sets one on a path of reasoning which is inescapably "complex, difficult and controversial". The outcome is a branch of the law which is "highly discretionary and unpredictable". Needless to say, this causes dissatisfaction to litigants, anguish for their advisers, uncertainty for judges, agitation amongst commentators and friction between healthcare professionals and their legal counterparts.

This volume addresses these serious concerns, and provides a framework for analysis of different theories of medical, scientific and legal causation as well as modes or tests relating to the proof of causation offered in different forensic and medical contexts.

Notions of risk in determining causation in criminal and civil law, the nature of proof in medicine and the law, issues of morality, responsibility and justice in the context of legal causation, as well as aspects of causation pertaining specifically to forensic medicine and coronial law are analysed from an interdisciplinary perspective. Several chapters contain an exposition of judicial and academic thinking regarding the underlying values and principles of legal causation, and the object and function of causal inquiry. Physicians explore issues of aetiology and pathogenesis in relation to medical assessment of probability of risk, the nature of proof in evidence-based medicine, and the function of perceptions and framing relating to death causation. In the process, conceptual uncertainties which beset medical and legal causation are clarified, and consideration is given to evidentiary principles that should govern the forensic process in this area of the law.

The collection is a comprehensive, illuminating, and at times controversial contribution to the current debates on the subject of medical, scientific and legal causation.

The Right Honourable Sir Zelman Cowen
AK, GCMG, GCVO, QC, DCI

Notes on Contributors

Professor Michael Ashby

Michael Ashby is the Professor of Palliative Care in the Department of Medicine, Monash University, Director of Palliative Care at McCulloch House, Monash Medical Centre, and Medical Director of the Cancer and Palliative Care Program of the Southern Health Care network in Melbourne, Australia. He trained in general medicine and radiation oncology in the United Kingdom and after fellowships at the Curie Institute and the Peter McCallum Cancer Institute was appointed the first Director of Palliative Care at the Royal Adelaide Hospital and the Mary Potter Hospice, Calvary Hospital, positions which he held until 1995. He has published on the subjects of ethics of care and decision-making at the end of life, as well as in the field of clinical pharmacology as it applies to palliative medicine.

The Honourable Justice Ian Callinan

Ian Callinan was appointed as a judge of the High Court of Australia in February 1998. At the time of his appointment he was a practising Barrister. Justice Callinan was educated at Brisbane Grammar School and the University of Queensland. He was called to the Bar in 1965 and subsequently appointed Queen's Counsel in 1978. He was President of the Queensland Bar Association between 1984 and 1987 and President of the Australian Bar Association in 1984 and 1985.

Justice Callinan is also a playwright and the author of two novels, a former Chairman of Trustees of the Queensland Art Gallery, and a former Honorary Chairman of the Brisbane Community Arts Centre. He was also formerly a director of a number of leading public companies, as well as a director of the Australian Broadcasting Corporation, and currently serves as the Chairman of the Australian Defence Force Academy.

Professor Stephen Cordner

Stephen Cordner graduated in medicine from the University of Melbourne in 1977. After his internship at the Royal Melbourne Hospital, he spent two years in the Department of Pathology at Geelong Hospital, which was headed by Vernon Plueckhahn, then Australia's foremost forensic pathologist. In 1981 he took up an appointment as a Lecturer, and later as a Senior Lecturer, in Forensic Medicine at Guy's Hospital in London where he stayed until 1987. He worked there with the Head of the Department, Keith Mant, and with Keith Simpson who, although retired, was still active in the field. During this period he became a Fellow of the Royal College of Pathologists of Australasia and gained his membership of the Royal College of Pathologists of Great Britain. He was appointed Foundation Professor of Forensic Medicine at Monash University and Foundation Director of the Victorian Institute of Forensic Medicine in 1987. During his time at Monash, close links between the Faculties of Medicine and Law have been developed, reflecting his interest in the interaction generally of these two disciplines.

The Honourable Chief Justice John Doyle

John Doyle was admitted to the degree of Bachelor of Laws from the University of Adelaide in 1966 and to the degree of Bachelor of Civil Law from Oxford University in 1969. He was the 1967 Rhodes Scholar for South Australia. He was admitted as a Barrister and Solicitor of the South Australian Supreme Court in 1970. He was a partner in an Adelaide firm of solicitors from 1970 to 1977. From 1977 until 1986 he practised at the Bar in Adelaide. His work at the Bar involved most branches of the law, with a substantial involvement in appellate work. He was appointed a Queen's Counsel in 1981 and in 1986 Solicitor-General of the State of South Australia. He was appointed Chief Justice of South Australia in May 1995.

For a number of years he was a part-time Lecturer and Examiner in the Faculty of Law at the University of Adelaide. From 1972 until 1979 he was a Member of the Council of the Law Society of South Australia. Chief Justice Doyle was a Member of the Legal Services Commission of South Australia from its establishment in 1978 until 1986, and at the time of his appointment as Solicitor-General he was Chairman of the Commission. He was President of the Bar Association of South Australia from October 1993 until his appointment as Chief Justice and had previously served a term as President of that Association from June 1989 until November 1990.

Dr Gary Edmond

Gary Edmond teaches torts, evidence and expert evidence at the School of Law, Adelaide University. His research interests include expert evidence, law and science, the history of evidence law, the public understanding of law and science, as well as the role of evidence in mass torts and miscarriages of justice. Recently he was awarded a PhD on *Scientific evidence and the construction of guilt and innocence: Textile evidence in the Azaria Chamberlain case* from the Faculty of Law, University of Cambridge.

Professor Ian Freckelton

Ian Freckelton is a Barrister in full-time private practice in Melbourne, Australia, having been called to the Bar in 1988. By night, he is also a Professor in the Department of Psychological Medicine, Adjunct Professor in the Law Faculty and an Honorary Associate Professor in the Department of Forensic Medicine at Monash University. He is also the Adjunct Professor of Law and Legal Studies at La Trobe University, the Vice-President of the International Institute of Forensic Studies, a Board Member of the Australian Institute of Health, Law and Ethics and a Past-President of the Australian and New Zealand Association of Psychiatry, Psychology and Law. He is a member of Victoria's Medical Practitioners, Psychologists Registration, Psychosurgery and Mental Health Review Boards. He is the foundation Editor of the *Journal of Law and Medicine,* the Editor-in-Chief of *Psychiatry, Psychology and Law* and an International Editor of *Behavioral Sciences and the Law.*

Professor Freckelton is the author and editor of some two dozen books on health law, compensation law, criminal law, evidence law, coronial law, policing, psychological profiling and involuntary detention of those with mental illnesses.

Dr Peter Greenberg

Peter Greenberg is the Clinical Director, General Medicine, at the Royal Melbourne Hospital, and a Principal Fellow in the University of Melbourne Department of Medicine. He graduated MBBS from Melbourne and undertook postgraduate studies in General Medicine and Endocrinology at the Royal Melbourne Hospital, in the University of Melbourne Department of Medicine and at the Royal Postgraduate Medical School, Hammersmith Hospital, London. Dr Greenberg works as a consultant general physician in a public hospital and in private practice, with clinical, teaching and research responsibilities. He has been President of the Australian Society of Consultant Physicians in General Medicine, and is currently Quality Convenor for the Royal Australasian College of Physicians, a Member of the Board of Directors of Western Health, Melbourne and a Member of the Case Committee of the Medical Indemnity Protection Society. His professional interests include clinical epidemiology, evidence-based medicine, and efforts to improve the quality of medical care.

Professor Robert Helme

Robert Helme is a past Director of the National Ageing Research Institute, North West Hospital, Parkville, Victoria, Professorial Associate, Department of Medicine of the Royal Melbourne Hospital, and Chairman of the Parkville Campus of the North West Hospital Special Clinical School. In 1974 he was the Australian-American Education Foundation Postgraduate Scholar (Fulbright Scheme) at Harvard University, and in 1984 Alexander von Humboldt Stiftung Fellow at the University of Heidelberg, West Germany. He is a member of the Faculty of Medicine, Dentistry and Health Sciences, at the University of Melbourne, has been President of the Australian Society for Geriatric Medicine, Australian Association of Neurologists, Behavioural Neurology Committee, Australian Association of Gerontology, and RM Gibson Scientific Research Fund Committee. He has worked and published in such fields as pain in the elderly, polymodal nociceptor function, pain measurement in people with dementia, "brain reserve" in nervous system physiology and pathology, particularly in relation to dementia and age-related cognitive decline, and medical education.

Professor Antony Honoré

Antony Honoré, a Fellow of the British Academy, is a legal philosopher, Roman lawyer and trust lawyer with a South African background. He served in the army during the Second World War and was severely wounded in the battle of Alamein. After the war he continued his studies at Oxford University. He has been teaching and writing about law for more than fifty years, mainly in the Oxford Law Faculty where he held positions as Regius Professor of Civil Law, Fellow and Acting Warden of All Souls

College, Fellow of Queen's College and Fellow of New College, Oxford. Professor Honoré has authored *Causation in Law* (2nd edition with Herbert Hart), *Making the Law Bind – Essays Legal and Philosophical, The Quest for Security, South African Law of Trusts* (4th edition published in 1992), *Ulpian* (2nd edition due to be published in 2002), *About Law - An Introduction, Tribonian, Concordance to the Digest Jurists* (with Menner), *Emperors and Lawyers, Sex Law, Law in the Crisis of Empire 379-455,* and *Responsibility and Fault.*

Professor David Lanham

David Lanham is a Professorial Fellow at the University of Melbourne. He was formerly Assistant Lecturer, Lecturer and Senior Lecturer at Nottingham University, Visiting Lecturer at Auckland University and Kenneth Bailey Professor of Law at the University of Melbourne. He is a former Assistant Editor of *Medicine, Science and the Law,* Editor of the *Criminal Law Review* and Member of the Editorial Board of the *Criminal Law Journal.* His books include: *A Study Guide to Criminal Law, Practical Forensic Medicine, Criminal Fraud, Taming Death by Law* and *Cross-Border Criminal Law.* He has published articles in a variety of journals on such subjects as property, blood tests, organ transplantation, issue estoppel, self-defence, provocation, felony-murder, euthanasia, consent to medical treatment, endangerment, accomplice liability, strict liability, vicarious liability and liability of corporations. He taught criminal law at the University of Melbourne from 1975 to 2000.

Professor Harold Luntz

Harold Luntz has been teaching in the Law School at the University of Melbourne since 1965. From 1986 to 1988 he was Dean of the Faculty of Law. He was educated in South Africa and at Oxford University. Professor Luntz is the author *of Assessment of Damages for Personal Injury and Death* (4th edition, in press), principal author of *Torts: Cases and Commentary* (5th edition, in preparation), and General Editor of the *Torts Law Journal,* which is now in its ninth year of publication. For several years he has taught a postgraduate course on Common Law Obligations of Health Professionals. In 2000 he was the inaugural recipient of the John G Fleming Memorial Award for Torts Scholarship.

Associate Professor Eric Magnusson

Eric Magnusson teaches in the School of Chemistry at the University College of the Australian Defence Force Academy of the University of New South Wales. It was for this University that he first taught and from which, in 1957, he was one of the first PhD graduates. In the same year he went to the University of London as an 1851 Exhibitioner, rubbing shoulders with the researchers using that University's first mainframe computer to refine the structure of DNA. He used it for computations in molecular quantum mechanics, his major research field, but he is equally fascinated by the study of science and the law. Associate Professor Magnusson is currently preparing for the first direct investigation of how courts with untrained jurors assess forensic science evidence in Australian criminal trials.

The Honourable Chief Justice David Malcolm

David Malcolm was appointed Chief Justice of Western Australia in 1988. In 1990 he was also appointed Lieutenant Governor of Western Australia. He was the Rhodes Scholar from Western Australia in 1960, and obtained a BCL with first class honours at Oxford in 1962. He was Chairman of the Law Reform Commission of Western Australia in 1976 and then from 1979 to 1982. During the same period, he was also a member of the Copyright Tribunal. He was Queen's Counsel from 1980 to 1988, President of the Western Australian Bar Association from 1981 to 1984 and Vice-Chairman of the Australian Bar Association in 1984. Since 1991 he has been the Chairman of the Judicial Section of the Law Association for Asia and the Pacific. He is the Chairman of the Advisory Board of the Crime Research Centre at the University of Western Australia, President of the Western Australian branch of the International Commission of Jurists and a Member of the Board of Directors of the Society for the Reform of Criminal Law.

The Honourable Justice Keith Mason

Keith Mason is President of the New South Wales Court of Appeal. He was appointed Queen's Counsel in 1981 and practised at the Sydney Bar as a private practitioner until 1985, when he was appointed Chairman of the New South Wales Law Reform Commission. Apart from general oversight and participation in all reports, he was the principal writer of reports on

Recovery of Payments Made under Mistake of Law and *Wills: Execution and Revocation*. Between 1987 and 1997, as Solicitor General for New South Wales he acted as the Senior Counsel and principal non-political legal adviser to the New South Wales Government and its instrumentalities. In his position, he represented New South Wales in many constitutional, criminal and civil cases in the appellate courts and in the High Court of Australia. He has published articles in Australian law journals, contributed chapters to books on restitution, law and government, morals and religious values in the Australian legal system, and co-authored the *Australian Law of Restitution*, published in 1995.

Dr Danuta Mendelson

Danuta Mendelson is a Senior Lecturer at the School of Law at Deakin University. She received MA, PhD and LLM degrees from Monash University. She is a joint Editor (Legal Issues) for the *Journal of Law and Medicine*. Dr Mendelson has authored books on *Metaphor in IE Babel's Short Stories*, published in 1982, *Interfaces of Medicine and Law: The History of the Liability for Negligently Caused Psychiatric Injury (Nervous Shock)*, published in 1998, and *Torts*, which won the 1997 Australian Award (joint) for Excellence in Academic Publishing (3rd edition, in preparation). Her articles on the law of consent and refusal of treatment, medical duty of confidentiality, withdrawal and withholding of medical treatment, palliative care and euthanasia, the "right to die" legislation, malingering and the function of expert medical witnesses, the law of rescue, and constitutional aspects of medical practice have appeared in Australian and international refereed journals.

David Mercer

David Mercer is a Senior Lecturer in the Science and Technology Studies Program at the University of Wollongong. He has taught across a wide variety of subjects ranging from the History and Philosophy of Science to Science and Technology Policy. He has published in a number of leading science studies journals, including *Social Studies of Science, Public Understanding of Science, Science Communication, Science as Culture, Prometheus, Social Epistemology* and *Metascience*. His research interests include the interaction of law and science, sociology of science, public understanding of science and science policy. He is currently writing on the EMF and mobile telephone debate and the uses and abuses of epidemiology in legal and regulatory settings. He is also currently a member of the editorial board of the international science studies "review journal" *Metascience*.

Professor Ralph Slovenko

Ralph Slovenko is Professor of Law and Psychiatry at Wayne State University in Michigan. He received BE, LLB, MA, and PhD degrees from Tulane University. He was Editor-in-Chief of the *Tulane Law Review*, and a varsity sports letterman at Tulane University. He served as Law Clerk to the Louisiana Supreme Court, and as Senior Assistant District Attorney under Jim Garrison in New Orleans. He was a Fulbright Scholar to France, and a Professor of Law at Tulane University from 1954 to 1964. He was also a member of the faculty of the Tulane University Department of Psychiatry and Neurology. At the invitation of Dr Robert G Heath, Chairman of the Tulane University Department of Psychiatry and Neurology, he did a residency in psychiatry, one of two persons to do so without a medical degree.

Professor Slovenko held a joint appointment, from 1965 to 1968, at the Menninger Foundation and at the University of Kansas School of Law. Since then, he has been at Wayne State University. He has lectured widely in the United States and also in Australia, Canada, France, Israel, Japan, Russia (Soviet Union), and South Africa. He was Visiting Professor in South Africa in 1976 and 1989, and he occupied the Rood Eminent Scholar Chair in 1991 at the University of Florida College of Law. He is a frequent visitor to Poland, Russia, and South Africa, and has written extensively about them. He has frequently served as an expert witness. Professor Slovenko is a Member of the American, Kansas, Louisiana, and Michigan Bar Associations, and a scientific associate of the American Academy of Psychoanalysis and amicus of the American Academy of Psychiatry and Law. He is the author of numerous books and articles. His book *Psychiatry and Law* received the Manfred Guttmacher award of the American Psychiatric Association and was a selection of the Behavioral Science Book Club. He is also the author of *Psychiatry and Criminal Culpability*, published in 1950 and *of Psychotherapy and Confidentiality*, published in 1998, as well as a number of other books.

Professor Dennis Smith

Dennis Smith was the Director of Rehabilitation at the Clinical Research Centre of the Medical Research Council in Harrow, England, before emigrating to South Australia in 1979. During this time he was, for a decade, engaged in clinical research and the development of appropriate outcome measures designed to determine the effectiveness of rehabilitation. He was the Foundation Professor of Rehabilitation Medicine at Flinders University, and the Repatriation General Hospital, from 1979 to 1992. He was President of the Faculty of Rehabilitation in 1994. In 1992 he established the Sydney University Motor Accidents Authority Chair of Rehabilitation at Ryde, and Royal North Shore Hospital. Professor Smith spent a sabbatical year in 1997 at Salisbury and Southampton as a Visiting Professor and has now returned to Flinders University in South Australia.

Professor Smith has considerable experience in the clinical management and rehabilitation of stroke and head injury, on which he has been an invited speaker at international conferences. He has written extensively on the determinants of disability He also has a continuing interest in the management of chronic pain syndromes affecting the back and neck, especially for those in which the consequence is an inability to return to work. Professor Smith is currently a consultant at the Griffith Rehabilitation Hospital in South Australia.

Professor Jane Stapleton

Jane Stapleton is currently a Professor within the Law Program of the Research School of Social Sciences at the Australian National University. She is also a Statutory Visiting Professor at Oxford University. Originally trained as a scientist, she resigned a postdoctoral post at Cambridge to study law, first at the Australian National University then at Oxford University. From 1987 to 1997 she was a Fellow in Law at Balliol College (where she remains a Fellow) and reached the position of Reader within the University of Oxford. She has held Visiting Professorships in the United States and at the European University Institute. Her interests cover the law of obligations, liability and compensation systems, ranging from product liability to philosophical foundations of the common law such as causation, duty and good faith. Her works include *Disease and the Compensation Debate,* published in 1986, and *Product Liability,* published in 1994. She has acted as consultant in major commercial, pharmaceutical and medical litigation in the United Kingdom, United States and Australia.

Associate Professor David Wells

David Wells is the Head of Clinical Forensic Medicine at the Victorian Institute of Forensic Medicine and Honorary Associate Professor of Forensic Medicine at Monash University. His other appointments include being Honorary Physician at the Child Protection Unit, Royal Children's Hospital, Melbourne, Honorary Specialist to the Sexual Assault Service, Royal Women's Hospital, Melbourne, and Visiting Specialist, Child Protection Unit, Monash Medical Centre.

Associate Professor Wells is an Examiner in Medical Jurisprudence for the Society of Apothecaries of London, a Board Member of the Australian Drug Foundation, a Member of the Advisory Panel, National Institute of Forensic Science, and a Member of the International Editorial Board of the *Journal of Clinical Forensic Medicine*. His professional interests cover the full span of clinical forensic medicine but current activities are centred on non-accidental injury of children, sexual assault, injury interpretation and medical education. He is coordinator of the Monash University postgraduate program in forensic medicine.

Acknowledgments

The idea for a book that would examine the concept of causation from a legal and medical perspective grew from discussions between Michael Ashby and the second editor and then between the two editors. What ensued was a non-adversarial forum for inter-disciplinary discussions and mutual education relating to medical and legal understanding of causation. A residential "round table" Symposium on Causation in Law and Medicine involving thirtyfour invited participants took place in November 1999. Sir Zelman Cowen, who graciously agreed to be the Patron of the Symposium, delivered the opening address. The core of the book comprises the edited papers delivered by the speakers at the Symposium but a number of other chapters have been included in the collection to ensure that a rounded coverage has been given to the subject matter. We are grateful to the Symposium participants and to the authors who were prevailed upon to contribute further chapters to the collection for their generosity, patience and co-operativeness with queries and requests from the editors, sometimes in difficult circumstances.

We also wish to thank Professor Philip Clarke, Dean of the Faculty of Business and Law, Professor Jean du Plessis, the Head of School of Law, and Roger Gamble, the Associate Head of the School of Law, Deakin University respectively for their generous assistance, without which the Symposium would not have eventuated. We are also indebted to Dr Heather Wellington through whose good offices the Commonwealth Department of Health and Aged Care agreed to co-sponsor the Symposium. Professor Jane Stapleton provided Dr Mendelson with guidance throughout this undertaking and she is deeply grateful for her encouragement and advice. As ever, the support and counsel of Professor George Mendelson, and the insights derived from the dinner table discussions with Hannah and David Mendelson have been invaluable.

Our heartfelt thanks go out to Mrs Lorna Frick who has prepared the manuscript for publication, weeding out inconsistencies, standardising citations, fonts, and English expression. She has also prepared the Table of Cases and the Bibliography.

Professor Freckelton also records his ongoing appreciation for the tolerance and good will shown by his wife, Helen Maloney, and his children, Leo and Julia Freckelton, as well as for the helpful suggestions of his colleague Marilyn McMahon at La Trobe University.

Most of all, we are grateful to the authors whose book this is.

Ian Freckelton and Danuta Mendelson
May 2001

Introduction

DANUTA MENDELSON AND IAN FRECKELTON

Analysis of causation underpins both medical and legal practice, just as it pervades day-to-day functioning by members of the general community. Doctors, lawyers and people generally adopt rules of thumb and function on the basis of both assumptions and expectations in relation to what has caused things and what is likely to generate results in the future. Within clinical and research medical practice, though, causation in the form of aetiology or diagnostic or prognostic process is governed by rules and cultural norms that are significantly at variance with those prevalent within the legal system when it focuses upon the making of litigation findings.

Under the law, the imperative of dichotomous decision-making constantly requires determinations of causation. The law is often not particularly interested in influences, impacts, or relationships. In criminal law, civil law, even coronial law, the question posed is whether an act has been proved to have caused or to be likely to cause something else. Because decision-making requires a finding about whether a fundamental issue such as causation is proved or not proved, the existence or non-existence of proof of causation is consistently fundamental to the outcome of litigation. It is surprising then that the law has struggled for so long with not just what constitutes "causation" but with how it can be proved. This has resulted in a series of different tests, rules and procedures, making evaluation of litigants' prospects of success difficult and hard to explain to persons from a non-legal background.

A particular aspect of the difficulty is that "causation" often means different things to representatives of different professions; this has impacted adversely upon the success of the law's search for resolution of different strands of thinking about causation. This book grapples with the conceptual complexities in a selection of different forensic contexts, employing perspectives from leading thinkers in medical, scientific, philosophical and jurisprudential backgrounds in an effort to locate both reconciliation and principles that can be applied across different categories of dispute.

The book includes medical/scientific contributions and legal contributions. The legal chapters identify and discuss conceptual uncertainties embedded in the substantive law of causation and evidentiary and procedural principles that govern the forensic process involving medico-legal issues. The medical chapters define pertinent issues of aetiology and pathogenesis, the nature of proof in medicine, the concept of evidence-based medicine, and issues of medical morality. The book is divided into five parts.

In part A, which examines different understandings of causation in law, medicine and science, the authors focus on particular aspects of this concept. Tony Honoré points out that since inquiries into the processes by which things happen, or have happened, are predicated on the concept of cause, the notion of causation, in the sense of objectivity, regularity and the possibility of cognition, is the same in law, medicine, science and everyday life. To establish a causal connection between events presents greater difficulty in the organic (including the medical) sphere than in the inorganic, purely physical, owing to the greater complexity of organic processes. The problem confronting the law is that of striking a balance which takes account of the complexity of organic processes and is at the same time fair to the wrongdoer. At their jurisprudential core, causation and legal liability are linked by the notion of responsibility for good or bad outcomes of human conduct.

The application in Hippocratic medicine and the Roman law of delict of the Aristotelian theory of efficient or triggering and latent causes is discussed by Mendelson. The relationship between efficient causes (that can be determined on the basis of factual evidence drawn from sensory observation and experience), and the latent or underlying causes (which explain scientifically or philosophically why something has happened) is as controversial today as it was in classical Greece and Rome, though the language of the discourse may be different. In the modern common law of negligence, the causal connection between the defendant's wrongful act and the plaintiff's harm is considered to be one of the elements essential to the attribution of legal responsibility.

Stapleton analyses conceptual implications of the rejection by the common law courts of causation as a scientific and philosophical concept in cases where there exists the so-called "evidentiary gap" in relation to past facts or about the weight to place on agreed facts in issue. Stapleton suggests that in such cases the courts should recognise the dispute as revolving around competing views of legal responsibility. Consequently, the courts should refuse to accept a formulation as being about "causation" and "causal tests", and instead insist that the parties argue directly about the issues of policy and principle relevant to the question of responsibility. If adopted by the courts, this approach would mean that other approaches to causation, including the modern scientific and medical models of causation, would be able to enter the arena of legal discourse. Mendelson is less certain, arguing that whereas modern medicine has developed scientific methodology to discover many causes, which Hippocratic medicine classified as "latent" or underlying causes, modern jurisprudence has failed to develop an equivalent legal methodology of ascertaining causal origins of wrongful events.

Greenberg explains how causal methodology works within the model of "evidence-based" medicine whereby a cause is linked with a particular condition if a number of preconditions are satisfied. These preconditions include data gathered from statistical studies showing that the cause in question precedes the physiological or psychological outcome; that this cause/outcome association is consistent across time as well as patient groups and settings; that the cause/outcome relationship is biologically plausible, by demonstrating, for example, that there exists a relationship between the likelihood or severity of disease and the magnitude of the cause and that this relationship is independent of observational study bias. Yet the scientific methodology is far from fail-proof, for, as Greenberg demonstrates, "even when group studies show unequivocal relationships between causal factors and disease, it may be difficult to extrapolate conclusions to *individuals*", which, of course, is what the courts have to determine in medico-legal litigation. At the same time, taking up the strands of Stapleton's exposition, Greenberg notes that lay, including legal, perceptions about medical causation depend partly on scientific and technological knowledge of the time and partly on philosophical, cultural, religious, political and sociological beliefs that "frame" the questions which are asked about the illness or disease.

Edmond and Mercer analyse the relationship between medical and scientific approaches to causation on the one hand and those found in legal settings on the other. They observe that the law tends to place greater emphasis on the apportionment of responsibility and explaining specific instances – the case at hand – rather than, as is often the case in science where the tendency is to make generalisations, about classes of relationships. However, they maintain that findings of a legal causation have social implications and should not be approached as a "simplistic or textbook-style" set of definitions and comparisons. They argue that decision-makers should strategically construct images of scientific and legal causation drawing from a variety of epistemic domains, policy considerations and practical contingencies. Specifically addressing what constructively can be done to ease the task of decision-makers, they argue that attempts to initiate change need to be systemic. In particular, the changes need to assist decision-makers' and witnesses' ability to marshal resources effectively.

Part B focuses on different aspects of causation in the law of torts. Callinan examines judicial approaches to tests of causation, chronicling the climate of disagreement amongst the judiciary, legal commentators and the community about not only how rules of causation and responsibility should be applied, but even what rules should apply, particularly in such difficult factual situations as palliative care. He queries whether there is a tendency for lawyers to believe that all is controllable; that scientific development has replaced biological uncertainty. He notes the tension between the law's demarcation between lawful palliative care and unlawful homicide on the basis of the intention of the medical profession administering the treatment. Determination of causation in this context raises fundamental ethical and legal problems, which are yet to be resolved. That uncertainty, however, must inevitably result in very difficult decisions regarding responsibility of medical practitioners practising in the field.

The theme of cause and legal responsibility discussed by Honoré from a jurisprudential and philosophical perspective is further examined by Mason, who concentrates on the "staggering march" of negligence. This cause of action has opened up new areas of responsibility for omissions, careless advice, pure psychiatric injury and pure economic loss. In particular, Mason examines judicial application of the notion that tort law is an instrument of corrective justice and that negligence at common law is still a fault-based system (though he also provides case law instances where principles of distributive justice have been influential). He argues that until recently the extent of the tortfeasor's moral responsibility has usually been explained through the concept of causation with control devices such as effective cause, remoteness of damage and *novus actus interveniens*. However, although causation principles continue to occupy a central role in the resolution of litigation, they have been affected by the need for greater transparency in enunciating reasons for the "hard" choices in tort liability. Like Stapleton, Mason argues that although the courts tend to emphasise that questions of causation are not answered in a legal vacuum, their approach remains normative and impressionistic.

One of the "hard choices" in torts law, which also involves the issue of "evidentiary gap" is the loss of chance doctrine, discussed by a number of authors in different contexts. Luntz analyses the caselaw relating to this doctrine in the context of medical negligence litigation which would allow compensation where the only loss involves the loss of a chance at a favourable opportunity to have a medical condition treated at an early stage or of a chance of avoiding a detrimental event, such as the possibility of a cure. Luntz argues that loss or diminution of such chance, when caused by a medical practitioner's negligence, should be compensable, irrespective of whether the chance was greater or less than even, as long as it was more than speculative. This should be so despite the fact that whereas damages for past and present events which the parties allege are proved on the balance of probabilities (to have or to have not occurred), a loss of chance, is at best a hypothetical event, which could only be established as a possibility. Admittedly, the *but for* test of causation involves a hypothetical question of what would have happened had the defendant not been negligent in an identical set of circumstances. Whether obtaining damages for a loss of a hypothetical event can be equated with a test which utilises hypothetical reasoning, and which is not the sole test of causation, is another question.

Another issue relating to the loss of chance doctrine which the courts are yet to resolve concerns the effective inversion of legal causation in negligence by shifting the legal burden of proof from the plaintiff, who traditionally is required to establish that the defendant's breach of duty of care had caused or materially contributed to his or her injury, to the defendant who has to prove not the absence of a legal nexus between the breach and injury but the absence of such nexus between the breach and the loss of a chance. This means that the defendant is expected to disprove a negative, namely that the breach of duty did not deprive the plaintiff of a chance not to suffer loss or of a possibility to minimise that loss. This is a question explored by Freckelton in the Epilogue to the book. In his chapter, Smith develops Greenberg's analysis of causation in the medical context by analysing the complex relationship between aetiology and perceptions in the context of pain and injury in cases of low back pain – a compensable injury that is often at the centre of forensic controversy in torts litigation.

In Part C Lanham explains that the approach of the criminal law to determination of liability for causing death involves asking two questions: first, is there a factual link between the defendant's conduct and the victim's death; secondly, is the link sufficiently substantial to make the defendant's conduct the cause of death? The factual link is sometimes described as the *but for* requirement or *causa sine qua non* test. According to this test, causation is established if the death would not have occurred but for the act of the defendant. Conceptual and jurisprudential difficulties in the application of the *but for* test in torts and in criminal law have long been recognised. Lanham provides a number of examples where the *but for* test would result in acquittal, yet a wider analysis would suggest the presence of a causative link. Even if the factual link is established, the law has to test whether that link is sufficiently strong to attribute the death to the defendant's action. Lanham questions the appeal to common sense in resolving issues of causation, noting that although it is true that common sense or sound judgement will need to be applied in assessing any matters of degree in which the legal tests present, it is neither a substitute for these tests nor does it provide an independent legal test. Lanham analyses different tests of causation, which include the general formula that to found liability a cause must be a substantial and operating cause; special sub-rules; and the issues of intention, foresight and foreseeability. He argues that the formula of "substantial and operating cause" is deficient in capturing the basic principle in causation, for there must be a point at which a cause is still operating but is so insubstantial that it should not result in liability. At the same time, a cause cannot be substantial unless it is operating. This was the issue that the Roman jurists found difficult to resolve. Lanham argues that in the case where there is an original injury and a second and more direct cause of the death, like poor medical treatment, only if that second cause is so overwhelming as to make the original wound part of the history can it be said that death does not flow from the wound.

The question whether the underlying illness or palliative care involving administration of high doses of opioid medication should be regarded as a cause of death, examined by Callinan from the perspective of criminal law, is analysed by Ashby from the point of view of a physician. Ashby notes that dialogue between medicine and the law is hampered by the fact that the term "causation" is usually employed in medicine and science in a narrow empirical sense, whereas in law causation is a complex phenomenon which encompasses the facts *and* determination of legal liability. Most people without a legal background, and hence most health care practitioners, will have first resort to the medical view of causation, which approximates to the *but for* test of causation without the over-arching test of common sense and experience.

Like Stapleton and Greenberg, Ashby discusses the issues of perceptions and framing, but he does so in relation to death causation in palliative care. He asks why medicine itself has failed to deal with ethical and legal problems of causation in this context, and discusses such reasons as the anxieties experienced by physicians about responsibility for causing death, as well as questionable assumptions by health care professionals and the public concerning the established international medico-legal view of palliative care interventions and death causation. Ashby demonstrates that many doctors still believe that they are causing or hastening the death of their palliative care patients by the administration of pain-controlling medication, despite the absence of any clinical scientific evidence that morphine causes death, if used with appropriate skill to palliate symptoms.

Palliative care is an excellent example of the inadequacy of the operative cause test as the sole determinant of legal causation, for, as Callinan and Ashby point out, it leaves out the issue of intention. Whilst a doctor's therapeutic intention may not always be easy to validate, evaluation of intention and motive are fundamental to legal analysis, and many would argue that intention is also determinative of the moral character of medical interventions. According to Ashby, the notion that there is agreement about a "high" dose of an opioid drug such as morphine beyond which timing and possibly causation might be in question has permeated medicine and found legal reflection in the 1957 instruction to the jury by (later) Lord Devlin in *R v Adams*. Ashby argues that although incorporation of the double-effect doctrine into the legal system is supportive of palliative care, much has changed in medicine (and society) since 1957. He discusses the deficiencies of the "double-effect" doctrine when viewed from the medical perspective.

Malcolm also critically analyses different legal bases for Lord Devlin's doctrine of "double effect". He examines various judicial interpretations of this doctrine, including its consideration as a discrete legal precedent in the form of a test that focuses on the defendant's intention rather than a causal link, or a specific principle of causation. Again, he demonstrates how the determination of causal link for death that occurs following administration of high doses of pain-relieving drugs will depend on a particular interpretation of the doctrine that the court adopts.

Another aspect of medical treatment where the issue of causation may arise involves refusal of life-saving or life-sustaining treatment. Malcolm discusses the approaches of North American, English and Australian courts to the right of a competent adult to refuse life-saving or life-sustaining treatment and doctors' liability for causing death, noting that the acceptance of this "right" in the law of tort may also provide an excuse at criminal law. As he puts it, where competent patients who have been fully informed of available treatment options refuse to give consent, medical practitioners are relieved of their duty to these patients. This principle is particularly significant in the context of the criminal sanctions that apply to an omission to provide such treatment, for in the absence of a duty to the patient, a medical practitioner may not be held liable for his or her failure to provide "necessaries".

While Malcolm's discussion of liability of doctors for omissions and positive acts relating to withholding or withdrawal of medical treatment and life supports is predicated on the assumption that the refusing patient is a competent adult, Helme and Mendelson examine medical aspects of competency in relation to patients with Alzheimer's Dementia. This condition has profound implications for questions of decisional competence not only with regard to refusal and withdrawal of medical treatment, but also to issues of competence and decisional capacity relating to *inter vivos* and testamentary dispositions in the context of the equitable doctrines of unconscionability and undue influence. When severe, the diagnosis of dementia is easily made. In its earliest stages, however, even the most skilled clinicians remain unsure. Yet, it is at this relatively early stage that many elderly persons make decisions both about their health and their wealth. Helme and Mendelson query the appropriateness of applying a strict cognitive test to persons with Alzheimer's Dementia, and point out problems with medical and legal assessment of competence. This makes the task of those concerned with the judgement of competence particularly difficult when in issue is the refusal of life-saving treatment and exercise of the "right to die".

In cases of persons diagnosed with dementia, their *inter vivos* and testamentary dispositions may be open to challenge on the ground that, due to "defective faculties", the disposing or transacting party was incapable of understanding their significance and purpose. Alternatively, dementia may be pleaded as the cause of the inability of the disposing party to consider his or her best interests, and the unfair exploitation of this circumstance by the defendant. Yet, the issues involved are much more complex. Helme and Mendelson argue that considerable care must be taken in making judgements based on personal or strictly juridical interpretations of observed behaviour. Rather, these behaviours should be interpreted from the subjective point of view of the affected person's brain and in the context of his or her social and personal situation.

Part D of the book grapples with issues concerning death and injury investigation, again from both a medical and a legal perspective. Cordner describes the role of the forensic autopsy conducted by pathologists. He contrasts the Hume and Mills approaches and examines a variety of circumstances in which the causes of death are indirect, multiple and complex. He notes too that on occasions determination of causation of death from a medical point of view is entirely dependent upon circumstances. He contends that if there is operating at the time of death a disease or condition capable itself of causing or accelerating death, and in the circumstances of the particular death its effects apparently exerted themselves, then the disease or condition should be regarded as part of the cause of that person's death. Cordner also argues that if a disease or condition (whether or not a potentially fatal condition) aggravates or complicates another disease or condition (whether or not a potentially fatal condition) such that death occurs, then both diseases or conditions should generally be viewed as part of the cause of death.

Wells addresses the issue of causation within the clinical forensic medicine context. He recognises that a range of factors is capable of contaminating the accurate assessment of the factors that, for instance, have caused injuries or that provide evidence in relation to sexual assaults upon either adults or children having taken place.

Freckelton analyses coronial law to evaluate whether it has evolved its own distinctive jurisprudence in relation to causation. In the context of contending that causation assessment is intrinsically context-dependent, he argues that the orientation of modern coronial law toward findings that have a potential for avoiding avoidable death has affected the tests employed for causation at inquests. He argues that there is considerable social merit in causation being viewed broadly within the coronial context, thereby encouraging investigation of both direct and indirect factors that have brought about deaths, fires and other phenomena involving risk to the community.

Part E deals with a number of different issues of causation as they manifest in forensic practice. Slovenko deals with the complex series of areas where psychiatric evidence seeks to assist courts in understanding causation issues in relation to mental health. He divides his chapter into sections dealing with behaviour that takes place as a result of mental illness, and mental illness that ensues as a result of a stressor. He poses the question: what does it mean to say that certain behaviour is a product or a feature of mental illness? He concludes that the terms used by legislatures and courts such as "product of", "a result of", "causal connection", "because of", "causative factor" are unsatisfying and impenetrable. He reviews a series of psychiatric theories about why people act in ways which may bring them into contact with the criminal justice system and argues that behaviour is a unitary process, but, with licence, it is spoken of in terms of either its subjective elements or its outward appearances. This can be like talking about the mind and body as though they had separate existence; we do it, he contends, because we do not have language expressive of continuous interactions with multiple or circular causality. He argues that the decision of whether behaviour is a "product" or a "result" of mental illness is not a matter of scientific expertise but a matter of social policy.

In analysing "psychiatric injury" Slovenko traces the evolution in the attitudes of United States courts toward the phenomenon, as well as the evolving thinking of psychiatry, in particular in relation to post-traumatic stress disorder ("PTSD"). He reviews another attribute of modern litigation involving mental health matters, the syndrome phenomenon, which is often associated with PTSD. He argues that in the law-psychiatry relationship, public policy plays a major role in determining whether certain kinds of behaviour will be considered to be the result of mental illness, or whether mental illness will be considered to be the result of a particular stressor.

Like Callinan, but from a different perspective, Doyle analyses the tests for causation in tort. He argues that "a function", or perhaps "the function", of the concept of causation in negligence, is to define the outer limits of harm or loss suffered by other persons for which the defendant may be held liable, if found to have been negligent. He locates the law's interest in causation in the civil context in the need to allocate legal responsibility for harm or damage suffered by a plaintiff. He makes the point that the making of a finding of causation gives rise also to a number of other considerations which can have significant consequences beyond the decision between the immediate parties. He argues that it is legitimate to take into account these other considerations when considering the soundness of the concept. Doyle reviews Australian law in relation to causation in the contexts of failure to advise and failure to warn of risks. He observes that the "but for" test and the common sense tests will continue to test the courts in particular applications.

Magnusson develops an aspect of Doyle's chapter by analysing a crucial aspect of proof of causation in a forensic setting – that sought to be done by the use of statistics. Statistical reasoning is employed increasingly frequently in the forensic context, in two ways – by the explicit presentation of statistical argument and, more broadly, by taking advantage of the conceptual approach inherent in statistical reasoning. Magnusson comments that statistical methods allow scientists and engineers to apply common sense to data that, like data of any other kind, are inexact. He accepts though that the potential for misunderstanding statistical proof of causation is substantial and illustrates the risk of mis-estimation by a series of worrying examples. He argues that the challenge for the courts is to ease the task for decision-makers by making statistical reasoning more accessible.

In his Epilogue, Freckelton analyses a selection of issues that occur at the practical end of forensic assessment of causation. He argues that many of these issues arise out of expert evidence. Some are statistical, as outlined by Magnusson; others go to the capacity of decision-makers to apply the kinds of tests outlined by Doyle. The evidence given by patients that had they been properly informed of the potentially adverse consequences of medical intervention, they would not have undergone it, can be particularly problematic. The role of hindsight revision can be substantial, whether an objective, subjective or modified subjective test is utilised. Freckelton argues that broad notions of "common sense" pose significant difficulties for decision-makers when they have to decide whether an act caused an outcome or might at some stage in the future produce an outcome.

Freckelton also discusses a number of difficult dilemmas faced by decision-makers when they have to evaluate epidemiological evidence, evidence about the aetiology of currently suffered psychiatric conditions and evidence about conditions that may have multiple aetiologies or that were prodromal at the time of a tortious or criminal act. He argues that difficulties exist both in criminal and tort law, resulting in a need for consistency and guidance for decision-makers if the sheer complexity of causation assessment in practice is not to retreat into impressionistic and unreliable fact-finding.

The book therefore is cross-disciplinary and views issues concerning causation through a number of different lenses. It does not purport to provide an overarching "solution" to the complexities faced by the courts when dealing with causation evidence. Its concentration is upon identifying difficulties and incompatibilities amongst the approaches of different disciplines to causation and upon grappling with what these differences and lack of conceptual consistency mean for the practical conduct of litigation. We are convinced that the integrity and regard in which the law is held within the general community depend upon its being responsive, and being seen to be responsive, to the values and enriching approaches of other disciplines. This book airs those values and approaches, while commencing the process of exploring how, consistently with its own objectives, the law can draw upon them in defining causation and how causation is established within the legal domain. In this regard, *Causation in Law and Medicine* is a beginning, not an end.

PART A:
THE CONCEPT OF
CAUSATION IN LAW,
MEDICINE AND SCIENCE

1 Principles and Values Underlying the Concept of Causation in Law

ANTONY HONORÉ[*]

Introduction

What principles and values underlie the concept of causation in law? This brief discussion of a far-ranging question will concentrate on values. Of special interest to the consideration of causation in law and medicine is whether different values underlie the concept of causation in the two disciplines. I argue that the values underlying the concept are the same in both, but that the values underlying law and medicine differ. A consequence of this is that law and medicine are concerned with different types of cause and use the concept for different purposes.

Some values hold good outside law and medicine. They are important in everyday life even in areas which are no concern of either. Others are values of the legal system, in particular of adjudication. An example is procedural fairness. Without procedural fairness adjudication is unjust. And healing and the relief of suffering is a value specific to medicine. In my view, however, no value underlies the concept of causation in law or causation in medicine as such. The notion of cause is the same in law, medicine, science and everyday life. This point is one that common law judges have often stressed, when they say that causation in law is a matter of common sense. Whether one thing has caused another is to be judged by criteria that prevail outside the law.

Three topics will be dealt with in the light of this distinction between values that mark everyday life and those specific to law or medicine. These

---

[*] Fellow of the British Academy, Formerly Regius Professor of Civil Law, Fellow and Acting Warden of All Souls College, Fellow of Queen's College and Fellow of New College, Oxford.

topics are causation, responsibility and legal liability. The concept of cause dominates our inquiries into the processes by which things happen, or have happened. Responsibility for good or bad outcomes of human conduct forms the link between causation and legal liability. It is central to the assessment of people's lives and doings, their successes and failures. But both causation and responsibility, though important in law, are concepts drawn from everyday life. The third topic is specific to law. It concerns the conditions that, in the interests of fairness, limit the extent to which people can be made liable for causing harm.

It may help to list at the outset the values that will be mentioned. In my view those that underlie causation concern the external world, which is, within limits, conceived as objective, regular and knowable. The knowledge that we acquire with its help enables us to survive in an uncertain world. That we should be responsible for our conduct and its outcome serves a different set of values. It encourages people to act in a way that will lead to good outcomes and it promotes a sense of personal identity. The restrictions on legal liability for harm caused to others rest on various aspects of fair adjudication, especially fair procedure. Fair adjudication is obviously not a medical value. Though the concept of cause is also not specially medical, its role in providing explanations of disease and recipes for cure is crucial to medical science and practice.

Values Underpinning the Concept of Cause

To take Kant as a starting point, causation can be thought of as a category, like space and time, built into our make-up. We cannot help conceiving the external world in terms of it. If Kant is right, it follows that it is an across-the-board notion, applied not only in law but in science, medicine, history, ethics, politics and, if it comes to that, cricket. The concept of cause is the same in every sphere of life. That the moon's shadow caused the eclipse of the sun; that the defendant's speeding caused the plaintiff's trauma; that the Plasmodium parasite caused the patient's malaria; and that Steve Waugh's leadership was the cause of Australia's victory in the World Cup – all apply the same notion. Causation is an all-purpose tool for inquiring into the relation between one event and another.

Some philosophers and lawyers conceive the cause of an event as a necessary condition *(sine qua non)* of the outcome, others as a condition that, along with others, is sufficient for the outcome. Whichever view is preferred,[1] a cause is something like an ingredient in a recipe: an element in a combination that, if repeated, will yield a similar outcome. Both views presuppose that we can generalise about the way things happen. We can say that when conditions A, B and C are present together this will lead in stages to D but that if A is absent and only B and C are present D will not follow, at any rate not by the same stages. Observation and experiment pick out the conditions that in combination consistently give rise to processes that yield a given outcome. The recipe idea has been refined to such an extent that with its help a rocket can be dispatched to Jupiter in the reasonable expectation that it will get there at a given moment. At a more mundane level the recipe idea applies to medical therapy. Given the patient's condition (A and B) doctors try to find a treatment (C) that will result in a cure. And if causation can be used in a forward-looking way to provide recipes it can also be used in retrospect to explain events, for example to diagnose illness.

To say that one thing caused or will cause another is therefore to refer indirectly to what happens in general. But in practice the sort of A,B,C formula just set out is not easy to discover or to apply to a given sequence of events, partly because the relation of particular to general varies with the type of process analysed. In the world of physics we can specify rather precisely what conditions will lead to what outcomes. Otherwise we could not send a rocket to Jupiter. Organic matter is less easy to analyse in terms of causal sequences because living creatures are complex. Members of a species do not react in a uniform way. The confidence that can be placed in judgements of cause in medicine differs from that in physics even though the concept of cause remains the same. A doctor may believe that, given complete knowledge of the relevant conditions, he could predict exactly the outcome of treating a patient with a certain drug, yet in practice seldom be able to do so. Patients do not react in the uniform way in which rockets do. Medical science of course assumes that the condition from which a patient is suffering has a determinate cause and that the therapy will have a determinate effect. But often this does not make it possible either to diagnose or to treat the condition with confidence. Doctors have to go by probabilities, based for example on the frequency with which a certain drug is followed by a cure, even when the details of the process are unknown. It was reasonable to assume that penicillin attacked streptococcal infection and that most of the patients suffering from this infection to whom penicillin was given recovered because of it, long before anyone could

---

[1]   In favour of sufficiency, see T Honoré, "Necessary and Sufficient Conditions in Tort Law", in DG Owen (ed), *Philosophical Foundations of Tort Law*, Oxford, 1995, pp363-85.

show how this happened. Lawyers need, I think, to bear this in mind when weighing medical evidence that is couched, as it often has to be, in causal terms. The causes of most diseases lie in a complex of factors any one of which can be said only to contribute to the pathology.

If the concept of cause is hard to apply in the organic world of living matter it is not clear that it applies at all to the way in which human beings decide what to do. When people decide what to do they have reasons for deciding. But we need not and often do not think that these reasons would persuade everyone in a similar situation or that they would persuade the same person on another occasion. It is not clear that, if we knew all there was to know about the person who has to decide what to do, we could predict their decision with certainty. The decision need not be seen as an instance of a general law about the way in which human beings in general, or that particular person, react. For this reason the law, which is deeply concerned with human decision and action, often employs concepts that are only loosely analogous to causal connection in the world of inorganic or organic matter. The difference between human decision-making and the material world is marked by speaking of reasons for deciding and acting rather than causes. Advising someone to invest in a certain stock, even if they take the advice, is not the same as causing them to invest in it. But there is an analogy between deciding to act for a certain reason and being subject, as we all are, to the principles of physics and biology. To be satisfied that a person acted for a given reason, say that they invested on the advice of their stockbroker, we must believe that in the mind of the person to whom the stockbroker's advice was given it was sufficient to induce them to make the investment.[2]

What values, then, does the concept of causation serve? It presupposes three features of the external world that help us to survive. It assumes that the world we live in is within limits objective, regular and knowable. To the extent that this is true we can understand what happens around us and achieve at least some of our aims. The external world is conceived as objective in that it exists independently of us. But it does not follow that the way in which we conceive it is independent of our make-up and situation. For example, according to the theory of relativity certain data are relative to the position and motion in space and time of the subject observing them. Though there is an external world independent of us, it is plausible to think with Kant that the way we are made, and with Darwin that our need to survive, structure the way in which we see it.

A second value presupposed by the concept of cause is regularity. We are aware not merely of an objective world but of one in which patterns

---

[2]   Honoré, above n1, pp380-4.

repeat themselves so that when similar conditions are present in different times and places similar outcomes follow. The universe treats like cases alike. But, as noted, our access to reliable generalisations is greater in the world of physics than in the world of living matter. This is not because causal regularities are not present in the organic world, if we can get at them, but because it is more difficult to get at them. It is less clear that causal regularities govern human decision-making and action. We do not and perhaps cannot know if determinism is true. So, even if causation is a category from which we cannot escape when we analyse the external world, it does not follow that we have to analyse everything that happens in terms of cause.

A third value presupposed by the concept of cause is that the way in which things happen is within limits knowable. Even if we cannot know how things are in themselves – and Kant thought we could not – we can know them as they appear to us human beings. That is in practice enough for us to find our way around and to survive. It does not follow that everything that happens is in principle knowable and, if known, would be seen as an instance of an objective and regular sequence of events. The point is worth making because thinkers such as Newton and Einstein conceived their inquiries into how events happen as an effort to understand the mind of God. Access to that would, they thought, yield a set of principles that operate with complete objectivity and regularity. That belief may or may not be correct. Many scientists think that it is not true at the level of fundamental particles or cosmology. But it is in any case separate from a belief in the value of the concept of cause. The value attaching to causation remains even if some events have no cause and if our makeup is such that we are tempted, by a sort of evolutionary overkill, to use the concept in unsuitable contexts.

Values Underlying the Concept of Responsibility

Human responsibility links causation and the law. But responsibility is not a purely legal concept. That people are responsible for their actions and the outcome of their actions is central to everyday life. We judge ourselves and others on the basis that we are responsible for what we do and bring about irrespective of whether what we did was legal. Only in a limited class of cases are we not only responsible for the harm we bring about but also legally liable for it. But these cases are common and important enough for causation to feature prominently in legal argument.[3]

The mention of "harm" may mislead. We are responsible not only for the bad things we do and bring about but also for the good things. Being responsible for good actions and outcomes is important in everyday life but not often in law. We are, and wish to be seen as, responsible for our successes. But we cannot take credit for them without also incurring discredit for our failures. Responsibility cuts both ways.

In ordinary language there is a close link between causation and responsibility even when natural events are concerned. The Plasmodium parasite was "responsible" for the patient's malaria. But human responsibility for outcomes is a narrower notion and rests on different values. It is used to pick out a certain type of cause, namely the person, if any, whose conduct explains what has happened. It focuses for example on the person who exposed the patient to the malaria parasite, rather than on the parasite itself. The outcome, welcome or unwelcome, is then attributed to that person and they must account for it, as the term "responsible" implies. So responsibility, and at one remove legal liability, are concerned with a different type of cause from the causes of disease and cure with which medicine is concerned, but not with a different concept of causation.

What values underlie the use of the concept of cause to fix responsibility? If the world is to be a good place to live in we must be alert to the difference people make to it, for better or worse, by their interventions.[4] People change the world. So do malaria parasites. But malaria parasites cannot be called to account. Holding people responsible is requiring them to account for the changes they bring about.

We need the concept of cause to decide what changes a person's conduct has brought about. For this purpose we compare the world as it is after the person has intervened with the world as it would have been had they not intervened. To make the comparison we must know what the person did, the circumstances in which they did it, and the relevant causal generalisations. These together tell us what would have happened (or more often what would probably have happened) if the person concerned had not done what they did. We then know what changes, if any, the person in question has to account for. If the motorist had driven at a reasonable speed the pedestrian would (or would not), given distance and speed of reaction, have been able to cross the road in time to avoid being hit. If the doctor had

---

3   In insurance law and some other contexts responsibility for harm caused by events such as riot, war and shipwreck is in issue.

4   Also with the changes they have failed to bring about by not intervening in the world when they were called on to do so.

not advised against it, the patient would have had the inoculation and avoided (or not avoided) the disease. Causation is an essential tool for holding people responsible for the changes they make in the world.

Why should we want to hold people responsible? Responsibility has a pragmatic value. Holding people responsible for the changes they make encourages them to change the world for the better and discourages them from changing it for the worse. To credit people with the good they bring about and debit them with the harm they do provide incentives to do good and avoid harm. The consequences of treating people as responsible are likely to be better than if they were treated as automata.

A second value is, in my view, more basic. If people are made responsible for their actions and the outcome of their actions they acquire a history of actions, achievements and failures which are genuinely theirs. This history helps to form their character and identity. It gives them a sense of themselves and others as individuals, each unique, because each has done or brought about different things. So the process by which we come to think of ourselves and others as distinct, unique people depends indirectly on our grasp of causal generalisations. Given this, when the patient who has undergone a difficult operation recovers, the surgeon who operated can be credited with a success. When a burst tyre causes a road accident this can be attributed to the clumsy way in which the garage mechanic fixed it. It is his failure, for which discredit attaches to him.

But the use of causal principles in the context of responsibility carries with it a built-in limit. We are responsible because we have intervened in the world. Consistently with this idea, what is attributed to us as part of our intervention extends only to the later events that our intervention explains. It explains the sequels that happen in the normal course of events but not what happens when some other person or coincidental event later intervenes in a way that serves to explain what happens thereafter. The patient's recovery is attributed to the surgeon's intervention. But if on recovering the ex-patient takes up a successful career in computing that is not the surgeon's doing, though he made it possible. The mechanic's clumsiness is responsible for the burst tyre and the accident that ensues but not for the fact that the owner then decides to buy a more expensive car. The decision to buy an expensive car, like the decision to take up computing, begins a new chapter of events that serves to explain what happens afterwards. It is not conceived as part of the earlier sequence of events, since these do not serve to explain it, though they provided the opportunity or occasion for the later decisions to take up computing or buy the expensive car. This idea of a later intervention (sometimes described in law by the ugly and pretentious but not inaccurate phrase *novus actus interveniens*) does not imply any break in the physical continuity of events.

But it does mark a break in the explanatory power of the earlier cause. It fits in with the idea of a cause as a recipe or explanation.

It also serves to limit human responsibility so that each person can be credited with achievements and debited with failures that are uniquely their own. If our responsibility extended to everything that would not have happened had we not done what we did, we would share responsibility with many other people and the sense of personal identity that responsibility serves to foster would be eroded. So to understand how the concept of causation applies to problems of human responsibility we need to be conscious of the functions that being responsible fulfils in our lives. Responsibility for outcomes is limited in such a way that it retains the power to explain events and at the same time fosters our sense of ourselves and others as individuals.

Values Underlying Limitations on Legal Liability

Law does not punish people or make them pay compensation for all the losses they inflict or all the harm they do. Often we intervene in the world and cause loss to others without incurring either legal liability or moral blame. Competitors in business, love, politics and sport cause loss to and even humiliate their rivals, but unless the successful competitor resorts to cheating, success is neither illegal nor immoral. Even when harm is inflicted – and I mean by harm something like bodily injury which in principle no one should inflict on another except in self-defence – special legal values must be satisfied before the person responsible for causing the harm is made subject to sanctions.

Law limits liability for harm caused out of regard for justice in adjudication. This takes the form on the one hand of corrective justice, which requires the person who causes harm to another without justification to make the harm good. On the other hand, it takes the form of procedural justice or fairness to the person on whom the sanction of punishment or compensation may be imposed. Fairness suggests that at least three conditions should be met before a person who is said to have caused harm can be made legally liable for it. The person must have had notice that if they did so-and-so and thereby caused such-and-such harm they would be liable to such-and-such a sanction. The sanction must be roughly proportional to the conduct. And the connection between conduct and harm must be proved. These values do not apply in quite the same way in criminal and civil law but they have always to be kept in mind.

These legal values balance regard for the doer with regard for the victim. In civil law the principle of corrective justice makes the doer morally responsible for harm caused without justification but leaves open what is due by way of reparation. To turn the duty to made amends for the harm into a legal duty to pay money involves a form of state intervention in the victim's favour. It needs to be balanced by measures to protect the defendant. One measure that fairness requires is that the defendant should have been able to choose whether to run the risk of incurring the sanction.

To respect freedom of choice, the law should define in advance, at least in general terms, the type of conduct and outcome that may entail liability and the sanctions that may be imposed on the person responsible. Hence in law we are almost never faced, except at a preliminary stage, with the open-ended inquiry What caused this harm? The question is rather "Did so-and-so's unlawful conduct[5] cause this harm?" Law prescribes what must be shown to have caused what. If a person causes harm by doing something that the law does not forbid, or else does something that it forbids but thereby causes harm for which it gives no remedy, the doer obviously incurs no legal liability. If the doer causes harm without fault in jurisdiction in which fault is condition of liability, or causes harm of a sort which is not the subject of compensation (for example, pure economic loss or psychological trauma in a jurisdiction that does not recognise these as grounding compensation) there is no recovery at law. Both ends of the causal chain, conduct and harm, have to satisfy legal criteria.

Fairness also requires that a sanction should not be disproportionate to the gravity of the conduct for which it is imposed. In civil law this serves to exclude liability for harm of an unforeseeable type even when caused by the defendant's wrongful conduct, for example for the result of an explosion when only a collision was to be feared. That the sanction would be disproportionate to the gravity of the conduct is a distinct ground for limiting liability. It can justify refusing compensation even when the harm was caused by the wrongful conduct and not by a later intervention. This point is sometimes obscured by the use of the umbrella term "remoteness of damage". To take a familiar example, a motorist negligently runs someone over. When the victim is taken to hospital, the hospital is struck by lightning and the victim suffers burns in the resulting fire. The burns will be regarded as caused by the lightning, a later intervention, rather than the negligent driving. The motorist's intervention in the world does not explain the burns though it forms part of the history of how they came about. But if the motorist runs into the boot of a car that is unexpectedly carrying explosives and the resultant explosion causes widespread damage, the motorist's negligent driving undoubtedly caused the widespread damage. But to make the motorist liable for the explosion might be

---

[5]   Or some person or thing for whom he is vicariously responsible or some thing for which he is strictly liable.

disproportionate to his fault and hence unfair. In legal terms it would be damage of an unforeseeable type.

A third value that law insists on in the interests of fairness to the person potentially liable is that the unlawful conduct must be proved to have caused the damage claimed. Here, I think, it is easy for lawyers and physicians to misunderstand one another. To be fair to the person potentially liable, causal connection between conduct and harm must be proved according to the appropriate standard of proof, whether on a balance of probabilities or to a more rigorous standard. Whatever the standard, there will be cases when, from a medical point of view, the connection between, say, physical injury and psychological trauma seems clear but the evidence fails to persuade the judge or jury because the onus of proof lies on the victim. The rules about onus of proof in civil law rest on the view that money should not be transferred from one person to another without a good reason. It must be fair to the defendant to order money compensation. Hence there are injuries that go uncompensated not because lawyers and doctors have differing conceptions of causation but because in treating patients doctors, even if they are practising "evidence based medicine", often have to act on probabilities that fall short of the standard of proof required by courts.

There is also the point noted earlier, that causal generalisations are more difficult to establish for organic biological processes than for inorganic ones. Thus "the pathogenesis of PTSD (post-traumatic-stress disorder) and a number of other affective disorders still remains to be solved".[6] This problem might be alleviated by altering the rules about proving causal connection. Sometimes there is a statistical correlation between trauma type A and trauma type B (say a physical injury and psychological sequel), but causal connection between them is not established, because we do not know the stages, if any, by which one leads to the other. If that is so, the law could perhaps retain the need to prove causal connection, but put on the person alleged to have caused trauma B the burden, once trauma A is established, of producing evidence to show that B was not caused by A. If it is desirable to extend compensation in this way – and to my mind the theory of compensation needs rethinking – it would be better to change the rules of proof in this way rather than to create a cause of action for exposing another to a statistical risk of injury of a given type, such as trauma type B. It is important to keep the law aligned

---

[6]   D Mendelson, *The Interfaces of Medicine and Law: The History of the Liability for Negligently Caused Psychiatric Injury (Nervous Shock)*, Dartmouth, Ashgate, 1998, p288.

as far as possible with the values that prevail in everyday life, and to insist on proof of causal connection is one way of doing this.

Conclusion

In the upshot, this brief survey leads to the conclusion that causation, responsibility and adjudication all embody different values that have a bearing on the extent to which a person who has caused harm to another should be made liable in law to pay compensation. There is no single key to the solution of the complex problems involved, no guiding star. As in many areas of life, values conflict, and the law must try to adjust the conflicts so as to promote, to the limited extent that it can, a harmonious and stable society.

2 Scientific and Legal Approaches to Causation

JANE STAPLETON[*]

Introduction

I should like to make a provocative claim. Causation is not a concept at all. Causation is simply a term we sometimes use to answer one question about some transition that has happened in the world, and sometimes to answer a quite different question about such a transition.

When we think about some transition that has happened in the world, there are two questions we might ask.[1] These two inquiries are:

- First, how did the transition come about ... this is a factual question about history, though there may be value choices about how we should frame this history question, as I will explain later.
- The second question is, of all the myriad of factors that we know came together to produce that transition, which ones seem, in our individual opinions, to be important for the particular purpose we have at hand. Clearly our answer to the second inquiry will vary according to what it was we perceived our purpose to be in asking the question and the perspective on that purpose each of us individually took in the light of our experience and common sense.

---

[*] Professor within the Law Program of the Research School of Social Sciences at the Australian National University in Canberra, and a Statutory Visiting Professor at Oxford University.

[1] For a more detailed explanation of these levels of inquiry and my overall thesis with regard to causation in legal disputes, see, J Stapleton, "Perspectives on Causation" in J Horder (ed), *Oxford Essays in Jurisprudence*, 4th series, Oxford University Press, Oxford, 2000, pp61-84; "Legal Cause: Cause-in-Fact and the Scope of Liability for Consequences" (2001) 54 *Vanderbilt LJ* 942-1009; "Unpacking 'Causation'" in P Cane & J Gardner (eds), *Relating to Responsibility*, Hart Publishing, Oxford, 2001.

14

When we come to express our answers to these two questions, we might well happen to use causal language, although in both we might alternatively choose non-causal language.[2] When causation is being discussed among lawyers and scientists, a basic source of difficulty they have in understanding one another is that, when scientists use causal language they are always pursuing facts, whether this is in the shape of the exhaustive historical inquiry or in the shape of a more focused inquiry. If a scientist knows all the facts of how a transition came about, he or she would not consider that there was any room for a dispute labelled as one about the "causation" of the transition. In contrast, when lawyers use causal language, they sometimes are applying it to cases where the parties agree about all the facts, but have nevertheless framed their dispute as one about "causation".

The Scientist

Let me explain. Imagine a scientist is investigating why a wheat crop unexpectedly fell over before the time for harvest. In the context of the exhaustive first, historical, inquiry about how the transition came about, gravity must be included as a factor in the answer; and the scientist may choose to express this in terms of gravity being one of the "causes" of the crop falling over. Though the scientist always has in mind this exhaustive, indeed infinitely long, list of factors which would satisfy this inquiry, in the real world scientists must narrow their inquiries to the practically manageable. They do this by focusing on a particular, usually very specific, hypothesis: for example, was the absence of rainfall in the preceding month a relevant factor in explaining the fall of the crop? That scientific inquiry is narrowed in this way to provide a short cut to practical knowledge does not mean that it is not concerned with the discovery of facts, or is inevitably riddled with bias and opinion. The validity of the scientific results of such a narrowed study are preserved by the strictures of scientific method which requires the assiduous and clear acknowledgment of the purpose and assumptions of the study (the specification of its narrow limits), and the specification of the hypothesis that it is testing.

It is important to realise how labile and shifting can be one person's use of causal language. Take our wheat scientist: she may well use causal language in answering the exhaustive historical, inquiry about how the transition came about and say gravity was a "cause" of the crop fall, and

---

2   For example that a factor "produced an outcome"; that an outcome "resulted from" a factor.

yet in the more focused purposive inquiry of whether the absence of rainfall had made a relevant explanatory difference she might dismiss gravity as not being a "cause" because relative to the hypothetical world she will have explicitly or implicitly specified, namely one in which a wheat crop does not fall over, the factor of gravity has not varied. Clearly, our scientist *means* quite different things by the same word, "cause", in the two contexts. In the focused context her causal usage is different, not because she has forgotten that gravity is part of the factual history of how the fall of the crop came about, but because she has used scientific method to structure her inquiry, confining her explicit analysis to factors which are potential *variables* relative to the implicitly assumed alternative universe, only against which a transition appears to be a transition.

The wheat crop example not only confirms the labile nature of causal usage, but it also illustrates a number of important points about scientific inquiry. First, it is always directed at the discovery of facts and facts alone. Ideally, a desire or "bias" for a particular answer to the inquiry should be absent. Ideal scientific method requires that any choices made by the scientist, for example in the specification of the alternative world against which the question of explanatory relevance is asked, must be disclosed. Secondly, a scientist has no difficulty, as some philosophers seem to have, in identifying an absence or *omission* of a factor as being part of the history of the transition. Indeed, a great deal of experimental method employs a comparison of simple differences between systems, in one of which a factor is present and in the other the system is identical save for the absence of that factor.

Yet a third feature of scientific inquiry may be illustrated by an extension of the wheat crop example. There may be an alternative hypothesis of practical relevance about the history of the fallen wheat. Perhaps in the preceding month not only was there an absence of rainfall but also a rare series of severe frosts. The scientist's aim will be to determine, by suitably controlled experiments, whether either factor (drought; frosts) was alone capable of producing the effect observed. She will consider all possibilities: that neither was capable of producing the effect alone and that only in combination were the factors capable of producing the effect; or that each alone would have been sufficient. This latter possibility produces a phenomenon, sometimes described by lawyers as "multiple sufficient causation" and by philosophers as "over-determination": the crop has fallen over after the operation of two factors either of which without the other would have been sufficient to produce the effect. Importantly, the scientist is in no way troubled by this possibility: if the experiments show it to be the case, then the factual history of the crop fall is understood: the scientist would not consider there was any room thereafter for a dispute labelled as one about the "causation" of the transition.

When scientists disagree in the course of such inquiries, they are disagreeing about the experimental design or theoretical techniques (such as the appropriate statistical method) by which facts are discovered or deduced, how to eliminate bias and so on: it is worth emphasising that scientists simply do not have disagreements about what this word "causation" means, or the role the but-for idea should play as a so-called "causal test": causal theory does no work for them. Of course, as Dr Greenberg explains in his chapter, scientists often have to deal with the problem of gaps in knowledge. But the processes they study are the consequence of natural laws. As he succinctly puts it: here "teleological notions are irrelevant".

The Lawyer

Lawyers also use causal language in different contexts and it therefore also has a shifting meaning in their mouths. In some cases, lawyers are concerned with the first, historical, question: for example, was the heart seizure the result of the drug the patient ingested? Was it part of the history of that seizure? Though the context here concerns a fact, the difficult problem for the law is not a question of fact in the sense the scientist, or indeed the citizen, would understand it. The task of weighing evidence, judgment, is not itself conceptually problematic. What really confronts the law as a critical problem in cases of this kind is the legal policy question of how to proceed when the evidence about the facts of past transitions is patchy. Courts cannot order experiments to fill evidentiary gaps. At most they can take expert evidence. Yet if there had been agreement between experts there would be no legal dispute on the issue. This means that the first, historical, inquiry is only presented to a court when there is a dispute between witnesses, some testifying that the relevant factor, let us say the defendant's breach of obligation, was a part of the history of the plaintiff's condition (ie that aspect of it of which she is complaining) and some testifying that it was not. The problem here is that, as we will see, appellate courts need to choose rules about how to resolve these disputes arising from evidentiary gaps, what should be required of the plaintiff in order to prove her case and so on. Ideally these choices will be guided by the overall purpose of the law in these contexts, namely the allocation of legal responsibility. Specifically, they should be guided by what the court perceives to be moral and policy goals of the particular rule of obligation.

But it is also true that in many of the contexts where lawyers use causal terms, they are in fact dealing with the second, purposive, inquiry (namely, which of the factors that, it is agreed, brought about the transition seem important in the context of a legal dispute about responsibility) and are asking it for the purpose of how legal responsibility *should* be allocated in the context of a legal dispute.[3] Where, as in law, the purpose at hand is the moral or policy evaluation of human conduct, this second inquiry can never be reduced to a question of fact. Indeed, it is only reached after the facts have been agreed or decided. This is why it is so misleading when lawyers couch disputes about the answer to the second inquiry in causal language and why courts mystify ordinary people when they describe the dispute as a question of fact. The distinction between the historical inquiry and the purposive legal inquiry is implicit in a well-known dictum of Lord Reid:

> The question [of legal causation] must be determined by applying common sense to the facts of each particular case. One may find that as a matter of history several people have been at fault and that if any one of them had acted properly the accident would not have happened, but that does not mean that the accident must be regarded as having been caused by the faults of all of them. One must discriminate between those faults which must be discarded as being too remote and those which must not.[4]

Earlier I argued that in cases formally concerned with whether the breach of obligation by the defendant had anything to do with the history by which the plaintiff's misfortune came about, the critical problem for the law is not a question of fact even though the context concerns a fact. It is the legal policy question of which rules to choose when confronting evidentiary gaps. I have now argued that where the legal dispute arises from agreed facts and concerns the weight to put on a particular historically relevant factor in allocating legal responsibility, courts must also use the moral and policy goals of the particular rule of obligation to resolve the issue. The important conclusion from this is that in both contexts in which disputes might be presented to appellate courts in causal language, the critical task of the court is to choose which legal rule best fits the perceived goals of the law. In both contexts it is bizarre and highly misleading to the average citizen for the court to assert they are confronting questions of fact. In this important sense, appellate problems of "causation in law" are not questions of fact.

---

[3]   This is why lawyers who seek or offer some singular "legal notion of causation" do law a disservice because this conflates usages from two quite separate inquiries.

[4]   *Stapley v Gypsum Mines Ltd* [1953] AC 663.

The Double Hunters' Illustration: *March v Stramare*

A startling example of the different goals pursued by lawyers and scientists is their reaction to what I will call the "double hunters' case". Here two hunters carelessly shoot into a wood, both bullets hitting a beater who dies, the medical evidence being clear that either shot would have been sufficient to kill the beater: in philosopher's jargon, the death was "over-determined". Scientists see no difficulty in this case because it is quite clear how the death came about. If forced to give an answer to the exhaustive first question, the scientist will include the decision of the great grandmother of Hunter No 1 to have children because that is certainly a factor in the prior history of the death of the beater. If asked the more focused explanatory question of what made a difference here, relative to the normal experience of human society (a qualification scientific method would require to be made clear), the scientist would be able to select the unusual features of both hunters' negligence. Relative to the observed manners of human society, this was unusual, a variable.

But lawyers regard the case as very problematic: some arguing that each hunter would be able to deny he was a "cause" because "but for" his act the death would still have occurred. Others argue that the law should not apply the "but for" "test of causation" but a different "test", known as the NESS test (the "necessary element in a sufficient set" test first formulated by Hart and Honoré), which compares the prospects of the victim to a world where the other hunter did not behave carelessly.[5] The NESS approach is the correct one for determining whether a factor played a role in the history of the outcome,[6] so the dispute here is not about what happened, but about the appropriate approach to the second, purposive, inquiry. That is when and why, in a context where the relevant purpose is the allocation of legal responsibility, the law *should* hold a defendant responsible for a transition that would have happened anyway.[7] The

---

[5]   See Hart and Honoré, *Causation in the Law*, 2nd edn, Oxford University Press, Oxford, 1985, discussed in "Perspectives on Causation" op cit, n1. Their NESS approach was popularised by R Wright, "Causation in Tort Law" (1985) 73 *Cal L Rev* 1735; R Wright, "Causation, Responsibility, Risk, Probability, Naked Statistics and Proof: Pruning the Bramble Bush by Clarifying the Concept" (1988) 73 *Iowa Law Rev* 1001. Liability for over-determined outcomes is one of the examples underlying statements such as that of Mason CJ in *March v Stramare (E & MH) Pty Ltd* (1991) 171 CLR 506 at 509 that "the legal concept of causation differs from philosophical and scientific notions of causation".

[6]   See J Stapleton, "Unpacking 'Causation'" in P Cane & J Gardner (eds), *Relating to Responsibility*, Hart Publishing, Oxford, 2001.

[7]   See J Stapleton, "Legal Cause: Cause-in-Fact and the Scope of Liability for Consequences" (2001) 54 *Vanderbilt LJ* 942-1009.

confusing thing is that under our unfortunate current structures of legal rhetoric this dispute is typically paraded as one about the correct causal "tests" to apply to the agreed facts, rather than a direct investigation of the opposing arguments about responsibility and about legal policy.

Exactly the same divergence of approach can be seen in responses to the facts of *March v Stramare (E & MH) Pty Ltd*,[8] one of the leading High Court authorities on causation in law. Here a drunk driver had been injured when at night his speeding car hit a truck that had been parked (by an employee of the defendant) straddling the centre line of a 6-lane road with its hazard lights on. The scientist has no problem with this case: it is clear how the injury came about and no past facts are in dispute. But there *was* a legal dispute. In the case this was, unfortunately, framed in causal language: here the litigants described the issue as whether the plaintiff-driver's conduct was something called *a "novus actus interveniens"*: and whether it broke something called the "chain of causation". But, again, this is an unfortunate configuration for legal reasoning to adopt because it tends to mask the real nature of the dispute: which is one about competing values and policies concerning what responsibilities citizens *should* be held to owe one another in relation to their control of vehicles.

Instead of discussing this slippery non-concept called "causation", I am going to go back to discuss the two types of inquiry that can be made about a transition in the world and give examples of how medico-legal disputes can arise within them. In so doing I want first to make brief comments about how lawyers and scientists might better make themselves understood to one another.

Advice to the Two Professions

As I have just been suggesting, courts would make themselves clearer to scientists and other citizens if they explicitly distinguished between these two types of inquiry: historical involvement; and purposive relevance. In particular, when courts are presented with cases where the substance of the dispute is about the rules governing how to fill evidentiary gaps in relation to past facts, or where the substance of the dispute is about the weight to put on agreed facts, courts should openly recognise the case is really about competing views of legal responsibility. Courts should refuse to accept a formulation of the dispute as one about "causation" and so-called "causal tests", but instead insist that the parties argue directly and in non-causal

---

8   *March v Stramare (E & MH) Pty Ltd* (1991) 171 CLR 506.

terms about the issues of policy and principle relevant to the question of responsibility.

For their part scientists should remember that judges face three major constraints. First, a court must reach a clear decision in a case and do so within a tight time frame. A court does not have the option of waiting and seeing, or of delivering a merely interim opinion. Where there are gaps in our knowledge of the world, including both gaps in our knowledge of past events as well as gaps in our knowledge about what would have happened in a hypothetical situation, the court must form a final view. In a sense it must make an informed guess. The court cannot postpone its decision until the results of conclusive empirical research become available, if ever. Clearly, in many cases medical practitioners are constrained in similar ways.

Secondly, since judgments of appellate courts constitute binding or persuasive precedents for future courts they should enunciate clearly the principles and policies that have guided those guesses. This is why a judgment in favour of one side of a legal dispute cannot convincingly turn on mere assertions that it is a pragmatic matter of "common sense". This approach manages to be both patronising and mystifying to ordinary people because it suggests that if the decision goes against what the particular observing citizen believes is fair this is because he or she is too obtuse to grasp what lawyers like the judge can see as pragmatic common sense.

Thirdly, the scientist should remember that the law must itself construct a firm framework within which legal findings are finally determined: for example, it must construct a rule relating to the appropriate burden of proof in a case, whether the actionable damage can be constituted by the loss of a chance, rules for assessment of damages and so on.

The First Historical Inquiry: Did this Factor Play a Role in the History of this Outcome?

Evidentiary gaps concerning past facts: McGhee's case

The first set of problems that can arise here is that it may not be clear what happened. This can be illustrated by what I will call the "single hunter's problem". This is like our earlier "double hunters' case", but now only one of the two bullets hits the beater and there is no evidence to tell from which hunter's gun that bullet came. Exactly such cases have been presented to appellate courts in North America[9] and parallel cases have also arisen elsewhere.

The classic example of these latter cases is a case presented to the House of Lords in 1973 called *McGhee v National Coal Board*.[10] Here the victim contracted dermatitis after two types of exposure to brick dust: exposure during work; and exposure after work as he travelled home caked with the dust of the day on his skin. It was only in relation to the second period of exposure, that is on the way home, that a legal complaint was pursued against the employer.

The medical evidence was clear that exposure to brick dust seemed to increase the probability of dermatitis. So in this case each period of exposure, the period at work and the period as the victim travelled home, could be said to have materially increased the probability of the dermatitis. Now, in an appropriate case, the law has no objection to a fact being proved merely by statistics based on the level of exposure to risk. If we know that a particular surgical error quadruples the risk of post-operative cardiac arrest, and a patient suffers that error and then post-operative arrest it may well be that the court will accept the statistic as evidence that the arrest was due to the error. Indeed, it may be held that the assessment of the level of material contribution to risk may need be no more precise than that it "more than doubled" the existing risk: for this is evidence that can go to establish that, on the balance of probabilities, the misfortune was more likely than not due to that source of added risk.

Moreover, courts are prepared to be quite rough and ready about these things. For example, in a case where it is known that the misfortune occurs through an instance of infection and that the risk of infection during two exposures is at the same level of intensity, courts may well be willing to take a temporal approach and regard the fact that the longer period of exposure was that due to the defendant's breach of obligation as evidence towards showing that, on the balance of probabilities, the infection occurred during that period. Of course, the temporal approach is also the rough and ready way courts handle medical conditions that are known to be cumulative in the sense that it is known that every exposure to the source of harm precipitates some deterioration in the condition. Thus, in the landmark industrial disease case of *Thompson v Smiths Shiprepairers (North Shields) Ltd*[11] each exposure of the employee to industrial noise was known to have increased his deafness: the court was then prepared to use the length of employment with the various employers to apportion between

---

9   See eg *Cook v Lewis* [1951] 1 SCR 830.
10   *McGhee v National Coal Board* [1973] 1 WLR 1.
11   [1984] QB 405.

them legal responsibility for the total level of deafness presented by the employee at trial. The case is also illuminating for its illustration of the legal principle that to succeed in establishing liability against a particular defendant the plaintiff need not show that his entire condition was the result of that defendant's breach: it is sufficient if he can establish that the breach "contributed" to that total condition. Indeed it is a much better illustration of this principle than the case usually cited for it: *Bonnington Castings Ltd v Wardlaw*,[12] a problematic precedent because, although the medical condition there was the result of a cumulative mechanism, apportionment was not discussed or applied, leaving the defendant liable to pay for a loss which had not been produced by his breach of obligation (that due to those periods of exposure not due to his breach).

McGhee's case was, however, different from these cases because here not only could the medical experts not put a figure on the level of contribution to risk presented by the period of exposure due to the defendant's breach, they could not even say whether or not it was more likely to have operated to produce the dermatitis than the other source of risk.[13] The reason for this major evidentiary gap was that the aetiology of this particular form of dermatitis was simply not known. As we have seen, had there been evidence that the biological relation of exposure to condition had been cumulative (as it is for deafness) the law might have been willing simply to apportion between the two periods of exposure on the basis of their length: holding the employer liable only for that proportion of the total condition corresponding to the proportion that the period after work was of the total exposure time. But, as the Law Lords implicitly accepted, the evidence did not allow them to assume a cumulative mechanism.[14] This was because the mechanism might just as easily have been a "trigger" type of mechanism akin to the "isolated incident of infection" mechanism. If this had been the case *and* the level of risk of triggering rose exponentially over time so that, say, a 20 minute exposure at the end of a 8 hour exposure created more risk than the entire first 8 hours, the pursuer (for *McGhee's* case was an appeal from a Scottish decision) might have been able to win and recover damages for his entire

---

[12] [1956] AC 613. Compare *Holtby v Brigham & Cowan (Hull) Ltd* [2000] 3 All ER 421.

[13] For another important and striking scenario consider a claim for nervous shock where "the psychiatric expert witnesses could not distinguish between the shock associated with the crash in which she was involved and the trauma brought about by the plaintiff's concern for the injuries suffered by her husband": D Mendelson, *The Interfaces of Medicine and Law*, Ashgate/Dartmouth, London, 1998, at p233.

[14] This was what generated the problematic "evidentiary gap". In general, see J Stapleton, "The Gist of Negligence, Part II: the Relationship between 'Damage' and Causation" (1988) 104 *LQR* 389 at 401-6.

condition using orthodox legal ideas. This is because the evidence of contribution to risk might have showed that the risk posed by the period of exposure at work was less than the risk posed by the period of exposure as the employee cycled home, even though the latter was very considerably shorter in time. But the evidence did not point to a trigger mechanism any more than it pointed to a cumulative mechanism.

What the Law Lords did with the problem in *McGhee's* case was to allow the pursuer to leap what they recognised was an "evidentiary gap". The technical argument for the workman was that: since he could prove that the fault of the employer (in not providing showers after work) had materially increased the risk of dermatitis, this material increase in risk should, *in the circumstances*, be accepted by the law as sufficient to establish a material contribution to the dermatitis from which he suffered. As we have seen, a material increase in risk may well be enough to be accepted by the law as establishing the appropriate historical connection if there is simply enough evidence to show that it adds more than the existing risk. What was so extraordinary here was that the pursuer could not even show this crude relation. Yet the Law Lords chose to allow the pursuer's argument. Moreover, they allowed him to recover damages for his total condition, a result that is a radical departure from orthodoxy, and would have been so even *if* the pursuer had been able to establish a cumulative mechanism.[15]

One might be tempted to dismiss *McGhee* as a peculiar case that should be confined to its facts. Certainly that is what a later generation of Law Lords tried, unsuccessfully, to do in a medical negligence case called *Wilsher v Essex Area Health Authority*.[16] But in terms of practice and litigation, the decision in *McGhee's* case has proved to be exceptionally important. It has, for example, come to haunt much of the asbestos litigation in Australia where an influential dictum of Dixon J has been thought, mistakenly in my view, to give it added importance.[17] Even more strikingly, it was critical to the success, in 1998, of the largest personal injury claim in British history, a case concerning ex-miners suffering from

---

[15]   See Stapleton, 1988, op cit, n14, at 405. Contrast *Wilsher v Essex Area Health Authority* [1988] 2 WLR 557.

[16]   [1988] 2 WLR 557. In general see J Stapleton, 1988, op cit, n14.

[17]   In *Betts v Whittingslowe* (1945) 71 CLR 637 at 649 Dixon CJ said, albeit in relation to a statutory duty: "breach of duty coupled with an accident of the kind that *might* thereby be caused is enough to justify an inference, *in the absence of any sufficient reason to the contrary*, that in fact the accident did occur owing to the act or omission amounting to the breach" (emphasis added). Clearly the presence of another potential source of risk of that same accident should constitute "sufficient reason to the contrary".

a range of chest illnesses linked to exposure to coal dust other than pneumoconiosis (eg bronchitis, asthma, emphysema and small airways disease).[18] The success of these cases depended on the trial judge agreeing to apply the approach to medical evidence approved by the Lords in *McGhee's* case. For political reasons – Tony Blair described the compensation settlement as "a debt we all owe to the ex-pitmen"[19] – that trial decision was not appealed. As a result, in 1999 a record settlement was agreed for the benefit of 100,000 ex-pitmen of £2 billion. This sum, payable by the taxpayer, is more than the sum the Conservative Government had received from the privatisation and associated asset sales of the coal industry.[20] So, at least in terms of socio-economic impact, *McGhee* must now be recognised as one of the most important post-war decisions of the common law.

In the context of this chapter, the point to emphasise about *McGhee* is that the Law Lords were faced with an issue they could not postpone until science had discovered the mechanism of dermatitis. Moreover, though the central issue arose from the first, historical, inquiry that can be made about a transition to an outcome, the real issue for the Lords was not what had or had not happened in the past in the sense that a scientist would be interested. It was about what rules the law should select to deal with evidentiary gaps concerning what happened in the past. What moral ideas and what legal policies should guide those choices was the question before that tribunal. Only when non-lawyers understand this will the ruling in the case be intelligible to them. And only when courts openly face and assess the moral and policy disputes at the heart of *McGhee* will they begin to construct coherent boundaries for its use in the future.[21]

Loss of a Chance: Redefining the "Damage" forming the "Gist" of the Action

The dilemma for the Law Lords in *McGhee* arose from the difficulty of knowing what physical processes occurred in the past. Another example of this phenomenon is *Hotson v East Berks Area Health Authority*,[22] a so-called pure loss of a chance case, where the plaintiff formulated his complaint in terms of the chance of avoiding an outcome. In this classic

---

18   Judgment of Turner J in *Griffiths v British Coal Corporation* (23 January 1998, QBD).
19   *Telegraph*, 27 March 1999.
20   *Guardian Weekly*, 4 April 1999.
21   On possible special policy justifications for a limited application for *McGhee* see Stapleton, 1988, op cit, n14, at 406.
22   [1987] AC 750, on which see also Stapleton, 1988, op cit, n14.

example a boy fell from a tree and suffered a particular injury to his hip. The medical evidence was that of people injured in that way 75 per cent would suffer necrosis. The boy went to hospital but was treated in such a careless way that even had he not been one of these doomed people he would have suffered the necrosis complication. Now, if the boy had formulated his legal complaint of "damage" in terms of the necrosis he would have lost. The law would have applied its traditional but-for test and the critical fiction associated with it in this context: namely the law would have asked but for the hospital's negligence would the boy have suffered the necrosis. This question is evaluated *as things stood just before the boy reaches hospital*. Now at that time, of 100 boys in his position 75 were doomed and 25 were not. But we will never know, certainly not in the time-scale of the litigation, whether our plaintiff was one of the doomed or one of the not doomed. So the law resorts to a fiction based on the statistics of groups: and because it is more likely he was one of the doomed, the law then adopts the *fiction* that he *was* doomed: hence the hospital's conduct is treated as having had no effect on him.

The plaintiff can avoid this dead-end if he formulates his complaint in terms of the "damage" of a loss of a chance (to avoid the necrosis) and persuades the court to adopt a *competing fiction*: under this fiction every boy arriving at the hospital has a 25 per cent chance of avoiding necrosis. Since this boy contracted necrosis, it is clear that the hospital took away that chance and thus the boy is treated as having suffered the injury of "the loss of his chance of avoiding the necrosis". If the plaintiff is allowed to reformulate the "actionable damage", or as I have called it elsewhere the "gist damage",[23] in this way he will then be able to reformulate the historical inquiry (which depends on that formulation) into one which he can easily satisfy: was the defendant's fault part of the history by which the plaintiff lost the chance of avoiding necrosis?

The dilemma underlying the debate about the loss of a chance argument is again an example of the wider phenomenon I have been discussing: the law having to choose which rules are appropriate where there are evidentiary gaps as to what happened in a case. The choice is not about causal theories but about what policies might be thought to justify expanding the way legal complaints can be formulated, what can form the subject-matter of complaint: can it extend to a "pure" loss of a chance. It is worth noting that in *Hotson's* case the Court of Appeal embraced the fiction underlying the loss of a chance reformulation of the gist damage while the House of Lords, in an unsatisfactorily reasoned set of speeches,

---

[23] See also Stapleton, 1988, op cit, n14.

seemed to prefer the fiction underlying the traditional formulation of actionable damage.

How to Define History? Choice of Parallel Worlds

The problems in *McGhee* and *Hotson* arose from the gaps in our knowledge of what physical processes occurred in the past when the evidence of those processes is sketchy. But there is an even more difficult aspect to our historical inquiry of how a transition came about and what factors were and were not involved. This is that the inquiry can only be made in relation to some fictional world.[24] Yet there may be more than one parallel world we can envisage and so the question becomes: relative to which parallel universe should our questions of history be framed?

For the physical scientist trying to establish whether a factor was part of the history of an outcome, this problem of the parallel universe against which the history question is asked is ameliorated by the ability to run multiple experiments and draw on known physical relations. As noted earlier, it is also ameliorated by the very nature of scientific method, which requires that the scientist state implicitly or explicitly the assumptions of the study. These define and confine the history question internally to those parameters.[25]

But consider the difficulties that may confront judges. The law is centrally concerned with human behaviour and often needs to make a decision about whether a piece of human conduct was part of the history of an outcome about which the plaintiff is complaining. But in the legal context there are many potential near-parallel worlds that could be used when it comes to human behaviour because there are many potential shapes[26] the court could give to the relevant obligation in issue. Typically, because there is disagreement between the two parties before the court

---

[24] In other words, the perception of historical involvement is relative. It is only seen as history because we can envisage another world. This has both a proof aspect and a policy aspect. We can only establish that something bore a but for relation to a transition if we can imagine a world without that factor. Until gravity was a factor in the world that we noticed, no one would have thought to ask whether part of the history of an event was the presence of gravity.

[25] Thus an exhaustive description of the history of any meteorological process on earth would cite the presence of gravity: the scientist can now envisage a world without gravity, and is thereby prompted to ask whether gravity was a necessary or duplicative force producing the meteorological process.

[26] By "shape" here I mean not only the incidence of the obligation (in the duty of care sense, a relational issue) but its content in the sense of what is the type of conduct required for its discharge.

about the shape of the obligation, there is no agreement about which near-parallel world should be used to determine whether the conduct of the defendant was part of the history of the injury of the victim. Logically, the dispute about the shape of the obligation must be resolved before the historical issue can be addressed because until then the relevant hypothetical cannot be crystallised.

Moreover, even once the court has chosen the shape of the obligation and therefore which parallel world it is appropriate to envisage, it may not be clear what would have happened there. Specifically, it may not be clear what a particular individual would have done in certain circumstances. The court never has the option of ordering an experiment modelled on the hypothetical world. At best it is going to make a guess based on evidence, often evidence relating to hypothetical human behaviour that a scientist would regard as very weak or speculative.

(i)   Harness case

Say on one particular occasion an employer carelessly fails to provide a safety harness that would have saved a workman from tumbling to his death.[27] The estate of the victim might well be able to establish that the employer was in breach of a duty of care in not providing the harness. But unless it can also establish that this failure was part of the history of the death of the victim the claim will fail. Now say that the workman was well known not to have used the harness on those occasions when the employer had actually provided it. The defendant will urge the court that the appropriate alternative universe to use when asking if the defendant's omission of the harness was a part of the history of the death is simply these other occasions when the harness was provided but not used by the workman. If the court confines the shape of the employer's obligation to the provision of the harness it will use this hypothetical and the estate will lose because, even if the defendant had not failed to provide a harness, the victim would have died anyway.

But this is not the only available near-parallel universe that might be used. As I have noted, logically we do not get to this question until we decide what the shape of the defendant's obligation was and there are many choices here. The estate might urge the court to construct the obligation on employers to include not only the provision of harnesses but vigorous surveillance to ensure that they were used. If the court chooses to impose an obligation of this shape, the estate has a much greater chance of showing that the employer's conduct was part of the history of the death

---

27   See eg *McWilliams v Arrol* [1962] 1 WLR 295.

because now the alternative universe in play is one where the employer not only provided harnesses but also was assiduous about the workers using them.

What these cases show is that a court often faces a choice of the context in which it asks the first, historical, inquiry of whether the defendant was part of the history of the victim's misfortune, and that this choice arises directly from the antecedent choices the court has in moulding the shape of the defendant's obligation. His Honour Keith Mason discussed this inter-relationship[28] and it is one that Lord Hoffman has touched on in a series of recent judgments.[29] It is also a central issue in the palliative medicine and euthanasia contexts, a point confirmed by Professor Ashby.[30]

(ii)   Failure to warn cases

Sometimes a legal dispute arises not because there is any dispute about the shape of the obligation but because there is a dispute about what limits the law should put on the extent of liability for the consequences of breach of that obligation. It is a bizarre feature of traditional legal rhetoric that this dispute about responsibility and policy can be concealed by being presented to the court as a matter concerning which near-parallel universe to use to decide if the breach of the defendant was part of the history of the injury.

Let me illustrate this with two failure to warn cases from the Canadian Supreme Court. In *Dow Corning Corp v Hollis*,[31] a claim against a product manufacturer, the majority held that the plaintiff needed only to show that, had the defendant warned her, she herself probably would not have used the product. In other words, the hypothetical used to address the historical inquiry was the subjective hypothetical of what this specific plaintiff would have done if warned. She did not have to show that a reasonable person receiving the warning would have declined the product. However, in *Arndt v Smith*,[32] a claim against a physician, the majority adopted a more demanding test[33] for the historical hypothetical: namely, the plaintiff must

---

28   See Mason, Chapter 7, below.
29   *Empress Car Co (Abertillery) Ltd v National Rivers Authority* [1998] 1 All ER 481; *Reeves v Commissioner of Police for the Metropolis* [1999] 3 All ER 897.
30   See Ashby, Chapter 11, below.
31   [1995] 4 SCR 634.
32   (1997) 148 DLR (4th) 48. For another critical perspective on the *Arndt* case see T Honoré, "Causation and Disclosure of Medical Risks" (1998) 114 *LQR* 52.
33   The so-called "modified objective test" from the earlier case of *Reibl v Hughes* (1980) 114 DLR (3rd) 1.

show that a reasonable person, albeit one sharing the reasonable beliefs, fears, desires and expectations of the patient, would not have agreed to the medical procedure.[34]

Now my point about these contrasting cases is that, although the Supreme Court described what they were doing as setting the appropriate "test of causation" in failure to warn situations, that terminology obscures what was really going on. What was really going on was a competition between different conceptions of responsibility and the different extent of liability for consequences these conceptions produce. The rule in *Arndt* truncates the liability of the physician for losses that were precipitated by the defendant-physician's breach of obligation more narrowly than the rule in *Hollis* truncates the liability of manufacturers. Under *Hollis* it was regarded as appropriate that the scope of liability for breach extended to include losses that would not have happened had the plaintiff been given the warning. Thus, if even if the psychological response of the plaintiff was so unreasonable that no one else would have declined the product on receiving the warning, if *she* would have declined use and thereby avoided the loss that loss fell with the extent of the *Hollis* obligation. In contrast, the *Arndt* obligation was held to extend only to those losses which would have been avoided by someone sharing the reasonable beliefs, fears, desires and expectations of the plaintiff. My point is that these are not disputes about matters of past fact or evidence. In both cases the failure to warn played a role in the history of the outcome suffered by the particular plaintiff. They are disputes about responsibility and policy. In other words, they are disputes about the second, purposive, inquiry: namely whether the loss to the plaintiff (in the history of which the defendant's tortious conduct played a role) *should* be held to be within the *appropriate* scope of liability for consequences of the tortious conduct. Causal language is simply not the appropriate vehicle for these determinations because it may suggest the dispute is one of objective fact when it clearly is not, as these two contrasting decisions illustrate.

---

[34]   The majority of the court adopted this line for policy reasons. Yet if couched as an approach to the history inquiry in the case, it seems very odd to be asking what someone else might have done. How should that be relevant to what happened to this patient?

The Second Inquiry: Is this Historical Factor Relevant to our Purpose?

Novus actus cases

The same problem arises when courts use casual language to address other types of dispute where the facts are agreed. This is because they are all really disputes about what answer the law should give to the second inquiry: about which factors making up the history of an injury *should be regarded* by the law as being relevant in terms of this type of legal responsibility. A very common form of this responsibility question is whether an intervening event provides a reason for truncating the responsibility of a defendant.

For example take cases where: a defendant carelessly breaks the plaintiff's leg but:

- on the way to hospital in an ambulance the victim is struck by lightning and killed; or
- at hospital a careless doctor maltreats the leg, necessitating amputation; or
- the victim has a rare allergy to some part of the medicinal treatment and dies; or
- the victim refuses a blood transfusion and dies; or
- the victim later becomes depressed by the accident and commits suicide or murder or rape.

Here, as in the double hunters' case and *March v Stramare (E & MH) Pty Ltd*, there is no dispute about the facts or about the history of what happened. The dispute is about the answer to our second purposive inquiry and our purpose is allocating legal responsibility. To couch the dispute in any of these cases as being about whether the intervening event was or was not a *novus actus* simply tends to mask the real issue here: an issue about what limits the law should choose to place on the scope of the legal responsibility of the defendant and why it should do so.[35] Lord Steyn

---

[35] In contrast to Professor Honoré, I am skeptical about the utility of examining, in the context of legal *disputes*, the patterns of how ordinary people use causal words. In my view this is too variable, unstable and opaque to serve the goals of the law. Moreover, even when an ordinary person uses such language he would be able to give his reasons for how and why he has used it a certain way in a particular context. As the comment from Lord Steyn emphasises, this underlying reasoning needs to be laid bare by judges resolving legal disputes.

succinctly emphasised this point in the recent "unwanted baby" case of *Macfarlane v Tayside Health Board*, where the facts would have allowed the argument, made in earlier parallel cases in other jurisdictions, that the decision of the parents to proceed with the unwanted pregnancy had been a *novus actus* breaking some "chain of causation":

> My Lords, to explain decisions denying a remedy for the cost of bringing up an unwanted child by saying that there is ... no causative link ... is to resort to unrealistic and formalistic propositions which mask the real reasons for the decisions. And judges ought to strive to give the real reasons for their decision.[36]

Chappel v Hart

Finally, let me turn to two troublesome features of Australian High Court jurisprudence in this area. In *March v Stramare (E & MH) Pty Ltd* Mason CJ said this:

> A factor, which secures the presence of the plaintiff at the place where and at the time when he or she is injured, is not causally connected with the injury, unless the risk of the accident occurring at that time was greater.[37]

With respect, the problem with this statement is that, by being couched in causal language it gives a misleading impression of the role that the concept of "risk" plays in our understanding of the world.[38] We use the concept of risk as a way of dealing with lack of information. If, after an event, we understand exactly how it came about and all the factors relevant to its history, there is no role for the idea of risk *when we are asking the historical question of what happened*. Put crudely, once such an injury has happened we know for certain that "a factor, which secured the presence of the plaintiff at the place where and at the time when he was injured" was indeed part of the history of how the injury came about. Far from the relation between that factor and the outcome being one of risk, we now know the relation to have been one of certainty:[39] because given that we now know all the other factors were going to be present, we can see that

---

36   [1999] 4 All ER 961 at 977.
37   *March v Stramare (E & MH) Pty Ltd* (1991) 171 CLR 506 at 516.
38   A less ambiguous term is "probability": see J Stapleton, "Unpacking 'Causation'" in P Cane & J Gardner (eds), *Relating to Responsibility*, Hart Publishing, Oxford, 2001.
39   Except in the case of over-determined events such as the double hunters' case.

the existence of the factor in question had in fact *doomed* the person to suffer the injury.

But while risk plays no role in the historical inquiry in such a case, it often plays a critical role in the *second* inquiry about relevance to our legal purpose. This is because when we ask what factors were important in our dispute about legal responsibility we often tend to think that it *is* relevant to know whether the defendant could foresee that what he or she was doing was increasing the apparent risks the plaintiff faced. This is very neatly illustrated by an example given by Mahoney JA in *Alexander v Cambridge Credit Corp Ltd*:

> If a defendant promises to direct me where I should go and, at a crossroads, directs me to the left road rather than the right road, what happens to me on the left road is, in a sense, the result of what the defendant has done ... But ... if, being on the left road, I slip and fall, the fact alone that it was the defendant's direction, in breach of (his obligation), which put me there will not, without more, make the defendant liable for my broken leg. I say "without more": if ... the left road was known to be dangerous [the defendant] may be liable.[40]

In other words, it is relevant to the responsibility issue to ask whether the defendant could reasonably foresee that he was exposing me to an increased risk relative to that which I would otherwise face. If there had been no such foreseeability then, on our current moral views about fault-based responsibility, the defendant would not be held responsible.

In the context of our discussions about "medical causation" this scenario is very important because it is very like that in the recent High Court case of *Chappel v Hart*.[41] Let me simplify the facts of that case to these: a patient suffers from a progressive throat condition which will sooner or later require an operation which, no matter how carefully performed, carries a slight but foreseeable risk of permanent damage to the vocal cords. The defendant does not warn of the risk, and though he performs the surgery carefully the vocal cords are damaged.

There is no question here of how the injury occurred and that the defendant's failure to warn was part of that history because the evidence was that had she been warned Mrs Hart would have gone to a different surgeon at a different time and so on. The dispute relates only to the second, purposive, inquiry: was that failure to warn relevant to the type of legal responsibility in question. It is critical to observe that, like the person giving me directions in the Justice Mahoney example, Dr Chappel had no

---

40   Mahoney JA in *Alexander v Cambridge Credit Corp Ltd* (1987) 9 NSWLR 310 at 333.
41   *Chappel v Hart* (1998) 195 CLR 232; 156 ALR 517.

reason to foresee that the injury would actually happen when he operated. As far as he or anyone knew, or could have known, the woman needed the operation at some time and so long as the operation was carried out carefully there would be no greater risk to the vocal cords if Dr Chappel operated rather than another doctor. Dr Chappel did not foresee and could not reasonably have foreseen that his failure to warn might expose the women to any greater risk than she would have faced anyway.

A 3:2 majority of the High Court found the doctor liable to compensate the woman for the damage to the vocal cords. In the context of this book, I want to make only a short comment about the case. It is that, although this legal dispute raised a number of difficult issues (and I have certainly simplified the facts for the sake of discussion), the High Court was prevented from really getting to grips with them because the parties couched their dispute in causal terms.

Put shortly, the first problem here is that the only rationale for requiring the doctor to give a warning in such a case (at least on the facts as I have simplified them) is to preserve the autonomy of the patient in being able to choose when and where she ran the relevant risk. We must remember that the law often ignores our interest in this sort of autonomy. For example, in the situation described by Justice Mahoney the law does not require the person giving me directions to tell me that both the left and right turnings seem to carry an equal risk of my slipping on the pavement. Typically we are not required to warn of such "apparently equal risks". So the first issue the High Court did not get to analyse because the parties in *Chappel v Hart* presented their dispute in terms of a dispute about causation *was when and why duties to warn should be imposed merely to protect the autonomy of decision-makers*. Clearly a critical issue here would be whether the decision-maker had questioned the adviser about the relevant type of risk.[42]

Of course, there is nothing to prevent the law protecting such an interest by imposing an obligation on one party for the benefit of another. But, as we saw in the harness case, it is only once we know what the obligation is that we can determine whether the behaviour allegedly in breach of that obligation injured the interest protected by the obligation. Yet it is not convincing for the court merely to assert that a warning of the "apparently equal risk" was the "very thing" the obligation was imposed to ensure, or was "called into existence because of the forseeability of that very risk".[43] There must be an explanation of why it is imposed in this

---

[42]   Originally an issue of contention in *Chappel v Hart* (1998) 195 CLR 232; 156 ALR 517 esp at p542.

[43]   156 ALR 517 at 520 (per Gaudron J).

situation when in other situations obligations to warn of "apparently equal risks" are typically not imposed.

The other problem with liability here is that if the obligation is aimed at protecting autonomy, then one might expect the damages to be assessed in relation to the injury to that interest in autonomy, however that is to be assessed.[44] But here Mrs Hart recovered for injury to another interest, namely the injury to her vocal cords, even though no one at the time the defendant failed to warn would have foreseen that his conduct was exposing her to any increased risk of injury to this interest at all. Again, the problem with the parties having delivered the dispute to the High Court as one about causation is that it hampered open scrutiny and analysis of this radical basis of recovery of damages.

Causation in Criminal Law

It is worth noting that one area in which the slippery idea of causation produces particularly intractable problems at the interface of law and medicine is in the criminal law. Chief Justice Malcolm[45] and Professor Lanham[46] both address this area in their chapters, so my comment will be brief.

There are twin sources of difficulty here. First, in criminal cases of importance the fact-finders are the members of the jury, and they give no reasons for their decision. It is they who must, within the legal principles of responsibility explained to them by the judge, apply the law to the case. Yet, unlike the law of tort, those principles do not allow a separation of the question of historical relevance from the question of whether a particular historical factor (the defendant's wrongful conduct) is relevant to the law's purpose in the situation. Thus, while the existing analytical categories of tort might be used to accomplish this – with "causation in fact" being reserved for the historical relevance issue, and the "remoteness" category accommodating the issue of the degree of relevance an historical factor has for responsibility purposes, specifically for the scope of responsibility for consequences[47] – there is no equivalent conceptual opportunity in the conceptual apparatus of the criminal law as it is currently constructed. The two functions or issues are at present compounded in the one step.

---

[44]   This is itself problematic because, as with injury to reputation, injury to autonomy cannot be directly calculated in dollar amounts.

[45]   See Malcolm, Chapter 12, below.

[46]   See Lanham, Chapter 10, below.

[47]   This is one of the themes of "Perspectives on Causation" op cit, n1, where I argue for the renaming of the "remoteness of damage" analytical category.

This gives rise to judicial statements in which causal language intertwines with responsibility language. For example in *Campbell v The Queen* Burt CJ said:

> It would seem to me to be enough if juries were told that the question of cause for them to decide is not a philosophical or a scientific question, but a question to be determined by them applying their common sense to the facts as they find them *appreciating that the purpose of the inquiry is to attribute legal responsibility in a criminal matter*.[48] (emphasis added).

Similarly in *Royall v The Queen* Deane and Dawson JJ wrote:

> ... it may assist the jury if the trial judge points out not only that there must be a causal connection between the acts (or, more rarely, omissions) of the accused and the death of the deceased, but that *the causal connection must be sufficiently substantial to enable responsibility for the crime to be attributed to the accused*.[49] (emphasis added).

What these quotations illustrate is that while some normative principles governing the attribution of criminal responsibility will rest openly with the judge whose exposition of them will be subject to the control of the appellate courts, the jury's decision will also turn on other normative issues of principle where the jury is free to apply their own choices, though unable to enunciate them. This phenomenon is masked, however, because the language of "causation" with which the jury is charged by the judge fuses these normative issues of responsibility with the factual question of historical relevance. Thus, for example, while the motive and intention of a doctor in administering or withdrawing medical assistance will have no effect on the question of whether this conduct was of historical relevance, it will typically be critical to one's attitude to the question of his or her criminal responsibility. The same can be said of other factors that form the focal point of competing approaches to "causation" in criminal law[50] such as forseeability.

Of course, we may well be content with this robust arrangement, at least in the delicate areas of palliative care and so on. Perhaps we think juries will always manage to, or appear to, "do the right thing" in relation to medical-defendants while not giving unsettling symbolic messages in detailed written judgments to a society unclear about the appropriate way to resolve the underlying moral and policy dilemmas such situations throw

---

[48]   *Campbell v The Queen* (1981) WAR 286 at 290.

[49]   *Royall v The Queen* (1991) 65 ALJR 451 at 465.

[50]   See the fine exposition of these by Malcolm, op cit, n45.

up. My point is that such a state of affairs is only achieved by our willingness to pack into the idea of "causation" issues of great controversy and by the chameleon-like ability of that concept to mean vastly different things to different people.

Conclusion

These few examples illustrate just some of the ways a gap in understanding can sometimes open up between lawyers and scientists. One step courts could take to help close that gap is by relying less on the causal packaging of legal disputes and by paying more attention to the responsibility and the policy disputes that lie at their heart.

3   The Cause of Disease and Illness: Medical Views and Uncertainties

PETER GREENBERG[*]

Studies concerning the cause of "disease" (pathological state) and "illness" (subjective state) reflect our needs to comprehend, prevent, treat, prognosticate and accept. Assumptions about causation are made by individuals and society, both to attribute blame and to provide a rational basis for compensation. In this chapter, the strengths and limitations of scientific approaches to causation and the differences between medical and legal approaches are reviewed.

Historical Background: Scientific Knowledge Versus Popular Beliefs

Contemporary medical views about "cause" are founded on the ancient Greek principle of determinism.[1] All events, including diseases, are perceived as consequences of natural laws and earlier circumstances. Teleological notions about fundamental purpose, which were felt to be of great importance before the Renaissance, are no longer considered relevant. The development of empiricism in Britain during the eighteenth century meant that concepts of causation were subsequently based on observation and experience, not just hypothesis.

Perceptions about causation at various times throughout history only partly depend on scientific and technological knowledge. The obvious contributions of diet, physical and chemical injury and inheritance to

---

[*]   Clinical Director, General Medicine, at the Royal Melbourne Hospital, and a Principal Fellow in the University of Melbourne Department of Medicine.
[1]   B Russell, *History of Western Philosophy*, 2nd edn, Routledge, London, 1961.

disease and illness were recognised from the dawn of time. Epidemics of infectious diseases especially were sometimes attributed to incorrect causes. Syphilis, the "French Pox" of 1492, first had astrological and astronomical explanations. Some believed syphilis was due to divine intervention, "a just and proper sentence for sins".

Scientific knowledge does not exist in isolation. It is "framed" by current philosophical, cultural, religious, political and sociological ideas.[2] Beliefs are stronger with recently recognised diseases and when scientific foundations are weak. In the early 1980s, when the cause of AIDS was unclear, as with syphilis 400 years before, there was speculation about divine intervention. When "cures" by surgery became technically possible, it was considered that a "wandering womb" explained hysteria and that "focal sepsis" in the tonsils or colon caused systemic disease. A current belief is the popular view, not supported by scientific evidence, that "stress" plays a significant causal role in cancer.[3]

Framing contributes to differences in beliefs about causation between individuals and communities and their advocates, including courts of law, in spite of the scientific evidence. Furthermore, beliefs may lag behind or ignore scientific progress. Consider "chronic fatigue syndrome". Although patients with similar symptoms were described in the second half of the 19th century,[4] the condition only attracted widespread medical and lay interest following apparent epidemics. In 1987 it was given this particular diagnostic label at the time that HIV and AIDS were attracting public interest. Similarities with HIV/AIDS were noted. It was felt, with minimal scientific evidence, that "chronic fatigue syndrome" also had an infectious and immunological basis. Another example is the idea that disease and illness are caused by "multiple chemical sensitivity". The validity of "multiple chemical sensitivity" is debated, but beliefs persist.[5]

Sometimes even the *name* of a disease determines myths about causation. "Multiple chemical sensitivity" implies there is no alternative explanation. Repetitive strain *injury* (RSI) implies that injury is the cause. The substitution of this name for an earlier name, "tenosynovitis", at least removed the implication of an inflammatory basis.

---

[2]   CE Rosenberg & J Golden, *Framing Disease: Studies in Cultural History*, Rutgers University Press, New Jersey, 1992.

[3]   R McGee, "Does Stress Cause Cancer?" (1999) 319 *Brit Med J* 1015.

[4]   E Jones & S Wessely, "Case of Chronic Fatigue Syndrome after Crimean War and Indian Mutiny" (1999) 319 *Brit Med J* 1645.

[5]   GE Simon, W Daniell, H Stockbridge, K Claypoole & L Rosenstock, "Immunologic, Psychological, and Neuropsychological Factors in Multiple Chemical Sensitivity: A Controlled Study" (1993) 119 *Ann Intern Med* 97.

Nosological constructions themselves can be causes of illness. Psychosomatic "memes", which are based on constructions of otherwise unexplained diseases or illnesses, may spread amongst susceptible individuals, rather like infectious diseases.[6] Under such circumstances, the *naming process* can be the main cause of the disease.

Factors determining discrepancies between lay and scientific views include the strength of entrenched beliefs, the dissemination and acceptance of both scientific knowledge and beliefs, and the zeal of stakeholders. The media play a critical role in dissemination of both scientific knowledge and of beliefs. The media are much more influential now than they were in Caxton's time, when syphilis first became widely recognised.

Cause can never be unequivocally proven in a scientific sense. The scientific method involves creation of hypotheses, which are then tested and sometimes rejected. It is the *failure of rejection* of hypotheses that confirms scientific validity. As in all applications of science to medical thought and practice, the issue is not the *absolute* likelihood of cause, but rather the *probability* of a particular factor being relevant to cause. Reichenbach extended David Hume's concept of *coincidental occurrence*: "The happenings of nature are like rolling dice rather than like revolving stars; they are controlled by probability laws, not by causality, and the scientist resembles a gambler not a prophet".[7]

Questions about causation can always be regressed until a more fundamental question that cannot be resolved is reached. Although genetic constitution and external influences must ultimately account for all disease, subtle interactions and complexities mean that scientific knowledge can approach the target of 100 per cent certainty regarding causation but can never reach it. Scientists take a pragmatic approach. "When we think we have found an approximation to the truth, in the form of a scientific theory which has stood up to tests better than its competitors, we shall, as realists, accept it as a basis for practical action, simply because we have nothing better (or nearer the truth)."[8]

An important limitation of the scientific approach is that currently accepted "causes" may not explain all cases. An example is ischaemic heart disease. Known "risk factors" such as family history, high blood pressure, smoking, and high blood lipid levels account for only about half of the prevalence.

---

[6]   SE Ross, "Memes as Infectious Agents in Psychosomatic Illness" (1999) 131 *Ann Intern Med* 867.

[7]   H Reichenbach, *The Rise of Scientific Philosophy*, University of California Press, Berkeley, 1951.

[8]   K Popper, *Unended Quest*, Fontana-Collins, Glasgow, 1976, at p151.

Single or Multiple Causes?

Scientific knowledge framed by beliefs does not completely explain disagreements about causation. In discussing cause of death, Cordner has helpfully described philosophical differences in the views about causation.[9] Hume (1711-1766) felt that a cause must be *both* necessary and sufficient, but JS Mill (1806-1873) argued that the concept of cause should comprehend the *totality* of conditions in which an event occurs.

The views of individuals and communities are also shaped by the importance attached to "reductionist" rather than "holistic" approaches. Reductionism attributes disease to its individual components. An example of a reductionist approach is Occam's razor: "It is vain to do with more what can be done with fewer." In contrast, holism acknowledges the complex and sometimes occult interactions between the various individual components. One holistic model, the biopsychosocial model,[10] views disease as a very complex interaction of a number of *systems*, both above (eg couple, family, culture) and below (eg organs, tissues, cells) the system level of the individual person (Figure 1). Alternative and equally compelling explanations for disease and illness often reflect the relative weighting given to reductionist versus holistic approaches.

There may also be disagreement about the relative contributions of multiple possible components to causation. Estimations of relative contributions are often sought to quantify "blame". Even the very best combinations of reductionist and holistic approaches produce only crude estimates, especially when known causal factors do not account for all cases, and when some causal factors are controversial.

Additional considerations apply when there are multiple causal factors. Causes may be linked with one another. It may then be necessary to dissect out the more fundamental and independent factors. An example is that both obesity and physical inactivity may be seen as causes of maturity-onset diabetes, but inactivity itself aggravates the tendency for obesity. Furthermore, some causes may only be apparent when other causal factors are present. A meal of fava beans may result in sudden anaemia due to red blood cell destruction, but only in persons who are genetically predisposed.

Questions about causation need to be specific. Do we require an estimation of the *relative* contribution of possible causal factors, or an assessment of the contribution of one particular factor to the *totality* of factors relevant to causation?

---

[9] SM Cordner, "Deciding the Cause of Death after Necropsy" (1993) 341 *Lancet* 1458.

[10] GL Engel, "The Clinical Application of the Biopsychosocial Model" (1980) 137 *Am J Psych* 535.

Scientific Views of Causation

Current scientific views on causation arise from hypotheses based on clinical observations made in individuals and groups. Hypotheses are confirmed using hypothetico-deductive reasoning by the application of epidemiological methods.[11] In studies of causation, the following criteria, some of which were suggested by JS Mill ("Mill's Canons") and consolidated by Bradford Hill,[12] strengthen the likelihood of a linkage between a possible cause and the subsequent development of a disease (Figure 2).

None of these criteria are sufficient on their own. Exceptions can be found for each. It is the strength of the individual criteria, as well as the strength of their combinations, which determines the likelihood of a cause-disease relationship. The cause precedes the outcome.

This is clearly inadequate as a sole criterion. It is problematic when there is lengthy interval between exposure to a causative event and the development of a disease. Consider two conditions: mesothelioma, a malignancy of the tissue lining the surface of the lung, and the human equivalent of "mad-cow" disease. There are many years between exposure to asbestos or to infectious material in brain tissue before either condition develops. Such long *latent periods* may obscure causal relationships.

The cause/outcome association is consistent across time, and consistent in different patient groups and different geographical and other settings

The greater the number of examples of the association, and the more reproducible it is in different circumstances, the greater the likelihood of a linkage between a cause and a disease.

There is a relationship between the likelihood, and/or the severity of the disease, and the magnitude of the cause

A "dose-response" relationship clearly increases the strength of the association. Examples are the relationships between the number of cigarettes smoked and the subsequent risk of lung cancer, and the level of

---

[11]   AS Feinstein & RI Horwitz, "Double Standards, Scientific Methods, and Epidemiological Research" (1982) 307 *N Eng J Med* 1611; B Russell, *History of Western Philosophy*, 2nd edn, Routledge, London, New York, 1961.

[12]   AB Hill, "The Environment and Disease: Association or Causation?" (1965) 58 *Proc R Soc Med* 295.

serum cholesterol and the likelihood of coronary heart disease. But a dose-response relationship is not invariable. Some causes have a *threshold effect,* in which the chance or severity of disease is not increased once a critical threshold has been passed, such as anaphylaxis (severe allergic response) from penicillin.

The cause/disease relationship is biologically plausible

Plausibility makes causal factors more likely to be correct, but only if associated with other criteria. There is a real danger, especially when conclusions are based on weak criteria, in accepting conclusions largely from the theoretical possibility of a plausible mechanism, which *could* account for the association. Plausibility may reflect fashions, which wax and wane. It was quite plausible in the Salem of 1692 to consider possession by demons as the cause for curious behaviour of young women. Another problem with relying on plausibility is that one plausible mechanism may be accepted whilst others are overlooked. Even if psycho-social stress contributes to coronary heart disease, there could be two plausible mechanisms, a direct effect of "stress" and an independent effect mediated by the chemical substances in cigarettes smoked in response to "stress".

The apparent cause/outcome relationship is not a reflection of bias and confounding

There have been few experiments where people are randomly allocated to "experimental" or "control" groups and then deliberately exposed to possible harms in order to prove that a potential cause was indeed responsible for a disease. Most of the scientific evidence about causation therefore comes from observational studies, although randomised studies of interventions likely to be beneficial sometimes provide sound evidence of harm as well. Critical appraisal of data is needed to ensure that the apparent linkage between cause and disease does not have alternative explanations, which reflect weaknesses of observational compared to experimental studies.[13] The essential problem is that an association between an apparent

---

[13] KS Trout, "How to Read Clinical Journals IV: To Determine Aetiology or Causation" (1981) 124 *Canad Med Assos J* 985; M Levine, S Walter, H Lee, T Haines, A Holbrook & V Moyer, "Users' Guides to the Medical Literature IV: How to Use an Article about Harm" (1994) 271 *J Am Med Assoc* 1615; MA Levine, "Readers' Guide for Causation: Was a Comparison Group for Those at Risk Clearly Identified?" (Jan-Feb 1992) 116 *Am Coll Phys Journal Club* A-12.

cause and a disease does not necessarily imply cause/disease linkage. There may be other explanations.

For instance, it was noted that some patients who had breast augmentation by the introduction of chemical substances into the breast area seemed to develop connective-tissue diseases. One way of establishing a cause-disease relationship would be a "cohort" study which compares the prevalence of connective-tissue diseases in patients following breast augmentation with "controls", who are similar in other respects, but who did not have the procedure. Alternatively, cause-disease relationships could be established by a case-control study. Patients with connective-tissue diseases and a control group are studied and the prevalence of the augmentation procedure in the cases and controls noted. In drawing conclusions from either of these observational studies, it is essential to ensure that the cases and controls were indeed similar in all other respects, including their predisposition to "connective-tissue" disease. Otherwise an alternative explanation, unrelated to the augmentation procedure might account for the differences observed between the groups. In addition, the possibility that it is whatever makes a woman choose to have chemical augmentation, rather than the augmentation procedure itself which causes the problem, needs to be excluded.

There is a specific relationship between the apparent cause and the subsequent effect

Cause could be firmly established if one cause was always followed by one disease, and if one disease was always a consequence of a particular cause, but there are notable exceptions. In tuberculosis and AIDS, for example, infected patients always harbour the relevant micro-organism yet many people exposed to the organism do *not* develop the disease. The micro-organism is therefore necessary but *not* sufficient. In the past, tuberculosis was considered to be *caused* by particular socio-economic circumstances. A similar case could now be made for HIV disease in socially deprived urban areas of the United States.

The same cause may also result in different expressions of disease. During poliomyelitis epidemics some people do not become infected at all. In others, infection can be demonstrated by tests and yet the person can be unaware of any symptoms. Some infected persons may have an influenza-like illness yet others develop paralysis. The determinants of the differences in the way the same disease is expressed are unclear, and there are many possible explanations.

Depending on the specificity of names used to describe diseases, there are examples of diseases having multiple apparent causes. Thus "hepatitis" may be caused by Hepatitis A, B, or C virus, or by Epstein-Barr virus, which more commonly produces the clinical syndrome we recognise as glandular fever. "Purpura", a descriptive term rather than a disease, may have many causes. "Chronic fatigue syndrome" is much more likely to be a common response to a variety of causal contributions than a single disease entity.

Prevention or specific therapy directed to the cause prevents or cures the associated disease

Examples include the prevention of infectious diseases like smallpox and influenza by immunisation, and the correction of diseases due to lack of hormones (eg under-active thyroid gland) by administering the deficient substance. This finding alone is certainly not sufficient to establish causation. Many diseases and illnesses resolve spontaneously and so improvement cannot be necessarily attributed to interventions.

The scientific studies of causation are applicable to this particular person[14]

Subtle, and often occult, differences between individuals may mean that scientifically-defined causes that have been found to be relevant in a group of persons studied may not apply to a particular person. Thus perhexilene, a drug sometimes used to treat angina pectoris (chest pain) in patients with ischaemic heart disease, is likely to cause side-effects in only some patients, those who metabolise it slowly.

Evidence Based Medicine

Although medicine has always had a scientific basis, there has been a recent re-emphasis on these foundations. The Evidence-Based Medicine (EBM) movement,[15] which originated in Canada and in the United States, has now been embraced internationally. As a consequence, physicians

---

[14] AL Dans, LF Dans, GH Guyatt & S Richard, "Users' Guides to the Medical Literature XIV: How to Decide on the Applicability of Clinical Trial Results to Your Patient" (1998) 279 *J Am Med Assoc* 545.

[15] Evidence Based Medicine Working Group, "Evidence Based Medicine: A New Approach to the Teaching and Practice of Medicine" (1992) 268 *J Am Med Assoc* 2420.

expect an even firmer requirement for evidence regarding diagnosis, prevention, treatment, prognosis and causation.

Proponents of EBM indicate a paradigm shift away from a hierarchical and dogmatic approach based largely on physiological and pathological considerations and experience, to a paradigm based mainly on evidence. Judgments about the value of opinions are now made less on the status of the opinion-holder, intuition and historical precedents, and more on the scientific evidence. The value of experience is not completely ignored as the practice of EBM involves integration of the practitioner's clinical expertise and judgment with the best available evidence.

Evidence is classified according to its *level* (Figure 3).[16] Thus evidence on causation which is based on only one or several anecdotes is judged as less valuable than evidence based on a larger series. Evidence obtained from comparative studies with historical controls is at a higher level. Case-control studies and studies with concurrent controls are at a higher level again. Although the level of evidence is even higher if there is pseudo-randomisation, or better still, formal randomisation, such high levels of evidence are seldom achieved in studies of causation because of ethical requirements to avoid deliberate harm.

An evidence based approach to causation involves the following four steps:[17]

Asking the right question about this cause and this disease

Questions should be specifically directed to the current problem. For example: Is there *any* possible causal link between this cause and this disease? How *likely* is a causal link between this cause and this disease? If there are many possible causal factors, what is the likely contribution of *this* particular causal factor? Does this factor act independently of other factors?

Searching for the evidence

An important outcome of the EBM movement has been consensus concerning the value of the particular elements selected from the wide

---

[16]   National Health and Medical Research Council, *A Guide to the Development, Implementation and Evaluation of Clinical Practice Guidelines*, NHMRC, Ausinfo, Canberra, 1999.

[17]   DL Sackett, SE Strauss, WS Richardson, W Rosenberg & RB Haynes, *Evidence-based Medicine. How to Practice and Teach EBM*, 2nd edn, Churchill Livingstone, London, 2000.

range of evidence sources.[18] Books are limited by their publication date. Readily updatable electronic versions of texts, both "on line" (eg "Harrison's on line") and on CD (eg "UpToDate") are now available. Primary sources of published data (eg *Medline),* are very comprehensive but relatively difficult to search. Highly valuable and more easily searched secondary sources such as "Best Evidence" ("on line" and on CD) provide useful information on causation. A systematic search involves retrieval of all relevant publications. This can be time consuming as it involves searching numerous texts and databases including publications in many languages.

Critical appraisal of the evidence

In order to answer questions about causation, material obtained through comprehensive searches must be critically appraised for validity. Essential criteria for validity include consideration of whether groups being compared were indeed similar except in regard to the possible cause, whether outcomes and exposures were similar in both groups, and whether meaningful time and dose-response relationships apply. In addition, the *strength* of the association between cause and disease and the precision of the estimation of risk are important in interpreting results.[19]

Applying the general evidence to a particular person

"Applicability" refers to the implications of evidence obtained from other people in different settings to a particular person in a particular setting.[20] One cannot assume that the results of a study linking a possible cause with a disease apply to the particular person under consideration. It is useful to begin by asking if there are compelling reasons why the results of the study should *not* apply to this particular patient. Possible reasons include differences in genetic predisposition, gender, age, inclusion and exclusion criteria, settings, use of medications, and other "co-morbidities" (eg medical, social and psychological circumstances). Additional reasons are differences in the degree of exposure to the possible cause and how the disease outcome was measured and detected.

---

[18] Ibid.
[19] M Levine, S Walter, H Lee, T Haines, A Holbrook & V Moyer, "Users' Guides to the Medical Literature IV: How to Use an Article about Harm" (1994) 271 *J Am Med Assoc* 1615.
[20] AL Dans, LF Dans, GH Guyatt & S Richard, "Users' Guides to the Medical Literature XIV: How to Decide on the Applicability of Clinical Trial Results to Your Patient" (1998) 279 *J Am Med Assoc* 545.

For all of these reasons it is more difficult to express an opinion about cause/disease linkage for an individual than for a group.

The contemporary emphasis on evidence in medicine increases the likelihood that possible causes and their relative contribution to disease are considered, detected and correctly weighted. It is acknowledged that EBM approaches have limitations. They should be seen as absolutely necessary although sometimes insufficient to establish firm cause/disease relationships.

Changing Concepts of Causation

Scientific information concerning causation is not static and can expand dramatically over short periods of time.

Causes

In recent years the combination of sophisticated technological advances and epidemiological studies of populations has strengthened knowledge about the critical influence of both genetic predisposition and infection as causes of diseases.

Genetic constitution is now seen to be a much stronger causal factor than previously recognised. It is relevant in conditions as diverse as bipolar affective disorder, maturity-onset diabetes, osteoporosis, cardiomyopathy and "auto-immune" diseases. Genome analysis is progressing rapidly. There are now known to be specific genes for some relatively rare diseases and several genes determining risks for more common diseases like ischaemic heart disease. Even when a specific genetic factor is found, estimates of its likely contribution to a disease may change over several years. A genetically determined vitamin D receptor is considered to account in part for osteoporosis, but initial estimates of its contribution were excessive.

The manner in which genes can influence causation is diverse. Genes may not only determine behaviours (eg excessive alcohol consumption) that increase the probability of certain diseases, but also the extent and manifestations of consequences of behaviours, such as the spectrum of diseases resulting from alcoholism. Genetic composition can protect individuals against infection (eg HIV[21] and tuberculosis).[22]

---

[21]   G Stewart, "Chemokine Genes – Beating the Odds" (1998) 4 *Nature Medicine* 275.

In addition to newly recognised infectious diseases (eg Legionnaires disease, Lyme disease, HIV), a new role for infection in conditions not previously known to have an infective basis is now established. Helicobacter pylori infection underlies the predisposition to peptic ulcer disease. There is strong but inconclusive evidence to suggest that infection plays a significant role in common chronic inflammatory joint diseases and even in ischaemic heart disease. There may be direct interactions between micro-organisms and genetic structures: retroviral particles like HIV become incorporated into host cell nucleotides and replicate when cells divide.

Diseases

Tuberculosis

Infection with specific mycobacteria is essential for the development of tuberculosis. Both the risk of developing and the clinical expression of tuberculosis depend on factors in the micro-organisms and the potential host, as well as in the environment where host and micro-organisms meet. Tuberculosis strains vary in virulence.[23] Individual risk for and expression of tuberculosis depends on genes[24] and on immunological responses. These are partly genetically determined but may be modified by present (eg HIV) and possibly past infections. Medications (eg glucocorticosteroids like "cortisone"), immunisation and nutritional status may also affect responses.

Mycobacterial infection is necessary but far from sufficient to cause tuberculosis. Environmental factors such as access to suitable food, overcrowding and ventilation are important. Death rates from respiratory tuberculosis in England and Wales began to decline from the middle of the nineteenth century, 50 years before the causal mycobacterium was recognised, and 100 years before specific immunisation and treatment became available.[25]

---

[22] R Bellamy, C Ruwende, T Corrah, KPWJ McAdam, C Whittle & AVS Hill, "Variations in the NRAMP1 Gene and Susceptibility to Tuberculosis an West Africans" (1998) 338 *N Eng J Med* 640.

[23] SE Valway, MPC Sanchez, TF Shinnick, I Orme, T Agerton, D Hoy, J Scott Jones, H Westmoreland & IM Onorato, "An Outbreak Involving Extensive Transmission of a Virulent Strain of Mycobacterium Tuberculosis" (1998) 338 *N Eng J Med* 633.

[24] Bellamy, Ruwende, Corrah, McAdam, Whittle & Hill, op cit, n22.

[25] T McKeown, *The Modern Rise of Population*, Edward Arnold, London, 1976.

Ischaemic Heart Disease

Although there are many contributory causes for ischaemic heart disease (eg genes, hyperlipidaemia, cigarette smoking, sedentary life style, obesity, and other diseases such as hypertension and diabetes), recognised "risk factors" only account for about 50 per cent of its prevalence. In recent years the possible role of micro-organisms (eg chlamydia) and the likely contribution of specific types of psycho-social stress in the workplace, such as lack of control over decision-making, have been considered to be causal.[26] At present it is not known how these complex factors interact to "cause" disease and illness in any individual.

Summary of Medical Views concerning the Cause of Disease and Illness

Studies across the spectrum of disease and illness suggest the following aphorisms:

- Disease results from a subtle and complex interaction of multiple causes. Disease and possibly illness as well may be modified by psychosocial experiences, especially early-life experiences;
- Genetic constitution contributes significantly to the range, risk, severity and response to disease, as well as to interactions with environmental causes;
- Causal factors in "illness" and "disease" may operate at all biopsychosocial[27] system levels;
- Given an inherent genetic constitution, physical, chemical, infectious and psychosocial causes interact to produce disease. The response is then subsequently modified by individual endocrinological, immunological and other responses. The experience of disease as *illness* is further modified by psychological and sociological responses.

---

[26]   H Hemingway & M Marmot, "Evidence Based Cardiology: Psychosocial Factors in the Aetiology and Prognosis of Coronary Heart Disease: Systemic Review of Prospective Cohort Studies" (1999) 318 *Brit Med J* 1460.

[27]   Engel, op cit, n10.

Differences Between Medical and Legal Views about Causation

Diversity in views about linkages amongst causal factors and disease has been referred to previously. There are differences between individual practitioners from the same profession and between professional groups. Differences between legal and medical views sometimes reflect the historical characteristics of systems that have evolved to resolve disagreement. Although the necessity for courts to provide pragmatic and timely resolutions is clear, it is sometimes difficult for the scientific medical practitioner to comprehend legal decisions regarding causation. This is especially so when decisions with extensive repercussions are apparently made without scientific evidence or in spite of it. The problem is accentuated if previous decisions are not revised as new evidence becomes available.

Consider the possible health risks of breast implants and the "interplay between medical science, law and public opinion".[28] Breast augmentation was initially undertaken by direct injection and then by inserting silicone-gel implants. About twenty years afterwards, anecdotes about connective tissue diseases affecting implant recipients were reported. Legal proceedings followed. Large settlements in the United States were made against implant manufactures on the basis of anecdotes in the absence of more scientific evidence. Soon after this the United States Food and Drug Administration banned breast implants, not because of demonstrable health risks, but because the manufacturers were unable to produce evidence that prostheses were safe. Two years later, as a result of more expensive settlements against them, the implant manufacturers agreed to a $US4.25 billion class-action settlement. The largest manufacturer, Dow Corning, filed for bankruptcy protection and in late 1999 a United States District bankruptcy judge approved Dow Corning's plan to settle for $3.2 billion. In 1996 in an outstanding review of this case Angell concludes: "For now, however, we can say that the accumulated evidence that shows any link between breast implants and a variety of systemic diseases and symptoms is very small, if it exists at all."[29] Recent publications support this view.[30]

Sometimes the fear of litigation, possibly because of doubts about the capacity of legal processes to address scientific material fairly, may have

---

[28] M Angell, "Evaluating the Health Risks of Breast Implants: The Interplay of Medical Science, the Law, and Public Opinion" (1996) 334 *New Eng J Med* 1513.

[29] Ibid.

[30] C Cooper & E Dennison, "Do Silicone Breast Implants Cause Connective Tissue Disease?" (1998) 316 *Brit Med J* 403; EC Janowsky, LL Kupper & BS Hulka, "Meta-analyses of the Relation Between Silicone Breast Implants and the Risk of Connective Tissue Diseases" (2000) 342 *N Eng J Med* 781.

striking consequences. "Bendectin" ("Debendox" in Australia), a drug mixture containing several constituents, was extensively used to treat nausea in pregnancy. It was withdrawn by the manufacturers when case-reports suggested possible foetal malformations. Although by current standards its efficacy is equivocal, a drug of probable value to many pregnant women is no longer available. The data on possible toxicity were only anecdotal.[31]

What are the fundamental differences between legal and scientific standards for proof of causation? The medical approach, especially in this era of Evidence Based Medicine (EBM), is to review the available evidence, graded according to its scientific level, and then to apply this to the case at hand. The legal approach is quite different: "In contrast, a court may approach the issue from the standpoint of the *presumptive inference* which a sequence of events inspires in the mind of any common sense person."[32] Although there is no absolute certainty about the validity of either approach, the scientific approach often requires more "hard" evidence than the legal utility of "presumptive inference", and is less subjective.

The present legal paradigm is more like the medical paradigm that preceded EBM. It is relatively hierarchical and based more on authority than scientific evidence. "Medicine is a science and law is not. Developments in medicine are made by experiment and observation; in law they are made by the decisions of legislatures and judges. A medical fact is one which can be empirically supported or clinically determined; a legal fact is one which is more probable than other countervailing facts."[33]

There are three elements of contemporary British, United States and Australian legal systems which tend to accentuate disagreement:

The adversarial nature of the systems

Contesting parties have no obligation to present *all* relevant evidence. They are entitled to present *selected* and potentially favourable evidence to the court. Furthermore, in contrast to the European inquisitorial model, the vision of the court, except in exceptional circumstances, is limited by the material presented by the adversaries. The judge cannot "... ferret out the truth in any absolute sense ... In our system the question is not 'What is the

---

[31]   LB Holmes, "Teratogen Update, 'Bendectin'" (1983) 27 *Teratology* 277.

[32]   H Gerber, "Lipovac v Black: was Dr Black Negligent?" (1999) 170 *Med J Aust* 550.

[33]   G Samuels, "Medical Truth and Legal Proof: Changing Expectations of the Expert Witness" (1998) 168 *Med J Aust* 84.

truth of the matter?' ... because the issue is whether the party carrying the burden of proof has discharged it".[34]

The selection, qualifications and roles of expert witnesses

Experts may be specifically chosen to present favourable opinions: "These witnesses are usually required to speak, not to facts, but to opinions; and when this is the case, it is often quite surprising to see with what facility, and to what extent, their views can be made to correspond with the wishes or the interests of the parties who call them".[35] The capacity of the expert may be seen as very broad indeed. "... it follows that a medical practitioner nearly always is permitted to give evidence on any branch of medicine."[36] Problems arise when "experts" undertake the very difficult task of extrapolating from the general issue to the particular case in the absence of significant past or ongoing clinical experience, and when the main emphasis in court is about their qualifications and status, rather than their *evidence*. The role of the expert is quite clear. "The expert's task is twofold. First, to furnish basic scientific or technical data. Second, to present inferences and conclusions from the facts which the judge or jury, for lack of specialised knowledge, cannot draw themselves. The expert is introduced to carry the proof to the conclusion for which the party presenting the evidence contends."[37]

The relationship between the expert and the court is also unequivocal. "The expert evidence should give the medical or scientific basis and if appropriate the statistical likelihood of the requisite connection but it is then up to the jury to say whether the connection is established to their satisfaction."[38]

The way in which the quality of evidence is assessed

Structures to ensure that evidence is sound may be seen as fairly fragile: "Up to the present, Australian law has not contained any criterion for evaluating the quality of expert evidence as a threshold element to be satisfied as a test for admission. In the average case, where there is a conflict of medical evidence, the dispute is most often about a commonplace medical condition in which specialised support for any of

---

[34]   Ibid.
[35]   Ibid. See generally I Freckelton & H Selby, *Expert Evidence: Law, Practice and Procedure*, 2nd edn, Law Book Co, Sydney, 2002.
[36]   G Samuels, op cit, n33.
[37]   Ibid.
[38]   *Dahl and Anor v Grice* [1981] VR 513, Young, Kaye, Gobbo.

the assertions that might be made are readily found. In the unusual case, the most novel proposition will have its adherents, who may compensate in vehemence for what they lack in scientific authority."[39] The clear communication of evidence about causation remains problematic. "There is the obvious danger that an expert when asked to provide an opinion as to whether a causal link exists may do so in terms of scientific proof that may be altogether too exacting for the degree of satisfaction necessary in a legal proceeding."[40]

Resolving Differences in Views about Causation

Responsibilities to our communities might be improved and professional disagreement reduced by:

- Accepting the historical evolution, strengths and weaknesses of current approaches to causation;
- Understanding the process of disease-framing and the role of influential stakeholders;
- Re-defining the role of the "expert witness";
- Evaluating the scientific quality of evidence presented in legal proceedings, and clearly distinguishing facts from opinions; and
- Improving communication both between professional groups and between professionals and the broader community.

---

[39]   G Samuels, op cit, n33.

[40]   *Tubemakers of Australia Ltd v Fernandez* (1976) 50 ALJR 720, per Stephen J.

Figure 1

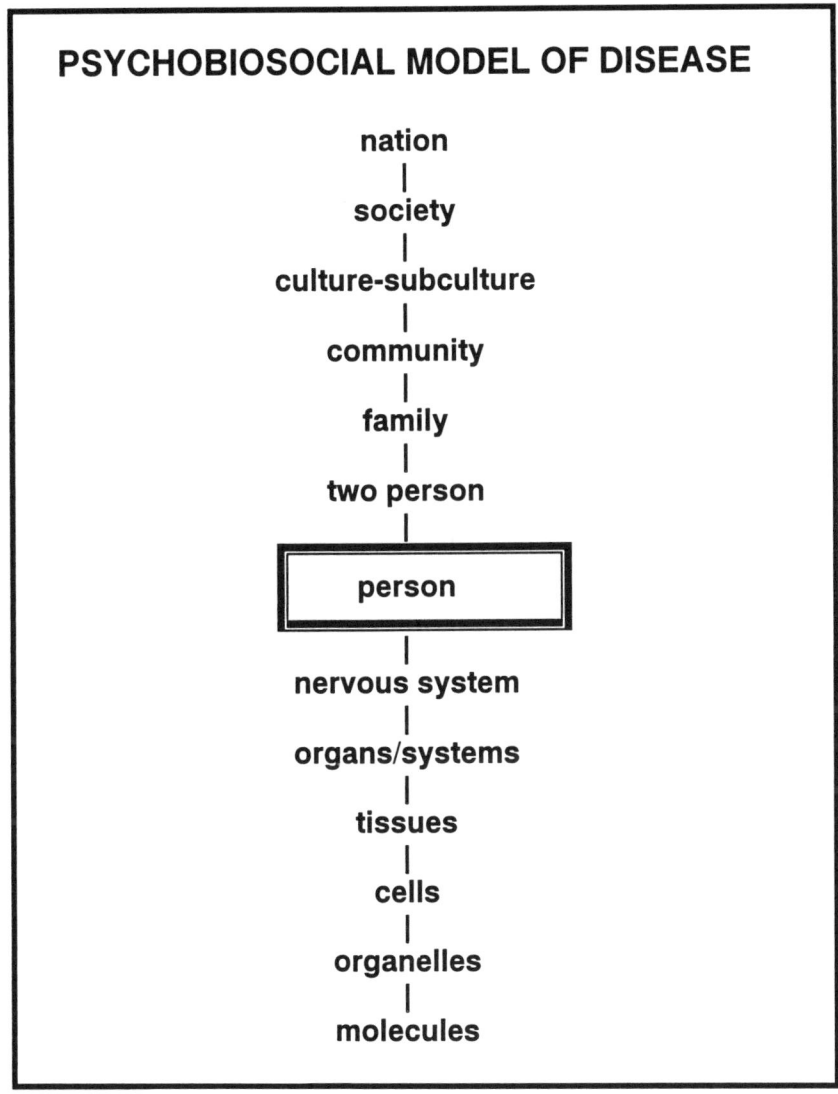

Adapted from GL Engel 1980.[41]

---

[41]   Engel, op cit, n10.

Figure 2

CRITERIA FOR CAUSE/DISEASE RELATIONSHIPS

- **cause precedes disease**

- **cause/disease link consistent**

- **magnitude of cause related to severity of disease**

- **biologically plausible**

- **link not due to bias or confounding**

- **specific relationship between cause and disease**

- **removal of cause prevents, improves and cures disease**

Adapted from RB Hill.[42]

---

[42]   Hill, op cit, n12.

Figure 3

GRADING OF LEVELS OF EVIDENCE

Level I: systematic review of all relevant randomised controlled trials

Level II: at least one properly designed randomised controlled trial

Level III: 1. pseudo-randomised controlled trial

2. cohort study, case control study, interrupted time series

3. historical controls

Level IV: case series

Adapted from NHMRC 1999.[43]

---

[43] National Health and Medical Research Council, op cit, n16.

4 Aspects of Causation in Hippocratic Medicine and Roman Law of Delict

DANUTA MENDELSON*

Introduction

The notion of causation is pivotal to law as well as to medicine, yet the concept of causation is one where legal and medical minds do not necessarily meet. The reason may lie in the two-faceted nature of this concept, for causation can be defined as referring to either origins of phenomena or to the consequential relationship between two events, one of which is claimed to have brought about the other. Therefore, how the nature and function of causation is understood depends on whether emphasis is placed on causation in the sense of sources and constituent elements, or on causation in the sense of a relationship between occurrences. This is why concepts of legal and medical causation, though they seem similar, have different contents. As a result, dialogue between the two disciplines tends to be in parallel, with messages between them interpreted in each profession's own, different way.

The question is whether this was always so, and how did these two ancient disciplines approach the concept of causation historically during their greatest periods of flowering and influence. Classical Greek medicine between the 5th and 2nd century BCE developed many concepts of scientific epistemology and causation that survived well into the nineteenth century, moulding modern medical and scientific thinking. Likewise, notions of legal causation developed by the Roman Law of delict from the

---

*   Senior Lecturer at the School of Law at Deakin University. I acknowledge with deep gratitude the help of Professor Antony Honoré who made a number of extensive comments on an earlier draft of this chapter. They have changed my understanding of the structure and the internal logic of the *Digest* and, hence, the Roman law of delict.

Republican *lex Aquilia* in c287-286 BCE to the promulgation of the *Digest*[1] and *Institutes*[2] by Justinian (527-565) in 533 CE still influence the legal discourse of causation.

Hippocratic Medicine

Many classical Greek concepts of medical epistemology and causation form part of modern medical and scientific thinking. In particular, Greek physicians developed a notion of rational aetiology, which involves correlation of disease to cause. The aetiology of a condition or disease would be arrived at through the process of diagnosis. The texts in the *Hippocratic Corpus*, reflect Greek physicians' clinical methods of physical examination: asking the patient about his or her symptoms; social and family history; observing the signs of the condition; and, if appropriate, performing such additional diagnostic tests as listening to the patient's chest, examination of urine, faeces and sputum.[3] This was done in order to group signs and symptoms into "descriptions of familiar, more or less standard clusters called syndromes",[4] with the final syndrome constituting the diagnosis in accordance with the medical theory acceptable at the time. Medical theory enabled the physician to decide "what is a significant sign and what helped to correlate symptoms with syndrome, syndrome with disease, and disease with its cause".[5] Although diagnostic techniques and evaluation of the findings have changed, the actual process of arriving at diagnosis and its correlation to aetiology has remained essentially constant. At least since the time of Hippocrates (460-377 BCE), at the beginning of the therapeutic process, physicians would invariably ask the question "why", in the sense of what is the source or what are the sources of the patient's complaint. The answers would often depend on the prevailing medical theory.

---

[1] The *Digest* comprises fifty books of excerpts from the writings of the classical jurists dating from the late Roman Republic to the beginning of the 3rd century CE. All quotations are from *The Digest of Justinian*, translation edited by Alan Watson, vol 1, University of Pennsylvania Press, Philadelphia, 1985.

[2] *Institutes* was envisaged as an elementary textbook for law students, based in large part on the *Institutes* of Gaius.

[3] Results of diagnostic tests also fall within the category of signs. It is acknowledged today that the process of diagnosis is not a one off event, but effectively continues through each stage of therapy.

[4] N Laor & J Agassi, *Diagnosis: Philosophical and Medical Perspectives*, Kluwer Academic Publishers, Dordrecht/Boston, 1990, at p32.

[5] Ibid.

In the classical Greece of the 5th and 4th century BCE, medical beliefs about the nature of sickness and health were closely linked to philosophical theories about the nature and order of the universe. Pythagoras of Croton (c530 BCE) suggested that the universe is governed by a dynamic balance of contraries, based on the opposition of odd and even numbers. The human body was seen as a microcosm of the universe (macrocosm),[6] whereby, according to Parmenides of Elea (c515-450 BCE), health and disease were affected by processes of change and stability within the universe.[7] Empedocles of Sicily (*fl* mid-5th century BCE) posited that nature was composed of four basic elements – earth, air, fire, and water – that combined into temporarily stable mixtures. Having further developed the ideas of Parmenides, and applied them to physiology, he argued that the source of living processes, including digestion, was an innate heat, with the heart as the furnace. Consequently, the function of breathing was to cool the body, and the function of the liver was to produce blood to nourish the tissues.

Hippocratic medicine, conceived as "a science of hidden things or causes (episteme), on the basis of which one could reason in therapeutic terms",[8] looked to philosophy for epistemic explanations of the human condition. For example, Alcmaeon of Croton (*fl* 470 BCE)[9] explained the fundamental principles governing health and disease through the Pythagorean notion of "pairs of bodily powers – hot and cold, sweet and sour, wet and dry. Seated in the blood, marrow or brain, illness could arise from an external cause or internal imbalance, caused by too much or too little nutriment."[10] This blend of medico-philosophical ideas, combined with scientific observation of nature and clinical experience of physicians led to creation of the humoral theory of medicine.

This medical theory, articulated in the writings of the *Hippocratic Corpus*,[11] involved a symmetrical grid of binary oppositions, and was

---

6 Roy Porter, *The Greatest Benefit to Mankind: A Medical History of Humanity From Antiquity to the Present*, Harper Collins, London, 1997, at p54.

7 For example, Parmenides of Elea (c 515-450 BCE). Roy Porter, op cit, n6, at p54.

8 Danielle Gourevitch referring to *Definitiones Medicae* in the Galenic corpus in "The Paths of Knowledge", in MD Grmek, *Western Medical Thought from Antiquity to the Middle Ages*, Harvard University Press, Cambridge, Massachusetts, 1998, at p104.

9 Alcmaeon was the first to scientifically establish that the brain was the chief organ of sensation.

10 See Porter, op cit, n6, at p55.

11 The *Hippocratic Corpus* consists of about 60 treatises, the collection of aphorisms, the *Oath* and the *Canon*. Some of the treatises and aphorisms were written by Hippocrates himself. However, the *Corpus* as a whole is the work of a large number of medical writers of ancient Greece compiled between 430 and 300 BCE, with subsequent interpolations.

based on a notion that the body was composed of four essential body fluids.[12] These fluids, *chymoi*, or "humours" – which gave the theory its name – were blood *(sanguis)*, phlegm *(pituita)*, yellow bile *(chole)*, and black bile *(melanchole)*. The four physiological humours met in binary combination with the Pythagorean pairs of bodily powers to constitute the four "essences" (air, earth, fire and water). In turn, these essences were the constituents of all matter.[13] Thus, humours were integrated within a wider schema of natural order. Black bile was linked to the essence of earth, the season of autumn, and melancholy temperament.[14] Its opposite was blood, related to the essence of air, spring, and sanguine temperament. Yellow bile was linked to the essence of fire, summer, and choleric temperament. Its opposite was phlegm, connected with water, winter, and phlegmatic temperament.[15] The scheme was supplemented by four ages of man (childhood, youth, adulthood, and old age) and the notions of moderation and excess in moral behaviour.[16] The author of *The Sacred Disease*, for example, wrote that the cause of epileptic convulsions was cold phlegm from the brain being discharged into blood-vessels, thus chilling the warm blood, obstructing its flow, and blocking the air-ways.[17]

The function of medicine was defined as "the complete removal of the distress of the sick, the alleviation of the more violent disease and the refusal to undertake cure of cases in which the disease has already won the mastery, knowing that everything is not possible to medicine".[18] The person's well-being and illness – and hence the general question of aetiology in Hippocratic medicine – was framed in terms of imbalances, be they physiological, environmental or moral. Once the cause of the harmful

---

[12] This theory was developed by the pupil of Hippocrates, Polybus. Much later, it was adopted by Galen.

[13] C Singer & EA Underwood, *A Short History of Medicine*, 2nd edn, Clarendon Press, Oxford, 1962, at p46.

[14] Black bile was associated with leprosy, malaria, melancholic madness and cancer.

[15] Based on each individual's unique temperament, history, and the season of the year associated with the complaint, treatment was specifically tailored to restore the balance appropriate to any given patient.

[16] In Roman times, the Greek model was augmented by humours of the four periods of day, four types of fever, four tastes, and four colours. The humoral model became more complex and unscientific when in medieval times four musical tonalities, and the four Evangelists were added; V Nutton, "Medicine in the Greek World, 800-50 BC" in LI Conrad, M Neve, V Nutton, R Porter & A Wear, *The Western Medical Tradition 800 BC to AD 1800*, Cambridge University Press, Cambridge, 1995, pp24-5.

[17] Hippocrates, "The Sacred Disease", GER Lloyd (ed), (trans J Chadwick & WN Mann), in *Hippocratic Writings*, Penguin Classics, Harmondsworth, 1983, para 10, at p245.

[18] "The Science of Medicine", ibid, n17, para 3, at p140.

condition was ascertained, physicians would strive to heal their patients by restoring the humoral equilibrium.[19]

Triggering and Latent Causes

The complex theory of humoral medicine was scientific.[20] It provided rational explanations of verifiable causes of diseases, as against ascribing them to an undifferentiated chance or a divine ordinance.[21] It was a Hippocratic credo that knowledge of natural causes would enable physicians to provide correct treatment.[22]

Aristotle (384-322 BCE) furnished the humoral model with epistemological framework. His epistemology was based on a teleological view of the world, which considered that everything in nature has its purpose, aim or goal *(telos)*, including all bodily organs and functions.[23] Aristotle identified four different categories of explanation, which he called causes:[24] "formal" (defining characteristics),[25] "material" (constituent elements),[26] "efficient" (origin or source of transition from one state or occurrence to another),[27] and "final" (in the sense of aim or goal).[28]

---

[19]   "Pain occurs when one of the substances [blood, phlegm, yellow and black bile] presents either deficiency or excess, or is separated in the body and not mixed with the others." Hippocrates, "The Nature of Man" in (trans J Chadwick & WN Mann), *The Medical Works of Hippocrates*, Springfield, Ill, Charles C Thomas, 1950.

[20]   Today, however, the paradigm of humoral medicine would be regarded as pseudo-scientific because its causal framework that cannot be falsified within its own terms. In other words, the model was capable of explaining the cause of any illness in terms of imbalance – a surfeit or deficit of humours and their associated qualities: see Nutton, op cit, n16, at p25.

[21]   "Every phenomenon [in nature] will be found to have some cause, and if it has a cause, chance [being a cause of cure] can be no more than an empty name. The science of medicine is seen to be real both in the causes of various phenomena which occur and in the provisions which it takes to meet them...". "The Science of Medicine", supra, n17, para 6, at p141.

[22]   "To know the cause of a disease and to understand the use of various methods by which disease may be prevented amounts to the same thing in effect as being able to cure the malady". "The Science of Medicine," supra, n17, para 11, at p145.

[23]   The famous example provided by Aristotle was the duck's webbed feet, which he explained were for the sake of swimming, an activity that supports the goal of a duck's existence, which is to find food in the water so as to stay alive.

[24]   Aristotle, *Metaphysics* [1013a][1] (b) 33.

[25]   Ibid, [994a][1]; [1013a][1] (g).

[26]   Ibid, [1013b][1].

[27]   Ibid, [1013b][1]; [1013a][20] (a).

[28]   Ibid, [994b][1].

Aristotle's concept of *final causality* was an integral dimension of the teleological approach to the natural order in the universe, which was regarded as divine.[29] However, Hellenistic physicians left to philosophy the ultimate search for the final or "first causes of all nature" within a teleological framework of the universe.[30] Nevertheless, they adopted the Aristotelian distinction between material and efficient causes, as well as a further distinction between *essential* or *significant* causes and *accidental* or *insubstantial* (trivial) causes. This analysis of causes was further refined by distinguishing evident or triggering causes from the latent or underlying causes, in the sense of being natural rather than supernatural, yet hidden from sensory knowledge.[31] Aristotle, and later, physicians belonging to such Hellenistic medical schools as Herophilean and Erasistratean, endeavoured to discover latent or underlying causes of diseases through systematic study of biology, anatomy, pathology and physiology.[32] They used scientific inquiry as means of ascertaining causal origins, *episteme*, of humoral imbalances. Epistemology of medical causation enabled them to understand not only how,[33] but also why diseases occur.[34]

But within its theoretical framework, the clinical art of humoral medicine was concerned with individual suffering to which practical solutions had to be found and applied. These solutions depended on the accurate identification of efficient or triggering causes that incorporated formal and material causality. Galen's description of different kinds of inflammations[35] provides a good example of the use of medical reasoning in terms of causes. In his *Cancer and Related Diseases*, Galen pointed out that although physicians did not know latent causes of inflammation, they

---

[29]   Ibid, [994a][1]; [994b][1]. Aristotle's teleological approach was later adopted by Christian philosophers, which led to the symbiosis between religion and medieval science, including medicine (medieval physicians regarded all causes of disease as being of divine origin). This link was only severed by Cartesian philosophers of the 17th century, who rejected the concept of final causality.

[30]   M Vegetti, "Between the Knowledge and Practice: Hellenistic Medicine" in Grmek, op cit, n8, at p78.

[31]   J Jouanna, "The Birth of Western Medical Art" in Grmek, op cit, n8, at p50.

[32]   See Vegetti, supra, n30.

[33]   The medical school of Empirics considered that for the practice of medicine, only knowledge of triggering causes, obtained through empirical experience was of any importance.

[34]   Apart from anatomy and physiology, modern medicine looks to biochemistry, neurosciences, genetics, etc, to provide scientific explanations for medical pathologies and diseases.

[35]   "The word [inflammation] is customarily used by the Greek [physicians] to refer to fleshy parts in a large swelling that occurs with tension, resistance, throbbing pain, heat and redness." Galen (trans J Reedy), "On Cancer and Related Diseases" (1975) 10 *Clio Medica* 229.

were nevertheless able to create a systematic humoral theory for diagnosis of swellings caused by inflammation. Formal causes such as body temperature and influx of blood with consequent exclusion of air[36] were important because:

> A major swelling never comes to any part of the body unless it suffers one or the other of these two things relative to its substance: either it is suffused with too much heat and is boiling hot, so to speak, or it has recently acquired some substance from without.[37]

Clinical observation enabled them to classify the inflammation in terms of material causes. These included swellings consequent upon a wound, an abscess or spontaneous growth. Hippocratic physicians would also observe the colour, size, mutations, secretions (clear serum or pus) and smell of the affected part, and then attribute the inflammation to such triggering causes as the high density of blood (an impacted humour) or bilious humours (bitter and black bile). Thus in clinical practice, identification of triggering causes was essential in diagnosing syndromes, which were ascertained from signs and symptoms. In this sense, the primary function of causation in medicine was "adjectival" or classificatory. Modern medicine, just as its Hippocratic ancestor, differentiates between the epistemological search for latent causes and efficient causality, which often provides sufficient explanation for diagnosis, prognosis and treatment.

Delictual Actions in Roman Law

In his *Nicomachean Ethics*, Aristotle developed theory of justice that was to profoundly influence the concept of legal causality in Western jurisprudence. In particular, Aristotle defined the concept of corrective justice as one that "plays a rectifying part in transactions between man and man".[38] This sentence was later interpreted as referring to "judicial justice" whereby the judge restores the just equilibrium in a "bipolar relationship"

---

[36]   Ibid, at 229.

[37]   Ibid.

[38]   "Of particular justice and that which is just in the corresponding sense, (A) one kind is that which is manifested in distributions of honour or money or the other things that fall to be divided among those who have a share in the constitution (for in these it is possible for one man to have a share either unequal or equal to that of another), and (B) one is that which plays a rectifying part in transactions between man and man." Aristotle (trans W D Ross), *Nichomachean Ethics,* Clarendon Press, Oxford, Book V, 2.

of rights and entitlements that have been wrongfully disturbed.[39] It is a moot point whether his concept of corrective justice was influenced by the Hippocratic notion of disease as an imbalance of humoral properties.[40]

Aristotle did not distinguish between crimes and torts.[41] Private law, as we understand it today, was developed by the Romans.[42] Classical Roman law, including delict,[43] was underpinned by a binary paradigm – with moral undertones. The Aristotelian notion of corrective justice is reflected in Ulpian's definition of the two basic principles of the right conduct: "... not to harm any other person, [and] to render to each his own."[44] Jurisprudentially, the binary paradigm of corrective justice[45] required that plaintiffs be restored to the position they enjoyed before sustaining loss or injury occasioned by the defendant's wrongful conduct.[46] This concept is not dissimilar to the humoral theory whereby the aim of medical intervention is to return the patient's homeostatic balance by treating the cause of the imbalance. In law, the forensic process focused on restoring the balance of equities through rendering "each his due". In determining the balance of equities – rights and obligations – causation played an

---

[39]   EJ Weinrib, "The Gains and Losses of Corrective Justice" (1994) 44 *Duke LJ* 277. Judicial rectification of wrongs in a particular case is predicated on understanding of the underlying rights that conform to the notion of distributive justice. RA Epstein, "Symposium on Causation in the Law of Torts: Causation – in Context: an Afterword" (1987) 63 *Chi-Kent L Rev* 653 at 654.

[40]   Aristotle (384-322 BCE), a son of the court physician from Stagira in Thrace, was very well familiar with the theory of humoral medicine.

[41]   ARW Harrison, "Aristotle's *Nichomachean Ethics*, Book V, and the Law of Athens" (1957) 77 *Journal of Hellenic Studies* 42 at 43. Though he did seem to distinguish between obligations arising out of voluntary and involuntary involvement between parties. Harrison, at 45; *Nichomachean Ethics*, Book V, 113.1a.2.

[42]   See generally RW Lee, *The Elements of Roman Law*, 4th edn, Sweet & Maxwell, London, 1956, at 371 (discussing the development of third party liability by the Romans); R Zimmerman, *The Law of Obligations*, Clarendon Press, Oxford, 1996.

[43]   In Roman law delicts included theft, robbery, injury to property, and wilful injury to the person or reputation.

[44]   D.1.1.10.1; *Inst.* 1.1. pr. This affirmation of right conduct, which begins with "To live honourably", was formulated in the late third century in a work wrongly attributed to Ulpian (- 223 CE). It was influenced by philosophical thought of the following generation, perhaps from the circle of Origen. See T Honoré, *Ulpian*, Oxford University Press, Oxford, 1982, 111-13; D Liebs, "Ulpiani Regulae – Zwei Pseudepigrapha" in *Romanitas-Christianitas. Untersuchungen zur Geschichte und Literatur der römischen Kaiserzeit*, 1982, pp282-92.

[45]   The Roman notion of corrective justice under *lex Aquilia* was not only compensatory, but also extended to penalties in a multiple of the loss in cases where, if the defendant denied liability, twice the loss would be payable to the victim.

[46]   Neither the Aristotelian notion of justice, nor the Roman ideal of just and fair legal system extended to slaves. Slaves were *res mortales* (mortal objects), and their death or injury was regarded as a proprietary loss for the plaintiff-owner.

important part at the procedural level, in substantive law, and at the policy level.

Though the development was gradual,[47] in general, depending on the legal context, Roman jurists tended to differentiate between:

- *ratio naturalis* – reasoning derived from nature and "rooted in facts of life, in objective reality"[48] and
- *civilis ratio* – technical legal reasoning that used analogy from the precedents, or general principles of the Roman civil law[49] to attribute legal responsibility for the plaintiff's harm. The arguments were drawn from a jurisprudential system of rights and obligations, which, in turn, tended to be determined by moral and social policy considerations.

At the same time, the modern distinction between factual causation and legal causation, which depends on a contrast between causal conditions (generally but-for conditions) and proximate causes,[50] was foreign to the Roman sources. To the Roman lawyers, causes were, in Aristotle's language, efficient causes. Within efficient causes, the jurists distinguished between direct and indirect causes, especially in relation to Aquilian liability (discussed below), which was where medical problems were most likely to arise.

Procedurally, under the Roman *lex Aquilia*, causation determined whether a remedy was available. At the substantive law level, again, factual causation helped to determine whether or not the conduct complained of was wrongful.

---

[47]   V Palmer, "A General Theory of the Inner Structure of Strict Liability: Common Law, Civil Law, and Comparative Law" (1988) 62 *Tul L Rev* 1303 at 1313 argues that under *Twelve Tablets* liability was strict and determined solely by the issue of causation, namely whether a person or thing was in fact the cause of an unlawful result.

[48]   P Stein, "The Development of the Notion of *Naturalis Ratio*" in A Watson (ed), *Daube Noster,* Scottish Academic Press, Edinburgh, 1974, at pp312-13.

[49]   Ibid.

[50]   In the modern tort of negligence, the legal issue of causal connection between the defendant's conduct and the harmful result is also split into two questions: (i) the "factual" causation known as the *causa sine qua non* ("but for") test, which effectively tests a hypothetical cause (would the damage have happened but for the defendant's negligence in an identical set of circumstances?); and (ii) "proximate causation" based on various normative tests that involve considerations of right, wrong and economics as understood by the judiciary of the time. For an elegant critique of these concepts see HLA Hart & T Honoré, *Causation in the Law,* 2nd edn, Clarendon Press, Oxford, 1985, pp98-108.

Causation as a Determinant of Delictual Remedies

Unlike the Hippocratic system of medicine, where there existed from an early stage an integral link between philosophy and medical theory, Roman jurisprudence, initially, that is until the advent of republican jurists,[51] seems to have developed without a systematic body of philosophical assumptions and principles.[52] Remedies *(actiones)* for delictual wrongs evolved gradually, from punitive prescriptions in the *Twelve Tablets* dating from c450 BCE, to republican *lex Aquilia*,[53] praetorian policy actions, and actions on the facts in Justinian's *Digest* and *Institutes*. The availability of Roman delictual actions was predicated on whether the plaintiff's financial harm *(damnum)* was classified as directly or indirectly caused by the defendant.[54] Consequently, the two types of efficient cause (direct or indirect) had a classificatory function in relation to the threshold question of the appropriate remedy.

The statutory *actio legis Aquiliae* provided for penal[55] and restorative[56] damages. To recover, the plaintiff had to establish both a direct causal

---

[51] Until 300 BC, the interpretation of the law, in particular, the *Twelve Tablets* was the prerogative of the College of Pontiffs, a quasi-religious body of public officials who passed down the law orally without providing reasons for their rulings. Pontifex Quintus Mucius Scaevola published the first systematic legal treatise, *De iure civili*, in the 80s BCE.

[52] Roman jurisprudence seems to have had close interaction with Roman rhetoric, which discussed concepts of proximate and remote cause as well as principal and antecedent causes. D Nörr, "Causam Mortis Praebere" in N MacCormick & P Birks (eds), *The Legal Mind: Essays for Tony Honoré*, Clarendon Press, Oxford, 1986.

[53] *Lex Aquilia* was a *plebiscite*, which was eventually incorporated into *Corpus Juris Civilis*. The statute contained three Chapters. Chapters I and III dealt with remedies for wrongfully caused *(damnum iniuria datum)* financial loss and damage to property. Chapter II, which became obsolete after the beginning of the 2nd century CE, provided a remedy for stipulators who were victims of fraud. For a discussion of the origins and nature of *lex Aquilia*, see Reinhard Zimmerman, supra, n42, at 955-7.

[54] Roman actions were litigated in two stages. The parties would go before the magistrate, the praetor, who would decide whether the dispute raised an issue recognised by the civil law, and which remedy should apply. Then, the *iudex*, a layman chosen by the parties from a list of qualified citizens, would conduct a trial and make determination. P Stein, "The Development of Law in Classical and Early Medieval Europe: Interpretation and Legal Reasoning in Roman Law" (1995) 70 *Chi-Kent L Rev* 1539.

[55] See n45. *Lex Aquilia* replaced fixed penalties for wrongful acts imposed under *Twelve Tablets* with a more flexible assessment of the damages suffered by the victim. There were also noxal actions, whereby a master who was sued for acts of a slave or a parent for the acts of a child, could hand over the slave or child to the plaintiff, either to be sold for compensation or to suffer private vengeance.

[56] A restorative *(rei persequendae)* action was intended to compensate the plaintiff for the actual loss he had suffered (an award in excess of the loss would be regarded as

connection between death or injury of a slave or four-footed grazing animal, and *iniuria*,[57] that is, the wrongful nature of the defendant's conduct. Initially, establishing efficient causation under *lex Aquilia* was not difficult, because the law required the cause of injury to be a direct and positive act "by the body to the body" *(corpore datum)*.[58] With time, liability was extended to blameworthy conduct causing death of the plaintiff's slave indirectly by dropping something on him, or drowning a slave by throwing him or her from a bridge. According to Celsus,[59] in drowning cases, it was irrelevant whether the immediate cause of the slave's death was the immediate impact with the water, exhaustion, or the force of current.[60] Nevertheless, while the requirement of direct positive action remained,[61] where the positive action led indirectly to loss, as when the defendant pushed someone who fell against and killed the plaintiff's slave,[62] the causal link would be regarded as too indirect[63] for it to be a case of "killing". However, Ulpian, writing at the time of Caracalla (211-217CE), commented that an action on the facts *(actio in factum)* would be granted for causing death.

It was in the final decades of the Republic,[64] that delictual liability was extended to indirectly caused wrongful death of slaves under praetorian policy actions[65] "in the spirit of the law"*(actiones utilis legis*

---

penal): E Metzger (ed), *A Companion to Justinian's Institutes*, Cornell University Press, Ithaca, New York, 1998, at pp224, 253.

57   The term *"iniuria"* had a number of meanings in Roman law. Ulpian distinguished the meaning of "iniuria" in the sense of insult (giving rise to an action for insult) from wrongful or illegal conduct which constituted fault for the specific purpose of Aquilian liability: D.9.2.5.1.

58   *Actio directa corpore corpori:* RW Lee, *The Elements of Roman Law*, 4th edn, Sweet & Maxwell, London (1956) at p395. Julian, writing under the Antonines, provided the following legal definition of killing: "A person is generally said to have killed if he had furnished a cause of death in any way whatever, but so far as the *lex Aquilia* is concerned, there will be liability only if the death resulted from some application of force, done as it were by one's own hand." D.9.2.51.pr.

59   Celsus worked in the time of Hadrian.

60   D.9.2.7.7; *Inst.* IV, 3, 16.

61   *Actio utilis corpori non corpore (quasi ex legis Aquilia)* D.47.2.51.

62   D.9.2.7.3.

63   For example, Julian disputing Proculus, pointed out that in relation to a defendant who set his dog against the plaintiff's slave, the form of action would depend on whether the defendant had actually held the dog at the time of attack or left the dog to perpetrate the attack without any physical assistance: D.9.2.11.5.

64   The Republic came to an end in 27 BCE.

65   Policy actions *(actiones utilis)* were formulated by analogy with the standard action, where the facts set out in the formula reflected the same policy underlying the standard action: Metzger, supra, n56, at p246.

Aquiliae)[66] and actions "on the facts" *(actiones in factum)*.[67] These actions were also used to expand liability under Chapter III of the *lex Aquilia* to include indirect conduct causing actual (physical) harm or loss to property.[68] Celsus distinguished between directly causing death, and furnishing an indirect cause of death.[69] He gave two examples: administration of poison instead of medicine, and handing a sword to a "madman" who, presumably, killed himself with it.[70] Labeo[71] observed that where an abortifacient was administered directly by pouring it down the woman's throat and she died, the conduct amounted to killing *(occidere)*, and fell within the *lex Aquilia*. By contrast, if the woman was handed the drug for self-administration and died, the person giving the abortifacient had not "killed" her, but had "caused her death" indirectly, since a voluntary act on her part intervened in the chain of events. This conduct was in the course of time treated by the lawyers and praetors as sufficient for liability *(mortis causam praestare)*, and action on the facts would be granted.[72] In other words, an indirect efficient cause came to be accepted as sufficient for liability.

Thus efficient causation became central to the question of liability under actions on the facts for *"mortis causam praebere"*, which extended delict to cover indirect loss occasioned without harmful physical contact.[73] A person would be liable to an action *in factum*, if by making smoke he killed or drove away another's bees.[74] An action on the facts for damages

---

[66] In post-classical law (ie, post Ulpian), *actio utilis legis Aquiliae* provided also a remedy to free persons who were wrongfully injured. D.9.2.13.pr.

[67] Praetorian edict allowed the formulation of actions on the facts *(actiones in factum)* sometime in the latter part of the 2nd century BCE. In these non-standard actions, the judge's verdict was determined by findings of fact. Gaius (G.3.219) did not mention action on the facts *(actio in factum)*: Reinhard Zimmerman, supra, n42, at pp981-2. In the *Digest*, the terms *actio in factum* and *actio utilis* are used interchangeably.

[68] Actionable loss included alteration of property, like causing wine to turn into vinegar. The term for the relevant damage, introduced by Celsus, was *"corrumpere"* (corrupted, spoiled). The defendant would be liable under an *actio in factum*: Zimmerman, supra, n42, at 984-5.

[69] Under actions on the facts, defendants were liable for "furnishing a cause of death". Celsus quoted by Ulpian in D.9.2.6.

[70] D.9.2.7.6.

[71] Labeo (- 10/11 CE). His *Libri posteriores* was an authoritative and systematic exposition of Roman law.

[72] D.9.2.9.pr.

[73] *Actio in factum nec corpore nec corpori (ad exemplum legis Aquiliae)*. For a discussion of *mortis causam praebere*, see Nörr, op cit, n52.

[74] Ulpian, *Digest*, 9.2.49.pr. Two millennia later, this Roman doctrine seems to have been the basis for a decision in *Sneesby v The Lancashire and Yorkshire Rly Co* [1875] 1 QB 42. In *Sneesby*, the English Court of Appeal found the defendant railway company liable in negligence to the plaintiffs for the loss of six head of cattle. The plaintiff's

would also lie against a defendant, who out of compassion, unchained the plaintiff's slave and enabled him to escape.[75] The action would lie, even though the plaintiff's loss of the slave amounted to merely economic and not to physical harm.[76] But then, economic loss *(damnum)* was regarded as being of the essence of the *lex Aquilia* and actions based on the analogy to it.[77]

Accordingly, as with humoral clinical medicine, the role of causation in the context of delictual remedies was adjectival – its identification and characterisation as either direct or indirect (furnishing the cause of death or loss) classified the conduct, which in turn, determined the nature of remedy.

Attribution of Liability

In addition to causation, fault was needed for Aquilian liability. Liability would be attributed to the defendant only if the additional element of *iniuria*, in the sense of unlawfulness associated with fault, was present. Ulpian provided two interrelated tests for establishing *iniuria*: *non iure*, that is absence of right (justification),[78] and fault *(culpa)*.[79] Broadly, the notion of fault or blameworthiness[80] was the determining criterion of liability. Broadly, the notion of blameworthiness involved either: deliberate, intentional fault, as when someone intentionally maimed or

---

employees were driving the cattle across a level crossing operated by the defendants, when several railway trucks were negligently allowed to run down the tracks, separating the beasts from the drovers. As a result, the cattle "became infuriated", rushed away, and were eventually found lying dead or dying on another part of the railway.

75   Justinian's *Institutes*, 4.3.16. R Evans-Jones & G MacCormack, "Obligations" in Metzger, supra, n56, at p189.

76   Ulpian provided an example of an actionable indirect cause of material loss in the case of a plaintiff who hired a plasterer to mend a vat. The plasterer punctured the side of the vat and, as a result, the wine contained therein ran out, to the plaintiff's loss. Ulpian, D.9.2.27.35.

77   Antony Honoré, personal communication.

78   Justinian's *Institutes*, 4.3.2: "to kill unlawfully is to kill without any right". When the Aquilian Act was enacted, the legal connotation of *"iniuria"* was *non iure* (without right). The liability was strict, but the defendant would be exonerated if he established that he was exercising a legal right such as self defence. Moreover, no liability would accrue under *lex Aquilia* in cases of killing by misadventure, providing there was no fault or carelessness on the part of the defendant: Justinian's *Institutes*, 4.3.3.

79   Gaius in the 2nd century CE defined "wrongful" exclusively in terms of fault: G.3.211.

80   D.9.2.5.1.

killed a slave, or, alternatively, unintentional but unreasonable[81] or careless[82] (negligent)[83] causing of harm.

The Romans, required both causation and culpability for responsibility under the *lex Aquilia* and its extensions. However, they distinguished between "causation" (culpability) and responsibility. Hence a problem arose when there was fault on both sides. If the slave killed was at fault and so was the defendant, then the act of each could be regarded as an efficient cause of the death or wound. In such cases, the plaintiff was barred unless the defendant intended the death etc, in which case the predominant fault was regarded as lying with the defendant, who could be regarded as both an efficient and a final cause of the death.

The defendant accused of having caused an injury could argue that though he caused (was responsible) for the harm, his conduct was not culpable (he was not at fault) because he had the right to perform the injurious act. In such case (an irrebuttable presumption would arise that) the defendant was not liable, and consequently, the harm caused to the plaintiff was not compensable. For example, if a defendant threw a javelin and accidentally killed the plaintiff's slave, his liability would depend on the presence or absence of justification and fault. If the defendant was a soldier practising in a place reserved for military exercises,[84] there would be no liability because he had the right to do what he did at the particular location. Conversely, if the defendant was not a soldier, liability may attach,[85] since a civilian would not have the right to practise javelin-throwing at a military training field. Likewise, a soldier practising javelin throwing in a non-designated area could be liable, for he had no right to practise in a public place.[86]

Moreover, *iniuria* through *culpa* could attach to either the injurer or the injured. For example, in the case of a killed slave, if the accident happened where the slave had no right to be, the slave's fault was regarded as cancelling out the defendant's fault, so that there was no liability on the defendant's part. The cause of death would be attributed to the slave's own fault. A slave possessing the right to be in the javelin training field, might

---

[81] Ulpian, D.9.2.5.2-3; Paul 9.2.6.
[82] Ulpian, D.9.2.7.2, 8.
[83] Gaius, D.9.2.8.
[84] Justinian's *Institutes*, 4.3.4.
[85] Ibid.
[86] Ibid. The echo of attributing fault according to the appropriateness of place in which the harm-producing activity took place can be found in *Mitchell v Allestry* (1676) 1 Vent 295, 3 Keb 650, where the court held that "It was the defendant's fault, to bring a wild horse into such a place [Little Lincoln's Inn Fields] where mischief might probably be done, by reason of the concourse of people."

still be adjudged to be at fault (contributory negligence),[87] on the basis that he failed to take care for his own safety.[88]

In the javelin throwing examples, the act causing accidental death remained the same. The analysis focused on the parties' respective legal rights and culpability of their conduct, which determined fault and consequent attribution of liability for the killing. However, whenever killing was deliberate, moral policy considerations dictated that the Aquilian action would lie irrespective of the right to practise javelin or the slave's contributory negligence.[89]

Direct and Indirect Causation in Multifactorial Settings

The example of the javelin throwing accident illustrated how the attribution of legal causality between two events depends on parties' perspectives. The plaintiff, whose slave had the right to be at the place where the accident had occurred, would attribute cause of death to the defendant's careless action in throwing the javelin. However, the javelin thrower arguing contributory negligence, would attribute the slave's death to the latter's careless walking into the javelin's trajectory. Medicine would attribute the cause of death to the piercing wound occasioned by a sharp instrument.

The issue of attribution of causal responsibility is even more difficult in cases with multifactorial causation. Roman jurists did not develop jurisprudence relating to direct and indirect causation in a multifactorial setting, even when they provided examples of it, as in the following passage from Ulpian:

> Further, Mela writes that, when some people were playing with a ball, one of them hit it hard and knocked the hands of a barber with the result that the throat of a slave whom the barber was shaving was cut by the jerking of the razor. In which of the parties does the fault lie? For it is he who is liable under the *lex Aquilia*. Proculus says the blame is the barber's, and surely, if he was doing shaving in a place where people customarily played games or where there was much going to and fro, the blame will be imputed to him; but it is no bad point in reply that if someone entrusts himself to a barber who has his chair in a dangerous place he has only himself to blame for his own misfortune.[90]

---

[87]   Contributory negligence was a complete defence: A Borkowski, *Textbook on Roman Law*, Blackstone Press, London, 1994, at p308.

[88]   D.9.2.9.4.

[89]   D.9.2.9.4.

[90]   D.9.2.11.pr.

Both Proculus[91] and Mela[92] argued the issue of fault and consequent liability on the basis that the direct, positive, though unintentional, action of the barber was the efficient (legal) cause of the slave's death. According to Proculus, since the barber's jerking motion was unintentional, his liability for causing the slave's death would rest on the attribution of fault to his conduct of setting up a stall in a dangerous place. Mela posited that the cause of the accident should be ascribed to the victim's own fault in acquiescing to be shaved in a dangerous place. Neither jurist asked whether the person who hit the ball "hard" and thus sparked the chain of events was at fault. This omission naturally followed the right-as-justification reasoning, because as long as the ball-player had the right to play ball in that place, he was not at fault. Yet, hitting the ball hard in the direction of a nearby barber's stall could amount to a careless, or even reckless act.[93]

It might be that Mela and Proculus purposely did not discuss possible liability of the ball-thrower because they focused on the *lex Aquilia* rather than praetorian actions and actions on the facts, concentrating on direct rather than indirect causation. Nevertheless, it is odd that they did not analyse the chain of causation in this case. Some 1800 years later, in the case of *Scott v Shepherd*,[94] the Court of Common Pleas would grapple with a not dissimilar case. The defendant, Shepherd, threw a lighted squib made of gunpowder from the street into the market-house. The squib landed on the stall of Yates. Willis, who was close by, instantly picked it up and, to prevent an injury to himself, threw the squib across the market-house onto the stall of Ryal, who in order to save his goods, at once picked up the still lighted squib and threw it away. It struck the face of the plaintiff, Scott, exploded, and blinded him in one eye. Three out of four judges found Shepherd liable in battery because Willis and Ryal acted under a compulsive necessity, and not as free agents. Consequently, their actions did not break the chain of direct causation. Likewise, it could be arguable that in Ulpian's example, the razor's cut was caused by the ball's impact on the barber's hands and thus was directly attributable to the thrower.

In *Scott v Shepherd*, William Blackstone dissented, saying that Scott's injury was indirect, and therefore should sound in action on the case – a common law remedy for indirectly caused injuries. Again, this conclusion would have been open in the ball-thrower's case, for, in contradistinction to the javelin-thrower's act which directly caused the slave's death, the ball-thrower's act was an indirect cause of the slave's throat being cut by the

---

91 Proculus, jurist and law teacher worked in the middle of the 1st century CE.
92 Mela, an Augustan jurist contemporary of Labeo.
93 Ulpian does not mention whether the player was aware of the nearby barber's stall when he hit the ball.
94 *Scott v Shepherd* (1773) 2 Wm Bl 892; 3 Wils 403; [1558-1774] All ER 295.

barber. Though it has to be acknowledged that whereas Shepherd clearly did not have the right to throw the lighted squib into the market, one must assume that the ball-player did have the right to play ball in the street – at any rate the possible fault on the ball-player's part is not discussed by Mela and Proculus.[95]

It has been suggested that Roman jurists concentrated on analysis of fault because "it was easier to decide difficult cases by pinpointing the incidence of fault than by asking who had actually caused the loss."[96] But it is also arguable, that while the Romans recognised the possibility or even likelihood of more than one efficient cause of the death or injury, they held that as a matter of corrective justice the plaintiff could not recover if one of the causes was the fault of himself or his slave.[97] The above examples suggest that the practical result of Roman legal reasoning may have been the same as that envisaged by the Aristotelian concept of corrective justice, even though Aristotle probably placed an emphasis on evening out "losses" and "gains" in terms of causation, whereas Romans approached the balance of justice in terms of fault.

Multiple Sufficient Causes: Mortal and Fatal Wounds

Determination of liability in cases where an assailant mortally wounded a slave who died from a subsequently inflicted fatal wound raised the question of multiple sufficient causes.[98] This question was examined in the *Digest* by three Roman jurists. Ulpian attributed to Celsus the following passage:

> Celsus writes that if one attacker inflicts a mortal wound on a slave and another person later finishes him off, he who struck the earlier blow will not be liable for a killing, but for wounding, because he [the slave] actually perished as the result of another wound. The latter assailant will be held liable because he did the killing.[99]

---

[95]   A point made by Antony Honoré in personal communication.

[96]   R Evans-Jones & G MacCormack, supra, n75, at p88.

[97]   Professor Antony Honoré, personal communication.

[98]   JS Kortmann in *"Ab alio ictu(s)*: Misconceptions about Julian's View on Causation" (1999) 20 *Legal History* 95, refers to this passage of Ulpian as dealing with the issue of "supervening cause", which is not entirely accurate in view of the fact that Ulpian describes the first wound as "mortal" *(mortifero)*, indicating that the slave was certain to die from it.

[99]   D.9.2.11.3.

Likewise, according to Ulpian, the attacker who mortally wounded a slave whose death was subsequently accelerated by the collapse of a house or a shipwreck, or a blow, would be liable merely for wounding.[100] Julian,[101] while discussing a case very similar to Ulpian's, provided a conclusion inconsistent with the first two examples, when he wrote that:

> ... it is not only those who wound so as to deprive at once of life who will be liable for a killing in accordance with the *lex* but also those who inflict an injury which is certain to prove fatal. Accordingly, if someone wounds a slave mortally and then after a while someone else inflicts a further injury, as a result of which he dies sooner than would otherwise have been the case, it is clear that both assailants are liable for killing.[102]

Both Ulpian and Julian assumed that the conduct of the first assailant in each of the three cases was blameworthy, and thus culpable. In issue, therefore was the culpability of the supervening fatal event. The function of efficient causation in the three examples was classificatory. However, this time, its purpose was to determine the scope of legal responsibility in relation each event for the slave's death (rather than the type of appropriate remedy). The three "wounding" cases provide a classic example of the interplay between medical causal uncertainty and its legal consequences. In each example, it was assumed that both the "mortal" and the "fatal" wound was sufficient to cause death, but medicine could not determine which wound was a significant and which was an insubstantial cause of death. In other words, medicine could probably explain the organic reasons of death, but could not apportion the causative legal factors. The law had to find its own way of solving this conundrum.

The Roman jurists adopted two distinct approaches. Ulpian's approach was to dissect the facts and to draw therefrom strict logical conclusions. The mortally wounded slave was still alive when an independent supervening event killed him. It was not known – and could not be known – for how long he would have lived. Ulpian therefore attributed the cause of death to the supervening event, which left the original attacker with legal liability merely for wounding. It was irrelevant to the scope of the first assailant's legal – as against moral – liability, whether or not the

---

[100] D.9.2.15.1.

[101] Julian (Iulianus Salivius), working under Hadrian, wrote 90 volumes of *Digesta*.

[102] D.9.2.51.pr. According to A Watson, *The Law of Obligations in the Later Roman Republic*, Clarendon Press, Oxford, 1965 at 245, the proposition contained in D.2.51.1: "This rule has the authority of the ancient jurists, who decided that, if a slave were injured by several persons but it was not clear which actually killed him, they would all be liable under the lex Aquilia" is an interpolation by Justinian for which there is no authority.

independent supervening event was blameworthy. If it was blameworthy, then *lex Aquilia* would apply.

Julian resolved the issue in policy terms. On the basis of essentially identical facts, he attributed legal liability for the killing to both assailants, though he stated that each of the culprits would have to pay the owner a differentiated amount in damages.[103] From a causal point of view, Julian seemed to have assumed that the inevitability of the slave's imminent death justified the imposition of liability even if the slave did not in fact die of the first wound. Since the first wrongdoer has not in fact killed the slave, the extension of liability was based on policy grounds. Thus, Julian's conclusion did not stem from an investigation of the causative factors; rather, it was based on a broad notion of blameworthiness and the social consideration that "Misdeeds should not escape unpunished, and it is not easy to decide if one is more blameworthy than the other."[104]

Julian was not entirely satisfied with his analysis, for he ruefully observed that "Indeed, it can be proved by innumerable examples that civil law has accepted things for the general good that do not accord with pure logic".[105]

The appeal to a greater social or moral good as an excuse for the failure to rigorously investigate and determine causation also tends to underlay the modern law of causation in the context of negligence.

Loss Caused Through Careless Performance of Duty

Apart from harm caused by careless positive direct conduct, *actio legis aquiliae* provided a remedy for careless performance of duty. Fault would be attributed to someone who negligently performed services under a contract or for a fee.[106] In general, the standard of care for the purposes of

---

[103] D.9.2.51.2. In the 20th century, a similar approach to compensation for wrongfully inflicted personal injuries, which are aggravated or exacerbated by subsequent tortious events, was adopted by the House of Lords in the controversial case of *Baker v Willoughby* [1970] AC 467.

[104] D.9.2.51.2.

[105] D.9.2.51.2. (Julian, *Digest*, Book 86).

[106] Rendering of services for a fee *(locatio conductio operarum)* was regarded as "mercenary activity", and limited to services that were usually performed by slaves *(opera illiberales)*, and lower class artisans or craftsmen. In the Republican Rome, the majority of doctors were either slaves *(servi)* or freedmen *(liberti)*. The minority of wealthy Roman citizens who practised medicine *(medicus ingenuus)*, would do so under a contract of *mandatum*. On Roman law of contract, see: A Borkowski, supra, n87, at p267.

delictual liability was very high.[107] The *Digest* stated that "under the *lex Aquilia* even the slightest degree of fault counts".[108] This meant that liability attached once damage was shown to follow directly from wrongful failure to attain the required standard.

In contradistinction to Classical Greece, where the law absolved from blame a physician whose patient died while under his care, both the *Digest* and *Institutes* provide examples of medical culpability. The difference in approach to medical liability may have been due to the fact that although Greek rational medicine became known to the Romans in the third century BCE, it was never popular.[109] Preference was given to traditional Roman medicine: a combination of folk remedies and magical incantations invoking the help of the supernatural.[110] The rational Roman lawyers, must have regarded these healing practices with unease.[111] Indeed, Ulpian, discussing claims for fees, distinguished between proper doctors, including specialists, who can sue for their fees, and those who resort to incantation or exorcism. He called the latter impostors, though, he added, there are those who say that the incantations etc have done them good.[112] Be that as it may, Ulpian quoted Proculus saying that if a surgeon operated negligently on a slave, the owner could have an action either under contract or under the *lex Aquilia*.[113] Gaius observed that "the law is just the same if one [doctor] misuses a drug, or, if having operated efficiently, the aftercare is neglected; the wrongdoer will not go free, but is deemed to be guilty of negligence".[114]

Ulpian's statement regarding negligently performed operations, and Gaius' instance of misuse of drugs would fall within Aquilian liability because of the requirement of wrongful positive conduct causing loss to the plaintiff was fulfilled. However, Gaius' example of the failure to provide post-operative care involved an omission, rather than positive conduct.

---

[107] The parties could vary the standard of care by terms of the contract.

[108] *Digest*, 9.2.44.pr.

[109] This may have been due to the fact that majority of Greek physicians in Rome were slaves or freedmen. V Nutton, "Healers in the Medical Market Place: Towards a Social History of Graeco-Roman Medicine" in A Wear (ed), *Medicine in Society*, Cambridge University Press, Cambridge, 1992, at p39.

[110] Under the Empire (31 BCE - 493 CE), cultic, frequently Oriental in origin, and superstitious faith healing practices were widespread. DW Amunden & GB Ferngren, "Evolution of the Physician/Patient Relationship: Antiquity Through Renaissance" in EE Shelp (ed), *The Clinical Encounter*, D Reidel Pub Co, Dordrecht, 1983, at p13.

[111] Not all Romans were scornful of Greek physicians. In 46 BCE, Julius Caesar presented all free-born Greek physicians on Roman soil with the right of Roman citizenship.

[112] *Digest* 50.13.1.3.

[113] Ulpian, *Digest*, 9.2.7.8.

[114] Gaius (130-180 CE) probably wrote his *Institutes* around 161 CE. *Digest*, 9.2.8.pr; Justinian's *Institutes* 4.3.7.

Omissions, as a general rule, did not give rise to an action in delict in classical law,[115] except under *actio in factum* or *actio utilis legis Aquiliae*, where the defendant had previously made a positive undertaking and then failed to carry it out.[116] Admittedly, this part of the commentary in the *Digest* is dealing with the fault rather than causal issues of what amounts to killing or wounding. Nevertheless, Gaius would have assumed that the doctor's fault was a cause of injury or death, since otherwise the action would not lie.

The example of post-operative care presages some contemporary conceptual problems involving the issue of fault and external as against inherent causes of harm. Many medical malpractice suits turn on the question whether liability for the plaintiff's harm should be attributed to the nature of the medical condition or to the conduct of the medical attendant. In other words, in determining causation, should the law examine why the slave died or should it merely consider how he died, thus conflating fault with causation.[117]

The structure of the *Digest* whereby key words in the law were discussed in turn, led the Roman jurists to focus separately on the different elements in the action – the defendant's conduct, including its relation to the outcome; the issue of fault, including the fault on the part of the plaintiff's slave; the right to sue; the damages or penalty recoverable. Ulpian's and Gaius' commentary on medical negligence occurs at point where fault *(iniuria)* is being analysed.[118] Consequently examination of liability for medical negligence is confined to the question whether the doctor was at fault, leaving aside the question of what his fault, if shown to be present, may or may not have caused. The inquiry into causal processes, so far as contemporary medicine allowed of it, fell under the discussion of what constituted killing, wounding, etc. Naturally, there may have been a tendency to suppose that the doctor, had he not been at fault, could have cured the patient or improved his or her condition.[119]

The question "how" did the slave die could be answered by stating that he died without having received a visit from the surgeon, thus causally linking slave's death with the surgeon's failure to attend him. The question "why" did he die would have pointed the legal inquiry in the direction of

---

[115] Roman law did not recognise the concept of pure nonfeasance: R Evans-Jones & G MacCormack, supra, n75, at p190.

[116] PJ Thomas, *Introduction to Roman Law*, Kluwer Law and Taxation Publishers, Deventer, Netherlands, 1986, at p125.

[117] Inquiry into how the patient died is more appropriate for determining fault than causation.

[118] *Digest* 9.2.4 to 9.2.11 pr.

[119] Antony Honoré, personal communication.

the slave's medical condition. For example, his death might have been caused by post-operative heart failure or septicemia – both conditions were described in the *Hippocratic Corpus*,[120] and both were fatal until the 1940s. Admittedly, there is a suggestion that the surgeon might have escaped liability if he could establish that he did provide some aftercare. This is because he would then be able to argue that the death was due to a cause other than his own neglect. Since he fulfilled his obligations under the terms of agreement, no fault should be attributed to his conduct.

Confined, though it is to the issue of fault – "what amounts to *culpa*?" – the discussion of post-operative care did not exclude entirely the issue of causation. It would have been known in Roman times, just as it is today, that some patients may die with the best of care while others will survive with none. Gaius thus provided an early example of attribution of causal liability based on policy considerations involving general creation and enforcement of acceptable normative standards under the law of obligations,[121] rather than through determination of particular medical causes.

Conclusion

The examination of the approach to causation in Hippocratic medicine and Roman law of delict suggest that in both disciplines, identification of material causes had a classificatory function. In medicine, ascertainment of the efficient or triggering causes was vital to the diagnosis and treatment of humoral imbalances. In law, classification of a cause as direct or indirect determined the cause of action, be it Aquilian, praetorian, or on the facts. In both disciplines causal analysis was directed backwards – from the present medical condition or legal set of circumstances to the source or act that caused the transition from the state of physical, psychological or economic well-being to illness, harm or loss.

Moreover, in both disciplines triggering causes were considered to be a matter of factual evidence drawn from observation and experience. In medicine, latent causes were only accepted if based on facts. But, unlike the ascertainment of triggering causes, knowledge of latent causes was not always essential for efficacious treatment. For example, humoral medical

---

120 There is no indication in the *Digest* whether the surgeon was practising classical Greek medicine or traditional Roman medicine, which essentially involved use of herbs and domestic remedies.

121 Roman concept of obligation connoted a legal relationship between two individuals under which one acquired a right and the other the correlative duty. R Evans-Jones & G MacCormack, supra, n75, at p127.

theory held that the heart was a furnace generating and distributing heat throughout the body. Consequently, ancient Greek physicians, who meticulously observed the signs and symptoms of heart failure did not correlate them with disordered cardiac function. Instead, the syndromes were attributed to the phlegm (cold humour) moving from the brain to the chest.[122] This notwithstanding, they were able to distinguish between many different syndromes, and in the case of pleural effusion, prescribe treatment to drain fluid in the chest, a procedure which did not differ too much from contemporary techniques.[123]

In modern medical practice, the diagnostic process would still proceed from symptoms to diagnosis of syndromes, disease entities and aetiologies. Though today, the medical theory requires that the correlative reasoning regarding medical diagnosis and causation be based on estimates of statistical probability.[124] However, application of statistical probabilities to diagnosis, aetiology and prognosis in the context of a particular condition presented by the patient is still to be fully worked out. Moreover, even today, not all causes of medical conditions are known and not all factual information is totally reliable.

In the face of causal uncertainty, modern physicians, just like their ancient Greek counterparts concentrate on alleviating symptoms. For instance, hypertension or high blood pressure may be caused by a number of medical conditions including kidney disease and uraemia or other toxic conditions; endocrine disorders such as hyperthyroidism and acromegaly; artery disease which reduces elasticity, and tumours of the central portion (medulla) of the adrenal gland.[125] However, primary or "essential hypertension" has no apparent specific organic cause. If a known organic cause cannot be found, the diagnosis will be that of primary or "essential hypertension", and the condition will be treated symptomatically.

Roman law focused on the circumstantial or factual connection between the defendant's conduct and the plaintiff's harm, but determined the ultimate question of liability on the basis of both causation and fault,

---

[122] Hippocratic Corpus, *The Sacred Disease* IX (18); AM Katz, "Evolving Concepts of Heart Failure: Cooling Furnace, Malfunctioning Pump, Enlarging Muscle" (1997) 3 *Journal of Cardiac Failure* 319 at 322.

[123] "Incise over the third rib, down to the bone, then drill through the rib with a trephine. The perforation completed, remove a little water and after evacuation, put in a plug of raw flax, and over this a soft sponge: you must then apply a bandage so that the plug does not fall out. You must take off the water over a period of twelve days, once daily; ... on the thirteenth [day] evacuate all of the water. For the remaining time if more water forms, you must remove it." Cited by AM Katz, op cit, n122, at 322.

[124] N Laor & J Agassi, supra, n4, at p35.

[125] RL Memmler, BJ Cohen & DL Wood, *The Human Body in Health and Disease*, JB Lippincott Co, New York, 1992, at p228.

neither being sufficient by itself for liability. This meant that efficient causality was ascertained by asking how rather than why the harm and its alleged legal causes were linked. In the modern law of torts, the distinction based on direct and indirect causation is nominally preserved in the divide between trespass and action on the case. The distinction is clearest in torts of trespass to land and nuisance, but it has become rather fuzzy in the tort of negligence.[126] Moreover, in the classic delictual paradigm, the wording of the *lex* and the *formulae* to give effect to it suggest that the *iniuria* issue and the causal issue were taken together *(iniuria occiderit)*. In Ulpian's commentary *iniuria* was discussed before *occiderit*.[127] This paradigm was followed in the tort of negligence. Fault, measured in terms of the defendant's response to foreseeable risk of harm,[128] is determined first, and then legal nexus in terms of causation may or may not be found between the culpable conduct and the alleged harm. For example, when a modern plaintiff complains about an injury in the form of hypertension allegedly due to the wrongdoing of the defendant employer, the defendant's lawyer, while admitting the client's fault may deny liability on the grounds of causation.[129] This is because legal liability will be attributed to the defendant only if the plaintiff can show that it was the defendant's wrongful conduct rather than such factors as death of a loved one, stressful divorce, gambling or other addiction, that on the balance of probabilities, caused or materially contributed to the risk of the injury by way of hypertension.[130] Therefore, although scientific causal explanations are considered, ultimately, the decision is reached on the basis of policy considerations rather than a logical extrapolation from established facts. The analysis of "wounding" and medical malpractice cases in the *Digest* illustrates how Roman jurists approached the issue of causation and fault.

---

[126] In *Gray v Motor Accident Commission* (1998) 73 ALJR 45, the High Court of Australia accepted that a case where the defendant deliberately drove his motor car into the plaintiff could be litigated in negligence.

[127] Antony Honoré, personal communication.

[128] The High Court of Australia in *Nagle v Rottnest Island Authority* (1993) 177 CLR 423; [1993] 67 ALJR 426 at 429, stated that: "A risk may constitute a foreseeable risk even though it is unlikely to occur. It is enough that the risk is not far-fetched or fanciful." Notably, the adjective "reasonable" which used to accompany the notion of foreseeability was not included in the definition of a foreseeable risk.

[129] In the process of determining to whom or to what event responsibility for the plaintiff's injury should be attributed, the law has regard to both "causing harm" and "enabling others (or other things) to do harm." See HLA Hart & T Honoré, *Causation in the Law*, 2nd edn, Clarendon Press, Oxford, 1985, at p133.

[130] *McGhee v National Coal Board* [1973] 1 WLR 1; cf *Wilsher v Essex Area Health Authority* [1988] AC 1974; in Australia, see *Chappel v Hart* (1998) 195 CLR 232; *Kavanagh v Akhtar* (1998) 45 NSWLR 588.

The shift in emphasis from factual causation to legal causation has been exacerbated in the modern law of negligence by the test of fault defined as failure to foresee the risk of harm. Romans adopted the standard of diligence and foreseeability. Paul,[131] quoting Sabinus[132] wrote that: "there is a fault when what could have been foreseen by a diligent man was not foreseen ..."[133] Modern law has incorporated the notion of risk into this test. The notion of foreseeability of the risk of harm, as against foreseeability of harm, is inchoate at best, but where the harm is known to have eventuated, asking whether the risk of it occurring was foreseeable amounts to foretelling the past.[134] This kind of reasoning makes the question of factual causation, in the sense of inductive reconstruction of past events, superfluous. Yet it is important for the intellectual credibility of the law, if not for the higher goal of achieving corrective justice, that a careful analysis be explicitly undertaken as to how the defendant's conduct and the plaintiff's harm are causatively linked. At the same time, the general question why something has happened belongs to the realm of sociology, politics, philosophy, and medical science. It is not the issue with which either Roman or modern courts have grappled. Their task has always been to determine whether some defined harm has been caused by some particular wrongful act.

---

[131]   Paulus Iulius, wrote many commentaries, including *ad Sabinum*, in the first decades of the 3rd century CE.

[132]   Sabinus Massurius, contemporary of Augustus, wrote an extensive and systematic treatise on *ius civile*, which was commented on by later jurists in works entitled *"Ad Sabinum"*: A Berger, "Encyclopedic Dictionary of Roman Law" in (1953) 43(2) *Transactions of the American Philosophical Society*, Philadelphia, at 687.

[133]   D.9.31.

[134]   For example, in *Rogers v Whitaker* (1992) 175 CLR 479, the High Court of Australia found that the risk of sympathetic ophthalmia that may occur in one out of 14,000 rarely performed procedures was foreseeable.

5 Rebels Without a Cause?: Judges, Medical and Scientific Evidence and the Uses of Causation

GARY EDMOND AND DAVID MERCER[*]

Introduction

If we aim to improve our understanding of the relationship between legal causation and scientific or medical causation, then attempts designed to identify epistemological essences or focus on the putatively discrete categories of law, science and medicine are likely to provide only limited assistance. From observations of law and science in practice, images of causation would seem to be epistemologically confusing and inconsistent. The following discussion is intended as an exploratory examination of how judges in a variety of legal settings (primarily personal injury cases) construct accounts of legal and scientific causation against a background of rhetorical resources and practical constraints. As an empirical generalisation, determining matters of causation in legal settings involves the management of a more heterogeneous assortment of concerns, constraints and resources, than is usually the case with the treatment of causation in scientific and medical contexts – perhaps with the exception of scientific controversies. In particular, those in the legal system tend to place greater emphasis on the apportionment of responsibility and explaining specific instances – the case at hand – rather than, as is often the case in scientific settings, making generalisations about classes of

---

[*]   Gary Edmond, School of Law, Adelaide University. David Mercer, Senior Lecturer in the Science and Technology Studies Program at the University of Wollongong. The authors thank John Keeler for his comments on a draft of this chapter.

relationships.[1] However, as we shall see, on occasion even the causal pronouncements in specific legal settings and judgments appear designed to have more general social implications.

Images of causation are not homogeneous among the sciences. Scientific and legal textbooks propose, often in ideal philosophical terms, standards by which an explanation may be classified as causal. Notwithstanding these idealised descriptions, in practical contexts different scientific sub-disciplines may hold different visions of the types of explanations that can be classed as causal. In these diverse scientific settings essential methodological and philosophical categories may be of little relevance or utility. Among the sciences as well within scientific sub-disciplines there may be differing perceptions about what constitutes an adequate causal explanation and even a relevant area of inquiry.

Historian of science Robert Proctor identifies differences among medical and scientific explanations for the cause of cancer (an area of legal and scientific causation we will explore more fully below). For example, in epidemiology causes for cancer may be sought by looking at the "variations in the practices of specific populations to identify agents or circumstances that might cause cancer".[2] Debates over the adequacy of the identification of a cause often involve considerations of the statistical strength of association between the suspected agent and the cancer, latency periods, consistency between studies, dose-response correlations and general assessments of biological plausibility. If the statistical associations are considered sufficiently compelling, then detailed explanation and the identification of specific biological processes may not need to be understood in depth before a causal relationship will be confidently attributed. For molecular biologists, however, the question of the causes of cancer may by focused quite differently:

> The questions of interest in molecular biology are often questions that abstract from particular causal agents. The questions are typically: What makes a cancer cell begin to grow? What genetic loci are altered in the process, and what does this do to cellular function? Why does the body's immune system not reject a tumor as foreign, and how might immunity be reversed? The molecular approach generally looks to processes

---

[1]   HT Engelhardt, "Relevant Causes: Their Designation in Medicine and Law" in S Spicker, J Healey & H Engelhardt (eds), *The Law Medicine Relation: A Philosophical Exploration*, D Reidel Publishing Company, Dordrecht, 1981, at p123; T Halper, "Time, Law and Responsibility: Additional Thoughts on Causality" in S Spicker, J Healey & H Engelhardt (eds), *The Law Medicine Relation: A Philosophical Exploration*, D Reidel Publishing Company, Dordrecht, 1981, at p129.

[2]   R Proctor, *Cancer Wars: How Politics Shapes What We Know and Don't Know About Cancer*, Basic Books, New York, 1995, at p257.

underlying a broad spectrum of cancers – and not just to causes of specific tumors (asbestos induced mesothelioma for instance). Molecular biologists may question the entire notion of cause, as when Harold Varmus of the National Institutes of Health cautioned that "You can't do experiments to see what causes cancer. It's not an accessible problem, and its not the sort of thing scientists can afford to do."[3]

Even within similar areas of scientific practice, some scientists may accept a particular form of explanation as causal whilst others may only adopt it conditionally and display a degree of agnosticism as to whether or not such an explanation is epistemologically warranted. Drawing upon an historical example, Newton's theory of universal gravitation provided a causal explanation which quickly dominated natural philosophical thought with respect to explanations of celestial and terrestrial motion. It was elegant and efficacious. Nevertheless, the idea of gravitation working by "action at a distance" without a clear mechanical entity to explain its operation contravened a range of contemporary commitments and troubled many of the proponents of the mechanical natural philosophy, who were trying to expunge – from natural philosophical endeavours – forms of causal explanation which did not rely on the more mechanically plausible direct physical interaction of atoms and corpuscles.[4] Eventually gravitation came to be understood as a satisfactory causal explanation, and influenced the sorts of explanation that were conceived as theoretically acceptable.

Writers such as Thomas Kuhn and Barry Barnes have argued that what is classed as a causal explanation in the sciences is invariably linked to how it conforms to existing theoretical frameworks and commitments as well as its perceived practical and theoretical utility. Abstract philosophical and scientific formulations (or canons) about what can be considered as a cause are of limited guidance. As Kuhn explained:

> To describe the cause or causes of an event is to explain why it occurred. Causes figure in physical explanations, and physical explanations are generally causal. Recognizing that much, however is to confront again the intrinsic subjectivity of some of the criteria governing the notion of cause ... [and] ... new canons of explanation are born with new theories on which they are to a considerable extent, parasitic.[5]

---

[3] Ibid.

[4] For an overview and introduction to some of the literature consider B Easlea, *Witchhunting, Magic and the New Philosophy: An Introduction to the Debates of the Scientific Revolution 1450-1750*, Harvester Press, Brighton, 1980.

[5] T Kuhn, "Concepts of Cause in the Development of Physics" in T Kuhn, *The Essential Tension*, Chicago University Press, Chicago, 1977, pp21, 29-30. See also B Barnes, "Belief Action and Determinism: the Causal Explanation of Scientific Change" in

Like notions of scientific causation, legal causation has a body of literature and some overlapping abstract philosophical canons but, as in the sciences, these idealised and frequently abstract categories provide resources and malleable constraints – not binding guides to practice.

Rather than try to extract the essences or classify the similarities and differences between causation in science and medicine and causation in law, we intend to illustrate some of the rhetorical processes, dilemmas and challenges, confronting judicial attempts to establish satisfactory causal explanations utilising scientific and medical evidence. In examining the assessment of expert evidence in legal settings it is useful to avoid the *a priori* demarcation of the legal elements of a causal explanation from the scientific elements. These types of demarcation are usually among the areas of active contestation, definition and "boundary working" undertaken by the protagonists in any particular litigation.[6] Instead, it is more useful to conceptualise images of scientific causation and legal causation as resources and constraints that the participants (judges in the following analysis) strategically deploy and resist.

Images of legal causation provide a more formal and less flexible set of resources than images of scientific causation because it is ultimately in the legal domain that legitimacy is most important. This is not to suggest that images of scientific and medical causation are completely malleable in legal settings. Because both judicial and scientific authority are premised upon images of rationality, where legal decisions involve the use of scientific or medical evidence there are invariably pressures for the decision to appear consistent with what is usually characterised as reliable scientific knowledge.[7] Any deviations, apparent or otherwise, require careful explanation, disclaimers, or skilful deflection. A decision which appears to arbitrarily dismiss scientific authority or blatantly assert the primacy of legal authority may have difficulty in maintaining its

---

B Barnes, *Scientific Knowledge and Sociological Theory*, Routledge and Kegan Paul, London, 1974, pp71-4: "The background of normality forms the set of unchanged necessary conditions against which the causal story stands out and operates as an intelligible communication the cause is a necessary condition in which we are interested; in labelling it, we define a taken for granted background of normality in terms of which our utterance makes sense ... in science it is a crucial function of theoretical entities that they are invoked as causes, to explain events or phenomena."

6 T Geiryn, *Cultural Boundaries of Science: Credibility on the Line,* Chicago University Press, Chicago, 1998; G Edmond, "Science in Court: Negotiating the Meaning of a 'Scientific' Experiment during a Murder Trial and Some Limits to Legal Deconstruction for the Public Understanding of Law and Science" (1998) 20 *Sydney Law Review* 361.

7 G Edmond, "Deflating *Daubert*: *Kumho Tire Co v Carmichael* and the inevitability of *general* acceptance *(Frye)*" (2000) 23 *University of New South Wales Law Journal* 31.

legitimacy.[8] This seems particularly applicable to mass torts, high profile litigation and cases involving well resourced parties. Social and institutional concerns, questions of policy and responsibility as well as the outcome of the specific case continuously inform the construction of legally acceptable causal explanations.

Law, Science, Judges, Society and Causation: Some Themes

Judges endeavouring to determine the adequacy of causal evidence in particular legal settings are engaged in acts of creative reconstitution and synthesis, requiring the alignment and management of various narrative themes and practical concerns. Some of these narratives and practical concerns are captured beneath the following rubrics:

- Alignment with the law;
- Evaluating scientific and medical knowledge;
- The specific contingencies of the case; and
- Responsibility and social policy.

These overlapping categories, intentionally more indicative than exhaustive, will be developed in more detail below.

Alignment with the law: precedent and the anticipated legal reception

Legal images of causation involve assessments and representations of similarities and differences between the present case and previous cases, consideration of the implications of particular representations of causation, and the relationship between scientific or medical evidence and the specific legal issue. In order to satisfy these requirement for the purposes of establishing legal causation, judges have at their disposal an extensive range of legal and other resources. Celebrated legal texts such as Hart and Honoré's *Causation in the Law*,[9] legal and folk philosophies of science, earlier judgments and common sense can all be invoked to strengthen the authority of legal decisions. Ideally, the construction of images of causation in legal settings should be "superficially transparent" and

---

8   R Smith & B Wynne (eds), *Expert Evidence: Interpreting Science in the Law*, Routledge, London, 1989; S Jasanoff, *Science at the Bar: Law, Science and Technology in America*, Harvard University Press, Cambridge, 1995.

9   H Hart & T Honoré, *Causation in the Law*, 2nd edn, Clarendon Press, Oxford, 1985.

"reflective". However, because legal constructions of causation are infused with policy considerations and more general conceptualisations of responsibility at law, transparency and reflection sometimes appear qualified or absent. Aligning questions of legal causation to medical and scientific causation and the specific evidence at hand is also rendered complex, both rhetorically and practically, because in many, perhaps most, contexts scientific and medical evidence presented to the court is packaged in anticipation of legal and judicial (sometimes appellate) expectations.[10] In mass toxic torts, such as the United States Bendectin litigation considered below, the process of integrating scientific, policy and legal considerations, may become highly refined. Some commentators have suggested that the integration of legal concerns with scientific and/or medical orientations is a major problem confronting contemporary legal systems and that the *two* domains should remain discrete.[11] Other commentators, most notably Roger Smith and Brian Wynne, have suggested that in it is quite unrealistic to expect such strict demarcations.[12] In fields like epidemiology, forensic pathology, forensic psychiatry, intellectual property and patent law, the growth and epistemological texture of scientific and medical knowledge, including practical concerns about what is eligible to be considered as a satisfactory causal explanation, have evolved concurrently with legal rules, processes and values.

This tendency toward what might be described as forms of hybridised law-science knowledge, with legal concerns entering into the practice and representations of science and medicine, provide interesting challenges for judges and commentators endeavouring to explain legal causation in relation to specific circumstances where there are competing expert opinions. To some extent it provides judges with a range of pre-assembled resources enabling them to more easily link legal and scientific concerns. However, it may also put pressure on judges to appear to address more general issues of scientific causation or appeal to common sense models of causation in order to differentiate their views from those of the experts. These two themes are addressed below, and in the case study which forms the second half of this chapter.

---

[10]   See below.
[11]   See below. P Huber, *Galileo's Revenge: Keeping Junk Science out of the Courtroom*, Basic Books, New York, 1991.
[12]   Smith & Wynne, op cit, n8; G Edmond & D Mercer, "Trashing 'Junk' Science" (1998) *Stanford Technology Law Review* <http://stanford.edu/STLR/Articles/Index.htm>.

Evaluating scientific and medical knowledge: comprehension, interpretation and reconstitution

Judges frequently endeavour to align the rhetorical domains of science and law with policy sensitivities. Consequently, the practice of constructing reliable scientific evidence in such settings can assume a variety of forms. At one level the perceived need for alignment encourages judges to show that they comprehend the general parameters of the scientific and/or medical evidence of causation presented by expert witnesses. This involves assessing not only general models of scientific and medical causation but also the scientific and medical knowledge relevant to ascriptions of specific causation. For example, has the specific plaintiff established causation between their condition and the harm allegedly flowing from the defendant's act or omission? Judges then, regularly need to provide tractable simplifications of scientific arguments presented before them. The existence of such simplified reconstructions of scientific and medical knowledge provides a ready source for recriminations, from experts outside the legal setting, who can claim that the simplification is a debased legal distortion, and for dissenting judges to criticise the understanding of scientific medical evidence by their peers.[13] (In the case study below, the trial judge was criticised by some of the appellate judges for his assessment of the scientific and medical evidence.)

It is presumably easier for judges, determining matters of scientific and/or medical causation, to produce and legitimate closure when expert disagreement is "shallow" and there are few conspicuous policy or social implications associated with the instant case. In contrast, in case congregations, class actions and where policy matters are sensitive, and scientific disagreement more intense, judges may find themselves being called upon to make difficult, *de facto* scientific, judgments about causation. This may provide some insight into judicial requests for alternative, usually more technocratic, fact-finding mechanisms including the use of expert panels in mass torts in the United States and court-appointed experts in civil litigation in the United Kingdom.[14] In areas of

---

[13] S Hilgartner, "The Dominant View of Popularisation: Conceptual Problems, Political Uses" (1990) 20 *Social Studies of Science* 519; G Edmond & D Mercer, "Scientific Literacy and the Jury: Reconsidering Jury Competence" (1997) 6 *Public Understanding of Science* 329.

[14] See below. With respect to expert panels, compare S Jasanoff, "Expert Games in Silicon Gel Breast Implant Litigation" in M Freeman & H Reece (eds), *Science in Court*, Dartmouth, Aldershot, 1998, at p83 and L Walker & J Monahan, "Scientific Authority: The Breast Implant Litigation and Beyond" (2000) 86 *Virginia Law Review* 801. In relation to court-appointed experts see G Edmond, "Judicial Representations of

long-standing scientific controversy, the legal system may become one of the primary locations for the resolution of debates about scientific and medical causation. In this context, the example of the litigation surrounding Bendectin is instructive.

Over the decade or so of Bendectin litigation in the United States, there was considerable debate around the types of scientific evidence best suited to determining questions of medical and scientific (and legal) causation in relation to the plaintiffs' injuries. The plaintiffs alleged that their birth defects were caused by the maternal ingestion of the anti-nausea (morning sickness) drug Bendectin (Debendox in Australia) during the first trimester of pregnancy. Assessments of the plaintiffs' claims involved not only assessments of the credibility of various experts but extended to include the credibility and comparative value of different types of scientific knowledge and their causal relevance.

The ability to shift the appropriate locus of relevant causation provided the parties and the judges with multiple sites to contest causation and explain its legal significance. Epidemiological debates were not restricted to general causation but included assessments of the appropriateness of extrapolations to the circumstances of specific individuals. The number of studies undertaken, their type, the degree of consistency between them and the status of meta-analyses were also subjected to debate and enrolment as resources informing and explaining legal representations of causation. Further, the role and significance of non-epidemiological evidence was also contested and frequently weighed against the epidemiological record.[15] The judicial balancing of different types of scientific evidence is captured in the following extract from an appeal in the case of *Richardson by Richardson v Richardson-Merrell, Inc*:

Scientific Evidence" (2000) 63 *Modern Law Review* 216 at 241-50; I Freckelton & H Selby, *Expert Evidence*, Law Book Co, Sydney, 1993-...; I Freckelton, *The Trial of the Expert*, Oxford University Press, Melbourne, 2002 (forthcoming).

[15]   M Green, *Bendectin and Birth Defects,* University of Pennsylvania Press, Philadelphia, 1996; J Sanders, *Bendectin on Trial: A Study of Mass Tort Litigation*, University of Michigan Press, 1998. An example of an appellate court, early in the Bendectin litigation cycle, recognising and attributing weight to the non-epidemiological evidence is provided by DC Court of Appeal in *Oxendine v Merrell Dow Pharmaceuticals, Inc*, 506 A 2d 1100 at 1104 (1986). This case was reversed in the mid 1990s according to what was then described as the weight of the evidence supporting the safety of Bendectin rendering the plaintiff's evidence inadmissible, in *Oxendine v Merrell Dow Pharmaceuticals, Inc*, No 82-1245, 1996 WL 680992 (DC Super 1996). That determination was inseparable from the emergent judicial consensus about the legal implications of Bendectin consumption.

These three types of studies then – chemical, in vitro, and in vivo – cannot furnish a sufficient foundation for a conclusion that Bendectin caused the birth defects at issue in this case. Studies of this kind, singly or in combination, are not capable of proving causation in human beings in the face of the overwhelming body of contradictory epidemiological evidence.[16]

The degree of (scientific) pro-activity displayed by courts in the Bendectin litigation continued beyond merely prioritising the significance of epidemiology in settling questions of scientific and medical causation.[17] It extended to the influential *Daubert v Merrell Dow Pharmaceuticals, Inc* judgment where United States Supreme Court judges actually stipulated the types of methodological strictures scientists should adopt in producing their knowledge for it to be classed as scientific and sufficiently reliable for admissibility in legal proceedings.[18] In this context it was not only judges seeking alignment with a set of scientific experts – witnesses who may have provided evidence and opinions – but rather an instance of judges seeking rhetorical alignment with meta-scientific experts such as sociologists, philosophers and historians of science.[19]

In summary, when constructing legal versions of scientific causation, judges need to engage in processes of simplification and synthesis to show they comprehend the scientific and medical controversy but also to provide an intelligible and tractable model of the evidence that can be applied to the construction and justification of their decisions. The role of courts in mass litigation has shown judges going further and in a sense actually constructing more overt models of legal-scientific knowledge about causation, relying on a diverse assortment of meta-scientific resources.[20]

---

[16] 857 F 2d 823 at 830. Here epidemiological evidence is used as if it precluded the insights produced in or among other scientific domains, compare the approach discussed in note 54, below.

[17] G Edmond & D Mercer, "Litigation Life: Law-science Knowledge Construction in (Bendectin) Mass Toxic Tort Litigation" (2000) 30 *Social Studies of Science* 265.

[18] 113 S Ct 2786 (1993).

[19] The US Supreme Court referred to the work of philosophers Popper and Hempel and the sociologist Jasanoff in their discussion of the nature of science in the *Daubert* decision.

[20] K Foster & P Huber, *Judging Science: Scientific Knowledge and the Federal Courts,* MIT Press, Cambridge, 1998, but compare G Edmond & D Mercer, "Juggling Science: From Polemic to Pastiche" (1999) 13 *Social Epistemology* 215; M Berger, "Eliminating General Causation: Notes Toward a New Theory of Justice and Toxic Torts" (1997) 97 *Columbia Law Review* 2117.

The specific contingencies of the case: "reflexive realism" and "judicial scepticism"

As well as responding to images of law, the evidence and what might be conceived as social and policy concerns, judges also shape their assessments of legal, medical and scientific causation in ways that correspond with the contingencies of the specific case. In such instances, overt reference to policy considerations, or making scientific judgments, or pronouncing on causation as a matter of law may in themselves fail to provide adequate legitimacy for the judgment. In particular, the peculiarities of the individual case – including evidence pertaining to the case – can be employed by judges to explain apparent inconsistencies among decisions or to allow recovery where the general evidence might prevent other plaintiffs from achieving similar level of success.[21]

Tony Ward argues that in some instances judges may revert to impressionistic assessments of the credibility of the witnesses and the coherence and plausibility of narratives. According to Ward, the appeal to contingency may reflect evidence of judges developing, to use the terminology of Ulrich Beck,[22] a degree of reflexive postmodernity – that is, a degree of ambivalence toward scientific explanations and some awareness of their limitations. Regardless of whether we fully accept Ward's thesis,[23] there would appear to be instances where, if nothing more, in response to the complexity and intransigent difficulties involved in establishing other rationales for causation, sceptical realism would seem to become a viable judicial option. The difficulties encountered in attempts to articulate causal evidence, capturing some of the nuances and tensions involved, can be formidable. Ward quotes Lord Hoffman, from a case involving a disputed genetic engineering patent, to capture some of these themes:

---

[21] An example is provided by Beazley JA's brief comments in the mesothelioma case of *EM Baldwin & Son Pty Ltd v Plane; Jsekarb Pty Ltd v Plane* (1999) Aust Tort Reports 81-499 at 65,622. Endeavouring to distinguish her earlier decision in *Bendix Mintex Pty Ltd v Barnes* (1997) 42 NSWLR 307, Beazley JA agreed with Fitzgerald AJA's proposition that: "differences of opinion which emerge in those cases: '... are, for the most part, less related to questions of principle and more attributable to conflicting views of the primary facts, and in some instances at least, the conclusions to be drawn from expert evidence.' This case is different from Bendix and Walsh because in this case there was medical evidence which supported the respondent's case. Thus my agreement with Fitzgerald AJA."

[22] U Beck, *Reflexive Modernization: Politics, Tradition and Aesthetics in the Modern Social Order*, Polity, Cambridge, 1994.

[23] For a discussion of some of the limitations of Beck's thesis see, B Barnes, *The Elements of Social Theory*, UCL Press, London, 1995, at pp109-11.

[Specific] findings of fact, even by the most meticulous of judges, are an inherently incomplete statement of the impression that was made upon him by the evidence. His expressed findings are always surrounded by a penumbra of imprecision as to emphasis, relative weight, minor qualification and nuance ... which time and language do not permit exact expression, but which may play an important part in the judge's overall evaluation.[24]

It may well be that judicial fatigue, a lack of resources, pressures of expedition, consistency and reflexivity all influence the construction of legal categories and decision-making in relation to questions of medical and scientific causation.

Responsibility and social policy: differentiation, deflection and incorporation

Regardless of whether they are articulated, judgments in cases involving scientific and medical evidence of causation inescapably involve a range of institutional, social and policy considerations. Invariably, questions of causation become linked to images of duty of care, foreseeability, the costs of compensation, public policy concerns, the worthiness of plaintiffs, the reprehensibility of the defendant's conduct and the social implications of the particular outcome and its explanation. In some contexts this may lead judges to differentiate explicitly between the nature of legal, as opposed to the nature of scientific and medical causation.[25] On other occasions, apparent differences or gaps between legal and scientific approaches will be downplayed or ignored.

In an analysis of judicial endeavours at establishing medical and legal causation, where there may have been multiple agents linked to the injury, Helen Reece examined the South Australian case of *Birkholz*.[26] In that case the plaintiff claimed that he had contracted Brucellosis (an infectious disease) through work in the defendant's abattoirs. In the Supreme Court his claim had been rejected on the basis that although he may have been infected through his employment, there was no way to determine by which, of a number of possible paths, he had been infected, or by what method the

---

24   T Ward, "Law's Truth, Lay Truth and Medical Science: Three Case Studies" in H Reece (ed), *Law and Science: Current Legal Issues*, vol 1, Oxford University Press, Oxford, 1998, at p263; *Biogen Inc v Medeva plc* [1997] RPC 1 at 45.

25   See below.

26   H Reece, "*Pedro Juan Cubillo v Commonwealth of Australia*: Right Result, Wrong Method" in H Reece (ed), *Law and Science: Current Legal Issues*, vol 1, Oxford University Press, Oxford, 1998, at pp81, 95.

employer could have removed the risk. On appeal, the Supreme Court (in banco) found in favour of the appellant. It was held, not only that it was more probable than not that he had contracted the disease through handling infected animals, but if the plaintiff had been provided with better information and protective clothing he could have avoided infection. King CJ suggested that even if the precise method of infection had not been ascertained, the court could have found in favour of the appellant. King CJ's reasoning provides an example of the rhetorical differentiation between legal and medical causation in the light of notions of responsibility and justice:

> Has the failure to take those precautions been shown to have caused or materially contributed to the contracting of the disease by the appellant? It might be argued as a matter of strict logic, that the fact that the given precautions would substantially diminish the risk, does not prove that failure to take those precautions materially contributed to the appellant's infection unless it can be established how that infection occurred. But the law's view of causation is less concerned with logical and philosophical considerations than with the need to produce a just result to the parties involved.[27]

The differentiation of medical and legal causation may also follow from burdens of proof entailed by explicit policy frameworks such as strict liability, the balance of probabilities (civil), beyond reasonable doubt (criminal) and in the case of emerging precautionary principles entailed by environmental risk management, where the possible harm may be seen as sufficient to warrant the development of a low threshold (but not one which eliminates the need for scientific evidence) for establishing causation.

Jane Holder and Sue Elworthy, provide an example of this type of precautionary rationale in their discussion of a decision by the European Court of Justice in relation to the proof of causation required to justify a ban on beef exports from the United Kingdom in 1996 at the time of the BSE crisis:

> Scientist have as yet only an imperfect knowledge of Creutzfeldt-Jakob disease and more particularly, its recently discovered variant. Its fatal consequences were reiterated several times at the hearing. There is at present no cure for it. Death ensues several months after diagnosis. Since the most likely explanation for this fatal disease is exposure to BSE, there can be no hesitation. Whilst acknowledging the economic and social difficulties caused by the Commission's decision in the United Kingdom,

---

[27]   *Birkholz v Gilbertson Pty Ltd* [1985] 38 SASR 121 at 130 per King CJ.

the court cannot but recognize the paramount importance to be accorded to the protection of health.[28]

There are also circumstances where social and policy considerations circumvent the effects of scientific and medical evidence of causation. Sometimes its relevance is deflected rather than confronted or differentiated by judges. A fairly extreme, but nonetheless instructive example can be drawn from the reluctance displayed by some courts in the United States to use blood testing to determine paternity disputes in divorce cases. Shari Rudavsky traces numerous cases from the 1930s to the 1990s where several courts evinced a strong reluctance to "bastardise" children.[29] Once a child was born within marriage, courts were often unwilling to allow the child to be submitted, during subsequent divorce proceedings, to blood tests which might reveal that their legal father was not in fact their biological father. Rather than challenge the scientific accuracy or veracity of blood testing *per se* there was a tendency to deflect its ultimate relevance to the causal issues that courts were adjudicating. Rudavsky quotes the judgment of a 1963 appeal in Pennsylvania, to illustrate her point. Judge Woodside explained:

> it is cruel for the law to inject such doubts [of paternity] into a child's mind when there are no circumstances to support the doubts except an allegation by an irate man who previously had been known to the child and the world as its father. It is the taking of the blood and not the result of it, which does the harm. ... Pricking the skin to get the blood is an act which plants indelibly upon the mind of a child the doubt as to its paternity which it will carry thereafter forever.[30]

Rudavsky traces the origins of this presumption to social policies underpinning United States divorce law designed to protect children from the social stigma of illegitimacy and potential financial hardship flowing from the withdrawal of "paternal" child support.

The impact of social factors in shaping standards of proof for medical causation may also be less overt. On some occasions there may be a tendency for legal, scientific and medical concerns to be incorporated or fused together. In some contexts such as, to use Joseph Sanders' terminology, case congregations, where the determinations by courts take

---

[28] J Holder & S Elworthy, "The BSE Crisis" in H Reece (ed), *Law and Science: Current Legal Issues*, vol 1, Oxford University Press, Oxford, 1998, p145.

[29] S Rudavsky, "Separating Spheres: Legal Ideology v Paternity Testing in Divorce Cases" (1999) 12 *Science in Context* 123 at 131.

[30] *Commonwealth ex rel Ivory Weston v John Weston*, 193 A 2d 782 at 783 (1963).

on a cumulative character, establishing not only legal but scientific precedent, courts may be far more circumspect in acknowledging a gap between legal and scientific assessments of causation.[31] This is regular feature of high profile mass tort litigation where tremendous human and economic stakes and public interest place considerable pressure on judges to make sure "they get it right". The usual judicial resources of insulation and deflection tend to be less effective when placed within the scrutiny of numerous well resourced and interested constituencies. For instance, while judges in the United States Bendectin litigation commented on the policy significance of the litigation – including the need for judicial rationing and accepting the authority of earlier decisions – there was also a strong impulse to establish an authoritative declaration about the state of "Bendectin science". The production of an authoritative statement involved procedural innovations such as bifurcating proceedings to separate causation from other issues such as liability and damages (in the Multi-District Litigation), epistemological "innovations" establishing the primacy of epidemiological studies over other types of evidence and the adoption of restrictive models of statistical significance and relative risk as criteria for determining the admissibility of epidemiological evidence and establishing medical causation in legal settings.[32]

Returning to the example of the *Richardson* appeal. Drawing authority from earlier decisions in other circuits, the DC Circuit Court of Appeal combined legal precedent with an implicit scientific assessment of their preference for causal explanations to be consistent with epidemiological evidence:

> The court (*Lynch*: an earlier appeal) noted the growing body of law recognizing the importance of epidemiological evidence in establishing causation in cases in which no direct evidence is available.[33]

As a resource to close the Bendectin litigation, these innovations seem to have been influenced by policy concerns, but their authority was simultaneously dependent upon emphasising and defending a close alignment with a particular version of the scientific record.[34] The pro-active role of judges in constructing, reconstructing and deconstructing scientific

•

---

[31]   J Sanders, "The Bendectin Litigation: A Case Study in Life Cycles of Mass Torts" (1992) 43 *Hastings Law Journal* 301.

[32]   Edmond & Mercer, 2000, op cit, n17.

[33]   *Richardson by Richardson v Richardson-Merrell, Inc*, 857 F 2d 823 at 831 (DC Cir 1988).

[34]   Further examples are considered below.

and medical approaches to causation in specific institutional settings overlaps with our previous discussion.

The foregoing discussion has developed a variety of heuristic categories outlining some of the major epistemological resources and concerns negotiated by judges confronted with contests over medical and scientific evidence influencing the development of legal causation. Depending on the circumstances of the case, the history of similar types of litigation and a range of other contingencies, it is possible to imagine greater priority or emphasis being ascribed to some of these considerations rather than others. So far we have attempted to provide some sense of these resources and constraints in a somewhat impressionistic manner, drawing upon examples from a range of legal encounters. In the remainder of this chapter we intend to elaborate upon these observations in the context of a more detailed case study of one asbestos related appeal.

Case Study: *Seltsam Pty Ltd v McGuiness*; *James Hardie & Co Pty Ltd v McGuiness*[35]

This case study focuses upon a recent application to the Court of Appeal from the Dust Diseases Tribunal (NSW). The (largely) uncontested facts presented at the trial and appeal are roughly as follows. The plaintiff, McGuiness, was 62 years of age at the time of the trial. Between 1950 and 1991 he had worked in factories owned by the defendants (Seltsam and James Hardie) and been exposed to asbestos through the manufacture and delivery of fibro-cement sheeting. In the early years McGuiness may have been exposed to both crocidolite (blue asbestos) and chrysotile (white asbestos), though predominantly chrysotile.[36] In 1997 McGuiness was diagnosed with renal cell carcinoma (RCC) of the left kidney. This malignancy was fast growing and at the time of an expedited trial McGuiness had only a short time to live.[37]

At the trial, the issues of duty, foreseeability as well as the extent of exposure were all resolved in favour of the plaintiff.[38] The defendants owed a duty of care to their former employee and foreseeability was resolved on the basis that risks associated with asbestos exposure had been known for

---

[35]   [2000] NSWCA 29; see I Freckelton, "Epidemiology Evidence" (2000) 8 *Journal of Law and Medicine* 133; C Miller, "Coal Dust, Causation and Common Sense" (2000) 63 *Modern Law Review* 763.

[36]   *Seltsam*, at [270].

[37]   At [191].

[38]   At [192], [259].

decades.[39] Judge McGuire, the trial judge in the Dust Diseases Tribunal, found that McGuiness' exposure to asbestos had been "heavy".[40] Because of these determinations, in combination with disagreements around the scientific record, argument was focused on the issue of causation.[41] The legal question to be answered, or proved, was: On the *balance of probabilities,* did exposure to asbestos *cause or materially contribute to* McGuiness' kidney cancer? One factor confounding this assessment was a known association between RCC, obesity and smoking among men of the plaintiff's age. The plaintiff, McGuiness, had been overweight and a moderate smoker.

Below, it is our intention to provide several examples from what we contend are the interrelated domains of law, science and society to illustrate how they were strategically composed to not only rhetorically distance or align legal discursive formations from other professional discourses but also enable judges confronted ostensibly with the same law and evidence to produce decisions with quite distinct legal implications. By focusing on the leading judgment of Spigelman CJ and the dissent of Stein JA we hope to provide a tentative phenomenology of the judicial production and recognition of causal knowledge(s). We accept certain, perhaps intractable, difficulties in proving some of our contentions, but think our overall approach offers a plausible and contextually sensitive means – consistent with some contemporary theorising about the sciences and legal practice[42] – of conceptualising judicial approaches to the complex and refractory issues raised through the use of scientific and medical evidence of causation in civil litigation and judicial decision making.

Seltsam: Alignment with the law

Abstract legal formulations of causation tend to allow considerable flexibility in application. Recognising that the appellate judges in the *Seltsam* appeal all agreed on the precise, admittedly abstract, legal formulation (developed below) confers limited expository benefit because it is through their application, that is their interaction with the evidence and a range of social, policy and institutional assumptions that the consensual

---

[39]   At [259]-[263].

[40]   At [24], [26], [161], [162], [254].

[41]   At [19], [189], [265].

[42]   Consider M Lynch & S Jasanoff (eds), "Contested Identities: Science, Law and Forensic Practice" (1998) 28 *Social Studies of Science* 675; S Fuchs & S Ward, "What is Deconstruction, and Where and When Does it Take Place? Making Facts in Science, Building Cases in Law" (1994) 59 *American Sociological Review* 481; Smith & Wynne, op cit, n8; Jasanoff, 1995, op cit, n8.

legal standard(s) actually achieves its various meanings and their social implications in this particular setting. In this way judicial consensus around the relevant legal principle hardly constitutes a defence of (legal) positivism or the repudiation of a range of more critical hermeneutic approaches to legal practice.[43] All of the judges agreed that the appropriate formulation was that the plaintiff, McGuiness, was required to prove that *on the balance of probabilities* his exposure to asbestos *caused or materially contributed to* his renal cell carcinoma. The phrase "caused or materially contributed to" already possessed a considerable lineage in Anglo-Australian common law.[44] In addition, the question of whether something had caused or materially contributed to an injury was to be decided using "common sense". Again, all of the judges agreed on this approach, citing the Australian High Court authority of *March v Stramare*.[45] Determinations of causation, even those involving complex scientific and medical evidence were to be undertaken with the aid of common sense. Recourse to "common sense" affords a degree of insulation to judges: they do not have to become amateur scientists.[46] Despite agreement on the relevant law at a level of generality, in the judgments of Spigelman CJ and Stein JA the application of the phrase "caused or materially contributed to" to the evidentiary array would prove more heterogeneous.

In his judgment Spigelman CJ devoted considerable attention to a review of the evidentiary requirements for an action in tort. Citing a number of earlier cases, and pre-figuring his own decision, he explained that evidence of a mere possibility had never been sufficient to sustain the causal component of a tort claim.[47] Notwithstanding this commitment, both Spigelman CJ and Stein JA accepted that judges were empowered to translate a scientific (or evidentiary) possibility into a legal probability. It

---

[43] Consider S Fish, *Doing What Comes Naturally: Change, Rhetoric and the Practice of Theory in Literary and Legal Studies*, Duke University Press, Durham, 1989.

[44] *Seltsam*, at [81], [201], [269].

[45] *March v E & M H Stramare Pty Ltd* (1991) 171 CLR 506. Appeals to common sense, even in the evaluation of scientific evidence, resonates with Rehnquist CJ's dissent in the *Daubert v Merrell Dow Pharmaceuticals, Inc*, 509 US 579 at 600-1 (1993), where he dismisses the suggestion that judges should be called upon to become amateur scientists.

[46] A Irwin & B Wynne (eds), *Misunderstanding Science: the Public Reconstruction of Science and Technology*, Cambridge University Press, Cambridge, 1995; G Edmond & D Mercer, "What Judges Should Know about Falsification" (1997) 5 *Expert Evidence* 29.

[47] *Seltsam*, at [78]-[120]; see also Stein J at [201] agreeing with Spigelman CJ.

was within the discretion of the judge to conclude that "the possible was the actual cause".[48]

> But if medical science is prepared to say that it is a possible view, then, in my opinion, the judge after examining the lay evidence may decide that it is probable. It is only when medical science denies that there is any such connection that the judge is not entitled in such a case to act on his own intuitive reasoning.[49]

And,

> There are cases in which medical science cannot identify the biological or pathological mechanisms by which disease develops. In some cases medical science cannot determine the existence of a causal relationship. Such a state of affairs is not necessarily determinative of the existence or non-existence of a causal relationship for purposes of attributing legal responsibility.[50]

The concept of a legal probability would not be automatically equated with a scientific or philosophical probability. Both Spigelman CJ and Stein JA endorsed the position outlined in the previous extracts, accepting that judges were not generally constrained by the opinions of medical science.

For Spigelman CJ, epidemiological studies, in conjunction with other evidence of causation were to be treated as circumstantial evidence that could cumulatively, if not individually, meet the necessary legal burden of proof even if they were understood only to suggest the possibility of an association among medical or scientific experts. Implicitly, judges were competent to translate evidence of individual or combined possibilities into legal probabilities. Finding that the expert evidence did not disprove the plaintiff's contention, Spigelman CJ was nonetheless unwilling to translate what he described as a medical possibility into a legal probability and thereby apportion liability and damages.

Basically, Stein JA adopted the same legal approach as Spigelman CJ, but concluded that the evidence before the Dust Diseases Tribunal and the Court of Appeal was sufficient to warrant a finding that "on the balance of probabilities, exposure to asbestos can cause or materially contribute to the contraction of RCC".[51]

---

[48] At [96].

[49] At [94].

[50] At [93]. Both statements, approved by Spigelman CJ, are drawn from the case of *EMI (Australia) Ltd v Bes* [1970] 2 NSWR 238 at 242.

[51] *Seltsam*, at [250].

Additionally, both Stein JA and Spigelman CJ referred to a principle espoused in the earlier High Court appeal of *Chappel v Hart*[52] where McHugh J had explained that "If a wrongful act or omission results in an increased risk of injury to the plaintiff and that risk eventuates, the defendant's conduct has materially contributed to that injury occurring."[53] For Stein JA, the plaintiff's evidence was sufficient to warrant finding that an increased risk of injury – that injury (RCC) having materialised – had, for legal purposes, caused the plaintiff's injury.

In responding to the respondent's (plaintiff) assertion that some evidence of a relationship between a cause and a realised risk was enough to base a legal finding of causation, Spigelman CJ explained that the likelihood of the increased risk had to be proved to the level of on the balance of probabilities or higher:

> The starting point of McHugh J's analysis was that it had been established on the balance of probabilities that the conduct did create or increase the risk of injury, "and *that* risk had eventuated".

> This starting point is the very matter in issue in the present case. Was there evidence on the basis of which the trial judge could conclude, on the balance of probabilities, that there was an increased risk of injury and that *that* risk had "eventuated" in the specific disease of the Respondent?

> If there was such evidence then ... the tribunal of fact was "entitled" to find that the conduct which increased risk, materially contributed to the injury – entitled, but not, of course, required to so find.[54]

That position was explicitly endorsed in the judgment of Stein JA.[55]

The mere possibility of an increased risk was insufficient to support an action in tort unless judicially transformed to the status of a legal probability. According to Spigelman CJ, finding the relationship between asbestos exposure and RCC to constitute only a legal possibility functioned to distinguish the case of *Seltsam* from the circumstances of the earlier cases of *Chappel v Hart*, *Naxakis v Western General Hospital*[56] and *McGhee v National Coal Board*.[57] In those cases there had not been expert disagreement about whether the increased risk actually caused or materially

---

52   *Chappel v Hart* (1998) 195 CLR 232.
53   *Seltsam*, at [203].
54   At [107]-[109].
55   At [201].
56   (1999) 73 ALJR 782.
57   [1973] 1 WLR 1.

contributed to the injury on the balance of probabilities.[58] Similar issues had also been addressed in considerable detail in the jurisdiction through the earlier appeal from the mesothelioma (another asbestos related illness) case of *Bendix*.[59]

In finally disposing of the matter Spigelman CJ drew upon extrinsic legal commitments to resolve what he acknowledged was a difficulty:

> There is a tension between the suggestion that any increased risk is sufficient to constitute a "material contribution", and the clear line of authority that a mere possibility is not sufficient to establish causation for legal purposes. The latter is too well established to be qualified by the former.[60]

Another way in which the articulation of legal standards influenced the reception, expression and interpretation of the evidence was through the strategic framing of expert testimony. Once again "gaps" between scientific and legal images of causation are purposively managed. Some conspicuous examples of evidence shaped for use in a legal setting sensitive to articulated legal standards and burdens of proof are recorded among the *Seltsam* judgments. The hybridised nature of law-science knowledges – involving processes of extraction, simplification, emphasis, modification and translation – seems to be exemplified in the following ostensibly scientific opinions. Although polemical ascriptions are always available, there seem to be few reasons to characterise the strategic framing as evidence of "junk science", charlatanism or some debased or unreliable form of scientific evidence designed exclusively for the exigencies of litigation.[61] First, experts appearing for the plaintiff testified in the following terms:

- McCredie: "*On the balance of probabilities*, obesity *and exposure* to asbestos *materially contributed to the causation* of renal cell carcinoma *in this case.*"[62] (emphasis added)
- Burns: "In my opinion *on the balance of probabilities*, his asbestos exposure while working with Wunderlich & Hardies in the period 1950

---

58 *Seltsam*, at [105]-[120].
59 *Bendix Mintex Pty Ltd v Barnes* (1997) 42 NSWLR 307. Spigelman CJ acknowledged that in *Bendix* there had been some division over whether an increased risk was capable of causing or materially contributing to an injury on the balance of probabilities. He contrasted the positions of Mason P and Beazley JA.
60 *Seltsam*, at [119].
61 Edmond & Mercer, "Trashing 'Junk' Science", 1998, op cit, n12.
62 *Seltsam*, at [35].

to 1984 *contributed to* the development of his renal carcinoma."[63] (emphasis added)

- Nankivell: *"On the balance of probabilities* this past exposure to asbestos *could* have made a *material contribution* to the development of his renal cell carcinoma."[64] (emphasis added)

Without exception, all of these examples present evidence in the contextually sensitive terms of legal causation and the burden of proof. Only Nankivell's qualified "could" is independently incapable of fulfilling the required legal standard, although it was susceptible to redemption through judicial conversion – particularly if combined with other evidence.

Expert witnesses

For the plaintiff	*For the defendants*
Dr Burns – thoracic surgeon	Professor Berry – epidemiologist
Dr McCredie – epidemiologist	Professor Henderson – pathologist
Dr Nankivell – nephrologist	Dr Lee – thoracic surgeon
	Professor McLaughlin -- epidemiologist
	Dr Katelaris – urologist

Whereas the plaintiff's experts framed their opinions in legally sensitive terminology, the defence experts called to challenge the association between asbestos exposure and RCC tended to utilise an ostensibly non-legal register, or at least this was how their testimony is selected and represented in Spigelman CJ's judgment. These expert opinions pertaining to causation provide few indications of translation into legally relevant terminology. The defence held an interest in encouraging the trial and appellate judges to align legal causation with their version of scientific causation, that is, to make legal and scientific images of causation isomorphic thereby naturalising the defendant's position. (This is not intended to substitute the defence representation for a putatively proper approach to the evidence.) In this way, the following scientific opinions provide support for the defendant's case without requiring the judge to explain and legitimate any apparent differences between the legal decision and scientific authority:

---

63   At [39].
64   At [48].

- McLaughlin: "The epidemiological evidence for an association between asbestos and an increased risk of renal cell cancer is *scanty and problematic.*"[65] (emphasis added)
- Lee: "... concluded that the epidemiological evidence was *limited and of insufficient strength to permit a conclusion* that a causal relationship existed."[66] (emphasis added)
- Katelaris: "... asserted that the link between asbestos exposure and renal cell carcinoma *had not been proved.*"[67] (emphasis added)

We should not forget that Spigelman CJ had endorsed earlier decisions empowering judges to locate legal causation on the basis of a limited record, with scant and problematic evidence and even in the absence of scientific proof. Notwithstanding the strategic benefit of ostensibly scientific – that is, non-legal – posturing, the defence experts were also capable of translating their evidence into highly contingent, legally inspired terminology:

- Henderson: "It is certainly my view that this *does not equate to a probability of causation or material contribution* by asbestos *at the level of 50% or greater* (in other words the relationship at this time is no more than *speculative or possible* and it does not achieve *probability* status)."[68] (emphasis added)

Having accepted, like Spigelman CJ, that judges could epistemologically transform scientific and medical possibilities to render them capable of satisfying the legal burden of causation, Stein JA sought to distinguish and contain some of the scientific statements in order to control their legal implications. This was the converse to Spigelman CJ's presentation of a range of scientific opinions as if they were self-evidently appropriate, without any modifications, to resolve the legal determination. Assessing whether the term "confidently concluded" appended to the end of an epidemiological study had direct legal bearing, Stein JA indicated that: "Professor Berry also said that when the Mandel authors mentioned 'confidently concluded', they would not have had the *balance of probabilities* in mind."[69] (emphasis added).

---

65 At [50].
66 At [54].
67 At [53].
68 At [58].
69 At [236], [249]. D Rier, "The Versatile Caveat Section of an Epidemiological Paper: Managing Public and Private Risk" (1999) 21 *Science Communication* 3.

Confident conclusions are the language of science. Professors McLaughlin and Berry agreed, the former assuming that the words connoted a higher standard than the balance of probabilities.[70]

In the legal forum, Stein JA was not bound to accept the scientific language and apparent implications of a scientific study. Significantly though, he felt compelled to explain modifications and qualifications.

Seltsam: Evaluating scientific and medical knowledge

Before proceeding to consider the treatment of the evidence, just one caveat. We do not intend to suggest that the approaches adopted by either Spigelman CJ or Stein JA were (im)plausible, (un)persuasive, right or wrong. Indeed, without dismissing one approach as simply mistaken, the concurrent plausibility of two quite different judgments may be their most interesting and analytically demanding feature.[71]

The party-oriented presentation of evidence in adversary legal systems exposes trial and appellate judges to two (or more) purposive evidentiary arrangements organised according to perceptions of legal standards, tacit and experiential skills and to some extent the anticipation of rulings and areas of perceived strength, weakness and conflict.[72] Interestingly, it seems that the contest surrounding the issue of causation in relation to the epidemiological record was perceived as an area of strength by both defendants and plaintiffs.

Testimony from the trial and the appellate judgments in *Seltsam* suggests continuous struggles and negotiations around the level of scientific support for a causal association between asbestos exposure and RCC and its assessment in terms of legal causation. But the contest over the sufficiency of the scientific evidence was not restricted, as in the discussion in previous section, to the legally sensitive conclusions of scientists and their representation in judgments. All of the appellate judges provided a review of the expert evidence against formulations of the legal backdrop. Having examined the basic agreement between Spigelman CJ

---

70 *Seltsam*, at [248].
71 The foundational argument, in the sociology of scientific knowledge, for the value of avoiding sociologies of error – that is, seeking more general sociological explanations for the generation of all beliefs whether characterised as "right" or "wrong" rather than focusing disproportionate sociological attention on sources of deviance in the production of error or pathological knowledge – see D Bloor, *Knowledge and Social Imagery*, 2nd edn, University of Chicago Press, Chicago, 1991.
72 This is not to suggest that processes of selection, application and interpretation could be avoided by other institutional or procedural arrangements, although it may displace some of them into a less visible "background".

and Stein JA over the appropriate law, it is also of interest to examine their assessments of the evidence, its relative strengths and weaknesses and its legal significance. It is not our intention to suggest that the legal standards, imprecise or flexible as they may have been, necessarily pre-exist and determine the judicial interpretation of the evidence. Rather, it is our contention that the interpretation of the evidence, like the identification and interpretation of the relevant legal principles, allows (or introduces) degrees of indeterminacy and interpretative flexibility. Without contending that the legal standards are meaningless, the following account might be used to support our contention that what counts as "the law" and "the evidence" are to varying degrees mutually constituting in legal settings. Their representation affords freedom and constraints.[73] The framing and description of what might be represented as "the law" and "the evidence" are closely related and purposively combined to support particular outcomes. In contrast to the judicial implication, we would contend that the outcome of the *Seltsam* litigation can be interpreted to suggest that the law and the evidence are rarely as constraining as the judges would seem to indicate. Differences in the assessments provided by Stein JA and Spigelman CJ would seem to suggest that the actual verdict was not the only plausible outcome.

Finding in favour of the defendants on the basis that the plaintiff's evidence of a cause or material contribution did not rise above a *possibility* – scientifically or legally – Spigelman CJ explained the decisions on the basis of what was described as a comprehensive examination of the scientific evidence. Like Davies AJA, the other judge forming the majority, Spigelman CJ obliquely criticised the trial judge for failing to undertake a more detailed examination of the evidence, especially the defendants' criticism of the plaintiff's epidemiological evidence. Spigelman CJ's discussion of the evidence is structured around and supplemented – but not determined – by the legal standards articulated in his judgment. Despite a number of references to a range of non-scientific, social and policy considerations influencing legal approaches to causation, Spigelman CJ's analysis of "the evidence" and its application to "the law" appear as if they actually determine his decision-making. If there were policy reasons shaping his view of causation they were not made explicit, other than an obscure reference to the trial being conceived as some kind of test case.

Very briefly, Spigelman CJ found (or represented) the defendants' evidence (as) convincing and the plaintiff's evidence only capable of supporting the possibility of an association between asbestos exposure and

---

[73] D Kennedy, "Freedom and Constraint in Adjudication: a Critical Phenomenology" (1986) 36 *Journal of Legal Education* 518.

RCC. Despite emphasising the need to examine the evidence in its entirety, most of Spigelman CJ's analysis was directed toward the epidemiological evidence. Even though he placed stress on the need to assess the "strength and quality" of the epidemiological studies, Spigelman CJ nevertheless emphasised the number of studies reporting no significant association between asbestos exposure and RCC.[74] Spigelman CJ privileged the cohort studies and dismissed much of the plaintiff's evidence for an association by drawing upon the Bradford-Hill postulates to suggest that McGuiness' epidemiological evidence lacked consistency with other studies and did not demonstrate a dose-response relationship.[75] While Spigelman CJ did not, as some United States courts had, require studies demonstrating a relative risk (RR) of 2.0 or higher, he expressed a preference for studies approximating that standard.[76] That preference offered the judiciary the following advantages. It could simplify legal determinations – to some extent judges could defer to the epidemiological record – and might encourage out-of-court settlements.

According to Spigelman CJ, the plaintiff could offer few studies suggesting more than a moderate association between RCC and asbestos exposure. In addition, the claim was compromised by a range of confounding factors such as the plaintiff's obesity and history of smoking. Evidence of a biopsy of the plaintiff's kidney had revealed no asbestos fibres even though a biological mechanism – accepted as plausible by most of the experts – had been proffered. Animal studies were accorded little weight and two epidemiological studies indicating strong associations between asbestos exposure and RCC were inoculated through reference to those results as merely curious. Ultimately, Spigelman CJ relied upon what he characterised as the great majority of epidemiological studies demonstrating no convincing association – that is beyond the level of a legal or scientific possibility.

In contrast, Stein JA found that the same evidence was capable of supporting the legal requirement that on the balance of probabilities the plaintiff's exposure to asbestos had caused or materially contributed to his illness. Even though Spigelman CJ had acknowledged the need to assess

---

[74] *Seltsam*, at [29], [31].

[75] *"Dose Response Effect.* If the risk of the disease rises with increasing exposure, a causal interpretation of the association is more plausible ..." (at [139]).

[76] *Seltsam*, at [137], [175]. "Most epidemiological studies identify the strength of an association by a measure called relative risk (RR). RR is defined as the ratio of the incidence of disease in exposed individuals compared to the incidence in unexposed individuals. If the relative risk equals 1.0, the risk in exposed individuals is the same as the risk in unexposed individuals. If the relative risk is greater than 1.0 the risk in exposed individuals is greater than the risk in unexposed individuals." (at [67]).

the strength and quality of the epidemiological record,[77] in actuality he made few endeavours to do so, preferring a weight of numbers approach. That assessment, however, is a feature of Stein JA's judgment.[78] Stein JA did not simply divide the epidemiological evidence between cohort and case control studies and then apportion weight on the basis of the larger number of cohort studies demonstrating no association.[79] Instead, he distinguished between the studies and, like McGuire below,[80] accorded considerable weight to one particular epidemiological study, the Mandel Study, undertaken by two of the experts (McLaughlin and McCredie) retained by the parties and engaged in the proceedings.

The Mandel study was a large international case-control study. It was the most recent epidemiological attempt to assess the relationship between asbestos and RCC. The Mandel Report concluded:

> Several investigators have found increased risks of kidney cancer associated with exposure to asbestos. ... Case-control studies not showing an association with asbestos exposure had small numbers of exposed workers. ... *Our study, with 200 exposed cases provides additional evidence that asbestos increases the risk of kidney cancer. Nevertheless, further research of asbestos-exposed workers is needed to demonstrate a relationship with either duration of employment or amount of exposure before a causal association can be confidently concluded.*[81] (emphasis added)

Like Stein JA's judgment, the Mandel Report distinguished among epidemiological studies and different types of evidence, drawing attention to the small size and limited participant exposure of some epidemiological studies (including some of those performed by McLaughlin) that had reported no association between asbestos exposure and RCC. Stein JA stressed that the Mandel Report concluded that "an association with asbestos was confirmed." The Mandel Report found a RR of 1.4 over six population groups in 5 countries. Moderate associations, those involving RR in the order of 1.4-1.7 were, in conjunction with the other evidence, for Stein JA, adequate to fulfil the "material contribution" component of legal causation.

For Stein JA, the importance of the Mandel study was closely associated with the participation of the epidemiologists McLaughlin and

---

[77]   At [29], [31],[32], [178].
[78]   At [250].
[79]   All of the experts accepted that cohort studies were the most reliable (#51, 221, 240).
[80]   *Seltsam*, at [199].
[81]   At [215], [285] and [71].

McCredie.[82] Indeed, their involvement led Stein JA to produce a number of strategic contrasts. Recalling that McLaughlin had been critical of case-control studies, Stein JA found it curious that he had been involved in the Mandel study, acting as one of its principals.

> The Professor was highly critical of case-control studies. Given this position, one might ask why he associated himself, as one of the authors, with a multi-national case-control study in six centres spread among five countries. Indeed, as I have mentioned, he agreed that he was the co-ordinator of the Mandel study and set the parameters and methodology for it. It is apparent that he was among the principal authors, if not *the* principal author.[83]

In the judgment of Stein JA, McLaughlin's in-court testimony is characterised as strangely inconsistent with his published scientific opinions: "as different as chalk and cheese".[84] Elsewhere, Stein JA, criticised McLaughlin for improprieties in his approach to peer review in medical publications.[85] Throughout the trial, the dominant expert contest had been fought around the meaning of the epidemiological record. The judgment of Stein JA provides some sense of the importance of, and relationship between, the representation of scientists, judicial images of scientific propriety and the status accorded to particular testimony. McLaughlin's evidence, unlike the testimony of McCredie, was apparently shaped for the exigencies of litigation. This stigmatised and purportedly inferior knowledge is sometimes referred to by the more pejorative label "science for litigation".[86] Having identified these "aberrations", the evidence of McLaughlin was rendered highly questionable or unreliable, indeed sufficiently questionable for Stein JA to dismiss it as unconvincing.

Like Spigelman CJ, Stein JA also drew upon the Bradford Hill postulates to explain his decision. Unlike Spigelman CJ, however, Stein JA thought there was sufficient consistency among the plaintiff's epidemiological evidence and particularly across the population centres covered in the Mandel study.[87] Stein JA accepted McCredie's opinion that a dose-response relationship was a desirable but non-essential feature of

---

82   At [240].
83   At [229].
84   At [243]-[247].
85   At [228], [242].
86   The issue of "science for litigation" was discussed in one of the US judgments referred to (though incorrectly cited) by Spigelman CJ, the case of *Daubert* on remand: *Daubert v Merrell Dow Pharmaceuticals, Inc*, 43 F3d 1311 (9th Cir 1995). For a critical appraisal consider Edmond, 2000, op cit, n7.
87   *Seltsam*, at [221], [227], [246].

epidemiological analysis.[88] In addition, Stein JA suggested that the non-epidemiological evidence assisted the plaintiff's claim. The availability of a plausible biological mechanism supported by animal studies and tests on the urine of workers, cancer produced through injecting asbestos into the kidneys of rats, and an appropriate latency period all provided what Stein JA characterised as common sense support for the attribution of a causal relationship between asbestos exposure and RCC.[89] He also referred to judicial authority, the decision in *Baldwin*, to account for complications in epidemiological evidence when associated with multiple causal factors, such as smoking and obesity.[90] But Stein JA went even further, questioning the reliance placed, particularly by the defendants, on epidemiological evidence.[91] Overall, Stein JA agreed with the position adopted by the trial judge, namely that the evidence supported the contention that asbestos had caused or materially contributed to the plaintiff's illness.

Significantly, none of these previous representations determines the appropriate manner in which to interpret the scientific evidence, or how to apply it to the relevant law, even if we were able to agree that either category was stable or could constrain its application or use. Instead, they provide some indication of the epistemic indeterminacy associated with the evidence and the law and their putatively principled interaction in the realm of legal causation.

Two further evidential matters also provide some additional insight into the special epistemic circumstances attending the use of expert opinion evidence in litigation. First, among their grounds of appeal, Seltsam argued that some of the evidence provided by McCredie and Burns was inadmissible because they had each strayed into domains where they were ineligible to testify because they possessed no "specialised knowledge" under s79 of the *Evidence Act* 1995 (NSW).[92] McCredie had apparently testified, without medical training, about the plaintiff's specific injuries and Burns, a medical practitioner, had expressed opinions about epidemiological studies. The Court of Appeal rejected this attempt at inter-scientific boundary working on the grounds that no objection had been taken at trial, the breaches were not serious and the defence

---

[88] At [221].
[89] At [254].
[90] At [209].
[91] At [251].
[92] *Evidence Act* 1995 (NSW) s79: "If a person has specialised knowledge based on the person's training, study or experience, the opinion rule does not apply to evidence of an opinion of that person that is wholly or substantially based on that knowledge."

epidemiologists had made similar incursions.[93] Boundaries developed because of the particular shape of litigation, the available evidence, tactical decisions made during the trial and the interpretation and application of rules can substantially influence the shape and availability of what constitutes evidence in legal settings.[94]

The second issue also concerns approaches to litigation which again illustrate some of the inter-relatedness of a number of domains. The other grounds of appeal provide some additional indication of the extent to which evidence, law and procedure are inter-related and actively contested and how well resourced defendants and plaintiffs are relatively free to contest their dispute across all sorts of legal-(and)-epistemic domains. On appeal, counsel for James Hardie made a brief submission against the trial judge's initial finding of foreseeability.[95] More fundamentally, other grounds of appeal included questions about the jurisdiction of the Dust Diseases Tribunal. *Seltsam* had also referred to the award of damages and procedural fairness as grounds of appeal. Even the diagnosis of the plaintiff's illness was contested.[96] These ongoing areas of contestation, not all of which were pursued, were capable of influencing not just the admissible evidence, and how it might be understood as relevant during the trial as well as its judicial assessment and the viability of the case but even the appropriate forum for their consideration.[97]

Seltsam: The specific contingencies of the case

So far most of the discussion of the evidence and the law – hopefully the categories will by now appear closely interdependent if not to some extent

---

[93] *Seltsam*, at [148]-[150], [255]-[258]. McLaughlin testified unequivocally that asbestos exposure "did not contribute to Mr McGuiness' renal cell cancer" (at [225]). Notably this representation appears in the judgment of Stein JA and not the judgment of Spigelman CJ. How it should be reconciled with Spigelman CJ's reference to McCredie's admission that epidemiologists were not competent to testify about individual cases and why he chose to cite the statement of McCredie (see text accompanying note 53) rather than McLaughlin seems consistent with the representations of the evidence and the standing of the scientists the judges were each endeavouring to establish.

[94] Geiryn, op cit, n6; Edmond, 1998, op cit, n6.

[95] Foreseeability was more actively contested in some of the earlier asbestos litigation such as the appeal in *Bendix*. Once judges had decided the issue of foreseeable in favour of plaintiff's some of the contestation became more sharply focused around causation.

[96] *Seltsam*, at [193].

[97] Some of the contests could be won procedurally. For a discussion of techniques employed in some of the earlier tobacco litigation, see R Rabin, "A Sociolegal History of the Tobacco Tort Litigation" (1992) 44 *Stanford Law Review* 853.

mutually constituting – has concentrated on fairly abstract or general legal and evidentiary issues. Despite the judicial framing, this overview of the law and the evidence does not appear to be undertaken independently from process(es) of decision-making and rationalisation. That which is characterised as evidence of the specific, and the application of the law, appear consistent with the articulated categories and standards purportedly used to decide the case. However, as we have argued, these very categories are to varying degrees shaped by both the development of the law and the specific evidential topographies presented during the trial and appeal. The ultimate decisions at the trial and appeal depend on the selective framing of the meaning of the evidence and its application to strategically articulated legal standards. Now we turn to consider some of the more case-specific factors – those relating specifically to the plaintiff – underlying the judicial rationalisations.

In the *Seltsam* appeal most of the discussion of the scientific and medical evidence and the application of the law focused on the general causal issues. To some extent that was a result of the emphasis placed on the epidemiological record by plaintiffs, defendants and judges. Distinguishing between specific and general causation, Spigelman CJ referred to McCredie's testimony in support for the proposition that epidemiologists were ineligible to testify about particular cases:

Q   I think you said earlier, doctor, that your speciality in epidemiology is one looking at statistics and populations and diseases and that your discipline does not permit you to make a particular diagnosis for a particular patient.

A   That's exactly right.[98]

Reliance on epidemiological evidence had the potential to cause difficulties when attention focused on the specific circumstances of the plaintiff's case. Significantly, both Spigelman CJ and Stein JA acknowledged these potential limitations although each represented their implications quite differently.

Although Spigelman CJ made no allowance for extrapolations from general causation to the particulars of the plaintiff's circumstances, preferring to rely on the strength of the general epidemiological record to

---

[98]   *Seltsam*, at [37]. Having decided that this type of incursion, an epidemiologist testifying about an individual case, did not render the testimony inadmissible under s79 of the *Evidence Act 1995* (NSW), Spigelman CJ nevertheless uses the very breach to support his position, particularly the purported strength of the epidemiological record in relation to general causation.

determine the case, he did cite an extract from the United States Federal Judicial Centre's *Reference Manual* outlining potential limitations to the application of epidemiological evidence to individuals:

> The discussion above assumes that the only evidence bearing on cause in fact is epidemiological. Such an assumption is unlikely, and a variety of additional pieces of evidence, although less quantifiable, affect a fact finder's assessment. Biases in the epidemiological studies might justify a conclusion that the real magnitude of increase risk is greater or lower than that revealed in the study. The dose to which the plaintiff was exposed might be greater or lesser than those in the epidemiological study, thereby requiring some extrapolation. In addition, there might be factors peculiar to the plaintiff – excess exposure to another known cause, pathological mechanism, family history of disease, or conflict in diagnoses – that modify any probability based solely on the available epidemiological evidence.[99]

These were some of the very factors introduced by Stein JA to distinguish among the epidemiological studies and infuse some with greater evidential and legal significance. In addition, Stein JA cited the case of *Baldwin* for authority (judicial bootstrapping) about the relevance of epidemiological studies to individual cases and the confounding effects of multiple causes on the value of epidemiological evidence.

Spigelman CJ made little effort to apply what he portrayed as a convincing epidemiological record to the plaintiff's circumstances. In the absence of general causal evidence, the plaintiff's cause was doomed. Accepting the defendants' representation of the epidemiological evidence as convincing, Spigelman CJ merely supplemented his assessment with a few case-specific non-epidemiological factors, operationalised to reinforce the thrust of his interpretation of the epidemiological evidence and mediate his conversion of general causation into a finding specific and definitive in relation to the plaintiff's action. The failure to find asbestos fibres during a fine needle biopsy of the plaintiff's kidney and the possibility that RCC was caused by obesity, smoking or some unknown aetiology all weakened the plaintiff's case.

In contrast, Stein JA suggested that the epidemiological evidence was open to alternative readings strengthened by the plaintiff's lengthy and heavy exposure to white, but also some blue, asbestos.[100] Heavy exposure, an appropriate latency period, the apparent biological plausibility and animal studies were all combined to strengthen the epidemiological

---

[99] *Seltsam*, at [122].
[100] At [254].

evidence supporting an association between asbestos exposure and the plaintiff's RCC.[101] Further, Stein JA differentiated among some of the epidemiological studies, discounting those suggesting no association where the participants had not, like the plaintiff, experienced extensive or heavy exposure to asbestos.[102] For Stein JA the negative result of the fine needle biopsy, like the lack of a dose-response relationship, was not interpreted as determinative.

Seltsam: Responsibility and social policy

Over the last few decades, judicial expressions of legal causation have regularly included debates around the extent to which judges should make social, moral and policy assumptions explicit. This was one of the features of the judgments in the leading Australian case of *March v Stramare* where a *common sense* approach to legal causation and putative commitment to judicial transparency were endorsed by a majority of the High Court. Acknowledging their sensitivity to a range of social and policy expedients, judges have repeatedly explained that their causal deliberations are not directly comparable with those undertaken in the supposedly epistemologically more pristine realms of science and philosophy. Such pronouncements tend to achieve a degree of judicial consensus and the tendency is exemplified in the *Seltsam* judgments. There, commenting on legal images of causation, Spigelman CJ explained:

> When assessing expert evidence on causation, the legal concept of causation requires the court to approach the matter in a distinctively different manner from that which may be appropriate in either philosophy or science, including the science of epidemiology.[103]

Judges frequently explain differences between law and purportedly more pure epistemic domains (such as philosophy and the sciences) in terms of the legal system having a range of constituencies beyond "truth". The legal system is not concerned exclusively with, nor is it possessed with the opportunity or resources to reflect upon, refractory epistemological matters. In addition to "truth", the legal system is sensitive to a range of other, often conflicting, considerations such as the pragmatic and expeditious resolution of disputes, policy implications, effects of liability, fairness, public acceptance of verdicts and limited resources. These types

---

[101] At [206], [254].
[102] At [239], compare Spigelman CJ at [179], [180].
[103] At [142], see also [202], [208].

of sentiments were expressed where Spigelman CJ explained that unlike philosophy or science: "In law, on the other hand, problems of causation arise in the context of ascertaining or apportioning legal responsibility for a given occurrence."[104]

So, the legal assessment and attribution of causation should not be understood as identical with conclusions derived for or within other contexts. This point has been developed in our discussion of the *Seltsam* appeal, where appellate judges explained that they were not constrained by medical opinions – even consensual medical opinions.[105] Judges are empowered, if such a decision is considered legally appropriate, to apportion (legal) causation where a physician or scientists might be tentative or reluctant.[106] Significantly, however, all of the judges in the *Seltsam* appeal explained their decisions on the basis of particular readings of the scientific evidence and the application of legal standards. In making and explaining such attributions, judges are not entirely insulated or sheltered from exogenous criticism from scientific fields and beyond.

Accepting that judicial representations of causation are not always consistent with scientific and medical approaches introduces a degree of vulnerability into legal decision making and rationalisations. This can require the judiciary to balance and defend a number of disparate legitimatory resources, such as the ability to recover damages, the valuing of scientific evidence, discouraging some types of social practices and determining the meaning of legal standards such as the burden of proof in relation to "uncertainty". Where judges appear to disagree with consensual scientific opinion, they are exposed to risk of criticism not only from scientists but also those concerned with specific outcomes and their implications.[107] Of course, accepting that judges are not entirely constrained by scientific and medical consensus or even expert majorities does not mean that they will or could readily reject such expert

---

[104] At [202], citing *March v Stramare* and *Chappel v Hart*.

[105] Despite the suggestion that judges were not empowered to accept expert evidence of a causal association that was explicitly excluded as a possibility by a field or fields, in practice this standard is always susceptible to manipulation. In the much earlier traumatic cancer case of *Commissioner for Transport v Adamcik* (1961) 106 CLR 292, a majority of the High Court recognised, as legally sufficient, the opinion of a single expert, even though he (and others) accepted that it was inconsistent with virtually all contemporary medical knowledge. The expert even described himself as somewhat of a visionary. For a critical response consider the dissent of Windeyer J.

[106] *Seltsam*, at [144].

[107] Such as insurance companies, manufacturers, pharmaceutical companies, certain professions as well as plaintiff and defence lawyers. Judicial differences over the value of scientific evidence have been a conspicuous feature of some high profile miscarriage of justice cases.

knowledges. Judges must skilfully manage the appropriation and/or rejection of expert knowledges pertaining to causation in ways which maintain institutional integrity and legitimacy.[108] Even though Spigelman CJ and Stein JA disagreed about the strength of the expert evidence and its legal significance they both endeavoured to produce a comprehensive assessment of that evidence to explain their respective positions. These judicial perspectives offer some indication of the status of scientific knowledge and its value as a legitimatory resource. Further, each produced a discursive formulation where the legal standards and the evidence are purposefully dove-tailed to support their preferred outcome. The legal standards were sufficiently flexible to support both readings as well as the decision of Davies AJA. Even though the decisions of Spigelman CJ and Stein JA are fundamentally incompatible, both are represented as the necessary combination of the law and the evidence rather than the rationalised preferences of judges confronted with degrees of legal and evidentiary indeterminacy or policy expedients.

Only rarely do judges reject the expert evidence in its entirety. More commonly, in adversarial settings, the evidence of one side is preferred. Sometimes that preference is signified by the application of an evidentiary threshold such as sufficiency or a burden of proof. Alternatively, the preferred expert evidence – the evidence purportedly underpinning the decision – is presented using different rhetorical tropes (usually empiricist framing) to the presentation of the evidence associated with the dispreferred side (usually contingent framing or a genre of uncertainty).[109] Invariably, such decisions require the strategic (re-)configuration of complex social, procedural and epistemic considerations.

In concluding the case study, it may be significant that Spigelman CJ indicated that the *Seltsam* appeal should be regarded as some kind of test case.[110] The *Seltsam* case may also be understood as legal authority for the recognition and use of epidemiological evidence in negligence cases in NSW (and beyond). Importantly, Spigelman CJ distinguished and rejected some of the more restrictive United States approaches to the admission and use of epidemiological evidence. In practice the differences between the United States and New South Wales approaches might be more illusory than real. Notwithstanding that judges in *Seltsam* (Spigelman CJ and Stein JA) and earlier cases had recognised difficulties associated with the use of epidemiological evidence – particularly in relation to specific causation and

---

[108] B Wynne, *Rationality and Ritual: The Windscale Inquiry and Nuclear Decisions in Britain*, British Society of the History of Science, Chalfont St Giles, 1982.

[109] N Gilbert & M Mulkay, *Opening Pandora's Box: A Sociological Analysis of Scientist's Discourse*, Cambridge University Press, Cambridge, 1984, at pp56-7.

[110] *Seltsam*, at [185].

adjusting the evidence to the circumstances of particular plaintiffs, the role of multiple causes, inconclusive records, the combination of epidemiological evidence with non-epidemiological evidence and hierarchising epidemiological postulates – epidemiology was conceived by the defendants, plaintiffs and judges to be the primary site of the evidential contest.[111] In that way legal expectations pertaining to proof, here in relation to causation, might be understood to have exerted a fundamentally epistemological influence. Reliance upon, or more accurately the privileging of, epidemiological evidence has been a conspicuous feature of toxic tort litigation in Australia but has been even more prominent in the United States.[112]

The *Seltsam* trial and appellate judgments might be conceived as a special case addressing difficulties associated with evaluating causation evidence in so-called toxic tort litigation. Earlier, in the same jurisdiction, in another case concerned with asbestos related illness (mesothelioma) and a range of epidemiological and non-epidemiological evidence, two appellate judges encouraged parliament to intervene in the resolution of cases involving extensive submissions of complex scientific and medical evidence.

> This case presents what appears to be the next evolutionary stage in a legal battle between employees and employers in mesothelioma cases. The Tribunal and this Court were confronted, not so much between experts of like disciplines but with experts in different disciplines ... There must also be considerable doubt as to whether the Tribunal should be the arbiter of the medical and scientific controversies which are fought out in these cases. However, as long as such cases must be brought within the normative rules of negligence, the Court is required to make findings as to causation on the uncertain and conflicting medical and scientific evidence which is presented. It is a matter for the Legislature as to whether this should remain the case.[113]

---

111 At [232]. The privileging of epidemiological studies dates has been a feature of a number of mass torts, including the prominent Agent Orange litigation: *In re Agent Orange Product Liability Litigation*, 597 F Supp 740 (DC NY 1984); *In re Agent Orange Product Liability Litigation*, 611 F Supp 1221 (DC NY 1985); *In re Agent Orange Product Liability Litigation*, 818 F 2d 145 (2nd Cir 1987). For some discussion of that litigation see P Schuck, *Agent Orange on Trial: Mass Toxic Disasters in the Courts*, Harvard University Press, Cambridge, 1986.

112 Edmond & Mercer, 2000, op cit, n17.

113 *EM Baldwin & Son Pty Ltd v Plane; Jsekarb Pty Ltd v Plane* (1999) Aust Tort Reports 81-499 at 65,623 per Beazley JA and 65,650 per Fitzgerald AJA. Judicial "unease" with cases such as *Baldwin* and *Seltsam* has received media coverage. A series of articles about the *Seltsam* case were featured in *The Sydney Morning Herald*, see W Bacon, "Experts on Trial" (5 July 2000) 1 and (6 July 2000) 11.

These comments provide some sense of a range of extra-legal considerations where cases are strategically fought and defended over time responding to earlier victories and defeats.[114] Beazley JA's request may signify both the difficulties involved in deciding and rationalising (closing) such disputes as well as judicial concern at the institutional vulnerability associated with such decision making, notwithstanding degrees of legal and evidential indeterminacy and the existence of a range of devices designed to insulate judicial fact-finding and deflect external criticism.

Seltsam: Overview

Notwithstanding the respondent's argument about the realised increased risk from *Chappel v Hart* or the trial judge's findings in the court below, Spigelman CJ and Stein JA basically agreed on the legal formulation appropriate to deciding the case. Both accepted that the possibility of a causal relationship was insufficient, by itself, to found an action in negligence. They also agreed that, in the absence of scientific evidence, or, where scientific and medical evidence only suggested the possibility of a causal relationship, the evidence might still support a finding of legal causation. They also accepted that the only circumstance preventing judges from transforming a scientific possibility into a legal probability was when the relationship had been effectively dismissed by *(all)* credible scientists or physicians. Spigelman CJ and Stein JA also agreed, in principle, that all of these assessments should be made according to common sense. However, as we have seen, Spigelman CJ and Stein JA did not agree about whether the scientific and medical evidence constituted a legal probability that asbestos exposure caused or materially contributed to the plaintiff's cancer. Spigelman CJ effectively decided the issue on the basis of general causation. In contrast, Stein JA indicated that the evidence was sufficient to support a finding of legal causation. We are not told, however, whether that threshold was achieved on the basis of the strength of the scientific and medical evidence or whether Stein JA elevated a scientific possibility and made it the basis for a finding of a legally significant causal relationship. Drawing attention to the process of judicial elevation – interpreting the scientific record to demonstrate a probable relationship between asbestos exposure and RCC – might have weakened the persuasiveness of Stein JA's judgment notwithstanding the legal commitment to a common sense approach. In contrast, Spigelman CJ explicitly aligned his judgment with what was characterised as the current scientific orthodoxy. Any association

---

[114] Sanders, 1992, op cit, n31.

between asbestos exposure and RCC never rose above a scientific or legal possibility.

A supplementary issue relates to the use of uncertainty and the burden of proof. We can imagine commentators criticising the foregoing discussion on the basis that knowledge about the cause of RCC, both specific and general, is limited and so the legal system is beset or constrained by scientific and medical uncertainties. Our response would be that the use of uncertainty, like the more fashionable concept trans-science,[115] does little to assist our understanding of the judicial uses of scientific evidence or to assist judges confronted with complex causal questions.[116] Judges, legal traditions, procedures and rules, case preparation and strategic configurations of evidence interact to influence what can be represented as (un)certain. In the absence of a range of possible legal-technical impediments – such as statutes of limitation or admissibility standards – that may determine the outcome of a case, judges ultimately have to decide whether an evidential record is sufficiently certain or uncertain (or trans-scientific) to meet a legal threshold of proof, however indeterminate. Recognising disagreement, questions of judgment, experience and interpretation in an area of uncertainty did not prevent Stein JA finding a causal relationship between asbestos exposure and the plaintiff's cancer on the balance of probability.[117] The use of certainty, like appeals to the weight (or consistency) of the scientific evidence and the possibility of judicial translation of scientific possibilities into legal probabilities, reveals little about how law, evidence and a range of social and policy concerns are combined to produce specific outcomes, or how these outcomes are connected to broader social concerns and legal developments.

---

[115] A Weinberg, "Science and Trans-science" (1972) 10 *Minerva* 209; W Wagner, "Trans-science in Toxic Torts" (1986) 96 *Yale Law Journal* 428; W Wagner, "The Science Charade in Toxic Risk Regulation" (1995) 95 *Columbia Law Review* 1613; S Jasanoff, "Contested Boundaries in Policy-Relevant Science"(1987) 17 *Social Studies of Science* 195.

[116] B Campbell, "Uncertainty as Symbolic Action in Disputes among Experts" (1985) 15 *Social Studies of Science* 429; S Shackley & B Wynne, "Representing Uncertainty in Global Climate Change Science and Policy: Boundary-ordering Devices and Authority" (1996) 21 *Science, Technology and Human Values* 275.

[117] *Seltsam*, at [253].

Conclusion: Minding the Gap(s)

Most directly, our assessment of the relationship between causation among the sciences and causation in legal settings would seem to caution against simplistic or textbook-style definitions, comparisons and recriminations. In the foregoing discussion we have emphasised an alternative approach, where judges, in a sense, strategically construct images of scientific and legal causation drawing from a variety of epistemic domains, policy considerations and practical contingencies. We also identified how the apportioning of responsibility, social and policy implications, and the specific details of the case were important to understanding the legal constructions produced in legal settings and judgments. These perspectives, and the call for a less philosophically orientated approach to exploring the complex and variable relations between scientific, medical and legal causation, were illustrated through the provision of a tentative framework and a case study.

Acknowledging that policy has not been the main focus of this chapter, our analysis does suggest some abstract yet rather interesting possibilities. First, following our outline of the multi-dimensional and epistemologically promiscuous nature of causal determinations, it could be suggested that attempts at regulation or reform of the ways in which issues of scientific and medical causation are addressed in courts would be advised to avoid reductionist or uni-dimensional approaches. Attempting to highlight or isolate any one hypothesised variable – such as expert witnesses, the scientific illiteracy of the judiciary and jury or limitations inherent to the adversarial system – as a recalcitrant source of law-science (here causal) difficulties, concedes too much ground to the ideal categories used to frame judicial decisions and their rationalisations without actually explaining how such decisions may have been produced.

Efforts at initiating change should probably be more systemic, working beyond the representations made by judges and expert witnesses, and actually influence their ability to manipulate the legal and scientific resources available, as well as influencing the relationship between expert witnesses and the court, and public expectations of the legal system. The multi-dimensional and epistemologically impure nature of legal determinations and representations of causation seem to have some tacit, or what might be better described as subliminal, acceptance in the evolution of various legislative initiatives such as the development of strict liability and compulsory insurance schemes. To varying degrees, these schemes internalise or displace some of the processes involved in aligning the rhetorics of law, medicine and science through the institutional provision of processes and interpretations which operate in a manner consistent with epistemic putty, able to be disguised with the paint of public policy. Even though such mechanisms may offer procedural advantages and appear tidy in operation, it is worth considering that contradictory epistemic glosses, judicial disagreement, the multifaceted nature and policy challenges associated with more traditional approaches to determining legal causation, continue to offer social value through their potential to allow some of the social processes and contingent judgments involved in the creation and dissemination of scientific/medical and legal images of causation to achieve, admittedly quite limited, visibility and public accountability.

PART B:
THE CONCEPT OF JUSTICE AND CAUSAL RESPONSIBILITY IN TORT LAW

6 Legal Rules Governing the Requirement of Causation in Tort Law

IAN CALLINAN[*]

It is not without significance that philosophy and science each attempt explanations of cause and effect. A body of scientists now subscribe to chaos theory. I sometimes think that that theory may have relevance to the legal theory of causation. The theory, as I understand it, is essentially that normal actions are not always productive of predictable consequences: they can cause random results. A mathematician wrote a book called *Does God Play Dice? The Mathematics of Chaos*. The most trivial of events he theorised, might, in combination with other trivial causes, contribute to major catastrophes – the butterfly wings theory. He wrote:[1]

> The flapping of a single butterfly's wing today produces a tiny change in the state of the atmosphere. Over a period of time, what the atmosphere actually does diverges from what it would have done. So, in a month's time, a tornado that would have devastated the Indonesian coast doesn't happen. Or maybe one that wasn't going to happen, does.

I will not dwell on the theoretical notions underpinning the requirement of causation. That is the task of others. I will merely focus on the legal rules, which are, in the end, those set by the court of which I am a member.

However, any discussion about the legal rules governing causation in tort would be incomplete without some reference to the piecemeal development of the law of negligence. It is open to question whether there is any underlying, universal principle. Each category of tort has a different

---

[*]   Justice of the High Court of Australia.
[1]   I Stewart, *Does God Play Dice? The Mathematics of Chaos*, Penguin, London, 1990, at 141.

history. Just as it is said of Roman Law, that to use the word "contract" is misleading for suggesting greater unity in the law than actually existed, to use the term "tort" may be similarly misleading.[2]

Developing in an unprincipled way, as actions on the case, torts were not underpinned by broader legal principles, as, for example occurred in other areas of the law, such as real and personal property. An example which springs to mind is the recent case of *Perre v Apand Pty Ltd*,[3] a case about pure economic loss which provoked an immediate critical response in an article in the *Australian Law Journal* by Justice Pincus of the Court of Appeal of Queensland.[4]

Until *Caltex Oil (Australia) Pty Ltd v The Dredge "Willemstad"*,[5] negligent cause leading to pure economic loss, although accepted as apparently falling within such principles as had evolved, was on policy grounds excluded as an enforceable cause of action. *Caltex* was the ground-breaking Australian case in this field. It has still not attracted the support of the House of Lords or the Privy Council.[6] In *Perre*, most Justices agreed that the appellants in that case could recover for losses which were purely economic. Seven separate judgments were published, none of which formulated the tests in exactly the same way, but all of which subscribed to a number of identical or similar themes.[7]

The High Court is, I can say, in my brief experience of it, not insensitive to the need for bright lines of demarcation and clear principle so that judges may apply, and the law schools may teach, the law with confidence. But a strength of the common law is that it does not seek to impose an inflexible principle when and before it is possible to do so: it acknowledges the need for building blocks of principle over time. This

---

2   B Nicholas, *An Introduction to Roman Law*, Oxford University Press, Oxford, 1962, at 165.
3   (1999) 73 ALJR 1190.
4   (1999) 73 *Australian Law Journal* 802-3.
5   (1976) 136 CLR 529.
6   See, respectively, *Caparo Industries Plc v Dickman* [1990] 2 AC 605; *Candlewood Navigation Corporation Ltd v Mitsui OSK Lines Ltd* [1986] AC 1.
7   The similar strains which can be identified in the judgments are as follows. A) the circumstances in which the common law recognises a duty of care such as will permit the recovery of pure economic loss are not yet governed by any definite general principle, but by other factors which are still developing. B) the law accepts the undesirability of imposing indeterminate liability on an indeterminate class of persons and the imposition of liability in the pursuit of legitimate commercial interests. C) factors of relevance are: common sense and practicality; avoiding interference or impairment of legal rights, freedoms and controls established by common law and statute; the plaintiff's vulnerability; whether the defendant knew or ought to have known that the plaintiff was likely to suffer loss; whether the tortfeasor should have had the interests of the plaintiff in mind; the defendant's capacity to avoid harm.

inherent common law protection should ensure that by the time a principle is articulated, its bases have been applied to a range of different factual circumstances throughout the country and throughout the common law world. I said in *Perre*:[8]

> [I]t must be accepted that this is an area of the law in which the courts should move incrementally and very cautiously indeed. It is not yet possible to identify a bright line of demarcation between those cases of pure economic loss in which damages are recoverable and those in which they are not. The law is still developing in the somewhat piecemeal fashion that Stephen J predicted in *Caltex*:[9]
>
>> "As the body of precedent accumulates some general area of demarcation between what is and is not a sufficient degree of proximity in any particular class of case of pure economic loss will no doubt emerge; but its emergence neither can be, nor should it be, other than as a reflection of the piecemeal conclusions arrived at in precedent cases."

People ought not be too ready to criticise final courts for adopting an evolutionary or incremental approach to causation because difficult problems not surprisingly sometimes provoke difficult solutions. The test of causation expressed in the very early cases, of "immediacy" and "remoteness" were deceptively simple and involved, in any event, value judgments.[10] Those tests are no less arbitrary than those presently applied. The very early cases, of course, were based not on negligence, but on an act causing damage. They were simple tests, "whether the person slain was nearer to death or further from life":[11] not much of a value judgment in that, but certainly more extensive liability. A man was said to act at his peril. Tests of that kind make our current problems seem small in comparison.

Causation, and especially causation in medical negligence cases, has been described as one of the most difficult tasks that the courts must undertake. There is little doubt that it has emerged as one of the most controversial and problematic in expression and application. But why is this problem exciting so much interest now? Causation is not a new doctrine. The concept of causation pre-dates negligence.

---

8   (1999) 73 ALJR 1190 at [405].
9   (1976) 136 CLR 529 at 576.
10   W Holdsworth, *A History of English Law*, 5th edn, Vol III, Methuen, London, 1942, at 379.
11   W Holdsworth, *A History of English Law*, 4th edn, Vol II, 1936, at 52.

One complicating factor is technological development. Theorists and philosophers have said that technology causes us to reconsider long-accepted notions: technology solves problems, but also creates new ones.[12] Although I think this is often overstated, it has an element of truth to it in the case of causation. Perhaps medical care is the field in which this is most evident. The philosopher Mesthene points to two relevant factors: first, the availability of treatments not before possible; and, secondly, delivery of medical care to the population at large as a matter of right, not privilege.[13]

Palliative care may provide a good example to illustrate this. Technology gives us a greater ability to control life, pain and death. With that enhanced ability comes the need to negotiate more difficult issues. As human endeavour breaks further boundaries, courts will be presented with new circumstances and choices of policy. Technology is important to causation because the more we can create, do, control and affect, the more we are able to "cause". I will return briefly to palliative care later. Professor Ashby's contribution to this book deals with that topic from a medical perspective.[14]

It was in the case of *March v Stramare (E & MH) Pty Ltd*[15] that the High Court rejected the so-called "but for" test as the exclusive test of factual causation. Instead, the but for test was to be accompanied or perhaps even superseded by a test of common sense principles. A passage from the judgment of Mason CJ is often cited to explain the logic of applying a test of common sense. The Chief Justice said:[16]

> In philosophy and science, the concept of causation has been developed in the context of explaining phenomena by reference to the relationship between conditions and occurrences.

In law, Mason CJ said, problems arise in the context of apportioning legal responsibility.[17] Therefore, the test becomes whether a particular act or omission can *fairly and properly* be considered a cause of the accident.[18] The implication of *March* is, in one sense, clear. Establishing causation in a but for sense is not sufficient to establish causation generally.

---

[12] See R Helme and D Mendelson, Chapter 13, below.
[13] E Mesthene, "The Role of Technology in Society" in A Teich (ed), *Technology and Man's Future*, 2nd edn, St Martin's Press, New York, 1977, at 160.
[14] See Chapter 11, below.
[15] (1991) 171 CLR 506.
[16] Ibid, at 509.
[17] Ibid.
[18] *Fitzgerald v Penn* (1954) 91 CLR 268 at 276; *Chappel v Hart* (1998) 195 CLR 232 at 243 per Gaudron J.

This reminds me of a parody of causation which appeared in the New Yorker in 1998. It went something like this:[19]

> Your dog ate my philodendron which depressed my mother who in a stupor voted for Marion Barry causing an upswing in crack sales that allowed Peru to maintain an embassy and accumulate parking tickets, encouraging me to stay a meter maid rather than become an Imagineer.

I accept that may be an overstatement of the "but for" test.

March may be the bridge between two conflicting views. The first was that satisfaction of the "but-for" test exhausts the causation issue, with policy considerations being considered at a different stage of the enquiry. The second view which, I should say, has prevailed, is that the but for test, will not of itself, usually be enough to make an act or omission a cause of damage for legal purposes.

The current generation of judges is certainly not the first to grapple with the problem of causation. The common sense test must be distinguished from the last clear chance rule which is said to have been formulated in *Davies v Mann*.[20] The test was that if both parties were negligent, but if one had a last clear chance of avoiding the harm, that person would be solely responsible for the harm. That rule has been trenchantly criticised, not only for being an inept way of giving effect to sensible policy, but also for masquerading as a common sense test and an excuse for throwing the whole blame on the defendant. The rule was abolished with the introduction of apportionment statutes.[21]

The High Court recently applied,[22] but with heavy qualification, the "but-for" test in the context of the *Trade Practices Act* 1974 (Cth) which provided for an examination of whether the applicant suffered damage *by* the conduct of the respondent. The provisions of the statute were held to require the identification of a causal link between loss or damage and conduct done in contravention of the Act. The Court noted the problems with the "but-for" test in *March v Stramare*[23] but preferred to resolve the case by comparing the position of the plaintiff with the position that the party would have been in but for the contravening conduct. On the facts of the case, it was held that no loss had been suffered as a result of the misleading conduct.

---

[19] S Martin, "Studies in the New Causality", *The New Yorker*, 26 October 1998.
[20] (1842) 10 M & W 546 [152 ER 588].
[21] J Fleming, *The Law of Torts*, 9th edn, Law Book Company, London, 1998, at 313.
[22] *Marks v GIO Australia Holdings Ltd* (1998) 73 ALJR 12.
[23] (1991) 171 CLR 506.

It is in the field of medicine, however, that causation poses special problems. I hardly need say, as Justice Kirby recently said, that causation, in the context of establishing a causal connection between medical negligence and damage, is often the most difficult task for a plaintiff in medical malpractice litigation. Fleming describes causation as "plaguing" the courts and scholars.[24] But courts do not even agree on that. Justice Gaudron, in *Naxakis v Western General Hospital*,[25] thought there was a tendency to exaggerate the difficulties associated with the proof of causation.

While the process is difficult and we have undoubtedly much further to go in arriving at a clear solution, the broad tension can be simply stated. Not all causes of damage should give rise to legal liability. Put simply, at what stage does cause become blame? What are the right rules to apply to limit legal liability appropriately?

By the time *Chappel v Hart*[26] came to be decided, the proponents of the stand-alone "but-for" test knew that the law had changed. The case was argued in the High Court on the basis of a lack of causal connection between the patient's injury and the doctor's conduct. It was argued as a loss of chance case. Loss of chance is now a well-settled basis for recovery in contract.[27] Its emergence as a basis for damages in tort[28] has occurred later. In *Naxakis* Gaudron J observed that the loss of chance approach is distinct from the "all or nothing approach involved in allowing damages for the actual harm suffered".[29] That feature of the doctrine has made it attractive to academics, some of whom are of the view that it also alleviates problems associated with causation,[30] especially, as Jansen observes, where there is "uncertain partial causation". Although the view that the difficulties associated with proof of causation may simply re-appear as difficulties in establishing the value of the chance in question must be taken into account,[31] I think, tentatively I might say, that the approach of

---

24   Fleming, op cit, n21, at 218.
25   (1999) 162 ALR 540 at 547.
26   (1998) 195 CLR 232.
27   *Chaplin v Hicks* [1911] 2 KB 786 (deprivation of all chance of obtaining a prize); cf *McRae v Commonwealth Disposals Commission* (1951) 84 CLR 377 at 412 (where the chance lay not in giving the plaintiff a chance, but in the nature of the thing contracted for itself); *Sellars v Adelaide Petroleum* (1994) 179 CLR 332 (loss of an opportunity to obtain a commercial advantage or benefit).
28   See Kirby J in *Chappel v Hart* (1998) 195 CLR 232 at 274-5 and Gaudron J in *Naxakis v Western General Hospital* (1999) 162 ALR 540 at 547-8.
29   *Naxakis v Western General Hospital* (1999) 162 ALR 540 at [30].
30   N Jansen, "The Idea of a Lost Chance" (1999) 19(2) *Oxford Journal of Legal Studies* 271.
31   See Gaudron J in *Naxakis v Western General Hospital* (1999) 162 ALR 540 at [32].

looking to just what damage was caused by the tort, rather than an "all or nothing" approach may have some attractions.

There are still, however, many differences of opinion to be overcome with respect to loss of chance. There is judicial authority to suggest it is simply a matter to be taken into account in assessing damages[32] and that loss of chance does not apply where the plaintiff sustains physical injury.[33] Many of the views are contradictory.

The second point I wish to make in relation to *Chappel v Hart* is this. I would not be overstating the position to say, perhaps not surprisingly, that *Chappel v Hart* has been trenchantly criticised and not dispassionately, by medical practitioners. They point to the inherent unpredictability of the human body, of tissue and of risks of infections.

There may be a tendency for lawyers to believe that all is controllable; that scientific development has replaced biological uncertainty.

If the courts apply a "plain person's" test of causation, then there are several very significant factors which must be considered when determining the extent to which legal responsibility will attach to tortious conduct.

The community generally has high expectations of professionals who hold themselves out as highly skilled, charge accordingly and have in part at least, been expensively educated by public subsidy. But it may now be another question whether public expectations may be tending to overreach the capacity (or indeed the public interest of the community) to match them. When the law of negligence started to assume its modern shape in 1932, concern soon mounted over the liability that manufacturers, and others in the community, might incur as a result of what they regarded as no more than mere mischance. There was always going to be a need for some kind of balancing exercise to ensure that a true victim was properly compensated, but that any burden upon the community to discharge liability, whether by increased insurance charges or higher prices for commodities and services, would not be intolerable.

In *Esanda Finance Corporation Ltd v Peat Marwick Hungerfords*,[34] McHugh J considered the importance of the willingness and ability of people to undertake the essential work of auditing, without the fear of being confronted by enormous claims for damages by people of whom they might be unaware. His Honour warned against the costs to society of too expansive a view of liability:[35]

---

[32]   *Chappel v Hart* (1998) 195 CLR 232 at [61] per Gummow J.
[33]   *Chappel v Hart* (1998) 195 CLR 232 at [16] per Gaudron J.
[34]   (1997) 188 CLR 241.
[35]   Ibid, at 285.

... it is likely that the public will have to pay, directly or indirectly, for the risk of those [economic] losses.

His Honour then went on to quote with approval Professor Siliciano:[36]

Both potential loss spreaders – the accountant and the third party – can expend resources to minimise the losses incurred; the accountant can attempt to audit more thoroughly, while the third party can audit the client independently or bear the investment risks. Both actors can theoretically pass on such costs, plus any residual losses, to the public: the accountant, through increases in the cost of its services; and the third party, through increases in the costs of its credit. Either way, the increased costs initially are imposed on the client class, which in turn passes it on to the public in the form of price increases.

McHugh J added:[37]

From the public's point of view, therefore, the primary question is, who is the more efficient absorber of the losses?

It is true that medical practitioners are paying very high insurance premiums. It is also true that some insurers have withdrawn from the market. It is worrying, as Mendelson has observed, that there is a perception that the law is imposing standards that are impossible to attain.[38]

These are no more than considerations which must be taken into account as the rules of causation are fashioned.

Causation in the criminal context arose for consideration in the recent case of *Osland v R*.[39] Since *Royall v R*,[40] there has been discussion of which of the various tests that were applied in that case would be adopted by the Australian High Court in future cases. In *Osland* the deceased had been drugged and then beaten to death. A mother and her son were the accused. They had jointly selected the weapon, the mother had drugged the deceased, and then the son beat him to death. The mother held the deceased down, either while he was being struck, or immediately after the blows had been administered. These acts were in pursuance of a preconceived plan.

---

36   Ibid, at 285-6 (footnote omitted).
37   Ibid, at 286.
38   D Mendelson, "The Breach of the Medical Duty to Warn and Causation: Chappel v Hart and the Necessity to Reconsider Some Aspects of Rogers v Whitaker" (1998) 5 *Journal of Law and Medicine* 312 at 317-18.
39   (1998) 159 ALR 170.
40   (1991) 172 CLR 378.

A majority of the court found that the mother was causally responsible as a principal for the death. The test preferred by McHugh J in *Royall* was applied, that is, whether the act or omission was "sufficiently significant", or the operating and substantial cause test. There was a difference, however, in the result that was reached on the application of the test. It does not mean that the other tests have been rendered inapplicable; they may still be applicable in appropriate circumstances.

Royall and *Osland* highlight the fact that there is nothing novel in courts disagreeing from time to time about the applicable test and its application.

On the horizon there may be looming problems, particularly with respect to, but perhaps not confined to medical cases, with respect to the proper measure of damages. I said earlier that in *Naxakis* Justice Gaudron referred to loss of chance as one method of avoiding the "all or nothing approach involved in allowing damage for the actual harm suffered".[41] It should be remembered, however, that loss of chance will not always work to the advantage of the plaintiff. I said in *Naxakis* that there is room for the operation of the loss of chance rule:[42]

> If the chance that has been lost is a 51 per cent or greater chance, why should not the plaintiff be taken to have proved his or her case on the balance of probabilities? I think that in such a situation, the plaintiff has, and should recover his or her damages in full. *Rogers v Whitaker*[43] is, in one sense, such a case. The Court there accepted on the balance of probabilities, that the plaintiff would not have had the operation to which she submitted, and which caused the problems for her that it did, if she had been warned of the risk that the Court thought material there. Perhaps the plaintiff's damages there might have been reduced, and indeed significantly so, if what had been established there, was that she might not have had, as opposed to, would not have had the operation.

> On the other hand, in other cases, there is a risk, it might be said, that in almost every instance there is a lost chance of some kind, perhaps even a 1 per cent or 5 per cent chance, and on that basis every plaintiff will succeed to some extent. The answer to this must be that the loss of a remote, or very slight chance should not attract an award of damages. The chance lost must be a real one and of some substance, even though less than a 50 per cent chance. In the practice of medicine, usually a definite, successful result will not be able to be guaranteed. Just as the practitioner should not suffer on that account, nor should the plaintiff, who is

---

41 *Naxakis v Western General Hospital* (1999) 162 ALR 540 at [30] per Gaudron J.
42 *Naxakis v Western General Hospital* (1999) 162 ALR 540 at [129]-[130].
43 (1992) 175 CLR 479.

precluded from saying what the outcome would have been had the procedure or treatment not performed been performed, for the very reason that it has not been performed.

I might tentatively suggest that some of the problems might be resolved if the necessity to keep the issues distinct is kept in mind, and the issues discretely treated. The first inquiry is did the act or omission cause non-minimal damage?[44] If that question is affirmatively answered, the plaintiff has a cause of action in negligence and the case can move to the second stage of inquiry. The second question then becomes what damage was caused by the act or omission?

Some people might even ask the question, what *actual* damage was caused by the act or omission, thereby reducing the possible measure of damages. Some people would say, measure the chance lost. To some it certainly would be anomalous that if you lose a 30 per cent chance you can nevertheless recover in full. To others, it may seem strange that if you lost 50 per cent chance, only nominal damages would be awarded.

None of this is to suggest any clear solutions. Indeed it would be wrong for me to generalise anyway because the outcome of particular cases will depend upon the arguments and the facts of them. Do not, however, be too critical of me. Cause and effect are not merely legal problems. They are problems, as I suggested in the beginning, which concern the philosophy of life itself. On one view, Nietzsche was one of the first deconstructionists and in his "The Will to Power" he spoke of cause and effect in terms of chronological reversal:[45]

> The fragment of the outside world of which we become conscious comes after the effect that has been produced on us and is projected a posteriori as its "cause". In the phenomalism of the "inner world" we invert the chronology of cause and effect. The basic fact of "inner experience" is that the cause gets imagined after the effect has occurred.

I mentioned earlier that palliative care is one area in which rules of causation are being tested. As is often the case with the intersection of law and medicine, approaches to causation and palliative care do not sit easily together. The spectre of criminal sanction for the administration of palliative care may produce defensive medicine with the consequence that patients do not receive adequate pain management. Equally, the law's demarcation between lawful palliative care and unlawful homicide on the

---

44   See *Cartledge v E Jopling & Sons Ltd* [1963] AC 758.
45   Quoted in JD Culler, *On Deconstruction*, Cornell University Press, Ithaca, New York, 1982, at 86.

basis of the intention of the medical profession administering the treatment does not always sit comfortably in the law of homicide. Of course this issue raises fundamental ethical and legal problems, which is undoubtedly one of the reasons that the present position is so uncertain. That uncertainty must inevitably result in very difficult decisions for the practising profession.

It is accepted that palliative care is concerned with the reduction of pain, an incident of which may be bringing about the death of the patient more quickly than otherwise. This can be distinguished from euthanasia, which seeks to relieve pain and suffering by inducing death. The difference, according to Casswell is between "intended consequences and unintended but foreseeable consequences".[46]

It is arguable that palliative care demonstrates some of the inherent limitations of the "but-for" test. Obviously, the underlying pathology of a terminally-ill patient can be said to be the cause of death: but for that illness, the patient would not die as he or she did. However, application of the same test could assign responsibility to a practitioner for causing death through the administration of large doses of morphine: but for the medical intervention, the patient would not have died when he or she did.

The legal approach to causation in palliative care, however, is not the application of the simple "but for" test, contrary to the views of some members of the medical profession. The line between homicide and death brought about by palliative care is drawn on the basis of intent − if the doctor deliberately gives a patient an overdose of narcotics for the purpose of bringing about death, this will constitute homicide. If the motivation is pain relief, then the fact that death is incidental will not be sufficient to attract the operation of the criminal law.

In *Airedale NHS v Bland*, Lord Goff noted the established rule:[47]

> A doctor may, when caring for a patient who is, for example, dying of cancer, lawfully administer pain-killing drugs despite the fact that he knows that an incidental effect of the application will be to abbreviate the patient's life. Such a decision may properly be made as part of the care of the living patient, in his best interests; and, on this basis, the treatment will be lawful. Moreover, where the doctor's treatment of his patient is

---

[46] DG Casswell, "Rejecting Criminal Liability for Life-Shortening Palliative Care" (1990) 6 *Journal of Contemporary Health Law and Policy* 127 at 130, citing "President's Commission for the Study of Ethical Problems in Medicine and Biomedical and Behavioural Research, *Deciding to Forego Life-Sustaining Treatment*" 82 (1983) 77.

[47] [1993] 2 WLR 316 at 379.

lawful, the patient's death will be regarded in law as exclusively caused by the injury or disease to which his condition is attributable.

It must be accepted that this is not a "but for" test.

Haugen notes that no doctor has ever been held liable in murder or assisted suicide for providing a patient with high doses of medication for pain relief.[48] An English case which dealt with the liability of a medical practitioner for the administration of life-shortening palliative care is *R v Adams*.[49] Implicit in the charge of Devlin J to the jury was the notion that administration of treatment with the intent to relieve pain does not attract the censure of criminal law:

> If the first purpose of medicine is the restoration of health, could no longer be achieved, there was still much for the doctor to do, and he is entitled to do all that is proper and necessary to relive pain and suffering, even if the measures he takes may incidentally shorten life.

His Lordship stated the distinction between culpable homicide and lawful medical conduct as being a deliberate cutting of the thread of life, as opposed to the administration of medical treatment which had the incidental effect of determining the exact moment of death.

But what are the remaining problems with causation in the context of palliative care? First, Haugen has observed that the greatest impediment to successful prosecution of medical practitioners for assisting the death of a patient through the administration of pain relief is causation. "Absent very aggravated factors, the prosecution always has an uphill battle".[50] Secondly, there is little clear guidance given by the law to physicians concerning possible criminal liability.[51] Thirdly, it has been argued that a strict application of the criminal law would result in far greater frequency of prosecution, because liability could be established where acts are committed with the knowledge that death will result: that hastening death is sufficient to constitute murder.[52] Clearly, there is a tension between the strict dictates of criminal law and the practice of palliative care. Fourthly,

---

[48] P Haugen, "Pain Relief for the Dying: The Unwelcome Intervention of the Criminal Law" (1997) 23 *William Mitchell Law Review* 325 at 329. However, since this article Dr Jack Kervorkian has been convicted in a Michigan court of second degree murder on 26 March 1999.

[49] Central Criminal Court, London, 1957, unreported, discussed in Palmer, "Dr Adams' Trial for Murder" [1957] Crim LR 365.

[50] Haugen, op cit, n48, at 356.

[51] Casswell, op cit, n46, at 137-8.

[52] See *Active Voluntary Euthanasia – A Timely Reappraisal*, University of Tasmania Law School Occasional Paper, 1991.

the misunderstanding in the medical profession about the nature of the correct test of causation to be applied may lead to defensive medicine, resulting in inadequate medication of terminally ill patients. It is even more ironic that if the profession understood the test of intent which is in fact applied, they may still practice defensive medicine in the knowledge that on a strict application of the criminal law, they may find themselves liable in homicide.

However, all this must be tempered by the recognition that palliative care and euthanasia are components of the same spectrum and that the Australian legislatures have responded to the problems. In the Australian Capital Territory, legislation ensures that patients have a right to receive adequate pain relief which is "reasonable in the circumstances"[53] and in South Australia, palliative care can be administered to people who are dying and to protect them from medical treatment which is "intrusive, burdensome and futile".[54]

---

[53] *Medical Treatment Act* 1994 (ACT) s 4.
[54] *Consent to Medical Treatment and Palliative Care Act* 1995 (SA) s 3(c).

7 Fault, Causation and Responsibility: Is Tort Law Just an Instrument of Corrective Justice?

KEITH MASON*

> *You look at where you're going and where you are and it never makes sense, but then you look back to where you've been and a pattern seems to emerge. And if you project forward from that pattern, then sometimes you can come up with something.*[1]

Like the Irish jury that were unanimous that they could not agree, the High Court of Australia laboured mightily in *Perre v Apand Pty Ltd*[2] before recognising lack of consensus or even a majority position about the essentials of the action in negligence for pure economic loss. Only Kirby J saw merit in the three stage framework favoured in England. Their Honours agreed that the animal exists. But proximity was rejected as a useful taxonomic guide. General reliance is no longer generally relied on by the hunters. The creature could not be identified by its foreseeability spots, but its known vulnerability was proposed as a working hypothesis.[3]

The lack of agreement is hardly surprising. The framework of modern tort law is elusive, perhaps inherently protean. Maybe Cooke P was correct in his gloomy prognostication that:

---

*   President of the New South Wales Court of Appeal.
1   Robert M Pirsig, *Zen and the Art of Motor Cycle Maintenance: An Inquiry into Values*, W Morrow, New York, 1983, p162.
2   [1999] HCA 36, 73 ALJR 1190, 164 ALR 606.
3   Support for this factor has firmed in *Crimmins v Stevedoring Industry Finance Committee* (1999) 167 ALR 1 at [3] per Gleeson CJ (agreeing with McHugh J), [43] per Gaudron J, [100], [104] per McHugh J, [233] per Kirby J.

Ultimately the exercise can only be a balancing one and the important object is that all relevant factors be weighed. There is no escape from the truth that, whatever formula be used, the outcome in a grey area case has to be determined by judicial judgment. Formulae can help to organise thinking but they cannot provide answers.[4]

Whether a new age of certainty will dawn in the High Court is unknown. In the meantime, the decision to proceed slowly and see what turns up was inevitable. It is hardly unprecedented. Even Sir Owen Dixon once confided to Chief Justice Latham:[5]

> In [s92] cases relating to transport ... I think it is almost clear that we must proceed by arbitrary methods. No doubt there will be limits but political and economic considerations will guide the instinct of the Court chiefly. In time the thing will work back to some principle or doctrine.

Perhaps Sir Owen had tongue in cheek, recognising the need for himself to mark time to allow his arbitrary brethren time to fall into line with his own clear logic.[6]

Very recently, in *Crimmins v Stevedoring Industry Finance Committee*,[7] McHugh J warned that incremental development by analogy must be rooted in principle and policy. Frank discussion about policy factors must not abandon the search for a linking chain of reasoning. His Honour stressed the merits of predictability and sought to confine the uncertainties of *Perre* to cases of pure economic loss. It may not be reading too much into his judgment to see it as a plea to his brethren not to revisit well-established areas of tort law in the quest to find and apply principles of general application.[8]

The concepts of "fault" and "responsibility" are part of the landscape of modern tort law, but they usually lie hidden. "Responsibility" covers a wide spectrum. It does not necessarily import legal liability or moral blame, although it is a condition of both. As Professor Honoré points out,

---

4   *South Pacific Manufacturing Co Ltd v New Zealand Security Consultants & Investigations Ltd* [1992] 2 NZLR 282 at 294. See also J Stapleton, "Duty of Care Factors: A Selection from the Judicial Menus" in P Cane and J Stapleton (eds), *The Law of Obligations: Essays in Celebration of John Fleming*, Clarendon Press, Oxford, 1998.

5   Letter dated 1 June 1937 quoted by Bennett, *Keystone of the Federal Arch*, p 67.

6   This, of course, happened. The new age of certainty dawned in *Hughes & Vale Pty Ltd v New South Wales* [1955] AC 241. It was to flourish for a time, before a new dark age, followed by a new age of certainty was to reappear (*Cole v Whitfield* (1988) 165 CLR 360) briefly (cf *Bath v Alston Holdings Pty Ltd* (1988) 165 CLR 411).

7   [1999] HCA 59 at [73]-[78].

8   Kirby J spoke to same effect at [226] n262.

human responsibility may relate to (a) our own conduct, (b) the responsibility that we choose to take on for other people, things and events; and (c) the responsibility that society thrusts upon us.[9] I shall confine myself to the field of *legal* responsibility as reflected in the law of *tort*, principally the expanding field of negligence. That area is more than large enough. Professor Honoré's three aspects of responsibility are still relevant. They remind us that liability may stem from omissions as well as acts, including the acts or omissions of a third party. And they show the fallacy of limiting duty of care to "assumption" of an obligation to control a person or situation.

The general rule is that a plaintiff bears the onus of proof on all matters.[10] Proving liability is one thing, getting all of the damages claimed is another. Academic lawyers tend to concentrate on the former. Practitioners and judges spend most of their time dealing with the latter. Many injured plaintiffs come with a history of other problems or acquire one after the tortious injury and before trial. The task of segregating the loss actually stemming from the tort may be complex and problematic. It is generally true that the tortfeasor takes the victim as found, but it is certainly not the corollary that the court ignores the victim's antecedent incapacities or potential disabilities and illnesses when assessing damages.[11] Nor does the victim get reparation for every loss stemming however remotely from the wrongdoer's fault. Many factual and legal issues require unravelling.

In *Perre*, McHugh J propounded the theses that tort law is "an instrument of corrective justice";[12] and that "negligence at common law is still a fault-based system".[13]

McHugh J's references to the law of tort being an instrument of corrective justice draw attention to a sophisticated debate occurring in North America.[14] At the broadest level, this theory sees tort law as grounded upon "correlativity", requiring those who have harmed others without justification to put the matter right by reparation (damages),

---

9   See T Honoré, *Responsibility and Fault*, Hart Publishing, Oxford, 1999, pp125-9. This book republishes essays written during the last decade, with an introduction drawing together the various strands.

10 A number of ostensibly procedural rules assist plaintiffs in their quest to prove a tort case against chosen defendants (see nn41, 42 below).

11 *Wilson v Peisley* (1975) 7 ALR 571, 50 ALJR 207.

12 *Perre* at [103], [151]. See also *Esanda Finance Corporation Ltd v Peat Marwick Hungerfords* (1997) 188 CLR 241 at 284, 289.

13 *Perre* at [131]. See also Gummow J at [171].

14 See, eg EJ Weinrib, "The Special Morality of Tort Law" (1989) 34 *McGill Law Rev* 403; RW Wright, "Substantive Corrective Justice" (1992) 77 *Iowa Law Rev* 625; Honoré, op cit, n9, pp73-6.

specific relief (eg return of a detained chattel) or other means (eg an apology). It requires proof of harm done to the plaintiff for which the defendant bears some causal responsibility.

But the wrongdoer may be impossible to identify or not worth suing. Exclusive adherence to corrective justice principles is not good enough for plaintiffs who go in search of "peripheral" parties.[15] An American newspaper headline summed it up:

> Can't sue the person who hurt you? Don't sulk. Hire a personal-injury lawyer and sue someone else.

Corrective justice does not fully explain the rules of tort.[16] Even within negligence, the silent but insistent demands of distributive justice may enlarge liability, for example by imposing strict or near strict liability upon classes of persons involved in risky undertakings or by favouring liability against insured defendants.[17] Conversely, they may restrict liability, for example by control devices in the field of nervous shock, that are difficult to justify in principle.[18] The highway non-feasance rule cannot be explained except according to principles of distributive justice.

Recently the House of Lords has given explicit recognition to distributive justice principles as reasons for limiting tort liability. *Frost v Chief Constable of South Yorkshire*[19] involved claims by police officers with respect to psychiatric injury suffered after helping victims at the Hillsborough disaster where 96 spectators were crushed to death at a soccer match. The negligence of the officers' employer was held insufficient to ground recovery for pure psychiatric injury.[20] Their Lordships expressed concern about the impact of a litigation explosion in this area, including concern about the burden of damages and the impact upon crowded court lists. It is also clear that they recognised the difficulty of justifying how it would be fair to award compensation to police officers when it had already been refused to family members of those killed or maimed at the disaster.[21]

---

15   See J Stapleton, "Duty of Care: Peripheral Parties and Alternative Opportunities for Deterrence" (1995) 111 *LQR* 301; *Crimmins* at [306] (Hayne J).

16   See generally P Cane, "Corrective Justice and Correlativity in Private Law" (1996) 16 *Ox Jo LS* 471; Honoré, op cit, n9, pp80-7.

17   At present the availability of insurance is, in theory, an irrelevant factor: see *Kars v Kars* (1996) 187 CLR 354 at 378-9; *Esanda* at 302-3.

18   See J Stapleton, "In Restraint of Tort" in P Birks (ed), *The Frontiers of Liability*, Oxford University Press, Oxford, New York, 1994, vol 2, p95.

19   [1999] 2 AC 455.

20   Whether this represents the Australian law is unclear. Cf *Mount Isa Mines Ltd v Pusey* (1970) 125 CLR 383.

21   *Alcock v Chief Constable of South Yorkshire Police* [1992] 1 AC 310.

Lord Hoffmann referred to competing proposals to scrap all "control mechanisms" in relation to psychiatric damage or alternatively to abolish recovery for psychiatric injury altogether. He continued:[22]

> The appeal of these two opposing proposals rather depends upon where one starts from. If one starts from the proposition that in principle the law of torts is there to give legal force to an Aristotelian system of corrective justice, then there is obviously no valid distinction to be drawn between physical and psychiatric injury. On this view, the control mechanisms merely reflect a vulgar scepticism about the reality of psychiatric injury or a belief that it is less worthy of compensation than physical injury: therein the patient must minister to himself. On the other hand, if one starts from the imperfect reality of the way the law of torts actually works, in which the vast majority of cases of injury and disability, both physical and psychiatric, go uncompensated because the persons (if any) who caused the damage were not negligent (a question which often involves very fine distinctions), or because the plaintiff lacks the evidence or the resources to prove to a court that they were negligent, or because the potential defendants happen to have no money, then questions of distributive justice tend to intrude themselves. Why should X receive generous compensation for his injury when Y receives nothing? Is the administration of so arbitrary and imperfect a system of compensation worth the very considerable cost? On this view, a uniform refusal to provide compensation for psychiatric injury adds little to the existing stock of anomaly in the law of torts and at least provides a rule which is easy to understand and cheap to administer.

In *McFarlane v Tayside Health Board*[23] the House of Lords held that damages were not recoverable for the maintenance of a healthy child born following a negligently performed vasectomy operation on her father. The child's mother was allowed general damages for the pain, suffering and inconvenience of childbirth. But the parents were refused their claim for the costs of maintaining and educating their healthy "unplanned" child. Lord Steyn said:[24]

> It is possible to view the case simply from the perspective of corrective justice. It requires somebody who has harmed another without justification to indemnify the other. On this approach the parents' claim for the cost of bringing up Catherine must succeed. But one may also approach the case from the vantage point of distributive justice. It requires a focus on the just distribution of burdens and losses among

---

22   At 503.
23   [1999] 3 WLR 1301.
24   At 1318.

members of a society. If the matter is approached in this way, it may become relevant to ask of the commuters on the Underground the following question: "Should the parents of an unwanted but healthy child be able to sue the doctor or hospital for compensation equivalent to the cost of bringing up the child for the years of his or her minority, ie until about 18 years?" My Lords, I have not consulted my fellow travellers on the London Underground but I am firmly of the view that an overwhelming number of ordinary men and women would answer the question with an emphatic "No". And the reason for such a response would be an inarticulate premise as to what is morally acceptable and what is not. Like Ognall J in *Jones v Berkshire Area Health Authority*, 2 July 1986, they will have in mind that many couples cannot have children and others have the sorrow and burden of looking after a disabled child. The realisation that compensation for financial loss in respect of the upbringing of a child would necessarily have to discriminate between rich and poor would, surely appear unseemly to them. It would also worry them that parents may be put in a position of arguing in court that the unwanted child, which they accepted and care for, is more trouble than it is worth. Instinctively, the traveller on the Underground would consider that the law of tort has no business to provide legal remedies consequent upon the birth of a healthy child, which all of us regard as a valuable and good thing.

It is interesting that in *Esanda Finance Corporation Ltd v Peat Marwick Hungerfords*[25] McHugh J effectively recognised that distributive justice could temper even "the most insistent demands of corrective justice". He saw the extension of auditor's liability to cover cases like *Esanda* as:

> ... likely to mean that courts and judges hearing such cases will be tied up for many months – sometimes for more than a year – to the detriment of other litigants. Only the most insistent demands of corrective justice should induce the common law courts to mould legal rules to cover cases that bring about this consequence in an era when court resources are already stretched to breaking point and courts are forced to send many cases out to private arbitrators for determination.

It is too early to declare corrective justice as the victor in the field. But it remains a predominating force.

Cutting across this corrective-distributive justice debate, but mainly within the corrective justice framework, lies the question of the role of fault.

---

[25]   (1997) 188 CLR 241 at 284.

Occasionally judges acknowledge the impact of fault and the way that moral responsibility is relevant in a marginal case.[26] In *Caltex Oil (Australia) Pty Ltd v The Dredge "Willemstad"*,[27] Stephen J referred to "a general public sentiment of moral wrongdoing for which the offender must pay" as a broad principle underlying liability in negligence.

Sir John Salmond denied the existence of a single law of tort. At the same time, he argued that a condition usually demanded for liability in an action of tort was either wrongful intention or culpable negligence on the part of the defendant. For him, there was no reason why a loss should be shifted from one person's shoulders to another's except, in general, to punish or deter wrongful intent or negligence.[28] Salmond was logically compelled to say of the decision in *Rylands v Fletcher*,[29] which is founded upon a theory of strict liability:[30]

> No decision in the law of torts has done more to prevent the establishment of a simple, uniform, and intelligible system of civil responsibility.

The High Court took note in *Burnie Port Authority v General Jones Pty Ltd*.[31] McHugh J's protest that "the common law holds no prejudice against strict liability"[32] did not sway the majority.

The overruling of *Beaudesert Shire Council v Smith*[33] in *Northern Territory of Australia v Mengel*[34] points in a similar direction. There have also been recent stern reminders that the action for breach of statutory duty does not exist in the absence of clearly expressed legislative intent to confer a personal right.[35] Other pockets of residual strict liability are being identified and exterminated in the "staggering march of negligence".[36]

---

26   See, eg *McLoughlin v O'Brian* [1983] AC 410 at 441 (Lord Bridge).

27   (1976) 136 CLR 529 at 575. The passage is cited by Gummow J in *Perre* at [171]. Stephen J was quoting from Lord Atkin's speech in *Donoghue v Stevenson* [1932] AC 562 at 580.

28   Sir John William Salmond, *The law of torts: a treatise on the English law of liability for civil injuries*, 6th edn, Sweet & Maxwell, London, 1924, pp12-13. See discussion by RFV Heuston & RA Buckley in *Salmond and Heuston on the Law of Torts*, 21st edn, Sweet & Maxwell, London, 1996, pp21-5.

29   (1866) LR 1 Ex 265, (1868) LR 3 HL 330.

30   *Salmond on Torts*, 6th edn, op cit, n28, at viii.

31   (1994) 179 CLR 520.

32   At 593. Only Brennan J joined him in dissent.

33   (1966) 120 CLR 145.

34   (1995) 185 CLR 307.

35   Ibid, at 343-4; *Byrne v Australian Airlines Ltd* (1995) 185 CLR 410 at 458-9; *Crimmins* at [157]-[158] (Gummow J).

36   See T Weir, "The staggering march of negligence" in Cane and Stapleton, op cit, n4. Professor Weir instances developments in relation to nuisance, trespass, defamation

But the trend is not all one-way. The desire to find identifiable and deep-pocketed defendants has pushed the boundaries of vicarious liability and non-delegable duties of care. Indeed, there are strong hints by McHugh J and Kirby J in *Northern Sandblasting Pty Ltd v Harris*[37] that the time is ripe for the High Court to consider adopting a principle of vicarious liability for the acts and omissions of independent contractors. It is impossible to fit these developments within the correlative framework of the corrective justice model.

"It's your fault, you should pay for it" represents the response of a primary school child whose treasured toy is broken by a playmate. Childish insights to ethical issues are not necessarily deficient. But complexities enter as the child matures, especially if he or she stands in the wrongdoer's shoes.

The childish response occurs where causation in fact is clear, at least to the child. There is a single wrongdoer whose responsibility stems directly from smashing the toy. To the naïve victim, the wrongdoer's capacity for self-discipline does not enter into the equation, nor the unexpected extent of the loss, nor its lack of proportion to the fault of the wrongdoer, nor the wrongdoer's capacity to pay. These things only occur as the growing child starts to perceive that standards set for others may be applied in reverse. Later comes the idea that it is more useful to lay the problem at the feet of the wrongdoer's parents.

Similar developments affect the mature common law as it is asked to make someone pay for every conceivable species of harm. Let me illustrate. P suffers blood poisoning in hospital where he is a temporary patient following a minor road accident. The simple example may throw up a plethora of issues:

- Which individuals are liable: the doctor, the nurses, the driver?
- Which organisations are liable because of vicarious liability or a non-delegable duty: the hospital, the driver's employer, the car owner, the highway authority?
- What damages are payable by each defendant? Does every person liable pay for both the bruising and the damage stemming from the blood poisoning?

---

and other areas where there are intrusions of negligence's concepts of reasonableness, foreseeability, proximity, remoteness etc.

[37] (1997) 188 CLR 313 at 366, 392. For recent cases illustrating difficulties with the existing law, see *Newcastle Entertainment Security Pty Ltd v Simpson* [1999] NSWCA 351, *Hollis v Vabu Pty Ltd (T/as Crisis Couriers)* [1999] NSWCA 334.

- Are damages reduced for contributory negligence?
- Can the defendants share the loss amongst themselves?

Several doctrines aid injured plaintiffs in their quest to find someone "to pay" and pay in full. These include substantive rules like the "egg shell skull" rule. There are also rules of procedure which aid plaintiffs uncertain whom to sue[38] or which allow (but do not compel) inferences of causation to be drawn against persons whose negligence is followed by an accident of the kind within the scope of the relevant duty.[39] Indeed there is a current debate about whether persons who create or increase a risk of injury should (without proof on the probabilities that the risk came home) bear legal responsibility if the risk comes home.[40] The plaintiff's task is eased by the need to show only that the injuries were "caused or materially contributed to" by the wrongful conduct of the chosen defendant or defendants,[41] and by the law's adherence to the concept of solidary liability.[42]

The fault notion may act as a control device. It is seen as unfair to place the burden of loss upon the shoulders of a tortfeasor whose fault is disproportionate to the loss claimed by one or many plaintiffs. To the extent that fault and degrees of fault influence findings as to liability or the extent of liability, there is a tempering of corrective justice in deference to a retribution principle in which there is proportionality between the gravity of the defendant's conduct and the extent of reparation.[43]

(Sometimes legislatures intervene to close floodgates. Occasionally defendants are given statutory immunity, which the courts construe

---

[38] See *Bendix Mintex Pty Ltd v Barnes* (1997) 42 NSWLR 307 at 317.

[39] See *Betts v Whittingslowe* (1945) 71 CLR 637 at 649; *Chappel v Hart* (1998) 195 CLR 232 at 238-9, 247-8, 257, 273-4; *Naxakis v Western General Hospital* [1999] HCA 22 at [31], [76], [127].

[40] The debate centres on the interpretation or re-interpretation of Lord Wilberforce's speech in *McGhee v National Coal Board* [1973] 1 WLR 1 at 6-7. Some propose effective reversal of onus of proof as distinct from the reasoning process referred to the authorities cited in the previous footnote. Cf *Bennett v Minister for Community Welfare* (1992) 176 CLR 408 at 420-1, esp fn (23) (Gaudron J); *Chappel* at 273-4 (Kirby J); J Stapleton, "The Gist of Negligence" (1988) 104 *LQR* 389 at 401-7. Within New South Wales much of the debate is focused on the correctness or otherwise of my reasons in *Bendix Mintex* in their application to mesothelioma cases.

[41] *March v E & MH Stramare Pty Ltd* (1991) 171 CLR 506 at 514.

[42] This enables the plaintiff to take action against one of many defendants and to receive full compensation from that defendant, leaving it to the defendant to seek to recover a share of the damages from any other liable defendant. See generally New South Wales Law Reform Commission, *Contribution Between Persons Liable for the Same Damages*, 1999, R99.

[43] See Honoré, op cit, n9, pp85-7.

narrowly.[44] More common are legislative caps which preclude certain heads of damages or limit their extent.)

Causation is a "central organising concept",[45] usually a control device, in tort law's quest to keep law (liability) and morality (fault) in step. Causation reasoning is often used to expand or to stem liability for particular losses flowing from an act of negligence.

Tracing tort law's use and abuse of causation discloses major developments in the quest to recognise fault but to stem its disproportionate outcome. Many hard issues have been hidden beneath the beguiling veneer of causation. In his introduction to *Responsibility and Fault*, Professor Honoré states[46] that "people are never legally liable *merely* because they have caused someone harm".

It may be possible to see four stages in the use and abuse of causation.

Like the child whose toy is broken, the ancient common law usually treated legal responsibility as a self-evident consequence of causation of damage, regardless of fault. This is hardly surprising since concern was focused on physical injury and since the action for trespass dealt with direct and intentional acts. Even the action on the case refused until the nineteenth century to recognise openly that absence of fault was an excuse.[47] So mechanistic was the early common law that it compensated for death by confiscation of the offending animal or object or requiring the owner to pay its value. In this institution of deodand, blame or fault was usually irrelevant, but juries sometimes imposed nominal deodands if fault was absent.[48]

By the nineteenth century a tort of negligence had emerged, but *Rylands v Fletcher* illustrates that strict liability remained well entrenched. *Re Polemis and Furness, Withy & Co Ltd*[49] epitomises the second stage of the role of causation in tort damages. Liability now depends, in the main, upon proof of lack of due care (fault) in established duty categories. But responsibility in damages (still almost invariably for physical loss and damage) extends to all of the direct consequences of a negligent act. On the plaintiff's side of the equation, contributory negligence is a complete defence.

---

[44] See, eg *Puntoriero v Water Administration Ministerial Corporation* (1999) 165 ALR 337, (1999) 73 ALJR 1359.

[45] Weinrib, op cit, n14, p404.

[46] Ibid, at p7.

[47] *Alford v Magee* (1952) 85 CLR 437 at 453. Generally, see C Peck, "Negligence and Liability Without Fault in Tort Law" (1971) 46 *Washington L Rev* 225 at 225-7.

[48] See T Sutton, "The Deodand and Responsibility for Death" (1997) 18 *Legal History* 44.

[49] [1921] 3 KB 560.

Ostensibly, causation reasoning provided answers for plaintiffs and defendants in this era. To limit liability for negligent defendants and to permit recovery by negligent plaintiffs judges developed metaphysical causation principles, using them like circuit breakers. Concepts such as *novus actus interveniens* were introduced as control devices to block Cardozo CJ's hideous spectre of liability "in an indeterminate amount for an indeterminate time to an indeterminate class".[50] In many cases, the judges were driven "to take refuge in metaphor or Latin".[51] Refinements such as *causa causans*, effective cause, proximate or legal cause and *novus actus interveniens* were introduced to reflect degrees of fault and to deal with difficulties presented by the distinction between acts and omissions and where the acts of third persons or natural forces are concerned. Negligent plaintiffs sometimes succeeded by showing that the defendant had the "last opportunity" to avoid an accident, and until at least the 1950s "last opportunity" was viewed in terms of breaking a chain of causation stemming from the plaintiff's own negligence.[52]

Wagon Mound (No 1) gave greater emphasis to the fault concept by overruling *Re Polemis* and offering foreseeability of damage as a control device.[53] However, Viscount Simond's test was really "a flexible concept deprive[d] ... of any fettering rigidity".[54] It warned not to take causation too far, but it did not change much. *Re Polemis* would probably be decided the same today. *Wagon Mound* has spawned its own complex distinctions between foreseeability as to kinds of damage and foreseeability as to the manner in which damage might occur.[55]

Around the 1960s and 1970s there was a determined effort by appellate judges to expel metaphysical theory with its attendant metaphors and latinisms. Windeyer J once joked that:

---

[50] *Ultramares Corp v Touche* 174 NE 441 at 444 (1931).

[51] *Environment Agency v Empress Car Co (Abertillery) Limited* [1999] 2 AC 22 at 29 per Lord Hoffmann.

[52] In *Alford v Magee* (1952) 85 CLR 437 the High Court exploded this view. But the proposition that the last opportunity rule was not a test of causation had to be reiterated in *Chapman v Hearse* (1961) 106 CLR 112 at 123-4. See also *March* at 511-4.

[53] *Overseas Tankership (UK) Ltd v Mort's Dock & Engineering Co Ltd ("The Wagon Mound")* [1961] AC 388.

[54] Sir Robin Cooke, "Remoteness of Damages and Judicial Discretion" [1978] *Cam LJ* 501 at 537. In *March* (at 510), Mason CJ explained that reasonable foresight was later to be rejected as a test of causation (in *Chapman v Hearse*) and as an exclusive criteria of responsibility (in *McKew v Holland & Hannen & Cubitts* [1970] SC (HL) 20 and *Mahoney v J Kruschich (Demolitions) Pty Ltd* (1985) 156 CLR 522).

[55] *Chapman* at 120-1; *Hughes v Lord Advocate* [1963] AC 837; *Commonwealth v McLean* (1996) 41 NSWLR 389 at 402-7.

those who would explain common law principles by exotic Latin maxims ought surely to remember that these are to be understood *secundum subjectam materiam.*[56]

What were we offered in its place? Enter the third phase. "Causation" was still seen as central, because reasonable foreseeability only "mark[ed] the limits beyond which a wrongdoer will not be held responsible for damage resulting from his wrongful act".[57] However, we were assured that causation problems could be solved by the robust application of "common sense". Thus, in *Alphacell Ltd v Woodward*[58] Lord Salmon said that:

> ... what or who has caused a certain event to occur is essentially a practical question of fact which can best be answered by ordinary common sense rather than by abstract metaphysical theory.

This robust approach was particularly suitable in the era when juries decided liability and damages.[59]

March v E & MH Stramare Pty Ltd[60] is the Australian authority still often cited for the glib submission that causation is a question of fact and a matter of common sense. It is frequently invoked in a context suggesting that hard questions of responsibility for fault can be solved once the causation issue is properly addressed. In fact, *March* is the modern turning point and the start of a fourth era in which causation reasoning becomes increasingly unfashionable. The CLR headnote reiterates the mantra that causation is essentially a question of fact to be answered by reference to common sense and experience. But this misrepresents *March*, which substantially qualifies or undermines this proposition by going on to emphasise that questions of policy and value judgments necessarily affect legal responsibility, measure of damages, contributory negligence and apportionment. The judgments in *March* acknowledge that the attribution of responsibility is a value-laden exercise even if the language of causation is used. Mason CJ was even critical of the view that value judgment has no part to play even in resolving causation as an issue of fact.[61]

---

[56] *Smith v Jenkins* (1970) 119 CLR 397 at 410.

[57] *Chapman* at 122 per curiam.

[58] [1972] AC 824 at 847. Lord Hoffmann describes this as being "in the best tradition of English anti-intellectualism" *Common Sense and Causing Loss*, lecture to the Chancery Bar Association, 15 June 1999, p2. See also *Clay v A J Crump & Sons Ltd* [1964] 1 QB 533 at 568-9 per Upjohn LJ ("... causation is almost entirely a question of fact in each case").

[59] See *Fitzgerald v Penn* (1954) 91 CLR 268.

[60] (1991) 171 CLR 506.

[61] At 515-7. See also Deane J at 523-4.

Building on *March*, there has been a further retreat in the last decade from the misplaced and misleading confidence that causation can be reduced to an opaque jury instruction about using common sense. Lord Hoffmann's speech in *Environment Agency v Empress Car Co (Abertillery) Ltd*[62] is a milestone. His Lordship put the matter bluntly in a recent paper:[63]

> The reason why courts get the wrong answer on questions of causation is not usually because they have misunderstood the facts or lack common sense but because they have got the law wrong.

We are now urged to ask necessary causation questions in their particular factual and legal context and, in the case of tort, from the point of view of the injured plaintiff and the wrong sued upon. Professor Stapleton helpfully describes this as the perspective through which the objective phenomenon of causation is judged.[64] Thus, in *Chappel*, Gaudron J said:[65]

> Questions of causation are not answered in a legal vacuum. Rather, they are answered in the legal framework in which they arise. For present purposes, that framework is the law of negligence. And in that framework, it is important to bear in mind that that body of law operates, if it operates at all, to assign a duty to take reasonable steps to prevent a foreseeable risk of harm of the kind in issue.

Cases such as *Medlin v State Government Insurance Commission*[66] applied this approach to mitigation issues. The last of the metaphysical latinisms using the language of causation *(novus actus interveniens)* was shown the door, without actually being booted out. The High Court there emphasised that the reasonableness of the plaintiff's conduct was to be judged, as between the plaintiff and the defendant, and from the perspective of the plaintiff's injured condition.

Appeals to common sense should nevertheless serve to remind us that the exercise is one in which judges and juries should have confidence in their personal sense of wisdom and reasonableness. But the task remains normative, because in the final analysis the various tests "allow the tribunal

---

[62] [1999] 2 AC 22.
[63] See footnote 58.
[64] J Stapleton, "Perspectives on Causation" in *Oxford Essays in Jurisprudence*, 4th series, Oxford University Press, Oxford 1999.
[65] (1998) 195 CLR 232 at 238.
[66] (1995) 182 CLR 1. In so doing, the court effectively applied what Mason CJ and McHugh J had said about *novus actus interveniens* in *March*. See *Kavanagh v Akhtar* (1998) 45 NSWLR at 597-9.

of fact to determine legal liability on broad grounds of moral responsibility for the damage which has occurred".[67]

In *March*, the High Court exposed the presence of policy values sheltering behind the glib language of causation. In later cases, that Court has commenced to articulate those values. The guidance from the recent cases is that ultimate questions such as "was there breach?", "did it affect the plaintiff's conduct?" and "did it cause the damage claimed?" must be asked in the context of the defendant's legal responsibility to the particular plaintiff. This may involve considering the scope of the risk in contemplation of the legal duty.

A cynical response to the title of my paper would be to propound the thesis that if a judge is moved by fault then he or she will find legal responsibility. But the books are full of cases "which show how shadowy is the line between culpability and compensation".[68] Recent decisions and recent academic writing have cast much light on the subject. The shadows remain, but the focus is clearer.

---

[67] *March* at 531 per McHugh J.
[68] *Wagon Mound (No 1)* at 418 per Viscount Simonds.

8 Loss of Chance

HAROLD LUNTZ[*]

> *McHUGH J: It might be that it is really a loss of chance case, is it not, rather than ...*
>
> *KIRBY J: At last we might ...*
>
> *MR BRERETON: Yes, it might be, your Honour. It has never been put on that basis.*
>
> *McHUGH J: No, I know. That seems to me probably the correct basis for putting that sort of case.*
>
> *MR BRERETON: But, essentially, what we are now faced with is something completely different from what was at trial and what was in the Court of Appeal.*
>
> *KIRBY J: One day we will get a good loss of chance case.*
>
> *MR BRERETON: I will see if I can find one, your Honour.[1]*

Introduction

So far the High Court of Australia has not been faced with a clear-cut case of loss of chance in a medical negligence appeal. Special leave to appeal was refused in the case from which the above extract is taken, mainly because the issue had not been litigated below and the necessary findings of fact had not been made. Cases will seldom be litigated on the basis of loss of a chance, because both plaintiff and defendant are hopeful of complete victory.[2] Nevertheless, experience in other jurisdictions suggests that Kirby J is right in saying that one day the court will have an opportunity to consider the issue.

The doctrine has been described in the Supreme Court of Canada as suggesting that "plaintiffs may be compensated where their only loss is the

---

[*] George Paton Professor of Law at the Faculty of Law, the University of Melbourne.

[1] Transcript of argument on special leave application in *Prosser v Eagle* [1999] 20 Leg Rep SL 2 (30 November 1999). See also the transcript of argument in *Green v Chenoweth* [1998] 19 Leg Rep SL 4 (20 November 1998).

[2] See G Masel, "Damages in Tort for Loss of Chance" (1995) 3 *TLJ* 43 at 52.

loss of a chance at a favourable opportunity or of a chance of avoiding a detrimental event."[3] A possible scenario might be as follows:

> *A patient presents for treatment with symptoms that should alert a medical practitioner to the possibility of cancer. The practitioner negligently fails to recognise the symptoms and to recommend tests that could confirm the presence of cancer. Six months later the patient is found to be suffering from cancer. Its state of growth and the earlier symptoms indicate that it was already present when the earlier examination was conducted. If the practitioner had then recommended the appropriate tests, the cancer would probably have been detected and treated. Had it then been treated, the patient would have had a 40 per cent chance of survival for another five years. Now that six months have elapsed without treatment, the chances of the patient's survival for five years are only 10 per cent.*[4]

In such a case, assuming that there is a contract between the medical practitioner and the patient, as there would ordinarily be even if no money passed directly from the patient to the doctor,[5] the patient would be entitled to nominal damages at least for the breach of the implied term requiring the exercise of reasonable care and skill. If there is no contract, nominal damages cannot be awarded, since any action would be in the tort of negligence and damage is the gist of the action. Beyond that, disputed territory lies.[6]

---

3 *Athey v Leonati* [1996] 3 SCR 458 at 474, cited by Gummow J in *Chappel v Hart* (1998) 195 CLR 232 at 260.

4 Cf *Herskovits v Group Health Cooperative*, 99 Wash 2d 609, 664 P2d 474 (1983), where the claim was brought by the patient's dependants after his death. In some ways, a Lord Campbell's Act claim simplifies the assessment of damages, but complicates other issues: cf JH King Jr, "Causation, Valuation, and Chance in Personal Injury Torts Involving Pre-Existing Conditions and Future Consequences" (1981) 90 *Yale LJ* 1353 at 1382, n100. For the sake of similar simplicity, I shall assume that the patient is alive at the date of the trial and that by "survival" is meant the ability to lead a relatively normal life with earning capacity unimpaired.

5 See *Breen v Williams* (1996) 186 CLR 71 at 78 per Brennan CJ; but cf at 123 per Gummow J; *Hotson v East Berkshire AHA* [1987] AC 750 (CA & HL) at 768 per Croom-Johnson LJ (assuming that claim against private doctor would be in contract and one against National Health Service one would be in tort).

6 Some of the voluminous literature on the topic is T Hill, "A Lost Chance for Compensation in the Tort of Negligence by the House of Lords" (1991) 54 *MLR* 511; W Scott, "Causation in Medico-Legal Practice: A Doctor's Approach to the 'Lost Opportunity' Cases" (1992) 55 *MLR* 521; E Adeney, "The Challenge of Medical Uncertainty: Factual Causation in Anglo-Australian Toxic Tort Litigation" (1993) 19 *Mon U Law Rev* 23; SR Perry, "Protected Interests and Undertakings in the Law of Negligence" (1992) 42 *Uni of Toronto LJ* 247; M Lunney, "What Price a Chance?" (1995) 15 *Leg Stud* 1; Hon Sir Anthony Mason, "The Recovery and Calculation of

On one view, the patient, if able to prove on a balance of probabilities that he or she suffered pain during the six months when the cancer was undetected, which would have been alleviated by treatment if the medical practitioner had not been negligent, may recover damages to compensate for that pain. Similarly, damages may be awarded for loss of earning capacity or any of the other heads of damage during that period if it is proved on a balance of probabilities that the patient suffered them and would not have if the medical practitioner had not been negligent. These losses may extend beyond the six months when the cancer was undetected in so far as it can be shown by the patient on a balance of probabilities that they have been, and will be, greater than if treatment had been given at the earlier stage. But no damages may be awarded for the loss of the chance of survival for five years, since on the balance of probabilities (60:40) the patient would not have survived for five years even if there had been no negligence on the part of the medical practitioner.

The analysis which is preferred in this chapter is that whether or not there was a contract between the patient and the medical practitioner, the patient would be entitled to compensatory damages for any pain and suffering, loss of earning capacity, etc during the six months when the cancer was undetected, subject to a discount for the chances that the pain and suffering and other losses would not in any event have been able to be alleviated.[7] Similarly, damages may be awarded for the chance that the patient will in the future suffer pain, loss of earning capacity and other losses, subject to a reduction for the chance that this would have occurred even if there had been no negligence on the part of the doctor.[8] In so far as there is uncertainty as to the extent to which the patient's underlying cancer would have brought the patient to a state similar to that which has thus far occurred and that is predicted to occur in the future, an evidentiary onus rests on the defendant to disentangle the causes,[9] though the ultimate onus rests on the plaintiff to satisfy the court that some damages should be awarded.[10] In other words, this chapter adopts the thesis of JH King Jr:

Economic Loss" in NJ Mullany, *Torts in the Nineties*, LBC Information Services, Sydney, 1997, p1 at pp32-3; H Reece, "Losses of Chances in the Law" (1996) 59 *MLR* 188; M Stauch, "Causation, Risk, and Loss of Chance in Medical Negligence" (1997) 17 *OJLS* 205; D Hamer, "'Chance would be a Fine Thing': Proof of Causation and Quantum in an Unpredictable World" (1999) 23 *MULR* 557; N Moshinsky QC, "Loss of Chance of Successful Treatment: *Naxakis v Western General Hospital* Considered" (2000) 8 *JLM* 216. Other articles will be referred to in the succeeding discussion.

[7] *Malec v JC Hutton Pty Ltd* (1990) 169 CLR 638.

[8] Ibid.

[9] *Watts v Rake* (1960) 108 CLR 158.

[10] *Purkess v Crittenden* (1965) 114 CLR 164.

Loss of chance should be compensable even if the chance is not better than even, and it should be recognized and valued as such rather than as an all-or-nothing proposition. Any other rule fails to satisfy the goals of tort law.[11]

Leaving aside medical negligence for the moment, the thesis may be illustrated by the decision of the House of Lords in the Scottish case of *McGhee v National Coal Board*.[12] Here the pursuer sought damages from his employer for dermatitis. He had been required to work in hot and dusty conditions in the defender's brick kilns. By the time the case reached the House of Lords it was accepted that this in itself was not negligent on the part of the defender. However, in breach of the duty of care owed to him, the defender had failed to provide showers with which he could wash off the accumulated dust at the end of his shifts. Accordingly, the dust had clung to him as he cycled home. Medical evidence was that this increased the risk of his developing dermatitis from the dust. But it was not known how this occurred. It could not be shown that more probably than not, he would not have developed the dermatitis if he had showered.

The lower courts held that the pursuer's action had to fail. The House of Lords unanimously upheld his appeal. The case was seen as either entitling the pursuer to all his damages for dermatitis or to none. There has been much subsequent debate as to whether their Lordships reversed the onus of proof or merely took a robust view in order to draw an inference of causation.[13] It is suggested that the case should have been seen as one involving loss of a chance: the failure to provide showers deprived the pursuer of the chance of avoiding the dermatitis, which was undoubtedly caused by the brick dust and not by any other factor. This was not a case such as where a plaintiff is negligently exposed to asbestos and also smokes and it is not known whether the lung cancer from which the plaintiff suffers was caused by the one or the other or the cumulative effect of both. There the plaintiff must prove on a balance of probabilities that the asbestos at least materially contributed to the cancer.[14] The plaintiff must

---

[11] King, n4 above. This article was relied on extensively by Deane J in his judgment in *Commonwealth v Amann Aviation Pty Ltd* (1991) 174 CLR 64.

[12] [1973] 1 WLR 1 (HL).

[13] See *Wilsher v Essex Area Health Authority* [1988] AC 1974 (HL) at 1086-91; cf *Bennett v Minister of Community Welfare* (1992) 176 CLR 408 at 422-3 per Gaudron J; *Chappel v Hart* (1998) 195 CLR 232 at 273 per Kirby J.

[14] *Bendix Mintex Pty Ltd v Barnes* (1997) 42 NSWLR 307 (CA), SLR 1 May 1998; *ICI Australia Operations Pty Ltd v Walsh* (1997) Aust Torts Reps 81-452 (NSW CA); *Wallaby Grip (BAE) Pty Ltd (in liq) v Macleay Area Health Service* (NSW CA, 18 December 1998, unreported, BC9806780), SLR [1999] 19 Leg Rep SL 2 (19 November 1999); *Seltsam Pty Ltd v McGuiness* (2000) Aust Torts Reps 81-547 (NSW

prove according to the ordinary standard of proof the fact of the loss and its source.[15]

It is not because the defender's negligence in *McGhee* consisted of an omission that the issue there should have been seen as one of valuation and not causation. Omissions may also be causes. As Mason J pointed out, a "gardener's failure to water the flowers may properly be regarded as a material cause of their dying for want of water, when it is his duty to water them".[16] The difficulty for the pursuer in *McGhee* was that the medical evidence would not sustain a conclusion that it was more likely than not in his case that the provision of showers would have prevented the dermatitis. The omission could not therefore in his case be said to have caused the harm itself. But if we recognise as a loss that he sustained the fact that he was deprived of the *chance of avoiding the dermatitis*, this loss was proved. It should then have become a matter of valuing that chance. If the chance was only 40 per cent, he should have received 40 per cent of the damages he ultimately received, since there was a 60 per cent chance that he would have developed dermatitis even if the employer had provided showers and so not been negligent. The court should not have been faced with the choice of awarding him 100 per cent of his damages or none at all.[17] Even if it was more probable than not that the provision of showers would have prevented the dermatitis, he should not have been awarded 100 per cent of his damages, because there was also a chance that he would still have incurred the dermatitis and such a chance should have been taken into account in the valuation of his loss.[18]

CA). See also *The Creutzfeldt-Jakob Disease Litigation, Straddlers Groups A and C v Secretary of State for Health* (1998) 54 BMLR 104; *The British Coal Respiratory Disease Litigation* (QBD, Turner J, 23 January 1998, unreported); as summarised at <http://wood.ccta.gov.uk/courtser/judgements.nsf/054a30dbaca8b75e8025683c004e82 de/2884ed31852fd3d9802568740038fa28/$FILE/qb_bcrdl.htm>.

[15] King, n4 above, at 1353-4 (drawing distinction between causation, which must be proved on balance of probabilities, and valuation, where chances are allowed); but cf at 1394-6 (opening up question whether all-or-nothing approach to causation should also be abandoned).

[16] *Sutherland Shire Council v Heyman* (1985) 157 CLR 424 at 467, citing HLA Hart and AM Honoré, *Causation in the Law*, 1st edn, OUP, Oxford, 1959, pp35-6; see now 2nd edn, 1985, p38.

[17] The percentages cited by Lord Salmon in *McGhee v National Coal Board* [1973] 1 WLR 1 (HL) at 12 should have led him to this conclusion.

[18] *Malec v J C Hutton Pty Ltd* (1990) 169 CLR 638; King, n4 above, at 1387. Cf *Naxakis v Western General Hospital* (1999) 197 CLR 269 at 312-13 per Callinan J (apparently favouring loss of chance where it is less than 51 per cent, but allowing plaintiff to succeed in full where it exceeds 50 per cent).

This chapter explores the case law in order to see whether it is possible to arrive at this solution in a medical negligence context. In other words, where there is little doubt that a plaintiff's physical or mental condition was caused by some pre-existing condition and the present state might have been prevented or alleviated in the absence of negligence on the part of a medical practitioner, may the failure to exercise reasonable care to prevent or alleviate the condition be itself treated as a loss to the plaintiff, damages for which may be assessed on the basis of the chances of success or alleviation? It is true that in all cases where the defendant is under a duty of care to act positively to prevent harm from another source, the issue of causation can be recast as one of valuation of a chance. For instance, someone who slipped and fell in a shop would be able to argue that the failure on the part of the shop to take care to provide a system for the removal of such substances deprived him or her of the chance of not slipping. This is contrary to the present law, which requires the plaintiff to prove on a balance of probabilities that such a system would have prevented the slip.[19] Ultimately, the issue is one of defining the scope of the rule that requires the defendant to act.[20] That is a question of policy.

Where It All Began: *Chaplin v Hicks*

The possibility of recovery for loss of chance may be seen as stemming from the decision in *Chaplin v Hicks*.[21] This unreserved judgment of the

---

[19] Eg, *Dulhunty v JB Young Ltd* (1975) 7 ALR 409; *Sleiman v Franklin Food Stores Pty Ltd* (1989) Aust Torts Reps 80-266 (NSW CA). In *Shoeys Pty Ltd v Allan* (1991) Aust Torts Reps 81-104 (NSW CA) Priestley JA called for law reform agencies to look at reversing the onus of proof in these cases. In the absence of such reform, the courts themselves are ready to draw an inference of causation: *Allcorp Cleaning Services Pty Ltd v Fairweather* (NSW CA, 29 June 1998, unreported, BC9804739). Rather than having an all-or-nothing solution here too, allowing loss of chance may be the better solution. However, the present paper is confined to considering the issue in the medical negligence context.

[20] See *Environment Agency (formerly National Rivers Authority) v Empress Car Co (Abertillery) Ltd* [1999] 2 AC 22 (HL) at 31 per Lord Hoffmann, cited by Gummow J in *Chappel v Hart* (1998) 195 CLR 232 at 256. Eg, *Lothian v Rickards* (1911) 12 CLR 165 at 194 per Isaacs J (whose dissenting judgment was affirmed, *Rickards v Lothian* [1913] AC 263 (PC)) (actual occurrence did not come within sphere of duty). See also The Rt Hon Lord Hoffmann, "Common Sense and Causing Loss" (1999) (unpublished Lecture to the Chancery Bar Association, 15 June 1999) (causation seldom at issue once one carefully defines scope of rule); J Stapleton, "Perspectives on Causation" in J Horder (ed), *Oxford Essays in Jurisprudence*, 4th Series, OUP, Oxford, 2000, p61.

[21] [1911] 2 KB 786 (CA).

English Court of Appeal, in which the respondent's counsel was not even called on to argue, has been enormously influential. Consequently, the facts are well known. The plaintiff entered a contest in which 12 women were to be offered theatrical engagement for a period of three years each. Her photograph was selected by readers of a newspaper in the region in which she lived as the most beautiful among the contestants from that region. This entitled her, along with 49 others, to be interviewed by the defendant and a committee for the purposes of final selection. In breach of the contract between them, the defendant failed to notify her in time of the interview and avoided giving her a subsequent interview. A jury awarded her £100 damages. The award was upheld by the Court of Appeal. Although her chances of being awarded one of the 12 positions may have been less than one in four, it was held that she had lost something of monetary value. Even though there was no market for the opportunity that the contract gave her and she could not have sold her right, damages were not unassessable. Precision was not necessary and the jury had to do the best it could on the evidence available.[22] The court could not interfere with the assessment it made.

This decision was ahead of the American practice of the time, which generally embodied a "rule of certainty".[23] It was described approvingly by an American text as "leading the way to a liberal practice", though attributed to the habit of English judges "of concealing problems of certainty under the cloak of 'remoteness'" and "their adherence to the tradition that questions of damages are for the jury's discretion".[24] Be that as it may, the decision was followed in Australia in *Howe v Teefy*.[25] In this case the plaintiff leased a horse from the defendant with the intention of training and racing him. The plaintiff claimed that he would have made a profit by betting on the horse himself and providing tips to others as to the horse and its prospects. In breach of the contract, the defendant withdrew the horse from the plaintiff. A jury having assessed the plaintiff's damages at £250, an appeal by the defendant was dismissed. The case for allowing the jury to evaluate the chance that the plaintiff would have made a profit

---

[22] Farwell LJ said that she had sustained a loss because "damage might result not only from the loss of the opportunity of winning a prize but also from the slur upon the plaintiff in her professional capacity, which might result in a diminution of the value of her services as an actress when she applied for an engagement": at 797. The other members of the court did not mention this additional loss that she might have sustained.

[23] CT McCormick, *Handbook on the Law of Damages*, West, St Paul, Minn, 1935, chap 4.

[24] Ibid, p121.

[25] (1927) 27 SR (NSW) 301 (FC).

from the use of the horse was said to be stronger than in *Chaplin v Hicks*, since the plaintiff here could probably have sold the right to lease the horse and had in any event paid for the right to lease it whereas the plaintiff in *Chaplin v Hicks* had paid nothing.[26]

In *Fink v Fink*[27] a wife claimed damages from her husband for breach of a contract which, she claimed, would have given her the chance of reconciliation with him. Dixon and McTiernan JJ denied her claim for damages, distinguishing *Chaplin v Hicks* on the ground that the loss here was, in the language of Vaughan Williams LJ in that case "so dependent on the mere unrestricted volition of another that it is impossible to say that there is any assessable loss resulting from the breach".[28] Latham CJ and Williams J, in their dissent, took the view that since *Chaplin v Hicks* it could not be said that the fact that an element in the contingency on which a contractual benefit depends is the exercise of the will of a particular person makes such benefit irrecoverable.[29] Deane J took a similar view in *Commonwealth v Amann Aviation Pty Ltd*,[30] being of the opinion that it was no answer to the plaintiff's claim in *Chaplin v Hicks* that there was a possibility that the defendant might arbitrarily have denied her a prize. Reconciliation between husband and wife is obviously something different from a commercial decision to offer employment as an actress or to renew a contract to provide surveillance for Australia's coastline and *Fink v Fink* should not be seen as standing in the way of awarding damages for loss of a chance in the medical context. Whether or not it depends on the husband's unrestricted volition to reconcile with the wife or on the grounds that reconciliation was so speculative that there was no reasonable chance of benefiting the wife, as was held in *Davies v Taylor*,[31] a Lord Campbell's Act action brought by a separated wife, a real chance of effecting a medical cure or alleviation is distinguishable. In *Amann* Brennan J, too, citing *Chaplin v Hicks*, recognised that in appropriate circumstances the loss of a chance is the proper subject of compensatory damages.[32]

Chaplin v Hicks was distinguished also in *McRae v Commonwealth Disposals Commission*.[33] The contract in *Chaplin* was said to be one "to

---

[26]   This latter ground of distinction is probably a correct reading of the authorised report of the case, but reference to the Law Times report, as reproduced in the All ER Reprint, shows that the plaintiff in *Chaplin v Hicks* paid a one shilling entry fee: see [1911-13] All ER Rep 224 at 225.

[27]   (1946) 74 CLR 127.

[28]   Ibid, at 143.

[29]   Ibid, at 135.

[30]   (1991) 174 CLR 64 at 133.

[31]   [1974] AC 207 (HL).

[32]   (1991) 174 CLR 64 at 104.

[33]   (1951) 84 CLR 377 at 411-12.

give the plaintiff a chance", whereas in *McRae* the plaintiff had no real chance of discovering a tanker which had never existed. An issue that we shall have to consider below is how it may be determined in a medical negligence case that the plaintiff had no real chance of a cure or alleviation if proper skill is exercised.[34] However, if the chance that still existed at the time of the treatment was a real one, *Chaplin v Hicks* and its acceptance in Australia should allow the plaintiff to recover for the value of the lost chance notwithstanding that the chance was less than an even one. We shall look later at the acceptance of the principle of *Chaplin v Hicks* in the High Court in a claim for breach of the *Trade Practices Act* 1974 (Cth), s52,[35] and at the dicta in the latest Australian High Court cases that consider the issue in the context of medical negligence,[36] but before doing so we turn to another area of professional liability in which loss of chance has been significant.

Solicitors

The principle of *Chaplin v Hicks* was applied without reference to the case in *Kitchen v Royal Air Forces Association*.[37] Like *Chaplin v Hicks,* this was also an unreserved judgment of the English Court of Appeal, but unlike the earlier case it was given after some 10 days of argument on a number of issues. Having upheld the trial judge's decision that the firm of solicitors was negligent in failing to issue proceedings in a Lord Campbell's Act claim, the court had to consider whether the trial judge's award of two-thirds of the maximum damages that could have been awarded in the original action should be upheld. Lord Evershed MR rejected the argument that if the plaintiff would on the balance of probabilities have succeeded in her original action, she was entitled to the damages that would have been awarded in that action in full; whereas if she would probably have failed, then she was entitled to nominal damages only. He took the view that she would have been entitled to the full damages if she must have succeeded in the original action. On the other hand, if she must have failed, in his view she would have been entitled to nominal damages only. He refused to countenance the argument that in the latter circumstances her claim would still have had a nuisance value and therefore she should be entitled to the

---

34 Cf *Hotson v East Berkshire AHA* [1987] AC 750 (HL).
35 *Sellars v Adelaide Petroleum NL* (1994) 179 CLR 332.
36 *Chappel v Hart* (1998) 195 CLR 232; *Naxakis v Western General Hospital* (1999) 197 CLR 269.
37 [1958] 2 All ER 241 (CA).

value of that.[38] The present case falling somewhere between the extremes, the court had to determine whether she had lost "some right of value" and to determine what that value was as best it could.[39] Parker LJ, too, said that unless the court was satisfied that the plaintiff's claim was bound to fail, something more than nominal damages were to be awarded.[40] All three members of the Court of Appeal regarded the trial judge's estimate of two-thirds as high, but as the particular percentage was not challenged they upheld the award.[41] There is no suggestion that if the trial judge had fixed the percentage at one-third (or anything less than 50 per cent), this would not have been upheld too. Indeed, such a suggestion would be contrary to the principle applied, namely that if the plaintiff had lost something of value the court had to do the best it could to evaluate it, just as in *Chaplin v Hicks* the plaintiff was entitled to a jury award even if her chances of winning a prize were less than one in four.

Kitchen's case was followed by Bray CJ in *Tutenkoff v Thiele*,[42] where it was held that in evaluating the chance of success in the original action the court could take account of evidence that would probably have been advanced on behalf of the original defendant, but which was not put forward in the action against the solicitor. Taking account of such evidence, which would probably have led to a greater reduction for contributory negligence or even possibly a finding of no liability, his Honour held that the damages as now assessed should be reduced by 40 per cent.

Kitchen's case and *Tutenkoff v Thiele* were cited as apparently correctly stating the law in *Johnson v Perez*.[43] This was a case where it was accepted that the plaintiff must have succeeded in the original action which the defendant solicitors had neglected to bring. The issue was whether the damages had to be assessed as at the time when the original action should have been brought or at the time of the action against the solicitors. It was accepted that the answer to the problem did not depend on whether the action was brought in contract or tort.[44] Only Brennan J dealt with the measure of damages in a case of uncertainty. He was of the opinion that the "value of the lost cause of action cannot be assessed as though there were a market for doubtful causes of action in damages for personal injury".[45]

---

38   Ibid, at 250.
39   Ibid, at 251.
40   Ibid, at 252.
41   See at 251 per Evershed MR, at 252 per Parker LJ, at 254 per Sellers LJ.
42   (1975) 11 SASR 148.
43   (1988) 166 CLR 351.
44   Ibid, at 363 per Wilson, Toohey and Gaudron JJ, at 389 per Dawson J.
45   Ibid, at 372.

Thus he refused to recognise that the plaintiff would be entitled to a percentage of the maximum damages that could be awarded. He required the court to find whether the plaintiff probably would have succeeded or failed or compromised the action and to award damages accordingly. He cited no authority for this and was alone in so thinking.[46]

In the companion case of *Nikolaou v Papasavas Phillips & Co*[47] Mason CJ, with respect, correctly cited *Kitchen* as authority for the proposition that on the retrial of the action, the order for which the High Court upheld, the court would "need to determine what the appellant would have recovered but for [the solicitors'] negligence and will need to discount that amount by the chance that he would not have been successful in that claim". He did not suggest that the discount could not be greater than 50 per cent. In the court below, from whose decision the appeal was dismissed, all three judges emphasised that the plaintiff's damages were for the loss of the chance of success in the original action.[48] Murphy J specifically stated that the damages to be assessed for the loss of this chance "are quite different from the damages which ought to have been assessed in" the original action.[49] He acknowledged that the amount of the likely award could provide a guide to the evaluation of the lost chance,[50] but that it would require adjustment in the light of the strength or weakness of the plaintiff's case on liability and quantum.[51]

This is the approach that has been taken in many such actions against solicitors.[52] In none has it been suggested that damages may be awarded

---

46 See also his Honour's judgment in *Sellars v Adelaide Petroleum NL* (1994) 179 CLR 332 at 362. The majority in *Sellars* at 353-4 cited these remarks of Brennan J, but noted that they were inconsistent with *Kitchen*. Cf *Norris v Blake [No 2]* (1997) 41 NSWLR 49 (CA) (rejecting trial judge's assessment of damages for loss of earning capacity on basis of weighted average of career paths open to plaintiff and requiring that most probable path be chosen, but adjusted for contingencies including those available from other careers), legislatively affirmed in *Motor Accidents Compensation Act* 1999 (NSW), s 126.

47 (1988) 166 CLR 394.

48 *Nikolaou v Papasavas, Phillips & Co* [1988] VR 682 (FC).

49 Ibid, at 703.

50 Ibid, at 704.

51 Ibid, at 709. An added factor that is relevant is the chance of the defendant being able to pay the damages. Little deduction need be made for this where the defendant to the original action would have been compulsorily insured or, as in this case, was the Incorporated Nominal Defendant. Cf *Instant Nominees Pty Ltd v Redman* [1987] WAR 218 at 226-7.

52 Recent applications of the principle include *Golec v Scott* (1995) 38 NSWLR 168 (CA); *Williams (t/as Harris Wheeler) v Bodewes* (1997) Aust Torts Reps 81-449 (NSW CA); *Feletti v Kontoulas* [2000] NSWCA 59 (NSW CA, 23 March 2000, unreported, BC200001286); *Harwood v Gayler & Cleland* (Qld CA, 1 November 1996, unreported, BC9605391); *Little v Suncorp Insurance and Finance [No 2]* [1994]

only if it was more probable than not that the original action, appeal or other proceeding that the solicitor failed to prosecute would have succeeded. Such an argument was advanced, but rejected, in what is now the leading English Court of Appeal decision on the point.[53] In some of the Australian cases the actual award has reflected the opinion that the plaintiff's prospects of success were not better than even.[54] There is an *obiter dictum* by Deane J that expressly recognises that the chance of success may be less than 50 per cent.[55]

In some cases it has been claimed that the negligence of the solicitors deprived the plaintiff not of the opportunity of success in litigation, but of the chance of acting in a particular way. In such circumstances the courts have usually denied the plaintiff damages on the basis of loss of chance, requiring instead that the plaintiff prove on a balance of probabilities that he or she would have acted differently if the advice given had not been negligent. Thus the proposition has been stated that "if the reality of the chance depends on some action that the plaintiff would need to have taken, he or she must establish on the balance of probabilities that the action would in fact have been taken".[56] We shall see below that the High Court has apparently accepted this distinction[57] and that a similar distinction has been drawn in the context of medical treatment.[58]

---

2 Qd R 273; *North Australian Aboriginal Legal Aid Service Inc v Liddle* (1994) Aust Torts Reps 81-300 (NT CA).

[53] *Allied Maples Group Ltd v Simmons & Simmons* [1995] 1 WLR 1602 (CA) at 1611-12.

[54] Eg, *Scott v Echegaray* (1991) Aust Torts Reps 81-120 (NSW CA); *Murphy v Miller* (NSW CA, 16 October 1998, unreported, BC9805397); *Garden State Packers v Lancken* [2000] NSWSC 139 (NSW SC, Windeyer J, 31 March 2000, unreported, BC200000826); *Green v Berry* [2000] QCA 133 (Qld CA, 5 May 2000, unreported, BC200002130); *Denkewitz v Hodgson* (Qld SC, Ambrose J, 6 November 1998, unreported, BC9805979); *Sloane v McDonald & Sutherland* (WA FC, 14 November 1997, unreported, BC9706153). For England, see *Motor Crown Petroleum Ltd v SJ Berwin & Co* [2000] Lloyd's Rep PN 438 (Eng CA) (40 per cent chance of successful planning appeal if proper advice given).

[55] *Commonwealth v Amann Aviation Pty Ltd* (1991) 174 CLR 64 at 119.

[56] B Coote, "Chance and the Burden of Proof in Contract and Tort" (1988) 62 *ALJ* 761 at 768, citing *Sykes v Midland Bank Executor & Trustee Co Ltd* [1971] 1 QB 113 (CA). See also *Daniels v Anderson* (1995) 37 NSWLR 438 (CA) at 528-9; *Allied Maples Group Ltd v Simmons & Simmons* [1995] 1 WLR 1602 (CA).

[57] *Sellars v Adelaide Petroleum NL* (1994) 179 CLR 332.

[58] *Tran v Lam* (NSW SC, Badgery-Parker J, 20 June 1997, unreported, BC9705945).

Loss of a Commercial Opportunity

The Australian High Court has twice held that a plaintiff may recover damages for loss of a commercial opportunity though the chance of the loss occurring was assessed at less than 50 per cent. As stated in *Sellars v Adelaide Petroleum NL,*[59] in *Commonwealth v Amann Aviation Pty Ltd*[60] four of the judges "concluded that a lost commercial advantage or opportunity was a compensable loss, even though there was a less than 50 per cent likelihood that the commercial advantage would be realized. Damages for breach of contract were assessed by reference to the probabilities or possibilities of what would have happened". In *Sellars* itself the trial judge had held that if not for a contravention of s52 of the Trade Practices Act 1974 (Cth), the plaintiff would have continued to negotiate an agreement, which had a 40 per cent prospect of being performed successfully. He awarded damages under s82(1) of the Act for loss of this opportunity. The High Court upheld this decision. It held that, as in tort, loss or damage is the gist of the action under s82(1).[61] The loss of the commercial opportunity that would have arisen if the agreement had been entered into was itself a loss that qualified for the purposes of s82(1). Thereafter, it was a matter of valuation and the trial judge's discount of 60 per cent from the full value of successful performance because of the various contingencies that attended such performance was upheld.

A similar view has been indicated in the House of Lords, in a case where the defendant was held liable for negligently giving the plaintiff a bad reference. In remitting the case for assessment of damages, Lord Lowry, citing *Chaplin v Hicks*, indicated that all the plaintiff had to prove was that he had lost a reasonable chance of employment.[62]

In New Zealand, too, the Court of Appeal has recognised on at least two occasions that damages may be awarded for loss of a commercial opportunity.[63] It need not be proved on the balance of probabilities that the opportunity would have had a successful outcome. All that need be proved

---

[59] (1994) 179 CLR 332 at 349.

[60] (1991) 174 CLR 64. This was a claim for breach of a contract that deprived the plaintiff of the chance of a renewal of the contract.

[61] (1994) 179 CLR 332 at 348.

[62] *Spring v Guardian Assurance Plc* [1995] 2 AC 296 (HL) at 327. This dictum was approved in *Allied Maples Group Ltd v Simmons & Simmons* [1995] 1 WLR 1602 (CA) at 1613. See also the discussion in *Bank of Credit and Commerce International SA (in Liq) (BCCI) v Ali (No 2)* [1999] 4 All ER 83 at 112-16.

[63] *Takaro Properties Ltd v Rowling* [1986] 1 NZLR 22 (CA) at 62-7 per Woodhouse P (Richardson concurring), at 68-70 per Cooke J, at 72 per McMullin J, at 74 per Somers J; *Craig v East Coast Bays City Council* [1986] 1 NZLR 99 (CA) at 108-9. See also *Gregory v Rangitikei District Council* [1995] 2 NZLR 208.

on a balance of probabilities is that the plaintiff had such a chance and was deprived of it.

The Court in *Sellars* distinguished several cases where proof on a balance of probabilities had apparently been required.[64] It thought that these turned "primarily on the issue of causation" and expressed the opinion that "[w]hen the issue of causation turns on what the plaintiff would have done, there is no particular reason for departing from proof on the balance of probabilities notwithstanding that the question is hypothetical".[65] It reiterated that "the general standard of proof in civil actions will ordinarily govern the issue of causation and the issue whether the applicant has sustained loss or damage. Hence the applicant must prove on the balance of probabilities that he or she has sustained *some* loss or damage".[66] For the purposes of proceedings under the Trade Practices Act the plaintiff had proved such loss by proof of the loss of the commercial opportunity, even though its valuation was less than 50 per cent of the full value of the agreement. There is no reason in principle why the court should not similarly recognise the loss of an opportunity to be cured as something that itself has value. All that the plaintiff need then prove on the balance of probabilities is that the defendant's negligence caused the plaintiff to lose a chance of cure that is not entirely speculative. Once that is proved, it is for the court to do the best it can to value the chance, even if cure is less probable than not. Whether that should be confined to cases where the chance does not depend on the plaintiff's own response to advice will be considered below.

Before leaving *Sellars* two points need to be made. First, the distinction between causation, which must be proved on a balance of probabilities, and valuation, where chances may be taken into account, is not one that is always easy to make.[67] Secondly, the court acknowledged in the first of the above quotations that proof of causation was required on a balance of probabilities "notwithstanding that the question is hypothetical". This recognises that hypothetical questions do not normally require proof on a balance of probabilities. The converse of this is that so-called questions of past (or "historical") fact do normally require such proof. It is to this distinction that we now turn.

---

64 *Gates v City Mutual Life Assurance Society Ltd* (1986) 160 CLR 1; *Norwest Refrigeration Services Pty Ltd v Bain Dawes (WA) Pty Ltd* (1984) 157 CLR 149; *Sykes v Midland Bank Executor & Trustee Co Ltd* [1971] 1 QB 113 (CA).

65 (1994) 179 CLR 332 at 353. Cf n56, above.

66 Ibid, at 355 (emphasis in the original).

67 Cf *Waribay Pty Ltd v Minter Ellison* [1991] 2 VR 391 (AD).

The Distinction between Past Facts and Future or Hypothetical Facts

In a well-known passage, Lord Diplock said:

> The role of the court in making an assessment of damages which depends upon its view as to what will be and what would have been is to be contrasted with its ordinary function in civil actions of determining what was. In determining what did happen in the past a court decides on the balance of probabilities. Anything that is more probable than not it treats as certain. But in assessing damages which depend upon its view as to what will happen in the future or would have happened in the future if something had not happened in the past, the court must make an estimate as to what are the chances that a particular thing will or would have happened and reflect those chances, whether they are more or less than even, in the amount of damages which it awards.[68]

This was approved by the High Court in *Malec v J C Hutton Pty Ltd.*[69] In this case the plaintiff was suffering from a neurotic condition induced by brucellosis that he had contracted owing to his employer's negligence. The lower courts found that he was also suffering from a degenerative condition of the spine that was equally likely to have caused him to suffer a similar neurotic condition. The majority of the intermediate appellate court held that he was not entitled to damages for economic loss after the time when the neurotic condition would probably have developed anyway. The High Court reversed the decision and referred the case back for further assessment of the damages. It went further than the statement of Lord Diplock in relation to past hypothetical events, saying: "The approach is the same whether it is alleged that the event would have occurred before or might occur after the assessment of damages takes place."[70]

This approach to hypothetical events that might or might not have occurred has since been applied almost daily where the plaintiff was suffering a condition, such as a natural degeneration of the spine, that might have affected him or her if the injury for which damages are being assessed had not been incurred. As the late John Fleming pointed out, however, this raises large questions in relation to causation, since causal

---

[68] *Mallett v McMonagle* [1970] AC 166 (HL) at 176.
[69] (1990) 169 CLR 638.
[70] Ibid, at 643. The only difference between the majority of the High Court and Brennan and Dawson JJ, who delivered a separate joint judgment, is that the latter thought it "undesirable for damages to be assessed on the footing of an evaluation expressed as a percentage" because "[d]amages founded on hypothetical evaluations defy precise calculation": at 639.

inquiries inevitably involve asking the hypothetical question of what would have happened if the defendant had not been negligent.[71] The High Court's response, as we have seen, was to suggest that proof on the balance of probabilities would continue to be required in relation to causation, at least in those cases that depend on the plaintiff's own response to advice.[72]

Strangely, two earlier High Court cases that might have been considered relevant to the problem it faced were not cited in *Malec*. These were *Watts v Rake*[73] and *Purkess v Crittenden*.[74] They were concerned with the onus of proof where the defendant has undoubtedly caused an injury to the plaintiff, but there is a dispute as to whether a natural condition or some other event would have resulted in the plaintiff suffering from a similar disability without the injury. The cases place an evidential onus on the defendant to show with some precision what would have been the effects if the plaintiff had not been injured by the defendant, but leave the ultimate onus on the plaintiff to prove that the defendant caused the harm for which damages are sought.[75] There is no suggestion in either of them that the plaintiff may recover damages for the full effects of the present condition, discounted by the chances that some of those effects may have occurred in any event. To reconcile these different lines of authority,[76] it is necessary to say that the plaintiff must prove on the balance of probabilities that the

---

[71] JG Fleming, "Probabilistic Causation in Tort Law: A Postscript" (1991) 70 *Can Bar Rev* 136 at 140-1 ("Postscript"). See also JG Fleming, *The Law of Torts*, 9th edn, LBC Information Services, Sydney, 1998, p228.

[72] *Sellars v Adelaide Petroleum NL* (1994) 179 CLR 332 at 355. See also n56, above.

[73] (1960) 108 CLR 158.

[74] (1965) 114 CLR 164.

[75] Cf *Franklins Self Serve Pty Ltd v Wyber* (1999) 48 NSWLR 249 (CA) at [24]; *Kessey v Golledge* (1999) 30 MVR 95 (NSW CA) at 106 (both referring to "persuasive burden" on defendant to disentangle consequences). This appears to be a misreading of *Purkess v Crittenden* at 171, which is cited in support. The term "persuasive burden", though itself open to criticism (see JD Heydon & DR Byrne, *Cross on Evidence*, Australian looseleaf edition, Butterworths, Sydney, [7010]), usually refers to the legal burden, not the burden of adducing evidence. Windeyer J in *Purkess v Crittenden*, who had concurred in *Watts v Rake*, on the previous page accepted the view of the majority that it is only the latter burden that rests on the defendant. The position is correctly stated in *Johnston v Cowra Shire Council* [2000] NSWCA 117 (NSW CA, 5 May 2000, unreported, BC200002214); see also *Expokin Pty Ltd v Graham* [2000] NSWCA 267 (NSW CA, 29 September 2000, unreported, BC200005756). Cf *Bridge Printery Pty Ltd v Mestre* [1999] NSWCA 342 (NSW CA, 5 October 1999, unreported, BC9906401) (unspecified onus on defendant to show when plaintiff's heart attack ceased to incapacitate him). Nevertheless, it may be desirable to place a legal onus on the defendant: King, n4 above, at 1390-4.

[76] Cf *Commonwealth v McLean* (1996) 41 NSWLR 389 (CA) at 410-11. The distinction there made between the occurrence of "an actual event", which is "an all or nothing issue", and a hypothetical event, does not seem a valid one on the facts.

defendant's negligence did contribute materially to the present symptoms (this is the legal onus that rests on the plaintiff). Once that is satisfied, there is an evidential onus on the defendant of proving that the alleged pre-existing or subsequent natural condition did exist and that this condition in its natural progression would have produced similar symptoms. If the defendant is unable to satisfy the evidential burden, the court will reduce the plaintiff's damages for contingencies to no greater extent than in the ordinary case. If, however, the defendant shows that there was a real chance that the plaintiff would have developed similar symptoms from a natural condition attaching to the plaintiff, the court will make a greater reduction than normal to reflect this increased chance.[77]

Malec was concerned with hypothetical facts, namely what would have happened in the absence of the defendant's negligence. The High Court held that such facts were to be evaluated according to the chances that they would have occurred. It also pointed out that where one contingency is dependent on another, the evaluation of the chance requires the multiplication of each by the other, so that the final chance is a reduced percentage.[78] It was not necessary to consider events that had happened in the past, but that were also attended by uncertainty. There was no dispute, at least before the High Court, that the diagnosis that the plaintiff was suffering from brucellosis was correct or that he had contracted the disease as a result of his employment. Facts of this nature would, in the view both of Lord Diplock in *Mallett v McMonagle*[79] and of the High Court,[80] if proved on the balance of probabilities, be treated as certain. This view was adopted by the House of Lords in *Hotson v East Berkshire AHA*.[81] Since this is the leading authority in English law on loss of chance in medical negligence cases, we must look at it closely.

---

[77] See *Wilson v Peisley* (1975) 7 ALR 571 at 574 per Barwick CJ (*Watts v Rake* and *Purkess v Crittenden* irrelevant because existence of pre-existing condition fully made out). Cf King, n4 above, at 1390-4.

[78] "If, for example, and only by way of illustration, there was a 75 per cent probability of his becoming unemployable by reason of his back condition even if he had not contracted brucellosis and a 75 per cent chance that that unemployability would have caused a similar neurotic condition, there was only a 56.25 per cent chance (75 per cent x 75 per cent) that, if he had not contracted brucellosis, he would have developed a similar neurotic condition": at 645 per Deane, Gaudron and McHugh JJ. See also King, n4 above, at 1387-90; Hon DH Hodgson, "The Scales of Justice: Probability and Proof in Legal Fact-finding" (1995) 69 *ALJ* 731 at 746-50.

[79] [1970] AC 166 (HL) at 176.

[80] *Malec v J C Hutton Pty Ltd* (1990) 169 CLR 638 at 642-3 per Deane, Gaudron and McHugh JJ.

[81] [1987] AC 750 (HL).

In *Hotson* a 13-year-old boy fell from a rope on which he had been swinging from a tree. He was taken to a hospital, where his knee, but not the upper part of his leg, was X-rayed. He was given an elastic bandage for his knee and sent home, with an instruction to return in 10 days. He continued to suffer excruciating pain. Five days later he returned to the hospital, his hip was X-rayed and a serious fracture discovered. The following day he underwent surgery. He was left with a permanent disability. The cause of the disability was avascular necrosis, a blockage of the blood supply to the upper femur. The hospital admitted negligence. The trial judge found that there was a high probability, which he put at 75 per cent, that the plaintiff would have suffered the same disability even if he had received proper treatment at the hospital. This was because the avascular necrosis had probably already set in. However, the hospital's negligence made the disability certain and deprived the plaintiff of the 25 per cent chance that he might have had that it had not already gone that far and could still have been avoided with the appropriate treatment. He awarded the plaintiff damages for the pain and suffering the plaintiff had undergone in the period immediately after he had been sent home by the hospital. In addition he awarded one-quarter of the damages that he would have awarded if the hospital had been fully liable for the disability. An appeal and cross-appeal were dismissed by the English Court of Appeal.[82] The House of Lords, however, upheld the defendants' appeal and set aside the damages in respect of the permanent disability.

The decision of the House of Lords depended on treating the existence or otherwise of avascular necrosis at the time when the plaintiff presented at the hospital as a past fact. Since the trial judge had found that there was a 75 per cent probability that it had already occurred, the members of the House of Lords treated it as certain. On this view, there was no chance that proper treatment could have averted the condition. Therefore, the plaintiff had not lost the benefit of any chance at all.[83] As they saw it, their Lordships did not have to deal with a pure case of a lost chance and they left the issue open, though with some discouraging remarks.[84]

Let us change the facts of *Hotson* slightly.[85] Assume that the plaintiff has a cause of action against a tortfeasor who caused him to fall from the

---

[82] Reported with the decision of the House of Lords, ibid.

[83] Cf King, n4 above, at 1395-6 (questioning whether accident victim probably dead on arrival at emergency room should not still recover damages for loss of chance of being treated without negligence).

[84] See ibid, at 782 per Lord Bridge, at 785-9 per Lord Mackay, at 793 per Lord Ackner. Lords Brandon and Goff agreed with all three. The dicta are considered below: see text at nn116-128.

[85] Cf SM Waddams, "Damages: Assessment of Uncertainties" (1998) 13 *JCL* 55.

tree. Assume also that because of his young age, treatment for one of the consequences of the fall cannot be performed until he is much older. We know that there is a 75 per cent chance of the treatment being successful. If the damages are assessed before the treatment, the plaintiff must be allowed damages for the 25 per cent chance that it will not be successful. Why, if he has not already recovered damages, should he not have a similar remedy against someone who later performs the treatment negligently so as to deprive the plaintiff of that 25 per cent chance? The distinction between past and future cannot account for a different outcome. It may be that the reason why only 75 per cent of the treatments are successful is that 25 per cent of patients are in fact untreatable due to their genetic constitution, but which patients are so untreatable is not presently known to medical science. When assessing the damages against the tortfeasor who caused the plaintiff to fall from the tree, the genetic make-up of the plaintiff is a past fact, which may really mean that it is 100 per cent certain that the treatment will not succeed, yet doing the best we can in the uncertain state of scientific knowledge all that we can say is that there is a 25 per cent chance of failure. As Waddams points out, much medical diagnosis and prognosis is a mixture of past "fact" and future predictions.[86]

Another illustration might be provided by the CJD litigation.[87] Assume that 100 people were injected with Human Growth Hormone after it became negligent to continue to do so. Some of the hGH was infected with a prion that transmitted the disease. All who received the infected hGH will eventually develop CJD if they do not die earlier from other causes. However, no tests can tell which of the 100 people received the infected hormone and which did not. If we were able to estimate from past experience that more than 50 will eventually develop the disease, each of the 100 people would be able to prove on the balance of probabilities that he or she received infected hGH. It is unlikely that any court would award damages on that basis alone.[88] On the other hand, if the estimate is less than

---

[86]   Ibid.

[87]   See, eg, *APQ v Commonwealth Serum Laboratories* [1999] 3 VR 633; AW Hurley, "Prospects of Recovery in Negligence and under Statute for Creutzfeld[t]-Jakob Disease resulting from Human Pituitary Gland Derived Hormone" (1996) 4 *TLJ* 60.

[88]   Cf the hypothetical blue and yellow cab (or blue and red bus) cases much discussed in the theoretical literature on probability: eg, Justice D Hodgson, "Probability: The Logic of the Law – A Response" (1995) 15 *OJLS* 51 at 59-60. The views expressed by Murphy J in *TNT Management Pty Ltd v Brooks* (1979) 23 ALR 345 at 351-2 and *West v GIO of NSW* (1981) 35 ALR 437 at 443 are unlikely to be followed: see the criticism in Justice DH Hodgson, "The Scales of Justice: Probability and Proof in Legal Fact-Finding" (1995) 69 *ALJ* 731 at 734-5; but see *Sinka v Mayne Nickless Ltd* [1964] VR 524 (jury required to be satisfied as to whose vehicle caused injury, but need not identify particular vehicle). The debate here is said to be as to the use of statistics to

that, none could succeed in proving this past fact. If some of the 100 developed psychiatric illnesses from fear of developing the disease and were awarded damages for the psychiatric illness,[89] a court would probably apply *Malec* and take account of the risk of developing the disease itself even if the probability was less than even, despite that risk being itself dependent on the past, but unknowable, fact that the plaintiff did or did not receive an infected dose. As will be suggested below, a better solution to this particular problem would be to award damages for the present illness and postpone the assessment of damages for the disease itself until it actually occurs, if it ever does.[90]

A further illustration of the futility of trying to distinguish between past and present facts in some circumstances has been suggested by recent events in Florida. Assume that someone sets fire to a polling station immediately after an election has been held. One of the candidates is inside the station at the time and is permanently disabled as a result of the fire. The ballot box is also destroyed in the fire. The candidate sues the person who started the fire. The candidate's earning capacity has been affected, but by how much? If the outcome of the election had been successful for the candidate, the earning capacity would have been assessed on one basis; if the candidate had lost, the earning capacity would have been assessed on a different basis. The outcome would have been dependent on the votes cast and that is a past fact. Yet, we can now never know how many votes were cast for the candidate and how many for the opponents. We would have to assess damages based on the chances of success, estimated as best we can.

It should be noted that events that lie in the future at the time the cause of action arises are taken into account on an all-or-nothing basis when they have occurred by the time of the trial. If a candidate for political office were killed before polling day and the election were postponed, we would assess the damages for the dependants on the basis of the probabilities of election if the death had not occurred. The probabilities may be less than even, as long as they are not entirely speculative.[91] But if the death occurs, say, just as polling closes, the court would probably take into account the actual votes cast, even if they are nullified by the death, and assess the damages on the basis that the candidate would or would not have been elected. Since facts are preferred to prophecies, where a surviving spouse

---

prove liability, not causation: Stauch, n6 above, at 220-1 (pointing to confusion by American judge quoted by Lord Mackay in *Hotson* [1987] AC 750 (HL) at 789).

[89] Cf NJ Mullany, "Fear for the Future: Liability for Infliction of Psychiatric Disorder" in NJ Mullany (ed), *Torts in the Nineties*, Law Book Co, Sydney, 1997, p101.

[90] See text at nn109-113 below.

[91] *Davies v Taylor* [1974] AC 207 (HL).

has died or remarried before the trial of a Lord Campbell's Act action, the damages are assessed with regard to the now known fact;[92] whereas, if they had not already happened, these matters would be assessed as contingent and the chances of their occurring would be estimated.[93] In the earlier illustration varying the facts of *Hotson*, so that the claim was brought against someone who caused the boy to fall from the tree, the damages are assessed at 25 per cent of the loss if there is a 75 per cent chance of medical treatment avoiding particular consequences. However, if the medical treatment has already been given and the outcome is known, the damages are assessed on the basis of that outcome, which is all or nothing. Facts that are knowable must, of course, be proved on the balance of probabilities. In the case of the death or remarriage of a plaintiff in a Lord Campbell's Act action, the party bearing the onus of proof on the issue would have to establish the fact of the surviving spouse's subsequent death or remarriage on the balance of probabilities or it will be ignored. The court cannot reduce the damages on the basis of a chance that the death or remarriage has already occurred.

The distinction between facts that are knowable, and that must therefore be proved on a balance of probabilities, and those that are not, where allowance can be made for chances, is not always clear cut. In the *Hotson* variation, the medical treatment might already have been given, but the outcome might still be precarious at the time of the trial. In such circumstances, it would be appropriate to assess the damages on the basis of the chance of a successful outcome, whether that is more or less than 50 per cent.

Support for the view that too much should not be made of the distinction between future and past events may be found in some dicta of Deane J in *Commonwealth v Amann Aviation Pty Ltd*. Under the heading "Loss of a chance", his Honour dealt at some length with the need, in order to do justice, to assess damages by reference to chances where facts related to the future or to what would have happened in the past.[94] He concluded:

> It is true that Lord Reid's reasons for rejecting the balance of probability test in the circumstances of *Davies v Taylor* could be applied equally to some categories of case in which a court is concerned with the determination of past events. That does not mean, however, that the traditional approach for determining past facts should be applied to a case requiring the assessment of damages on the basis of what would have

---

[92] *Willis v The Commonwealth* (1946) 73 CLR 105 (remarriage of widow); *Williamson v John I Thornycroft & Co Ltd* [1940] 2 KB 658 (CA) (death of widow).
[93] Eg, *Jones v Schiffmann* (1971) 124 CLR 303.
[94] (1991) 174 CLR 64 at 118 ff.

happened or will happen. To the contrary, it lends support for the view that there is a need for modification or reassessment in some categories of case of the conventional approach that, in assessing damages for what has occurred in the past, a court decides on the balance of probabilities and assumes certainty where none in truth exists.[95]

On the facts of the case before him, he found it unnecessary to pursue this further. Although some of his citations indicate that he might have been prepared to measure even past "facts" by the chances that they might or might not have occurred, his first citation may indicate only a relaxation of what amounts to proof on a balance of probabilities, where a "robust" approach to the finding of a causal link enables a court to treat as certain otherwise doubtful connections.[96] But, as Waddams has pointed out, the odds on a roll of dice are the same whether the roll is about to take place or the dice have already been rolled and the dice are covered.[97] Damages should be similarly assessed.

That does not mean, of course, that every disputed fact is to be taken into account according to the chances that it occurred. In some of the cases dealt with below, disputes arose as to whether the plaintiff told the medical practitioner of symptoms that should have led to a particular diagnosis. If relevant, the judge has to resolve such disputes on the balance of probabilities. Once so resolved, the fact is taken as certain.[98] A plaintiff cannot recover damages for the chance that he or she might have told the doctor, even though often the trial is many years after the event and no-one can know for certain whether or not the doctor was told. The plaintiff must prove on the balance of probabilities that he or she did lose a chance[99] and where that turns on what the doctor was told, that must be established on the balance of probabilities. This is the explanation of the decision in *Hotson*: the plaintiff simply failed to prove that there was a chance of any

---

95   Ibid, at 123-4. He cited in support *Snell v Farrell* [1990] 2 SCR 311 and *Herskovits v Group Health Cooperative* 99 Wash 2d 609, 664 P2d 474 (1983), as well as Fleming, Postscript, n71 above, and JH King Jr, n4 above, though he noted dicta in *Hotson* as being to the contrary.

96   *Snell v Farrell* [1990] 2 SCR 311. See also *McGhee v National Coal Board* [1973] 1 WLR 1 (HL), as "explained" in *Wilsher v Essex Area Health Authority* [1988] AC 1974 (HL).

97   Above n85. See also Reece, n6 above (distinguishing between "deterministic" and "indeterministic" cases, loss of chance being allowable in the latter); Stauch, n6 above (criticising Reece for applying loss of chance to human volition, but also rejecting distinction between past facts and hypothetical ones); C Miller, "Coal Dust, Causation and Common Sense" (2000) 63 *MLR* 763 (criticising Reece's test of indeterministic).

98   Eg, *Tran v Lam* (NSW SC, Badgery-Parker J, 20 June 1997, unreported, BC9705945).

99   *Sellars v Adelaide Petroleum NL* (1994) 179 CLR 332. See also T Honoré, "Medical Non-Disclosure, Causation and Risk: *Chappel v Hart*" (1999) 7 TLJ 1 at 6-7.

sort of preventing the disability. Nevertheless, it is the sort of case where justice requires the relaxation of the strict rule. A rigid application of the rule in a case that turns on whether the plaintiff's cancer had already developed secondary cancers elsewhere in the body at the time when the doctor should have detected it, so that treatment would have been comparatively futile, would mean that the plaintiff would fail altogether if the proof shows that there was a 51 per cent probability of it having done so, but would succeed wholly if there was only a 49 per cent probability.[100] It would be better to allow the plaintiff to succeed and to reduce the damages by the percentage probability that it had already occurred.[101] As Professor Waddams has put it, "[w]here the primary significance of a past fact is what it indicates about the future it should ... be treated as a hypothetical fact, and uncertainty assessed according to the probabilities rather than on an all-or-nothing basis".[102]

"Open" and "Closed" Cases

It is suggested that in the interests of justice, courts should draw a distinction between what might be called "open" and "closed" chance cases. Fleming has correctly observed that "[l]oss of chance is the mirror image of the proposition that exposure to risk should be compensable. Just as chance quantifies the probability of a positive outcome (cure), risk describes the probability of a negative occurrence".[103] However, mirror images are not identical. Let us deal first with exposure to risk. These can be said to be "open" cases.

A plaintiff who has been exposed to a risk, which may or may not occur, is confronted with a dilemma resulting from the once-and-for-all rule of assessment of damages.[104] First, if the plaintiff waits to see whether the risk will occur before suing and the court recognises that some damage has already been suffered, the plaintiff might find that the limitation period

---

[100] These percentages are indicative only: cf *Davies v Taylor* [1974] AC 207 (HL) at 213. Mathematical precision is almost always spurious in such cases: see, eg, *Tran v Lam* (NSW SC, Badgery-Parker J, 20 June 1997, unreported, BC9705945).

[101] See the quotation from *Sturch v Willmott* (Qld SC, Thomas J, 13 April 1995, unreported, BC9505737) after n182 below; and *Talbot v Lusby* (Qld SC, Fryberg J, 14 July 1995, unreported, BC9506006), citing the last sentence of Deane J's statement quoted in the text at n95 above.

[102] Waddams, n85 above.

[103] JG Fleming, "Preventive Damages" in NJ Mullany, *Torts in the Nineties*, LBC Information Services, Sydney, 1997, p56 at p69. See also *Torts*, n71 above, p229.

[104] See *Todorovic v Waller* (1981) 150 CLR 402 at 412.

has run before the risk eventuates.[105] Secondly, if the plaintiff sues before the risk occurs, the plaintiff will be awarded damages only on the basis of the chance that the risk will eventuate. While the plaintiff then receives a windfall if it never does, the plaintiff is likely to be much undercompensated if the risk does eventuate.[106]

To avoid these problems, the law may simply state that the risk is not itself damage sufficient to satisfy the gist of an action in negligence.[107] This way of avoiding the problem cannot be adopted where the plaintiff suffers some recognised damage and the uncertain future risk is a consequence. As long as the once-and-for-all rule remains in place, the court must assess the damages on the basis of its estimate of the chances of the risk eventuating. Inevitably then, the plaintiff is over- or undercompensated.[108]

There is a solution here. That is to adopt legislation for what are known as provisional damages. Their introduction in England in 1985 by Rules of Court[109] made pursuant to the Supreme Court Act 1981 (Eng), s 32A, followed recommendations by the Law Commission.[110] They are intended, according to the Commission, to provide for what it calls "chance" cases, as opposed to "forecast" cases where a deterioration in the plaintiff's condition is probable, but its severity is uncertain.[111] The provisional damages are then assessed at the time of the trial without regard to the possibility of the loss occurring, but the event that will authorise a return to

---

[105] Cf *Cartledge v E Jopling & Sons Ltd* [1963] AC 758 (HL). There has been some questioning of this authority recently: see *Nixon v Philip Morris (Australia) Ltd* (1999) 165 ALR 515 at 535-6; *Wilson v Horne* (1999) 8 Tas R 363 (FC) at 385-6 per Evans J. Legislation in most jurisdictions also overcomes the problem to some extent, but that legislation will not always protect plaintiffs: see *Brisbane South Regional Health Authority v Taylor* (1996) 186 CLR 541.

[106] *Jones v Griffith* [1969] 2 All ER 1015 (CA) at 1020 per Harman LJ (risk of epilepsy); G Glasgow & ME Casey, "The Problem of Monetary Compensation for Post-traumatic Epilepsy" [1968] *NZLJ* 9 and 56; *Cowan v Kitson Insulations Ltd* [1992] PIQR Q19 (mesothelioma).

[107] J Stapleton, "The Gist of Negligence: Part II" (1988) 104 *LQR* 389 at 392 ff. See also Stauch, n6 above (advocating damages for loss of chance, but not for exposure to risk).

[108] *Lim v Camden & Islington Area Health Authority* [1980] AC 174 (HL) at 183. See also *Todorovic v Waller* (1981) 150 CLR 402 at 457-8 per Aickin J.

[109] RSC Ord 37, rr 7-10. See also Practice Direction (Provisional Damages: Procedure) [1985] 2 All ER 895. There are similar rules in the County Court. For interpretation of the rules, see *Hurditch v Sheffield Health Authority* [1989] QB 562 (CA); *Willson v Minister of Defence* [1991] 1 All ER 638; *Molinari v Ministry of Defence* [1994] PIQR Q3.

[110] *Report on Personal Injury Litigation – Assessment of Damages* (Law Com No 56, 1973), paras 239-44.

[111] In its latest review the Law Commission has recommended against extending the provisions to cases of gradual deterioration: Law Commission, *Structured Settlements and Interim and Provisional Damages* (Law Com No 224, 1994), paras 5.6-5.8.

court for further assessment is specified with particularity. A similar provision was adopted in the Dust Diseases Tribunal Act 1989 (NSW), s 11A.[112] The New South Wales Law Reform Commission has recommended that, with some modifications, legislation such as that under the Dust Diseases Tribunal Act be introduced for general application in personal injury actions in the State.[113] It should be adopted everywhere.

Whether or not such recommendations are adopted to deal with these "open" chance cases, the problems with "closed" chance cases are not the same. Although the issue remains whether loss of chance on its own should be regarded as damage for the purpose of a negligence action, the reasons for not so recognising it in the "open" chance cases do not apply. Where a medical practitioner has simply failed to diagnose a condition for which there was a chance of cure if treated at the time, the lack of a cure will already have eventuated at the time of any trial. Limitation problems are no different from any other case of professional negligence. They are linked to discovery of the fact of negligence, not to reasons for awaiting the eventuation of a risk.[114] The court will be in no better position to assess the damages for the missed chance if the assessment is postponed. Of course, the uncertainty as to what would have happened if the chance had not been missed and what will now happen remains. That uncertainty is inevitable, but plagues all personal injury litigation.

Medical Practitioners

What the courts or legislatures do with "open" cases of exposure to risk is not directly relevant to the issue of whether medical practitioners should be held liable for the loss of a chance of preventing or alleviating a medical condition for which the practitioner is not responsible. Before considering the Australian authorities, we shall refer briefly to those in the United Kingdom, Canada and the United States.

---

[112] As of September 1996, the provision had not been used: NSWLRC, *Provisional Damages* (Report 78, 1996), para 3.20.

[113] Ibid, paras 5.6-5.17. The Commission endorsed most of the modifications proposed by the Law Commission in its report, op cit, n111, Pt V, but was opposed to the listing in the legislation of matters to which the court should have regard in making its order. One such recommendation of the Law Commission, relating to provisional damages and fatal accident claims, is already in force in England: Damages Act 1996 (UK), s 3.

[114] Cf *Wardley Australia Ltd v Western Australia* (1992) 175 CLR 514; *Scarcella v Lettice* [2000] NSWCA 289 (NSW CA, 1 November 2000, unreported, BC200006725).

Overseas Authorities

United Kingdom

The issue arose comparatively early in Scotland. In *Kenyon v Bell*[115] a child fell and cut her eye. She was taken to hospital, where she was treated. Some months later the eye had to be removed. She alleged among other things that she had been deprived by negligence of the chance of saving the eye. In interlocutory proceedings it was held that such an allegation was insufficient, the pursuer being required to prove on the balance of probabilities that the defender's negligence had caused her loss. The matter was allowed to go to trial on her other allegations, but she failed, since the judge held that "no treatment could have made any difference because the initial injury involved a perforating wound of the sclera with consequent haemorrhaging into the interior of the eye".[116]

The finding that damage had probably already occurred and was therefore to be treated as certain, so that no treatment would have made any difference, lay also at the heart of the decision of the House of Lords in *Hotson v East Berkshire AHA*,[117] which has already been discussed. There it was held that the issue of loss of chance did not arise. In the Court of Appeal, however, the trial judge's award of damages based on loss of a 25 per cent chance of being treated successfully had been upheld.[118] Sir John Donaldson MR there said:

> As a matter of common sense, it is unjust that there should be no liability for failure to treat a patient, simply because the chances of a successful cure by that treatment were less than 50 per cent. Nor, by the same token, can it be just that if the chances of a successful cure only marginally exceed 50 per cent, the doctor or his employer should be liable to the same extent as if the treatment could be guaranteed to cure. If this is the law, it is high time that it was changed, assuming that this court has power to do so.[119]

His Lordship went on to suggest that the use of the word "chance" confused the distinct processes of identifying the loss and valuing it.[120] He

---

[115] 1953 SC 125.
[116] *Hotson v East Berkshire AHA* [1987] AC 750 (HL) at 784 per Lord Mackay, who wrongly refers to the child as a boy.
[117] [1987] AC 750 (HL).
[118] The judgments of the Court of Appeal are reported along with those of the House of Lords at [1987] AC 750.
[119] Ibid, at 759-60.
[120] Ibid, at 760-1.

preferred to say that the plaintiff had lost the benefit that he would have derived from the treatment that should have been given to him. This seems to be no more than a semantic distinction. Dillon LJ, too, thought it to be contrary to common sense that if a patient has only a chance of cure and loses that chance through a doctor's negligent failure to diagnose or treat, the patient can only recover damages if the chance were more than 50 per cent. He observed that medicine does not deal only in certainties.[121] Croom-Johnson LJ emphasised that it is a chance personal to the plaintiff that must be shown to have been lost, not merely a statistical chance.[122]

In the House of Lords Lord Bridge saw the analogy with *Chaplin v Hicks* and *Kitchen* as attractive, but superficial. Although he left the matter open, he saw formidable difficulties in the way of accepting the analogy.[123] He did not explain what he perceived those difficulties to be. Similarly, Lord Mackay considered it unwise to lay down a rule that a plaintiff could never succeed on loss of a chance in a medical negligence case.[124] He set out at length passages from *Herskovits v Group Health Cooperative*,[125] in order to demonstrate that a variety of views is possible in "this difficult area of the law".[126] Lord Ackner took the view that liability has to be established on a balance of probabilities and once so established, the loss which the plaintiff has sustained is paid in full. He disapproved of the decision in *Bagley v North Herts HA*,[127] where damages awarded for causing a child to be stillborn were discounted by 5 per cent because of the chance that it would have been stillborn without negligence.[128] This is clearly inconsistent with the decision of the High Court of Australia in *Malec*.[129]

Despite the matter having been left open by the House of Lords, there appears to be only one subsequent medical negligence case in England in which the damages were assessed on the basis of loss of chance. This was *Judge v Huntingdon Health Authority*,[130] where the failure to diagnose the plaintiff's breast cancer when it should have been identified was held to have deprived her of an 80 per cent chance of a full expectation of life and

---

[121] Ibid, at 764.
[122] Ibid, at 769-70.
[123] Ibid, at 782.
[124] Ibid, at 786.
[125] 99 Wash 2d 609, 664 P2d 474 (1983).
[126] [1987] AC 750 (HL) at 790.
[127] (1986) 136 NLJR 1014.
[128] [1987] AC 750 (HL) at 793.
[129] See Fleming, Postscript, above n71, at 141. See also *Veivers v Connolly* [1995] 2 Qd R 326 (damages for failure to diagnose rubella discounted by 5 per cent for chance that plaintiff would have been unable to obtain abortion).
[130] (1994) 27 BMLR 107.

the damages were assessed accordingly. The judge relied on the statement of Lord Diplock in *Mallett v McMonagle*,[131] quoted above, and a similar statement of Lord Reid in *Davies v Taylor*[132] and found nothing in *Hotson* to the contrary. Since, however, the judgment shows confusion between the issue of whether a chance is itself damage and cases where there is undoubtedly damage, but the consequences are dependent on contingencies, it is not of much value, even though its outcome is in accordance with the contention put forward here.

Canada

The Supreme Court of Canada rejected the doctrine of loss of chance in a medical negligence case in *Laferrière v Lawson*.[133] The defendant performed a biopsy of a lump in the plaintiff's breast, which the pathology report showed to be cancerous. However, he did not inform her of this finding or arrange any follow-up. She became aware of cancer in her system only some three and a half years later. Despite treatment, she died from it. The trial judge was not persuaded that treatment at the earlier stage would probably have prevented the spread of the cancer and gave judgment for the defendant. The intermediate Court of Appeal, however, by majority, awarded damages of $C50,000 for loss of a real and serious chance of benefiting from earlier treatment so that she might have survived longer. An appeal by the defendant to the Supreme Court was upheld and the damages reduced to $C17,500, being $C10,000 for the plaintiff's psychological suffering as a result of not being informed of the original detection of cancer and $C7,500 for the improvement in the quality of her life during her last months had the treatment been undertaken sooner. La Forest J dissented and would have upheld the award below for the reasons of one of the majority.

This case came from Quebec, where a civil code is in force. The Supreme Court began its analysis with a lengthy consideration of the law on loss of chance in France and Belgium. It attributed the fact that "French and Belgian courts have been especially alert to the contingency of lost chances" to a different approach to causation from that adopted in Quebec. Holding that proof of causation must be established on the balance of probabilities, it rejected the application of loss of chance to medical negligence cases. Loss of chance should, in its opinion, be confined to

---

[131] [1970] AC 166 (HL) at 176.
[132] [1974] AC 207 (HL) at 212-13.
[133] [1991] 1 SCR 541.

exceptional situations, of which destruction of a lottery ticket was the purest example.

The present Chief Justice of Canada was a member of the court that gave this decision. Clearly, she does not see it as foreclosing the issue in the common law jurisdictions of Canada. She has since written: "Although recovery for loss of chance has been considered in the context of Quebec civil law, it has not been evaluated under the common law."[134]

United States

We have seen that *Chaplin v Hicks*[135] was regarded as an advance on the insistence by courts in the United States on certainty.[136] The article by J H King Jr, to which frequent reference has been made above, was very influential in changing the attitude of many courts.[137] There remains a division of opinion as to whether to recognise the doctrine of loss of chance. A 1992 article, itself opposed to the use of loss of chance, claimed that "a majority of jurisdictions have declined to relax the standard of causation or create a new compensable injury".[138] Yet, in listing the jurisdictions still adhering to the "reasonable medical probability standard", the article shows that they are in the minority.[139] By 2000, at least two of those jurisdictions had adopted the loss of chance doctrine.[140] The debate

---

134   Hon Justice Beverley M McLachlin, "Negligence Law – Proving the Connection" in NJ Mullany & AM Linden (eds), *Torts Tomorrow: A Tribute to John Fleming*, LBC Information Services, Sydney, 1998, p16 at pp25-6. See also K Cooper-Stephenson, *Personal Injury Damages in Canada,* 2nd edn, Carswell, Scarborough, Ont, 1996, pp764-76 (*Laferrière* and *Hotson* would be persuasive, but not conclusive, in common law Canada); *Athey v Leonati* [1996] 3 SCR 458 at 474 (unnecessary to consider loss of chance doctrine and these reasons neither approve nor disapprove it).
135   [1911] 2 KB 786 (CA).
136   Above n23.
137   King is said to have drawn his ideas from LL Wolfstone & TJ Wolfstone, "Recovery of Damages for Loss of a Chance", *Personal Injury Annual 1978*, p744: see TS Aagard, "Identifying and Valuing the Injury in Lost Chance Cases" (1998) 96 *Michigan L Rev* 1335, n10.
138   L Perrochet, SL Smith & U Collelo, "Lost Chance Recovery and the Folly of Expanding Medical Malpractice Liability" (1992) 27 *Tort & Ins LJ* 615.
139   Ibid, Appendix A. See also JD Hodson, "Annotation, Medical Malpractice: 'Loss Of Chance' Causality" 54 ALR 4th 10 (1987, as supplemented to September 2000).
140   See *Roberts v Ohio Permanente Med Group, Inc,* 668 NE 2d 480 (Ohio SC, 1996); *Jorgenson v Vener*, 616 NW2d 366 (SD SC, 2000). On the other hand, at least one legislature has overturned its courts' decision to adopt loss of chance and has laid down a requirement of 50 per cent probability: Michigan Compiled Laws Annotated, Chapter 600, Revised Judicature Act of 1961, s 2912a(2) ("In an action alleging medical malpractice ... the plaintiff cannot recover for loss of an opportunity to survive

appears to have moved on to the question of *how* the chance is to be valued.[141] This latter debate will not be considered here. It is often tied up with what the jury is to be allowed to do.

Australian Cases

High Court dicta

In *Naxakis v Western & General Hospital*[142] the plaintiff schoolboy had been hit over the head in a minor scuffle with one of his friends. He was taken to hospital, where he was kept for nine days. Two days after he was discharged, he suffered a burst aneurism, which led to serious brain damage. In his action against the school principal, those who would be vicariously liable for her, the doctor who treated him and the hospital, the trial judge withdrew the case from the jury. His decision to do so was upheld by the Victorian Court of Appeal, in a judgment delivered by Hayne JA (as he then was).[143] The High Court granted special leave to appeal only in respect of the action against the doctor and the hospital. It upheld the appeal and ordered a new trial. Its decision was based on there having been sufficient evidence of negligence and causation of the injury to have been left to the jury. The judges found it unnecessary to deal with the argument that had been put in the alternative that the plaintiff had been deprived of a chance of avoiding the burst aneurism and the jury should have been allowed to assess the value of the chance.[144] Before the retrial the Victorian Supreme Court had to consider whether to allow an amendment to the pleadings so that this argument could be advanced. Hedigan J declined to do so, being of the opinion that a majority of the High Court was opposed

---

141   or an opportunity to achieve a better result unless the opportunity was greater than 50%.")

Eg, *Smith v State of Louisiana, Dept of Health and Hospitals*, 676 So 2d 543 at 549 (1996); Aagard, n137 above. Cf King, n4 above, at 1381-7. See MJ McMahon, "Annotation, Medical Malpractice: Measure and Elements of Damages in Actions Based on Loss of Chance" 81 ALR 4th 485 (1990) (as supplemented to September 2000). The weighted average method advocated by King has been rejected in NSW in the context of damages for loss of earning capacity resulting from motor accidents: see n46 above.

142   (1999) 197 CLR 269.

143   *Naxakis v State of Victoria* (Vic CA, 5 September 1997, unreported, BC9704282).

144   See counsel's argument briefly reported at (1999) 197 CLR 269 at 271. A transcript of the argument presented on 16 November 1998 may be found at http://www.austlii. edu.au/au/other/hca/transcripts/1998/M43/1.html. See also Moshinsky, above n7, at 218.

to the doctrine of loss of chance.[145] For this, he relied on dicta in *Chappel v Hart*[146] and *Naxakis* itself, which we shall investigate shortly. He also relied on the article by Perrochet *et al*,[147] which he said showed that a majority of jurisdictions in the United States did not apply loss of chance,[148] which "strongly criticised" King's theory, and which "caution[ed] against recognition of the lost chance as a compensable injury, on policy grounds".[149] Leave to appeal was refused by the Court of Appeal, mainly because of the length of time that had elapsed,[150] but also because of the possibility of amending the pleadings at the trial if the evidence justified it. The case was settled after the hearing of the retrial had begun. So it provided no answer to whether Australian law will recognise loss of chance in medical negligence cases.

The dicta in the High Court are far from conclusive in favour of rejecting loss of chance. Most strongly opposed to the notion have been Brennan and Gaudron JJ in cases not concerned with medical negligence, though the latter has reiterated her stance in this context. We have already seen that Brennan J took a more uncompromising attitude than the rest of the court in the solicitors' negligence cases dealt with above.[151] In *Sellars* he quoted and expressly agreed with the following passage in Gaudron J's judgment in *Bennett v Minister of Community Welfare*:

> It might be said that, where questions of causation depend on hypothetical considerations, allowance should be made, as in the assessment of damages, for the possibility that some event would not have occurred. Possibilities, if they are not fanciful, must be taken into account, at least in a general way, whenever causation or the related issue of prevention is in issue. But questions of that kind are not answered "maybe" or, even, "more probably than not". They are answered "yes" or "no" depending on the probabilities for or against. In this respect, they are indistinguishable from the question whether an event happened where possibilities are taken into account but, once the question has been answered, those possibilities have no further bearing on the matter.[152]

She was, however, a party to the joint judgment of all but Brennan J in *Sellars* and must therefore recognise that if the loss itself constitutes harm

---

145   [1999] VSC 389 (Vic SC, Hedigan J, 15 October 1999, unreported, BC9906720).
146   (1998) 195 CLR 232.
147   See n138 above.
148   This is doubtful: see n139.
149   These will be considered below: see text at nn220-224.
150   The injury was sustained in 1980.
151   See text at nn43-51.
152   (1992) 176 CLR 408 at 422-3 (omitted footnotes refer to *Malec*).

that satisfies the requirement of the gist of the action, then one can quite readily answer "yes" or "no" to the question whether the defendant has caused the plaintiff to suffer that harm. Possibilities must then come into the evaluation of the loss, just as in *Sellars* it was accepted that there was a 40 per cent chance of successfully negotiating the contract that the defendant deprived the plaintiff of the chance of doing.

Say that a plaintiff has a less than 50 per cent chance of not having a leg amputated if a surgeon takes reasonable care in treating it. The surgeon fails to take care and the patient loses the leg. In *Bennett* Gaudron J took the view that one might infer causation whenever a defendant fails to take required precautions against a particular risk, which then eventuates, in the absence of evidence that the breach had no effect or the harm would have occurred anyway.[153] On this view, one might infer that the surgeon's negligence deprived the patient of the chance of saving the leg, but one could not infer that it caused the loss of the leg, since more probably than not that would have happened even if the surgeon had not been negligent. The plaintiff should be entitled to damages for that loss. Otherwise, according to those who believe that the law of torts operates as a significant deterrent, medical practitioners can be as negligent as they like when treating seriously ill patients who have less than a 50 per cent chance of survival, since the doctors would never be liable if the patient did not survive. A similar point has been made by Professor Waddams in relation to *Hotson*: if the doctor in that case had four patients annually, only one of whom had a chance of not developing permanent incapacity, the doctor could treat all four of them negligently and would not be liable to any of them.[154]

In *Chappel v Hart* Gaudron J categorised the plaintiff's loss as "clearly ... not the loss of a chance − valuable or otherwise − but the physical injury which she, in fact, sustained".[155] This is questionable. To some extent it may depend on a view of the facts that was not accepted by all the judges. In this case, the plaintiff was not warned of a risk that her voice might be affected by an operation which she needed to undergo at some stage. By the time the case reached the High Court, it was not contested that in the circumstances of her having expressed concern that she should not have a "voice like Neville Wran" after the operation, it was negligent on the part of the defendant, who carried out the surgery with all due care and skill, not to warn her of this risk. The risk did eventuate. Gaudron J held that on

---

[153] (1992) 176 CLR 408 at 420, citing, among others, *Betts v Whittingslowe* (1945) 71 CLR 637 at 649 per Dixon J. See also her judgment in *Chappel v Hart* (1998) 195 CLR 232 at 238-9.

[154] Above n85.

[155] (1998) 195 CLR 232 at 238.

the evidence it had to be accepted that the risk to which the plaintiff was exposed would have been less if the operation had been performed by a more experienced surgeon, to whom she would probably have resorted if she had been warned.[156] Her Honour pointed out that if there had been evidence that even if when performed by a more experienced surgeon the risk was a "probability", it would have had to be taken into account.[157] Since she cited part of the judgment in *Malec*,[158] to which she was a party, she must have meant a possibility that was more than speculative. Be that as it may, since the chance of the risk occurring on any other occasion than the one when it did was extremely small, the damages would have been reduced only by a small amount under the *Malec* doctrine.

As commentators have pointed out, the plaintiff did lose a chance by not being warned. She lost the chance of going into the operation metaphorically with her eyes open. For being deprived of this chance, she should have been compensated, at least by a conventional figure, for the intangible harm to her autonomy and dignity.[159] But this was not an argument that was put. The chance for which she contended, as McHugh J saw it, was an opportunity to seek a higher standard of care or better treatment from another surgeon, or even in effect a guarantee of the absence of a perforation of the oesophagus. In his Honour's dissenting opinion, there was nothing in the doctor-patient relationship to require the defendant to provide the plaintiff with such opportunities.[160]

Gummow J pointed out that the plaintiff did not put her case as one for loss of a chance at all; that it was the defendant who sought to reduce his liability by reference to the doctrine.[161] His Honour made reference to the Canadian cases, but gave no indication of his own approach to the question. Kirby J, too, referred to the defendant having raised loss of chance at a late stage and the plaintiff not having done so at the trial. Since the evidence might have been different, he thought a new perspective on the case should not be adopted.[162] Earlier, however, he referred to his own judgment in *CES v Superclinics (Australia) Pty Ltd*,[163] where, he now said,

---

156 Ibid, at 241.
157 Ibid, at 241-2.
158 (1990) 169 CLR 638 at 642-3.
159 SM Waddams, "Causation, Physicians and Disclosure of Risks" (1999) 7 *Tort L Rev* 5; Hoffmann, n20 above. See also Hon Justice I Englard, "Informed Consent – The Double-faced Doctrine" in NJ Mullany & AM Linden (eds), *Torts Tomorrow: A Tribute to John Fleming*, LBC Information Services, Sydney, 1998, p152. Cf Honoré, n99 above (court justified in overriding causal principles to vindicate plaintiff's rights).
160 (1998) 195 CLR 232 at 252.
161 Ibid, at 258-60.
162 Ibid, at 278-9.
163 (1995) 38 NSWLR 47 (CA) at 56-7.

he had indicated his "attraction to this approach as a more rational and just way of calculating damages caused by established medical negligence".[164] It is difficult to find so strong an expression in favour of the alternative way in which the plaintiff could have, but did not, put her case in *CES* in the report of his Honour's judgment. Whether or not what he said in *Chappel* are first or second thoughts, he cannot be regarded as opposed to the doctrine. Finally, Hayne J thought it neither necessary nor appropriate, for reasons he gave, to analyse the case as one for loss of chance.[165] He did point to the difficulty of evaluating a lost chance when one is dealing with very small risks, such as an increase in risk from one in 200 to one in 100, or even more so from one in 20,000 to one in 10,000. It is in the context of the facts of the case itself that one should understand his remark that "the loss of chance analysis is flawed and should not be adopted". Immediately after this remark, he went on to say that he need not and did not "express any view on the difficult questions that arise where a plaintiff claims damages for negligence, as opposed to contract, and contends that the damage suffered is the loss of a chance".[166]

The dicta in *Chappel*, which have been analysed here, show, as to is to be expected, that the judges of the High Court have open minds on the question of loss of chance in medical negligence. If Gaudron J is unsympathetic, Kirby J is in the opposite camp and the other three are neutral. *Naxakis* adds little to the picture, other than introducing an odd preliminary view from Callinan J. Gleeson CJ expressly refrained from commenting on the alternative argument based on loss of chance.[167] Earlier, when sitting in the New South Wales Court of Appeal, he had shown that he was at least open to an argument based on loss of chance, even though it was in the least likely context for such an argument to be successful, namely where the causal issue is what the plaintiff's own response would have been to a warning or notice.[168] Gaudron J elaborated on her views for rejecting loss of chance.[169] She correctly said that the doctrine of loss of chance would not necessarily benefit individual plaintiffs.

> If damages were to be awarded for the chance lost, rather than the actual injuries or disabilities suffered, consistency would require that damages be assessed according to the value of the chance, not the injury or

---

[164] (1998) 195 CLR 232 at 274.
[165] Ibid, at 288.
[166] Ibid, at 289.
[167] (1999) 197 CLR 269 at 272.
[168] *Public Trustee v Sutherland SC* (1992) Aust Torts Reps 81-149 (NSW CA) at 61,141.
[169] (1999) 197 CLR 269 at 277-81.

disability. Thus, a chance which is 51% or greater but less than 100%, must result in an award of damages less than would be the case if damages were awarded for the injury or disability which eventuates.[170]

But Gaudron J failed to recognise the extent to which *Malec* now reduces damages below 100 per cent on account of chances that might have occurred, even where the plaintiff proves on a balance of probabilities that the defendant did cause harm in the form of a risk that eventuated. This will be illustrated by some of the cases dealt with below.

McHugh J was silent on the point. Kirby J expressly said that he did not need to deal with the alternative argument relating to loss of a chance and added nothing further.[171] Callinan J did deal with the matter and expressed the view that there is a place for the doctrine, "particularly in cases involving the practice of what is even today said to be an art rather than a scientific skill".[172] He apparently did not see the need for consistency between cases where the plaintiff can prove on a balance of probabilities that the harm would not have occurred without negligence, in which he thought that the plaintiff should recover in full, and cases of less than an even chance. He observed that there would be a small chance in nearly every case and was concerned to confine the plaintiff's right to recover for the loss of a chance to a substantial one. In relation to the plaintiff's recovering in full where the plaintiff proves on a balance of probabilities that the defendant's negligence did cause the harm, he cited *Rogers v Whitaker*,[173] a case where the causal issue depended on what the plaintiff's own response to a warning would have been. This may well be a case where loss of chance is excluded, as we shall see below.

From this, possibly tedious, recitation of the dicta of the present High Court Justices in Australia, it should be apparent that Hedigan J should not have concluded "that with respect to a case of alleged medical negligence in the course of treatment (as distinct from advice) the law would not and should not entertain a claim for damages for loss of a chance".[174] All one can say is that Gaudron J is opposed and Kirby and Callinan JJ are probably sympathetic.

---

[170] Ibid, at 279.
[171] Ibid, at 296.
[172] Ibid, at 312-13 (citation to Hippocrates omitted).
[173] (1992) 175 CLR 479.
[174] [1999] VSC 389 (Vic SC, Hedigan J, 15 October 1999, unreported, BC9906720).

Intermediate appellate court cases

In *Sullivan v Micallef*[175] the plaintiff was awarded substantial damages for the consequences of the defendants' negligent failure to diagnose her cancer when they should have. Those consequences led to her early death. On appeal, it was argued that the damages should be reduced because they should have been assessed on the basis that there was only a chance that her cancer, if diagnosed when it should have been, would have been successfully eradicated. This was so, it was urged, even if the chance was a high one. The court acknowledged that the argument raised interesting "questions which, were this the appropriate occasion, could be pursued at length".[176] However, it held that there was evidence justifying the trial judge's conclusion that the cancer would have been successfully treated if it had been diagnosed when it should have been and there was no justification for interfering with this finding. Since this was a finding of a hypothetical fact – what would have happened if there had not been negligence – it seems that some allowance should have been made for the chance that the treatment would not have been successful.

Some consideration was given to the issue in *Board of Management of Royal Perth Hospital v Frost*.[177] There a plaintiff complaining of chest pains had been allowed to go home prematurely. This was held to be negligent. He had thereafter suffered a heart attack. The trial judge's "modest" award of damages was upheld. Wallwork J, with whom Malcolm CJ and Rowland J agreed on this issue, said:

> [T]he respondent had to establish on the balance of probabilities that the contravening conduct caused the loss of an opportunity for treatment which had some value, that value being ascertained by reference to the degree of probabilities or possibilities. His Honour found that the respondent lost the chance of having his heart muscle damage minimised or reduced by timely thrombolytic therapy. The respondent did not have to prove on the balance of probabilities that the treatment would have been effective, because in such a case as this that is too theoretical. Once it was established that the respondent should have been given a second ECG, which was not given to him, he had established on the balance of probabilities that he had lost a valuable chance of getting some treatment

---

[175] (1994) Aust Torts Reps 81-308 (NSW CA).

[176] Ibid, at 61,791 per Mahoney AP.

[177] WA FC, Malcolm CJ, Rowland & Wallwork JJ, 26 February 1997, unreported, BC9700642. See now also *Gavalas v Singh* [2001] VSCA 23 (22 March 2001, unreported, BC200101238) (law will allow claim for damages for lost chance of a more favourable outcome from treatment resulting from doctor's negligent failure to diagnose, though precise boundaries of such claims await future determination).

which may have improved his position. He had therefore suffered loss or damage.

First instance decisions

The "loss of a chance factor" was recognised by the judge in another case of failure to diagnose cancer, *Locher v Turner*.[178] However, he declined to reduce the damages by at least 40 per cent, as counsel urged, because the damages were already conservative in significant areas and already made some allowance for loss of a chance.[179] Two more similar Queensland cases did more explicitly reduce damages on this account. In *Sturch v Willmott*[180] the trial judge began the assessment of damages with a clear recognition of the task:

> It is important to remember that the defendant did not cause the plaintiff to suffer from cancer. The consequences for which he is liable to pay damages are for the extent to which he deprived her of the chance of making a better recovery than is now the case. The evidence suggests that early diagnosis and treatment would have given her a good chance of a successful outcome. There are however no certainties, and the present case is a good example of one in which the prospect of some degree of trouble in any event must be brought into account.

The judge noted that the first issue that arose was whether the first episode of bleeding from which the plaintiff suffered was caused by a benign polyp or a growth that was already cancerous. Although this was a past fact, no-one could answer that with certainty or even confidence.[181] He questioned the applicability of statements that past facts are treated as certain when proved on a balance of probability and referred to King's "useful discussion of the relationship between pre-existing condition and the exercise of assessment of damage".[182] Having referred to *Sellars*, his Honour concluded:

> I reject the submission of counsel for the plaintiff which would urge me to shut my eyes to the substantial chance, perhaps of the order of forty

---

[178] (1994) [1995] Aust Torts Reps 81-336 (Qld SC), appeal dismissed *Turner v Locher* (Qld CA, 21 April 1995, unreported, BC9505744).

[179] [1995] Aust Torts Reps 81-336 (Qld SC) at 62,350.

[180] Qld SC, Thomas J, 13 April 1995, unreported, BC9505737. An appeal by the plaintiff was successful in having one head of damages increased: *Sturch v Willmott* [1997] 2 Qd R 310 (Qld CA). The question of loss of chance was not dealt with on the appeal.

[181] Cf text at nn83-97 above.

[182] Citing King, above n4, at 1354, 1356, 1363-4, 1368-9, 1373, 1381 et seq, and 1397.

per-cent, that the growth may already have been cancerous when the plaintiff first consulted the defendant. That possibility will not enable me to make any specific mathematical calculation, but it is a factor that I must take into account in discounting damages so as to take into account the level of problems that the plaintiff may have had to face even without any omission on the part of the defendant.

In *Talbot v Lusby*[183] the judge said:

> Mrs Talbot might not have been diagnosed as having cancer until it was too late, even if she had been sent for an ultrasonic scan, or the aspiration needle had been sent for cytological examination, in August 1989. There might have been a false negative result again. Moreover even if the diagnosis had been made, she might have turned out to be incurable, even at that early stage.

Under the heading "Discounting for Loss of a Chance" the judge noted that it was common ground between the parties that these contingencies should be allowed for by discounting of the damages, which he proceeded to do by 15 per cent. The same principle was applied in *Veivers v Connolly*,[184] a case of failure to diagnose rubella in a pregnant woman. Here the damages were reduced by 5 per cent because of the chance that, even if the condition had been diagnosed, the plaintiff might have been unable to obtain a termination of the pregnancy.

In each of these Queensland cases the judge held that the chance of successfully avoiding the harm if the defendant had not been negligent was better than even. Yet in each the damages were not the full damages that would compensate the plaintiff for the actual loss, but such a sum discounted by the probability (which was less than 50 per cent) that the harm would not have been avoided even if the defendant had not been negligent. In some recent New South Wales cases, damages were awarded for loss of a chance where the probability of avoiding the harm was not better than even.[185] Contrary to the view of Callinan J in *Naxakis*,[186] it

---

[183] Qld SC, Fryberg J, 14 July 1995, unreported, BC9506006.

[184] [1995] 2 Qd R 326.

[185] *Tran v Lam* (NSW SC, Badgery-Parker J, 20 June 1997, unreported, BC9705945) (judge declined to put precise mathematical figure on it, but seems to have regarded the chance as small); *McInnes v Ahluwalia* [1999] NSWSC 818 (NSW SC, Davies AJ, 11 August 1999, unreported, BC9904583) (damages reduced by 50 per cent because chance of recovery if defendant had advised plaintiff's mother to see specialist only 50 per cent); *Bourke v MacNeil* [2000] NSWCA 144 (NSW CA, 14 June 2000, unreported, BC200003177) (chance that plaintiff would have had substantial recovery if not operated on 40 per cent and damages assessed on this basis, but judgment

should make no difference once one accepts that damages may be awarded for loss of a chance in these cases whether the chance is estimated at more or less than 50 per cent, as long as it is not purely speculative.

In *Tran v Lam*,[187] Badgery-Parker acknowledged that in an earlier case[188] he himself had set too high a standard in refusing to recognise loss of a chance. He now stated the law as being that:

> when the chance which the plaintiff claims to have lost was a chance that an event would have occurred, conferring a benefit upon the plaintiff, over the happening of which event the plaintiff had no control ... what the law requires the plaintiff to prove on the balance of probabilities is the existence of the chance. Upon proof of that, the cause of action is complete and the court may proceed to the assessment of damages in the manner recognised in *Malec*.

His Honour distinguished a different class of case:

> Where the chance lost was a chance that the plaintiff may have acted in such a way as to receive a benefit or avert a detriment, the plaintiff must prove on the balance of probabilities that there was such a chance and that the plaintiff would have so acted.

It is to this class of case that we now turn.

Chances Dependent on the Plaintiff's Response

In the leading Australian case on loss of a chance, *Sellars v Adelaide Petroleum NL*,[189] the High Court distinguished three cases in which it was argued that proof had been required on the balance of probabilities when what was at issue was really the loss of a chance.[190] The joint judgment of the majority of the court accepted the distinction in *Hotson* between proof

---

overturned because CA found that on evidence plaintiff had failed to prove that he was suffering from particular condition).

[186] See text after n172 above.

[187] NSW SC, Badgery-Parker J, 20 June 1997, unreported, BC9705945.

[188] *Woods v Lowns* (NSW SC, Badgery-Parker J, 9 February 1995, unreported on this point, BC9504451) (finding that brain damage would probably not have occurred but for negligence excluded any allowance for chance that it would have occurred anyway).

[189] (1994) 179 CLR 332 at 351-3.

[190] *Sykes v Midland Bank Executor & Trustee Co Ltd* [1971] 1 QB 113 (CA); *Gates v City Mutual Life Assurance Society Ltd* (1986) 160 CLR 1; and *Norwest Refrigeration Services Pty Ltd v Bain Dawes (WA) Pty Ltd* (1984) 157 CLR 149.

of causation and damages. It said that these cases may have turned on the issue of causation, "which is ordinarily governed by the general civil standard of proof".[191] Although it noted the criticism by Professor Waddams of the first of these cases,[192] it concluded: "When the issue of causation turns on what the plaintiff would have done, there is no particular reason for departing from proof on the balance of probabilities notwithstanding that the question is hypothetical."[193] This also explains cases such as where an employer has failed to provide safety equipment and the issue has been raised as to whether the employee would have used the equipment if it had been supplied.[194] In such cases Professor Atiyah long ago pointed to the hypothetical nature of the inquiry and its resemblance to the questions involved in the estimation of future probabilities.[195] Unless it is proved on the balance of probabilities that the equipment would have been used and the injury averted, the plaintiff has failed to prove that the failure caused the injury. Similarly, where the defendant's negligence consists in failing to erect a warning sign, it is generally required that the plaintiff establish on the balance of probabilities that he or she would have responded to the warning in such a way as to avert the danger.[196]

The issue of loss of chance was considered at some length in the English Court of Appeal in *Allied Maples Group Ltd v Simmons & Simmons*,[197] a solicitor's negligence case. The case bore some similarity to *Sellars*, though no reference was made to it. The outcome was, however,

---

[191] (1994) 179 CLR 332 at 353.

[192] Citing *Law of Damages*, 2nd edn, Canada Law Book, Toronto, 1991, §13.360; and "The Principles of Compensation" in P Finn (ed), *Essays on Damages*, Law Book Co, Sydney, 1992, pp10-12. See also Waddams, n85 above.

[193] (1994) 179 CLR 332 at 353.

[194] Eg, *Duyvelshaff v Cathcart & Ritchie Ltd* (1973) 1 ALR 125.

[195] PS Atiyah, *Accidents, Compensation and the Law*, 1st edn, Weidenfeld & Nicolson, London, 1970, pp124-6, referring to *McWilliams v Sir William Arrol & Co* [1962] 1 All ER 623 (HL). The discussion is omitted in P Cane, *Atiyah's Accidents, Compensation and the Law*, 6th edn, Butterworths, London, 1999, p95, where the law is regarded as settled, unsatisfactorily, by placing the burden of proof on the plaintiff.

[196] Eg, *Nagle v Rottnest Island Authority* (1993) 177 CLR 423; *Council of the Municipality of Waverley v Bloom* (1999) Aust Torts Reps 81-517 (NSW CA); *Secretary to the Department of Natural Resources and Energy v Harper* (2000) 1 VR 133 (Vic CA) at 152-3, citing *Romeo v Conservation Commission of the Northern Territory* (1998) 192 CLR 431 at [134] per Kirby J and *Qantas Airways Ltd v Cameron* (1996) 66 FCR 246 (FC) at 293-4 per Lindgren J. Cf *Public Trustee v Sutherland SC* (1992) Aust Torts Reps 81-149 (NSW CA) at 61,141 (contemplating possibility of treating such cases as for loss of chance); *Lilley v Alpine Resorts Commission* (1998) Aust Torts Reps 81-475 (Vic CA) (where it was held that plaintiff failed to prove what response of third party to notice would have been).

[197] [1995] 1 WLR 1602 (CA).

the same. The defendant solicitors negligently failed to advise the plaintiffs in relation to the takeover of certain assets. Had the correct advice been given, the plaintiffs would probably have negotiated further with the vendor. The majority held that there was a realistic chance that the negotiations would have been successful. The solicitors were held liable for the loss of that chance. The leading judgment of Stuart-Smith LJ, with which Hobhouse and Millett LJJ (as they then were) agreed on the law, though the latter dissented on the facts, made a number of points:[198]

- There is a distinction between positive acts and omissions. In relation to positive acts, the question of causation is one of historical fact and must be proved on a balance of probabilities. If so established, the fact is taken as certain and "[t]here is no discount because the judge considers that the balance is only just tipped in favour of the plaintiff".
- Questions of quantification often depend on future uncertain events. These are not decided on a balance of probabilities, but on the court's assessment of the risk, which is often expressed in percentage terms.
- "If the defendant's negligence consists of an omission, for example to provide proper equipment, or to give proper instructions or advice, causation depends, not upon a question of historical fact, but on the answer to the hypothetical question, what would the plaintiff have done if the equipment had been provided or the instruction or advice given. This can only be a matter of inference to be determined from all the circumstances. ... Although the question is a hypothetical one, it is well established that the plaintiff must prove on the balance of probability that he would have taken action to obtain the benefit or avoid the risk. But again, if he does establish that, there is no discount because the balance is only just tipped in his favour."
- If the plaintiff's loss depends on the hypothetical action of a third party, the plaintiff does not have to establish on a balance of probabilities that the third party would have acted to confer a benefit on, or avoid a risk to, the plaintiff.
- There is no difference in principle between the chance of gaining a benefit and avoiding a liability.
- The chance of success need not be more than 50 per cent.

The distinction made by the English Court of Appeal between positive acts and omissions cannot be completely supported.[199] It is true that where there are competing possible causes the plaintiff must prove on the balance

---

198 Ibid, at 1609-14.
199 See Stauch, n6 above, at 219, n48.

of probabilities that the defendant's negligence did at least contribute materially to the harm.[200] But once that is established, the possibility of other causes having a like effect in the absence of the defendant's negligence must also be taken into account.[201] In the case of a surgical operation which is only sometimes successful if done with all due care, we cannot know, in a particular case where it is performed negligently, whether or not it would have been successful if done without negligence. The issues should be the same as in a case where the negligence consists in failing to diagnose the condition or to perform the operation at all.

The other points made in the judgment in *Allied Maples Group* have been followed and endorsed in many subsequent English cases.[202] They are valid and are consistent with Australian law. It has at least been assumed in cases such as *Rogers v Whitaker*[203] and *Chappel v Hart*[204] that where the issue is whether the plaintiff would have acted so as to avert the harm or detriment, this must be proved on a balance of probabilities. This was so held in *Green v Chenoweth*,[205] where the onus was held not to have been discharged. If the onus had been discharged, the plaintiff would have recovered the damages in full.[206] Only Professor Waddams appears to dispute this.[207] Although theoretically there is much to be said for his view, the authority for distinguishing cases dependent on the plaintiff's own response seems too firmly entrenched to be challenged now. On the other hand, where what would have happened in the absence of negligence by the defendant depends on the response of a third party that is not completely one of that party's volition, authority favours the view that the plaintiff may rely on loss of chance, so long as the chance is real and not purely speculative.

Where the plaintiff's response to a failure by a medical practitioner to give warning is in issue, some North American cases have said that this is

---

[200] See n14 above.
[201] Cf *Malec v J C Hutton Pty Ltd* (1990) 169 CLR 638.
[202] Some of them are discussed in *Bank of Credit and Commerce International SA (in Liq) (BCCI) v Ali (No 2)* [1999] 4 All ER 83 at 110-12. See also *Motor Crown Petroleum Ltd v SJ Berwin & Co* [2000] Lloyd's Rep PN 438 (Eng CA).
[203] (1992) 175 CLR 479. This was noted by Callinan J in *Naxakis v Western General Hospital* (1999) 197 CLR 269 at 313.
[204] (1998) 195 CLR 232. See now also *Rosenberg v Percival* (2001) 178 ALR 577.
[205] [1998] 2 Qd R 572 (CA); SLR [1998] 19 Leg Rep SL 4 (20 November 1998). Cf *Keeys v State of Queensland* [1998] 2 Qd R 36 (CA) at 39-40 per McPherson JA, at 41 per Davies JA, at 44 per Moynihan J.
[206] Cf *Kite v Malycha* (1998) 71 SASR 321 (having no doubt that plaintiff would have sought and obtained treatment, judge refused to treat case as one for loss of chance; however, allowance should have been made for chance that treatment would have been unsuccessful).
[207] See nn192 and 85 above.

to be judged objectively.[208] It is clear that in Australia it is judged subjectively, but as McHugh J has pointed out, this may make little difference, since the court will not accept the plaintiff's evidence given with hindsight unless backed up by objective features:

> Human nature being what it is, most plaintiffs will genuinely believe that, if he or she had been given an option that would or might have avoided the injury, the option would have been taken. In determining the reliability of the plaintiff's evidence in jurisdictions where the subjective test operates, therefore, demeanour can play little part in accepting the plaintiff's evidence. It may be a ground for rejecting the plaintiff's evidence. But given that most plaintiffs will genuinely believe that they would have taken another option, if presented to them, the reliability of their evidence can only be determined by reference to objective factors, particularly the attitude and conduct of the plaintiff at or about the time when the breach of duty occurred.[209]

Policy

In a more rationally organised society there would be no medical negligence litigation.[210] People who were ill would have their needs met and be compensated for permanent disability from a social insurance fund.[211] Medical standards would be maintained through education, guidelines, disciplinary proceedings and, as a last resort, the criminal law.[212] Disputes that occurred would be resolved through mediation by the offices of the Health Services Commissioner or their equivalent in each State. It seems, however, that these rational views will not prevail for some

---

[208] See *Chappel v Hart* (1998) 195 CLR 232 at 246 n64 per McHugh J, citing *Canterbury v Spence* (1972) 464 F 2d 772 at 791 and *Reibl v Hughes* (1981) 114 DLR 3d 1 at 16. See also the so-called "modified objective approach" adopted in *Arndt v Smith* [1997] 2 SCR 539, criticised by M McInnes, "Failure to Warn in Medical Negligence – A Cautionary Note from Canada" (1998) 6 *TLJ* 135 and by T Honoré, "Causation and Disclosure of Medical Risks" (1998) 114 *LQR* 52. Cf *Hollis v Dow Corning Corp* [1995] 4 SCR 634.

[209] *Chappel v Hart* (1998) 195 CLR 232 at 246. Cf *Allied Maples Group Ltd v Simmons & Simmons* [1995] 1 WLR 1602 (CA) at 1623-4 (considering how a third party would have acted).

[210] See H Luntz, "Mrs Whitaker's Gothic Cathedral" (1996) 4 *TLJ* 195.

[211] Cf the proposals of the National Committee of Inquiry into Compensation and Rehabilitation in Australia (Chair: Sir Owen Woodhouse), *Report* (1974).

[212] Cf Final Report of the Review of Professional Indemnity Arrangements for Health Care Professionals (Chair: Fiona Tito), *Compensation and Professional Indemnity in Health Care* (1995). For a summary of this report see GJ Reinhardt (1996) 4 *TLJ* 173.

time.[213] Instead, the torts system must continue to serve the ends of compensation, deterrence, maintenance of standards and moral judgment.[214] On all these scores, there can be little doubt that the law should impose liability for loss of a chance brought about by medical negligence. It is a real loss, something that people would give money for.[215] Corrective justice arguments seem to require that the wrongdoer compensate the person who has suffered.[216] As the House of Lords emphasised recently when abrogating the advocate's immunity, wrongs must be righted unless there are good reasons to the contrary.[217] There are no strong distributive justice reasons for denying the remedy beyond the fact that many people who fall ill are left without any remedy if they cannot prove negligence.[218]

The article that Hedigan J in *Naxakis*[219] found persuasive does advance reasons of policy for denying the extension of liability to loss of chance.[220] One is obviously spurious. The article refers to two commentators and two courts that have pointed out that loss of chance leads to statistically more wrong decisions than right ones. In a group of 99 cases, of which only 33 would have survived, allowing recovery for all 99 means that 66 are wrongly decided. This is like saying that a clock that has stopped is better than one that is a minute fast, since it is right twice a day, whereas the one that is fast is never right! Most people would prefer the fast watch to the stopped one as being much more useful. In this example, the defendant would, if loss of chance were denied, never pay any compensation despite repeated acts of negligence. By requiring the defendant to pay 33 per cent of the assessed damages to all, the defendant compensates exactly the total damage that has been caused by negligence.

The other arguments against extension of liability have more validity. The article contends that it would have an adverse effect on health cost

---

213 Cf Law Reform Committee of Victoria, *Legal Liability of Health Service Providers* (1997).
214 Cf RL Abel, "A Critique of Torts" (1990) 37 *UCLA L Rev* 785 (summarised in (1994) 2 *Tort L Rev* 99).
215 Waddams, n85 above.
216 See, eg, RW Wright, "Right, Justice and Tort Law" in DG Owen (ed), *Philosophical Foundations of Tort Law*, Clarendon Press, Oxford, 1995, p159.
217 *Arthur JS Hall & Co (a Firm) v Simons* [2000] 3 WLR 543 (HL). See also *Giannarelli v Wraith* (1988) 165 CLR 543 at 588 per Deane J (dissenting).
218 Cf *Frost v Chief Constable of South Yorkshire* [1999] 2 AC 455 (HL) at 504 per Lord Hoffmann; *McFarlane v Tayside Health Board* [2000] 2 AC 59 (HL) at 83 per Lord Steyn; T Honoré, "The Morality of Tort Law – Questions and Answers" in DG Owen (ed), *Philosophical Foundations of Tort Law*, Clarendon Press, Oxford, 1995, p73.
219 See text at n149 above.
220 See Perrochet *et al*, n138 above.

containment. This is probably true. In so far as there will be increased litigation and recovery of damages, the costs will in most cases be borne in the first instance by the hospital's or medical practitioner's insurer or medical defence organisation. In Australia, it will ultimately have to be passed on to the community in increased costs for Medicare. Nevertheless, the floodgates are unlikely to be opened. People who are seriously ill already have all sorts of deterrents to launching litigation. They are seldom keen to add to their existing worries the burdens and anxieties of doubtfully successful litigation. The vast majority of adverse events in hospitals do not give rise to any litigation at all even in the United States.[221] The same seems to apply in Australia.[222] Proof of negligence is always difficult in such cases and, where the rewards are likely to be comparatively small, litigation will not lightly be embarked on.

It is also contended that extension of liability will increase the incidence of defensive medicine. Some commentators think that increased care on the part of practitioners, even if manifested in tests and procedures that would not otherwise be undertaken, would be a good thing.[223] Nevertheless, one should accept that tests and procedures undertaken not for the benefit of the patient, but for the protection of the medical practitioner against litigation, are expensive and not in the community interest when funds for medical treatment are limited. It is difficult to know what is the present incidence of defensive medicine.[224] There seems no reason why a medical practitioner should increase defensive tactics because of the extension of liability from cases of proof on the balance of probabilities of the actual harm to cases of loss of chance. The only plausible theoretical explanation is that some doctors do not presently conduct tests on patients with a less than even chance of survival, but

---

[221]   PC Weiler *et al*, *A Measure of Malpractice*, Harvard Univ Press, Cambridge, Mass, 1993, p70, Table 4.1 (ratio of negligent injuries to number of claims in NY State, 1984, more than seven to one).

[222]   See Tito Report, n212 above, para 2.55 ("clear that few people suffering even a highly preventable adverse event with significant resultant disability ever sue their health professional").

[223]   See D Hoffman, "Doctoring the Evidence" (1990) 15 *Leg Serv Bull* 76.

[224]   See L Hancock, *Defensive Medicine and Informed Consent* (1993) (commissioned by the Tito committee), who concluded that "whether or not defensive practices are beneficial or detrimental to patient care and to the health system generally" is an "unanswered question": para 8.46. Cf MJ Trebilcock, DN Dewees & DG Duff, "The Medical Malpractice Explosion: An Empirical Assessment of Trends, Determinants and Impacts" (1990) 17 *MULR* 539 at 550-61; D Dewees & M Trebilcock, "The Efficacy of the Tort System and its Alternatives: A Review of Empirical Evidence" (1992) 30 *Osg Hall LJ* 57 at 80-1; PC Weiler, *Medical Malpractice on Trial*, Harvard Univ Press, Cambridge, Mass, 1991, pp85-8, 104.

would be induced to do so if there was potential liability for loss of a chance. This has little realistic credibility.

One should also recognise that there might be some direct saving of costs. If courts currently award full damages whenever the plaintiff proves on the balance of probabilities that the harm would not have occurred and do not make any deduction for the chance that the harm might have occurred even in the absence of negligence, recognition of the fact that the claim is really for loss of chance may lead to a lesser award of damages.[225] The apparent view of Callinan J that full damages will continue to be awarded in such cases is insupportable.[226] Furthermore, if the law does have any real deterrent effect, medical practitioners can be expected to be more careful. Although prolonging someone's life does not necessarily save the community money and may even increase its costs, preventing disability and thereby increasing productivity might actually save costs indirectly. Certainly, such increased care can be expected to reduce the total level of pain and suffering in the community.

Conclusion

Where a medical practitioner fails to exercise reasonable care, the aim of the law generally is not to reposition the plaintiff as though no treatment had been given, but as though proper treatment had been given.[227] It does not matter whether the claim lies in contract or tort. In many instances proper treatment could have done no more than give the plaintiff a chance of cure or alleviation of a pre-existing condition. This is something of value, something for which many people would give money. The law should treat such a chance as worthy of protection. The scope of the medical practitioner's duty of care should be taken to extend to not detrimentally affecting that chance. Loss or diminution of the chance as a result of the practitioner's negligence should be recognised as a legal injury for which the patient may recover damages, whether the chance was greater or less than even, as long as it was more than speculative. The court should be required to do the best it can to assess the damages accordingly.

---

[225] Cf *Sullivan v Micallef* (1994) Aust Torts Reps 81-308 (NSW CA), text at n175 above.

[226] See text at nn172-173 above.

[227] J Stapleton, "The Normal Expectancies Measure in Tort Damages" (1997) 113 *LQR* 257.

9 Causality and Spinal Pain: The Problem of Back Pain

DENNIS SMITH[*]

Introduction

Recently, there has been a plain word approach in medicine to public and clinical debate on common medical problems. Stroke, and low back pain are two examples in these areas of concern. The term, "low back pain" is now used to characterise lower spinal pain, and its variety of syndromes.

This chapter will limit itself to those features of low back pain related to morphological changes in the joints and discs of the lumbar spine. It will not consider those serious causes of back pain which are inflammatory or malignant in nature. Nor will it discuss back pain referred from other organs. All of these serious causes of back pain are relatively easy to distinguish from the commonest types of low back pain, which, it is assumed, arise from the ligaments, joints and discogenic structures making up the lumbar spine.

Clinical Epidemiology

The clinical epidemiological approach to medical management pioneered by Sackville, Haynes and Tuckwell[1] at McMaster University, Hamilton, Canada, is largely responsible for many recent conceptual changes in the evolution of back pain diagnosis and management during the two last decades. Their approach to clinical diagnosis is worth highlighting. They recognise that sickness has three elements:

---

[*]   Former Foundation Professor of Rehabilitation Medicine at Flinders University, South Australia, and a consultant at the Griffith Rehabilitation Hospital in South Australia.
[1]   J Biddle, *Lumbar Disc Pathology*, Medical Report Council Special Report No 1, HMSO, London, 1930.

1. The disease, or target disorder, the objective of the diagnostic process;
2. The illness, or cluster of symptoms and signs exhibited by the patient and elucidated by the doctor;
3. The predicament, or the social, psychologic, and economic context in which the patient is situated.

In most patients with acute back pain, the target disorder is difficult, if not impossible, to define with clarity in exact pathological terms. The illness is also vague and often extremely non-specific.

The predicament is that the patient is in pain, and often finds it difficult to work. This predicament is added to by the wide variety of often conflicting advice to which the patient may have been subjected.

Morphology

There are few conditions so common and poorly understood as persistent or repetitive low back pain. This type of back pain is ubiquitous. The reason for it may well be related to human evolution.

In anthropological terms man is a large ape. However, we differ from our closest cousins, the Orang-Utan, the Gorilla, and the Chimpanzee, in that we have, in recent developmental terms, adopted an upright posture, which has freed our upper limbs for skilled manipulation, throwing, and uniquely human activities, such as art and craft. We also utilise our extremely well developed binocular vision as a result of our stable neck and head posture, particularly when running. All of this comes at a cost.

The vertebrate spine is not, in evolutionary terms, a weight-bearing organ. It originated in reptiles and fish. Most other mammals are like cats and dogs, in that they have a horizontal back which is flexible, strong in construction in order to contain the essentially delicate spinal cord, and equipped with muscles and spinous processes which are both protective and mechanically designed to facilitate energy transfer between the fore and hind limbs when walking or running. The vertebrate spine also enables safe and efficient rapid changes of direction and movement when running or hunting.

The upright human posture is probably developmentally less than a million years old. Cro-Magnon man, our immediate ancestor, may be less than 40,000 years old, and is indistinguishable from Homo Sapiens.

A direct result of this recent evolutionary adaptation is that the vertebral discs of the spine, particularly the lower (lumbar) spine, degenerate in early adult life. This is almost certainly directly related to the severe transmitted vertical weight-bearing pressures to which these structures are inevitably exposed. Lifting, carrying, jumping and running, all subject these structures to compression and shearing forces of up to 500 kilograms. This results in mechanical damage to the external part of the disc, and subsequently to partial extrusion of the *nucleus pulposus* of the disc through tears in the annulus fibrosus. These changes have been known for at least 80 years.

Schmorl in Germany first described them, in the 1920s.[2] He had access to spines removed at *post mortem* following fatal accidents, and was able to accumulate data on many hundreds of spines across a wide range of ages and conditions. Biddle,[3] an anatomist from England, was given access to this material in 1930 and, in an elegant and careful series of histological microscopic and macroscopic studies, was able to demonstrate the degenerative process in considerable detail.

These were published in the first report of the newly created Medical Research Council of England, demonstrating that this process of disc degeneration was eventually almost universal and was related to the age of the individual, coming to a maximum prevalence of some 80 per cent, in those specimens studied, between the ages of 30 and 40.

The changes consist of extrusions of the central nucleus pulposus of the lumbar disc through the annulus fibrosus, which itself shows tearing and rupture of its intertwined collagenous fibres. This process is accompanied by considerable local infiltration of cells such as lymphocytes and macrophages. This is part of the healing or repair process, but does not lead to a restoration of the premorbid situation. Hence the term "degeneration". This implies healing with scar tissue and loss of function, and can be looked upon as a specific part of the ageing process.

This imperfect repair process leads to a resolution of these changes such that the degenerative process is complete by the 6th and 7th decade. By this stage, the liquid centre *("nucleus pulposus")* in most of the specimens of this age, has broken down and migrated through the degenerative fibres of the annulus fibrosus of the disc, the result being that the functionally well designed lumbar disc becomes a flattened fibrous remnant, with loss of movement and elasticity. A consequence is secondary osteoarthritic changes in the facet joints of the spine. These are often, but by no means always, the cause of symptoms such as stiffness, local pain, and associated muscle spasm.

An equally important, but much later study by Hult[4] in Sweden in the 1950s, was a retrospective incidence analysis of a large population. This

---

[2]   G Schmorl & H Junghanns, *The Human Spine In Health And Disease,* Grune & Stratton, New York, 1971.

[3]   See Biddle, 1930, op cit, n1.

[4]   L Hult, "The Munkfors Investigation" (1954) *Acta Orthop Scand* (Supp 16) 1.

important study related the first severe attack of back pain to the age of the patient. His findings included data showing that the initial symptoms of acute back pain had an age distribution essentially the same as in Biddle's study carried out some 25 years earlier.

From these two well-designed studies, it would be reasonable to hypothesise that acute incidents of back pain are therefore probably closely related to the degenerative changes now known to occur in the spine in adult human life. This conclusion is now generally accepted. What is still not clear is the exact immediate cause of the acute symptoms in the individual patient.

Hadler, in his monograph, *Medical Management of the Regional Musculoskeletal Diseases*,[5] elaborates on the ubiquity of low back pain as a problem. He does this in an important section entitled: "The Interface between the Clinical Concept of Low Back Pain, and the Workers Compensation and Social Security Disability Insurance Programs." He points out that it is "unparalleled in its morbidity". We know that in the western world, for which good data are available, 70 per cent of the population suffer from acute disabling back pain at some time in their lives, and 10 per cent in the previous two years.

Clearly, according to Hadler, the problem of the relationship of pain to injury is complex. The public perception of acute back pain is in general that it is caused by injury. This simplistic view is defendable up to a point, in that an incident of bending, or picking up, or lifting, often has a strong temporal relationship to the acute episode. The reality is that the well-known proverb, "It's the last straw that breaks the camel's back", is somewhat closer to the truth: This is, that the lower back is prone to acute episodes of pain and disability, often triggered by minor incidents, such as bending down to pick up an envelope. It is also prone to acute episodes related to lifting heavy objects, or repetitive lifting, or unexpected additional mechanical stress during a lift. This spectrum of "causes" is of considerable importance in the work environment because of the fact that most acute back pain incidents occur at work, and many of them are disabling, and some of them are prolonged. It is also important to be aware that the precise clinical and pathological nature, in structural anatomical terms, of these acute attacks is still uncertain.

Taken together, these observations and the lack of precision in the diagnosis, mean that back pain in the work environment is a major social, economic and productivity concern. It is also a growing concern, or was up until the last year or so in most industrial countries or environments.

---

5   NM Hadler, *Medical Management of the Regional Musculoskeletal Disorders*, Grune & Stratton, Orlando, Florida, 1984.

The epidemiology of back pain in industry has been well recorded in Australia, the United States and in Western Europe. Since the end of the 1950s, the point prevalence (numbers at any one time) of back pain resulting in more than a week's time off work has increased from 3 per cent of the work force to 20 per cent of the work force. This is in spite of the recorded incidence of acute back pain being fairly stable. It is also certainly true that the nature of much industrial work has also changed, and may now be less arduous and better structured in ergonomic terms. Despite this, time off work with back pain disability has become more common.

The explanation for these alarming statistics is complex. It is almost certainly related to changes in the management of back pain, including its perception as a disability with particular consequences.

Disability and Back Pain

Disability is an essential concept in this area of concern, and has been well defined in the WHO publication, *The International Classification of Impairments Disabilities and Handicaps*,[6] as in the context of health experience, any restriction or lack (resulting from an impairment) of ability to perform an activity in the manner or within the range considered normal for a human being. Disability is characterised by excesses, or deficiencies of *customarily expected activity, performance and behaviour*. It may be temporary or permanent, reversible or irreversible, and progressive or regressive.

Disabilities may arise as a direct consequence of impairment, or may be a psychological or learnt response to a physical sensory or other impairment. Disability is the objective behaviour at the level of the person in response to impairment, and is concerned with abilities in the form of composite activities and behaviours, generally accepted as being essential components of everyday life. This includes work disabilities.

It is also important to consider the relationship of disability to the interface between disease and illness. A common variety of illness behaviour is related to the "sick role". This is an adaptive, or learnt response to being acutely ill, well described and defined by Parsons.[7] Essentially, it is an abrogation of responsibility in return for being looked after when ill. The implied contract means that the ill patient is compliant and passive, doing as he or she is told. This is a reasonable form of

---

6   International Classification of Impairments, Disabilities and Handicaps, World Health Organisation, Geneva, 1980.

7   T Parsons, *The Sick Role: The Social System*, The Free Press, Glencoe, Illinois, 1951.

behaviour when acutely ill, as with, for example, influenza or acute appendicitis. It is short term and socially sophisticated.

Acute back pain is rarely accompanied by a feeling of illness. The pain may be severe, but is more in the nature of a mechanical problem than an acute debilitating illness. If it is managed by the forced or voluntary adoption of the sick role, then it leads to disability, in association with deconditioning. It is only 20 years ago that acute back pain was regularly managed by confinement to bed for between a week and 10 days initially, and by the accompanying use of tranquillisers such as diazepam in doses of up to 20 or 30 mgms a day. It is now clear that this form of management leads to significant disability.

This is not to say that it is never appropriate. It may be of value in gross degrees of disc prolapse in which the contents of the spinal canal are compromised, but this is rare in the extreme – perhaps one in a thousand cases of back pain, perhaps less. Unfortunately, variants on this form of management are still common, and the lay view is also still somewhat in favour of rest as the primary approach to acute back pain.

Management

Inappropriate management itself may well cause and certainly can prolong disability in association with the majority of patients with persistent back pain. There is, as yet, little uniformity in the management of patients with acute back pain, but there is now consensus in the medical profession. An excellent review article: "Low Back Pain" by Andrew Frank[8] was published in the 1993 *British Medical Journal*, and is still difficult to improve on. His description of differing types of management concludes that active mobility exercises and fitness training are associated with better recovery. Hadler's[9] approach is essentially the same, and Waddell's[10] recent approach to management also emphasises the value of simple exercises such as walking regularly and swimming in a warm pool. To this I have recently advised that a snorkel and mask are useful when swimming, because their use helps the patient to avoid twisting, or hyper-extending the back, both often painful activities during acute episodes. The logic of this active management approach is related to the limited blood supply to the lumbar disc. It may well be that its normal nutrition is more related to the

---

8   A Frank, "Low Back Pain: Regular Review" (1993) 306 *British Medical Journal* 901.
9   Hadler, op cit, n5, pp30-1.
10   G Waddell, G Feder, A McIntosh, L Lewis & A Hutchinson, *Low Back Pain Evidence Review*, London Royal College of General Practitioners, 1996.

alternate compression and relaxation, with dynamic fluid interchange, which occurs during walking, sitting and standing, rather than to its haemodynamics.[11]

Historically, the management of back pain has always been a matter of energetic debate. Mixter and Barr's 1934 paper[12] describing the prolapsed intervertebral disc was sufficiently convincing at the time to result in a preferred surgical approach to be fashionable for decades. Not until Barr's excellent retrospective studies in the 1960s[13] did it become clear that surgery is only strongly indicated in those patients with major neurological problems – less than 5 per cent of patients. There is, even now, no convincing evidence that spinal fusion is effective in relieving symptoms and disability in more than a very small minority of patients.

The preferred management, based upon the studies by Waddell, Frank, and Hadler is that a conservative, informed and optimistic approach is appropriate. Bed rest for more than a day is of no value. In practice, prolonged bed rest causes physical deconditioning and increases disability.

The Problem of Pain

The most difficult to manage problems in this field of practice are without doubt the group of chronic back pain sufferers whose symptoms have been present for more than a year. There are a number of characteristics, which define the group. In my experience, these are the patients who are referred to multidisciplinary pain clinics with non-cancer pain. They are usually unable to work. Most previous modes of management have either made them worse or were of no help. Analgesics, including opiates are generally of little help. They are usually able to carry out activities of daily living (dressing, feeding, toilet care) without any major problems, but work is not possible, or travelling to work is disabling. Their lives are totally dominated by the recalcitrant pain. They talk and think of little else. They often have a history of multiple surgical interventions, none of which have helped. They often have an unsettled compensation problem. They are frequently clinically depressed. A full psychological assessment defines certain persistent behavioural traits.[14]

---

[11] Ibid.

[12] WJ Mixter & JS Barr, "Rupture of the Intervertebral Disc with Involvement of the Spinal Canal" (1934) 211 *New England Journal of Medicine* 210.

[13] JS Barr et al, "Evaluation of End Results in Treatment of Ruptured Lumbar Disc" (1967) 125 *Surgery, Gynaecology and Obstetrics* 250.

[14] GA Waddell, "A New Clinical Model for the Treatment of Low Back Pain" (1987) 12 *Spine* 632.

Physical examination is uncomfortable, and may demonstrate inconsistencies, related to position. The process of undressing, and then getting onto the examination couch, may be slow and distressing. It usually is not painful, but may appear to be grossly abnormal, and sometimes bizarre, if the patient is carefully instructed not to move beyond the point of discomfort. Palpation of the region in which the pain is found is often described as burning or knife like. A few of these patients are exaggerating their symptoms consciously, but an equal or greater number are not. They are often depressed; some of them have post traumatic stress disorder ("PTSD"). Many may have been inappropriately managed at an earlier stage. This is at times related to their own insistence on continuing with therapies of little value or benefit. Many of them have what Pilowsky[15] has defined as "abnormal illness behaviour". This is a learnt phenomenon, and can be characterised as acquired disability, usually and specifically including an inability to carry out work-related activities.[16]

Effective management depends upon a sympathetic approach by a multidisciplinary team, which needs to include a psychiatrist, a psychologist, a physiotherapist, a social worker, a pain consultant, and a specialist in vocational rehabilitation. The assessment may take a number of days. All members of the team are specifically and professionally trained in the management and assessment of chronic pain.

The model I have described is based upon the University of Washington Multidisciplinary Pain Centre, which was set up by John Bonica and Wilbert Fordyce in 1960. Similar centres are now functioning in the United Kingdom, Canada and Australia, using the same essentially pluralistic model, and a cognitive behavioural approach to management, based upon an informed contract between the centre and the client. Even so, of those patients referred to clinics of this nature, only about 15 per cent are assessed as being likely to improve with the program, which is both behavioural, that is to say, designed to alter illness behaviour and physical, that is to say designed to produce realisable improvements in both perceived strength and fitness.[16] The pain clinic needs effective linkage with competent vocational selection and rehabilitation services. It also often needs to be in enlightened and informed touch with the clients employer, if this is agreed by the client, and if they still have one. It is necessarily an expensive process, but for this extremely difficult group, is the only form of management demonstrated to be effective in both the short

---

15   I Pilowsky & N Spence, *Manual for the Illness Behaviour Questionnaire*, University of Adelaide, 1981.
16   JD Loeser & J Egan Kelly, *Managing the Chronic Pain Patient*, Raven Press, New York, 1989.

and long term, but only for the small percentage of those referred and accepted as suitable for the programs.

A New Zealand study by Feyer and her co-workers in Dunedin and Sydney Australia has recently looked at risk factors related to the development of low back pain in health care workers. They found that a previous history of back pain predicted further attacks, but pre-existing psychological distress, as measured by the General Health Questionnaire,[17] was the only other factor which preceded new attacks of lower back pain. This finding suggests that the management of the onset of occupational low back pain might be improved by the management of psychological stress in those with a previous history of low back pain.

Osteoarthritis of the Facet Joints, Goniometry and Impairments

Compared to the previous problem of so-called discogenic back pain, osteoarthritis of the facet joints is conceptually a relatively simple condition. It is both straightforward to diagnose, and clear in its symptomatology. It is usually related to, and a consequence of prolonged hard physical work. There are, as always in medicine, exceptions to this statement. Infrequently, it can be related to specific inflammatory diseases such as variants of rheumatoid arthritis, or it may eventually develop following childhood or adolescent trauma or illness.

Miners, professional athletes, labourers and farmers are characteristically subject to the condition which is usually of gradual onset, associated with pain and stiffness, and localised to the affected segment of the spine. The physical and radiological signs are eventually "hard". This means objective and persistent. It is usually possible to quantify the level of impairment in terms of loss of movement and increased pain and weakness, and for this the American Guides are a useful tool.

It is useful to have regard to the fourth edition of the American Medical Association Guides to the Evaluation of Permanent Impairment.[18] The purpose of these Guides is to render objective the assessment of permanent impairment. They use an odd definition of impairment, which, while exclusively related to loss at the level of the organ, as in the ICIDH I[19] is defined in terms of how they affect the patient's daily

17 DP Goldberg, *The Detection of Psychiatric Illness, by Questionnaire*, Oxford University Press, London, 1972.

18 American Medical Association, *Guides to Permanent Impairment*, 4th edn, AMA, Chicago, 1993.

19 International Classification of Impairments, Disabilities and Handicaps, WHO, Geneva, 1980.

activities, including work, that is to say, implied disability. Not everyone's daily activities and work are the same, so there is a conceptual problem with the scoring, which would disadvantage the concert pianist as compared to the professional footballer in the case of loss of finger movements in the dominant hand. This example is only one, and exposes a fundamental weakness of the Guides.

However, if the scores are looked upon as impairment scores only, then they are both useful, generally repeatable and thus reliable. They are an expanded and comprehensive system of quantifying what used to be called "maims". According to the Oxford English Dictionary this archaic word meant the loss of a limb or its use. The term "maims" has been used in law to indicate a specific loss of function. In low back pain they have value in the quantification of the loss associated with loss of spinal joint range, in those with facet joint and discogenic osteoarthritis. They can be taken in conjunction with the 1937 Schöber test,[20] which is reliable and often used as a single measure. Schöber found that a simple measurement, using a ribbon tape measure, of forward flexion from a fixed skin mark at the level of the sacrum, defined osteoarthritic stiffness in the back with excellent reliability and simplicity. The normal range is from 10-15 cms. Anything less than 12 cm is deemed to be pathological.

Even so, it is important to be aware that findings of restricted movements in the lumbar spine relate very little to a history of low back pain. Goniometry, or measurement of restriction of movement, as mandated under the second edition of the *American Medical Association Guides to Permanent Impairment*, is appealing, because of its objectivity in terms of mensuration, but its relationship to impairment is arguable, and it certainly has little to do with disability. There have been many critiques of this aspect of medical measurement.[21] For instance, in spite of the seductiveness of accurate measurement of movement, mobility variations occur significantly from day to day and year to year, without having any value other than to quantify normal variations, rather than function. They are useful in watching progress in individual patients, and may be of value in monitoring fitness and mobility training.

---

[20] P Schöber, "The Lumbar Vertebral Column and Backache" (1937) 84 *Munchener Medizinische Wochenschrift*, Munich 336.

[21] For instance, see D Smith, "Measurement of Joint Movement: An Overview" (1982) 8(3) *Clinics in Rheumatic Diseases* 523.

Summary

The cause of low back pain is multifactorial, and relates to morphology, psychology, behaviour and culture. The relationship to trauma is often temporally convincing as a cause of the subsequent pain and disability. In the individual case, without a history of previous back pain, and in which the strain on the back is clearly extreme, then cause is likely to be perceived as being consequential to the incident. The minor incident, followed by a prolonged period of disabling pain and limited function is a different matter, and cause might be attributed to fortuitous chance. If the subsequent pain is aggravated by work, then the pendulum swings back towards compensability. Modern management would encourage return to slightly modified work as being the best form of therapy. It may well be that with the increased interest in maintenance of fitness, as a way of life, that we will now begin to see a different attitude to back pain in both the public and occupational domains. It will always be a common problem, but it is now clearly less threatening to health and fitness with the right approach to diagnosis and care. The concept of use it or lose it contains more than a grain of truth.

PART C:
ISSUES OF CAUSAL RESPONSIBILITY, AGENCY AND HARM IN CRIMINAL LAW

10 Principles of Causation in Criminal Law

DAVID LANHAM*

Introduction

Questions of causation in the context of crimes involving personal injury can present themselves across the whole spectrum of such offences, from the causing of transitory pain to the infliction of death. Most of the major reported cases have been decided in the context of homicide. The principles emerging from those cases are, in general, and with appropriate allowance for the different level of harm caused, applicable to crimes involving non-fatal injuries. From this point, however, in order to keep the explanation reasonably simple the discussion will focus on causing death.

In that context, causation resolves itself into two questions: first is there a factual link between the defendant's conduct and the victim's death, secondly is the link sufficiently substantial to make the defendant's conduct the cause of death?[1]

In the main, the proving of the factual link raises questions of evidence rather than theory. So in *R v White*,[2] the defendant placed poison in his mother's drink. She consumed the drink and died, but the medical evidence showed that she died of a heart attack unconnected with the poison. As no factual link was made out the defendant could not be found guilty of murder.

---

* Professorial Fellow at the Faculty of Law, the University of Melbourne.
[1] A person's act may be a cause of death even if it is justified, as in a case of self defence – see *Keown v Khan* [1999] 1 VR 69. Problems such as the administration of painkillers which may shorten life are also better dealt with under a theory of defences than by overloading the rules of causation: see D Lanham, "Euthanasia, Painkilling, Murder and Manslaughter" (1994) 1 *J of Law and Medicine* 146.
[2] [1910] 2 KB 124.

The factual link may be indirect. In *Sirinjui Biagwei v R*[3] two natives J and S cast spears into the victim. J threw four spears and then S threw his four. It was not clear whose spear caused the death nor was it a case of aiding and abetting. Each native was acting independently, but there was a native custom under which natives who joined in a killing gained prestige. The court held that J was guilty but S was not.

The result can be explained as follows. There was not enough evidence to establish a factual link between S's action and the death. The victim may have been dead by the time S threw his first spear. J however could be held guilty on either of two hypotheses. If his spear caused the death there would be no problem. If S's spear caused the death, J could be held liable since his action induced S to act. The factual link was established.

It may be objected that even though there was a factual link, the link was too weak to justify holding J guilty because S was an independent actor. This goes to the strength rather than the existence of the link, a matter to be taken up below. For the moment it seems that the native custom was regarded as strong enough to overcome the objection that S's act was independent.

What I have called the factual link is sometimes described as the "but for" requirement or *"sine qua non test"*. According to this test, causation is not established if the death would not have occurred but for the act of the defendant. In many cases this way of describing the requirement will work well enough. In *R v White*,[4] the poisoning case, the mother would have died even if the defendant had not poisoned her drink. It could not be said that she would not have died but for the defendant's action.

But other cases which seem to cry out for liability would yield the wrong result under a "but for" test. Suppose A and B independently place two grains of poison each into V's drink, and that the fatal dose is two grains. V dies of the poison. There is clearly a factual link between A's act and the death, but it would be wrong to say that V would not have died but for the action of A. If A had done nothing V would still have died. The same is true of B. The result of a "but for" test would be that both would have to be acquitted even though each contributed in a substantial way to the death. Such a result would be intolerable and its avoidance justifies the wider factual link test. Professor J Andenaes suggests that both would be liable under Norwegian criminal law[5] and the same should be true of Australian law. Both should also be liable where neither act is enough by itself to cause death but in combination the two acts do. Suppose in the poison case the fatal dose is 3 grains. A's 2 grains

---

3   (1962) 36 ALR 9 (High Court) and (1962) 1967-68 PNGLR 209 (retrial).
4   [1910] 2 KB 124, above.
5   *The General Part of the Criminal Law of Norway*, Fred B Rothman, South Hackensack NJ, 1965, at p118.

would not have killed nor would B's. But their combined four grains would be enough.[6]

A more borderline case would be that where A gives 3 grains (the fatal dose) and B gives 2. Andenaes notes a conflict of opinion in Norwegian law on this point.[7] There might be room for a distinction between cases where the whole of the drink was consumed and those where something less was taken. But this could lead to complicated questions of medical proof and it would seem better to hold both guilty.

Once the "but for" requirement is abandoned other cases which might cause difficulty can be more easily solved. Hart and Honoré[8] adapting a problem set by McLaughlin,[9] pose a problem along these lines: V is entering a desert. A secretly places poison[10] in V's water keg, B steals the keg and V dies of thirst. The "but for" test would lead to the acquittal of both A and B. But there is a clear factual link between A's act and V's death, but no factual link between B's act and the death. V has died because of the absence of drinkable water. It cannot matter whether the death is due to poisoning or thirst.[11] Suppose B had not intervened but V had somehow discovered the water was poisoned. V might throw the poison away, preferring the risk of death by thirst to the certainty of death by poison. A could not complain that the death occurred in a manner different from that contemplated. B's intervention makes no difference. There is no factual link between B's act and V's death. B has unwittingly prolonged V's life. The withdrawal of drinkable water by A remains the cause of V's death.

Where causation is a matter for the general (common) law the "but for" test creates no difficulties because there is nothing to require the courts to apply it. But where causation has been embodied in legislation there may be less room for a sensible result. Section 153(2) of the Tasmanian *Criminal Code* for example expressly adopts the "but for" test. It would do well to abandon it.

If the factual link is established, the next question is whether that link is sufficiently strong to attribute the death to the defendant's action. Three matters need to be considered: first the general formula, secondly special sub-rules and thirdly the significance of intention, foresight and foreseeability.

---

6   Andenaes, op cit, n5, at p121.

7   Ibid.

8   *Causation in the Law*, 2nd edn, 1985, at p239.

9   JA McLaughlin, "Proximate Cause" (1925-6) 39 *Harvard Law Review* 149 at p155.

10   To avoid ambiguity we need to assume that the poison would kill instantaneously so that the poisoned water would not postpone death by overcoming thirst for a short while: see J Stapleton, "Perspectives on Causation" in J Horder (ed), *Oxford Essays in Jurisprudence*, 4th Series, Oxford Uni Press, Oxford, 2000, at p84.

11   M Hale, 1 PC 617.

General Formula

Australian law adopts the view that to found liability a cause must be a substantial and operating cause. This was the test set out in the English decision of *R v Smith*,[12] where a person who had been stabbed by the defendant was dropped by stretcher bearers and given poor medical treatment. The Court of Criminal Appeal held that the defendant was guilty as his act was a substantial and operating cause of the death. This test has been adopted by Australian state full courts.[13] The position taken by the High Court of Australia is more obscure. A rather special aspect of the law of causation arose in *Royall v R*[14] where the problem was whether one who frightens another into killing herself accidentally can be held to have caused the death. This question was the main focus of the judgments but there were some, largely conflicting, views expressed about causation more generally. It is virtually impossible to find a majority position. Only McHugh J attempted an overall theory of causation, based upon foreseeability,[15] but this led him into dissent on the main question before the court, and this approach was in effect rejected by the other judges. But not much positive was put in its place. There is a majority appeal to common sense,[16] but it is clear that common sense provides no test at all. It is true that common sense or sound judgment will need to be applied in assessing any matters of degree which the legal tests present, but common sense will not provide those tests. We need look no further than the main legal point at issue in the *Royall* case itself to see that common sense can lead to either of two different rules. At its simplest the question was: if the victim reacts unreasonably to the defendant's threats and in doing so accidentally kills herself, has the defendant caused the death? Most of the judges said no, but McHugh J said maybe. Both answers are consistent with common sense.

Three judges referred to a significant contribution.[17] Deane and Dawson JJ appear to have regarded "significant" as meaning the same as "substantial", as does McHugh J.[18] There certainly seems no good reason to reject the learning based on the word "substantial" and introduce doubts based on the slightly different word "significant". The majority judgments on the reasonable reaction question suggests no desire to widen the rules of causation through the adoption of the word "significant". The result seems to

---

[12] [1959] 2 QB 36.
[13] Eg *R v Hallett* [1969] SASR 141; *R v Evans and Gardiner (No 2)* [1976] VR 523.
[14] (1991) 172 CLR 378.
[15] At p449.
[16] Mason CJ at p387, Dean and Dawson JJ at pp411-12; Toohey and Gaudron JJ at p423.
[17] Brennan J at p298; Deane and Dawson JJ at p411.
[18] At p449.

be that the basic approach taken in England and adopted by State courts in Australia remains.[19]

Do we need two words to capture the basic principle in causation? In *R v Malcherek*,[20] an English case involving the withdrawal of life support from victims injured by the defendants and close to death, the Court of Appeal said that the operating cause did not need to be substantial. As there was no doubt in the case that the original injury was a substantial cause of death the question did not arise for decision, but the comment looks wrong. There must be a point at which a cause is still operating but is so insubstantial that it should not result in liability. If either of the words is to be rejected it should be the word "operating", but simply on the ground that it is superfluous. A cause cannot be substantial unless it is operating. But that is clear from the further explanation of the formula adopted in *R v Smith*.[21] Speaking of the case where there is an original injury and a second and more direct cause of the death, like poor medical treatment, the court said that only if the second cause is so overwhelming as to make the original wound part of the history can it be said that death does not flow from the wound. This test seems to reflect the requirement of substance rather than mere operational quality, and seems an equally appropriate test whether the word "operating" appears in the formula or not.

The substantial cause test is flexible enough to cover most causation questions, but there are recurring situations where some sort of additional rule is advisable either to exemplify, qualify or supplement the basic test.

Special Rules

(i) *Physical infirmity*

Cases can occur where a fairly minor blow can cause death because the victim suffers from an unusual physical condition like an egg-shell skull or haemophilia. In such cases it might be argued that the pre-existing physical condition rather than the blow is the substantial cause of death. The criminal law deflects this line of reasoning by adopting a notion that defendants take their victims as they find them. On the question of causation they cannot avoid liability on the ground that their attack would not have killed a person

---

[19] The substantial cause test seems to have been approved by the High Court of Australia in *Osland v R* (1998) 73 ALJR 173 but there the defendant was also acting in concert.

[20] [1981] 2 All ER 422 at 428.

[21] [1959] 2 QB 193 at 198.

within the normal range of health. So in *R v Hayward*,[22] a husband chased his wife, threatening violence. She was suffering from a persistent thymus gland so that the combination of physical exertion and fright was enough to kill her. Ridley J told the jury that the threats were a sufficient cause of the death. The jury convicted the husband of manslaughter. *The Laws of Australia*[23] accept the general rule but suggest that it applies only to the pre-existing condition of the intended victims and not to those unintentionally harmed. The author relies upon *Timbu Kolian v R*,[24] where a husband aimed a blow of moderate but illegal chastisement at his wife in the dark. She was carrying a baby in her arms and the blow hit the baby on the head killing him. The husband was held not guilty of manslaughter, but the ground of acquittal was that the mental or fault element of the crime was not made out, not that the husband's act had not caused the death of the child.[25]

(ii)   Victim's reaction to threats

Another case where the defendant's physical contribution to the death might be regarded as minimal is that where the defendant threatens the victim who reacts in such a way as to cause her own death. There is no problem with the factual link in these cases, but how is the requirement of substantial cause to be satisfied? There are three main tests: substantial consequence, foreseeability and reasonable response.

Under the substantial consequence test, apart from the question of degree, nothing more would need to be shown than that the threat was the substantial cause of the victim's killing herself. In *R v Halliday*,[26] a husband made threats against his wife's life and to escape him she got out by a window and injured herself. The husband had made frequent threats of violence before but had not used actual violence. The Court for Crown Cases Reserved held that he was liable for her injuries. The court adopted a wide principle.

> If a man creates in another man's mind an immediate sense of danger which causes ... such person to try to escape and in doing so he injures himself the person who creates such a state of mind is responsible for the injuries which result.

---

[22]   (1908) 1 Cox CC 692. See also *Mamote Kulang v R* (1964) 111 CLR 62 (Papua New Guinea Code).

[23]   *Criminal Law, Homicide*, para 2[17].

[24]   (1968) 119 CLR 47.

[25]   This is also the case of the majority judgment of the High Court of Australia in *R v Van Den Bemd* (1994) 179 CLR 137. See also J Blackwood, "Humpty Dumpty Was Pushed Off the Wall ..." (1996) 15 *Univ of Tasmania LR* 306.

[26]   (1889) 61 LT 701.

The strength of this case is diminished by the fact that the trial judge had expressed the law in a way more favourable to the defendant. He did so by requiring that the fear of the victim should be well grounded and the action of the victim reasonable.[27] It may be that the appellate court's wide statement needs to be understood in the light of the facts which were consistent with the trial judge's narrower approach to causation. Even so, the appellate judgment at face value may show that there is no inflexible rule that the reaction must be a reasonable one and founded on a reasonable belief.

The second approach, that of foreseeability, would lay down a narrower test of causation, but would not necessarily demand that the victim's belief or response be reasonable. This was the line taken by McHugh J in *Royall v R*.[28] The facts were unclear but one possibility was that the defendant had made threats against the victim's life and that the latter had jumped out of a window to escape, killing herself. The High Court of Australia upheld the defendant's conviction for murder, but the judges differed on the test of causation. McHugh J favoured a reasonable foreseeability test. On this basis a defendant could be held guilty of causing the death even if the victim's fear was not reasonable or if the victim's reaction was unreasonable. Reasonableness either of belief or action on the part of the victim would be merely a factor in assessing reasonable foreseeability. There are however difficulties in relying on reasonable foreseeability as the dominant approach to questions of causation. These will be considered later, but the possibility that unreasonable beliefs or actions may be foreseeable argues against a universal rule that unreasonableness breaks the chain of causation.

The third approach takes just that line. This is the approach favoured by modern English cases[29] and by most of judges of the High Court of Australia in *Royall v R*.[30] While some of the majority judges recognised that foreseeability lay behind at least some rules of causation,[31] they preferred to adopt a rule which made the reasonableness or unreasonableness of the victim's belief or action the crucial test of whether the threat caused the death.

If unreasonable conduct on the part of the victim does break the chain of causation in these cases, there is room for considering whether a distinction should be made between unreasonable beliefs and unreasonable reaction.[32] A victim may have a reasonable fear of great harm but may select an

27 At p702.
28 (1991) 172 CLR 378 at p450. Contrast Brennan J who seems to have equated reasonable response with foreseeability (at p394).
29 Eg *DPP v Daley* (1979) 69 Cr App R 39; *R v Williams and Davis* (1992) 95 Cr App R 1; *R v Mackie* (1973) 57 Cr App R 453; *R v Marjoram*, *The Times*, 3 December 1999.
30 (1991) 172 CLR 378.
31 Eg Mason CJ at 390; Deane and Dawson JJ at 412; Toohey and Gaudron JJ at 425.
32 A point left open by Mason CJ at 339.

unreasonable method of escape. Even where there is only one escape route, it may be one that leads inevitably to death so that the mode of escape is unreasonable. This distinction could lead to a salutary narrowing of the requirement of reasonableness but it would be better to drop it altogether as an automatic requirement in establishing causation.

(iii)   Reaction to injuries

If an unreasonable reaction to a threat breaks the chain of causation, what about an unreasonable reaction to an actual injury? Cases before *Royall v R*[33] reject any hard and fast rule that unreasonable conduct by the victim breaks the chain. A modern case is *R v Blaue*.[34] The defendant stabbed the victim piercing her lung. She was a Jehovah's Witness and refused to have a blood transfusion which was necessary to save her life. The defendant argued that her refusal was unreasonable and so broke the chain of causation. The Court held that attackers must take their victims as they find them and so the defendant caused the death. This reasoning may go too far, but the case supports a proposition that there is no automatic rule that intervening unreasonable conduct by the victim will break the chain of causation in this kind of case. *Blaue's* case was approved by the Victorian Court of Criminal Appeal in *R v Evans and Gardiner*.[35]

At one level there is an inconsistency between the cases in this section and those in the last. In both cases there is a factual link between the defendant's action and the death, but the immediate cause of death is unreasonable conduct on the part of the victim. This breaks the chain of causation in the case of threats, but not in the case of injuries. The best solution would be to bring the threats cases into line with the injuries ones so that unreasonable conduct would not break the causal link, but the two lines of cases can be reconciled on the basis that by itself a threat cannot (except where a person is literally frightened to death) be the cause of death, whereas an injury of any seriousness may be. This might explain a difference between the two situations.

---

33   (1991) 172 CLR 378.
34   [1975] 1 WLR 1411. See also *R v Wall* (1802) 28 State Tr 51; *R v Holland* (1841) 2 Mood and R 351.
35   [1976] VR 523 at 527. See also *R v Bingapore* (1975) 11 SASR 469.

(iv)   *Third party reaction to threats*

The direct cause of death may be an act by a third party who reacts to a threat by the defendant. In *R v Pagett*,[36] the defendant shot at armed police and used the victim as a shield. The police returned the fire, killing the victim. The defendant was held guilty of causing the death. The court held that a reasonable act in self defence or in the execution of a legal duty did not break the chain of causation. What if the police officers had acted unreasonably, for example by using excessive force or by unduly risking the victim's life where no one was in immediate danger? The situation would then be analogous to that in *Royall v R*, discussed in section (ii) above.

(v)   *Negligent intervening conduct by a third party*

The typical case is negligent medical treatment, though any negligent action in response to the original attack would raise the same principle. Until relatively recently intervening negligence by a third party seems to have broken the chain of causation, at least if the original injury was not itself life threatening. In the 17th century, Hale[37] said that if the injury was not mortal and the victim dies of the ill application of unwholesome medicine which causes the death the original assailant is not guilty. This view was followed in the United States decision of *Bush v Commonwealth*[38] where a wound was treated by a doctor suffering from scarlet fever. The victim died of this fever and the original assailant was held not guilty. The court seems to have regarded the scarlet fever as a wholly independent instrumentality, but that seems doubtful as it was carried by a physician treating the wound. The case was rather one of negligent medical treatment[39] and so stands for the proposition that, in the case of non-mortal injuries, such treatment breaks the chain of causation. The same principle seems to have been applied as one of the grounds of decision in *R v Jordan*.[40] The defendant stabbed the victim, but after the wound had largely healed the victim was given medical treatment to which he was intolerant and which the appeal court said was palpably wrong. The court held in effect that the treatment broke the chain of causation. Though on one view it was the abnormality of the treatment which broke the chain of causation, the case must be seen in the context of an original wound that had almost healed. On this latter basis, the original wound had ceased to

---

[36]   (1983) 76 Cr App R 279.
[37]   1 Pleas of the Crown 428.
[38]   78 Ky 268 (1880).
[39]   See p271.
[40]   (1956) 40 Cr App R 152.

be a substantial cause of death so that the case supports no general principle that abnormal treatment or negligent treatment breaks the chain of causation.

This is the way *R v Jordan* has been treated by later English and Australian cases which have held that medical negligence does not necessarily break the chain of causation.

In England the turning point came in 1959 in the shape of *R v Smith*.[41] The defendant soldier stabbed the victim, another soldier, with a bayonet. The wound might not have been fatal, but the victim was dropped while being carried to the medical centre and at the centre he received inappropriate medical treatment. The Courts-Martial Appeal Court refused to regard the intervening negligent treatment as something breaking the chain of causation and held the defendant liable on the basis that the stabbing was a substantial and operating cause of the death. This approach was approved and the *Jordan* case was confined to cases of insubstantial cause by the Jehovah's Witness case *R v Blaue*[42] and by *R v Malcherek*,[43] a case which involved the withdrawal of a respirator when there was no hope of recovery from the defendant's attack. Not surprisingly, the withdrawal did not break the chain of causation.

The operating and substantial cause approach in *R v Smith* was adopted by the Full Court of Victoria in *R v Evans and Gardiner (No 2)*.[44] Here the victim received a bowel resection operation for a stab wound inflicted by the defendant. The operation was initially successful but about eleven months later, the victim suffered pain and vomiting. He received treatment but died from a stricture in the bowel. There was evidence that this should have been diagnosed and could have been rectified by operative treatment. Nonetheless the Full Court held that the alleged negligent medical treatment did not break the chain of causation.

Though intervening medical negligence, or other negligent third party conduct will not necessarily break the chain of causation, it will do so if it renders the defendant's action a less than substantial cause. In *R v Cheshire*[45] the Court of Appeal said that it was wrong for the judge to tell the jury that only reckless medical treatment would break the chain of causation. Negligent treatment would do so if independent of the defendant's acts and so potent as to make the contribution of those acts insignificant.

---

41 [1959] 2 QB 35.
42 [1975] 1 WLR 1411.
43 [1981] 1 WLR 690. For a similar case under the *Queensland Criminal Code*, see *R v Kinash* [1982] Qd R 648.
44 [1976] VR 523.
45 (1991) 93 Cr App R 251. See also *R v McKechnie* (1992) 94 Cr App R 51.

In Australia it is possible that a narrower view of causation will be held as a result of the decision of the High Court in *Royall v R*.[46] There the majority held that an unreasonable reaction to a threat would break the chain of causation. If this reasoning were extended to the intervening medical treatment context, negligent treatment would break the chain. This would overturn cases like *R v Evans and Gardiner* and restore *R v Jordan* to centre stage. That case however has rightly had few champions and some limit to the *Royall* case is desirable. Recognition that medical negligence may, where independent and potent, break the chain of causation would be an appropriate way of limiting the effect of the *Royall* case, while it stands.

The criminal codes of Queensland,[47] Western Australia,[48] Tasmania[49] and the Northern Territory[50] contain variations on these themes, the main thrust of which is to hold that the chain of causation is broken where the immediate cause of death is improper medical treatment.[51] This seems an unduly restrictive approach to causation.

(vi)   Suicide by the victim

If any reaction to the defendant's conduct is going to break the causal link, a deliberate act of self destruction seems a prime candidate. But there is no blanket rule that even a deliberate suicide will of necessity break the chain of causation. In *R v Hallett*[52] the Full Court of South Australia considered whether suicide by a victim after a severe beating would break the chain of causation, but left the matter unresolved, save to refer to United States cases discussed in *Howard's Criminal Law* text.[53]

One of the American cases cited by Professor Howard does support the view that suicide breaks the chain of causation. In *State v Angelina*[54] the defendant inflicted a serious wound which could have itself caused death, but the victim committed suicide. The court held that if the suicide was the act of an independent responsible agent, it broke the chain of causation, but that if the victim was rendered irresponsible by the wound inflicted by the defendant, the chain was not broken. The court equated a responsible act of

---

46   (1991) 172 CLR 378.
47   *Criminal Code* (Qd) s298.
48   *Criminal Code* (WA) s275.
49   *Criminal Code* (Tas) s154(b).
50   *Criminal Code* (NT) s160.
51   Treatment includes a medical decision not to give treatment: *R v Cook* (1979) 2 A Crim R 151.
52   [1969] SASR 141.
53   C Howard, *Australian Criminal Law*, Law Book Co, Melbourne, Sydney, 1965, pp32-3.
54   80 SE 141 (1913).

suicide with negligent medical treatment and with the independent act of deliberate killing on the part of an intervening third person.[55]

This case is in line with the early 20th century thinking on intervening medical negligence but is weakened by later developments which hold that medical negligence does not automatically break the chain of causation. Even so, suicide is a stronger basis for breaking the chain than negligence and there is some merit in the principle laid down by the court. Much depends, however, on the meaning of "independent" and "responsible".

The notion that a non responsible act of suicide will not break the causal link was taken further in *Stephenson v State*.[56] The defendant brutally raped the victim and bit her all over her body. She poisoned herself. On the trial for murder the defendant argued that the victim's suicide broke the chain of causation. At the appeal court two judges would have held that the victim's suicide broke the chain unless the victim was irresponsible in the sense of insane within the meaning of the defence of insanity. But the majority took a wider view of non-responsibility. The fact that the victim was distracted by pain and shame was enough to remove her responsibility for the act of suicide and so render the defendant liable for her death.

But even this may be too narrow a rule. A third American case focuses more on the question of independence than on that of the responsible nature of the act of suicide. In *People v Lewis*[57] the defendant shot the victim who then cut his own throat, hastening the death. It was unclear why the victim killed himself. It may have been because of the pain from the gunshot wound, from remorse or from a desire to shield the defendant who was the victim's brother in law. The Supreme Court of California held that the defendant was guilty of murder, whichever of the three reasons was the true reason for the suicide. The court seems to have been persuaded by the fact that the original gun shot wound was mortal in the sense that it would inevitably have led to death within the hour. It took the view that if the wound had been merely painful and not mortal and if the victim knew this, the suicide would have broken the chain.

What is noticeable about the *Lewis* case is that what is regarded as important is not whether the suicide was a responsible act, but whether it was caused by the wounding. This seems a better test than that in the other two American cases, but the application of the principle may have gone too far on the facts of the case. If there really was a reasonable doubt whether the victim killed himself out of remorse, the defendant should have been acquitted of the

---

[55]   At 142-3.
[56]   179 NE 633 (1933).
[57]   57 P 470 (1899). See also *US v Hamilton*, 182 FS 548 (1960).

full crime.[58] The remorse reason suggests that the victim killed himself because of his own earlier blameworthy actions (the two men had quarrelled) rather than the defendant's act of wounding. But the reference to remorse is brief in the extreme and the point is not examined. It is possible that, despite mentioning remorse as a possible motive, the court did not take the possibility at all seriously. On either of the other (more plausible) possible motives, the causal potency of the wound on the suicide seems substantial. On that basis the case is in line with most of the Australian cases on causation. Certainly, it does not seek to erect a hurdle of reasonableness. While the motive of pain might have made the self destruction a reasonable act, the desire to shield the assailant from the law could hardly have been regarded as reasonable. Yet neither motive would have led to a break in the chain of causation.

(vii)   Intervening deliberate act of killing by X

Perhaps the strongest case for recognising a break is that where the immediate cause of death is a deliberate act of killing by a third party. In a United States case, *State v Scates*,[59] the defendant inflicted severe burns on the victim but the immediate cause of death was a blow to the head by X, an unidentified third party. It was assumed that the act of X was independent of the infliction of the burns. The court held that the independent act of killing by X meant that the defendant had not caused the death. The court said that where the intervening act was independent, the original assailant could not be said to have killed the victim without involving the absurdity of saying that the victim was killed twice. This reasoning is unsatisfactory. It would apply equally to a case where the second act of killing was dependent on, in the sense of a reaction to, the first attack. We can ascribe two (among many) possible motives to killer X. One is that X wanted the victim dead for X's own purpose and was not willing to entrust the death to the burning. A sufficiently massive blow to the head might properly break the chain of causation. The second is that X found the victim in an apparently painful and hopeless condition and inflicted the blow to the head as an act of mercy. There would then be no good reason to deny the liability of the defendant.

A case from Papua New Guinea provides a more borderline example. As was seen earlier, in *Sirinjui Biagwei v R*,[60] the first defendant threw four spears at the victim and then the second defendant did the same. The second defendant acted in accordance with a native custom which accorded honour to those who joined in a killing. That custom removed the quality of

---

[58]   There is some support for this view in *R v Dear* [1996] Crim L R 595.
[59]   50 NC 409 (1858).
[60]   (1962) 36 ALJR 9 and [1967-68] PNGLR 209.

independence from the second defendant's acts so that they did not break the chain of causation.

Another situation in which the original assailant should be held liable is that where the original blow continues to be a substantial factual cause of death even though the second blow is given by a fully independent third party with his or her own reasons for wanting the victim dead. In *People v Lewis*[61] the Supreme Court of California said that in this situation both assailants could be guilty of homicide, and this seems the right solution.

(viii)   Independent intervening human actions which represent the sole or overwhelming actual cause of death

Quite a mouthful, but there seems little doubt that this kind of intervening action would break the chain of causation, whether or not the original injury was likely of itself to result in death. The principle is clearly stated in *Bush v Commonwealth*[62] and *State v Scates*,[63] cases referred to earlier, but neither the application of the principle in *Bush* nor the reasoning behind it in *Scates* is entirely satisfactory. The difficulty perhaps is not so much in stating the principle as in applying it. Independence lies not in the fact that the intervening actor may be criminally or civilly liable as the court in the *Scates* case seems to have thought, but in the fact that the intervening act is not a reaction to the original injury. It does not turn on the culpability or level of culpability of the intervening actor, as an act can be independent in the sense used here, whether it is deliberate, negligent or innocent, justified, excused or illegal.

Suppose in time of war or rebellion a fighter pilot aims a missile at what he believes is the enemy's headquarters but hits what turns out to be a field hospital killing dying patients and doctors. Whatever the legality of the pilot's act, it would break the chain of causation in relation to any patient killed solely by the missile. The killing would be in no way a reaction to the original injury. But were a patient in the far end of the hospital to die partly of the original wound and partly by some aggravation of that wound by shock from the missile, the chain of causation would not necessarily be broken. It would not be broken if the original wound was still a substantial cause of the death.

---

[61]   57 P 470 at 473 (1899).
[62]   78 Ky 268 (1880).
[63]   50 NC 409 (1858).

(ix) *Intervening act of nature*

Suppose the defendant's act leaves the victim vulnerable to the forces of nature which are the immediate cause of the death. Here the law draws a distinction between the ordinary course of nature and extraordinary events. So if the defendant knocks the victim unconscious and leaves him on the sea shore and he is drowned by the incoming tide, the defendant is liable, but if the victim is killed by an earthquake on a tidal wave, the chain of causation is broken.[64]

(x) *Intention, foresight and foreseeability*

There are two extreme views on the relationship between causation and intention, foresight and foreseeability. At one end of the spectrum is the notion that causation is a matter of objective fact and that questions of intention, foresight and foreseeability have nothing to do with this part of the case. This was the position taken by the Full Court of South Australia in *R v Hallett*.[65] At the other extreme, foreseeability is a, if not the, central test of causation. This was the approach taken by McHugh J in *Royall v R*[66] and by Smith and Hogan's *Criminal Law*.[67] The current position seems to be that foreseeability is not necessary for causation, but that intention, foresight or foreseeability may sometimes establish causation where otherwise it would be lacking.

If we take a case where normally causation would not be made out, we can see how intention might make a difference. Suppose the defendant knocks the victim unconscious and the victim is killed by an earthquake. *Hallett's* case contemplates that the defendant would not be guilty of causing the death. This would be so whether the defendant intended to kill the victim by the attack or was merely grossly negligent. But suppose the defendant knows that an earthquake is imminent and leaves the victim in a place where he or she hopes the earthquake will cause death. The defendant should be held liable. Though *R v Hallett* seems to deny liability even where this kind of intention is present, the High Court of Australia in *Royall v R*[68] would impose liability. Mason CJ said that state of mind could be relevant to causation for example where the defendant intended the injury should result in the way in which it

---

64 *R v Hallett* [1969] SASR 141 at 150.
65 [1969] SASR 141.
66 (1991) 172 CLR 378 at 451. See also S Yeo, "An Australian Evaluation of Causation in Fright Cases" (1943) *J of Criminal Law* 390.
67 (9th edn, 1999) at pp 339-44.
68 (1991) 172 CLR 378.

did.[69] Brennan J applied a similar principle to the case where the victim reacts unreasonably to the defendant's threat. If the defendant intended that the threat should cause the reaction, causation is made out.[70]

This principle extends to foresight.[71] Even if the defendant does not want the victim to die and is not virtually certain that she will, he may be liable if he foresees that death is likely to (or may as a real possibility) occur in the way that it does. The degree of probability has not yet been worked out, but real, as opposed to fanciful possibility should be enough to establish causation.

Where does that leave foreseeability? We saw earlier that in *Royall v R* only McHugh J was prepared to regard foreseeability as the appropriate criterion of causation to ask the jury to apply. The other judges rejected that approach. Implicit in that rejection are two consequences. First, that one can be held to cause death even if the manner of death is not reasonably foreseeable. The stabbing of a Jehovah's Witness who refuses a blood transfusion seems to fall into that category. Secondly, it is not generally appropriate to ask the jury to consider the foreseeability of the manner of death in deciding matters of causation. Leaving an unconscious person on the sea shore where she is drowned by the incoming tide is an example. It would be profitless to clutter up the issue with the question whether a reasonable person would foresee that the tide might come in and drown the victim. Better to have a fully objective rule which recognises the effect of the normal course of nature. So is there any room at all for foreseeability? There is one function it could perform. Like intention and foresight, it might be allowed to widen the notion of causation to cases it would not normally reach. But in order to play this part it would have to be something different from a reasonable person style of foreseeability. In order to justify a widening of the ordinary rules of causation, the foreseeability would have to be personal to the particular defendant. The point can be illustrated by reference to the reaction to threat kind of homicide. The rule that the reaction must be reasonable can be reframed as a rule that the reaction must be reasonably foreseeable together with a sub-rule that unreasonable reactions are not reasonably foreseeable. This last proposition could be restated in terms that a reasonable person would not foresee a real possibility that the victim would react in an unreasonable fashion. (It could not plausibly be stated that a reasonable person could foresee no possibility whatever that the victim would act unreasonably.) This way of expressing the law would simply be a clumsier, more convoluted and more confusing way of arriving at the same position as

---

69   At 390. See also *R v Michael* (1840) 9 C and P 356.
70   (1991) 172 CLR 378 at 400.
71   *R v Jemielita* (1996) 81 A Crim R 409.

the more direct rule that an unreasonable reaction breaks the chain of causation. So if foreseeability has any useful part to play it must be what this defendant could reasonably be expected to foresee. So if there is evidence to show that this defendant should, say by reason of past experience, have realised that the victim would act in an unreasonable way, that should be enough to prevent the break in the chain of causation.

Causation and the *Model Criminal Code*

The Commonwealth, States and Territories, through the Standing Committee of Attorneys-General, are working on a *Model Criminal Code* intended for adoption by all Australian jurisdictions. Clause 5.1.3 of the *Model Criminal Code* provides that a person's conduct causes death or harm if it substantially contributes to the death or harm. This is designed to codify Australian common law's preference for substantial cause over any test based on foreseeability.[72] It also seems designed to overrule *Royall v R*[73] on the point that an unreasonable reaction by a frightened victim would break the chain of causation.[74] The Committee did not consider the question whether intention, foresight or foreseeability might provide a basis for causation where objectively causation would not be made out, as in the predicted earthquake case. The formulation in clause 5.1.3 seems flexible enough to cater for such cases.

---

[72] Model Criminal Code Officers Committee, *Fatal Offences Against the Person*, Discussion Paper, 1998, at pp25-31.
[73] (1991) 172 CLR 378.
[74] Note 72, at pp27-31.

11 Death Causation in Palliative Medicine

MICHAEL ASHBY*

Introduction

Analysis of causation is central to any deliberative process which has as its object the determination of the moral character and legality of medical decisions or palliative interventions at the end of life, but there are semantic, evidential and argumentation difficulties which require elucidation.[1] The following quotation, from a 1996 judgment in the United States articulates (at its most extreme) the prevalent established international medico-legal view of palliative care interventions and death causation:

> as part of the tradition of administering comfort care, doctors have been supplying the causal agent of patients' deaths for decades.[2]

Whilst it is undoubtedly true that throughout history certain doctors have administered treatment to terminally ill patients with the covert or overt intention of shortening their lives, this is not the clinical or ethical

---

*   Professor of Palliative Care in the Department of Medicine, Monash University, Director of Palliative Care at McCulloch House, Monash Medical Centre, and Medical Director of the Cancer and Palliative Care Program of the Southern Health Care network in Melbourne, Australia.

[1]   See M Ashby, "Palliative Care, Death Causation, Public Policy and the Law" (1998) 6 *Progress in Palliative Care* 69; M Ashby, "Of Life and Death: the Canadian and Australian Senates on Palliative Care and Euthanasia" (1997) 5 *JLM* 40; and M Ashby, "The Fallacies of Death Causation in Palliative Care" (1997) 166 *Medical Journal of Australia* 176.

[2]   *Compassion in Dying v Washington*, 79 F 3d 790 (9th Cir 1996), quoted in GJ Annas, "The Promised End - Constitutional Aspects of Physician-Assisted Suicide" (1996) 335 *New England Journal of Medicine* 683.

position which is put forward by palliative care practitioners.[3] It is the central tenet of this chapter that death causation is a major factor influencing care and decision-making at end of life. There has been a failure within medicine itself to deal with causation in this context, and there are widespread anxieties about responsibility for causing death. As well, questionable assumptions by health care professionals and the public, concerning law and ethics, permeate practice and debate related to death and dying.

These problems are apparent in an influential study published by Kuhse et al in 1997.[4] They conducted a survey of a cross sectional sample of the Australian medical work force to study attitudes to end of life care and decision-making. Their work was based on the approach taken by Van der Maas and co-workers,[5] where a legal channel for such practices exists. In these studies euthanasia is categorised as a type of medical decision at the end of life (MDEL).[6] The term medical decision at the end of life, used by both groups of researchers, encompasses:

> all decisions by physicians concerning courses of action aimed at hastening the end of life of the patient or courses of action for which the physician takes into account the probability that the end of life of the patient is hastened.[7]

Two of the other categories (in addition to euthanasia) are: firstly, administration of "high doses of opioids" that "almost certainly would shorten the life of the patient" and secondly, decisions in which "life-prolonging" treatment was withheld or withdrawn.[8]

The Australian authors reported that some kind of end of life decision was made in 64.8 per cent of cases. The largest sub-group was "alleviation of pain and suffering through the administration of opioids in sufficient

---

3   J Gilbert & S Kirkham, "Double Effect, Double Bind or Double Speak" (1999) 13 *Palliative Medicine* 365.

4   H Kuhse et al, "End of Life Decisions in Australian Medical Practice" (1997) 166 *Medical Journal of Australia* 191.

5   J Van der Maas et al, "Euthanasia and Other Medical Decisions Concerning the End of Life" (1991) 338 *Lancet* 669; L Pijneneborg et al, "Nationwide Study of Decisions Concerning the End of Life in General Practice in the Netherlands" (1994) 309 *British Medical Journal* 1209; P Van der Maas et al, "Euthanasia, Physician-Assisted Suicide, and Other Medical Practices Involving the End of Life in the Netherlands, 1990-1995" (1996) 335 *New England Journal of Medicine* 1699.

6   Ibid.

7   P Van der Maas et al, *Euthanasia and Other Medical Decisions Concerning the End of Life*, Elsevier, Amsterdam, 1992.

8   Ibid.

doses to hasten death" – 30.9 per cent (with a stated intention to hasten death in 6.5 per cent), followed by "decision not to treat" – 28.6 per cent (with an explicit intention to hasten death stated in 24.7 per cent).[9] This study was based on doctors' perceptions and interpretations of their management and decision-making for the most recent patient who died under their care in the year prior to the completion of the study questionnaire. There was no attempt to validate these impressions, and the results should be viewed with caution. However, at the very least, they show that these general practitioners and non-palliative care specialists considered themselves to be making significant contributions to the cause of death of their dying patients, far in excess of what most palliative care specialists would expect.[10]

In a 1995 survey of specialist Victorian nurses, some respondents expressed the following views about causation in their practice:

> Surprisingly, even within the palliative care and cancer nursing communities, myths exist about the power of morphine to lead to respiratory distress and death in narcotic-tolerant patients. Of further concern is that some respondents consider the routine escalation of morphine doses in response to increasing pain, as active euthanasia. The knowledge and attitudes of nurses about euthanasia, and the use of morphine in particular, requires further exploration.[11]

So, within medicine and nursing themselves, there is no clear agreement on death causation with regard to palliative care interventions and treatment abatement decisions. The majority of palliative care practitioners, and all of their peak bodies, maintain the position that in clinical practice, provided that the prevailing standards of the field are adhered to, the process of dying is neither hastened nor prolonged. Death is therefore *natural*[12] in a *forensic* sense, that is it results from natural causes,

---

9   By the demonstration of a such a high incidence of so-called medical decisions at the end of life (65 per cent of the deaths studied by Kuhse et al, op cit, n4), that all have the same outcome of causing death, it is presumably hoped that the case for the legalisation of voluntary active euthanasia is advanced by undermining existing medical practice, which is thereby shown to be inconsistent in both its principles and processes. Euthanasia accounted for 1.8 per cent of cases, and in 3.5 per cent life was ended without the patient's request.

10   Kuhse et al, op cit, n4.

11   S Aranda & M O'Connor, "Euthanasia, Nursing and Care of the Dying; Rethinking Kuhse and Singer" (1995) 3 *Australian Nurses Journal* 18.

12   See Raymond Williams' invaluable book *Key Words: a Vocabulary of Culture and Society*, rev edn, Oxford University Press, New York, 1985, pp219-24 for consideration of the word "nature", which he views as perhaps the most complex word

ie there is no human agency involved. However, there is a growing view, particularly in the health professions, that there are now very few natural deaths because they are mostly orchestrated[13] by medical decisions. At the very least timing and mode of death, if not the main mechanism (disease or injury), are now determined, wholly or in part, by human intervention.

Palliative care literature and practice is infused with a notion of the "naturalness" of death in an *existential* sense, that is death is an inevitable consequence of living, and dying is emphasised as being a normal part of the life cycle. Palliative care practice is therefore based on the recognition of a natural dying process.

Opioid and Sedative Drugs in Palliative Care

Significant obstacles to the good care of dying people can be shown to arise from deeply entrenched myths that morphine causes addiction and death.[14] In countries like the United Kingdom and Australia, which have made substantial inroads into palliative care provision, access to opioids is good, but some bureaucratic hurdles still exist which generate inconvenience for prescribers. In many other countries, however, access to morphine is still limited or non-existent, and there is still serious concern that in global terms poor cancer pain control is commonly due, at least in part, to poor opioid access.[15] This is largely due to the regulation of opioid use by governments in order to control illicit drug use and its enormous attendant social and health problems.

---

in the English language. It is derived from the past participle (natura) of the Latin verb *nasci*, to be born. Williams shows that, historically, the word commences (like "culture") as a quality or process, defined by a specific reference, which later became a noun. Williams identifies three areas of meaning: (i) the essential quality and character of something, (ii) the inherent force which directs either the world or human beings or both; (iii) the material world itself, taken as including or not including human beings.

[13] See B Stoffell, "Orchestrating Death", in preparation.

[14] M Reidenberg, "Barriers to Controlling Pain in Patients with Cancer" (1996) 347 *Lancet* 1278; and, M Zenz & A Willweber-Strumpf, "Opiophobia and Cancer Pain in Europe" (1993) 341 *Lancet* 1075.

[15] See Rita Carter, "Give a Drug a Bad Name," (1996) *New Scientist*, 6 April, 14. The introduction reads: "Morphine is the world's most effective painkiller, yet because of its reputation as a dangerous drug it is rarely prescribed even to terminally ill patients." This is, of course, untrue, but nonetheless, the article highlighted the extent and depth of the negative attitudes and lack of knowledge concerning the safety and efficacy of opioids, even in the United Kingdom, where palliative care is well embedded, appearing in a scientific publication of the highest standing.

In two surveys conducted in 1991 for a parliamentary select committee of the South Australian parliament, general practitioners showed minimal concern about addiction to pain-killing drugs, but over 80 per cent of the community sample thought that addiction was a significant issue. A causal question concerning pain relief was asked in the public survey and showed a wide divergence of views, and much uncertainty.[16] Unfortunately, no such question was asked in the general practitioner study.[17]

In a large retrospective case note review of 11,882 hospitalised inpatients at Boston University Medical Center, two physicians reported that only four patients showed evidence of addiction to opioids prescribed for pain.[18] Marie Fallon (Glasgow, Scotland) and colleagues conducted a prospective comparative study of mood and drug use in three groups of patients receiving opioids for: cancer pain, chronic non-malignant pain and drug dependence. They found profound differences in opioid use between the groups. Whilst cancer and chronic pain patients mainly took opioids to relieve pain, those with drug dependence used them for mood elevation and sleep.[19] Although medical opinion is now clear that addiction is not an issue in cancer pain management and palliative care, opinion is divided about opioid use in non-malignant pain,[20] and patients and families in the wider community clearly still have a high level of concern about the potential for addiction.

Despite an extensive and sustained international campaign by the World Health Organisation,[21] many doctors still believe that they are

---

[16] Asked if too many pain-killers shorten life, the results were (n=462): very true 11.7 per cent, somewhat true 25 per cent, not at all true 28 per cent, don't know 35.3 per cent. M Ashby & M Wakefield, "Attitudes to Some Aspects of Death and Dying, Living Wills and Substituted Health Care Decision-making in South Australia: a Public Opinion Survey for a Parliamentary Select Committee" (1993) 7 *Palliative Medicine* 273.

[17] M Wakefield, J Beilby & M Ashby, "General Practitioners and Palliative Care" (1993) 7 *Palliative Medicine* 117.

[18] J Porter & H Jack, "Addiction Rare in Patients Treated with Narcotics" (1980) 302 *New England Journal of Medicine* 123.

[19] Fallon, personal communication.

[20] For the prevailing views on the use of opioids for non-malignant pain, from the Australian Pain Society see: P Graziotti & R Goucke, "The Use of Oral Opioids in Patients with Chronic Non-malignant Pain" (1997) 167 *Medical Journal of Australia* 30, and an editorial in that journal: A Molloy et al, "Role of Opioids in Chronic Non-cancer Pain" (1997) 167 *Medical Journal of Australia* 9. In Canada, see the website of the Canadian Pain Society: "Use of opioid analgesics for the treatment of chronic noncancer pain in a consensus statement and guidelines from the Canadian Pain Society" <www.pulsus.com/Pain/03_04/opio_ed.htm>.

[21] J Stjernsward & N Teoh, "The Cancer Pain Relief Programme of the World Health Organisation" (1989) 4 *Palliative Medicine* 1; R Twycross, *Pain Relief in Advanced*

causing or hastening the death of their palliative care patients, despite a lack of any evidence to support this view.[22] These deep-seated fears are based on the fact that opioids, used inappropriately, can cause respiratory depression, coma and death. In particular, the notion that there is agreement about a "high" dose of an opioid drug such as morphine beyond which timing and possibly causation might be in question has permeated medicine, and hence, every legal deliberation on this issue since the 1957 instruction to the jury by Devlin J in *R v Adams*:

> But that does not mean that a doctor who is aiding the sick and the dying has to calculate in minutes or even hours, and perhaps not in days or weeks, the effect on the patient's life of the medicines that he administers or else be in peril of a charge of murder. If the first purpose of medicine, the restoration of health, can no longer be achieved, there is still much for a doctor to do and he is entitled to do all that is proper and necessary to relieve pain and suffering, even if the measures he takes may incidentally shorten life. This is not because there is a special defence for medical men but because no act is murder which does not cause death. We are not dealing here with the philosophical or technical cause, but with the commonsense cause. The cause of death is the illness or injury, and the proper medical treatment that is administered and that has an incidental effect on determining the exact moment of death is not the cause of death in any sensible use of the term. But ... no doctor, nor any man, no more in the case of the dying than of the healthy, has the right deliberately to cut the thread of life.[23]

It is clear that expert medical evidence, given forty years ago has been incorporated into legal deliberations and public policy formulation ever since. Whilst the judgment is supportive of palliative care, and expresses double effect in law for the first time in this context, much has changed in medicine (and society) since the expert evidence which would have informed that judgment in 1957. The title for Patrick Devlin's 1985 book

---

Cancer, Churchill Livingstone, London, 1994; DF Zech et al, "Validation of World Health Organization Guidelines for Cancer Pain Relief: a 10-year Prospective Study" (1995) 63 *Pain* 65; Expert Working Group of the European Association for Palliative Care, "Morphine in Cancer Pain: Modes of Administration" (1996) 312 *British Medical Journal* 823; and R Twycross et al, "A Survey of Pain in Patients with Advanced Cancer" (1996) 12 *Journal of Pain and Symptom Management* 273.

22   M Ashby, "The Fallacies of Death Causation in Palliative Care" (1997) 166 *Medical Journal of Australia* 176; and D Mendelson, "Quill, Glucksberg and Palliative Care – Does Alleviation of Pain Necessarily Hasten Death?" (1997) 5 *Journal of Law and Medicine* 110.

23   *R v Adams* [1957] Crim LR 365.

as a result of the 1957 Bodkin Adams case, *Easing the Passing*,[24] is perhaps illustrative of the prevailing views on palliative care at the time. The widespread use of the Brompton's Cocktail[25] also shows that the view of dying was that rapidity of death and oblivion were the goals of palliative interventions, which were almost exclusively focused on terminal care. Palliative care has now expanded well beyond terminal care, and is seeing patients far earlier in the course of their illness. Patient expectations have also changed, and until the last few hours or days of life, most patients wish to have optimal pain management with minimal side effects; in particular, they do not wish to be drowsy or cognitively impaired. Ognall J in his summing up to the jury in *R v Cox*, shows that, in 1992, this perception of the fine line for medical practitioners between provision of pain relief and causing death was still operating:

> We all appreciate that some medical treatment, whether of a positive, therapeutic character or solely of an analgesic kind – by which I mean designed solely to alleviate pain and suffering – some treatment carries with it a serious risk to the health or even the life of the patient. Doctors are frequently confronted with, no doubt, distressing dilemmas. They have to make up their minds as to whether the risk, even to the life of their patient, attendant upon their contemplated form of treatment, is such that the risk is, or is not, medically justified. If a doctor genuinely believes that a certain course is beneficial to his patient, either therapeutically or analgesically, then even though he recognises that that course carries with it a risk to life, he is fully entitled, nonetheless, to pursue it. If in those circumstances the patient dies, nobody could possibly suggest that in that situation the doctor was guilty of murder or attempted murder.[26]

There is no clinical scientific evidence that morphine causes death, if used with appropriate skill to palliate symptoms. However, like any class of drugs, the opioids are dangerous if used inappropriately. There is now a substantial body of clinical experience in palliative care about safe

---

[24] P Devlin, *Easing the Passing: The Trial of Dr John Bodkin Adams*, The Bodley Head, London, 1985.

[25] Named after the Brompton Hospital (a famous London postgraduate teaching hospital which specialises in chest diseases). The mixture usually contained heroin, cocaine and alcohol, although its composition has varied from one institution to another over the years. It was very extensively used prior to the advent of the modern hospice/palliative care movement. The effects of these ingredients include pain relief, but also "pharmacological oblivion", an attempt to relieve emotional and "existential" pain and anxiety associated with the dying process by a seemingly contradictory combination of mood modification (elevation) and sedation.

[26] *R v Cox* (1992) 12 BMLR 38.

standards of practice, with particular regard to initial doses for "opioid-naïve" patients and subsequent dose titration according to the person's pain or symptom reporting. It is widely assumed that the morphine (or other opioid) dose per se, is the main determinant of whether the drug causes or hastens death. In fact there is no such determinative or threshold dose, and this approach is flawed. What matters is the present dose in relation to the previous dose. Gradual dose escalation by a factor in the region of 50-100 per cent of the previous dose is usual practice, although substantially higher increases can usually be well tolerated by patients who are not new to the drug (that is they are no longer termed "opioid-naïve"). It is therefore the size of the initial dose, and the rate of subsequent increases which are important.

Cancer pain management with morphine is unusual compared to most other forms of drug treatment in that there are no predetermined dose ranges to achieve satisfactory pain control for adults or children. Most adults will achieve initial pain control with a daily dose in the range of 30 mg to 200 mg (per 24 hours, orally), but the range of doses is very wide. The accepted practice is to adjust the regular dose upwards according to the requirements to keep the pain under control, balanced against incidence of side effects.

Terminal Sedation

Sedative drugs are commonly used in terminal care (when death is believed to be imminent), in order to maintain comfort and dignity (for patient *and* family) by alleviation of agitation, anxiety and so-called terminal restlessness. They are used proportionately to the patient's distress, and not to bring about death. It should incidentally be noted that patients are usually unconscious and/or cognitively impaired, and therefore incompetent at this stage. They are used proportionately to the patient's distress, and not to bring about death. It is clear that there is a robust disagreement within medicine itself, about whether such treatment contributes to the cause of death, and even what the therapeutic goals are or should be. There are those who contend that, within accepted palliative care practice, patients are sedated, and death is thereby caused, either through central nervous system and respiratory depression, or dehydration and starvation.[27] Billings and Block also contend that this is the result of

---

[27] See the article by a British geriatrician, Gillian Craig and the author's riposte. G Craig, "On Withholding Nutrition and Hydration in the Terminally Ill: has Palliative Medicine Gone too Far?" (1994) 20 *Journal of Medical Ethics* 139; and M Ashby & B

the use of morphine infusions.[28] Certainly, palliative care practitioners rarely use morphine for its sedative properties at any stage of an illness, especially when patients are trying to function as normally as possible, and sedation is usually unwelcome. In terminal care sedatives are titrated against agitation and distress, but occasionally also against another symptom (eg pain or shortness of breath) where other measures have failed and the patient may wish to be less aware of what they are going through. If patients are conscious and competent they are consulted about this and asked if they wish to be more sedated. However, patients in the terminal phase of their illness are often unable to give this consent due to incompetence as a result of unconsciousness and/or cognitive impairment. It is clearly not possible to state categorically that such sedation has no effect on time of death. The precise timing of death is unpredictable, and verification of the relative causal contributions to that timing of disease, physiological and pharmacological factors is not usually measurable. Outside the setting of terminal care, so-called "pharmacological oblivion" is not part of accepted palliative care practice, especially not as a way of ending a patient's life.

Causation

Dialogue between medicine and the law is hampered by the fact that the term "causation" in medicine and science is usually employed in a narrow empirical sense, a term which itself has a complex and interesting history,[29]

Stoffell, "Artificial Hydration and Alimentation at the End of Life: a reply to Craig" (1995) 21 *Journal of Medical Ethics* 135.

[28] J Billings & S Block "Slow Euthanasia" (1996) 12 *Journal of Palliative Care* 21. See also the palliative care riposte: B Mount "Morphine Drips, Terminal Sedation, and Slow Euthanasia: Definitions and Facts, Not Anecdotes" (1996) 12 *Journal of Palliative Care* 31.

[29] See Raymond Williams' invaluable book *Key Words: a Vocabulary of Culture and Society*, rev edn, Oxford University Press, New York, 1985, pp115-17, for an account of the various meanings of "empirical". Williams points out that the word is used, in English, in a medical context from the 16th century onwards, to refer to treatment based on assessment of individual patient response, rather than theory, which was the preserve of physicians. As such, the term had negative connotations, alluding to quackery and unqualified practice. In science and philosophy, the term is used to denote knowledge gained from experience, and hence experiment, rather than derived from reason. This distinction is complex and derives substantially from the work of the English philosophers Locke and Hume. In modern medical usage it can refer to treatment given on a "try and see" basis in individual patients (usually with some theoretical mechanistic basis, but perhaps without the existence of good supporting evidence – a practice which is also often seen as "unscientific" and lacking in rigour),

but taken here to mean the facts or data pertaining to a given situation, and their relationship to one another. Causation is a complex phenomenon in the law, and it might be reasonably argued that it is a misnomer in that context.[30] Legal causation is a process whereby courts look at the chain of events in a case, and then attempt to attribute legal liability. In legal usage the term therefore encompasses the facts *and* determination of legal liability.[31]

Most people without a legal background, and hence most health care practitioners, will have a narrow medical view of causation, which approximates to the but-for test of causation.[32] In fact the law, particularly in Australia, tends to recognise the multifactorial nature of causation, and does not use the "but-for" test as the sole legal standard for ascertaining or apportioning legal responsibility, which is over-arched or controlled by the test of common sense and experience:

> In law ... problems of causation arise in the context of ascertaining or apportioning legal responsibility for a given occurrence ... Thus, at law a person may be responsible for damage when his or her wrongful conduct is one of a number of conditions sufficient to produce that damage.[33]

With regard to palliative care, it can also be shown that in (at least) jurisdictions which follow the English common law tradition (eg, Australia, New Zealand, Canada, the United States, and of course, England and Wales), the leading reference case is still *R v Adams*, and, in particular, the famous passage on causation quoted above.

Although there has been no known case where this position has been put to the test as such, it is always quoted in judicial and parliamentary deliberations concerning end of life issues. Absent any prosecutions of medical practitioners, except where intention is clearly in question,[34] academic lawyers and parliamentary inquiries have continued to take the

---

or, perhaps paradoxically, it can refer to the scientific (experimental) tradition itself. In a legal context it appears to be used to describe facts of a case known through human experience, hence through the senses, a use in harmony with mainstream western scientific tradition.

30 Danuta Mendelson, personal communication.

31 D Mendelson, *Torts*, 2nd edn, Butterworths, Sydney, 2000.

32 The "but for" test in law asks whether the damage or harm would have occurred but for the (plaintiff's) wrongful act, and serves to eliminate matters which could not have been the causes of the (plaintiff's) damage (other expressions include *causa sine qua non*, literally "the cause without which", "proximate cause" or "real effective cause").

33 D Mendelson, "Medico-Legal Aspects of the 'Right to Die' Legislation in Australia" (1993) 19 *MULR* 112. For further reading, see D Mendelson, op cit, n31.

34 Eg, *R v Cox*, op cit, n26.

view that prosecution is at least theoretically possible, and various legal mechanisms have been put forward to allow lawful palliative care.[35]

The Australian Attorney General's Department gave this (confusing) legal advice to the senate inquiry about the meaning of the term "intentional killing" in the Euthanasia Laws Bill, and whether the passage of the bill would generate legal "uncertainty" about end of life decisions:

> The Attorney-General's Department noted that English cases refer to a rule that a doctor caring for a dying patient may lawfully administer pain-killing drugs despite the fact that he or she knows that an incidental effect of doing so will be to shorten the patient's life. The Department said it is uncertain whether the rule as stated is part of the law in all common law jurisdictions in Australia ... [and a] degree of further uncertainty exists as to code jurisdictions .... The Department said if the rule were to be adopted [in Australia], "which seems probable as to general principle, if uncertain as to reasoning and detail", many uncertainties remain on matters of significant detail.[36]

In a 1989 paper on criminal law reform, by the Law Reform Commission of Canada, it was proposed that criminal liability not attach to the administration of life-shortening palliative care "appropriate to the circumstances". In a commentary on this, David Casswell (an academic lawyer in British Columbia at the time) urged more specific criteria (terminal illness, pain and suffering). In his paper he agreed with Devlin J's instruction to the jury on causation in *R v Adams*, but stated that he:

> did not support as a generalized proposition his Lordship's reasoning that palliative care which has the "incidental effect of determining the exact moment of death, or may have, is not the cause of death in any sensible use of the term". If a factual causal connection between the administration of palliative care and the patient's death is proved and if the physician subjectively knew that the palliative care he or she was about to administer would likely be life-shortening, it would seem that causation would be established. Further, two causes may operate together, with each legally being a cause of an event. In the present context both the

---

[35] P Skegg, "Drugs Hastening Death" in *Law, Ethics and Medicine: Studies in Medical Law*, Clarendon Press, Oxford, 1984, 121; and P Skegg, "Pain-killing Drugs and the Law of Homicide" (1995) 4 *Otago Bioethics Report* 8.

[36] Parliament of the Commonwealth of Australia, *Senate Legal and Constitutional Legislation Committee, Consideration of Legislation Referred to the Committee. Euthanasia Laws Bill 1996*, Canberra, 1997, 29.

patient's illness and the physician's administration of life-shortening palliative care would be the causes of death.[37]

Casswell argued that Devlin J's "absence of causal analysis" in the case had led to reasoning by others that there was an absence of intent, or that the act was justified by necessity (to relieve pain).

Peter Skegg (Professor of Law, Otago University, New Zealand) has written that there is a theoretical possibility that the administration of pain-killing drugs which hasten death might lead to a prosecution of negligent homicide[38] in a New Zealand court, although no such thing has so far happened, and criminal liability would not be established, provided that intention is clear. Reliance on causation is thought to be preferable to a defence of necessity, as these do not have a very successful track record in English courts.[39]

It is of note that Skegg has contended that the principle of double effect has no standing in legal analysis. It has recently been subjected to penetrating intellectual assault by a number of writers, despite the fact that courts and parliaments have endorsed it.[40] Singer has suggested that it is a "figleaf" behind which decisions at the end of life, which will have the effect of ending life, are hidden. In the *Bland* case, he makes the surely strong and self-evident case that the intended outcome of the court's decision was Anthony Bland's death.[41] Jessica Corner, a prominent palliative care nurse, in commenting on the recent Annie Lindsell case in the United Kingdom, has made a plea for palliative care to recognise that there may be times when death is an intended outcome.[42] Quill and co-authors have argued that patient self determination is more important than doctors' intentions as a guide to action in end of life decision making.[43]

---

[37] D Casswell, "Rejecting Criminal Liability for Life-shortening Palliative Care" (1990) 6 *Journal of Contemporary Health Law and Policy* 127.

[38] Note the specific provision in the criminal law of New Zealand re negligent homicide (Freckelton, personal communication).

[39] P Skegg, op cit, n 35.

[40] M Otlowski, *Voluntary Euthanasia and the Common Law*, Oxford University Press, Oxford, 1997. C Corns, "Withdrawal of Life-support: Some Criminal Prosecution Aspects" in I Freckelton & K Petersen (eds), *Controversies in Health Law*, Federation Press, Sydney, 1999, pp44-59.

[41] P Singer, *Rethinking Life and Death*, Text, Melbourne, 1994.

[42] J Corner, "More Openness Needed in Palliative Care" (1997) 315 *British Medical Journal* 1242.

[43] T Quill, "The Rule of Double Effect – a Critique of Its Role in End-of-Life Decision-Making" (1997) 337 *New England Journal of Medicine* 1768.

This view has been shared by a South Australian palliative care specialist (Roger Hunt),[44] and another in Quebec (Marcel Boisvert).[45]

Keyserlingk,[46] in an argument against decriminalisation of assisted suicide based on an analysis of *Rodriguez*, proposes a move away from standard and "but-for" causality of death approaches in legal analysis, and the adoption of what he terms a normative causality approach, and what courts more commonly term the common sense and experience test of causation. He divides causality into three categories: standard, empirical and normative.

Standard causality entails the characterisation of treatments (eg ordinary v extraordinary) in order to allow abatement. Cause of death is usually ascribed to the underling disease rather than the decision or intervention in question. Any therapeutic intervention in palliative or terminal care may potentially affect the timing of death, but the cause remains the underlying condition from which the person is dying. Lord Goff appears to be articulating Keyserlingk's standard causality category in *Bland*:[47]

> As I see it, the doctor's decision whether or not to take any step must (subject to his patient's ability to give or withhold his consent) be made in the best interests of the patient. It is this principle too which, in my opinion, underlies the established rule that a doctor may, when caring for a patient who is, for example, dying of cancer, lawfully administer painkilling drugs despite the fact that he knows that an incidental effect of that application will be to abbreviate the patient's life. Such a decision may properly be made as part of the care of the living patient, in his best interests; and, on this basis, the treatment will be lawful. Moreover, where the doctor's treatment of his patient is lawful, the patient's death will be regarded in law as exclusively caused by the injury or disease to which his condition is attributable.

"But-for" or empirical causality relies on the scientific cause. Normative causality allows a more comprehensive analysis including normative considerations and empirical data:

---

44 R Hunt, "Palliative Care: the Rhetoric-Reality Gap" in H Kuhse (ed), *Willing to Listen, Wanting to Die*, Penguin, Melbourne, 1994, 115; and R Hunt, "Taking Responsibility for Affecting the Time of Death" (1999) 13 *Palliative Medicine* 439.

45 A Mullens, *Timely Death. Considering Our Last Rights*, Alfred A Knopf, Toronto, 1996.

46 E Keyserlingk, "Assisted Suicide, Causality and the Supreme Court of Canada" (1994) 39 *McGill L J* 708.

47 *Airedale NHS Trust v Bland* [1993] All ER 868.

(This) position emphasises not simple scientific causality, the cause-in-fact of a death, but normative or legal causality as well. This more nuanced and comprehensive analysis holds that empirical, scientific or "but-for" causality cannot alone account for what distinguishes assisted suicide from voluntary euthanasia, or what distinguishes both from withdrawal of life support or appropriate pain control resulting in death.[48]

This normative, or "common sense and experience" approach allows the "but-for" cause of death to be overridden if a society (via its legal or parliamentary institutions) decides that the intervention or non-intervention in question should not be viewed as a cause of death in law. Jane Stapleton has suggested that causation in legal analysis sometimes masks more important public policy considerations which may be the true issues at stake in certain cases.[49]

Margaret Somerville has given the most profound analysis of the difficulties which are encountered when those outside the law attempt to grapple with legal causation and its application to end of life issues.[50] She points out the important but nuanced distinctions between causation in criminal, and tort (civil responsibility) law. In criminal law, for causal analysis to be relevant, there would need to be conduct which would constitute a crime, *actus rea*, together with the *mens rea*, criminal intent, and the "but-for" test is not always applied. She writes:

> When multiple causes are present, there is a value judgement involved in choosing which formulation of the "but-for" test predominates in establishing causation-in-fact, and whether none of the causal factors, one, more than one, or all of them, each of which could attract legal liability, count as relevant in establishing criminal liability.[51]

Somerville points out the distinction between cause-in-fact and cause-in-law *(causa causans)* and its lesser emphasis in criminal compared to tort law. She cites this example:

> In a situation where one has a duty not to continue to treat the patient with artificial life support because the patient has refused this or because it is medically futile, then it is inappropriate to formulate the test of causation (even if it were relevant to assess causation, itself, which it is not if the

---

48   Keyserlingk, op cit, n46.

49   J Stapleton "Perspectives on Causation" in J Horder (ed), *Oxford Essays in Jurisprudence*, Oxford University Press, Oxford, 2000; and J Stapleton, Chapter 2, above.

50   M Somerville, "Euthanasia by Confusion" (1997) 20 *NSWLJ* 550-75.

51   Ibid, p564.

act of withdrawing treatment is legal) in terms of whether the cause of death was the withdrawal of the treatment. The physician cannot have a legal obligation to withdraw the treatment and not withdraw it and we must choose which of these duties predominates in a given situation. If the former, then the relevant test of cause of the patient's death is "but for" the patient's underlying condition would the patient have died; if the latter, "but for" turning off the respirator would the patient have died.[52]

Looking at withdrawal of life support, another approach is to see it as a situation of multiple causation, but here Somerville notes that courts, from the point of view of causation, where the act is legal, say turning off a respirator (for example) was not the cause of death, death resulted from "natural causes". Judges adopt this line of reasoning, she speculates:

> to avoid any possibility that they could be seen as setting a precedent to the effect that lethal injections would be legally acceptable.[53]

In the law of torts, tests for causation-in-law are of "varying degrees of stringency", and are of two sorts, "reasonable foreseeability" (a prospective test) and "substantive cause" (a retrospective test). So with a treatment withdrawal decision, death may be foreseeable, but not the "substantive" cause of death. In tort cases, Somerville also points out that judges will sometimes attempt to determine the proximity or remoteness of the damage from the cause, another way of looking at foreseeability.

The last test analysed by Somerville is that of public policy, which can be mobilised in tort law to provide immunity from legal liability, but not to impose it, and also has a special role in the criminal law to:

> characterise acts to which consent of the person affected by such acts may function as a defence. For instance, the intentional infliction of bodily harm, beyond a certain very limited degree, will be held to be contrary to public policy and, therefore at common law the consent of the person suffering that harm will not be a defence to such an act.[54]

Lastly, Somerville addresses the public policy stance on the importance of the provision of pain and symptom relief, albeit with the causal assumption about pain relief and death risk:

---

[52] Ibid.

[53] Ibid, p565.

[54] Ibid, p567.

This raises the issue of how necessary pain relief treatment given with the primary intention of relieving pain that could or will shorten life should be prima facie characterised from a public policy perspective. Just as the intent to relieve pain and not to kill justifies, through the doctrine of double effect, the administration of such treatment, likewise this same intent legitimates this treatment from a public policy perspective and, therefore, it can be given with the consent of the patient. Indeed, it should be considered contrary to public policy to fail to offer fully adequate pain relief treatment to persons who need this.[55]

A novel approach to these issues, in law, comes from South Australia. Double effect was put into statute law for the first time, with regard to the care of dying persons, with the *Consent to Medical Treatment and Palliative Care Act* 1995 (SA). In Division 2 of the Act, entitled "The Care of People Who Are Dying", there is a non-culpability clause which specifically states that medical treatment for the relief of pain or distress, and the non-application or discontinuance of life sustaining measures (for people who are dying) does not constitute "an intervening cause of death" (*novus actus interveniens*, ie a cause that breaks a pre-existing chain of causation). A saving provision was inserted stating that the provision does not allow euthanasia.[56]

The parliamentary select committee from which this piece of legislation emerged heard wide-ranging evidence, including assertions by palliative care physicians that death was not caused by palliative

---

[55] Ibid, p568.

[56] *Consent to Medical Treatment and Palliative Care Act* 1995 (SA): "The Care of People Who are Dying – 17. (1) A medical practitioner responsible for the treatment and care in the terminal phase of a terminal illness, or a person participating in the treatment and care of the patient under the medical practitioner's supervision, incurs no civil or criminal liability by administering medical treatment with the intention of relieving pain or distress – (a) with the consent of the patient or of patient's representative; and (b) in good faith and without negligence; and (c) in accordance with proper professional standards of palliative care, even though an incidental effect of the treatment is to hasten the death of the patient. (2) A medical practitioner responsible for the treatment or care of a patient in the terminal phase of a terminal illness, or a person participating in the treatment or care of the patient under the medical practitioner's supervision, is, in the absence of an express direction by the patient or the patient's representative to the contrary, under no duty to use, or to continue to use, life sustaining measures in treating the patient if the effect of doing so would be merely to prolong life in a moribund state without any real prospect of recovery or in a persistent vegetative state. (3) For the purposes of the law of the State – (a) the administration of medical treatment for the relief of pain or distress in accordance with subsection (1) does not constitute cause of death; and (b) the non-application or discontinuance of life sustaining measures in accordance with subsection (2) does not constitute a cause of death."

interventions and treatment abatement. Nonetheless, they heard sufficient professional and community concern about the issue to take the same view as the Canadian senate, namely that it was important to be specific in law, in order to prevent false perceptions of what the law had to say in this area from obstructing appropriate care of dying people. The House of Lords Select Committee on Medical Ethics, in 1994, also endorsed double effect but did not recommend any legislation.[57]

The objects sections of the four Australian State and Territory pieces of legislation which have been passed over the last decade on matters related to death and dying all have significant comment to make about the issue of proper pain and symptom control,[58] but only the South Australian Act specifically articulates and codifies the principle of double effect in this context. This is not to suggest that there have been prosecutions of doctors for treatment abatement decisions or palliative interventions, which there have not, nor to propose legal remedies for clinical problems. Rather, if the law specifically articulates, in statute, the priorities and parameters it sets for the care of dying people and differentiates palliative care from euthanasia,[59] this sends a powerful message to practitioners and their teachers which may fundamentally influence such care for the better. This holds even if the predicate about opioids and causation is inflated and unsubstantiated.[60]

The Ontario coroner seems to have captured the essence of palliative care practice, as the vast majority of its practitioners (internationally) see it, in laying down four conditions which apply for palliative care interventions to be legal in his jurisdiction, and these should be universally applicable:

> (1) the care must be intended solely to relieve suffering; (2) it must be administered in response to suffering or signs of suffering; (3) it must [be] commensurate with that suffering; and (4) it cannot be a deliberate

---

57 House of Lords, *Report of Select Committee on Medical Ethics*, HMSO, London, 1994.

58 See eg *Medical Treatment Act 1988* (Vic), Preamble: "(e) to encourage community and professional understanding of the changing focus of treatment from cure to pain relief for terminally-ill patients; and (f) to ensure that dying patients receive maximum relief from pain and suffering." *Consent to Medical Treatment and Palliative Care Act 1995* (SA), Part 1, s3: "(c) to allow for the provision of palliative care, in accordance with proper standards, to people who are dying and to protect them from medical treatment that is intrusive, burdensome and futile."

59 See Corns, op cit, n40.

60 This "educational" role for the law is interesting, an expanded role which the author thinks is worthwhile, but one that may trouble some legal "purists". See T Faunce & B McSherry, "Chinese Whispers: Judicial Narratives and the Regulation of Clinical Medicine" (1997) 4 *JLM* 326.

infliction of death. Documentation is required, and the doses must increase progressively.[61]

Modern palliative care practice standards are based on the notion that death is natural in the sense of being a universal and unavoidable consequence of having life, and that interventions or abatement decisions should neither hasten nor prolong the dying process. The intention is to relieve symptoms and suffering, not to bring forward the time of death. Whilst this position is sustainable in the palliative phase, it is susceptible to challenge in the terminal phase, when death is imminent (hours or days away).[62] Signals that death is approaching may consist of overt and covert acknowledgment by the patient that death is both inevitable and imminent, and anticipatory grief behaviour on the part of patient, family, significant others and carers. Clinical evidence may consist of declining appetite, weight loss, recumbency, lassitude, physiological systems failure and disease progression. There is an associated decrease in oral intake which usually ceases altogether as the patient's conscious state lapses. It is both philosophically and medically contentious to suggest that it is consistently possible to distinguish between patients who are dying, and those who are not, but in medical practice it is often necessary to attempt to do so.[63] The distinction is not made on religious or ethical grounds, but on biological and psychological observations, and no suggestion is inferred that the dying days are of lesser worth than non-dying ones, or that the dying have different rights to those which they previously enjoyed before they were dying.

It is acknowledged that as death approaches, abatement of life-sustaining treatment and terminal sedation may indeed alter the time of death, although this matter cannot be verified scientifically, one way or the

---

[61] Dr James Young, the Ontario Coroner in 1997 quoted in: Senate of Canada, *Of Life and Death: Report of Special Senate Committee on Euthanasia and Assisted Suicide* (Ottawa, 1995); and JV Lavery and P Singer, "The 'Supremes' Decide on Assisted Suicide: What Should a Doctor Do?" (1997) 157 *Canadian Medical Association Journal* 405.

[62] For a description of these three phases of illness and goals of care: curative, palliative and terminal, see: M Ashby & B Stoffell, "Therapeutic Ratio and Defined Phases: Proposal of an Ethical Framework for Palliative Care" (1991) 302 *British Medical Journal* 1322.

[63] Certain American writers who have expressed fairly strong conservative and religiously-based "sanctity of life" arguments against most treatment abatement decisions, such as Ramsey, Dyck, Grisez and Barry cited in Weir, pp271-4, nonetheless recognise the process of dying. R Weir, *Abating Treatment with Critically Ill Patients. Ethical and Legal Limits to the Prolongation of Life*, Oxford University Press, New York, 1989.

other, in a particular case, or in general. There are serious limitations to the use of clinical studies in this area, and the causal question itself cannot be directly asked in any interventional study for obvious reasons. We cannot know when a particular patient would have died in the absence of palliative interventions or treatment abatement, particularly during the final dying process, and it would be unethical to design randomised controlled trials to find out.

In the absence of formal training in palliative care, doctors' attitudes and clinical behaviour are complex and variable, ranging from abrupt cessation of treatment, minimalist palliative care and treatment directed at bringing about a rapid dying process, to excessive caution about being seen to be instrumental in causing the death, particularly with regard to the provision of pain and symptom relief, cessation or non-initiation of artificial hydration and alimentation and cardio-pulmonary resuscitation. Whilst a doctor's intention may not always be easy to validate, evaluation of intention and motive are fundamental to legal analysis, and many would argue that intention is also determinative of the moral character of medical interventions.

Conclusion

There is almost universal support for the relief of pain and suffering, and avoidance of prolongation of the process of dying. Public policy and the law have, without known exception, endorsed these common sense principles. There is also wide support for the cessation of life-sustaining measures in certain non-dying persons, where it is clear that the intention is to bring about death, as for instance those in a permanent and irreversible coma, or the persistent vegetative state, such as in the case of Anthony Bland.[64] However, there is deep division in societies about whether assisted suicide and euthanasia[65] should be made legal, and the fundamental question is causal. Those who advocate such changes often cite accepted palliative care practice in support of their position, on causal and consequentialist grounds. The line of argument runs something like this: "if you agree with the administration of opioids and sedatives, or treatment

---

[64] *Airedale NHS Trust v Bland* [1993] All ER 821.

[65] Defined by the peak body Palliative Care Australia as "the deliberate action to terminate life by someone other than, and at the request of, the patient concerned". Australian Association for Hospice and Palliative Care Inc (AAHPC), "Voluntary Euthanasia – Position Statement", 27 October 1995, The Association, Perth, 1995. (See appendix).

abatement which even have the potential to alter the timing, and therefore the cause, of death, how could you disagree with the administration of a lethal injection which has the expressed intention of causing death?".

It is concluded that, as argued by Keyserlingk,[66] narrow empirical causality, applied in the setting of terminal care, cannot alone account for the distinction between accepted palliative care practice and euthanasia. It is both false and unhelpful if appropriate and skilfully administered and monitored pain and symptom relief, together with the abatement of futile treatment in the context of a person's dying process, are seen as causing death. Self-willed and planned death, with or without third party assistance, surely has better arguments in its favour anyway.

In the experience of caring and being cared for, both intention and honesty are decisive. Palliative care must be clear about its intentions, and accept that there are some occasions when the process of death is hastened, either unknowingly or knowingly. Far from subverting its practice, this acknowledgment might liberate it from wider claims of ambiguity on causal issues.

Divergence about whether third party assistance (medical or non-medical) to die is permissible reveals a deep and complex fault line in modern western democracies, as they chart their courses based more on individual conceptions of liberty and autonomy than organised religion and deontological codes. This process is ongoing and will not come to a sharp resolution. Societal energy should be more focused on palliative care, about which we can nearly all agree and where modest investments have yielded excellent results for patients and families by improving care and decision-making at the end of life. There is much still to do. Euthanasia should remain narrowly defined as "the deliberate action to terminate life by someone other than, and at the request of, the patient concerned",[67] which is the matter at stake in the on-going societal debate.

The public needs to have complete confidence that there is a safe and morally sound body of modern palliative care practice which is clearly and unambiguously distinguished from euthanasia. Palliative care practitioners are confident to give this reassurance. However, no matter what one's view of euthanasia, it is important to unpack what is meant by the term "natural death".[68] Causation can be an important analytical and reflective

---

[66] Keyserlingk, op cit, n46.

[67] Weir, op cit, n63.

[68] The use of the term "natural" is ubiquitous in medicine, but its meanings are diverse and ill-defined: natural history means the course of a disease without treatment, natural causes means death absent human agency, natural therapy means treatment with natural (as opposed to man-made) substances. So-called "natural death" acts were passed in most states of the United States during the 1970-80s, starting with *Natural*

component of the process of determining whether palliative care is ethical and, therefore, legal. However, the concept of "natural" death, in the forensic sense of death without intervening human agency, which is intrinsic to the palliative care position of causal neutrality (neither hastening nor prolonging the process of dying), cannot be empirically defended in all cases. Natural death can be understood in a broader existential sense of inevitability, as a composite of causality, autonomy and dignity, and not solely in terms of the presence or absence of human agency. Perhaps one of contemporary medicine's biggest tasks is to embrace its limitations, so well articulated by the New Zealand judge Thomas J in *Auckland AHA v A-G*:

> Medical science and technology has advanced for a fundamental purpose: the purpose of benefiting the life and health of those who turn to medicine to be healed. It surely was never intended that it be used to prolong

---

Death Act 1976 (California) (for a comprehensive list of legislation in US jurisdictions as of 1992, see P Hill & D Shirley, *A Good Death. Taking More Control at the End of Your Life Choice in Dying*, The National Council for the Right to Die, Addison Wesley, New York, 1992). Two such statutes were passed in Australia: in South Australia, *Natural Death Act* 1983 (SA), and the Northern Territory of Australia, *Natural Death Act* 1988 (NT). The *Natural Death Act* 1983 (SA) was repealed by the *Consent to Medical Treatment and Palliative Care Act* 1995 (SA). The provisions of these "natural death" acts allow persons to make binding "living wills" to prevent them being subjected to life-sustaining medical treatment when incompetent, if the underlying condition is terminal and/or irreversible. There is an underlying theme of the need to bolster patients' rights to refuse treatment, redressing a past power imbalance, seen as being in favour of "paternalistic" doctors. The ethical and theoretical derivation of "natural death" in this context therefore appears to be focused on death absent human agency, and hence a causal construct. See also, for instance, the quote from the British Columbia Crown Counsel Policy Guidelines: "withholding or withdrawing treatment means ... discontinuing or not intervening with medical procedures to prolong life *beyond its natural length*." (emphasis added). Senate of Canada, *Of Life and Death: Report of Special Senate Committee on euthanasia and assisted suicide*, Ottawa, 1995, at 40. For a discussion of natural causes of death in a respirator withdrawal case see: B Schneiderman, "A Winnipeg Inquest: a Case of Natural Death or Physician Assisted Suicide?" (1996) 24 *Manitoba Law Journal* 365. See also B Stoffel & MA Ashby, "On Natural Death and Palliative care" in L Shotton (ed), *Health Care Law and Ethics*, Social Science Press, Katoomba, 1997, 163, at 164: "'Natural death' cannot be used without careful explication. It can be understood as a composite of two moral elements: patient self determination and avoidance of harm; that is, the priority of patient choice in determining what they personally find acceptable treatments in the terminal phase of an illness, plus the avoidance of certain obstructions to the process of dying. The first element is of course the one that the law is interested in protecting, whereas the latter will demand close scrutiny of treatment decisions ...."

biological life in patients bereft of the prospect of returning to an even limited exercise of human life. Nothing in the inherent purpose of these scientific advances can require doctors to treat the dying as if they were curable. Natural death has not lost its meaning or significance. It may be deferred, but it need not be postponed indefinitely.[69]

---

[69]   *Auckland AHA v AG* [1993] 1 NZLR 235.

Appendix to Chapter 11

The Australian Association for Hospice and Palliative Care Inc (AAHPC) issued the following position statement on voluntary active euthanasia on 27 October 1995.

The Australian Association for Hospice and Palliative Care:

1. defines Hospice and Palliative Care as a concept of care which provides coordinated medical, nursing and allied services for people who are terminally ill, delivered where possible in the environment of the person's choice, and which provides physical, psychological, emotional and spiritual support for patients' families and friends. The provision of hospice and palliative care services includes grief and bereavement support for the family and other carers during the life of the patient, continuing after death;
2. defines Voluntary Active Euthanasia (VAE) as the deliberate action to terminate life by someone other than, and at the request of, the patient concerned;
3. believes that dying is a natural process and that the refusal or withdrawal of futile treatment is not voluntary active euthanasia;
4. believes that legalisation of voluntary euthanasia is not a substitute for the proper provision of palliative care services to all Australians;
5. believes that public interest in voluntary active euthanasia reflects a concern about lack of adequate support for people who are dying, and will continue to campaign for improved services, education and research in all aspects of palliative care;
6. states that currently accepted palliative care practice does not include deliberate ending of life, even if this is requested by the patient;
7. asserts that palliative care experience shows that appropriate and effective use of morphine and other drugs for pain relief does not cause death;
8. recognises that there is a wide divergence of views about voluntary active euthanasia in Australian society, and also within the caring professions, including the palliative care community;
9. recognises and respects the fact that some people rationally and consistently request voluntary active euthanasia;
10. acknowledges that, while pain and symptoms can be addressed, complete relief is not always possible in all cases, even with optimal palliative care;
11. welcomes open and frank discussion within the community, and particularly with the health professions, about all aspects of death and dying, including voluntary active euthanasia;
12. nevertheless, due to the inherent risk to individuals and society, opposes all legalisation of euthanasia.

12 Euthanasia and the Criminal Law: What Will Sever a Causal Link?

DAVID MALCOLM[*]

The dread of something after death -
The undiscover'd country from whose bourn
No traveller returns.

Hamlet, Act III, Scene 1

Introduction

Advances in modern medicine have meant that that the twilight between when an individual enters a state of permanent unresponsiveness and death can be extended almost indefinitely. In circumstances where there is little likelihood of recovery, what is created is something that is after death, in practical terms, but before medical science and law agree that death has occurred. It is in this twilight world that medicine, law and community values have attempted to achieve some form of reconciliation over when it is appropriate to withdraw life-sustaining treatment. My analysis is directed to the question of causation in the context of euthanasia and the law. The moral and legal justification, or lack of justification, for the sanctioning of euthanasia by the State has received considerable attention in recent years. The debate over the passage of the *Rights of the Terminally Ill Act 1995* (NT) in the Northern Territory and the subsequent enactment by the Commonwealth Parliament of the *Euthanasia Laws Act 1996* (Cth), which effectively invalidated the Northern Territory legislation, is still fresh in the community's memory. It has been suggested that the introduction of

---

[*]   The Chief Justice of Western Australia.

legislation similar to that in the Northern Territory is the culmination of a steady retreat from the sanctity of life ethic which has, until now, been paramount in precedent and statute.[1]

Courts' Approach

In many cases the courts remain reluctant to hasten the death of an individual. The justification for such reluctance is as much based in a moral or cultural understanding of death as it is in the law. For example, one judge in the course of his summing up to jury on a charge of murder, arising out of what could be termed an act of euthanasia, said:

> However gravely ill a man may be ... he is entitled in our law to every hour ... that God has granted him. That hour or hours may be the most precious and most important hours of a man's life. There may be business to transact, gifts to be given, forgiveness to be made, 101 bits of unfinished business which have to be concluded.[2]

Even in those circumstances where a court has approved the withdrawal of life support facilities, judges have been at pains to point out that the question is not one of sanctioning death. As Taylor LJ said in *Re J (A Minor) (Wardship: Medical Treatment)*:

> The court never sanctions steps to terminate life. That would be unlawful. There is no question of approving, even in a case of the most horrendous disability, a course aimed at terminating life or accelerating death. The court is concerned only in which steps should not be taken to prolong life.[3]

The perception of a retreat from the primacy of the sanctity of life has been prompted largely by significant advances in medical technology. These have blurred the distinction between life and death. As one New Zealand judge has said:

> With the use of sophisticated life-support systems, life may be perpetuated well beyond the reach of the natural disease. The process of

---

[1]   R Magnusson, "The Future of the Euthanasia Debate in Australia" (1996) 20 *Melbourne University Law Review* 1108 at 1109.

[2]   *R v Carr* reported in *The Sunday Times*, 30 November 1986, p1 cited in J Mason & RA McCall Smith, *Law and Medical Ethics*, 4th edn, Butterworths, London, 1994, p317.

[3]   [1992] 3 WLR 782 at 786.

living can become the process of dying so that it is unclear whether life is being sustained or death being deferred.[4]

Definition of Death

In settling on a definition of "death" to determine when a patient has "died", the law has taken its lead from the medical profession. In 1968 a body called the Harvard Brain Death Committee published a report in the *Journal of the American Medical Association* in which the Committee noted that "responsible medical opinion" was prepared to adopt new criteria for pronouncing death in circumstances where an individual had suffered "irreversible coma as a result of permanent brain damage".[5] In 1977, the Australian Law Reform Commission recommended the introduction of a statutory definition of death that included the concept of "whole-brain death".[6] That recommendation was subsequently adopted in New South Wales,[7] Victoria[8] and Western Australia in relation to the donation of human tissue for transplant.[9] More recently, the courts have been called upon to consider the effective extension of this definition to encompass what could be termed "higher brain death" whereby the cortex has been damaged, but the brain stem continues to function.[10] The patient enters what has been termed a "persistent vegetative state" in which, while the patient may continue to breathe unaided, he or she remains unconscious and unresponsive. In those decisions, the emphasis has been placed on the quality of life which the patient can expect while he or she remains in that state, as against the argument that he or she could be pronounced "dead". This is a significant aspect of the ongoing discourse and one that I will return to shortly.

---

4   *Auckland Area Health Board v A-G* [1993] 1 NZLR 235 at 245 per Thomas J.
5   Ad Hoc Committee of the Harvard Medical School, "A Definition of Irreversible Coma" (1968) 205(6) *Journal of the American Medical Association* 85 at 87 cited in Magnusson, op cit, n1, at 1113.
6   Australian Law Reform Commission, *Human Tissue Transplants*, Report No 7, AGPS, Canberra, 1977, paras 133-7.
7   *Human Tissue Act 1983* (NSW).
8   *Human Tissue Act 1982* (Vic).
9   *Human Tissue and Transplant Act 1982* (WA), s24.
10 *Airedale National Health Services Trust v Bland* [1993] 1 All ER 821; see also *Auckland Area Health Board v A-G*, op cit, n4, dealing with Guillain-Barre Syndrome.

Freedom of Choice

Changes in medical science have also been accompanied by changes in our social or cultural approach to death. As a community, we have seen in recent years a greater emphasis placed on the importance of the freedom of choice of the individual over the responsibilities of the State. In an article in *The Age* in Victoria, one commentator noted that the debate over the Northern Territory legislation:

> [I]s about the limits of individual freedoms and the political power of the Baby Boomers, now at the age when they are beginning to contemplate their mortality. Its about an ageing population and a limited health dollar. It's about an increasingly educated population losing its awe of the medical profession.[11]

In the last thirty years there has been a rise in the acceptance of wide variations in private morality and the assertion of individual freedom of action. There has been a much greater emphasis on the rights of the individual, with correspondingly less emphasis on the obligations of the individuals to others or to society as a whole. Debates about moral questions in Australia are further complicated by a number of factors including a wide diversity of beliefs and values shared among members of our multicultural society. A common set of moral or social values has become harder to define.

While on its face, these issues appear unconnected with euthanasia, they will continue to influence the course of social, political and legal debate in the coming years. The law cannot be divorced from the community to which it is applied. In my view, in the years ahead, questions about our understanding of death and of the "quality of life" of patients, will be raised before the courts in an ever-increasing number. Suggestions that euthanasia should be available in respect of a range of illnesses or disabilities raise the possibility that it may be considered a legitimate treatment option, even for those individuals who may remain conscious of their surroundings. The position to be adopted in relation to those illnesses is of particular relevance. I note, for example, that the Human Rights and Equal Opportunity Commission has estimated that within the next four years, 200,000 Australians will be diagnosed with Alzheimer's Type Dementia. This figure will continue to increase as more and more "Baby Boomers" reach the age of 65. While the onset of dementia is distressing

---

[11] G Alcorn, "Marshall Law", *The Age* (Melbourne), 24 May 1995, p13 cited in Magnusson, op cit, n1, p1111.

for both the sufferer and his or her family, the same questions in relation to consciousness or pain do not arise as they do in relation to "whole-brain" death, or the onset of a persistent vegetative state. The challenge for the law is to strike a balance between the interests of the individual and the interests of the community.

Euthanasia

In order to understand the position that confronts the courts in determining questions of euthanasia, it is also necessary to understand the background against which such disputes are determined. It is trite that the administration of any medical procedure or treatment without first obtaining the consent of the patient may make a medical practitioner liable to criminal prosecution for assault. Where the treatment causes the death of the patient, the practitioner may be criminally liable for murder or manslaughter, regardless of whether he or she had obtained the consent of the patient. In Western Australia, apart from assault and murder, assisting a suicide is also an offence punishable by life imprisonment.[12]

In the context of "active euthanasia", that is, an act which is intended to bring about the death of a patient, the position in the United Kingdom has been put unequivocally by Lord Devlin: "If the acts done are intended to kill and do, in fact, kill, it does not matter if a life is cut short by weeks or months, it is just as much murder as if it were cut short by years."[13]

These basic principles apply regardless of the competency, the degree of disability or the seriousness of the illness of the patient.[14]

In addition to the risk of criminal liability of medical practitioners or others for actively taking steps to kill, or assist in the death of, another, in those States in which a *Criminal Code* exists, the *Code* imposes a duty on certain individuals to act to *prevent* harm to another.[15] For example, in Western Australia, s262 of the *Criminal Code* provides that:

> It is the duty of every person having charge of another who is unable by reason of age, sickness, mental impairment, detention, or any other cause, to withdraw himself from such charge, and who is unable to provide himself with the necessaries of life, whether the charge is undertaken under a contract, or is imposed by law, or arises by reason of any act,

---

12 *Criminal Code* (WA), s288.
13 H Palmer, "Dr Adams' Trial for Murder" [1957] *Crim LR* 365 at 375.
14 *Secretary, Department of Health & Community Services v JWB (Marion's Case)* (1992) 175 CLR 218.
15 See *Criminal Code* (Qld), ss285-287 at 290; *Criminal Code* (WA), ss262-264 and 267.

> whether lawful or unlawful, of the person who has such charge, to provide for that other person the necessaries of life; and he is held to have caused any consequences which result to the life or health of the other person by reason of any omission to perform that duty.

In the context of what has been termed "passive euthanasia", that is, the omission to act to prolong a patient's life, a medical practitioner may be liable for prosecution for murder or manslaughter under these provisions for failure to provide "necessaries" such as respiratory aids.

Against this background, courts have attempted to identify aspects of the act or omission leading to the death of another, which, in the case of euthanasia, would allow an accused to avoid criminal responsibility. One of the principal areas upon which the courts have focused is the causal link between the act or omission of the accused and the death of the patient or family member.

Causation and Euthanasia

Causation in criminal law is a question of fact to be determined by a jury. The jury is asked to consider, as a distinct element of the offence, whether the act or omission of the accused could be said to have caused the death of the victim.[16]

The question however becomes much more difficult where, as in the case of an act of either active or passive euthanasia, the victim's death could be attributable to more than one cause. There has been a significant divergence in the test to be applied in those circumstances to establish a causal link between the victim's death and any one action or omission. In *Royall v The Queen*,[17] McHugh J identified four different tests that had been applied in the United Kingdom without consistency, namely:

1. Whether the offender's act or omission is an "operating and substantial cause" of the victim's death.[18] In some texts, it has also been suggested that the accused's actions must be more than a *"de minimis* contribution".[19]

---

[16] *Pagett* (1983) 76 Cr App R 279 at 290-1; *Royall v The Queen* (1991) 65 ALJR 451 at 477 (per McHugh J).

[17] (1991) 65 ALJR 451 at 478.

[18] See for example *Smith v R* [1959] 2 QB 35 at 42-3 (per Lord Parker CJ).

[19] G Williams, *Textbook of Criminal Law*, 2nd edn, Stevens, London, 1983, p385.

2. Whether the victim's death is a "natural consequence" of the offender's act or omission.[20]
3. Whether the victim's death was a reasonably foreseeable consequence of the offender's act or omission.[21]
4. Whether an intervening act, or *novus actus interveniens*, could be said to have severed the causal link between the offender's act or omission and the victim's death.

In Australia, a similar degree of inconsistency is evident in some of the more recent cases on causation in criminal law. In *Royall v The Queen*,[22] for example, the majority of the members of the High Court adopted the first test identified by McHugh J but also adopted different approaches to the issue of the degree of responsibility which must be attributed to an accused in order to establish a causal link. I do not propose discussing the decision in detail as the court was not called upon to consider the question of causation as it applies to an act of euthanasia. What is of significance is the divergence of approaches to the issue of causation.

Toohey and Gaudron JJ avoided the approach of placing conditions on the assessment of a causal link. They adopted instead the approach in *Campbell v The Queen*[23] in which Burt CJ said:

> It would seem to me to be enough if juries were told that the question of cause for them to decide is not a philosophical or scientific question, but a question to be determined by them applying their common sense to the facts as they find them appreciating that the purpose of the enquiry is to attribute legal responsibility in a criminal matter.[24]

Deane and Dawson JJ also cited the judgment of Burt CJ but added a condition:

> No doubt in some cases of murder it may assist the jury if the trial judge points out not only that there must be a causal connection between the acts (or, more rarely, omissions) of the accused and the death of the deceased, but that the causal connection must be *sufficiently substantial to enable responsibility for the crime to be attributed to the accused.*[25] (emphasis added)

---

20 See for example *Beech* (1912) 7 Cr App R 197.
21 See for example *Roberts* (1971) 56 Cr App R 95 at 102 (per the court); *Mackie* (1973) 57 Cr App R 453 at 459 (per the court).
22 *Royall v The Queen* (1991) 172 CLR 378.
23 (1981) WAR 286, *Royall*, op cit, n22, at 470.
24 Ibid, at 290.
25 *Royall*, op cit, n22, at 465.

Brennan J adopted a similar approach to Deane and Dawson JJ, without making reference to *Campbell*, holding that the accused's acts or omission must "contribute significantly" to the death of the victim.[26] Adopting a more restrictive approach, Mason CJ suggested that the initial assault by the accused must be the *"primary cause* of sequential events causing death"[27] (my emphasis). In an approach that differed significantly from the other members of the court, McHugh J concentrated on the state of mind of the offender, rather than the degree of responsibility:

> In a criminal case, a person should not be held liable for a wrongful act or omission which has caused harm in a "but for" sense if that harm was the product of a novus actus interveniens or was not a reasonably foreseeable consequence of the act or omission. It goes almost without saying, however, that a person should be held liable for harm which is causally linked with his or her conduct and which he or she intended should be brought about by that conduct.[28]

The same divergent approach was again evident in the more recent High Court decision in *Osland v The Queen*,[29] although only two members considered the question of causation on that occasion. McHugh J referred to his reasons in *Royall* as the approach to be adopted in considering issues of causation.[30] Kirby J on the other hand found that the trial judge was correct in his direction to the jury that the accused's actions "should be a 'substantial cause of death'".[31]

Inconsistency or divergence on the question of causation may be a double-edged sword in the context of an act of euthanasia. The adoption of an approach that depends upon the "reasonable foreseeability" of harm may mean that, even though a patient is seriously ill, any act or omission that may hasten death would be sufficient to sustain a causal link. On the other hand, an approach that relies on an assessment of the "substantial", "significant" or "primary" cause of death may allow an offender to avoid criminal responsibility if he or she could demonstrate to a court that death was inevitable or imminent.

In the United Kingdom, the administration of pain-killers or other drugs as part of a course of palliative care, and which have the secondary effect of hastening a patient's death, has been found not to constitute a

---

26   Ibid, at 459 citing *Pagett* (1983) 76 Cr App R 279.
27   *Royall*, op cit, n22, at 457.
28   Ibid, at 481.
29   (1998) 73 ALJR 173.
30   Ibid, at 201.
31   Ibid, at 214.

criminal offence, even if the doctor knows that the death of the patient may be a likely outcome. This proposition has been attributed by some writers to the summing up by Lord Devlin in *R v Adams (Bodkin)*[32] and as having been accepted by the English courts as the doctrine of "double effect". The legal basis of the doctrine is unclear. Professor Glanville Williams suggests that Lord Devlin may have had in mind the first test identified by McHugh J in *Royall*, that is, whether the accused's actions were a "substantial cause" of the death. Professor Williams, however, adds somewhat disparagingly that "[w]e may applaud his attitude without enquiring too closely into its legal basis".[33]

The Doctrine of Double Effect

Two principal bases have been advanced as support for the doctrine of "double effect". The first basis, and one that is not without precedent, is more closely associated with the accused's intention than a causal link. Courts in the United Kingdom have accepted that an accused who does not intend, but may have reasonably foreseen the outcome of his or her act or omission, is not necessarily legally responsible for them. For example, in *Beatty v Gilbanks*,[34] the Court of Appeal found that members of the Salvation Army who regularly marched through Weston-super-Mare, were not responsible for the violent actions of others who gathered to watch.[35] At the time that *Adams* was heard, this basis also accorded with the opinion, expressed extra-judicially, of some members of the House of Lords.[36]

The approach focusing on intention has attracted criticism.[37] At common law, as it applies in the United Kingdom and in some states of Australia, an intention to commit murder may be constituted either by proof of an intention to achieve a desired result, or, proof that the offender knew that the result was a probable or likely outcome of his or her actions

---

[32] At first instance. Reported in H Palmer, "Dr Adams' Trial for Murder" [1957] *Crim LR* 365; see for example P Skegg, *Law, Ethics and Medicine*, Clarendon Press, Oxford, 1984, pp135-8; L Skene, *Law and Medical Practice*, Butterworths, Sydney, 1998, p210; I Freckelton & K Petersen (eds), *Controversies in Health Law*, Federation Press, Sydney, 1999.

[33] Williams, op cit, n19, p385.

[34] (1882) 9 QBD 308.

[35] Ibid, at 314 (per Field J).

[36] See for example the speech by Lord Jowitt, then Lord Chancellor, (1950) 169 *Parliamentary Debates*, (HL) 593 cited in Skegg, op cit, n32, 137.

[37] A Grubb, "Commentary: Attempted Murder of Terminally Ill Patient; R v Cox" (1993) 1 *Med Law Rev* 232 at 233.

and was indifferent to that probability.[38] This second aspect has been referred to as recklessness.[39] For example, the High Court in *The Queen v Crabbe*[40] held that:

> The conclusion that a person is guilty of murder if he commits a fatal act knowing that it will *probably* cause death or grievous bodily harm but (absent an intention to kill or do grievous bodily harm) is not guilty of murder if he knew only that his act *might possibly* cause death or grievous bodily harm is not only supported by a preponderance of authority but is sound in principle.[41]

Insofar as the doctrine of "double effect" would excuse a medical practitioner administering drugs in circumstances where he or she knew it was likely or probable, the approach by Lord Devlin in *Adams* is wholly inconsistent with that of the High Court in *Crabbe*. How this conflict in the authorities will be resolved remains to be seen. However, I suggest that the approach in *Crabbe* is the more persuasive decision.

Before leaving this particular issue, I note that in those states where a *Criminal Code* applies, the position is somewhat different. The concept of recklessness cannot be taken into account in dealing with the provisions relating specifically to murder.[42] Recklessness may provide the ground for a charge of criminal negligence.[43]

The Course of Illness

The second basis relates specifically to the question of causation. It is argued that the administration of drugs to a patient over and above what is required, or the active withdrawal of life-sustaining treatment, does not constitute an offence, because it is not the doctor's act which causes the death of the patient, but rather the patient's underlying illness which is the cause. The death of the patient, as a matter of law, was the natural course of the disease. This basis was discussed at length by High Court of New Zealand in *Auckland Area Health Board v Attorney-General*.[44] In that case, Mr L suffered from an extreme case of Guillain-Barre syndrome. The

---

38 *R v Nedrick* [1986] 3 All ER 1.
39 See for example *R v Jakac* [1961] VR 362.
40 (1985) 156 CLR 464.
41 Ibid, at 469 (per the court).
42 See *R v Wilmott (No 2)* [1985] 2 Qd R 406.
43 *R v O'Halloran* [1967] Qd R 1.
44 [1993] 1 NZLR 235.

effect of the illness is to sever brain functions from the rest of the body. While Mr L continued to breathe, and his circulation continued without assistance, he remained completely unresponsive. Mr L had existed in that state for 12 months and there was no likelihood of recovery. The Health Board made application for a declaration that by withdrawing life-sustaining treatment, and allowing Mr L to die, they would not be liable for prosecution for homicide. The question turned largely on the lawful excuse of doctors to withdraw life-sustaining treatment in the event that it no longer served a useful purpose in the patient's recovery. Justice Thomas endorsed the formulation of a doctor's duty in the context of palliative care by Professor Glanville Williams in his seminal text on criminal law:

> A doctor must never do anything to actively kill his patient, but he is not bound to fight for the patient's life forever. His duty in this respect is to make reasonable efforts, having regard to customary practice and expectations, and in particular having regard to the benefit of the patient to be expected from further exertions. He need not and should not crassly fix his attention upon mere heart-beats.[45]

Relying upon this formulation of a doctor's ethical duties, and in particular a duty to act in the best interests of his or her patient, Thomas J explained his analysis of the question of causation in the following terms:

> Most objective observers would accept that where a life-support system which has ceased to serve any medical purpose or benefit to the patient is withdrawn, the certain death which it had for a time arrested would be *the outcome of the original disease and not the withdrawal of the support.* To hold, therefore, that where a doctor is under no legal duty to provide that support and has a lawful excuse for withholding it, the discontinuance of the life support is not legally the cause of death is simply to make the law coincide with the perception dictated by good sense.[46] (emphasis added)

Justice Thomas makes the question of causation conditional upon, and secondary to, an assessment of the *bona fides* of the doctor's conduct. The question is not one specifically of causation, but is more closely related to "lawful excuse".

---

[45] Williams, op cit, n19, at p279 cited in *Auckland Area Health Board*, op cit, n4, p253.
[46] *Auckland Area Health Board v A-G*, op cit, n4, at 254.

Patient's Best Interests

The House of Lords adopted a similar approach in *Airedale National Health Service Trust v Bland*.[47] Their Lordships, however, expanded further upon the concept of the medical practitioner withholding treatment "in the patient's best interests". Young Anthony Bland suffered hypoxic brain damage as a result of being crushed against crowd control barriers during a riot at the Hillsborough football ground. As a result of his injuries, Anthony entered a persistent vegetative state. Although he continued to breathe, he remained unconscious and unresponsive. The bulk of his bodily functions were performed by machines or with the assistance of hospital staff. The medical authorities, with the support of Anthony's parents, had made application for approval to withdraw life-sustaining treatment, thereby hastening Anthony's death. At the time of the application, Anthony had remained unresponsive for a period of three and a half years. Lord Goff, with whom a number of the Lords agreed, made reference to the decision of Thomas J in *Auckland Area Health Board* and said:

> [I]t cannot be right that a doctor, who has under his care a patient suffering painfully from terminal cancer, should be under an absolute obligation to perform upon him major surgery to abate a condition which, if unabated, would or might shorten his life still further. The doctor who is caring for such a patient, in my opinion, cannot be under an absolute obligation to prolong his life by any means available to him, regardless of the quality of the patient's life. Common humanity requires otherwise, as do medical ethics and good medical practice accepted in this country and overseas.[48]

In the context of considering the question of causation, His Lordship went on to say:

> As I see it, the doctor's decision whether or not to take any such step must (subject to his patient's ability to give or withhold his consent) be made in the best interests of the patient. It is this principle too which, in my opinion, underlies the established rule that a doctor may, when caring for a patient, who is, for example, dying of cancer, lawfully administer painkilling drugs despite the fact that he knows that an incidental effect of that application will be to abbreviate the patient's life. *Such a decision may properly be made as part of the care of the living patient, in his best interests; and, on this basis, the treatment will be lawful. Moreover, where the doctor's treatment of his patient is lawful, the patient's death*

---

[47] [1993] AC 789; [1993] 1 All ER 821.
[48] Ibid, at 867; 868 (per Lord Goff).

> will be regarded in law as exclusively caused by the injury or disease to which the condition is attributable.[49] (emphasis added)

As in *Auckland Area Health Board*, the question of causation is linked with a question whether a medical practitioner has acted in the patient's best interests. What the decisions suggest is that if the court finds that the medical practitioner has acted against the patient's best interests, the action of the practitioner severs the causal chain between the patient's illness and death, introducing an intervening act which may be characterised as the cause of the harm.

Level of Patient's Disability

What characterises the jurisprudence to this point on euthanasia and the law is the significant level of disability or illness of the patient. Both *Auckland Area Health Board* and *Bland* highlight the futility of continuing life-sustaining care. For example, in *Auckland Area Health Board*, Thomas J noted that:

> Mr L's prognosis is now hopeless. It must be concluded that his condition is irreversible ... [A] current examination has confirmed that the degeneration is continuing and that there is no sign of improvement.[50]

Hoffman LJ in *Bland* drew attention to the quality of life of Anthony Bland:

> There is no question of his life being worth living or not worth living because the stark reality is that Anthony Bland is not living a life at all. None of the things that one says about the way people live their lives – well or ill, with courage or fortitude, happily or sadly – have any meaning in relation to him.[51]

In both cases the court was presented with a bleak prognosis of the patient's future. In one, the patient had been in a persistent vegetative state for more than twelve months. In the other, the patient had been in a similar state for more than three years. It is arguable that in both cases the patient was at the extreme end of the spectrum in terms of the seriousness of his illness. What of those situations in which the patient remains responsive,

---

49   Ibid.
50   *Auckland Area Health Board*, op cit, n4, at 240.
51   *Airedale National Health Service Trust v Bland*, op cit, n10, at 855.

but his or her quality of life is slowly deteriorating, as is the case in the context of motor neurone disease? Alternatively, what if the patient has a normal life expectancy, but his or her quality of life is seriously affected, as is the case, for example, where the patient suffers from severe quadriplegia or Alzheimer's type dementia?

In those cases where the patient lacks capacity to consent, or, as is more likely the case, to direct that treatment be withheld, the courts will carefully scrutinise a decision that is made by a person with impaired mental capacity. For example, in *Re C (adult: refusal of medical treatment)*[52] a 68 year old patient suffering from paranoid schizophrenia developed gangrene in one of his feet, but refused to consent to the amputation of his leg below the knee, notwithstanding medical advice that his chance of survival without amputation was only 15 per cent. The court upheld the patient's decision to refuse the treatment, but only after being satisfied that he had comprehended the treatment information which his doctor had given him, had believed it and had weighed it in the balance in arriving at the decision which he had made.[53]

Substitute Decision-Making

In addition to contemporaneous decisions or directions given by a mentally impaired adult, consent may be withheld or given either by the patient's court-appointed guardian or from a written instrument executed by the patient before he or she became incompetent.

In Australia, all states except Queensland have legislation allowing a guardian to be appointed to manage the affairs and property of an intellectually disabled individual. Whether the power to consent, or withhold consent, to a medical procedure would extend to a course of action which may lead to the death of the individual in whose interests they act is doubtful. The power has been limited in some respects by the courts. For example, in *Secretary, Department of Health and Community Services v JWB and SMB (Marion's Case)*, the High Court found that the parents of an incompetent child could not consent to her sterilisation, that consent being outside the scope of the parental power. Mason CJ, Dawson, Toohey and Gaudron JJ adopted as their starting point the fact that sterilisation was "invasive, irreversible and major surgery".[54] They then listed three principal factors which justified the court's role in sanctioning the

---

52 [1994] 1 All ER 819.

53 *Re C (adult: refusal of medical treatment)* [1994] 1 All ER 819 at 824.

54 *Marion's Case*, op cit, n14, at 250.

proposed procedure, namely, the complexity of the question of consent, the involvement of complex medical procedures and the possibility of conflict between the child's interests and the independent interests of the parents and other family members.[55] Subject to the overriding criterion of the welfare of the child, the interests of others, particularly the primary care giver, are relevant to the decision. The court's involvement ensures that in the case of conflict, the interests of the child will prevail.

Given the High Court's reluctance to allow parental consent to be given to a procedure not designed to bring about death, it is unlikely that the court will allow simple consent to be given by a parent or guardian for an act of active or passive euthanasia without a court's supervision. In the absence of that consent, I consider that the court would apply the same or similar principles to those that I have discussed in relation to *Marion's Case*.

The Right to Refuse Treatment

In the case of passive euthanasia or the withdrawal of treatment from *competent* adults, the starting point is the right at common law to refuse treatment. The clearest statement of that right is contained in the judgment of McHugh J in *Marion's Case* who observed that:

> It is the central thesis of the common law doctrine of trespass to the person that the voluntary choices of an adult person of sound mind concerning what is or is not done to his or her body must be respected and accepted, irrespective of what others, including doctors, may think is in the best interests of that particular person.[56]

The acceptance of this "right" at common law may also provide an excuse at criminal law. In Western Australia, where a competent patient has been fully informed of the options available in the context of their ongoing treatment, and refuses to give consent, a medical practitioner is relieved of his or her duty to the patient.[57] This is particularly significant in the context of the criminal sanctions that apply to an omission. In the absence of a duty to the patient, a medical practitioner may not be held liable for his or her failure to provide "necessaries".[58]

---

[55]   Ibid, at 251-2.
[56]   Ibid, at 309.
[57]   Western Australian Law Reform Commission, *Medical Treatment for the Dying*, Project No 84, (1991), paras 1.11 and 1.12.
[58]   See s262, *Criminal Code* (WA) and discussion above.

In the United Kingdom[59] and Canada,[60] the courts have given recognition to the provision of anticipatory or advance directives by individuals concerning the method of treatment to be adopted in the event of a terminal illness before they become incompetent. An assessment of the validity and weight of that direction is difficult. For example, in *Re: T (adult: refusal of medical treatment)*,[61] Lord Donaldson MR provided some guide with how best to deal with a contemporaneous direction by a patient:

> Doctors faced with a refusal of consent have to give very careful and detailed consideration to the patient's capacity to decide at the time when the decision was made. It may not be the simple case of the patient having no capacity because, for example, at that time he had hallucinations. It may be the more difficult case of a temporarily reduced capacity at the time when his decision was made. What matters is that the doctors should consider whether at that time he had a capacity which was commensurate with the gravity of the decision which he purported to make. The more serious the decision, the greater the capacity required. If the patient had the requisite capacity, they are bound by his decision. If not, they are free to treat him in what they believe to be his best interests.[62]

Some states in Australia have enacted legislation to provide a mechanism for competent adults to ensure that their right to refuse treatment is respected, even after they become incompetent.[63] Each model differs slightly, but what is common is that the statement must be in the correct, prescribed written form and witnessed by one or two other individuals, thereby providing some weight to the anticipatory direction. In Western Australia, similar legislation was introduced into Parliament in 1991 but not proceeded with after the Second Reading in the Lower House.[64] It was restored to the Notice Paper in 1996 and passed through the Committee stage. It has not since been taken any further.

In the United States, further developments have accompanied the recognition of a common law right to refuse treatment. Utilising the reference to a "right", recent decisions have canvassed the existence of an implied constitutional "right to die". The development is a significant one.

---

[59] *Airedale National Health Service*, op cit, n10; *Re T (adult: refusal of medical treatment)* [1991] 4 All ER 649.
[60] *Malette v Shulman* (1990) 67 DLR (4th) 321.
[61] [1991] 4 All ER 649.
[62] Ibid, at 661-2.
[63] *Medical Treatment Act 1994* (ACT); *Natural Death Act 1988* (NT); *Consent to Medical Treatment and Palliative Care Act 1995* (SA); *Medical Treatment Act 1988* (Vic).
[64] *Medical Care of the Dying Bill 1991* (WA).

It lends immeasurable weight to an advance directive that treatment is to be withheld in certain circumstances.

There is no express constitutional or common law "right to die" sanctioned by the courts in the United States. Both state Courts of Appeal and the Supreme Court of the United States have held that the touching of another person without his or her consent constitutes the tort of trespass or the tort of battery. In essence, the tort has been explained as arising out of a proprietary interest of the individual in his or her own body. For example, the Supreme Court has said that "[n]o right is held more sacred, or is more carefully guarded, by the common law, than the right of every individual to the possession and control of his own person, free from all restraint or interference of others, unless by clear and unquestionable authority by law."[65]

The "right" referred to by the Supreme Court has also been referred to as a "right of self-determination".[66] The notion of bodily integrity has since been embodied in the requirement that informed consent is generally required for medical treatment. The Court of Appeals of New York has stated the principle as follows:

> Every human being of adult years and sound mind has a right to determine what shall be done with his own body; and a surgeon who performs an operation without his patient's consent commits an assault, for which he is liable in damages.[67]

In the 1990 decision, *Cruzan v Director, Missouri Department of Health*, Rehnquist CJ observed that the doctrine of informed consent had become firmly entrenched in United States tort law.[68] A right to refuse treatment, or the right to withhold consent, with the potential that it may cause the death of the patient, has been found to be the natural corollary of the doctrine of informed consent.[69]

Until the late 1970s and early 1980s refusal of treatment cases were relatively rare. Where they did occur, they were largely based on the patient's right constructed at common law to withhold consent. In 1976, the direction of the development of this right underwent a reassessment. In *In Re Quinlan*,[70] the father of a woman who had entered what is termed a

---

[65] *Union Pacific R Co v Botsford*, 141 US 250 at 251 (1891).
[66] See for example *In re Conroy*, 486 A 2d 1209 (1985).
[67] *Schloendorff v Society of New York Hospital*, 211 NY 125 at 129 (1914) (per Cardozo J).
[68] *Cruzan v Director, Missouri Department of Health*, 497 US 261 at 269 (1990).
[69] Ibid, at 262.
[70] 355 A 2d 647 (1976).

"persistent vegetative state" following a car accident made application for judicial approval to disconnect his daughter's respirator. The New Jersey Supreme Court granted the application on the basis that Ms Quinlan's constitutional right to privacy, rather than a common law right to withhold consent, allowed her to refuse or terminate treatment.[71] There is no express right to privacy guaranteed by the United States Constitution. The Court acknowledged that:

> Although the Constitution does not explicitly mention a right of privacy, Supreme Court decisions have recognised that a right of personal privacy is guaranteed under the Constitution ... Presumably this right is broad enough to encompass a patient's decision to decline medical treatment under certain circumstances.[72]

The Court however recognised that the right was not absolute and balanced it against the state's interest in the preservation of life, proposing a "sliding scale" whereby the state's interest "weakens and the individual's right to privacy grows as the degree of bodily invasion grows and the prognosis dims."[73]

In *Superintendent of Belchertown State School v Saikewicz*,[74] the Supreme Court of Massachusetts relied on both a right to privacy and the doctrine of informed consent to permit the withholding of chemotherapy from a profoundly retarded 67 year old man.[75] It has been suggested that the decisions in relation to a right to privacy constitute a move away from the common law to a constitutional basis, thereby suggesting the creation of hybrid or "para" right to die.[76] A careful reading of the State decisions in the United States, however, reveals that this observation is incorrect. The extent of the right to privacy remains uncertain. The development of the law relating to refusal of treatment has proceeded largely on the basis of the tortious principles of trespass and battery and the so-called right to self-determination.[77]

More recently, the question of a right grounded in constitutional principles has been revived by reference to the Fourteenth Amendment of the United States *Constitution*, namely, the constitutional provision that no

---

[71] Ibid, at 662-4.
[72] Ibid, at 663.
[73] Ibid, at 664.
[74] 370 NE 2d 417 (1977).
[75] Ibid, at 424.
[76] A Meisel, *The Right to Die*, Wiley, New York, 1989, p49; see also R Dworkin, *Life's Dominion: an argument about abortion, euthanasia, and individual freedom*, Knopf, New York, 1993, pp218ff.
[77] See, for example, *In re Estate of Longeway*, 549 NE 2d 292 (1989).

State shall deprive any person of his or her life, liberty or property without due process of law. In *Cruzan*, the Supreme Court was called upon to decide whether the Fourteenth Amendment created a constitutional right to refuse unwanted medical treatment. The Supreme Court reviewed a number of its own decisions in relation to the Fourteenth Amendment and found that: "The principle that a competent person has a constitutionally protected liberty interest in refusing unwanted medical treatment may be inferred from our prior decisions."[78]

The elevation of the ability of an individual to refuse treatment to a constitutional right has not been accepted in any other jurisdiction, even where similar express constitutional rights exist. What this process does reflect, however, is the change in community attitudes which I discussed in my introduction. These influences will continue to be brought to bear, in even greater weight, in the coming years. How they will influence the development of the law in Australia is a matter of speculation. One thing is certain. This is a developing area of jurisprudence in which the courts, the medical profession and the community have a deep and continuing interest.

---

[78] *Cruzan*, op cit, n68, at 278.

13 Issues of Medical and Legal Causation Relating to Alzheimer's Disease

ROBERT HELME AND DANUTA MENDELSON*

Introduction

Biological, physical and environmental factors can cause or induce all kinds of medical conditions, including dementia, in humans, apes or mice. In contradistinction, only humans can cause or produce legally binding directives and instruments. In private law, these include testamentary and *inter vivos* dispositions, as well as directions about medical treatment. Thus, the discourse of causation differs in medicine and law. Issues of causation in the two disciplines intersect, however, when the validity of a transaction, a disposition or executed instrument is questioned on the ground of legal competence. The issue is complicated by the fact that the medical nature of dementia is yet to be fully ascertained, and that its progress and symptoms are often misunderstood.

The law presumes that adults of "sound mind" are legally competent. Consequently, an otherwise binding decision may not be followed when the presumption of "sound mind" is displaced. The terms "sound mind" and competence are not part of medical nosology. They refer to a person's legal status: his or her cognitive competence to make valid dispositions and binding decisions. Competence can only be determined by a judge or an administrative body empowered to make guardianship decisions. Psychiatrists or a psychologists may be called in to assist in ascertaining

* Robert Helme, Former Director of the National Ageing Research Institute, North West Hospital, Parkville, Victoria, Professorial Associate, Department of Medicine of the Royal Melbourne Hospital, Chairman of the Parkville Campus of the North West Hospital Special Clinical School. Danuta Mendelson, Senior Lecturer at the School of Law at Deakin University.

someone's decision-making capacity.[1] In the eyes of the law then, the cause of change in the validity of a person's dispositions and decisions is a lack of competence. Medicine may provide a diagnosis and an explanation of the condition that impaired the person's decision-making capacity, however, the aetiology – the precise medical cause of the condition, is usually only of secondary interest to this area of the law.

Yet an understanding of the nature of dementia and its nuances can be vital in determining a person's competence. This is because the concept of legal competence traditionally refers to the person's cognitive capacity "to understand and process information so that a decision can be made and communicated",[2] and dementia is a cognitive disorder characterised by gradual onset and continuing cognitive decline. However, the process of this decline fluctuates, and, as will be discussed below, a demented person may retain reasonable cognitive capacity in relation to certain life activities but not others.[3] Consequently, a mere diagnosis of dementia cannot not of itself pre-determine the issue of competence.

Alzheimer's disease is presently considered to be the most common cause of dementia.[4] The vast majority of persons previously labelled as suffering senility prove to have Alzheimer's disease. The prevalence of this disease in all countries where data are available, including Australia,[5] increases exponentially from 1 per cent of those aged 60 to more than 30 per cent of those aged 80. It is estimated that by 2021, there will be 2.26 million Australians aged over 65, or 12 percent of the population. The number of Australians over 80 years old has grown from 260,000 in 1991 to a projected 560,000 in 2001, and will grow to 790,000 in 2021.[6] The legal issue of competence involves a medical understanding of capacity to

---

[1]   PS Appelbaum & TG Gutheil, *Clinical Handbook of Psychiatry and the Law*, 2nd edn, Williams & Wilkins, Baltimore, 1991; S Crowe, "Forensic Neuropsychology" in I Freckelton & H Selby (eds), *Expert Evidence*, Law Book Co, Sydney, 1993-....

[2]   JE Rein, "Ethics and the Questionably Competent Client: What the Model Rules Say and Don't Say" (1998) 9 *Stanford Law & Policy Rev* 241 at 242.

[3]   Dementia usually leads to death in a severely debilitated, immobile state between four and fifteen years after its onset: American Psychiatric Association, *Diagnostic and Statistical Manual of Mental Disorders – DSM-IV-TR*, American Psychiatric Association, Washington, DC, 2000.

[4]   Alzheimer's Type Dementia is the major cause of dementia (70 per cent), however, dementia can also be produced by stroke, which damages patches of the brain and produces "multi-infarct" dementia. Dementia may also be caused by AIDS, Huntington's Chorea, Parkinson's disease, or by alcohol-induced brain damage.

[5]   AF Jorm & AS Henderson, *Dementia in Australia*, Department of Health and Family Services, Australian Government Publishing Service, Canberra, 1998.

[6]   Human Rights and Equal Opportunity Commission, *Human Rights and Mental Illness. Report of the National Inquiry into the Human Rights of People with Mental Illness*, Australian Government Publishing Service, Canberra, 1993, at p510.

consent to matters relating to medical treatment and decisions relating to wealth transfer through *inter vivos* and testamentary dispositions. The growing importance of such an understanding is highlighted by rapidly growing costs to society associated with the health and welfare of older people and the high proportion of wealth owned by this age group.[7] Health and welfare costs increase approximately five-fold for persons over 65 years of age over younger adults. Conversely, it is estimated that most of Britain's and Australia's wealth is owned by these same people.

In several jurisdictions legislative attempts have been made to deal with the issue of consent to and refusal of medical treatment by incompetent persons. The enactments usually provide for appointment of agents with enduring medical powers of attorney.[8] These instruments, however, can be executed only by persons of "sound mind". In cases where dementia has rendered the person incompetent, a legal guardian with power to make medical decision on behalf of the patient may be appointed by a superior court of record under its inherent *parens patriae* jurisdiction, a Guardianship Board or Tribunal. Issues of wealth transfer are regulated under succession and probate legislation. Some jurisdictions have provisions that enable courts to authorise wills for mentally incompetent persons.[9] Dispositions of vulnerable and mentally impaired persons are also protected by common law actions of duress and fraud, and by equitable remedies of unconscionability and undue influence. This chapter will focus on only two aspects of medical and legal causation relating to Alzheimer's disease – questions of decisional competence relating to refusal and withdrawal of medical treatment, and issues of competence and decisional capacity relating to *inter vivos* and testamentary dispositions in the context of the equitable doctrines of unconscionability and undue influence.

---

[7]   *OECD Economic Surveys, 1998-1999*, Australia, 1999.

[8]   Legislation providing for statutory agency under enduring powers of attorney for medical treatment have been enacted in Victoria, South Australia, Northern Territory and South Australia: Medical Treatment Act 1988 (Vic) s 6; Consent to Medical Treatment and Palliative Care Act 1995 (SA) ss 7 and 8; Natural Death Act 1988 (NT) s 4; Medical Treatment Act 1994 (ACT) ss 6 and 13. In New South Wales and Tasmania, as well as in Victoria, Guardianship Acts provide for surrogate decisions with respect to medical treatment to be made by especially appointed guardians on behalf of an incompetent patient.

[9]   Mental Health Act 1983 (UK) Part VII; Wills Act 1936 (SA) s 7; Wills Act 1997 (Vic) s 21.

Legal Tests of Competence

Not surprisingly, given its socio-economic importance, the jurisprudence of legal competence for the purposes of private law[10] was initially developed in the area of testamentary law. Sound mind is a prerequisite of testamentary capacity.[11] In *Greenwood v Greenwood*[12] and *Harwood v Baker*,[13] English courts provided an undemanding test of competence or "sound mind". It required testators to know: the nature and extent of their property; the natural objects of their bounty, and how the will disposed of their property. They also were required to have the ability to make a rational plan for the disposition of the property.[14] Once these criteria were met, testators were considered to be of sound mind, and were free to make eccentric or unusual dispositions. The notion of "sound mind" was negatively defined by Lord Cockburn CJ in *Banks v Goodfellow*.[15] His Lordship wrote that:

> It is essential ... that no disorder of his [the testator's] mind should poison his affections, pervert his sense of right, or prevent the exercise of his natural faculties – that no insane delusions shall influence his will in disposing of his property and bring about a disposal of it, which if the mind had been sound, would not have been made.[16]

Lord Cockburn thus defined testamentary capacity in terms of absence of two inter-related "disorders of mind". The first relates to the testator's emotional, moral and cognitive capacity ("poisoning of affections"; "perverting" of the sense of right; impairment in the exercise of "natural faculties"). The second, in the form of "insane delusions", relates to cognition, and could be described as a psychiatric disorder. More recently, "insane delusions" have been re-interpreted as beliefs and ideations that are

---

10 In criminal law, the rules of criminal insanity in *McNaghten's Case* (1843) 10 Cl & F 200; 8 ER 718 provide the legal test for the plea of insanity defence. See D Mawson, "Specific defences to a criminal charge: assessment for court" in R Bluglass & P Bowden (eds), *Principles and Practice of Forensic Psychiatry*, Churchill Livingstone, Edinburgh, 1990. O Wood & GL Certoma, *Succession. Commentary and Materials*, Law Book Co, Sydney, 1990.

11 The testator must be of sound mind at the time of signing the will: *Marquess of Winchester's Case* (1598) 6 Co Rep 23a; *Arthur v Bokenham* (1708) 11 Mod Rep 148.

12 *Greenwood v Greenwood* (1790) 163 ER 930.

13 *Harwood v Baker* (1840) 13 ER 117.

14 LA Frolik, "The Biological Roots of the Undue Influence Doctrine: What's Love Got To Do With It?" (1996) 57 *U Pitt L Rev* 841 at 849.

15 *Banks v Goodfellow* (1870) 5 QB 549; followed in Australia in *In Will of Wilson* (1897) 23 VLR 197; *Timbury v Coffee* (1941) 66 CLR 277.

16 *Banks v Goodfellow* at 565.

"not capable of rational explanation or amenable to reason, and ... not explicable by reference to the subject person's education and culture."[17] However, the mere presence of a "disorder of mind" is not sufficient to displace the presumption of "sound mind", and hence testamentary capacity.[18] To ground invalidity, such delusions, poisoned affections, etc, *must influence the person's will in disposing of the property*, in a way in which he or she would not have done otherwise. The standard for determining the existence of testamentary capacity is therefore subjective. The question is not how a reasonable person in the shoes of the testator would have decided to dispose of the property in question, but what the actual testator would have done, absent the "disorder of mind".

Thus the test of competence for testamentary capacity, involves the person's intellectual capacity to understand, weigh and consider the nature of the proposed course of action.[19] For example, in *Banks v Goodfellow*, the testator though convinced that he was pursued by evil spirits, nevertheless had the capacity to attend to his financial affairs and had given clear and rational instructions for his will, which left the greater part of his fortune to the niece who had looked after him. His will was challenged by other members of the family, but it was held that it was valid, on the basis that an "insane delusion" from which the testator suffered did not influence his capacity to make testamentary dispositions.[20]

Finally, "free will" in the sense of autonomy – the ability to form independent judgment – is also a prerequisite for both, valid property dispositions and binding directions regarding medical treatment.

Thus there are three cumulative legal standards which test the validity of binding dispositions and directions: absence of "internal" coercion of the will through "disorder of mind"; absence of external coercion of the person's will by other parties; and the cognitive competence to understand

---

[17] *Re Hodges* (1988) 14 NSWLR 698 at 706 per Powell J; applied in *Re Crichton*, (unreported, Supreme Court of New South Wales, Probate Division, 22 July 1994), and in *Re Crooks* (unreported, Supreme Court of New South Wales, Probate Division, 4 December 1994).

[18] See further J Devereux, "Competence to Make Decisions" in I Freckelton & K Petersen (eds), *Controversies in Health Law*, Federation Press, Sydney, 1999.

[19] HJ Bursztajn, HP Harding, TG Gutheil & A Brodsky, "Beyond Cognition: the Role of Disordered Affective States in Impairing Competence to Consent to Treatment" (1991) 19 *Bulletin of the American Academy of Psychiatry and Law* 383.

[20] In NSW, the court held that being a protected person under the Protected Estates Act 1983 (NSW) did not of itself raise a conclusive presumption of incompetence to make a will: *Perpetual Trustee Co Ltd v Fairlie-Cunninghame* (1993) 32 NSWLR 377. Likewise, in the American case of *In re Estate of Gentry*, 573 P 2d 322 (Or Ct App 1978), it was held that the testator who was suffering from schizophrenia and was under a guardianship was lucid, and therefore competent to execute and sign a will.

the subject-matter of the decision. Several major questions arise in relation to these tests. The first concerns the applicability of general legal standards for valid medical treatment decisions of persons with intricate cognitive and affective disorders caused by dementia. The second is a jurisprudential issue of the tension between the importance of individual autonomy in lawful decisions regarding one's property[21] on the one hand, and law's willingness to invalidate or vary *inter vivos* and testamentary dispositions on the other.[22] Underlying these questions is the problem of how the courts and physicians interpret behavioural, cognitive, affective and expressive aspects of dementia. The final legal question posed is whether the present tests of competence and sound mind are appropriate to safeguard the interests of persons diagnosed with dementia.

Medical Nature of Dementia

Alzheimer's disease is but one cause of dementia. Indeed, it has been postulated that there are a number of Alzheimer's diseases and that they occur simultaneously with other pathologic forms of dementia. When severe, the diagnosis of this and other dementias is easily made. In its earliest stages, however, even the most skilled clinicians remain unsure. This has led to a classification of severity of 0.5, 1, 2 and 3, where 1, 2 and 3 correspond to mild, moderate and severe degrees of the disease. The category of 0.5 is unsure territory, where the diagnosis may be that of normality within a wide range of functional ability; examples of which might include eccentricity, senile squalor syndrome and age-associated memory impairment. Once the examiner is sure that cognitive impairment is present, other diagnostic dilemmas arise. Firstly, there are the more than 150 documented causes of dementia to be considered. Some, such as depression, the effects of concomitant medication, and intercurrent illness which may lead to acute or subacute brain failure or delirium, must be excluded by history and laboratory investigation, and specific treatments need to be instituted.

The clinical course of a patient with Alzheimer's disease is most easily judged at a distance in place and time. The attentive observer, however, is always impressed by fluctuation in cognitive and emotional abilities,

---

21 JW de Furia Jr, in "Testamentary Gifts Resulting from Meretricious Relationships: Undue Influence or Natural Beneficence?" (1989) 64 *Notre Dame L Rev* 200 at 200 noted that "freedom of testamentary disposition has been described as one of the basic tenets of our social structure."

22 *Nattrass v Nattrass* [1999] WASC 77 (25 June 1999).

whether globally or individually, from moment to moment, hour to hour, day to day and week to week. Intercurrent reversible illnesses compound this fluctuation. This makes the task of judging competence particularly difficult. The final diagnosis of Alzheimer's disease depends on histological examination, a facility rarely present during life because brain biopsy is not generally accepted as a routine investigation in most western countries given the potential for serious associated morbidity. At best, clinical diagnosis is associated with only a ninety per cent sensitivity and specificity for assured diagnosis. The judgment of pathologists as the final gold standard arbiter has also been questioned, and found to be less than hundred percent reliable. This is not surprising when it is realised that the aetiology and pathogenesis of this disease remain uncertain.

Dementia is a behavioural syndrome best thought of as a consequence of chronic brain failure. There is an assumption that the affected individual has previously had sufficient intellectual capacity to function as a normal independent member of the community. Increasing age is associated with diminished organ structure and function (including brain function), which is a consequence of the biological processes of ageing, age-associated disease, disuse, and short and long term latent effects of environmental stimuli. Current medical understanding of the processes underlying these factors is limited. There is a limited capacity to measure the effects of each factor, the relative contribution one makes to the other, and any interactions between them. Clinical assessment and diagnosis depend on observation of the signs of the condition, asking the patient or a carer about symptoms; obtaining social and family history from the patient or a carer, and, performing physical examination and laboratory investigations. With a wide range of acceptable errors to each of these components, statistically inevitable multiplication of these errors in identifying a single cause for a decline in function, it is easy to understand that diagnostic precision and an ability to monitor the indicia of well being are low in the practice of medicine for older people. This situation is compounded by interaction of the several disease states, and discrete treatments for all or some of them, that are usually present in the older person.[23]

---

[23] DS Fairweather & AJ Campbell, "Diagnostic Accuracy: The Effects of Multiple Aetiology and the Degradation of Information in Old Age" (1991) 25 *J Royal College Physicians of London* 105.

Refusal, Withholding and Withdrawal of Medical Treatment

Patients with Alzheimer's disease and their carers are also faced with the effects of ageing biology, disuse and environment. One pertinent example is the paradox whereby the use of narcotic analgesics may worsen pain in such a person. Pain is a sensory, emotional and cognitive experience. We all make cognitive appraisals of noxious stimuli which are compared to beliefs we have about their influence. Generally, coping strategies that lead to positive behaviours tend to reduce pain: we wince, limp, go to the doctor, take analgesics and reason that the pain must not otherwise dominate our lives. These abilities are not so available to the patient with Alzheimer's disease. For example, patients working at the limit of their cognitive ability may refuse medication. In such cases, the side-effects of a narcotic on cognition, and thereby coping capacity, may outweigh its analgesic effect. A further complication is their manifestation in opposite ways in different patients, or even in the same patient: consistent screaming at one time, deathly silence and inactivity at another. Both are manifestations of suffering.

With regard to cognitive losses, inability to change concept is often the easiest loss to document objectively, and is usually associated with a particular decline in capacity for self-care. It also means that a person may well, and repeatedly, understand a line of reasoning at one point in time, but an examiner may be unable to demonstrate a similar understanding at a similar level of complexity when the patient is examined serially, or at another time. Understanding of these clinical features of dementia is particularly important in cases where the patient refuses life-saving medical treatment or requests euthanasia. Modern common law jurisprudence has developed a doctrine of inviolability of individual decisions regarding one's body.[24] Under the law of trespass to the person, a competent adult patient has the right to make a voluntary choice whether to refuse or consent to any medical intervention, including life-saving or life-sustaining treatment.[25] The right to refuse life-saving or life-sustaining medical treatment is commonly referred to as the "right to die". Lord Mustill in the *Airedale NHS Trust v Bland* expressed this rule in the following terms:

> If the patient is capable of making a decision on whether to permit treatment and decides not to permit it his choice must be obeyed, even if on any objective view it is contrary to his best interests. A doctor has no

---

[24] *Schloendorff v Society of New York Hospital*, 105 NE 92 at 93 (1914).
[25] *Secretary, Department of Health & Community Services (NT) v JWB and SMB (Marion's case)* (1992) 175 CLR 218.

right to proceed in the face of objection, even if it is plain to all, including the patient, that adverse consequences and even death will or may ensue.[26]

The rule is based on the notion that with regard to voluntary decisions of competent adults, "the principle of the sanctity of human life must yield to the principle of self-determination."[27] In relation to patients with mild to moderate dementia, the undemanding criterion of competence may well be fulfilled enabling them to make valid decisions to refuse medical treatment. Common examples of such decisions include requests for institution or withdrawal of mechanical life-sustaining treatments, the use of antibiotics, antidepressants, fluids and food, and restraint. Yet many patients with mild dementia have a syndrome known as "word-finding difficulty". They are often unable to articulate ideas (expressive aphasia), or to apprehend (internalise) ways of reasoning other than the one they have adopted. The vocabulary of such patients is very limited. Therefore, once they have articulated an idea, they keep reiterating it, as if "stuck" in the groove of their narrow and rigid conceptual framework. It is in this context that repeated requests for euthanasia or repeated denials of a medical condition and refusal of life-saving medical treatment need to be understood.

Frequently, mild to moderate dementia is co-morbid with depression, which is an affective disorder.[28] This raises an ethical dilemma associated with the first generation of medications known to influence cognition and behaviours in patients with Alzheimer's disease. These medications are only of partial benefit in that they do not arrest cognitive decline. Difficult medical decisions that must made include a judgment on whether it is appropriate to prolong depression in patients with mild to moderate disease who still have insight into their condition, and when to withdraw treatment in someone of moderate to severe impairment knowing that their decline will probably accelerate?[29] The legal causative conundrum is whether

---

26 *Airedale NHS Trust v Bland* [1993] AC 789 at 891.

27 Ibid, at 864 per Lord Goff of Chieveley. See also 826-7 (Hoffmann LJ).

28 A person's "affect" refers to his or her immediate emotional experience. In psychiatric practice, subjective affective sensations such as pleasure, displeasure, irritation, etc, as reported by the patient are equivalent to symptoms; the observed mood and affective display (anger, joy, sadness, hurt, etc) serve as objective signs. The term "mood" refers to a more sustained and less flexible mental state over a longer period of time. In depression, the affective sensations are often shallow, inadequate or flattened: R Ketal, "Affect, Mood, Emotion and Feeling: Semantic Considerations" (1975) 132 *Am J Psychiatry* 1215.

29 The rationale for the Commonwealth government, and hence our society, to underwrite the cost of these medications is currently the cost-savings in delaying and thus shortening residential care.

continuation of depression or acceleration of dementive process should be ascribed to the underlying illness or the medical decision to withdraw the medication. The common law's approach to causation is not settled.[30] However, it is agreed that "in the realm of negligence, causation is essentially a question of fact, to be resolved as a matter of common sense."[31] Consequently, the court, presumably, would regard dementia rather than the physician's decision to withdraw the medication to be the legal cause of the patient's condition.

With all patients who have early (0.5) to moderate (2) dementia, great caution is needed to ascertain whether their decisions and statements adequately reflect their affective state. Given the difficulties of psychiatric assessment, when a person refuses medical treatment while expressing the wish to die, the right to exercise this choice should be held paramount only after a very careful consideration of the way in which the decision was made, and its social, emotional and organic context. In the case of *In re T*,[32] Lord Donaldson MR suggested the following four rules pertaining to the patient's capacity to make legally binding choices concerning medical treatment:

> (1) Prima facie every adult has the right and capacity to decide whether or not he will accept medical treatment, even if a refusal may risk permanent injury to his health or even lead to premature death. Furthermore, it matters not whether the reasons for the refusal were rational or irrational, unknown or even non-existent. This is so, notwithstanding the very strong public interest in preserving the life and health of all citizens. However, the presumption of capacity to decide, which stems from the fact that the patient is an adult, is rebuttable. (2) An adult patient may be deprived of his capacity to decide by long-term mental incapacity ... (3) If an adult patient did not have the capacity to decide at the time of the purported refusal and still does not have that capacity, it is the duty of the doctors to treat him in whatever way they consider, in the exercise of clinical judgment, to be in his best interests. (4) Doctors faced with a refusal of consent have to give very careful and detailed consideration to what was the patient's capacity to decide at the time when the decision was made. It may not be a case of capacity or no capacity. It may be a case of reduced capacity. What matters is whether at that time the patient's capacity was reduced below the level needed in the case of a refusal of that importance, for refusals can vary in importance. Some may involve a risk to life or of irreparable damage to health. Others may not."[33]

---

[30]   *Chappel v Hart* (1998) 195 CLR 232.
[31]   *Bennett v Minister of Community Welfare* (1992) 176 CLR 408 at 412–413.
[32]   *In re T (Refusal of Medical Treatment)* [1992] 3 WLR 782.
[33]   Ibid, at 797.

In short, persons with dementia should not be treated against their will, but neither should life-saving treatment be withheld from them because their condition has made them incapable of expressing their actual wishes. The "facts" that contribute to a particular behavioural outcome in a patient with Alzheimer's disease should always be subject to close analysis to ensure that interpretations are not contaminated by unrealistic expectations of cognitive performance from a diseased brain. Indeed, behaviours in patients with Alzheimer's disease may be entirely the opposite of what might be expected from a normal adult. To complicate matters further, the demented person may have windows of lucidity when they may be judged competent to make decisions for themselves, or they may at various times during the course of the disease, be able to make decisions in some matters but not others.

In severe cases, losses associated with frontal lobe are often accompanied by positive physical signs of a reflex nature and which remain unrecognised or misinterpreted by observers. These include grasp reflexes, sucking responses, and blepharospasm or involuntary prolonged eye closure following visual threat. In cases where the patient is connected to life-supports, grasp reflexes whereby the patient pulls out alimentation tubes are often misinterpreted as an indication that he or she wishes to have them withdrawn. In fact, however, these patients are incompetent, and their movements do not reflect cognitive awareness or intellectual insight. In relation to persons with severe dementia, the decision to withdraw life-sustaining treatment should not be made on the basis that the patient "demonstrated" a wish to refuse further treatment, but in accordance with the doctrine of best interests, taking into consideration the appropriateness of the treatment and its therapeutic burdens and benefits.

Unconscionable Conduct and Undue Influence

As noted above, dementia manifests as a slowly progressive loss of cognitive ability over many months to as many as 15 years. The disorder is characterised by loss of cognitive and emotional control which are functions of the cerebral cortex, the largest component of the human brain. Thus memory, language, complicated motor and sensory tasks and visuo-spatial performance become noticeably impaired. Most of the cerebral cortex of the frontal lobes, however, is concerned with executive functions that underlie complex behaviours such as judgment, reasoning and ability to change concepts. The manifestations of dementia depend on intellectual and practical demands made of the individual. Early in the clinical course, and sometimes for years, external demands may imperceptibly reduce, so that decline in cognitive ability goes unrecognised. For example, a businessman may have put in place such a robust support system of colleagues that his cognitive losses remain hidden for remarkably long periods of time.[34] On the other hand, some individuals have such a large cognitive reserve that much erosion is required before cognition is manifestly impaired. This effect can be global or focal. For instance, an accountant may retain arithmetic skills well beyond the time when all other cognitive abilities are noted to be impaired by even the most casual observer.

As the population ages, challenges to validity of dispositions by those diagnosed with dementia either at the time, or soon after of making a disposition or will, became more frequent. A fairly common case scenario may provide a basis for further discussion. It involves a businessman who, during the period of two years after diagnosis of early dementia at 0.5 level, had given a business colleague large sums of money, including some significant family assets over which he had sole control. The colleague was aware of the businessman's cognitive impairments, but "covered" for him in running the business until the dementia became moderate to severe. The businessman's gifts were dispositions *inter vivos*, but often a similar scenario arises when testamentary bounties to friends, close neighbours and institutional and private carers of the demented testator are challenged by disgruntled relatives. Can these dispositions be invalidated on the ground that they were created by persons with dementia, and thus subject to the doctrines of undue influence or unconscionable conduct?

All dispositions may be open to challenge on the ground that, due to "defective faculties",[35] the disposing or transacting party was incapable of understanding their significance and purpose.[36] This will often be the case in moderate to severe dementia. However, in the example under discussion, the nature and effect of the dispositions was understood. Whether the dementia constituted a relevant "disorder of mind", either in the sense of impairment of "natural faculties", "poisoning of affections" or "insane delusions" would very much depend on the individual signs and symptoms. However, the competence challenge to the validity of the businessman's gifts would turn on whether they would have been made at all in the absence of dementia. At this point, the legal issue of causation becomes a chicken and egg question, since but for the dementia he would have required his colleague's help. Thus, but for the dementia the reason for the

---

[34] It is said that this situation has pertained to more than one head of state in the contemporary world.

[35] The High Court of Australia still refers to "defective faculties" in its judgments: see *Bridgewater v Leahy* (1998) 194 CLR 457 at 475 per Gaudron, Gummow, Kirby JJ.

[36] *Gibbons v Wright* (1954) 91 CLR 423 at 449; *Blomley v Ryan* (1956) 99 CLR 362 at 401.

gifts would not have arisen. Is it fair therefore to invalidate them on the ground that dementia made the businessman vulnerable to undue influence or unconscionable conduct by his colleague?

In the case of *Bridgewater v Leahy*,[37] the majority of the High Court of Australia reiterated the notion that undue influence and unconscionable conduct "may be seen as a species of that genus of equitable intervention to refuse enforcement of or to set aside transactions which, if allowed to stand, would offend equity and good conscience". Since neither the standard of "equity" or "good conscience" are defined, the courts have wide discretion in the interpretation and application of these two doctrines.

In the case of the businessman, early dementia was the factual cause of his decision to make gifts to his colleague, who was helping him to stay in business for an extra two years. Yet, one suspects that the dispositions would be open to challenge on the ground of unconscionability because, according to the majority of the High Court of Australia, a donor's disposition may be invalidated even though that person far from being "of weak mind", and was "perfectly competent to understand what she or he was doing, had done, or proposed to do, if the court finds that the intention [to execute the disposition] was produced as a result of undue influence or unconscionable conduct".[38]

In other words, factors associated with the person's ability to form an independent intention to dispose of property rather than his or her cognitive capacity will be determinative of the validity of the disposition. Thus, the businessman, possibly persuaded by his family, through a litigation guardian could ask the court to set aside his dispositions of the family assets on the ground of unconscionable conduct. He could plead that his early dementia placed him under a serious disadvantage when he was deciding that his best interests were served by staying on in business and making expensive gifts to a colleague rather than by retiring, and that the colleague-recipient knew of his impaired competence and took advantage of it. In *Bridgewater v Leahy*,[39] the High Court of Australia reaffirmed the general principle that the essence of unconscionable conduct is the combined inability of the disposing party to consider his or her best interests, and the unfair exploitation of this circumstance by another.[40] Mason J noted that:

---

[37] *Bridgewater v Leahy*, op cit, fn 35, at 477 per Gaudron, Gummow, Kirby JJ.
[38] Ibid, at 492 per Gaudron, Gummow, Kirby JJ.
[39] Ibid.
[40] "Whenever one party by reason of some condition or circumstance is placed at a special disadvantage vis-a-vis another and unfair or unconscientious advantage is then taken of the opportunity thereby created ...": *Commercial Bank of Australia Ltd v*

the disabling condition or circumstance is one which seriously affects the ability of the innocent party to make a judgment as to his own best interests, when the other party knows or ought to know of the existence of that condition or circumstance and of its effect on the innocent party.[41]

Would the action be successful? Historically, lack of intelligence,[42] alcoholic daze,[43] infatuation of an elderly solicitor with a younger woman,[44] and the emotional dependence of an elderly but competent uncle upon his nephew[45] have all been considered sufficient disabling conditions for the purposes of unconscionability. One of the symptoms of dementia is an impaired ability to change concepts. It is arguable that once the businessman decided to remain in the business, his medical condition prevented him from even contemplating any other alternative. On this analysis, it could be said that his actions, including making gifts to the colleague were subject to an "internal coercion". Yet, at the time of the dispositions the businessman had early dementia, suggesting only a slight cognitive impairment. This may not have involved conceptual rigidity, at least with respect to the dispositions.

Almost certainly, by the time the case reached the courts, the businessman's dementia would have been sufficiently advanced to render him an incompetent witness. In a way, the position would be practically the same as that of a challenged will. The difference between the colleague and beneficiaries under challenge is that having received the gifts, he is in a better financial position than they to defend the claim. The court would doubtless consider circumstantial evidence to determine whether dementia constituted a "disabling condition" in the context of his business activities. The determination would thus be based on inferences drawn from general medical theory and evidence provided by witnesses. The question of whether the colleague acted unfairly or took unconscientious advantage of the opportunity created by the early dementia would remain. The colleague enabled the businessman to continue to enjoy the status, respect and prestige. These norms of community approval unfortunately disappear once a diagnosis of dementia is made. Arguably, it was reasonable for the businessman to decide that the price – in the form of gifts – was worth paying for the help in retaining the community's esteem.

Amadio (1983) 151 CLR 447 at 462, per Mason J referring to Fullagar J in *Blomley v Ryan* (1956) 99 CLR 362 at 386.

[41] *Commercial Bank of Australia Ltd v Amadio* (1983) 151 CLR 447 at 462.

[42] *Wilton v Farnworth* (1948) 76 CLR 646.

[43] *Blomley v Ryan* (1956) 99 CLR 362.

[44] *Louth v Diprose* (1992) 175 CLR 621.

[45] *Bridgewater v Leahy*, op cit, fn 35.

But then, the definition of what constitutes unconscionable conduct is vague and open-ended. According to Lord Brightman unconscionable conduct is "victimisation, which can consist either of the active extortion of a benefit or the passive acceptance of a benefit in unconscionable circumstances."[46] Any human act as well as dynamics of any relationship can be interpreted negatively, so this definition invites challenges to dispositions along a wide spectrum of psychiatric and emotional conditions, as well as old age.[47] Motives that activate human conduct are intricate, and only rarely can be compartmentalised into purely angelic and purely devilish. In a society where greed is regarded as virtue, there are many who prey on the vulnerable and the lonely, including the demented. The elderly with even mild dementia are not great company. If they are lucky, their loving family and devoted friends will visit them regularly. But those who live away from the family have to rely on strangers. Again, if they are lucky, non-family carers, neighbours, new friends and partners may visit and help them out of the goodness of their heart. Alternatively, these legal strangers (like some family members) may do so for strictly mercenary purposes. However, if either way the result is that donors or testators are made to feel special, respected and cared for, then their dispositions – often by way of a codicil – should be analysed from their perspective. Accordingly, whereas moderate and severe dementia should always be regarded as a serious disadvantage and a disabling condition in relation to the doctrine of unconscientious conduct, this might not necessarily be the case with early dementia.

Although jurisprudential distinctions between unconscionable conduct and undue influence are somewhat blurred, the characteristic feature of the doctrine of undue influence is that a gift by a donor can be set aside even "where a donor is perfectly competent to understand and intend what he or she did."[48] This doctrine instead focuses on decisional independence or freedom within the relationship between two parties.[49] In relation to dispositions *inter vivos*, the gist of undue influence lies in the impairment of freedom and voluntary judgment of the donor by the stronger party to

---

[46] *Hart v O'Connor* [1985] AC 1000 at 1024. Cited with approval in *Bridgewater v Leahy* [1998] HCA 66; (1998) 194 CLR 457 at 479-80, per Gaudron, Gummow, Kirby JJ.

[47] In *Bridgewater v Leahy*, op cit, fn 35, the majority determined that testator's old age affected the quality of his consent or assent to the transfers.

[48] *Bridgewater v Leahy*, op cit, fn 35, at 479-80 Gaudron, Gummow, Kirby JJ, referring to Lord Eldon LC's statements in *Huguenin v Baseley* (1807) 14 Ves Jun 273 at 299-300; 33 ER 526 at 536.

[49] In *Mountain v Bennet* (1787) 29 ER 1200 the judge instructed the jury to invalidate a will if they believed that "the dominion or influence" of another prevented the exercise of independent discretion by the testator.

the relationship.[50] The court examines "the quality of the donor's intention or the means by which it [the intention] was produced,"[51] in the sense of ascertaining that the intention was not subject to the influence of a person in a position of dominance. Thus, the critical issue is not decisional competence, but whether the donor executed the dispositions "as the result of the free exercise of his independent will".[52] Evidence of diminished competence due to dementia may raise a presumption that the donee was in a position to influence the donor's intentions. It could be claimed on behalf of the businessman that, by definition, his early dementia made him a weaker party vis-a-vis the colleague, and thus open to undue influence. The conclusion that the businessman, like the uncle-transferor in *Bridgewater v Leahy*,[53] was emotionally and professionally dependant on the colleague may be well founded. Nevertheless, as a ground for legal challenge, the case in which such conclusion might be drawn sits uncomfortably with the principle that all of us, even the elderly, have the right to dispose of property in any lawful manner we wish.

Conclusion

Major misjudgments may occur as a consequence of not recognising the complexity of conditions that cause dementia together with the dynamic inter-relationship of brain and environment. Considerable care must be taken in making causal judgments based on personal interpretations of observed behaviour. Law, with the help of medicine, must strive to understand behaviours from the point of view of an affected person's brain. It must also recognise that even a seriously impaired brain may be able to provide a suitable response to current perceptions of external threat.

This area of interface between medicine and law can be expected to grow substantially over the next few years as we witness a major increase in the number of patients with Alzheimer's disease. Their families and

---

[50]   *Kinleside v Harrison* (1818) 2 Phillim 449; (1818) 161 ER 1196 established the principle that certain confidential relationships, such as member of the clergy and parishioner, parent and child, guardian and ward, solicitor and client, as well as physician and patient raise a presumption of undue influence. See also: *Commercial Bank of Australia Ltd v Amadio* (1983) 151 CLR 447 at 461, 474.

[51]   *Bridgewater v Leahy*, op cit, fn 35, at 475 per Gaudron, Gummow, Kirby JJ.

[52]   Ibid.

[53]   In *Bridgewater v Leahy*, op cit, fn 35, the owner of land entered into a contract to sell it to his nephew for a price of $A696,811 and at the same time executed transfers of the land and a deed of forgiveness for $A546,811 of the price. Although the Australian High Court acknowledged that at the time of execution of the transfers, the owner was of sound mind, it set aside the deed of forgiveness of price on sale of land.

carers are likely to have unrealistic expectations of the ability of both medicine and law to resolve the ethically and legally difficult questions that affect health and wealth, unless members of the legal profession specifically pay attention to the growing medical understanding of the nature and epistemology of cognitive disorders.

PART D:
CAUSATION IN FORENSIC MEDICINE AND CORONIAL LAW

14 Cause in Forensic Pathology: The Cause and Manner of Death

STEPHEN CORDNER[*]

Introduction

The attribution of "cause" in forensic pathology is a fascinating subject about which too little has been written.[1] It is one particular area, amongst many, of confusion at the dynamic interface of law and medicine. One reason for this confusion is that those involved have to grapple with (at least) two different conceptions of cause: that used in medicine and that in law. This chapter has been written from a medical perspective – and the lawyers amongst the readers will have to take from it what they can!

The chapter begins by outlining the terrain covered by forensic pathology and the main features in the landscape. It then briefly looks at the medical certification of the cause of death by doctors generally, before unwrapping some of the issues peculiar to forensic pathology. The main aim is to arrive at something like a coherent schema for the attribution of the cause of death following autopsy. While in most cases this is straightforward, in some it is not, and in those cases I do not think the discipline of forensic pathology has a uniform approach. This is not surprising as the attribution of cause, particularly in retrospect and in as complex and unpredictable field as biology, is essentially a philosophical question. During the course of this chapter examples of the issues arising in a number of cases will illustrate the breadth of the forensic pathologist's

[*] Professor of Forensic Medicine at Monash University and Foundation Director of the Victorian Institute of Forensic Medicine. Acknowledgment: Publishers of *The Lancet* for permission to reproduce much of the author's paper "Deciding the Cause of Death after Necropsy" (1993) 341 *Lancet* 1458.
[1] S Cordner, "Deciding the Cause of Death after Necropsy" (1993) 341 *Lancet* 1458.

contribution and the complexity of the associated causal issues, which, it must be said, are sometimes not appreciated by either pathologists or lawyers.

Forensic Pathology – The Terrain

Forensic pathology is the application of the principles and practice of pathology to the needs of the courts or, more generally, the law. Pathology is the study of disease and forensic pathology is a subdiscipline of anatomical pathology (or what was once known as morbid anatomy). Anatomical pathology has left its morbid anatomical roots and concentrates in the main on surgical and biopsy pathology. Forensic pathology on the other hand is a mortuary-based speciality which provides the knowledge base for the performance of autopsies in deaths reported to coroners (or their equivalents in countries with other forms of death investigation systems).

At the outset, it is important to appreciate the scope of the forensic autopsy. The aims of this part of a death investigation are:

- To discover, describe and record all the pathological processes present in the deceased and, where necessary, the identifying characteristics of the deceased;
- With knowledge of the medical history and circumstances of the death, to come to conclusions about the cause of death and factors contributing to death and, where necessary, the identity of the deceased;
- In situations where the circumstances of death are unknown or in question, to apply the autopsy findings and conclusions to the reconstruction of those circumstances. This will, on occasions, involve attendance at the scene of death, preferably with the body in situ; and
- To record the positive, and relevant negative, observations and findings in such a way as to enable another forensic pathologist at another time to independently come to his or her own conclusions about the case. As forensic pathology is essentially a visual exercise, this involves the use of good quality, and preferably colour, photographs.[2]

---

[2]   S Cordner, B Linehan, M El Nageh, D Wells & H McKelvie, *Ethical Practice in Laboratory Medicine and Forensic Pathology*, WHO Regional Publications, Eastern Mediterranean Series, WHO Regional Office for the Eastern Mediterranean, Alexandria, Egypt, 1999, p38.

Encapsulated in this approach to the forensic autopsy are two consequences at odds with a common perception of the specialty. Firstly, forensic pathology could be regarded as the "what happened" specialty (and not the "whodunnit" specialty). It is as part of this that the pathologist is concerned to come to the best conclusion about the cause of death. However, and this is the second consequence, in pursuit of answers to "what happened", conclusions about the cause of other findings on or in the body, or at the scene, or of events described in witness statements, may require the pathologist to attribute "cause" in areas other than the cause of death. Provided the pathologist keeps to his or her expertise, this is a quite proper exercise.

Certification of Cause of Death Without Autopsy

There is, however, a preliminary area which needs a little exploration. Every fully registered medical practitioner is imbued, by law, with the authority to "sign a death certificate". The function of the certification of the cause of death by doctors is poorly appreciated. In policy terms, it originated as part of the British Government's response in the 1820s and 1830s to the outrages of Burke and Hare. Together with a requirement to report deaths to coroners, the Registration of Births Deaths and Marriages Act 1836 (UK) meant that no body could be buried lawfully without a doctor certifying an opinion as to the cause of death. Thus, certification of the cause of death originated as a means of controlling or detecting hidden homicide. A side benefit (and a major one) was the collection of epidemiological data about why people were dying. As a tool for accurate information of this kind, however, death certificates are notoriously inaccurate, with numerous studies establishing error rates of as much as 20-30 per cent in the major condition reported as causing death.[3] These rates have not altered, either historically or more recently, with advances in investigative and diagnostic technology. Many people find this hard to believe, but forensic pathologists – amongst others – know it to be true. That such error rates exist is not to be critical of one's clinical colleagues. Concluding the cause of death without the benefit of autopsy means that one is relying on the medical history and little else. The clinician cannot

---

[3]   PM Nemetz, J Ludwig & LT Kurland, "Assessing the Autopsy" (1987) 128 *American Journal of Pathology* 362; PA McKelvie & J Rode, "Autopsy Rate and a Clinicopathological Audit in an Australian Metropolitan Hospital – Cause for Concern?" (1992) 156 *Medical Journal of Australia* 456; GDH MacLaine, EB MacArthur & CR Heathcote, "A Comparison of Death Certificates and Autopsies in the Australian Capital Territory" (1992) 156 *Medical Journal of Australia* 462.

take a history of the period immediately before death, which is often not witnessed, is limited to an external examination of the body and the only special test – an autopsy – is generally not available. It is perhaps surprising that clinicians certify correctly as many causes of death as they do.

Writing death certificates can be tricky in some circumstances, and the following example shows how confusions may arise.

CASE 1

Mr H was 75 years old and suffering from metastatic lung cancer; that is, cancer of the lungs which had spread, in his case, to involve brain, liver and ribs. These were the cause of convulsions (fits), hemiplegia ("stroke") and pain. He was admitted to a hospital for palliative care. At the time of admission a Refusal of Treatment Certificate, in the form of Schedule 1 of the Medical Treatment Act 1988 (Victoria), was properly completed. This recorded Mr H's decision to refuse both medical treatment generally and artificial hydration. He also requested complete relief of pain and suffering with analgesics and sedation. Combinations of varying amounts of these drugs were prescribed and administered. He appeared to be comfortable and deeply asleep, but rousable. On the third day after admission, he became unconscious (ie not rousable) and he died on the fourth day.

The treating doctor reported the death to the coroner believing it to be possibly a suicide. This was on the basis, it seemed, that Mr H had refused medical treatment including artificial hydration and that this, together with the drugs prescribed and administered at Mr H's request, had hastened death. The treating doctor gave the cause of death as:

CAUSE OF DEATH

I	
Disease or condition directly leading to death.*	(a) Dehydration
Antecedent causes (morbid conditions, if any, giving rise to the above cause, stating the underlying condition last).	(b) Refusal of fluids
II	
Other significant conditions (contributing to the death but not related to the disease or condition causing it).	(a) Sedation (b) Metastatic Carcinoma of Lung

*   This means the disease, injury or complication which caused death not only, for example, the mode of dying such as "heart failure, asthenia" etc.

One needs to understand the form of the cause of death to appreciate what the treating doctor is saying (whether wittingly or unwittingly). The cause is divided into I and II. "I" is the direct cause of death or the disease or condition directly leading to death. "I" is subdivided, if necessary, into a, b and c (and theoretically d and e etc if necessary; it very rarely is). "I(a)" is due to or a result of "I(b)" and so on. The last listed condition under "I" is the main, central or underlying cause of the patient's death. "II" represents those other significant conditions contributing to the death but not directly related to the disease or condition causing it.

This is the internationally accepted form that tends to want singular particular causes of death (which makes coding, classification and statistics easier) and does not invite multiple causes. There is an undefined distinction drawn between cause ("I(a), (b)" above) and contribution ("II(a), (b)" above) that is essentially arbitrary where the latter is some form of lesser cause of death.

On this basis, the treating doctor in this case is saying that the underlying cause of Mr H's death is his refusal of fluids. This clearly cannot be right. Any correct statement of the underlying cause of Mr H's death must refer to his terrible metastatic cancer. The doctor is probably correct that the refusal of fluids has hastened Mr H's death as did the sedation, but Mr H was already very seriously and terminally ill.

There is no doubt in my mind that the doctor could (and in my view, should) have completed a death certificate in this case, and not reported it to the coroner, as it was a death from natural causes. All the elements of the cause of death were the natural consequences of properly authorised sedation and pain relief, of properly authorised refusal of artificial hydration and of his underlying disease. The cause of death might have read:

I(a) Probable dehydration and bronchopneumonia following sedation in a man with metastatic carcinoma of the lung (brain, liver, ribs).

Admittedly this is a complicated example. It emphasises the gatekeeper role of medical practitioners generally in relation to the investigation of deaths and their causes. In doing so, they apply their own understanding of cause to the 90 per cent of deaths that never come to the attention of the forensic pathologist.

This understanding is sometimes imperfect. For example, the cause of death will on occasions be certified simply as "cardio-respiratory arrest". This is a manifestation or a description of the body's cessation of function, not the reason or cause underlying this cessation of function. Generally speaking, however, I believe the medical profession discharges its obligations in this area well and has a good instinctive understanding of those deaths which, because of their cause or manner, should be reported to the coroner and those in which a medical certificate of the cause of death can be completed. Only rarely will the latter result in issues for evaluation by lawyers or a court. The cause of death is not often a contentious issue in litigation, and when it is there will almost always have been an autopsy. It is to these cases that I now turn.

Deciding the Cause of Death Following Autopsy

Deciding the cause of death is a fundamental responsibility for all anatomical pathologists after autopsy. The responsibility is greatest for forensic pathologists, yet very little has been written about the criteria that need to be satisfied to make a decision. This issue causes confusion in some court cases because both pathologists and lawyers fail to appreciate the philosophy of causation. Leaving aside the minority of cases where the lesion observed at autopsy is incompatible with life (eg decapitation), what in fact usually happens in coming to a conclusion is that *a* cause of death discovered at autopsy, which accords with the medical history and circumstances, is elevated to *the* cause of death. In general terms, the pathologist makes a subjective decision that a certain autopsy finding is capable of leading to death, and that this is consistent with the deceased's medical history and circumstances of death. Furthermore, a conclusion about the cause of death (unlike many medical diagnoses) is retrospective and cannot be tested. These problems emphasise the need to discover all the pathological processes present in the deceased before considering them in relation to the medical history and the circumstances of death.

Causation: Philosophy and Problems

David Hume (1711-1776) believed that for something to be the cause it must be both sufficient and necessary for the effect: X is always followed by Y, and Y never occurs unless X occurred. John Stuart Mill (1806-1873) disagreed, and thought that the cause was the sum total of the conditions in which an event occurred: it was not correct to isolate *one* of the conditions in which an event occurred as the exclusive cause. To Hume, the statement "the rising of the sun causes daylight", would have been reasonable, since the rising of the sun is always followed by daylight, and daylight never comes about unless the rising of the sun has occurred. The statement is, in fact, incomplete because daylight could not occur unless there was an atmosphere. Mill's approach would include an atmosphere in any statement about what caused daylight because it is one of the conditions in which the event occurs.

The restrictiveness of Hume can be seen in the commonest cause of death in the western world: coronary atherosclerosis ("hardening of the arteries of the heart", "heart disease", "heart attack", "myocardial infarction"). The development of coronary atherosclerosis is not always followed by death, and death does not occur only when coronary atherosclerosis has developed. Yet clearly it is a reasonable proposition that coronary atherosclerosis has been the pathological basis for an enormous number of deaths. It seems that Hume's approach is suited more to those cases where the cause of death is incompatible with life. This is not to say that Mill's approach is necessarily the complete answer. Take the example of the heavy smoker who dies of carcinoma of the lung. One of the conditions in which the death occurred is smoking, but there are more: a person may smoke because of the effect of advertising, because of parents' smoking, because of particular personality traits, and so on *ad absurdum*. Pathologists (and in some cases, courts) have to make a practical decision that cause stops somewhere. In general, the line is drawn at the "medical" cause of death but, as the example shows, this may be unsatisfactory: smoking is increasingly noted on death certificates. This, of course, raises the interesting question of whether such deaths are truly "natural".

Pathologists have some instinctive understanding of these issues but there are particular sorts of cases where the difficulties are even greater. If Mill's approach is to be the basis of a coherent schema for the attribution of cause, let us see how it works in the various types of difficult cases that confront the forensic pathologist.

Types of Cases Where Concluding the Cause of Death is Difficult

Substantial delay between injury and death

CASE 2

Injury or disease not sufficient in itself to cause death, but death has occurred. One of the classical causal problems is that of pulmonary embolus and its relation to antecedent events.

> *Mr A was a postmaster of 57 with a history of chronic bronchitis and emphysema, associated with smoking. He was threatened in his office by a man with a knife and was stabbed in the back of the chest when he refused to hand over any money. Taken to hospital, he seemed in good condition and because of his past history of chronic airways disease, he*

was managed conservatively. Management included a chest drain and close observation. 24 hours after admission, he had a cardiovascular collapse from which he was resuscitated, but which left him with bilateral parietal lobe infarction. Intensive physiotherapy restored the patient to limited mobility, and he was discharged five weeks after admission. One week later he collapsed and died in his bathroom.

The autopsy disclosed:

1. Stab wound scar on the posterior pleura (ie the stab wound definitely entered the pleural – chest – cavity).
2. Massive bilateral pulmonary thromboembolism ("clot on the lung").
3. Deep vein thrombosis of calf ("clots in the leg").
4. Chronic bronchitis and emphysema (the consequences of smoking).
5. Diffuse myocardial fibrosis and coronary atherosclerosis (ie ischaemic heart disease, the commonest form of heart disease in the western world).
6. Unsuspected adenocarcinoma of the rectum with liver metastases (ie cancer which had spread).

The case was proceeded with as a homicide, the cause of death having been given as:

1(a) Pulmonary thromboembolism in a man with chronic bronchitis and emphysema and metastatic carcinoma of the rectum, six weeks after being stabbed in the chest leading to cardiovascular collapse and cerebral infarction.

Part of the opinion included in the necropsy report was that the stab wound initiated a chain of events which culminated in the pulmonary thromboembolism. This opinion was provided in the face of the knowledge that the first presentation of metastatic carcinoma of the rectum could well be deep vein thrombosis of the calf and pulmonary thromboembolism. (It is also important to appreciate that the stab wound and the subsequent cardiovascular collapse which it precipitated by virtue of some haemorrhage and a small pneumothorax on a background of chronic bronchitis and emphysema, could well lead to deep vein thrombosis and pulmonary thromboembolism.) The original thrust of the defence indeed was that the deep vein thrombosis and subsequent pulmonary embolus could have been caused by the carcinoma of the rectum, and it was unnecessary to attribute any contribution to death from the stab wound and its consequences. This is Hume's approach to causation, which seeks particular and singular causes. This approach is encapsulated in the following question to the pathologist relied upon by the prosecution: "But

Doctor, you cannot exclude, can you, that this man died from a complication of his metastatic cancer, a well-recognised complication I might add, and that the stab wound might have had nothing to do with it?"

The answer, based on Mill, is that there are multiple causes in this case, and no way of apportioning weight to each. A corollary of this is that no one cause (eg the stabbing and its consequences) can be discarded as having no weight. In this case, there is an interaction between various factors: a man with these pre-existing conditions (heart disease, chronic bronchitis, emphysema and metastatic cancer) who is stabbed in the chest would be more likely to get a deep vein thrombosis and die from pulmonary thromboembolism than one who was not stabbed in the chest. On this basis, a pathologist cannot agree to exclude the stabbing from the cause of this man's death. Responsibility cannot be apportioned between the stabbing and the cancer, but the opinion must be that both are involved in causing death. It is useful in such cases to have some idea of Hume's and Mill's principles, since difficulties that arise will tend to arise from an application of Hume's principles.

The accused in this case was tried for manslaughter at The Old Bailey. A defence submission at the conclusion of the prosecution case, that the prosecution had not established that the actions of the accused had caused the patient's death, was accepted by the judge. The submission at this stage was that the contribution of the stab wound was so minor compared to the metastatic cancer that it should be disregarded. When asked about this, the prosecution pathologist had declined to apportion any particular weight to either, simply emphasising that both had to be included in any statement purporting to encapsulate why death occurred. The defence submission was accepted. The accused was convicted of a wounding charge and sentenced to a term of 15 years imprisonment.

In some cases of a pulmonary thromboembolus following some time after an injury and period of immobilisation, the suggestion will be made that the condition can occur spontaneously and therefore the injury did not cause death. A deep vein thrombosis and pulmonary thromboembolus can only be considered spontaneous if an autopsy fails to discover an adequate explanation. If an adequate explanation is discovered, then there is no need to resort to calling the embolus spontaneous (in reality, a synonym for "idiopathic" which means "of no apparent cause").

Non-fatal injury precipitates death in a setting of natural disease

Sudden death during a fight where the only findings at necropsy are some bruises and coronary atherosclerosis is common. The pathological cause of death will be given as coronary atherosclerosis and the legal process will require an opinion about any relationship between the fight and the cause of death. Linking the death to exertion during the fight may have substantial legal consequences as the survivor, if the aggressor, may be charged with manslaughter (or, in other jurisdictions, a homicide-related offence). At the trial, the pathologist will almost certainly be asked the Hume-type question "But doctor, could not this man have died at any time?". While it can be agreed in general that a person with this degree of atherosclerosis is at risk from sudden death, in this particular case the death cannot be separated from the circumstances in which it occurred. That is, the exertion and emotional impact of being in a fight increased his heart rate and blood pressure, putting a stress on the diseased heart which it was unable to withstand. In this way, the fight (or the exertion and other physiological effects of being involved in the fight) precipitated or caused his death from his underlying heart disease. Again, it can be seen that this approach follows Mill's view that cause is the sum of the conditions in which the event occurred.

A peculiarity of the victim renders a survivable injury fatal

CASE 3

This is a variation of the preceding category. In English-derived legal systems, it has traditionally been a rule that assailants take their victims as they are.[4] This has the consequence that if the victim has a bleeding disorder which would turn a normally non-fatal injury into a fatal one, that does not diminish the responsibility of the assailant for causing death (although it will obviously affect the outcome of a trial or sentence).

> Mr J, 45, lived alone and was on warfarin (a "blood thinner") after cardiovascular surgery. He was sitting on a park bench when he was involved in an argument with the co-occupier of the bench. The description from eyewitnesses was that Mr J's face was pushed, causing him to fall off the end of the bench onto the grass. The assailant then left. Mr J was found unconscious at home two days later and was dead on arrival at hospital. The cause of death was subdural haemorrhage (bleeding over the brain). No scalp or facial bruises were present, but there were five large scattered bruises on the chest and legs. That the medication contributed to this man's demise could not be denied. In fact, the assailant was not even proceeded against in this particular case, since it was felt that even had Mr J survived and complained to the police the assailant would not have been charged with assault. (Not everyone would agree with that logic. A pickpocket taking a wallet in ignorance of its

---

[4]   See D Lanham, "Principles of Causation in Criminal Law", Chapter 10, above.

contents will probably be charged if it happened to contain $100,000 and may not even be chased if it was empty.)

Had this case gone to court there would also have been questions of fact making it difficult to relate the assault to the subdural haemorrhage. Unless there was good evidence that clinical deterioration could be related directly to the assault, it may have been difficult to refute the following argument by defence counsel: "Well, Doctor, we admit pushing Mr J off the bench, but you can't say whether or not he fell on the way home or possibly even turned his head sharply when something caught his eye. Because trivial trauma (which is the prosecution's case) could have precipitated his fatal subdural haemorrhage, it is possible that it was some other trivial trauma which initiated the fatal chain of events in this case."

Decomposition Obscures the Effects of Injuries or Disease

CASE 4

Forensic pathologists have encountered numerous cases where much or all of the pathological evidence has been obliterated by putrefaction. The greatest difficulties arise when there is the possibility of foul play.

> *Mrs B, a woman of 70, came to stay with her 45 year old daughter and son-in-law. The relationship between mother and daughter was stormy and included, over the fortnight of the stay, a number of scuffles. According to the daughter, one night Mrs B was unwell and she stayed downstairs in the armchair. In the morning, Mrs B was found dead, but because of the number of bruises from the scuffles, the daughter was afraid she would get into trouble. She decided not to tell anyone, covered her mother up with blankets and a sheet of plastic, and pulled the chair over towards the heater. Five days later, when the smell had become too much, she went to a lawyer who advised her to contact the police. Every scrap of paper in the house was covered with the daughter's description of her hate for her mother.*

The autopsy findings were:

1. Advancing putrefaction with greenish/purple discolouration of all body compartments and bloating.
2. Numerous abrasions and widely scattered bruises.
3. Severely fractured larynx:
   (a) Fractured right hyoid bone cornu.
   (b) Fractured right thyroid cartilage cornu.

(c) Bilateral fractures of the cricoid cartilage.

(These are the main cartilaginous and bony structures of the larynx or neck.)

4. Multiple fractured ribs and fractured sternum (breast bone).
5. Severe coronary atherosclerosis (ie the common form of heart disease in the western world).

None of the injuries to the larynx or chest was associated with bruising, and therefore they could not be differentiated from injuries occurring after death. The daughter specifically denied that she or anyone else interfered with the body after death. Nothing happened to the body on its way to the mortuary or in the mortuary, and the neck was dissected in situ to identify the fractures (obviating the possible criticism that the autopsy itself may have caused the fractures). The conclusion thus arose that the fractures occurred in life, precipitating death so quickly as to minimise the bruising in the neck, which was then altered by putrefaction. (It is known that putrefaction can so alter bruises that they are not detectable.) Death could have occurred rapidly either as a direct result of the neck injuries themselves or because the injuries and the circumstances of their occurrence put a severe strain on the already diseased heart resulting in death. The cause of death was given as:

> 1(a) Multiple laryngeal fractures, multiple rib fractures, and a fractured sternum in an elderly woman with severe coronary atherosclerosis.

The report stated that the cause was conditional upon nothing having happened to the body after death, and that the court would have to be satisfied about this before it could accept the cause of death as given. The prosecution felt that because of the daughter's mental state, it could not rely on her evidence that she had not interfered with the body after death. Having admitted assaulting her mother, she was sentenced to six months imprisonment. Had it been possible to perform the autopsy in this case before the onset of decomposition, the timing of the neck and chest injuries would probably have been apparent and the main issue in this case, an issue of causation, therefore would have been resolved.

The Humean approach, not actually followed by the defence in this case, would have been to propose the following:

> Look Doctor, the one thing you can say in this case is that the deceased woman had severe coronary artery disease. Depending on the circumstances the injuries could have occurred before or after death; you cannot actually say as a forensic pathologist that the injuries occurred in

life. Surely the only conclusion that you can properly come to is that this woman probably died of her heart disease.

A reasonable response from the pathologist might have been along these lines:

> I agree that a correct statement about the cause of this woman's death should make reference to her coronary artery disease. While it is true that I cannot say as a matter of pathology that the injuries observed occurred in life, the injuries are present. I simply put into the middle of the court room the obvious statement that if the injuries did not occur after death then they occurred during life and there are good reasons in this case why the appearance of the injuries is not what would normally be expected of those occurring in life. If the injuries occurred during life then, in my view, they are of such severity that they should be included in any statement purporting to accurately convey the cause of her death.

Cause is Completely Dependent Upon Interpretation of Circumstances

CASE 5

Occasionally, the cause of death is completely dependent upon an interpretation of the circumstances.

> *Mr A was a 29 year old man with no known previous illnesses. He was working with electrical machinery when he suddenly collapsed and died. His workmates thought he had been electrocuted although others in contact with the same machine had no shock. The results of the examination of the machinery were controversial; government inspectors saying that it was conceivable that the machine had been electrically alive, electrical engineers retained by the factory saying it was not. At autopsy, there were no marks of electrocution. The only positive finding was appreciable hydrocephalus ("water on the brain" or dilatation of the ventricles of the brain) but no acute cerebral oedema (or brain swelling). Some basal meningeal thickening suggested the hydrocephalus may have been secondary to meningitis in infancy or childhood. There were no abnormal histological or toxicological findings.*

If it is assumed that uncomplicated hydrocephalus (as in this case) can cause sudden unexpected death (a matter of some dispute at the inquest), it is easy to see that the cause of death is completely dependent on the assessment of the machinery by electrical experts. Even the assessment of the circumstances contained causal issues because the inspectors, who said it was conceivable that the machine could become electrically live, could not say that it actually had been.

CASE 6

> *Baby A was 3 months old and left in the care of a local authority nursery. It was windy and snow was on the ground. She was left outside in a pram unattended for 3 hours. When she was fetched in, it was found that she was dead. There were no significant pathological findings at autopsy.*

At the time, the definition of the Sudden Infant Death Syndrome (SIDS) was basically the sudden unexpected death of an infant in whom a thorough autopsy failed to find any adequate pathological cause for the death. The pathologist in this case accordingly gave the cause of death as SIDS. However, another pathologist at the inquest correctly pointed out that death from exposure (or hypothermia) in infants may leave no signs; the better conclusion, so the pathologist continued, would have been to say that the cause of death could not be ascertained, and then to have discussed the extent to which the exposure may have been involved in this death by a consideration of the circumstances. (The local authority in this case made a moderately sized ex gratia payment to the family following the inquest.)

CASE 7

While this case was not completely dependent upon the interpretation of the circumstances, it certainly played a large part.

> *Mr F was 33 years old and was severely overweight (Height: 1.85 M. Weight: 120 kgs). He was in receipt of benefits following a back injury at work causing him unremitting pain which was being managed by analgesic drugs. On this particular weekend his back pain was especially bad and he visited three different doctors receiving three different prescriptions of pain killers including pethidine, oxycodone and morphine.*

Subsequent events were described by his wife and can be summarised as follows:

- In the afternoon, Mr F appeared to her to be "really dopey". He was able to speak and eat but he was clearly affected by drugs and this was not uncommon when he self-medicated with pethidine.
- Later that evening when his wife returned from work, he was snoring very loudly.

- He was lying on his front on the bed with his head into the pillow.
- She was concerned with his position so she removed the pillow and moved his head to the side. He did not wake up.
- He continued to snore, did not respond to a nudge from her foot, so she went and slept elsewhere.
- She woke at 3.15 am and heard no snoring. She went to check on him and could not waken him. He was in the same position as when she had last seen him. He was too heavy for her to roll him over.
- An ambulance was called and she was told he was dead.

AUTOPSY

The relevant findings can be very briefly summarised. At autopsy, the only significant findings were:

- a heart weighing 510 g with thickening of the wall of the left ventricle and dilatation of the chamber of the left ventricle;
- 50 per cent occlusion of the anterior descending branch of the left coronary artery by atheroma.
- Samples of blood taken for toxicology showed the presence of the following drugs:

Morphine	0.2 mg/l
Oxycodone	0.1 mg/l
Pethidine	0.7 mg/l
Paracetamol	~5 mg/l
Naproxen	~2 mg/l
Diazepam	0.1 mg/l
Nordiazepam	0.2 mg/l
Sertraline	0.2 mg/l

The pathologist who performed the autopsy gave the cause of death as:

1. (the disease or condition directly leading to death)
   (a) Unascertained
2. (other conditions contributing to death but not to the condition causing death)
   Cardiomegaly, moderate coronary atherosclerosis.

The wife was concerned about this conclusion and the case went to inquest. The pathologist persisted with the view that the drugs had no part to play in the death because at the levels they were not sufficient to cause unconsciousness, let alone death.

A second pathologist gave evidence that there was a confluence of a number of events aggravating each other to produce the fatal outcome:

- the presence of drugs interacting with each other to render him, in the second pathologist's view, unconscious
- the level of unconsciousness may have been associated with a reduced respiratory drive
- his posture, associated as it was with snoring, indicated a degree of obstruction to breathing
- his size, being as overweight as he was, particularly when lying on his front would probably be associated with some reduction in the diaphragmatic component of his breathing
- his enlarged heart and moderate cardiomegaly.

The second pathologist viewed the course of events as follows. Any person who is unconscious is at serious risk of death from respiratory obstruction. A certain level of respiratory obstruction was present in any event as evidenced by the snoring. Respiratory obstruction would have reduced the oxygen and allowed the accumulation of carbon dioxide in the blood. His heart, being abnormal, would have rendered him more susceptible to a fatal outcome from the effects of respiratory obstruction. The lowered oxygen levels triggered a fatal disturbance of heart rhythm.

The cause of death was formally given by the second pathologist as:

> 1(a) Mixed drug toxicity causing unconsciousness in an obese man with cardiomegaly and moderate coronary atherosclerosis lying on his front.

The second pathologist also offered the following caution:

> The absolute essential in this cause of death is the unconsciousness. If it was found that the deceased was not unconscious, but simply asleep, then the cause of death and the analysis I have made obviously cannot be right.

Counsel for the doctors who had prescribed the drugs asked the second pathologist for the grounds that were relied on to conclude that the deceased was unconscious. The answer given was:

- the wife's view that earlier in the day he had been clearly affected by drugs
- the very loud snoring which did not awaken him
- the removal of the pillow and moving of the head by the wife which did not wake him

- the finding of him dead in the very same position
- nothing to positively suggest that he was just asleep.

The second pathologist re-iterated, that while it was proper for a pathologist to form a view about the circumstances in formulating the cause of death, it was clearly open to the court to have a different view in which case it would have a different conclusion about the cause of death.

Counsel was also concerned to understand the basis for the conclusion that the mixed drugs could result in unconsciousness or even death. The second pathologist pointed to experience in the form of a number of deaths – the complete reports of which were exhibited – where mixtures of similar drugs at similar levels had been concluded, by a variety of pathologists, to have resulted in death. This, the second pathologist stated, was sufficient basis for the conclusion that the drugs in Mr F's case were capable of causing unconsciousness, if not death.

This case then, is not only an example of the cause of death being dependent upon the interpretation of the circumstances, but also the subjectivity of whether a particular finding at autopsy is capable of causing death.

In the event, the coroner, having heard other conflicting evidence from anaesthetists and clinicians involved in pain management about the effects of the drugs, made no conclusion about the relationship between the drugs and the death.

Summary

What general rule, if any, can we formulate following all of this? In my view, if there is operating at the time of death a disease or condition capable itself of causing or accelerating death, and in the circumstances of the particular death, its effects apparently exerted themselves, then the disease or condition should be included as part of the cause of that person's death. (This formulation deals, amongst other things, with the situation where it would be nonsense to include coronary atherosclerosis in the cause of death of a man decapitated by a train having been seen by the driver to place himself on the line in the path of an oncoming train.) In addition, if a disease or condition (whether or not a potentially fatal condition) aggravates or complicates another disease or condition (whether or not a potentially fatal condition) such that death occurs then both diseases or conditions should generally be included as part of the cause of death.

This formulation has its weaknesses as it does nothing to help draw the line in the areas of remoteness of cause. The example given above of the smoking-related death and its causal connection to advertising and the parents' smoking habits is a good one. Courts should, and will, have a view about the remoteness of a particular cause.

Conclusions as to Manner of Death

For many, the cause of death is synonymous with the manner of death, for example, murder, accident, suicide or natural death. A chapter purporting to deal with the cause of death needs to canvas some of the issues in relation to manner of death as well.

It will have been apparent in many of the cases above that conclusions as to the cause of death often carry with them an implication as to the manner of death; but not always. Making conclusions as to the manner of death is a fundamental responsibility of medical examiners in the United States and of many coroners' jurisdictions around the world, but not all.

Making these conclusions can be a bit like pushing square pegs into round holes. So much so, that some jurisdictions have moved away from requiring such conclusions. In Victoria, the coroner must find who the deceased was, the medical cause of death and how the deceased died.[5] The last requirement is met in descriptive terms. For example: "The deceased, who was an intravenous drug addict, unemployed and depressed, was found on the floor in the kitchen of the house he was sharing with friends. Intravenous drug paraphernalia was found on the kitchen table, recent injection marks were identified on his forearms at autopsy and metabolites of heroin together with alcohol and a benzodiazepine were found on toxicology. The cause of death was 'Mixed Drug Toxicity'." The words "accident" or "suicide" are not used although on occasions reference will be made to apparent intentions on the part of the deceased to take his/her own life. This, of course, causes problems for those charged with compiling mortality statistics!

The reverse is true in England where coroners are required to classify the death into one of a number of categories:[6] for example, "natural cause", "industrial disease", "want of attention at birth", "dependence on drugs", "killed himself (while the balance of his mind was disturbed)", "accident", "misadventure", "murder", "manslaughter", "infanticide", "accident",

---

5   Coroners Act (Victoria) 1985, s19(1). See I Freckelton, "Causation in Coronial Law", Chapter 16, below.

6   RB Hill & RE Anderson, *The Autopsy – Medical Practice and Public Policy*, Butterworth, Boston, 1988, pp68-90.

"open verdict". Doing so may not be straightforward as some recent work from the United States has verified.

A study by Hazlick and Goodin[7] is interesting in demonstrating the high level of disagreement amongst the "experts" in this area. Twenty-three succinct, well described classical forensic pathology situations were presented to more than 700 medical examiners/coroners (ie forensic pathologists) who were members of the National Association of Medical Examiners, eliciting responses from 198 of them. The manner of death inferred from the ICD Code that was assigned by the (US) National Centre for Health Statistics matched the most common response of participants in 18 (78 per cent) of the 23 scenarios. Table 1 shows the percentage agreement for the most popular conclusion (homicide, suicide, accident, natural, undetermined, other/blank).

TABLE 1
Percentage of 198 forensic pathologists agreeing on the most popular manner of deaths in 23 scenarios

Percentage	No. of scenarios
41-50	2
51-60	4
61-70	5
71-80	1
81-90	7
91-100	4

In fewer than half the cases, admittedly chosen because they were at the boundary of different manners of death, was there greater than 80 per cent agreement. In other words, in only 11 out of 23 cases did more than 80 per cent of 198 United States forensic pathologists agree on the manner of death. There was considerable diversity of opinion amongst the relevant experts as to the manner of death in these examples. This points to different understandings even on the same facts, of the criteria to establish particular manners of death. Such differences commonly include:

---

[7]   R Hazlick & J Goodin, "Mind Your Manners Part III Individual Scenario Results and Discussion of the National Association of Medical Examiners Manner of Death Questionnaire, 1995" (1997) 18(3) *American Journal of Forensic Medicine and Pathology* 228.

- how certain the pathologist should be to make a conclusion (eg the special consequences of concluding suicide may be such as to mean some will require a higher standard of proof than others); and
- different understandings of intention (eg the reckless killing of another may be a homicide whereas the reckless killing of oneself will generally be considered an accident and not a suicide).

The differences amongst pathologists and between them and the health statisticians about the manner of death shows how contentious assigning this form of cause can be.

15 Forensic Medicine: Issues in Causation

DAVID WELLS[*]

Introduction

> While forensic pathology deals with examination of the dead, clinical forensic medicine deals with the living. It is principally concerned with the provision of medical advice in the investigation of crimes and other offences where medical knowledge and experience is essential to assist the legal process. Without accurate documentation and expert interpretation of injuries by forensic clinicians who can also properly evaluate medical history and circumstances, conclusions about how the injures occurred might be flawed. Such conclusions will affect investigations of both criminal and civil trials.[1]

Injury interpretation is very much "bread and butter" work for the forensic physician. Increasingly acknowledged as one of the special skills of this field of medicine, it remains one of the most fascinating and yet contentious areas of forensic medicine. There is often an unrealistic expectation, by the lay public, of what the forensic practitioner can derive from observing a wound; a process fuelled by a number of television dramas and detective novels.

The interpretation of injuries is a critical building block for forensic medical practice as it requires a unique inter-dependence of observations and interpretative skills. This is perhaps most clearly understood when reviewing cases where an incorrect observation is made. This observation is recorded and a false conclusion is reached by both the original observer and

---

[*] The Head of Clinical Forensic Medicine at the Victorian Institute of Forensic Medicine and Honorary Associate Professor of Forensic Medicine at Monash University.

[1] D Wells, M El-Nageh, B Linehan, S Cordner & H McKelvie, *Ethical Practice in Laboratory & Medicine & Forensic Pathology*, WHO Regional Publications, Eastern Mediterranean Series, Egypt, 1999, p41.

any subsequent reviewer. What then occurs is that mistaken evidence is provided and a verdict is reached not so much on the facts but rather on the basis of an error that occurred in the initial phases of the investigation.

It is regrettable that there are often flaws in the way that medical practitioners observe and interpret wounds. Why does this occur? Most medical assessments of wounds have as their end-point the medical consequences and treatment of that wound. In the Emergency Department, the practitioner's management is driven by a need to explore the extent of the injury (with particular reference to possible damage to underlying structures) and then treatment of that injury. The type of wound and the forensic implications are secondary to the management of that wound:

> ... clinicians do not think in terms of causation. The entire goal in the practice of medicine is treatment prevention of death and minimization of morbidity. To this end, a diagnosis is essential but does not address causation. (The clouded sensorium may be a result of a subdural haematoma. How the subdural haematoma occurred is of no real concern in the therapy regimen).[2]

Limited knowledge of the definition of injuries creates further problems. Frequently terminology is inaccurately applied (for instance, a "laceration" rather than an "incised wound") or may be used interchangeably for similar injuries. Whilst not affecting the management of the wound this may result in difficulties in interpreting causation when there is a medico-legal consequence of the injury.

There are other fundamental differences between forensic practice and other clinical practice that may further impact upon injury observation and documentation.

- In forensic practice *the history* of the incident may not be available from the injured party, (eg the head injured individual), may be unreliable or inaccessible (eg physically or sexually assaulted infants or intoxicated subjects). The heavy reliance on the history of symptoms or events, in clinical medical practice[3] and its frequent absence in forensic medical practice creates some unique challenges in this field.
- The practitioner may be confronted with considerable limitations in the desire to perform a thorough *examination*. Clinical forensic practice

---

[2]   I Root, "Head Injuries from Short Distance Falls" (1992) 13(1) *Am J Forensic Med Pathol* 85.

[3]   G Sandler, "The Importance of the History in the Medical Clinic and the Costs of Unnecessary Tests" (1980) 100 *Am Heart J* 928.

includes a large clientele who may be abusive or threatening (eg intoxicated or psychotic individuals), uncooperative (eg suspects in police custody), agitated (eg assault victims), or confused (individuals with intellectual disabilities). Further, there may be constraints in the physical surrounds (eg poor lighting).

- In many medical conditions the luxury of *review* may assist the diagnostic process. In forensic practice, healing, surgical intervention or bandaging may limit the value of this review. Nonetheless a review may be necessary to observe the delayed appearance or evolution of injuries.

- Practitioners limited *knowledge* of the medico-legal implications of a case may also create problems. For instance, the accurate aging of injuries is rarely possible; yet many practitioners, armed with factually incorrect information from old texts and a misplaced "desire to help" will be prepared to give an opinion regarding (say) the age of a bruise. In reality, one can rarely be specific in timing these injuries.[4] Practitioners often do not appreciate how much weight may be placed on such an opinion; for investigators it may influence a decision to charge, for a jury a verdict of guilt.

- *Impartiality*, a quality not tested in other clinical practice, is a critical component to the provision of all forensic services. Investigators, consciously or subconsciously, may bring considerable pressure to bear on practitioners to provide an interpretation that would resolve an issue. This is particularly so in cases where national security is threatened (eg terrorist activities), serious serial offences (eg multiple murders) or when public interest or anxiety is at a high level. These coercive forces may be direct and forceful, or subtle and insidious. They may be particularly strong where the practitioner has a formal relationship with the investigating authority (eg an employee of that authority), when a close personal relationship has developed between investigator and forensic practitioner or when the individual roles of the investigator and practitioner become blurred. Additionally, fairness may be compromised when the practitioner develops an unconscious or a misplaced "desire to help" the investigators.

- A further component to all forensic services is the need for *objectivity*: "Inappropriate expectation-laden observations can lead to observational

---

4   N Langlois & G Gresham, "The Ageing of Bruises: A Review and Study of the Colour Changes With Time" (1991) 50 *Forensic Science International* 227.

errors. Observational errors can lead to interpretive errors and interpretive errors can lead to inferential errors".[5]

Without malicious intent, false information may be provided to the practitioner. This information may influence the practitioner's approach to the case, to the point that some observations are disregarded or incorrectly interpreted and a false conclusion may be reached.

In this chapter, some of the specific issues relating to injury causation as they apply to clinical forensic medicine will be explored, albeit briefly. By necessity, such a review cannot be all-inclusive. Instead, focus will be directed to some of the principles of injury interpretation, particularly as they apply to allegations of sexual assault in both adults and children. For it is these fields that are frequently dogged by misinformation and misinterpretation by both medical and legal practitioners.

Injuries

There is a randomness to the distribution of assaultive injuries. This may result in a wide range of sites and structures being damaged. Injury interpretation requires a broad comprehension of anatomical, physiological and pathological principles. These principles may be utilised to address questions of type and quantification of force, timing of the injurious event or simply, the how, what and when.

Apparently minor injuries of the skin may result from the application of major forces (eg, blunt abdominal trauma). The maxim – no injury on the outside does not mean no injury on the inside – has implications for the medical assessment and the forensic interpretation.

The depth of anatomical knowledge required is, therefore, directed at describing the findings and interpreting the consequences. In forensic medical practice, there are some sites that may warrant particular attention: scalp, face, neck, forearms, hands and genito-anal region.

In the application of force to the body, there are a number of variables that may affect injury production.

- *Type.* Physical forces are the main factor applicable to forensic situations. The physical agents involved may produce disruption of

---

[5]   J Nordby, "Can We Believe What We See, If We See What We Believe? Expert Disagreement" (1992) 37(4) *Journal of Forensic Sciences* 1115.

tissues (eg an abrasion) or protein denaturation (eg thermal or electrical injuries). Chemical or biological agents are far less common.

- *Amount.* Accurate quantification of forces is not feasible in clinical situations. In blunt trauma there is a close relationship between force and resultive injury.

- *Duration.* The same amount of blunt force delivered over a shorter period will produce a greater transfer of kinetic energy and greater tissue damage.

- *Agent.* Exposure or contact with some weapons is more likely to produce trauma than others.

- *Extent.* Type of tissue involved. Issues of tissue vascularity, sensitivity to hypoxia, ability to regenerate may also influence outcomes of trauma.

What are the injuries that may result from an assaultive action?

Certain actions inevitably produce injuries. However, not all assaultive actions will result in injuries to the victim (Table 1). Further, there will be instances where the assailant may sustain an injury whilst the "victim" has no visible site of trauma (eg a punch or a bare-footed kick may be delivered with sufficient force to fracture a finger or toe without the recipient sustaining an observable injury).

There are multiple explanations for the absence of injuries in individuals alleging physical assault. Some of these are specific to the *complainant.* These may include an inaccurate or untruthful account or individual characteristics that make the application of force less likely to result in an injury. For instance, a young healthy person may show no stigmata of injury following the application of relatively trivial trauma whilst an elderly person may demonstrate extensive bruising. This in turn is due to lesser amounts of subcutaneous tissue and poorly supported vasculature in the older age group. Similarly certain diseases (eg clotting defects and a range of connective tissue disorders) or drugs (eg aspirin, corticosteroids) may increase the propensity of "easy bruising."

The type of assault is also a critical element in the injury outcome. Certain activities are inevitably associated with injury production (eg a stabbing) whereas others (eg slapping, hair-pulling) are infrequently physically injurious. The features of the tissue at the site of contact constitute a further factor. Hence blunt trauma to the optical orbit where the skin is loose, relatively poorly supported, highly vascular and overlying bone, is more likely to result in significant bruising or laceration than at sites where these conditions are absent, such as the abdominal wall or the palm of the hand. Clothing may also have some protective effects.

Examination techniques and timing will affect the likelihood of injuries being recognised. Poor quality examinations (particularly where examinations are performed for the specific purpose of treatment rather than documentation) have resulted in inadequate assessments. Blunt trauma may result in bruising that does not become evident until after the examination. Similarly, healing, particularly of minor injuries, may occur in the period between the assault and the examination.

Adult Sexual Assault

Considerable variations exist in the legal statutes prescribing what constitute sexual offences. Many jurisdictions are specific as to the elements required to be proven in the criminal offence of rape and these include:

- Occurrence of sexual penetration; and
- Absence of free agreement or consent.

Sexual penetration is also variously described but may include the introduction (to any extent) of a penis into a bodily orifice or an object into the vagina or the anus. Defences utilised by people accused of rape generally evolve around:

- A denial that sexual penetration occurred; and
- An acceptance that penetration occurred but with the complainant's consent, or a belief that it was with the complainant's consent.

Consent or broadly "free agreement" can only be provided in the absence of force, fear or coercion. Additionally, the subject must have the capacity to consent to the act.

From the forensic perspective, it follows that the role of the doctor is to seek, document and interpret information that may demonstrate whether:

- The complainant was able to provide competent consent to the act;
- Force was used during the alleged assault; and
- Sexual penetration occurred.

The presence or absence of consent to the act are appropriately judged by the court. There is no role for the medical practitioner in such decisions.

Nonetheless health practitioners may assist in the debate as to the complainant's ability to provide competent consent.

Competence in this setting will revolve around issues of temporary or chronic conditions that impact upon cognitive function. Drugs (including alcohol) and head injury are the more common conditions encountered that may produce short-term impairment. Psychiatric illnesses and intellectual disability tend to be of a more chronic nature with an increased likelihood of prior recognition of these conditions.

Conditions affecting cognitive function may have direct relevance to situations in which injuries were sustained and hence, their interpretation. Alcohol and other drugs affecting the central nervous system may impair balance and co-ordination. This will increase the likelihood of "bumps and falls" resulting in a range of blunt trauma particularly to bony prominences (eg shins, knees, elbows and face).

Restraint or handling injuries (eg grip marks in the form of fingertip bruises) about the upper arms and forearms may reflect "assistance" provided by others. Alternatively, they may also be associated with forceful restraint for the purposes of assault (eg arms or inner aspects of thighs).

Memory may be adversely affected by a range of acute and chronic conditions. Here complainants may not be able to recall details of an incident including the circumstances in which an injury was sustained. Alternatively, confabulation or a misplaced desire to assist investigators may produce a range of inaccurate responses.

Injuries (Non-genital). Consenting intercourse in its various guises rarely results in bodily injuries. Notwithstanding this, anecdotal accounts abound of individuals or couples who sustain injuries during coitus. These are usually in the setting of experimentation (eg sado-masochistic activities), intoxication or inappropriate settings (eg heights, surfaces etc). Relatively little is known about injuries sustained in this fashion. There is almost certainly significant under-reporting and non-publication, as the current literature amounts to little more than single case reports.

There now exists a significant body of literature documenting injury findings in adults reporting recent sexual assault. Some difficulties arise however in the interpretation and comparison of these various publications because of the considerable variations in study designs:

- *Age and gender.* Pre-pubertal children, adults, females and males are combined in some studies. The nature of the assault, the relationship to the offender and the injury pattern are significantly different in these groups.
- *Examination timing.* Whilst some studies include only individuals reporting assault within the previous twenty-four hours, others include

all reports (days or weeks after the assault). Healing or resolution of injuries may have occurred in the latter group.

- *Injury definition.* Even within this relatively specialised field, there exists considerable variation in the classification and definition of wounds. Some studies inappropriately include tenderness (as reported by the complainant) or redness (a subjective assessment by the examiner) as definitive indications of trauma.
- *Practitioner experience.* Studies include examinations conducted by inexperienced practitioners and others with considerable expertise in gynaecology and forensic medicine.
- *Study design.* Small numbers, retrospective studies, non-blinded design and the absence of control groups are limiting factors in some publications.
- *Bias.* It is generally accepted that the majority of sexual assaults are not reported. Hence those motivated to report may not reflect the characteristics of the majority of victims of these offences. Motivating factors may include serious injury (and in particular those requiring treatment), ready access to quality services, and a range of secondary gain issues.
- *Causation.* The studies record injuries without attempting to relate them to the allegations in each case. Hence the noted injuries have not necessarily been sustained during the assault, but perhaps prior or subsequent to the assault.

Notwithstanding these limitations it would be reasonable to conclude that between one half and two-thirds of adult women reporting sexual assault are found to have some form of non-genito-anal injury. The vast majority of these being classified as a minor injury (small abrasions and bruises) not requiring treatment. (Table 2) It follows that between one-third and half of women reporting sexual assault do not have any objective evidence of the use of force during the assault. The absence of injuries removes a very potent form of corroboration of a non-consenting act.

Paucity of injuries was a major factor dictating the approach of police and the courts, to allegations of sexual assault.

> Allow her to make her statement to a police woman and then drive a horse and cart through it. It should be borne in mind that except in the case of a very young child, the offence of rape is extremely unlikely to have been committed against a woman who does not immediately show signs of

extreme violence. If a woman walks into a police station and complains of rape with no such signs of violence, she must be closely interrogated.[6]

Here there was emphasis placed on the evidence of "resistance" because of the requirement that the act be committed "against the will of the victim" rather than without the consent.

> However the extent and visual impact of the injuries incurred were probably the principal reason for a conviction in this case. Photographs were shown of the victim with blackened eyes, swollen face and nose, and missing clumps of hair.[7]

In the minds of many, the absence of consent still equates to the use of force leading to an expectation that the complainant should have sustained assaultive or defensive injuries.

Genito-anal Injuries. In sexual assaults, injuries to the anus or to the female genitalia are generally the result of penetration or attempted penetration by a blunt object. Clearly, blows or an assault with a sharp object may produce wounds but these are generally readily identified by the history and the injury pattern.

The post-pubertal hymen is an elastic membranous structure that is quite capable of deforming or stretching without tearing. The anatomy of the hymen shows considerable variation; the hymenal orifice may be of different shapes and the margins may be irregular. Generally, the hymen is most prominent posteriorly and may be deficient anteriorly. Consequently, most injuries to the hymen are in the posterior segment.

It is to this author's dismay that considerable weight continues to be placed on the appearance of the hymen in post pubertal girls and adult women. Statements of virginity (or otherwise), *virgo intacta* or "intact hymen" regularly appear in medical reports and yet the factual basis for such statements is, in nearly all cases, absent.

> Contrary to public belief, no definite criteria have ever been established for deciding whether a woman is a virgin or not.[8]

---

6   Anon, "Police Review 1975" in T Williamson, "Police Investigations – Separating the False and Genuine" (1996) 36(2) *Med Sci Law* 135.

7   A Edwards & M Heenan, "Rape Trials in Victoria: Gender, Socio-cultural Factors and Justice" (1994) 27 *ANZ J Criminol* 213.

8   R Underhill & J Dewhurst, "The Doctor Cannot Always Tell – Medical Examination of the Intact Hymen" (Feb 1978) 18 *Lancet* 375.

Nearly a quarter of a century later *there has been little* advancement. What can be safely concluded is that:

- Acute injuries to the hymen (bruising, abrasions or lacerations) are indicative of recent penetrating blunt trauma;
- Acute injuries heal quickly (days or weeks) most frequently with no residual evidence of injury;
- Hymenal lacerations may remain as partial or complete transections. However, the finding of a deficiency in the hymen should not necessarily lead to a conclusion of past penetrating blunt trauma;
- Post-pubertal females may have penile vaginal penetration (even on multiple occasions) without sustaining any hymenal injuries; and
- The finding of hymenal remnants *(carunculae myrtiformes)* is indicative of repeated penetration or childbirth.

Few other conclusions can be safely drawn from hymenal examinations in the post-pubertal. The act of penetration causes the soft tissues around the orifice to stretch. The likelihood and extent of genito-anal injuries will thus depend upon:[9]

- The state of the tissues – Injuries are more likely when the genital orifice is small (eg, prepubertal girls) or has some co-existing pathology that makes it more susceptible to trauma (eg, infections, inflammation, neoplasia). The post-menopausal woman may be at higher risk of trauma because of atrophic tissue changes and diminished lubrication.
- The size and type of penetrating object. Clearly, very large objects have a higher likelihood of producing trauma but there is the potential for considerable distension of both orifices. Fisting or handballing (whereby the hand is inserted into the vagina or anus) may or may not be associated with injuries. Variation in penile size, is unlikely to be a factor in injury production.
- The amount of force used. This is undoubtedly one of the most significant factors in injury production. However, the act of intercourse is generally one of not inconsiderable vigour.

---

[9]   D Wells, E Ogden & S Young, "Child Abuse" in I Freckelton & H Selby, *Expert Evidence: Law, Practice and Procedure*, 2nd edn, Law Book Co, Sydney, 2002.

All of these factors need to be considered collectively in the assessment of genito-anal trauma. These principles have practical significance in the assessment of gynaecological trauma:

- Generally, it is not possible to differentiate the injurious effects of penetration with fingers, penis or a blunt, inanimate object. All are examples of blunt objects, creating similar effects upon the anus or female genitalia. Rarely will penetration with an inanimate object produce effects that will assist in identifying the object.
- Injuries to the genito-anal region may be asymptomatic. However, the rich vasculature and nerve supply will usually result in injuries being associated with symptoms of pain and bleeding. Less frequently, symptoms may include difficulty or pain with the passage of urine or faeces. The injuries producing symptoms are most commonly abrasions and bruising and less commonly, lacerations.
- Tenderness is a subjective phenomenon and whilst it may reflect tissue trauma, it is not by itself, indicative of injury. Clumsily performed examinations or anxiety about the examination procedure may invoke complaints of discomfort or pain.
- Inflammation (manifest by swelling, redness or discomfort) of either the genitalia or the anus may be the result of recent intercourse but the finding is not specific for recent penetration. Alternative causes of inflammation include infections or chemical or other physical irritants.
- The finding of blood in the genito-anal region requires from the examiner a careful inspection as to the possible source. Whilst trauma may be the source, other causes include haematuria, menstrual loss and haemorrhoidal bleeding.
- Scientific analysis of fluid found about or within the vagina or anus is required before any opinions can be provided as to its source.
- Consensual sexual activities may result in genito-anal injuries in the post-pubertal female. The frequency of injuries sustained in these circumstances is unknown but some may be severe enough to warrant treatment.

Child Sexual Assault

Background issues. There is no universal definition of child sexual assault with many variations incorporating social, legal, behavioural or medical models. Perhaps a useful starting point was that developed by the American Academy of Paediatrics.[10]

> Sexual abuse occurs when a child is engaged in sexual activities that the child cannot comprehend, for which the child is developmentally unprepared and cannot give consent, and/or that violate the law or social taboos of society. The sexual activities may include all forms of oral-genital, genital, or anal contact by or to the child, or non-touching abuses such as exhibitionism, voyeurism or using the child in the production of pornography.

The medical assessment of children alleging that they have been sexually assaulted remains one of the more problematic areas of paediatric practice. Few practitioners have received formal teaching in the genito-anal anatomy of pre-pubertal children. Even fewer have had training in the recognition of signs of either acute or chronic trauma to that region.

In recent years, there have been considerable advances in the knowledge of what constitute normal and abnormal genito-anal anatomy. This has been primarily driven by some major cases (where the knowledge of the practitioners was clearly found to be wanting), significant increases in the reporting of alleged abuse, new technology and the development of medical training in this specialised field.

The doctor must have an accurate knowledge of genital anatomy, experience in performing gynaecological examinations and be able to apply the pathological principles of trauma to the genital tract. It is perhaps worth reiterating the comments of the Cleveland Inquiry on this matter:[11]

> It was entirely proper for the two paediatricians to play their part in the identification of sexual abuse in children referred to them. They were responsible for the care of their patients. Nonetheless they had a responsibility to examine their own actions; to consider whether their practice was always correct and whether it was in the best interests of the children and their patients. They are to be criticised for not doing so and for the certainty and over-confidence with which they pursued the detection of sexual abuse in children referred to them. They were not solely nor indeed principally responsible for the subsequent management of the children concerned. However, the certainty of their findings in relation to children diagnosed by them without prior complaint, posed particular problems for the Police and Social Services.

---

[10]   American Academy of Paediatrics, "Guidelines for the Evaluation of Sexual Abuse of Children: Subject Review" (1999) 103(1) *Paediatrics* 186.
[11]   *Report of the Inquiry into Child Abuse in Cleveland 1987*, HMSO, 1988.

Visualisation and documentation of children's genito-anal regions has historically been a difficult and contentious issue. Previously naked eye, hand-held lenses or oto/ophthalmoscopes, Glaister's rods or catheters were utilised. Problems encountered with these methods include pain, limited angle of view, short focal length and unsatisfactory documentation. These factors, combined with the inappropriateness or inability to review the child, resulted in the development and application of newer technology.

Colposcopy was first utilised by Hinselmann in Germany in 1924. Struck by the limitations of naked eye examination in the diagnosis of early cervical cancer, he constructed the first colposcope using Leitz lenses mounted on a pile of books for his first colposcopic examination.[12]

In the early 1980s William Teixeira,[13] a Brazilian medical examiner, commenced utilising the colposcope to clarify what he called dubious diagnoses made on gross unaided visualisation. It was not until the mid 1980s that Woodling and Heger[14] at UCLA commenced systematic use of the colposcope in evaluating children who had allegedly been sexually abused.

Colposcopic documentation is obtained through either a 35 mm camera or video attachment. Colposcopic examination has specific benefits in that it allows for magnification, illumination and photo documentation. Recorded findings in the form of photographs or videotapes may be used for case presentation, peer review, teaching and research activities.

There is no doubt that colposcopic photo documentation has greatly contributed to the body of scientific knowledge of genital and anal findings in both abused and non-abused children.[15]

Genital findings in children are difficult to interpret and is not within the expertise of most medical practitioners. Whilst acute trauma may be readily recognised, other findings remain much more problematic. What is normal? Could it be accidental? What is the age of injury?

---

[12]   E Burghardt, *Colposcopy Cervical Pathology*, Teorg Thieme Verlag, Stuttgart, 1984.

[13]   W Teixeira, "Hymenal Colposcopic Examination in Sexual Offences" (1981) 2 *Am J Forensic Med Pathology* 209.

[14]   B Woodling & A Heger, "The Use of the Colposcope in the Diagnosis of Sexual Abuse in the Paediatric Age Group" (1986) 10 *Child Abuse & Neglect* 11.

[15]   J McCann, "Use of the Colposcope in Childhood Sexual Abuse Examinations" (1990) 37(4) *Pediatric Clinics of North America* 863; D Muram, K Arheart & S Jennings, "Diagnostic Accuracy of Colposcopic Photographs in Child Sexual Abuse Evaluations" (1999) 12 *J Pediatr Adolesc Gynecol* 58; C Hobbs, J Wynne, A Thomas, "Colposcopic Genital Findings in Prepubertal Girls Assessed for Sexual Abuse" (1995) 76 *Archives of Disease in Childhood* 465; M Finkel, "Technical Conduct of the Child Sexual Abuse Medical Examination" (1998) 22(6) *Child Abuse & Neglect* 555.

Current information allows us to reasonably conclude that:

- The *position* in which the child is examined is critical to the interpretation of observations. When hymenal abnormalities are observed in the dorsal position, the child should be re-examined in the knee-chest position to exclude gravitational effects on the tissues.
- A genital examination with *normal findings* does not exclude some forms of sexual contact. In the majority of cases, the medical examination will neither confirm nor refute an allegation of sexual assault.[16] Certain actions are unlikely to produce injuries (eg oro-genital contact) whilst others, (eg penetration of the anus or penetration of the labia but not the hymen) may not necessarily produce injuries. Again, the amount of force will be a central issue.[17] Other explanations for the absence of physical signs may include the absence of penetration[18] and the healing of minor injuries[19] (particularly as many disclosures are delayed for lengthy periods after the alleged assault).[20]
- *Falls* (eg astride an object) may produce genital injuries. Generally, these are confined to the labia and surrounding skin.[21] It is difficult to conceive of a situation where either the hymen or the vagina could be injured without evidence of trauma to the external genitalia.
- There is no evidence that a range of *sporting activities* produce hymenal disruption but this issue has not been the subject of specific study.
- There is considerable variation in the shape of the hymen. The *pre-pubertal hymen* is generally thin and relatively inelastic. In this age group, penetration into the vagina may be associated with tearing of the hymenal tissue. At a later time, this tearing may be manifest by a deep notching of the hymenal margin or by scarring of the hymenal tissue.

---

[16] D Moran, "Child Sexual Abuse: Relationship between Sexual Acts and Genital Findings" (1989) 13 *Child Abuse and Neglect* 211; D Moran, "Child Sexual Abuse – Genital Findings in Prepubertal Girls" (1989) 160 *Am J Obstet Gynaecol* 328.

[17] JA Adams & S Knudson, "Genital Findings in Adolescent Girls Referred for Suspected Sexual Abuse" (1996) 15 *Arch Pediatr Adolesc Med* 850.

[18] K Edgarth, G Von Krogh & K Ormistad, "Adolescent girls investigated for sexual abuse: history, physical findings and legal outcome" (1999) 104 *Forensic Sci Int* 1-15.

[19] D Moran & M Laufer, "Limitations of the Medical Evaluation for Child Sexual Abuse" (1999) 44(12) *J Reprod Med* 993.

[20] D Smith, E Letourneau, B Saunders, D Kilpatrick & H Resnick, "Delay in Disclosure of Childhood Rape: Results from a National Survey" (2000) 24(2) *Child Abuse & Neglect* 273.

[21] S Pokorny, W Pokorny & W Kramer, "Acute Genital Injury in the Prepubertal Girl" (1992) 166 *Am J Obstet Gynecol* 1461.

- Evaluation of the *post-menarchal hymen* warrants some specific comments. Oestrogen produces dramatic changes to the hymen at the time of puberty causing it to become more elastic, distensible, thick and irregular.[22] These features mean that the tissue is less likely to be damaged during penetration. It also means that the ability to reach a conclusion regarding past penetration is very limited as notching or even scarring or transections may become obscured in the physical changes to this structure.

Relatively little is known about what constitutes normal variations of the peri- and post- menarchal hymen. One study[23] of 300 non-abused adolescent girls with a mean age of 18 found:

- In the subgroup of 100 sexually active girls, 81 per cent had hymenal clefts compared to 11 per cent of non-sexually active tampon users and 5 per cent of non-sexually active pad users.
- 37 per cent of sexually active girls had narrowing of the hymenal rim to <1mm compared with 0 per cent (of 200 girls) who were not sexually active.

Caution should be used in interpreting the results of this single study and, in particular, whether narrowing is a particularly sensitive marker in this group and further, the reliability of self-identification of past sexual activity.[24]

In another study (204 girls with a mean age of 13 years), the authors concluded that:[25]

- Most of the subjects had a hymen of normal appearance after an episode of penetration of the vagina with a penis.
- Previous consensual sexual activity did not predict an abnormal finding.

---

[22]   S Pokorny, J Murphy & M Preminger, "Circumferential Hymen Elasticity: A Marker of Physiological Maturity" (1998) 43 *J Reprod Med* 943.

[23]   J Emans, E Woods, E Allred & E Grace, "Hymenal Findings in Adolescent Women, Impact of Tampon Use and Consensual Sexual Activity" (1994) 125 *J Paediatrics* 153.

[24]   F Goodyear-Smith & T Laidlaw, "Can Tampon Use Cause Hymen Changes in Girls Who have not had Sexual Intercourse? A Review of the Literature" (1998) 94 *For Sci Int* 147.

[25]   J Adams & S Knudson, "Genital Findings in Adolescent Girls Referred for Suspected Sexual Abuse" (1996) 150 *Arch Pediatr Adolesc Med* 850.

- *Repeated penetration* over a long period of time may result in attenuation and loss of hymenal tissue. The findings of hymenal scarring or the absence of hymenal tissue posteriorly is highly suggestive of blunt, penetrating trauma.
- Empirical studies have not found evidence of *congenital absence of the hymen*.
- *Hymenal orifice measurements* are of little diagnostic value in the assessment of penetrating trauma. Orifice size varies with the age, position and relaxation of the child and there is limited consensus regarding measurement interpretation.
- There are a considerable number of findings that, when seen in isolation, may be considered as being non-specific or, at best, suggestive but not diagnostic of *anal penetration*.[26] These findings include peri-anal inflammation, fissures, skin tags and reflex anal dilatation.[27] Reflex anal dilatation is a highly variable finding and cannot be considered diagnostic of anal penetration.
- The findings of *anal dilatation* at postmortem is not a marker for prior penetration. Postmortem perianal findings should be interpreted with caution.[28]
- *Lichen sclerosus* may produce findings that could be misinterpreted as being the result of genito-anal trauma.[29]

Genital trauma in young boys. Recent debate has centred around the interpretation of genital findings in prepubescent females and anal findings in both sexes. This has been appropriate given the controversy that certain cases have produced and the desire to develop a consensus of opinion in these fields. Relatively neglected in the debate has been the issue of genital trauma to male children.

Despite their external position, the genitalia of the male child should be relatively immune from injury. Mobility of the organs, the anatomical protection offered by buttocks and thighs and the likelihood of covering by

---

[26]   D Muram, "Anal and Perianal Abnormalities Seen in Prepubertal Victims of Abuse" (1989) 161 *Am J Obstet Gynecol* 278.

[27]   J McCann, M Simon, J Voris et al, "Perianal Findings in Prepubertal Children Selected for Nonabuse: A Descriptive Study" (1989) 13 *Child Abuse Negl* 179.

[28]   J McCann, D Reay, J Siebert, B Stephens & S Wirtz, "Postmortem Perianal Findings in Children" (1996) 17(4) *Am J Forensic Med Pathol* 289.

[29]   S Young, D Wells & E Ogden, "Lichen Sclerosis, Genital trauma and child sexual abuse" (1993) 22(5) *Australian Family Physician* 729-33; R Thomas, C Ridley, D McGibbon & M Black, "Anogenital Lichen Sclerosis in Women" (1996) 89 *J R Soc Med* 694; P Wood & T Bevan, "Child Sexual Abuse Enquiries and Unrecognised Vulval Licen Sclerosus et Atrophicus" (1999) 319 *BMJ* 899.

clothing (especially a nappy), shelters the organs from the majority of hazards to which this age group are exposed. Nonetheless, accidental trauma to the male genitalia is a well recognised, though infrequent, event.

Trauma to the male genitalia may result from the number of sources. In the adult male, the injury pattern ranges from the predictable to the bizarre; seemingly, the only limiting factor being the imagination of the perpetrator. Injuries produced by a range of household items such as vacuum cleaners, blades, drills and guns have been well-documented.[30] Additionally, sexual activity in its various guises has associated hazards with more than 70 per cent of penile injuries reportedly occurring during some form of sexual activity.[31] Traumatic fractures of the penis during intercourse, bites and bizarre entrapments are anecdotal in most Emergency Departments.

In young children, however, access to causative agents (either by physical restriction or prescribed by law) reduces the range of injurious agents. However, genital trauma in young children may be produced in a diversity of situations.

Iatrogenic – Although well described, the frequency of iatrogenic genital injuries appears to have reduced in recent years. Arguably, this is due to a lower incidence of circumcisions and improved surgical techniques. However, there may be some communities where this problem remains current.[32]

Blunt Trauma – Vehicular collisions and straddle falls may produce a range of blunt genital injuries. Additionally, such trauma may be associated with vascular and urethral damage. Other forms of blunt trauma may be the result of blows, pulling, pinching or crushing, producing abrasions, lacerations or bruising to the genitalia. A carefully obtained history from the child and eye witnesses, an assessment of the injury pattern, relevant medical investigations and an examination of the scene will usually assist in the analysis of that situation.[33]

Bites – The finding of a bite injury to the genitalia should be an immediate prompt for a thorough investigation. Any human bite sufficient to leave objective signs of trauma should be a clear indication of assaultive behaviour. Animal bites to male genitalia are rare.

---

[30]   A Cass, P Gleich & C Smith, "Male Genital Injuries from External Trauma" (1985) 57 *Br J Urol* 467.

[31]   J Prior, J Hill & D Packham, "Penile Injuries with Particular Reference to Injury to the Erectile Tissue" (1981) 53 *Br J Urol* 42.

[32]   ER Thatt, M Wagh & NI Kulkarni, "Identical Unusual Subtotal Amputation in Children: a Report of Four Cases" (1993) 46(6) *Br J Plast Surg* 535.

[33]   D Wells, "Genital Trauma in Young Boys" (1996) 3 *J Clin For Med* 129.

Incarceration – As an appendage, the male genitalia has the potential to be entrapped between objects or be the object of a tourniquet. In children, the ubiquitous zipper remains a potential source of injury. The child may present with his genitalia entrapped in the zipper or, alternatively, injury secondary to the entrapment may be seen. Generally, the child provides a good history of the event and the injury is usually limited to mild abrasions. Cases of strangulation by hairs, hidden threads or even a wrench have also been documented.[34]

Burns – Despite the relatively high incidence of burns in childhood, isolated burns of the genitalia appear to be a most unusual event. Whilst there is a considerable range of potential causative agents, the history and the burn pattern will usually assist in defining the circumstances of the injury.

Incised wounds – Incised wounds of the genitalia appear to be most unusual. Self-inflicted incised wounds are usually associated with a troubled adolescent and any other presentation demands a thorough investigation.

Non-accidental trauma to the male genitalia may be due to either sexual or physical forms of abuse. Interestingly, non-accidental trauma to the female genitalia is generally categorised as sexual abuse. This demarcation between sexually and physically assaultive behaviour raises a number of issues for medical practitioners and the criminal justice system.

Unless the circumstances of the assault are unequivocal, the distinction between physically or sexually assaultive behaviour may be difficult. It has been suggested that girls are more likely to interpret assaultive acts involving their genitalia as being sexually motivated.[35] Arguably, such an interpretation is just as likely to be made by the investigators and prosecutors of such offences. Sexually assaultive behaviour involving young boys' genitalia usually consists of an assailant handling, licking or sucking the genitalia; actions that are infrequently associated with the production of injuries.[36]

From a case management perspective, the distinction between sexually or non-sexually motivated assault may be of significant importance.[37] Medically, issues of disease transmission and counselling require addressing. For law enforcement agencies, knowledge of the causative circumstances may be critical to decisions of charging and penalties.

---

34   V Vahasarja, P Hellstrom, W Serlo & M Kontturi, "Treatment of Penile Incarceration by the String Method: Two Case Reports" (1993) 149 *J Urol* 372.

35   D Finkelhor & J Wolak, "Non Sexual Assaults to the Genitals in the Youth Population" (1995) 274 *JAMA* 1692.

36   D Wells, "Genital Trauma in Young Boys" (1996) 3 *J Clin For Med* 129.

37   W Holmes & G Slap, "Sexual Abuse of Boys: Definition, Prevalence, Correlates, Sequelae and Management" (1998) 280(21) *JAMA* 1855.

TABLE 1: Assaultive Injury Patterns[38]

Action	*Site*	*Possible Injuries*
BITE	NECK	• Bite marks: bruising, abrasions. • Suction type petechial bruising.
	BREASTS	• Bite marks, abrasions/lacerations to nipples.
BLOWS	SCALP	• Bruising, (including haematomas), lacerations.
	FACE	• Fractures (zygoma, jaw, nose). • Dental trauma. • Intra-oral bruises, abrasions, frenulum damage. • Facial bruises-slap marks.
	EYES	• Periorbital haematomas. • Subconjunctival haemorrhage. • Hyphaemas. • Traumatic mydriasis.
	EARS	• Tympanic membrane perforation (usually slapping). • Pinna bruises/lacerations. • Post auricular bruises.
	NECK	• Laryngeal skeleton trauma. • Voice changes (hoarseness, dysphonia), and dysphagia.
	HANDS	• Knuckle abrasions, (punching) bruising, lacerations or fractures.
	LIMBS	• Bruises, abrasions, lacerations & fracture.
	TRUNK	• Bruises, abrasions, fractures (especially ribs).
BURNS – CIGARETTE BURNS		• Circular burns between 5 mm and 15 mm in size, on any part of the body. • Partial or full thickness. Flame, scald, contact.

---

[38] (Modified from) A Welborn, *Adult Sexual Assault*, Monash University, Victoria, 2000.

Action	Site	Possible Injuries
DEFENSIVE RESPONSES	LIMBS	• Bruising (especially on medial and lateral aspects of forearms, hands), "warding off" type injuries. • Incised wounds (knife, bottle). • Lacerations and fractures (blunt implements).
	HANDS	• Incised wounds to palms and web space (grasping sharp weapon). • Incised wounds and bruises to dorsum (deflecting blows). • Nail damage (may also occur in counter-assault, eg scratching).
DRAGGING	LIMBS / TRUNK	• Abrasions and bruises on exposed skin surfaces. Embedded foreign material.
FALLS	LIMBS	• Abrasions and bruising especially to bony prominences; elbows, knees and heel of hands, lacerations, fractures.
FINGERNAIL SCRATCHES		• Linear scratch abrasions to any part of body.
FLIGHT	LIMBS	• Linear scratch abrasions due to contact with vegetation. • Bruises from contact with other objects, falls. • Abrasions and bruises on soles.
GRASPING	EARS	• Bruising. • Trauma secondary to earring contact/loss.
	LIMBS	• Fingertip bruises, especially to medial aspect of upper arms and forearms and medial thighs.
HAIR PULLING		• Hair follicle haematomas, bald patches, tenderness.
INJECTIONS	UPPER LIMBS	• Puncture site over the course of a vein. • Bruising.

Action	Site	Possible Injuries
LIGATURE / MANUAL COMPRESSION	NECK	• Ligature marks or imprint bruising (necklace, clothing). • Fingertip bruises, abrasions (due to fingernails). • Facial petechiae, intra-oral petechiae, conjunctival haemorrhages.
PENETRATION	MOUTH	Occasionally, • Pharyngeal bruising, palate bruising, frenulum trauma.
RESTRAINT	LIMBS	• Ligature marks (wrists and ankles), fingertip bruising.
SQUEEZING / PINCHING	BREASTS	• Bruising.
WHIPPING WITH ROPE / CORD	TRUNK / LIMBS	• Linear, curved or looped bruising, abrasions. • Tramtrack bruises.

TABLE 2: Adult Female Sexual Assault Studies

	Beh[39]	Bowyer[40]	Lenahan[41]	Cartwright [42]
No	350	83	17	405
Age	4-66	16-48 (mean 25)	>15	>10
Extragenital injuries	35%	82%	76%	40%
Genito-anal injuries	-	27%	6% naked eye 53% colposcopy	16%

	Slaughter[43]	Rambow[44]	Tintinalli[45]	Wells[46]
No	311	182	372	170
Age	11-85 (mean 24)	>16	13-78	>16
Extragenital injuries	57%	50%	32%	64%
Genito-anal injuries	68% (colposcopy)	10%	19%	27%

[39] PSL Beh, "Rape in Hong Kong: an Overview of Current Knowledge" (1998) 5 *J Clin For Med* 124.

[40] L Bowyer & ME Dalton, "Female Victims of Rape and their Genital Injuries" (1997) 104 *Br J Obstet Gynaecol* 617.

[41] L Lenahan, A Ernst & B Johnson, "Colposcopy in Evaluation of the Adult Sexual Assault Victim" (1998) 16 *Am J Emerg Med* 183.

[42] PS Cartwright & the Sexual Assault Study Group, "Factors that Correlate with Injury Sustained by Survivors of Sexual Assault" (1987) 70 *Obstet Gynecol* 144.

[43] L Slaughter, CRV Brown, MN Crowley & R Peck, "Patterns of Genital Injury in Female Sexual Assault Victims" (1997) 176 *Am J Obstet Gynecol* 609.

[44] B Rambow, C Adkinson, TH Frost & GF Peterson, "Female Sexual Assault: Medical and Legal Implications" (1992) 21(6) *Annals of Emergency Medicine* 727.

[45] JE Tintinalli & M Hoelzer, "Clinical Findings and Legal Resolution in Sexual Assault" (1985) 14 *Annals of Emergency Medicine* 447.

[46] D Wells & S Young, "Circumstances and Findings in Women Alleging Rape", Proceedings, International Conference on Emergency Medicine, Sydney, 1996.

16 Causation in Coronial Law

IAN FRECKELTON*

Introduction

The concept of causation is fundamental to the coronial function. In fact, society's need to determine the reasons lying behind unexpected, suspicious and violent deaths continues to this day as a principal reason for coroners having the role of conducting formal inquests. Coroners in England, Canada, Australia and New Zealand have as key parts of their role to determine the identity of persons who have died in prescribed circumstances, to make findings about how deaths have occurred and to rule upon what constituted the cause or causes of deaths. In some jurisdictions, the obligation to decide formally whether a person contributed to the cause of death is stipulated; in others it is regarded as subsidiary to other findings. In some jurisdictions, the coroner has additional but cognate responsibilities – to determine the origin and cause of fires, whether or not causing death; to ascertain the origin and cause of explosions; and to find out what caused certain kinds of accidents and other dangerous phenomena.

The obligation to determine causation, especially in relation to deaths, has proved, as a matter of law and fact, an extremely problematic exercise going to the very heart of the coronial function. Justice Nathan summed up the problem in *Harmsworth v The State Coroner*:[1] "the issue of causation ... has vexed philosophers and judges since Socrates was obliged to drink the hemlock." As McClemens J noted in *Ex parte Minister of Justice; Re Malcolm*,[2] too, the forensic difficulties posed by the need to make findings

---

* Barrister in full-time private practice in Melbourne, Australia, Professor in the Department of Psychological Medicine, Adjunct Professor in the Law Faculty and an Honorary Associate Professor in the Department of Forensic Medicine at Monash University, Adjunct Professor in the Department of Law and Legal Studies, La Trobe University.
1 [1989] VR 989 at 995.
2 [1965] NSWR 1598 at 1604.

about causation, in particular in the coronial context, will persist into the future.

In the latter quarter of the twentieth century the emergence of coronial law as an area of intense media and popular interest,[3] the glamorisation of the role of the forensic pathologist and of the coroner, together with the increased incidence of appellate litigation arising out of coroners' decisions, have shone a complex spotlight upon decision-making in relation to causation by coroners. While coronial law is part of the general law which deals with causes and results, it is a distinctive characteristic which has generated its evolution. Historically, coroners and coronial juries have been empowered to add "riders" to the formal records of their decisions. These "riders" or recommendations have generally been directed toward matters of health and safety or to the administration of justice. They evolved because of the potential to reduce the incidence of avoidable deaths and injuries.[4] As a formal part of the decision-making process, they are a unique component of this aspect of the law. The potential for riders, and, indeed, their growing importance as a factor influencing the scope and content of coronial inquests in some countries, in particular Australia, in turn has had a significant impact upon the construction of causation as a concept under coronial law.

Particularly problematic aspects of the coronial function occur in the fact-finding context of multi-factorial causes of death and fires, and also where it is contended that a death has been caused, at least in part, by a failure on the part of an institution to exercise proper care and supervision over a resident, such as a person who is intellectually disabled, mentally ill or confined within a penal institution. This kind of scenario has generated considerable jurisprudence in recent times, but the law in relation to causation in such contexts remains unresolved to a significant degree.

Concentrating on these difficult contexts in which causation has challenged both coroners and appellate courts, this chapter explores the notion of causation as it has evolved in the context of modern coronial law. It does so with reference to the function of coroners' courts as inquisitorial modes of investigation into death and associated phenomena.[5]

---

3   A point made by Australian High Court Justice, Ian Callinan, in his fictional work: I Callinan, *The Coroner's Conscience*, Central Queensland University Press, Rockhampton, 1999, at p9.

4   See D McCann, "The Range of Findings Open to the Coroner" in H Selby (ed), *The Aftermath of Death*, Federation Press, Sydney, 1992; G Johnstone, "Coroners' Inquiries and Recommendations" in H Selby (ed), *The Inquest Handbook*, Federation Press, Sydney, 1998.

5   See *R v South London Coroner, ex parte Thompson* (1982) 126 SJ 125; *In re Rapier* (1986) 150 JP 481.

Coroners as Fact-Finders: An Historical Perspective

The early role of the coroner

The history of coroners dates back at least to the Council of Eyre in 1194. The early duties of the coroner were essentially those of a tax gatherer, protecting the pecuniary interests of the Crown, in particular those arising from the administration of the criminal law,[6] by ensuring the safekeeping of fines, recognisances and treasure trove. Another important function in the early phase of the coroner was the taking for the Crown of deodands, which were the instruments that the coroner found to have been responsible for deaths. They could be ships, carts, oxen or axes, but they had one thing in common – all of such chattels had a value to the Crown. To the considerable financial advantage of the monarch of the day, the coroner was responsible for the confiscation of such goods from malefactors once he was satisfied that they had caused the death of a deceased person.

In due course, the administrative role of the coroner[7] developed so that when a person was found dead, the coroner was notified and a jury assembled from the local *hundred super visum corporis*[8] with the body being laid on a table and examined by the jury under the direction of the coroner. Evidence was taken and a verdict arrived at by the jury. An important element of the verdict was the determination of the cause of death.

Before the rise of area magistrates and local police forces, the coroner could properly be described as the principal agent for investigation of crime, especially homicide, and before the comparatively late introduction of medical evidence[9] about the aetiology of death and the subsequent development of forensic pathology, the coroner was the official whose duty it was to examine the body of the deceased and determine the cause of the person's death. If there was evidence to accuse someone of a homicide offence, the inquisition of the coroner's jury, naming the suspect, operated

---

6   See W Holdsworth, *A History of English Law*, Vol 1, 7th edn, Methuen & Co, London, 1964, 84-5.

7   See K Waller, *Coronial Law and Practice in New South Wales*, 3rd edn, Butterworths, Sydney, 1994, 1.

8   See DM Walker, *Oxford Companion to Law*, Oxford University Press, Oxford, 1980 for definition of "hundred" and "hundred court".

9   M Baden, *Unnatural Death: Confession of a Medical Examiner*, Sphere Books, London, 1989, at p48; DS Jones, *Speaking for the Dead*, Ashgate, Dartmouth, 2000.

as a bill of indictment and committed the suspect to trial, in exactly the same way as the grand jury did in England until its abolition in 1933.[10]

In the United States a variety of factors led to the abolition of the coronial role and the institution of a system of medical examiners. Going with this phenomenon was a concentration upon ascertaining from a medical, as well as a legal perspective, the causes of death. Prominent amongst the factors was the fact that early American coroners tended to be unqualified occupants of a minor political office, typically farmers, carters or undertakers. As Johnson has pointed out, "Political, not professional skills, were what was demanded of potential coroners".[11] While in the mid-nineteenth century, the role of the coroner was not dissimilar to that in England, urban coroners in the United States began to assemble significant political power and to command substantial police forces – some had prosecutorial powers rivalling those of the district attorney. Corruption became endemic and attempts at reform focused upon the need to change the nature of the coroner's office, to depoliticise it and thereby to remove the temptation for venery. Reformers

> saw coroners as furthering the breakdown of law and order by allowing crime to go unpunished, whether because of the inexperience of the coroner's physicians or simple cupidity. Physicians in particular vilified coroners for their errors in post-mortem diagnosis and regularly lambasted them in the medical press ... Socially and professionally elite urban physicians often led attempts to reform the coroner's office, which took two forms. The simpler expedient was to demand the election of a physician to the office, in the belief that medical science would be better served – or at least acknowledged – by a medical practitioner. The more thoroughgoing approach was to seek abolition of the coroner's office and its replacement by a medical examiner system.[12]

In due course, the medical lobby and the anti-corruption movement were successful and a system of medical examiners was instituted throughout most United States jurisdictions in place of the office of coroner.

---

10 See RH Vickers, *The Powers and Duties of Police Officers and Coroners*, TH Flood & Co, London, 1889, at p214.

11 J Johnson, "Coroners, Corruption and the Politics of Death: Forensic Pathology in the United States" in M Clark & C Crawford, *Legal Medicine in History*, Cambridge University Press, Cambridge, 1994, 269.

12 Ibid, at p272.

The modern role of the coroner

In recent times, the coronial function has evolved considerably in Australia, New Zealand and Canada, and to a lesser degree in England. This is so in many regards. A major development in Australia is that in most States and Territories[13] coroners sit without juries. This is a significant change in terms of the role that coroners now play not only in relation to conducting investigations and ensuring that inquest hearings run fairly and efficiently, but in terms of the complexity of evidence that can be dealt with by coroners possessed of an expertise in grappling with technical issues that is not shared by lay jurors.

Another important shift may be identified in the move toward the conduct of quasi-judicial inquiries into the circumstances of deaths and certain other phenomena with an increasing emphasis on making recommendations to prevent repetition of life-endangering conduct. This has led the inquest away from being a straightforward exercise directed toward determining identity of the deceased, medical cause of death, proximate circumstances giving rise to death and particulars necessary for registration of death. It has seen the inquest process change so that it explores and makes findings about a complex array of factors that have led to death, both indirectly and directly. Along with this transformation has come an increasing preparedness by coroners to investigate and make findings about a range of multifaceted factors leading to avoidable deaths. In New Zealand, this even constitutes a specific reason for the holding of an inquest. Section 15(1)(b) of the *Coroners Act* 1988 (NZ) provides that an inquest can be held for the purpose of:

> Making any recommendations or comments on the avoidance of circumstances similar to those in which the death occurred, or on the manner in which any persons should act in such circumstances, that, in the opinion of the coroner, may if drawn to public attention reduce the chances of the occurrence of other deaths in such circumstances.[14]

Controversies about the modern role of the coroner

The changes, though, and the challenges facing the modern coroner have not been without their critics. They have proved controversial. A Canadian decision, for instance, has pointed out that "an inquest is not a trial; an

---

13 See I Freckelton & D Ranson (eds), *Coronial Law and Medicine*, Oxford University Press, Melbourne, 2002 (forthcoming).

14 See also Law Commission of New Zealand, *Coroners*, Report No 62, Law Commission, Wellington, 2000.

inquest is not a Royal Commission; an inquest is not a public platform; an inquest is not a crusade".[15] This said, the role of the coroner in functioning as a means of public inquiry into how avoidable deaths can be avoided in the future is increasingly entrenched as a feature of the modern inquest. Such a shift is not so much the adoption by coroners of a significantly new function; it is a consolidation of a longstanding feature of coronial inquisitions and inquests, dating back to the earliest period of coronial decision-making.

Contextualising the modern role

For instance, coroners in fourteenth century England ordered that wells be filled to prevent further drownings.[16] A practical way to prevent further injury was also identified in a 1487 inquest:

> About 8pm on 6 Nov, when going home, John Aleyn of Rye, "hokemaker", by misadventure fell over "le clyff" near the east side of the Austin Friars in a great wind. Because "le clyff" was crumbling and the cause of his death, the land near it has been marked off 3 feet towards the king's highway there.[17]

Coroners' recommendations, reflecting a broad perspective and a pragmatic bent toward reducing the incidence and causes of injury and death, may be seen, too, in the investigation into the death of Thomas Drake in 1793 at Squirrel Farm, Ewan Field in Kemble. The coroner's roll records that:

> Drake – with another man standing on a stone at the top of a high precipice and quarry and moving and drawing a large stone at the bottom by means of a large wheel and cord, slipped and fell and was killed. Because the master of the works and the proprietor of the land were both at a distance and the employment appeared very dangerous in future without better contrivance and the addition of a stage, etc, it was adjudged highly requisite to adjourn and summon those with other evidence on 30 Aug., when the said alterations and additions were agreed on and promised to be effected.[18]

---

[15] See *People First of Ontario v Niagara (Regional Coroner)* (1991) 85 DLR (4th) 174, 187.

[16] See G Johnstone, "Coroner's Inquiries and Recommendations" in H Selby (ed), *The Inquest Handbook*, Federation Press, Sydney, 1998, 38.

[17] RF Hunnisett, *The Medieval Coroner*, Cambridge University Press, Cambridge, 1961.

[18] Ibid, at p34.

Similarly, in 1788 at Chippenham a William Deverill was lost on a river "supposed to have fallen in passing over a very narrow foot-bridge called Black-Avon Bridge". The Coroner found that the deceased:

> drowned by falling from a very dangerous and presentable foot-bridge over the Avon at the back of the town. As well by reason of many past accidents as the present and to prevent future ones, it was judged highly necessary to adjourn until after a convention by vestry of the chief inhabitants of Chippenham, the result whereof is to widen and strengthen the bridge and render it safer in time of floods.[19]

Coroners' inquests in England were investigated by a Parliamentary Select Committee in 1860. This occurred in the context of increasing hostility to the institution of coroners in the United States and tensions between coroners and magistrates on the one hand in England and between coroners and police forces on the other hand.[20] The scope of inquests was extended in an effort to address social problems evident in an aspect of urban deaths. The Committee accepted the view of the coroners and sanitarians that inquests should be held in all cases of sudden or accidental death "for denunciation of the guilty, for the comfort of the innocent, and for the information of the public, who should be taught the nature and extent of the dangers that surround them."[21]

Appellate perspectives on the modern role

A number of modern descriptions of the coroner's function have explicitly recognised this ancient function of the coroner to go beyond the circumstances of the individual death and to initiate and facilitate measures to reduce the likelihood of similar tragedies. Lord Lane CJ in *R v South London Coroner; Ex parte Thompson*,[22] for instance, stressed the need for the inquest process to uncover the facts sufficiently to enable the adoption of counter-measures, characterising the role of the inquest as being "to seek out and record as many of the facts surrounding the death as public interest requires".[23] Similarly, *in People First of Ontario v Niagara (Regional*

---

[19] Ibid, at p143.

[20] See J Sim & T Ward, "The Magistrate of the Poor? Coroners and Deaths in Custody in Nineteenth Century England" in M Clark & C Crawford, *Legal Medicine in History*, Cambridge University Press, Cambridge, 1994, 256ff.

[21] Registrar-General, *Nineteenth Annual Report*, PP, 1857-8, XXIII, 1, 198.

[22] (1982) 126 Sol Jo 625.

[23] *R v South London Coroner; Ex parte Thompson* (1982) 126 Sol Jo 625 (QB), Lord Lane CJ at 628.

Coroner)[24] it was held that, "The social and preventative function of the inquest which focuses on the public interest has become, in some cases, just as important as the distinctly separate function of investigating the individual facts of individual deaths and the personal roles of individuals involved in the death". However, it was acknowledged that "the narrow investigative function" of the coroner to lay out the essential facts surrounding a death "is still vital to the families of the deceased and to those who are directly involved in the death".[25]

Advantages to the modern role

The benefits of the broader form of the coronial inquest process can be summarised as follows:

- determining the medical cause of death, thus providing accurate statistical information on causes of death;
- advancing medical knowledge;
- investigating deaths to allay rumours or suspicion, and thereby to ensure no foul play or wrongdoing slips through the net;
- making recommendations to avoid future fatalities;
- checking on the death registration system; and
- enabling relatives to find out how the deceased died, which can assist in the grieving process.[26]

The increasing focus upon the role of the coroner as a vehicle for preventing causes of injury and death has become a characteristic of the evolution of coronial law in Australia and Canada, particularly, since the mid-1980s.[27]

---

[24] (1991) 85 DLR 174 at 183-4.

[25] Ibid, at p184.

[26] See P Matthews , "Involuntary Manslaughter: A View from the Coroner's Court" (1996) 60 *Crim LJ* 189 at 191. See also the Report of the Committee on Death Certification and Coroners, September 22 1971, Cmnd 4810, chaired by N Brodrick QC; H Hallenstein, "Coronership – the Practical Application of Law, Medicine, Science and Specialty Knowledge", paper presented to Australian Institute of Criminology Conference, Surfers Paradise, Institute of Criminology, 1993. The coronial hearing as a procedure for investigating controversial deaths has its detractors, however. In England, see for instance, G Robertson, *The Justice Game*, Random House, London, 1998, at p201.

[27] See, for example, G Johnstone, "An Avenue for Death and Injury Prevention", in H Selby (ed), *The Aftermath of Death*, Federation Press, Sydney, 1992; J Harrison & J Moller, "Learning from Experience – Toward Prevention", in H Selby (ed), *The Inquest Handbook*, Federation Press, Sydney, 1997. Concerns about the extent to which this may fundamentally change the role of the coroner have also been expressed:

The Scope of Coronial Inquiries

Direct and indirect findings as to causation

A tension can be discerned between the vision harboured by many coroners as to what should constitute the scope of the inquest process and the perception articulated by both superior court reviews of coronial hearings and a series of government-sponsored reviews of the modern inquest. The issue goes beyond a hegemonic assertion of authority by contemporary coroners. It revolves around an attempt by one component of the legal/bureaucratic process to fill a void left by deficits in both the civil and criminal law – to address constructively scenarios in which members of the community meet their deaths unnecessarily and prematurely. In good part it is a public health issue.

In spite of the evolution of inquests, which have resulted in Australia, in particular, in an avalanche of inquests taking in excess of 100 court days each, appellate cases which have had reason to determine the breadth and extent of the coroner's jurisdiction, and therefore, by inference the circumstances in which findings of causation should be made, have tended to do so relatively narrowly. A number of inquiries into the coronial jurisdiction have supported this approach and indeed given an historical justification for it. For instance. the 1936 English departmental committee on coroners under the chairmanship of Lord Wright[28] urged that, save in cases of murder and manslaughter, inquests should be limited in their scope to ascertainment of a finite number of statutorily mandated facts. It expressed concern that inquests were too readily being used as a vehicle to elicit facts and obtain riders for the purposes of imputing or escaping civil liability for acts or omissions causing death.

Similarly, the 1971 report of the committee reviewing the law and practice relating to death certification, under the chairmanship of Mr Brodrick QC[29] argued that coronial findings ought in no sense to function as surrogates for criminal or civil determinations. It argued that "In future the function of an inquest should be simply to seek out and record as many of the facts concerning the death as the public interest requires, without deducing from these facts any determination of blame." A result of the report was the removal from English coroners and their juries of the right

---

I Freckelton, "Expert Proof in the Coroner's Jurisdiction", in H Selby (ed), *The Aftermath of Death*, Federation Press, Sydney, 1992. For the view of the coroner in a "social context", see *R v Faber* [1976] 2 SCR 9 at 30 per De Grandpre J.

[28] Cmnd 5070.
[29] Cmnd 4810.

to prefer homicide charges.[30] Three years later, coronial juries were precluded from adding a rider to their findings by an amendment to the coronial rules.[31]

In Victoria, Australia, a similar inquiry took place under JG Norris in 1981,[32] this giving rise shortly afterwards to new legislation in that jurisdiction governing coroners.[33] Again a key recommendation of the inquiry was that coroners' determinations not trespass on either the civil or the criminal processes, rather confining themselves to making findings arising out of the statutorily mandated coronial obligations.

Appellate perspectives on the scope of inquests

However, this is not to suggest that coronial inquests are or should be of narrow compass. As the Ontario Supreme Court held in *People First of Ontario v Niagara (Regional Coroner)*:[34] "the social and preventative function of the inquest which focuses on the public interest has become, in some cases, just as important as the distinctly separate function of investigating the individual facts of individual deaths and the personal roles of individuals involved in the death."

Uncertainty as to findings about causation in all jurisdictions is fuelled by the fact that coronial law, while having its own identity and its own objectives,[35] exists in a nether world between criminal law and civil law. A key issue in this regard is the contemporary view of the purpose and legitimate scope of coronial inquests. These have been addressed both by governmental reports and by superior court decisions.

Appellate constructions of the coroner's obligation to find "how" the deceased died

A crucial constraint of the scope of coronial inquests and findings exists in the meaning to be given to the coroner's task to ascertain, if possible, how

---

[30]   *Criminal Law Act* 1977 (UK), s56(1).

[31]   See M Levine & J Pyke, *Levine on Coroners' Courts*, Sweet & Maxwell, London, 1999, at p145.

[32]   JG Norris, *The Coroners Act 1958: A General Review*, Law Printer, Melbourne, 1981.

[33]   *Coroners Act* 1985 (Vic). It proved to be a model for a number of Australian states and territories.

[34]   (1991) 85 DLR (4th) 174 at 183-4.

[35]   See *R v South London Coroner; ex parte Thompson* (1982) 126 Sol Jo 625; P Matthews, "Involuntary Manslaughter: A View from the Coroner's Court" (1996) 60 *Criminal Law Journal* 189 at 191; Report of the Committee on Death Certification and Coroners (chair: N Brodrick QC), Cmnd 4810, 1971.

a deceased died. The leading appellate decision on the subject is that of the English Court of Appeal *in R v HM Coroner for North Humberside and Scunthorpe; ex parte Jamieson*,[36] where the court read down in important ways the scope of inquests, affirming an earlier decision on a similar subject[37] in which Hutchison LJ had found that the obligation of a coroner to find "how" a deceased died[38] meant "by what means" not "in what broad circumstances" and holding that "lack of care" aggravated the cause of death only when there was a close connection between the lack of care and the death.

Sir Thomas Bingham MR held that the task of the coroner is not to ascertain "how the deceased died", which "might reach general and far-reaching issues but 'how ... the deceased came by his death', a more limited question directed to the means by which the deceased came by his death."[39]

The nub of the decision from a point of view of its impact upon the scope of future inquests lies in its narrow construction of the obligation of the coroner to determine "how" any given deceased passed away, this being the umbrella under which an inquest has the potential to analyse indirect factors suspected of contributing to the causal chain resulting in a death.

A similar approach to that of the Court of Appeal in *Ex parte Jamieson* was taken by Warren J of the Victorian Supreme Court in *Kahn v West and Keown*[40] in relation to the proper ambit of findings about "how" the deceased came by her death. The case was an appeal from a coroner's decision that police had not contributed to the cause of death of an intoxicated, tomahawk-wielding Aboriginal woman when they fatally shot her. Justice Warren held that the scope of the coroner's duty to find "how" the deceased died is narrow: in the case before her, it consisted in no more than the pulling of the trigger on the pistol held by a police constable. It did not encompass the surrounding issues which might or might not have affected whether the shooting was legitimate, namely in the exercise of lawful self-defence. Such matters could include, for instance, indirect issues such as police training and a range of reasonably direct causal

---

[36]   [1995] QB 1.
[37]   *R v HM Coroner for Birmingham, ex parte Secretary of State for the Home Department* (1990) 155 JP 107 per Hutchison LJ and Watkins LJ.
[38]   Under s11 of the *Coroners Act* 1988 (UK).
[39]   [1995] QB 1 at 8.
[40]   [1999] VSC 530.

factors particular to the circumstances in which the particular constable fired his weapon.[41]

Deaths in institutions: the closeness of required nexus and the role of the coroner

One of the contexts in which causation in coronial law has been vigorously contested and has fallen to be construed in terms of the sufficiency of nexus between act or omission and consequence has been in relation to deaths occurring in institutions such as prisons, psychiatric hospitals and residences for those with intellectual disabilities. Frequently such deaths are a result of the detainee's own actions, by reason of less than ideal care by the institution or in the context of an insurrection within the facility.

A typical and tragic example was canvassed before the Coroner's Court in Victoria in April 2001. An elderly resident of a supported rehabilitation facility was known to be psychiatrically ill, with a range of positive and negative symptoms of schizophrenia, as well as depressive symptomatology, for which he was receiving anti-psychotic and anti-anxiolytic medication. In certain circumstances, he would wander away from the facility, only later to be found confused and sometimes at considerable risk. Community visitors, who have a statutory mandate in Victoria to inspect such facilities, had commented of the facility where he resided that little attention was given to the construction of proper "service plans". Such plans, by force of statutory regulations,[42] are supposed to set out and plan the services given to vulnerable residents to assist in meeting their individual needs. One day the resident again left the facility for no known reason. The next day his body was found floating in a nearby river. The task for the Coroner was to determine not so much whether the deceased died as a result of foul play, for which there was no indication, but whether his death was caused by inadequate planning and care being devoted to catering to vulnerabilities that placed him at risk of avoidable death.[43]

One of the most significant judicial analyses of the issue has been that of the English Court of Appeal *in R v HM Coroner for North Humberside and Scunthorpe; ex parte Jamieson*[44] The decision came in the wake of a series of decisions in "lack of care" inquests where people had passed away

---

[41] Warren J's decision was successfully appealed to the Victorian Court of Appeal in *Khan v Keown* [2001] VSCA 137 but the general issue of the meaning of "how" was not finally resolved.

[42] *Health Services (Residential Care) Regulations* 1991 (Vic), Reg 303(1)(b).

[43] *Re David Nixon Deceased*, Victorian Coroner's Court, 2001.

[44] [1995] QB 1.

arguably because sufficient care had not been taken of them and they had died either directly by their own act or by reason of neglect by a facility.[45] The deceased, who was serving a lengthy custodial sentence, hanged himself in a single cell in the prison hospital after he had previously tried to commit suicide within the prison. The key issue in the inquest related to the care extended to the deceased by the prison authorities in the light of their knowledge of his mental state at the relevant time. The coronial jury was not invited by the coroner to consider whether the death of the deceased was caused or contributed to by lack of care.

Consistent with the Court of Appeal's decision as to when a coroner should make findings on "how" a person died is its determination that a verdict of "lack of care" is only legitimate when a failure on the part of authorities, such as those running prisons, is causally connected with a death, that is to say when evidence establishes a "close connection", rather than, for example, that the failure created the general environment within which a desperate act such as a suicide, occurred. What is necessary is a "clear and direct causal connection" between neglect or self-neglect and death.[46]

However, the difficulties of application of this requirement have persisted in the aftermath of the Court of Appeal decision in *Ex parte Jamieson*. In 2000, for instance, Tomlinson J[47] held that the requirement for a "clear and distinct causal connection" does not carry the sense that such words convey when a court considers a contract, a tort or an insurance policy. He held that the touchstone is the opportunity to render care, in the narrow sense of the word, and thereby to have prevented death. He found that the test of the Court of Appeal does not mean that a conscientious person would necessarily have provided the care but that the person had an opportunity to do something effective.

In the case before Tomlinson J, the deceased was an alcoholic who had been arrested and detained at the Tamworth Police Station, later suffering a series of fits that led to his death. Justice Tomlinson held that there was sufficient evidence to conclude that, in light of information already in the

---

[45] *R v HM Coroner for Birmingham, ex parte Secretary of State for the Home Department* (1990) 155 JP 107; *R v HM Coroner for East Berkshire, ex parte Buckley* (1992) 157 JP 425; *R v Coroner for Inner North London, ex parte Diesa Koto* (1993) 157 JP 857; *R v HM Coroner for South Yorkshire, ex parte Stringer* (1993) 158 JP 453; *R v HM Coroner for Western District of east Sussex; ex parte Homberg* (1994) 158 JP 357.

[46] *R v HM Coroner for North Humberside and Scunthorpe; ex parte Jamieson* [1995] QB 1 at 26; see also *R v HM Coroner for Swansea and Gower, ex parte Chief Constable of Wales* (199) 164 JP 191 at 197.

[47] In *R v HM Coroner for Coventry, ex parte Chief Constable of Staffordshire* (2000) 164 JP 665.

possession of the police, and in light of the deceased man's spilling of his tea on two separate occasions in the context of severely shaking hands, there existed circumstances in which, had the police promptly summoned medical aid, it was at least possible that the deceased would not have died. Thus, he found it legitimate for the coroner to have summed up to his jury in terms of there being a clear and direct causal connection between the deficits in care on the part of the police and the death of the deceased.[48]

Appellate rulings on the extent of the coroner's investigative responsibilities

By the time of the 1995 decision of the Court of Appeal in *Ex Parte Jamieson* and the 2000 decision of Warren J, the controversies about the depth of inquiry that the coroner should pursue were not new in Australia. An important analysis had been undertaken in the first of the major modern Australian decisions on coronial law, *Harmsworth v State Coroner*,[49] an appeal to the Victorian Supreme Court dealing with a coroner's inquest into the deaths of several men in a fire after the construction by prisoners of a barricade inside a high security section of a jail. Justice Nathan had been called upon to deal specifically with the propriety of a coroner inquiring into a number of matters which had the potential to shed light into how it was that prisoners in an electronically controlled, high security part of Melbourne's main prison had engaged in what was clearly risky and ill-considered behaviour, blocking up entrances and setting fire to bedding and other combustibles. Objection had been taken to the liberal response of the coroner to the attempt by relatives of the deceased to explore the background to the conduct of the prisoners. The dispute therefore was in substance as to the remoteness of the causal factors into which the coroner should inquire and as to which he should be entitled to make findings.

Justice Nathan conceded that the prisoners would not have died, had they not been in prison but found that a line had to be drawn in terms of the parameters of the coroner's inquiry. He held that the sociological factors which related to the causes of the men's imprisonment "could not be remotely relevant".[50] Justice Nathan had regard to how wide, prolix and indeterminate the inquest might be if each of the many facets of the individual personalities of all those involved were to be considered:

---

[48] See too *R v HM Coroner for Wiltshire, ex parte Clegg* (1997) 161 JP 521 at 529.
[49] [1989] VR 989.
[50] *Harmsworth v State Coroner* [1989] VR 989, Nathan J at 995. See also the analysis in *People First of Ontario v Niagara (Regional Coroner)* (1991) 85 DLR (4th) 174, 187.

A coroner would be confronted with a need to enquire into the personal peculiarities of all of the prisoners who barricaded themselves in. Both those who relented and those who did not. Whether, for example, one group or person suborned others, and if so why and how. The personalities of all of the prison officers who interacted with all of the prisoners could also be investigated. Even the interaction of all of the other prisoners at any time in Jika with the deceased.[51]

The irony was that these aspects of the decision of Nathan J carried an element of "tilting at windmills". What had been attempted in the inquest was an exploration of why it was that the prisoners had responded to grievances with those running the jail in the desperate and manifestly dangerous way that they had. While there had been some suggestions, for political reasons, no doubt, that the coroner should inquire generally into the deficits in the prison system, that had never been a serious option, so far as the coroner had been concerned. What had been taking place, though, from the perspective of the prison authorities was a broader-based analysis of the factors precipitating the conduct of the prisoners, which in turn resulted in their death, than they were comfortable with. Hence the attempt by the prison authorities to curtail this aspect of the inquest. Clearly enough the view of Nathan J was that the inquest had exceeded its proper parameters. Unfortunately, he did not enunciate clear criteria for delimiting the extent to which matters other than those absolutely proximate to the circumstances of death should be the subject of inquiry at inquest.

The key aspect of the decision of Nathan J lies within its rationale for the coroner's inquiry not being able to extend in the way that the presiding coroner contemplated: "Such an inquest would never end, but worse it could never arrive at the coherent, let alone concise, findings required" under the legislation. He conceded that such an inquest could certainly provide material for riders and comments, but he held that "[s]uch discursive investigations are not envisaged nor empowered. ... They are not within jurisdictional power."[52] He noted the existence of a legislative entitlement on the part of the coroner to make comments and recommendations, but held unequivocally that the "power to comment is incidental and subordinate to the mandatory power to make findings relating to how the deaths occurred, their causes and the identity of any contributory persons".[53] In this he was consistent with the approach taken in *Re Kelly, dec'd*,[54] an English inquest dealing with the death of an army

---

[51] *Harmsworth v State Coroner* [1989] VR 989 at 996.
[52] Ibid.
[53] Ibid.
[54] (1996) 161 JP 417 at 427.

captain in Kenya from injuries he sustained in the course of a live firing exercise. Lord Justice Pill and Newman J had emphasised that the power to make recommendations so as to endeavour to avoid repetition of an avoidable death is ancillary to inquest procedure, not its mainspring. Justice Nathan's decision narrowed the extent in Australia to which an inquest can be directed toward facilitating a coroner's preparedness to delve into the indirect circumstances contributing to the cause of death and to make recommendations or comments, the question being one of remoteness and not readily susceptible to definition.

What Nathan J's decision means in practice has not been clearly explicated. It has become clear that relatively little heed has been taken of the decision by coroners desirous of inquiring into matters some distance removed from why fires engulfed vulnerable people, how it was that police shot unarmed civilians, how persons in hospitals were treated in ways which resulted in deaths which should not have happened, and why objectively dangerous incidents, such as building implosions, took place, although contra-indicated by safety considerations. Justice Nathan's desire that coroners should not inquire far along the chain of causation beyond the immediate circumstances of death has not resulted in Australian inquests becoming either of confined dimensions or of short duration.

The Required Nexus Between Causative Factor and Death

Magnitude of nexus

A number of difficult decisions have grappled specifically with the proper scope of coronial findings on the issue of causation. As already indicated in the context of neglect and self-neglect cases, in England the need for a "clear and causal connection" between a causative factor and a death has often been emphasised by the Court of Appeal but never further defined.[55] In *R v Cato*,[56] it was confirmed in the criminal law context in England that if an act contributed significantly to the cause of death, that is sufficient – it need not be the sole or even the principal cause of death. Subsequently, in England, Lord Woolf MR in the Court of Appeal applied criminal jurisprudence on the issue and held that what is necessary under coronial

---

[55] C Dorries, *Coroner's Courts: A Guide to Law and Practice*, John Wiley & Sons, Chichester, 1999, at p223.

[56] (1976) 62 Cr App R 41 at 46.

law is that the act "more than minimally, negligibly or trivially contributed to the death".[57]

In Australian law, there is no clear authority on the issue, although it has been held that a coroner is obliged to endeavour to ascertain the "real cause" of death.[58] It seems under the criminal law that for a cause to be sufficient for criminal liability, it must be a substantial and operating cause.[59] As Lanham in this collection points out, the position taken by the High Court of Australia is not entirely clear, though different formulations being adopted in the leading decision of *Royall v R*,[60] where the question traversed was whether a person who frightens another into killing herself accidentally, could be held to have caused the death. Three judges referred to a significant contribution satisfying the test for causation,[61] and three (two of them the same) appear to have regarded "significant" as meaning the same as "substantial".[62]

The common sense test

In *Commissioner of Police v Hallenstein*,[63] Hedigan J examined the concept of causation in negligence and then sought to apply it to the coronial context. He expressly adopted the "common sense" test articulated by the High Court in *E & MH Stramare Pty Ltd*,[64] in particular the formulation of Deane J, the judgments of the court arising in the context of the law of torts. Justice Deane posed as the test whether "the question of causation arises in relation to attribution of fault or responsibility whether an identified negligent act or omission of the defendant was so connected with the plaintiff's loss or injury that, as a matter of ordinary common sense and experience, it should be regarded as a cause of it".[65]

---

57   *R v HM Coroner for Exeter & East Devon; ex parte Palmer*, unreported, Court of Appeal, 10 December 1997.
58   *Ex parte Minister of Justice; Re Malcolm* [1965] NSWR 1598 (SC), McClemens J at 1604.
59   *Eg R v Hallett* [1969] SASR 141; *R v Evans and Gardiner (No 2)* [1976] VR 523.
60   (1991) 172 CLR 378.
61   Brennan J at 298; Deane and Dawson JJ at 411.
62   Deane and Dawson JJ at 298; McHugh J at 449.
63   [1996] 2 VR 1.
64   (1991) 171 CLR 506 at 522.
65   [1996] 2 VR 1 at 17.

Causes and non-causes

In *Keown v Khan*[66] the Victorian Court of Appeal had reason to pursue the notion further. In the leading judgment of the court, Callaway JA distinguished between causes and what he classified as "background circumstances", which he defined as a "non-causal condition". His Honour held that in determining whether an act or omission is a cause or merely a background circumstance "it will sometimes be necessary to consider whether the act departed from a norm or standard or the omission was in breach of a recognised duty".[67]

This meant that it is appropriate for the coroner to find that a person who kills contributes to the cause of death, whether the person did so wrongfully or in lawful self-defence. He held that a finding in relation to the identity of a person contributing to a cause of death could then be made under the provision mandating such a finding, which in Victoria and the Australian Capital Territory, but not Tasmania, has now been repealed, or, as in England, under the umbrella of the obligation to find how a deceased came by his or her death.

Multiple causes

The question, therefore, will often be one of degree in determining the extent of the causal link. This is most problematic in the common situation where there are multiple causative factors. An example is to be seen in recent British Columbia coronial findings on causation:

> The debris flow occurred progressively, commencing on a steep section of a naturally unstable slope. ... An investigation team was organized by the Ministry of Forests to determine the causative factors. Members of the team were specialists in slope stability, forest hydrology, soil science, forest engineering and watershed management. The investigation reveals that the 42 days preceding 12 June 1990 were the wettest on record. This situation created wet soil moisture conditions that set the stage for a precipitation event. Along with this, the terrain in the vicinity of the initial debris flow is inherently unstable. This is evident by the presence of pistol butt trees and old stump scarps on a hillslope of 34 degrees. There

---

[66]   (1998) 101 A Crim R 503.

[67]   Ibid, at p511. Compare the so-called "NESS test": a person's breach is a cause of death or injury if it is a necessary element of a set of conditions sufficient to bring about the death or injury: R Wright, "Causation, Responsibility, Risk. Probability, Naked Statistics, and Proof: Pruning the Bramble Bush by Clarifying the Concepts" (1988) 73 *Iowa Law Review* 1001; see also D Hamer, "Proof of Causation and Quantum in an Unpredictable World" (1999) 23 *Melbourne University Law Review* 557.

is a clearcut area above the debris flow. This absence of trees changed the timing and the amount of water delivered to the soil. The network of roads and ditches here increased the drainage source areas above the debris flow. All of these factors although not singly causative, when combined the effect was potentiated.[68]

A leading decision on the subject is that of McClemens J of the New South Wales Supreme Court who was called upon in 1965 to grapple with the issue in the context of a worker who had been admitted to hospital after taking ill at work in suspicious circumstances suggestive of his having been the victim of chemical poisoning in the workplace. He died after a lengthy period in hospital, the terminal cause of death being pneumonia that he contracted shortly before passing away.[69] Justice McClemens expressly adopted the following passage in the then current edition of *Jervis on the Office and Duties of Coroners*:

> [O]steomyelitis, which is a septic disease of bone, may occur naturally or may, for instance, be caused by an injury from a fall: tetanus, which is an infection, proceeds from a wound: an old lady may die in a hospital from hypostatic pneumonia months after a fall which injured her hip. It is suggested that in so far as the terminal cause of death directly and consequentially follows from a definable event the death should be regarded as being caused by the definable event.

He went as far as to hold that the approach of the coroner in the case before him of only focusing upon the terminal cause of death was erroneous and misconceived the function of the coroner. He found that what the coroner was obliged to do was to address the "real cause" of death, namely the disease, injury or complication, not the mode of dying, such as, for instance, heart failure, asphyxia or asthenia. In the case before him, he found that the pneumonia suffered in his last days of hospitalisation was not the real cause of death of the deceased; this was merely a final result operating on a man who was suffering from a bed sore, bladder infection, secondary infection from the bed sore, who was inert, vegetative, and incontinent of urine and faeces. He found that if what brought the deceased to such a pass was "poisoning", then poisoning could be said to be the real cause of death.

From an international perspective, the leading decision on the subject of causation in a multi-factorial coronial context savours more of the malice of a legal academic, setting an impossible problem for his or her

---

[68]   *Kozub v HMTQ* [2000] BCSC 0194 at [5].
[69]   *Ex parte Minister of Justice; Re Malcolm* [1965] NSWR 1598.

students, than of real life. However, although the facts explored in *R v Poplar Coroner; ex parte Thomas*[70] were quite extraordinary, they allowed an opportunity for important consideration of where lines should be drawn in terms of remoteness or, put another way, insignificance of certain of multiple factors contributing to a cause of death.

Miss Thomas, a young woman of 17, suffered a severe attack of asthma at 1.00am. Her family telephoned for an ambulance when the attack began but only received a recorded message, "There is no-one here at present. Please hold on and we will answer your call as soon as we can". When the message was repeated, they decided to take Miss Thomas to hospital in their car. On the way, she deteriorated and the car was stopped. She was laid out on the pavement, alive but unconscious and the police urgently requested an ambulance once more at 1.15am. Two further calls were made at 1.17am and 1.32am. An ambulance arrived at 1.33am but before it arrived, Miss Thomas had suffered a cardiac arrest. Attempts by ambulance personnel to revive her were fruitless.

The analysis of the Court of Appeal was directed toward whether Miss Thomas' death was unnatural. For these purposes, though, the analysis was relevant because the court held that the determination of whether the deceased's death was natural or unnatural depended on what was the cause of death. The argument mounted on behalf of the relatives of Miss Thomas was that the chance of saving her life was unacceptably diminished because such a long time – 33 minutes – elapsed between the first abortive emergency call and the time when finally the ambulance arrived. In essence, the reasoning pressed upon the Court of Appeal was a version of lost chance reasoning.[71]

Lord Justice Dillon commented that:

> It is easy to think of a variety of different scenarios as a result of which an ambulance could have arrived too late to save a patient who had suffered a severe attack of asthma like Miss Thomas's, eg (i) the distance from the ambulance centre to the patient's home was too great for there to have ever been any chance of the ambulance arriving in time to save the

---

[70]   [1993] QB 610.

[71]   For "loss of chance reasoning" in the economic loss context, see *Hotson v East Berkshire Area Health Authority* [1987] AC 750 at 759-60; *Sellars v Adelaide Petroleum NL* (1994) 179 CLR 332 at 355; in the context of medical negligence, see *Naxakis v Western General Hospital* (1999) 162 ALR 540; *Chappel v Hart* (1998) 156 ALR 517; *Gavalas v Singh* [2001] VSCA 23; N Moshinsky, "Loss of a Chance of Successful Treatment" (2000) 8 *Journal of Law and Medicine* 216; I Freckelton, "Malpractice Actions Against Health Care Professionals" in I Freckelton & K Petersen (eds), *Controversies in Health Law*, Federation Press, Sydney, 1999. See also Luntz in this collection.

patient, (ii) there was much more traffic than normal in the locality and so the ambulance was delayed and arrived just too late, (iii) the ambulance was diverted on its journey and had to take a much longer route because of flooding caused by a burst water main, which may have been due to lack of proper maintenance by the water company, (iv) a newly installed computer installed by the ambulance service to handle emergency calls more efficiently malfunctioned, as newly installed computers are prone to, or (v) the ambulance came late because the ambulance crew were inefficient and the management was slack.[72]

On each of these scenarios, he (with Farquaharson LJ agreeing) found that the cause of death was the asthmatic attack. Lord Justice Simon Brown was more hesitant in his concurrence, specifically accepting that courts often find there to have been multiple causes to a given eventuality. He commented that if a civil action were brought, it could not be doubted that Miss Thomas' death was in part caused by the late arrival of the ambulance. Thus, his inquiry was into what view should be taken of causes that were secondary but were "not self-evidently irrelevant". He provided this example:

> Take a medical condition between the two extremes postulated by the coroner in this case – neither a condition like a strangulated hernia or ectopic pregnancy which clearly ought never to result in death and which, if it does, will require an inquest, but not a condition as serious as this deceased's asthma with its considerable risk of natural mortality rate; assume that consequent upon some clear failure of the emergency services the condition, unusually, proved fatal. Would not common sense dictate that that was an unnatural death?[73]

He concluded that the circumstances before him would have constituted a cause if the arrival of the ambulance had constituted a more extreme failure of the service than it did.

Standard of Proof of Causation in Coronial Law

Findings as to causation, as in relation to other matters in respect of which coroners are statutorily obliged to make findings, are on the criminal standard of beyond reasonable doubt in England,[74] at least in respect of

---

[72] At All ER 386.
[73] Ibid, at p388.
[74] See *R v West London Coroner's Court; ex parte Gray* [1988] 1 QB 467; *R v Wolverhampton Coroner; ex parte McCurbin* [1990] 2 All ER 759.

matters such as homicide, including suicide,[75] but on the balance of probabilities in Canada[76] and Australia.[77] In Australia, this analysis is affected by the so-called *"Briginshaw* principle"[78] which results in a coroner needing to factor into his or her determination both the seriousness of allegations against a person and the likely impact of a finding that the allegations are made out. Thus, in *Anderson v Blashki*[79] Gobbo J held that because of the gravity of an assault allegation in the coronial context, proof of what in fact constituted a criminal act had to be "cogent and exact and when considering such proof, weight must be given to the presumption of innocence."[80] In addition, he held that the extremely deleterious effect that an adverse finding would have on the character of the person accused, as well as upon his reputation and employment prospects, meant that that weight of evidence was necessary which was commensurate with the gravity of the allegation against him. In practice, this means that in some circumstances, where, for instance, the allegation is tantamount to murder, the coroner needs to arrive at a high level of satisfaction before making a finding about contribution in relation to cause of death. The law in Canada is not dissimilar, proof where there are serious allegations being to "a high degree of probability".[81]

Conclusion

In *Environmental Agency v Empress Car Co (Abertillery) Ltd*,[82] Lord Hoffmann observed that: "[C]ommon sense answers to questions of causation will differ according to the purpose for which the question is asked." To a similar effect, Gaudron J in *Chappel v Hart*[83] has pointed out that "Questions of causation are not answered in a legal vacuum. Rather, they are answered in the legal framework in which they arise." The unique nature of the coronial jurisdiction has generated its own substantial

---

[75]   See *R v HM Coroner for Solihull; ex parte Nutt* [1993] COD 449; *R v HM Coroner for Northamptonshire, ex parte Tomkinson* [1996] COD 191.

[76]   *Re Beckon* (1992) 93 DLR (4th) 161 at 175.

[77]   See *Anderson v Blashki* [1993] 2 VR 89; *Secretary, Department of Health and Community Services v Gurvich* [1995] 2 VR 69; *Chief Commissioner of Police v Hallenstein* [1996] 2 VR 1.

[78]   *Briginshaw v Briginshaw* (1938) 60 CLR 336.

[79]   [1993] 2 VR 88 at 95-6.

[80]   Citing *Cuming Smith & Co Ltd v Western Farmers Co-operative Ltd* [1979] VR 129 at 147.

[81]   *Re Beckon* (1992) 93 DLR (4th) 161 at 175.

[82]   [1999] 2 AC 22 at 29.

[83]   (1998) 195 CLR 232 at 238 [7].

jurisprudence in relation to causation. Much of it is affected by the emerging role of the modern coroner as an inquirer and maker of recommendations about avoidable death.

It has become apparent that the call in the common law of Australia to have resort simply to common sense has not proved adequate. The need for causation findings to be made in all inquests has brought about many analyses of difficult issues such as the criteria for attributing not just causation but causation framed in such a way as to denote or imply fault. In addition, many cases have had to confront where the cut-off should be made in terms of proximate causation and indirect causation. No consistent or coherent approach can readily be discerned, the most substantial set of analyses being present in the English jurisprudence concerning neglect and self-neglect, where the demand of the appellate courts has been that the nexus between the unsatisfactory conduct and the death be close, namely clear and direct. Inevitably, some room remains open for subjectivity, but the message from the English Court of Appeal is that the connection cannot in any sense be remote.

In Australia the criminal law appears generally to have been adopted in coronial law, meaning that the connection between the act or omission and the death must be "real" or perhaps "significant" or "substantial". Confidence in relation to a coroner's finding of causation must be beyond reasonable doubt in England but on the sliding scale of the balance of probabilities in Australia and Canada. Clear criteria for differentiating amongst differently contributing causative factors where they exist in numbers have not been identified, save that in respect of any given causative factor the tests in the criminal law seem to be applied.

For coroners the core function of identifying both the circumstances around a death, in particular, those which gave rise to a death, and attributing a causative role to them, are unresolved. This is highly problematic as determination of causation is so central to the coronial function as to leave unclear the extent to which it is proper for coroners to inquire into, and make decisions about, indirect factors giving rise to deaths and other phenomena. This has been addressed in New Zealand's coronial legislation with s15 of the *Coroners Act* 1988 (NZ) permitting a coroner to inquire into matters that he or she concludes are likely to result in recommendations conducive to public health and safety. There is much to be said for such a revised conceptualisation of the coroner's role.

It is likely, and a constructive development, that the increasingly recognised role of the coroner as an instrument for identifying, developing and promoting community safety will lead to the adoption of an approach along the lines of that in New Zealand. It assists the community little to identify by formal coronial findings only the proximate or terminal events around deaths. Frequently, it is as to the environment within which the acts and omissions which resulted in a death, as well as in relation to the potentiating and exacerbating nature of factors leading to the death, that analysis needs to be undertaken if the incidence of avoidable death is to be reduced. Often it is intangible factors such as workplace culture, longstanding practices of neglect or insensitivity, lack of awareness of options different from those adopted that need to be identified if important changes are to be made which will reduce unsafe practices. It is coroners who are best positioned as a result of the formal hearing process of inquests to discern such issues, to make findings about them and to make recommendations about how they can be changed. A range of public policy reasons, distinct and separate from those operating in the civil and criminal contexts, suggest that the notion of causation needs to be construed more broadly in the coronial context than in most others within the contemporary legal system.

PART E:
CAUSATION, EVIDENCE AND PROOF IN LAW AND MEDICINE

17 Causation in Law and Psychiatry

RALPH SLOVENKO[*]

In the law-psychiatry intermix, causation involving mental illness can, broadly speaking, be categorised: (1) behaviour as a result of mental illness, and (2) mental illness as a result of a stressor.

Behaviour as a Result of Mental Illness

People rarely ask if praiseworthy behaviour is a product of mental illness, though it is sometimes asked about the creativity of artists (as in the case of Vincent van Gogh), but on the other hand, when a person harms someone, the question is invariably raised whether the behaviour is a result of mental illness. If the behaviour is a result or product of mental illness, society will act one way; if not, society will take a different stance. Social convention brings sick people to doctors; evil people, on the other hand, go to jail.

Time and again, forensic experts are asked to say whether the behaviour of the individual is fundamentally the result or product of mental illness or merely representative of a lifestyle. Put another way, the question is raised whether the person's behaviour or thoughts are ego-dystonic or ego-syntonic (that is, viewed by the self as repugnant or inconsistent with the total personality, or as acceptable and consistent with the total personality).

Every test of responsibility, whether in criminal or civil law, contains a product or "on account of" mental illness question. That is, was a pathological condition, like a human agent, the motivating force behind the

---

*   Professor of Law and Psychiatry at Wayne State University in Michigan, a member of the American, Kansas, Louisiana, and Michigan Bar Associations, a scientific associate of the American Academy of Psychoanalysis, and amicus of the American Academy of Psychiatry and Law.

act? A person compelled to commit an act (crime or contract) at gunpoint is not held responsible. Likewise, according to logic, mental illness may threaten a person and force him or her to do things he would not ordinarily do. Not long ago, the blame was put on the devil.

In Edward Oxford's trial in 1840, Lord Denman instructed the jury, "If some controlling disease was, in truth, the acting power within him which he could not resist, then he will not be held responsible".[1] Under the M'Naghten Rules set out by the House of Lords in 1843, the accused, to be deemed not responsible, must suffer from a disease of the mind so severe as to render him or her incapable of knowing the nature and quality of the act or of knowing that the act was wrong.[2] The American Law Institute's test of 1955, which has also been widely adopted, provides that a "person is not responsible for criminal conduct if at the time of such conduct *as a result of mental illness or defect*, his capacity either to appreciate the criminality of his conduct or to conform his conduct to the requirements of law is so substantially impaired that he cannot justly be held responsible" (emphasis added).[3] The Federal Insanity Defense Reform Act exculpates a defendant when as *"as a result of a severe mental disease or defect*, he was unable to appreciate the nature and quality or wrongfulness of his act" (emphasis added).

An act is not the result of mental illness merely because of the presence of mental illness. Looking at a movie is not a pathological act although, at the time, the person viewing the film may be pathologically depressed. Correlation is not causation – there is correlation but not causation of summertime with an increase in crime. Correlation and causation can be distinguished by experimentation.

The interactions between mental illness and criminality may be summarised: (1) Mental illness may simply coexist with criminality, without having any causal significance; (2) mental illness may predispose toward criminality, as in the case of M'Naghten's delusion that he was the victim of persecution by the Prime Minister of England, or it may be due to a compulsion, ranging from paraphilias, impulse disorders, Tourette's syndrome, post-traumatic stress disorder (eg, "Vietnam syndrome") to automatism; and (3) the mental illness may inhibit criminality, as catatonia would inhibit a person who otherwise would commit a rape.[4] The

1   *R v Oxford* (1843) 9 CNP 525.
2   *M'Naghten Case* (1843) 10 Clark & Fin 200, 8 ER 718.
3   ALI Model Penal Code §4.01 (1955).
4   See P Dietz, "The Mentally Disordered Offender: Patterns in the Relationship between Mental Disorder and Crime" (1992) 15 *Psych Clin North America* 539; J Monahan & HJ Steadman, "Crime and Mental Disorder: An Epidemiological Approach" in M

commission of a crime, it must also be noted, may cause mental illness rather than mental illness being the cause of the crime; facing prosecution or punishment is a significant stressor and potentially pathogenic.

In 1954, in *Durham v United States* Judge David Bazelon of the United States Court of Appeals for the District of Columbia formulated a "disease-defect-product" test. Trial judges attempted to instruct juries on the meaning of the rule. Three years later, seeking to clarify it, the DC Court of Appeals said:

> When we say the defense of insanity requires that the act be a "product of" a disease, we mean that the facts on the record are such that the trier of the facts is enabled to draw a reasonable inference that the accused would not have committed the act he did commit if he had not been diseased as he was. *There must be a relationship between the disease and the act, and that relationship, whatever it may be in degree, must be. . . critical in its effect in respect to the act.* By "critical" we mean decisive, determinative, causal; we mean to convey the idea inherent in the phrases "because of", "except for", "without which", "but for", "effect of", "result of", "causative factor"; the disease made the effective or decisive difference between doing and not doing the act. The short phrases "product of" and "causal connection" are not intended to be precise, as though they were chemical formulae. They mean that the facts concerning the disease and the facts concerning the act are such as to justify reasonably the conclusion that "But for this disease the act would not have been committed."
>
> To the precise logician deduction of the foregoing inference involves a tacit assumption that if the disease had not existed the person would have been a law-abiding citizen. This latter is not necessarily factually true and can rarely, if ever, be proved, but in the ordinary conduct of these cases we make that tacit assumption. For ordinary purposes we make no mention of this logician's nicety. (emphasis added.)[5]

The widely adopted formula set out in 1955 in the ALI Model Penal Code, which contains a combination of the right-wrong test and an updated version of irresistible impulse, does not resolve the questions presented by the *Durham* formula. The issues persist. The ALI formula, as we have noted, provides that the impairment of cognition or control must be "a result of mental disease or defect". The *M'Naghten* test asks the same about impairment of cognition. The *Durham* formula brought "result" or

---

Tonry & N Morris (eds), *Crime and Justice; An Annual Review of Research*, No 4, University of Chicago Press, Chicago, 1983, 145.

[5] *Carter v United States*, 252 F 2d 608, 617 (DC Cir 1957).

"product" to centre-stage. It asked a more direct question: was the defendant's conduct itself the "product" of mental illness?

Causal nexus between behaviour and illness is asked as well in other areas of the law. The test on competency to stand trial asks whether the incompetency was a result of mental illness. The law on civil commitment asks whether on account of mental illness the person is dangerous or in need of care or treatment. The law of contracts provides that certain people should not be held responsible for their agreements if they were mentally ill and as a consequence did not know what they were doing. The law on testamentary capacity asks whether mental illness prevented the testator from realising the nature and extent of his or her property or the natural objects of his or her bounty. A testament that is "the direct unqualified offspring of a morbid delusion" is null and void.

The question arises: does major mental disorder equal violent tendencies? From early times, a relationship between mental disorder and violence was recognised. The Talmud said, "No man commits a crime except when a spirit of madness has entered into him". On the other hand, it has been claimed that psychotic people are not particularly prone to be assaultive. Following the Kennedy assassination, an American Psychiatric Association study claimed that the incidence of criminal behaviour among discharged patients of mental institutions was not significantly higher than among the general population.[6] Another study estimated the probability of violent behaviour in this category of seriously mentally ill persons at five in 10,000.[7] The MacArthur Risk Assessment Study found that 27 per cent of released male and female patients committed at least one violent act within a mean of four months after discharge.[8] Dr E Fuller Torrey points out that, contrary to claims by advocates attempting to decrease the stigma against mental illness, random community surveys indicate that seriously mentally ill individuals are significantly more dangerous than the general population. He observed: "The frequency with which individuals with schizophrenia reported having use a weapon in a fight – 21.5 times more than individuals with no psychiatric disorder – is especially noteworthy."[9]

---

6 Reported in JR Rappeport (ed), *The Clinical Evaluation of the Dangerousness of the Mentally Ill*, Thomas, Springfield, IL, 1967; see also SB Guze, *Criminality and Psychiatric Disorders*, Oxford University Press, New York, 1976.

7 H Hafner & W Boker, *Crimes of Violence by Mentally Abnormal Offenders*, Cambridge University Press, Cambridge, 1982.

8 Cited in J Monahan, "Mental Disorder and Violent Behaviour/Perceptions and Evidence" (1992) *American Psychologist* 47.

9 M Moran, "Seriously Mentally Ill Do Have Higher Rates of Violence, Torrey Reports" (19 November 1993) *Psychiatric News* 5.

Current research points to a high incidence of mental disorder among individuals who have committed violent crimes. Although there is general agreement that individuals with certain characteristics of mental disorder are more prone to violence than other individuals, there is still debate concerning the prevalence of violent behaviour among various diagnostic groups. Current data suggest that schizo-affective diagnosis, paranoid features, psychotic symptoms, and substance abuse may all be associated with greater risk of serious violence.[10]

When, then, is it justified to posit a causal nexus between behaviour and illness? How does one distinguish between behaviour that is a product of illness and behaviour that is a reaction to it? When is mental disorder "causative" or merely "correlated with" criminal behaviour? Does mental disorder "cause" behaviour in the same sense that epilepsy "causes" seizures? What does it mean to say that certain behaviour is a product or a feature of mental illness? Is the answer anything more than opinion? The French philosopher Voltaire, a fervent believer in free will, satirised the way people would excuse their brutal actions by attributing them to a providential command. One could say that mental illness tinges all aspects of the thought processes of the mentally ill individual, and that every act of the individual is at least partially affected by mental illness. There may be sick and healthy aspects of mental functioning within the same person. The terms used by the legislatures or the courts – "product of", "a result of", "causal connection", "because of", "causative factor" – are unsatisfying and impenetrable.

There is the "bad seed" hypothesis. One belief is that criminals suffer a physiological dysfunction that may be hereditary or result from trauma. Brain lesions or tumours, temporal lobe epilepsy, blood chemistry changes, glandular abnormality, and hypoglycemia are among the organic factors linked to criminality. Is there a connection among genes, mental disorder, and violence? Biological psychiatry holds that mental illness stems from a chemical imbalance in the brain, and that many human traits are genetically influenced. In the past few decades, the majority of researchers have endeavoured to show that psychiatric disorders are triggered by chemical imbalances in the brain that can be rectified with medication. *The American Journal of Psychiatry* is now almost entirely organic psychiatry; it used to be biopsychosocial and before that, psychosocial. Limitations on insurance coverage and developments in neuroscience technology propel that direction.

With the focus increasingly on the organic, and on psychopharmacology, the term "organic disorder" is eliminated from the

---

[10]   S Hodgins (ed), *Mental Disorder and Crime*, Sage, Newbury Park, CA, 1993.

American Psychiatric Association's Diagnostic and Statistical Manual (DSM-IV) on the grounds that it is misleading in implying that other psychiatric disorders do not have an organic component.[11] In the 1960s a controversy arose over whether criminals have special chromosome patterns. Some criminal defendants (presumably those with no better alibi) presented expert testimony that they possessed an extra Y chromosome, causing them to be legally insane at the time of the crime.[12] The defence in the trial of John Hinckley Jr, the would-be assassin of President Reagan, submitted CAT scans to show a slightly shrunken brain.[13] Andrei Chikatilo, who murdered 52 people over a 12-year period in Russia, requested that, following his execution, his brain be dissected to learn why he committed the crimes.[14] Advances in neurology, many neurological experts say, enable them to probe the brain's anatomy and function to reveal abnormalities caused by disease or trauma that may spark violence. They buttress a defence of not guilty by reason of insanity ("NGRI") with brain scans and other tests that underscore claims of derangement in a seemingly direct and objective way.

The nature-nurture controversy asks whether genetics (nature) or cultural and experiential factors (nurture) is the more important determinant of human behaviour. The nature-nurture debate became highly politicised in the early part of the twentieth century. In 1933, shortly after assuming chancellorship of Germany, Adolf Hitler convinced the Reichstag to pass the Law for the Prevention of Genetically Diseased Offspring, a law closely patterned after a 1922 model statute drawn up in America. By that time the United States had carried out about 20,000 sterilisations, most of them involuntary.

Nazi Germany's program evolved into "the destruction of unworthy life." The Nazi program, with strong support from the medical community, was represented as "applied eugenics" – the Nazis were carrying out "purification." In America, as eugenicists and others favouring a genetic view of human behaviour became linked in the public mind with events taking place in Germany, those favouring a cultural view of human behaviour grew progressively stronger. Nature was silenced, and nurture was Freudianised, as illustrated in the writings of Franz Boas, Ruth

---

[11] RL Spitzer, MB First, JBW Williams, K Kendler, HA Pincus & G Tucker, "Now Is the Time to Retire the Term 'Organic Mental Disorders'" (1992) 149 *Amer J Psychiatry* 240.

[12] PJ Farrell, "The XYY Syndrome in Criminal Law: An Introduction" (1969) 44 *St John's L Rev* 217.

[13] AP news release, "Witness Talks of Hinckley's Brain Scans," 2 June 1982.

[14] W Sloane (AP news release), "Russian Cannibal Convicted in Killings," 15 October 1992.

Benedict and Margaret Mead. The name "Freud," once merely a euphemism for sex, turned into a broader symbol of non-genetic approaches to human behaviour.

The nature-nurture debate ended in 1946 at Nuremberg. Nature was put on trial along with the Nazi leaders. Henceforth, theories, including Freud's, extolling nurture as the primary antecedent of human behaviour would take centre stage and encounter little intellectual opposition. Nurture ruled, but instead of a competition against nature there was a debate among supporters of nurture as to whether early childhood experiences or cultural factors were more important determinants of human behaviour. By the mid-1950s the flow of Freud's ideas through popular magazines reached fluvial proportions. On the paediatric frontier, Dr Benjamin Spock was the Freudian missionary. Spock taught that early childhood experiences, particularly those sexual in nature, are crucial determinants for personality development.

The arguments about criminal behaviour became part of the broader nature-nurture debate. By the early 1920s, Freudian theory was widely discussed in criminology and forensic science. The question was whether criminals were born as such or whether they were the products of early childhood experiences and social forces. In Nazi Germany genetic theories of criminality had been prominent, but in the aftermath of the Second World War, theorists about crime in America could talk only about its social, economic and familial antecedents. Treatment facilities to "cure" prisoners of their criminal behaviour were opened in various states.

Experts nowadays frequently argue a neurological defense, even in cases of seemingly calculated violence. They argue that the violence was actually the uncontrollable by-product of damage to a specific region of the brain, caused genetically or by years of physical abuse during childhood, but neurologists have yet to demonstrate a necessary correlation between a non-limbic (frontal lobe) abnormality in the brain and violent behaviour. Individuals convicted of violent crimes do show a higher incidence of certain factors associated with brain damage – abuse, head injuries, malnutrition, lower IQ, seizures, and subtle neuropsychological deficits – than do people in control groups, but most people thus afflicted do not commit violent crimes. In a number of writings, neurologist Richard Restak has pointed out that the more complex and symbolically meaningful the behaviour, the less likely it can be linked to a specific region of the brain. The line of causation is hard to draw for premeditated acts of violence. Neuropsychological examinations do not account for motivation.[15]

The kind of violent behaviour that results from damage to the limbic system, unlike a non-limbic abnormality, is relatively easy to identify. People who suffer from episodic dyscontrol – also known as intermittent explosive disorder – display spells of violence grossly out of proportion to any preceding event. These intermittent paroxysms of aggression strike out of nowhere, and the individual expresses a genuine sense of regret when the spells pass.[16]

The appropriate insanity defence on these types of cases requires specification and corroboration of symptoms of loss of reality-related cognition, or loss of control during the crime, or both. For the needs of the courts, the important questions are: What was the nature of the violent act and the circumstances surrounding it? Does the defendant exhibit signs of neurological damage? If so, is it likely with a reasonable degree of medical certainty that, absent the neurological impairment, the violence would not have taken place?

Speculations about the relations between brain dysfunctions and behavioural aberrations, however, do not form a proper basis for asserting, with the degree of certainty required by the law, that a violent act was committed on the basis of some form of neurological dysfunction. But that has not stopped experts from testifying on the slimmest evidence. People who kill others often report disturbances in consciousness, including depersonalisation and feelings of unreality. It is not to be assumed that all such people are suffering from neurological damage, especially since the same experiences are regularly reported by people suffering from disturbances that are not considered neurological and may occur in anyone. Assuming neurological damage simply because a person has undergone some impairment in consciousness ignores studies that report 65 per cent of all murderers have amnesia for the act itself.[17] It is always questionable whether the dissociation took place before, during, or after the killing.

Tracing criminal violence to a specific region in the brain is reminiscent of ancient times when it was believed that demon possession caused mental illness, and, in turn, unlawful behaviour. "The devil made me do it" is the old saying, or in the Talmud's phrasing, "No man commits a crime except when a spirit of madness has entered into him". Demonic possession is with us still, even if the label is different. The various tests of

---

[15] RM Restak, "See No Evil/The Neurological Defense Would Blame Violence on the Damaged Brain" (July-August 1992) *Sciences* 16.

[16] Ibid.

[17] Reported in R Restak, "Violence and the Brain" (November-December 1992) *Sciences*, p4.

criminal responsibility are grounded on something like a demon possession theory. Although the criminal law tests do not mention demons, mental illness, as used in these tests, is regarded essentially as a form of demoniacal manipulation. Under the *M'Naghten*, *Durham*, or ALI rule, it is necessary to establish that a disease or defect of the mind exists and impairs cognition or control. The operational use of the concept illustrates what the philosopher Alfred North Whitehead called "misplaced concreteness", that is, an abstraction is reified: a process is turned into an entity. Restak pointed out how, in our vocabulary, we tend to describe the mental processes mediated by our brain as a machine. "He had a mental crack-up." "His mind is 'rusty' or unable to 'grind out' solutions to problems." At other times, our mind is "sharp as a razor" or "really revved up", "the wheels are turning" within our heads. "His ego is easily bruised." "His mind was shattered." "He went to pieces." "His mind just snapped from the shock of it all."[18]

The terms "result of" and "product" in the test of criminal responsibility denote separateness and imply a lineal causation. Behaviour is a unitary process, but, with licence, it is spoken of in terms of either its subjective elements or its outward appearances. It is like talking about the mind and body as though they had separate existence. We do it because we do not have the language expressive of continuous interactions with multiple or circular causality. Our language limits us to a lineal step codification of reality and to a world of single one-to-one causality. Dr Philip Q Roche wrote in his Isaac Ray award book:

> In the language of the law, *cause* is regarded as an event which has direct or proximate connection in sequence with another event. ... [W]e can recognize that, when viewed within a moral system, out of our own psychological needs and design we are impelled arbitrarily to dichotomize behaviour into subjective (motivational) and objective elements. This dichotomy sets and maintains the alignments of the adversary system of resolving moral problems. At the same time, however, the dichotomy opens the door to the realm of infinite differences which may come less out of actual differences in nature, and more out of the differences in the persons who report and evaluate them. ... Seemingly, by an inner psychological necessity we are impelled to abstract the outward act from the hypothetical subjective element and to regard the act as a "product."[19]

---

[18] R Restak, *The Brain Has a Mind of Its Own*, Crown, New York, 1991, p18.

[19] PQ Roche, *The Criminal Mind/A Study of Communication Between the Criminal Law and Psychiatry*, Greenwood Press, Westport CT, 1958, pp259-60.

The way society labels a particular cluster of mental characteristics corresponds to how it feels about the individual, and society is constantly changing its mind to accommodate competing policy interests. Society's representatives may benefit from psychiatric expertise in determining which cognitive and emotional characteristics are features of a diagnostic category, but it is up to society, through its representatives, to decide whether a behaviour is a product of mental illness or not. The decision of whether behaviour is a "product" or a "result" of mental illness is not a matter of scientific expertise but a matter of social policy.[20] Under an amendment of the Federal Rules of Evidence, as provided by Congress as part of the Insanity Defense Reform Act of 1984,[21] the expert may be asked whether the individual suffers a mental illness but the expert may not be asked: "Was the accused able to appreciate the nature and quality of his act?", "Was the accused able to appreciate the wrongfulness of his acts?", or "Was the act the product of that disease or defect?" Taken literally, under the amendment, the jury is to decide causation issues without the assistance of expert testimony.

Mental Illness as a Result of a Stressor

Traditionally in a tort action, recovery at law for emotional distress was only recognised as an additional or parasitic element of damages. Thus, where the tortious conduct inflicted bodily harm, the ensuing emotional distress could be taken into account in assessing damages. Emotional distress could be the sole basis of a claim only in cases of intentional wrongdoing for assault, defamation, false imprisonment, invasion of privacy, and malicious prosecution. In the mid 1950s, the courts in various states of the United States began to allow an action for the intentional infliction of emotional distress, as when a jokester tells a woman that her son has been mutilated in an accident.

In cases of negligence resulting in fright, shock, or other mental suffering, the various jurisdictions have required proof of physical impact or injury. Over the years, the law has been concerned about a flood of litigation or fraudulent claims if compensation were awarded in cases of negligence alleging mental distress without accompanying physical impact or injury. The physical impact or injury would establish causal nexus. Of course, in all torts in which there is physical injury, be it an intentional tort or negligence, damages are awarded for pain and suffering.

---

20   B Bursten, *Beyond Psychiatric Expertise*, Thomas, Springfield, IL, 1984.
21   Federal Rules of Evidence 704(b), as amended.

Beginning in the mid-twentieth century, an increasing number of states in the United States, one by one, removed the physical impact or injury limitation in negligence actions. The law in a near majority of states has moved from that of requiring physical impact or injury to allowing claims without insisting either that the victim feared for his or her own safety or even suffered physical injury, such as a heart attack or miscarriage. In 1968, a trend began in allowing an action for mental distress even for bystanders witnessing negligent injury. That year, in the famous case of *Dillon v Legg*,[22] the California Supreme Court set out standards for a bystander action: a close relationship to the person injured, close proximity to the scene, and "sensory and contemporaneous observation" of the accident. A number of jurisdictions have loosened the requirement that the plaintiff has to be at the scene of the alleged act that caused the mental suffering. In the *Dillon* case, the distressed mother was outside the zone of danger – there was no possibility that she would be hit by the car that killed her daughter, but she was at the scene.

Fear, when well founded, of becoming ill at a later date may also be compensable. The question has arisen in litigation over toxic torts and latent diseases, as in lawsuits brought by those who have been exposed to asbestos or by the daughters of women who took the drug diethylstilbestrol (DES).[23] In a Wisconsin case, the plaintiff claimed damages for a physical injury and for her phobia that she might develop a cancer from broken pieces of a catheter that could not be removed from her body. The court said, without further explanation, that "although there is no question about there being in fact a fear of future cancer, the claim of damages (by way of cancer) is so remote and is so out of proportion to the culpability of the tortfeasor that, as a matter of public policy, we conclude that the defendants are not to be held liable for this element of damages."[24]

The most frequently cited public policy factors a court will consider when deciding whether liability should not attach to damages caused by a defendant's negligence are: (1) The injury is too remote from the negligence; (2) the injury is wholly out of proportion to the defendant's culpability; (3) in retrospect, it appears extraordinary that the negligence would have brought about the harm; (4) allowing recovery places an unreasonable burden on the defendant; (5) allowing recovery is too likely

---

[22]   68 Cal 2d 728, 441 P 2d 912, 69 Cal Rptr 72 (1968).
[23]   See, eg, *Gideon v Johns-Manville Sales Corp*, 761 F 2d 1129 (5th Cir 1985) (asbestos-related cancer); *Techalloy Co v Reliance Ins Co*, 338 Pa Super 1, 487 A2d 820 (1984) (toxic chemicals); *Payton v Abbott Laboratories*, 386 Mass 540, 437 NE 2d 171 (1982) (diethylstilbestrol).
[24]   *Howard v Mt Sinai Hosp*, 63 Wis 2d 515, 219 NW 2d 576 (1974).

to open the way for fraudulent claims; (6) allowing recovery will enter a field having no sensible or just stopping point.

A psychiatric diagnostic category is not essential to a cause of action, but the listing of stress reactions in the DSM has tended to give the claim more legitimacy. Forensic psychiatrists pushed the listing of post-traumatic stress disorder (PTSD) in the DSM. With the inclusion of PTSD, victims of trauma have increasingly used that formulation in civil and criminal cases. As expert witnesses, psychiatrists embrace PTSD to explain the psychological sequelae of trauma in personal injury cases.

In tort litigation, PTSD is a favoured diagnosis in cases of emotional distress because it is incident specific. It tends to rule out other factors important to the determination of causation. Thus plaintiffs can argue that all of their psychological problems issue from the alleged traumatic event and not from myriad other sources encountered in life. A diagnosis of depression, in contrast, opens the issue of causation to many factors other than the stated cause of action.

Questions asked on direct examination and cross-examination reflect the concern over causation and malingering. "What is the relationship, if any", the expert is asked, "between the trauma and the plaintiff's mental disorder?" "Can the plaintiff work?" "What is the type and length of treatment required?" "What part does litigation play in the plaintiff's mental illness?" "How do you know that the plaintiff is not faking?" If the expert has concluded that the plaintiff is suffering from PTSD, he or she is asked to explain it, at which time the plaintiff's history is used to illustrate the DSM criteria for PTSD.

Wholly aside from the question of how far the law should go in protecting against emotional disturbance, there are difficult evidentiary questions not only of causation, but also of fault and assessment of damages. The vulnerability of the victim is considered differently in each of these various elements that together constitute a tort.

For fault, the risk reasonably to be perceived determines the duty of care. Foreseeability is the traditional test. Thus a greater duty of care is imposed on a motorist when he or she sees a handicapped person or child crossing the street. When the vulnerability of a person is not reasonably apparent, he or she may fairly be assumed to be an ordinary individual. Negligence is failing to observe the care of a reasonable person in like circumstances.

For causation, the law looks for proximate cause. There is no litmus test for determining proximity, and there may be more than one proximate cause. Some courts use the foreseeability test in determining causation, as is done in determining fault, but usually the courts say that for causation it is a question of the objective evidence. For causation, there is the well-known expression, "the tortfeasor must take his victim as he finds him", so peculiar vulnerability to harm does not excuse. It may be argued, however, sometimes successfully, that "the straw that broke the camel's back" is not a proximate cause.

So-called delayed PTSD may be the result of a cumulation of events resulting in a crisis. (In law, the limitation period begins when the injury is made known.) The proximate cause may arguably be either the earlier or a later event. The term "proximate" has connotations of nearness in time, but that is not its meaning in law. Legal cause and responsible cause are more appropriate terms, but those terms also leave much room for vagaries in decision-making. In a number of cases, the courts have said that the determination of proximate cause is the province of judges, not juries, but more often than not, it is a decision left to the jury.

In days gone by, when the term "traumatic neurosis" was used, psychiatrists distinguished between a true traumatic neurosis in which a healthy individual suffers emotional distress as a result of an overwhelming stress, and a triggered neurosis, in which a vulnerable individual decompensates as a result of stress that would be quite inconsequential to a healthy individual. Theoretically, in law, however, the distinction is one without a difference, but in the case of a triggered neurosis, the argument is made that a triggering event is not a proximate cause.

Trauma, of course, is a relative concept – stimulus in relation to the coping ability of an individual – but when a stressor is not outside the range of common experience, the evidence tends to support a finding that it is not a proximate cause. Also, when a stressor is not outside the range of common experience, suspicion arises of malingering.

In assessing damages, testimony of the condition of the claimant before and after the occurrence of the stressor is crucial to the case. (Punitive damages are another matter.) The forensic examiner is called on to make a long-term assessment of impairment. The before-and-after testimony dwells on difference in personality, character traits, and behaviour, such as outgoing versus withdrawn, loving versus indifferent, mild-mannered versus abusive, reliable versus erratic, and clean versus slovenly. When pre-existing psychological problems are aggravated, accelerated, or reactivated by trauma, a court may have qualms about ascribing the full injury to the defendant. As a matter of law, a jury is to discount what would have happened anyhow.[25]

Actually, what difference does a diagnosis make when before-and-after determines the measure of damage? In fact, a diagnosis is not necessary to establish what the claimant was able to do before and after the trauma. Lay

---

[25]   *Steinhauser v Hertz Corp*, 421 F 2d 1169 (2d Cir 1970).

witnesses can attest to that, but the DSM is state-of-the-art, and the forensic expert is invariably asked to label the claimant's suffering.

Theoretically a diagnosis informs about prognosis. In general, claimants have an obligation to minimise their damages. In some cases, PTSD symptoms diminish over time, in association with many differing factors, whereas in other cases, they do not diminish and in fact may worsen in the absence of treatment. A wide variety of factors may affect the course of PTSD, including coping mechanisms, social support, type and duration of stress, family functioning, personality, other disorders and so on.

Syndrome Evidence

The search for evidence, particularly in child abuse cases, has led to a new species of medical evidence: the "syndrome" diagnosis. This type of evidence, designed to establish a stressor, apparently originated historically in radiology and clinical observation. John Caffey, the father of paediatric radiology, spent 20 years trying to fit the bony abnormalities seen on childhood x-rays into known syndromes. He noted abnormalities that must be associated with child abuse as they were not seen in any known disease.[26] In 1962, Dr C Henry Kempe drew the attention of the medical profession to a set of presenting symptoms for which he coined the term "battered child syndrome".[27]

The term "syndrome" is well known in the medical community as being "a running together", a *"sundromos"* in the Greek, or as the *Oxford English Dictionary* puts it, "a concurrence of several symptoms in a disease". Normally a syndrome is regarded as being identifiable when a collection of symptoms occurs together so often that they provide a recognisable clinical entity. There is controversy, however, over the admissibility of "syndrome" evidence in criminal or tort cases to establish either that a particular traumatic event or stressor actually occurred or to explain the behaviour of the victim. In a child abuse case a psychiatrist or psychologist is presented to testify that the child exhibits the characteristics of a sexually abused child and that, by implication, the child was sexually abused.[28] (Experts use the term "rape trauma syndrome" in the case of a

---

[26] J Caffey, "Pediatric X-Ray Diagnosis," in *Yearbook*, Medical Publishers, Chicago, 7th edn, 1978, p1335; J Caffey, "The Parent-Infant Traumatic Stress Syndrome" (1972) 114 *Am J Radiology* 218.

[27] CH Kempe, FN Silverman, BF Steele, W Droegemueller & HJ Silver, "The Battered Child Syndrome" (1962) 181 *J Am Med Assn* 17.

[28] See, eg, *People v James*, 451 NW 2d 611 (Mich App 1990).

young girl as well as in the case of an adult woman, and they tend to use the term "sexually abused child syndrome" in the case of a child of tender years or when the offender is a family member.)[29] Because the defence in these cases is usually that the abuse did not occur and that the child is making it up, the testimony is designed to bolster the credibility of the child.[30]

Proponents of syndrome evidence argue that it is probative and logical. After all, what could seem more sensible than to look for patterns? In medical diagnosis, of course, the symptoms of an individual are compared with a pattern and a conclusion is drawn about aetiology. As the comedian Jimmy Durante once put it, "If something looks like a duck, walks like a duck, and quacks like a duck, it must be a duck". Some courts call it the "the duck test". Its application should be cautious, however, when it is based only on symptoms. Dr Albert Drukteinis put it thus: Medical conditions, generally, can be defined on different levels, depending on structural pathology, etiology, deviation from some physiological norm, observable signs or symptom presentation. As definitions move from more objective criteria of identifiable and measurable pathology to symptom presentation only, they change from disease to syndrome. Therefore, a syndrome is more likely to include arbitrary or subjective criteria, and to lie in a more gray area of certainty. However, by using the term "syndrome", a word which has its roots in medicine, the symptom pattern described gains medical legitimacy.[31]

Certain assumptions about psychological evidence to ascertain a stressor are particularly questionable. One is the assumption that a certain post-traumatic stress syndrome is the pathway of a particular kind of stressor. In actuality, a wide variety of stressors may result in the trauma. Second is the assumption that victims of a particular stressor react in the same manner. Moreover, it would be surprising for someone to have no other stressors in his or her life other than the one associated with the alleged event.

In actuality, the impact of stressors depend upon the interaction between predisposition and environmental influence. One person may break down; another may be stoic. In short, not all victims react with the same characteristics, and many persons with these characteristics have not

---

[29] See, eg, *People v Bledsoe*, 36 Cal 3d 236, 203 Cal Rptr 450, 681 P 2d 291(1984); *State v McCoy*, 400 NW 2d 807 (Minn App 1987).

[30] RJ Roe, "Expert Testimony in Child Sexual Abuse Cases" (1985) 40 *U Miami L Rev* 97.

[31] AM Drukteinis, "Overlapping Somatoform Syndromes in Personal Injury Litigation," presented at the annual meeting on 30 March 2000 of the American College of Forensic Psychiatry in Newport Beach, CA.

been abused but instead, may be suffering from something else, or they may be malingering or acting hysterically.[32]

Freud's patients recalled their trauma "with all the feelings that belong to the original experience". In 1895-96, Freud, in listening to his female patients, felt that something dreadful and violent lay in their past. The psychiatrists before Freud who had heard seduction stories believed their patients to be hysterical liars and dismissed their memories as fantasy. Freud believed that his patients were reporting the actuality. However, some nine years later he publicly retracted his theory about the aetiology of hysteria. His patients, he now said in an about-face, had been deceiving themselves and him, "I was at last obliged to recognize that these scenes of seduction had never taken place, and that they were only fantasies that my patients had made up."[33] Other therapists, however, find that the incest fantasies of their patients are based on a history of incest.[34] "Revival of memory" therapists link problems of depression, eating disorders, and multiple personality disorder to childhood sexual abuse.[35]

Therapists who "uncover" dissociative identity disorder claim that its genesis is childhood abuse, so in every case of dissociative identity disorder, they say, an allegation of child abuse is warranted. In a 1988 article in *Psychiatric Annals,* Daniel Hardy, a psychiatrist who also holds a law degree, wrote, "The psychiatrist or therapist must be alert to the potential danger of a malpractice suit arising from failure to diagnose multiple personality disorder".[36]

As it turned out, just the opposite has happened, to wit, diagnosing or uncovering dissociative identity disorder has been regarded as malpractice, which follows the proposition that dissociative identity disorder is treatment-created or sometimes the result of self-hypnosis. Dr Paul McHugh, chairman of the Department of Psychiatry and Behavioural Science at Johns Hopkins, wrote, "[Dissociative identity disorder] is an

---

[32] See PR McHugh, "How Psychiatry Lost its Way" Commentary, December 1999, p32; Note, "Unreliability of Expert Testimony on Typical Characteristics of Sexual Abuse Victims" (1980) 74 *Georgetown L J* 429.

[33] See JM Masson, "Freud and the Seduction Theory" (February 1984) *Atlantic*, p33. See also DP Spence, *Narrative Truth and Historical Truth/Meaning and Interpretation in Psychoanalysis*, Norton, New York, 1982.

[34] Reported by Dr Bertram Karon of Michigan State University in an address on delusions presented at a meeting of the Detroit Psychoanalytic Society, 11 April 1987, in Ann Arbor, MI.

[35] See WM Grove & RC Barden, "Protecting the Integrity of the Legal System: The Admissibility of Testimony from Mental Health Experts Under *Daubert/Kumho* Analyses" (1999) 5 *Psychology, Public Policy and Law* 224.

[36] DW Hardy, "Multiple Personality: Failure to Diagnose and the Potential for Malpractice Liability" (1988) 18 *Psychology Annals* 543.

iatrogenic behaviour syndrome, promoted by suggestion and maintained by clinical attention". He noted that multiple identities disappear when the therapist does not ask about them, take notes about them, or otherwise take an interest in them.[37]

So, out of concern for relevance, comes the legal question: Does the victim's clinically observed emotional trauma support the allegation about the stressor? In the usual tort or criminal case, an act is not in dispute – say, an automobile accident – but rather causation and damages are in dispute. In a turnaround, in cases involving syndrome evidence, symptoms are offered as evidence that a certain act occurred, but is trauma stressor specific? Is there something peculiar about the trauma suffered by a victim of a tort or crime that is different from the trauma suffered as a result of other stressors such as a hurricane or an automobile accident? Are subcategories of PTSD warranted – such as "sexually abused child syndrome", "rape trauma syndrome", "battered spouse", "battered elderly", or "incest trauma"?[38] These terms have developed to encompass the recurrent pattern of certain victims. Should they be elevated to the level of diagnostic nomenclature? Should they simply all be called PTSD? They are not listed as separate syndromes in the *DSM*, the state of the art, but who knows, perhaps some day they will.

A number of appellate decisions have been rendered on syndrome evidence. For some purposes, some appellate courts have recognised a number of categories of PTSD and have allowed testimony on them.[39] In rulings followed by many other courts, the California Supreme Court has admitted testimony on the battered child syndrome to prove child abuse but has excluded the rape trauma syndrome to prove that a rape had occurred. In *People v Bledsoe*,[40] the California Supreme Court made an attempt at explanation, saying that expert testimony concerning the battered child syndrome is admissible because that concept was devised for the purpose of determining whether a child's injuries were intentionally inflicted.

Dr Kempe's formulation of the syndrome, however, was based on physical evidence. Put another way, the physical injuries sustained by the child do not form any injury pattern normally sustained by children in day-to-day activities. The "battered child syndrome" indicated that the injuries

---

[37]   P McHugh, "Psychiatric Misadventures" (Autumn 1992) *American Scholar*, p497.

[38]   For a discussion, see DW Shuman, "The Diagnostic and Statistical Manual of Mental Disorders in the Courts" (1989) 17 *Bull Amer Acad Psych & Law* 25.

[39]   Evidence of rape trauma syndrome was allowed in *State v Marks*, 231 Kan 645, 647 P 2d 1292 (1982), but was rejected in *State v Saldana*, 324 NW 2d 227 (Minn 1982). See Annot, "Admissibility, at Criminal Prosecution, of Expert Testimony on Rape Trauma Syndrome," 42 ALR 4th 879 (1985).

[40]   36 Cal 3d 236, 203 Cal Rptr 450, 681 P 2d 291 (1984).

suffered by the child were not the result of an accident. Following Dr Kempe's formulation, courts in various jurisdictions allowed an expert medical witness to express an opinion that a child exhibits the battered child syndrome. In these cases the expert is permitted to give an opinion as to the cause of a particular injury, either on the basis of the expert's deduction from the appearance of the injury itself of from the syndrome.

Sexual child abuse, on the other hand, often leaves no physical injuries on which a diagnosis of "battered child syndrome" could be based. And what about an alleged rape? Should a rape counsellor or other mental health professional be permitted to testify to an individual's post-incident emotional trauma – "a constellation of symptoms experienced by the victims of sexual assault" or "rape trauma syndrome" – in order to prove that a rape in fact occurred (or a "sexual abuse syndrome" to prove that molestations occurred)? In a rape case, it is argued that the complainant would not suffer the symptoms if she had consented to the sexual act.[41] (Consent is no defence, of course, in cases of sexual abuse involving children. In these cases, the issue is whether it occurred or whether the accused is the perpetrator.)

In *Bledsoe,* the California Supreme Court noted that the rape trauma syndrome is a fundamentally different concept from the battered child syndrome because the "[the rape trauma syndrome] was not devised to determine the truth or accuracy of a particular past event". Rather, the court said, it is "a therapeutic tool" used to treat victims by counsellors who consciously "avoid judging the credibility of their clients".[42] The distinction has been widely but not always followed.[43] Actually any of the

---

[41] In *United States v Wesson*, 779 F 2d 1443 (9th Cir 1986), the Ninth Circuit allowed a doctor's testimony that the alleged rape victim's injuries were not consistent with consensual intercourse to "aid the jury in determining the credibility of the alleged victim's claim that the intercourse was nonconsensual." 779 F 2d at 1444. Similarly, in *Henson v State*, 535 NE 2d 1189 (Ind 1989), the Indiana Supreme Court held that "fundamental fairness" required that the defense be allowed to present rape trauma syndrome evidence to show that the victim's behaviour was inconsistent with that of a rape victim. See also *United States v Rivera*, 43 F 3d 1291 (9th Cir 1995); *State v Wilkerson*, 295 NC 559, 247 SE 2d 905 (1978); *People v Whitfield*, 425 Mich 116, 388 NW 2d 206 (1986).

[42] The *Bledsoe* case involved a 28-year-old offender and a 14-year-old victim.

[43] In *Spencer v General Electric Co*, 688 F Supp 1072 (ED Va 1988); *Commonwealth v Zamarripa*, 379 Pa Super 20, 549 A 2d 980 (Pa Super Ct 1988). There are decisions to the contrary. See, eg, *State v Allewalt*, 308 Md 89, 517 A 2d 741 (1986). See TM Massaro, "Experts, Psychology, Credibility and Rape: The Rape Trauma Syndrome Issue and its Implications for Expert Psychological Testimony" (1985) 69 *Minn L Rev* 495; D McCord, "Syndromes Profiles and Other Mental Exotica: A New Approach to the Admissibility of Nontraditional Psychological Evidence in Criminal Cases" (1987) 66 *Oregon L Review* 19; D McCord, "The Admissibility of Expert Testimony

PTSDs are treatable without regard to the nature of the stressor or even whether a stressor actually occurred. (The "rape crisis centre" could be "crisis centre" for all people in emotional distress.)

While courts have more often rejected than accepted "rape trauma syndrome" in establishing the stressor, they have allowed evidence of a "child sexual abuse syndrome" to show that the child was sexually abused. As a result of the concern about child abuse, in the trial of accused child molesters, many courts in recent years in the United States have allowed mental health professionals to testify that the psychological problems of a child are evidence that abuse has in fact occurred.[44] Other courts draw a distinction without a difference, saying that an expert may testify that the particular behaviour of the child was characteristic of, or "consistent with", the behaviour pattern of child sexual abuse victims generally, but the expert may not testify about whether the victim's allegations are truthful or whether sexual abuse did occur.[45]

In proving the rape of an adult, however, many courts like the California Supreme Court in *Bledsoe*, have concluded that rape trauma syndrome does not meet the standard of general acceptance in the scientific community.[46] The court emphasised, however, that while such testimony is not admissible for the purpose of proving that a rape occurred, it may be admissible for other purposes, such as explaining to the jury certain popular myths concerning rape victims. It may be used to explain a delay in reporting. Likewise, in battered spouse cases, prosecutors call mental health professionals as expert witnesses to explain the individual's failure to make a timely report for fear of reprisal, fear of being blamed, and fear of terminating the relationship.[47] Quite frequently the prosecutor seeks to

---

Regarding Rape Trauma Syndrome in Rape Prosecutions" (1985) 26 *Bost Coll L Rev* 1143.

[44] *People v Lukity*, 596 NW 2d 607 (Mich 1999); *State v McCoy*, 400 NW 2d 807 (Minn App 1987).

[45] *People v Beckley*, 434 Mich 691, 456 NW 2d 391 (1990); *In re Brimer*, 191 Mich App 401, 478 NW 2d 689 (1991). The rule applies to child protective proceedings as well as to criminal prosecution.

[46] See *Frye v United States*, 293 Fed 1013 (D C Cir 1923).

[47] See *Ibn-Tamas v United States*, 407 A 2d 626 (DC 1979); *Commonwealth v Craig*, 783 SW 2d 387 Ky (1990). For discussion of the "battered woman syndrome," see L Walker, *The Battered Woman Syndrome*, Springer, New York, 1984. The prominent Australian barrister Ian Freckelton argues against the role of syndrome evidence in the legal system and questions whether "battered woman syndrome" and "rape trauma syndrome" merit the status that they have been accorded by some courts: I Freckelton, "Contemporary Comment: When Plight Makes Right – The Forensic Abuse Syndrome" (1994) 18 *Criminal Law Journal* 29. See also AL Hyams, "Expert Psychiatric Evidence in Sexual Misconduct Cases Before State Medical Boards" (1992) 17 *Am J Law & Medicine* 171.

introduce evidence to explain behaviour unique to victims of sexual assault in order to enhance the credibility of its witnesses. Some child or adult victims of sexual assault, for example, may fear retaliation and may delay reporting the crime for a longer period than the victims of other crimes. Others may delay out of shame; still, others may recant their earlier allegations. The "child sexual abuse accommodation syndrome" (developed by Dr Roland Summit) has as its premise that children do not lie about sexual abuse, but change their stories for other reasons.[48]

Promptness in the report of a crime tends to be taken as evidence of reliability. It is regarded as an indication that the accusation is not a concoction. Indeed, the law of evidence regards spontaneity of a statement as an indicium of trust or trustworthiness and makes an exception for it in the rule against hearsay.[49] How can a prosecutor deal with a delay in reporting, or with a recanting of the story? In *Bledsoe*, the court said: "[I]n such a context expert testimony on rape trauma syndrome may play a particularly useful role by disabusing the jury of some widely held misconceptions about rape and rape victims, so that it may evaluate the evidence free of the constraints of popular myths."[50] Thus, in another case, in Washington, a worker at a "sexual assault centre" was allowed to testify that in over 50 per cent of sexual abuse cases involving children there is a delay in reporting.[51]

Syndromes are multiplying. In the 1970s, there was much publicity about a disorder called the "Stockholm Syndrome." The presenting symptom of this affliction affected hostages who, showed signs of sympathy for the captors who had terrorised them. This condition was offered as an explanation for Patty Hearst's taking part alongside her former captors in a bank robbery. Not much is heard now about the "Stockholm Syndrome"; but we hear a lot about many others. The Montana Supreme Court upheld an award to a farmer because the state's nearby highway construction was stressful to his pigs. A veterinarian gave expert testimony about "porcine stress syndrome".[52] After a few days in Jerusalem, the Holy City, apparently normal pilgrims imagine they are

---

48 RC Summit, "The Child Sexual Abuse Accommodation Syndrome" (1983) 7 *Child Abuse & Neglect* 177; see SJ Ceci & H Hembrooke (eds), *Expert Witnesses in Child Abuse Cases*, Washington, DC, American Psychological Association, 1998; see also TG Gutheil & PK Sutherland, "Forensic Assessment, Witness Credibility and the Search for Truth through Expert Testimony in the Courtroom" (1999) 27 *J Psychiatry & Law* 289.

49 Federal Rules of Evidence, Rule 803 (2).

50 681 P 2d at 298.

51 *State v Petrich*, 101 Wash 2d 566, 683 P 2d 173 (1984).

52 *State of Montana v Howery*, 204 Mont 417, 664 P 2d 1287 (1983).

biblical figures. The Holy City derangement is labelled "Jerusalem Syndrome".

In *Werner v State*,[53] Judge Marvin Teague of the Texas Court of Criminal Appeals described the proliferation in this way: "Today, we have the following labels: 'The Battered Wife Syndrome'; 'The Battered Child Syndrome'; 'The Battered Husband Syndrome'; 'The Battered Patient Syndrome'; 'The Familial Child Sexual Abuse Syndrome'; 'The Rape Trauma Syndrome'; 'The Battle Fatigue Syndrome'; 'The Vietnam Post-Traumatic Stress Syndrome'; 'The Policeman's Syndrome'; 'The Whiplash Syndrome'; 'The Low-Back Syndrome'; 'The Lover's Syndrome'; 'The Love Fear Syndrome'; 'The Organic Delusional Syndrome'; and 'The Holocaust Syndrome.' Tomorrow, there will be additions to the list, such as 'The Appellate Court Judge Syndrome'."

Werner involved the admissibility of evidence on the "Holocaust Syndrome", offered in support of a plea of self-defence (just as evidence of "battered spouse" is offered to establish a lower threshold of self-defence). The syndrome is one exhibited by children of survivors of the Nazi Holocaust who grew up hearing the stories from their parents of how entire Jewish families perished in the concentration camps during the Second World War without resisting. These children have formed a firm determination that if their lives are ever threatened, they will immediately resist forcibly and not permit injustice to be foisted upon them. This mind-set makes them vulnerable to precipitous use of deadly force in what they believe is self-defence when confronted with assaultive behaviour.

In this case, a psychiatrist would have testified (if allowed) that the defendant showed "some" of the characteristics of the syndrome associated with children of survivors of Nazi concentration camps. He would also have testified "that one does not need to be thinking of an event for another event in one's life to have an effect, a subconscious effect on him". The State objected to the proffered testimony on the ground of relevancy; that is, if self-defence is urged, the test to be applied is "the standard of an ordinary and prudent person in the defendant's position at the time of the offence". The majority of the Texas Court of Criminal Appeals, agreed; but Judge Teague, while mocking the proliferating phenomenon of syndrome evidence, argued in dissent that the "Holocaust Syndrome" should be given the same deference as the "Battered Spouse Syndrome", or other syndrome, that is allowed to explain the effects of abuse on the condition of a defendant's mind.

It remains a controversial issue whether syndrome evidence should be admissible as evidence to establish that a specific stressor has in fact

---

[53]   711 S W 2d 639 (Tex Cr App 1986).

occurred. Because symptoms of a psychological nature are not stressor-specific, the "duck test" is of questionable value. These symptoms do not imply aetiology. With few exceptions, the DSM does not set out the aetiology of the disorders.[54] A wide variety of stressors may give rise to a given symptom, which may also be attributable to normal developmental variations.[55] During a therapy session, the poet Anne Sexton asked, "Do I make up a trauma to go with my symptoms?"

As we have noted, a number of courts have allowed evidence of PTSD to explain the behaviour of the victim in delaying a report or in recanting, while they have been divided on allowing it to establish the nature of a stressor or whether any stressor in fact occurred. To disallow syndrome evidence to directly prove an occurrence but to allow it to indirectly prove an occurrence by proving the complainant's credibility is to draw a distinction without a difference.[56] In either case, the aim in the last analysis is to establish the occurrence of a stressor, either directly or through the truthfulness of the complainant. Explaining the delay in reporting by syndrome evidence is to enhance the credibility of the complaining witness and thereby, in effect, to establish the stressor. It is yet another way around the bar on credibility testimony.

To sum up

In the law-psychiatry intermix, public policy very much determines whether certain behaviour will be considered to be the result of mental illness, or whether mental illness will be considered to be the result of a particular stressor. Quite often psychiatric input is allowed to assist in reaching a decision. Forensic experts are asked to say whether the behaviour of the individual is fundamentally the result or product of mental illness and they are asked to say whether mental illness is the result of a particular stressor.

---

54   For example, the most common childhood diagnosis – attention deficit/hyperactivity disorder – describes behaviour without in any way explaining its origin.

55   In *United States v Charley*, 176 F 3d 1265 at 1281 (10th Cir 1999), the Tenth Circuit ruled that a mental health counsellor's opinion that the child's symptoms were more consistent with symptoms of children who have been sexually abused than with the symptoms of children who witness physical abuse of their mother was erroneously admitted. The court made its decision, citing *Kumho Tire Co v Carmichael*, 119 S Ct 1167 (1999), because no sufficient foundation was laid for this kind of expert's analysis, and no reliability inquiry was undertaken.

56   In *State v Hall*, 330 NC 808, 412 SE 2d 883 (1992), evidence that a victim's symptoms are consistent with those of the typical sexual or physical abuse victim was held admissible, but only to aid the jury in assessing the complainant's credibility.

18 Causation in the Context of Medical Practitioners' Liability for Negligent Advice

JOHN DOYLE*

Introduction

The law to be applied in Australia in deciding issues of causation in the law of tort is settled by *March v Stramare*.[1] In most situations, a sufficient causal connection between an act of negligence and an injury is established by showing that the plaintiff would not have sustained the injury complained of but for the negligence of the defendant, or had the defendant not been negligent. That test, however, is neither a comprehensive nor an exclusive criterion for liability. There are situations in which a closer analysis of the question of causation must be made.

The judgments in *March v Stramare* indicate that the "but for" test can be applied as a negative or exclusionary test of causation in almost all cases. If the plaintiff cannot satisfy the "but for" test, then in most cases the plaintiff's claim will fail. The fact that the plaintiff can satisfy the "but for" test does not mean that the plaintiff's claim will necessarily succeed. The "but for" test cannot be applied as a negative criterion of causation in cases where there are two or more acts or events which would each be sufficient to bring about the plaintiff's injury.[2] Later decisions of the High Court, for example *Bennett v Minister of Community Welfare*[3] and *Chappel v Hart*[4]

---

* The Chief Justice of South Australia.
[1] (1991) 171 CLR 507.
[2] Mason CJ at 516.
[3] (1992) 176 CLR 408.
[4] (1998) 195 CLR 232.

demonstrate that difficult issues in the area of causation will continue to arise.

Particular problems can arise in the area of negligent advice by medical practitioners. The extent of the duty to advise has been settled by the High Court in *Rogers v Whitaker*,[5] but the application of this duty gives rise to practical problems. Issues of causation are complicated by the fact that there are risks inherent in most procedures.

In *Chappel v Hart*, in relation to establishing causation in connection with medical negligence, Kirby J observed that the state of the law:

> causes dissatisfaction to litigants, anguish for their advisers, uncertainty for Judges, agitation among commentators and friction between health care professionals and their legal counterparts.[6]

Whether that rather gloomy diagnosis is correct I do not know, but there can be no doubting the difficulty of the legal and medical issues that can arise. In this commentary I do not intend to analyse the case law in detail. My aim is to raise for consideration some issues in relation to the workings of the principles of causation in the context of liability for negligent medical advice.

I propose to comment on two aspects of the relevant principles: first, the duty to advise about the risks involved in undergoing surgery and secondly, the circumstances in which liability is imposed for risks inherent in surgery, after a failure to provide advice when it should have been provided.

Causation in Context

The importance of the concept of causation in the law of tort, and in the law of negligence in particular, is obvious. A function, or perhaps the function of the concept of causation in negligence, is to define the outer limits of harm or loss suffered by other persons for which the defendant may be held liable, if found to have been negligent.

Causation is concerned with allocating legal responsibility for harm or damage suffered by a plaintiff. That process of allocating legal responsibility has various aspects. A claim for damages is a claim to attribute legal responsibility, on the basis of fault, to another person for harm suffered by the plaintiff and, by an award of damages, a claim to shift

---

5   (1992) 175 CLR 479.
6   (1998) 195 CLR 232 at 264.

the loss from the plaintiff to the defendant. Such a claim does not raise only technical legal considerations. It also raises fundamental issues of justice. Such a claim should be disposed of by applying clearly articulated legal principles, principles that reflect coherent policy considerations, and principles that accord with community conceptions of justice.

As well, we need to recall that the concept of cause and effect is applied in everyday life. There is an everyday notion of cause, and of limits to the result of what we do. The law needs to keep an eye on the everyday notion.

A claim against a medical practitioner for negligent advice requires the court to make an assessment of the competence of the practitioner. A finding of negligence will be significant for the medical practitioner, quite apart from its financial implications, and even if the defendant is fully insured. A finding of negligence will usually involve a significant reflection on the medical practitioner concerned.

No doubt many plaintiffs regard a favourable verdict as some kind of vindication of the plaintiff's complaints, and an unfavourable verdict as an adverse reflection on the plaintiff. A decision on such a claim may well affect the manner in which a particular aspect of medical practice is conducted. Various judgments refer to the capacity of the law in this area to deter or discourage bad practice, and proceed on the assumption that a function of the law is to promote good practice.

The other side of the coin is that the prospect of liability may encourage an approach to treatment which is excessively cautious, or which results in unnecessary costs being incurred by patients and by public funds.

There are also claims that the risk or fear of liability, as a result of decisions in widely publicised cases, leads to medical practitioners withdrawing their services from high risk areas of practice, to the general detriment of the public. The literature suggests that well publicised findings of liability in particular cases, based on evidence given in a particular case, can cause the public to believe that particular medical procedures or approaches are unsafe, when that is not so. The result can be a loss of faith in procedures that offer real benefits to the public. Finally, most would agree that as far as possible the law should be reasonably comprehensible by lawyers and by those to whom it is applied.

These observations are intended to make the point that the concept of causation, when applied to the liability of a medical practitioner for negligent advice, plays an important part in a process that is directed to the allocation of legal responsibility for identified harm or loss, but the process gives rise to a number of other considerations and can have significant consequences beyond the decision between the immediate parties. It is legitimate to raise these other considerations when considering the soundness of the concept.

In this commentary, it is not possible to canvass all these issues. But they cannot be ignored. At the end of the day, the state of the law in this area must be assessed by taking account of considerations of this sort.

A Diversion

A claim for medical negligence necessarily involves a very close examination of the facts of a particular case. It is only that case that the judge is called to decide. But in deciding the case, the judge must apply the standard of a reasonably competent practitioner, and so must apply a standard which is capable of general application. However, in deciding the particular case, it is very difficult, perhaps impossible, for the judge to assess adequately the impact of the particular decision if applied to medical practice generally.

There is no obvious solution to this problem. The duty of the judge is to decide the particular case. Inevitably, others will generalise from the decision of the court. There is an obvious risk of a judge imposing a particular standard of practice, in the context of a particular case, which will have untoward consequences when applied to medical practice generally.

Another difficulty in litigation over medical negligence is the dependence of the court upon the expert evidence presented by the parties. The court is in the hands of the parties. It is quite possible that, in the context of a particular case, a judge will be persuaded to accept the views of a medical expert even though, unknown to the judge, those views are in conflict with views generally held within the profession, or are even wrong. Much can depend upon the skill with which the respective cases are presented, and the apparent quality of the expert medical evidence presented to the judge. Once again, there is no escape from this. Our system relies upon the parties to present the best evidence.

Finally, the judge must decide the particular case presented to the judge for or against the plaintiff, on the evidence presented and on the balance of probabilities. The judge cannot defer a decision, awaiting scientific developments. The judge cannot decline to make a decision, or record a draw.

Neither of these points has anything in particular to do with the principles of causation. I mention them merely to highlight some sensitive aspects of litigation over medical negligence, and to emphasise that it is not surprising that medical practitioners should, at times, be critical of the processes of the courts and of the results of particular cases. These criticisms are likely to surface in the consideration of causation cases.

I mention them also as an introduction to a related point made by Professor Fiona Stanley in the second Eleanor Shaw lecture[7] when she said:

> Litigation, by use of selective or misleading evidence and fanned by a media whose aim is to sell rather than to inform, can drive us away from making the best decisions in medicine – those which have the potential to help the majority that rarely may harm or not benefit the individual.
>
> The modern sciences of public health ie epidemiology and statistics are now of enormous importance, they have a population focus. They determine, as rigorously as possible, whether associations are real and whether they are likely to be causal. Courtroom trials are quintessentially singular, framing facts in isolation and demand that scientific truths be rediscovered anew every time. They often are influenced by biased expert witnesses, who present an extreme and outrageous view which is not the general consensus of knowledge.

Professor Stanley went on to illustrate her point by reference to four areas in which she asserted that litigation has had a negative effect on the practice of medicine or public health. I will mention one only, to illustrate her point.

Cervical cancer is the seventh commonest cancer in Australian women, with 1,700 new cases per year. Screening healthy women is an attempt to identify abnormalities in women who have no symptoms, and thus give them and their doctors an idea of their risk status. Such tests are not diagnostic of cancer. The tests can give false positives and false negatives. According to Professor Stanley, publicity has been given to recent litigation involving women who have claimed that their cancers were not picked up by the screening process. She maintained that this is not a failure of the screening program, nor a result of negligence on the part of the laboratory. It is to be expected that in rare cases a false negative will occur. Professor Stanley said that this litigation, and the publicity given to it, have had negative effects on public health. There has been a marked increase in referrals for slightly abnormal smears, with increased cost and anxiety to women. The cost of the program has increased, because of more repeat tests, more examinations and so on. Fewer women are attending for screening, having been put off the screening program by adverse publicity.

---

[7]   29 August 1995, Melbourne, "Litigation versus Science: What's Driving Decision Making in Medicine?"

Trained people have left the relevant areas of medical practice, because they do not like being sued. There is an encouragement to search for new technologies or tests which may bring very small gains of increased accuracy, but carry with them considerable increases in cost.

I am unable to comment on Professor Stanley's observations. I refer to them in this context to make the point that it is important that, putting it colloquially, the courts get it right. Although a judge sits to decide a case between particular parties, the principles that the judge applies, and the outcome of the case, can have far-reaching effects.

Perhaps in the development and application of the relevant legal principles, we need to be better informed about issues like this. But there is a problem. The principles of causation are applied in all areas of negligence, and more generally in the law of tort. We cannot fashion the relevant principles by reference to their impact in the area of medical negligence. And, as will be evident, some of Professor Stanley's concerns relate to the adversarial process, although her concern about attributing responsibility for false negatives might involve issues of causation.

At the end of the day, it may be that we can do no more than acknowledge that the principles that we apply and the decisions that the courts make have important ramifications for those who must and do adjust their conduct by reference to the decisions of the courts.

How Does One Assess the Legal Concept of Causation?

Once one moves beyond a critical consideration of the approach to causation, it is not easy to say how best to assess the adequacy of the existing concepts. I suspect that in the ordinary case the approach of the courts to causation has been quite satisfactory, by and large. In the ordinary case, the issue of causation is straightforward. If this is so, one could say that the fact that there are hard cases, causing the sort of dismay to which Justice Kirby alluded, is of no great significance. The other approach is to say that the measure of an approach to causation is how well it grapples with the hard case. In the straightforward cases one can get to the right answer almost intuitively, and what we need is a sound test for the hard cases. That is how I am proposing to approach the matter in this commentary.

The "But For" Test

What follows is just a brief description of the approach affirmed in *March v Stramare*. It is drawn mainly from the judgment of Chief Justice Mason. The High Court has emphasised that the legal concept of causation differs from philosophical and scientific notions of causation. Those concepts were developed in the context of explaining phenomena by reference to the relationship between conditions and occurrences. In a court, on the other hand, problems of causation arise in the context of determining legal responsibility for a given occurrence.

What this seems to mean is that the law determines causation for a particular purpose, namely the attribution of legal responsibility. The reason or purpose for attributing responsibility should therefore shape the approach to the concept of causation.

The legal approach to causation is likely to differ from the medical approach. A doctor looks for causes in the interests of prevention and cure. The law looks for a cause, or the cause of an event, with a view to attributing liability for the event. We should be able to say that the legal concept of causation is one which attributes responsibility when it is appropriate to do so, and does not attribute responsibility when it is not appropriate to do so. But appropriate to do so or not appropriate to do so by what measure or standard? An obvious, if circular one, is by the standard of doing justice as between the parties. More debatable is the question of whether and to what extent some of the wider considerations identified by me are relevant here. It may be that Sir Anthony Mason's statement about the context in which causation arises is really a truism. Perhaps it means nothing more than that the law must set some limits to the concept of causation, when attributing legal responsibility. That is not contestable. How it sets the limits is critical.

The legal concept of causation is a question of fact, to be determined by applying common sense to the facts of each case. This statement may also be something of a truism. In jurisdictions in which civil juries are used, the question of causation is one for the jury. But much of the reasoning in the High Court cases looks like reasoning in terms of rules of law to me. The emphasis in the judgments here seems to be that the application of the but for test must be tempered by common sense considerations, and also by the making of value judgments and infusion of policy considerations.

In *March v Stramare* Mason CJ referred with approval to remarks of Dixon CJ, Fullagar and Kitto JJ in *Fitzgerald v Penn*[8] to the effect that "it

---

[8]   *Fitzgerald v Penn* (1954) 91 CLR 268 at 277.

is all ultimately a matter of common sense", and "In truth the conception in question [ie, causation] is not susceptible of reduction to a satisfactory formula".[9] When one sees the emphasis put upon the role of common sense in determining issues of causation, and the emphasis upon value judgments and the infusion of policy considerations, one is forewarned that in the difficult and unusual cases things are going to get difficult.

Things are going to get difficult because, in the end, the judge will have to attribute legal responsibility for a putative consequence, or refuse to attribute legal responsibility. And in making that choice the judge will have to decide that particular facts or aspects of the case are a reason to make that decision. It is making that choice, and explaining it, and justifying it by policy considerations, that is difficult in the hard cases. It is important that talk about causation should not mask the selection of reasons for attributing liability.

It is no criticism of judges to say that in the hard cases they will sometimes differ about what is a common sense result and what is a sound policy outcome. The decision in *Chappel v Hart* is a sufficient illustration of this. There, in what is undeniably a difficult and unusual case, a decision finding that the defendant had caused the relevant loss was upheld by a three-two majority. Each group invoked arguments based on policy and common sense. One of the things that I find interesting about the more difficult cases is that, despite what Sir Anthony Mason said, one does not find much overt reference to value judgments and policy considerations. My impression is that, by and large, the judges are endeavouring to apply a "but for" approach, but to do so in a common sense and practical fashion. In *Chappel v Hart* Kirby J observed that in deciding the question of causation "there is usually a large element of intuition in deciding such questions which may be insusceptible to detailed and analytical justification".[10] But he went on to say that the losing party has a right to know why it has lost, and that this imposes an obligation upon the courts to elaborate their reasons for reaching a conclusion. I suspect, with respect, that there is a good deal of truth in what Kirby J says, and that many judges are trying to articulate reasons for a result which intuitively they think is right and just.

In *March v Stramare* Deane J said that: "The question whether conduct is a 'cause' of injury, remains to be determined by a value judgment involving ordinary notions of language and common sense."[11] We also know that the "but for" test will generally not provide a satisfactory answer

---

9   At 278.
10   (1998) 195 CLR 232 at 269.
11   (1991) 171 CLR 507 at 524.

in cases in which a supervening event, deliberate or negligent, is said to break the chain of causation or to terminate the liability of the defendant for a consequence.

In this area there are some propositions that seem reasonably well established. If the defendant's negligence merely secures the presence of the plaintiff at the time when, and the place where, he or she is injured, it will not be causally connected with that injury, unless the risk of the accident occurring at that time was greater. Unless the risk was greater, the supervening injury will usually terminate the chain of causation. The causal connection between a defendant's negligence and injury to a plaintiff may also be negatived by deliberate conduct of another person, or a deliberate omission, which is intended to exploit the situation created by the defendant. Negligent or unreasonable conduct by another person, causing injury to the plaintiff, may also terminate the chain of causation, but will not do so if the possibility of such an event was the sort of thing against which is it was the duty of the defendant to safeguard the plaintiff.

A later act of negligence causing injury will also not terminate the chain of causation if it was in the ordinary course of things the kind of thing that was likely to happen. For that reason, if a plaintiff is negligently treated and seeks further treatment from another doctor, and that doctor treats the plaintiff negligently, usually the original doctor will remain liable for all of the foreseeable consequences. However, the cases suggest that if the negligence of the second doctor is extreme or is quite out of the ordinary, then the chain of causation may be terminated.

What we see here is a number of signposts or guides to decision-making. But the manner in which the particular rules are expressed, indicates that there is plenty of leeway for differences of opinion when applying the rules.

The Duty to Advise

In *Rogers v Whitaker* the surgeon in question was found to have conducted an operation on the plaintiff's eye with the required level of skill and care. Nevertheless, a condition ensued which, on the evidence, occurred once in approximately 14,000 such procedures. The plaintiff was an anxious patient, and addressed many questions to the surgeon about possible complications. She was not warned about the particular complication which occurred. This was devastating for the plaintiff. She had virtually no sight in one eye. The operation was being performed on her good eye. The end result was that she was virtually blind.

In the area of advice, the decision makes two important points. The first is that it is for the courts to decide what is the required standard of care, and not for medical practice or opinion to do that. Evidence of acceptable medical practice is a useful guide, but no more than that. Accordingly, the question of the advice that should be given to a patient was not to be determined solely by reference to medical opinion.

The High Court held that:

> The law should recognise that a doctor has a duty to warn a patient of a material risk inherent in the proposed treatment; a risk is material if, in the circumstances of the particular case, a reasonable person in the patient's position, if warned of the risk, would be likely to attach significance to it or if the medical practitioner is or should reasonably be aware that the particular patient, if warned of the risk, would be likely to attach significance to it. This duty is subject to the therapeutic privilege.[12]

This requirement is an onerous one, emphasised by the fact that the risk of which the plaintiff was not informed was one of an adverse outcome in one in 14,000 such procedures.

Advice about Risks

All surgery involves risks. Without any lack of care, something can go wrong. We read that merely being admitted to a hospital carries with it a not insignificant risk of infection. It appears that a material risk of which a doctor must warn a patient may be a risk that is quite remote. The doctor must consider what a reasonable person would think, but also has to consider the anxieties and concerns of the particular patient. It is no criticism of the approach taken by the High Court to say that it is likely to give rise to some difficult questions.

Presumably all inherent risks of a procedure should be canvassed, except those that are so remote that no reasonable person would take account of them, and as to which there is no reason to think that the particular patient would have a concern. How does a doctor decide the point at which a risk becomes so remote that it can be disregarded? Presumably, in deciding that, the doctor has to weigh up the incidence of the risk and the nature of the outcome should it eventuate. A difficult judgment is involved here. The answer might depend upon refined statistical analysis. It will be tempting for doctors to play safe and to advise of almost all conceivable risks. Ironically, this could either deaden the impact of advice about significant risks, or alternatively paralyse the

---

[12]   (1992) 175 CLR 479 at 490.

patient with fear. And is a doctor bound to deal with what might be called associated risks? What about the risk of the anaesthetist making a mistake? What about the risk of infection in the hospital? There are also difficulties with the question of how the advice is to be given. How much time is the doctor required to spend explaining what might be quite difficult issues to the patient? How do doctor and patient cope with the statistics, or can the doctor use every day expressions such as "highly unlikely" or "a remote possibility"?

Does the doctor have to go to the extent of canvassing with the patient alternative methods of conducting the relevant procedure? Must the doctor canvass his or her own level of skill, and the existence, if it is the case, of practitioners who have a higher level of skill or experience in relation to the particular procedure?

There is plenty of scope for debate about the scope of the duty to advise of risks. But advice on risks is only one matter for the medical practitioner to address. In giving the advice, the doctor should consider and canvass medical factors, the impact of different courses of action on the patient's quality of life, the patient's own wishes, and the cost, certainly to the individual and probably as well to the State. Presumably the prudent practitioner, in particular a specialist, must keep abreast of the literature that deals with these matters.

It seems to me that there are some unresolved issues about the scope of the duty to advise. As I have already said, they are not to be resolved by medical practice, although evidence about the nature and extent of the risks, the feasibility of explaining them to patients, and actual medical practice in this respect will be relevant. Focusing on the duty to warn about risks tends to obscure the fact that many other matters must be considered.

A Hard Case

Chappel v Hart[13] was undoubtedly a hard case. The plaintiff underwent surgery for removal of a pharyngeal pouch in her oesophagus. She was not warned of the risk of injury to her pharyngeal nerve and the consequent risk of partial or total loss of her voice. The court found that the operation was carried out with an appropriate level of care and skill. During the operation the oesophagus was perforated. This was one of the inherent risks of the procedure. It could happen without any lack of care and skill. In the event of perforation, there was a chance that if bacteria were present in the oesophagus, those bacteria could, as a result of the perforation, cause

---

[13]   (1998) 195 CLR 232.

infection. It was a matter of random chance whether bacteria were or were not present at the crucial time. Infection from the escape of bacteria, and consequent injury, was a very rare complication, but it ensued. This resulted in some loss of voice for the plaintiff. The plaintiff claimed that the surgeon had been negligent in failing to warn her of the risks of the operation. She said that if she had received such a warning she would have explored the possibility of having the most experienced surgeon available conduct the operation. She would have deferred the operation. She asked specific questions about the possibility of damage to her vocal chords. On the other hand, on the evidence, the plaintiff had to have the operation sooner or later. The condition from which she suffered was progressive.

The application of the principles enunciated in *March v Stramare* led the majority and the minority in different directions. The majority approach was, in substance, that there was a duty to inform the patient of the possible consequences in the event of the perforation of her oesophagus and subsequent infection, notwithstanding the relatively remote nature of that risk, and its random nature. That duty was not performed, and the relevant risk eventuated. The plaintiff had given evidence that if warned of the risk, she would have acted to avoid or minimise the risk of injury, by seeking a more experienced surgeon. The majority judgments seem to accept that the risk of injury would have been reduced had the patient consulted a more experienced surgeon. To what extent it would have been reduced, is not made clear. The majority also seem to proceed on the basis that, the risk being remote and random, and having eventuated in the case in question, had the patient had the operation at a later time, the risk of injury then would have been minimal.

In other words, the majority proceeded on the basis that the damage that the plaintiff suffered was reasonably foreseeable. There should have been a warning about it. The very risk of which the patient should have been warned materialised. If the surgery had been performed at a different time, or by a more experienced surgeon, in all likelihood the patient would not have suffered the random chance of injury. That summation is drawn from the reasons of Gummow J[14] who went on to consider whether there was any good reason to deny the plaintiff recovery upon the basis that injuries of the nature sustained by the plaintiff might be caused without negligent performance of the procedure. He found that there was no such reason. His conclusion was that it would be unjust to absolve the doctor from legal responsibility "by allowing decisive weight to hypothetical and problematic considerations of what could have happened to Mrs Hart at the

---

[14]   At 257.

hands of some other practitioner at some unspecified later date and in conditions of great variability".[15]

The dissenting view was, in essence, that the failure by the doctor to warn the patient of the risk did not materially increase the risk of the plaintiff suffering the injury. The negligent failure to warn had done no more than expose the patient to a class of risk to which she would have been exposed in any event. In the opinion of the minority, the plaintiff's claim should fail because she had not established that there was any surgeon available of such skill that he or she would never perforate the oesophagus. Nor did the evidence establish that there was any other surgeon whose skills were so superior that an operation by that surgeon carried with it a statistically significantly lesser risk of perforation than an operation by the defendant. In the opinion of the dissentients the case was a "time and place" case. That is, the negligence of the defendant had brought the plaintiff to the time and place where the injury had occurred, but had not caused it.

My impression is that a point of distinction between the majority and the minority is the firm view of the minority that nothing that the plaintiff would or might have done if warned would have reduced the likelihood of the complication occurring. My impression is that the majority were of the view that the plaintiff might have reduced the risk, although they did not state the extent to which she might have done so. It may be that that difference is the whole basis of the departure in the reasoning.

The other strand in the majority reasoning is that it was the risk of which the patient was not warned which eventuated and which caused injury, and that that being so an evidentiary onus lay upon the doctor to displace the inference of causation which thereupon arose, and that inference had not been displaced. In the reasoning of Gummow J there is also a reference to the injustice of absolving the medical practitioner from legal responsibility by reference to hypothetical and problematic considerations. This shifting of the evidentiary onus is likely to influence the outcome in borderline cases, and so has some practical significance. The justification for this rule seems to be policy considerations.[16] Whether this rule is really fair, or does reflect sound policy, is open to argument.

We have to accept that there will be hard cases, but where does this one leave us? The decision emphasises the onerous nature of the duty imposed on a doctor to warn or advise a patient about the risks of surgery. The risk which eventuated was remote, and pretty well unknown. The other point which emerges from the case is that if the warning is not given, and

---

[15]   At 262.
[16]   See the discussion by Kirby J at 273.

the very risk not the subject of warning eventuates, a court is likely on grounds of common sense or justice or policy to find that the resulting injury is caused by the failure to give the warning, even if the plaintiff finds it difficult to prove that he or she could have done anything to reduce the risk of the relevant injury. My impression is that the evidence for the plaintiff in *Chappel v Hart* that was said to show that, if warned, she might have followed a course that would have reduced the risk of injury, was slender indeed.

So what this seems to tell us is that considerations of policy or justice may indeed play a significant part in ascribing responsibility.

A Hypothetical Case

In order to focus on the two matters to which this commentary is directed, I will now postulate a hypothetical case, based on *Chappel v Hart*.

Assume that patient A consults doctor B with a view to undergoing a surgical procedure. First of all, B must advise A about the procedure. As I have pointed out, there are many factors to be considered when giving that advice. A particular matter which must be covered is the risk associated with the procedure. Certainly, the doctor must deal with the risk associated with the doctor's own work. It is unclear whether and to what extent the doctor must deal with risks involved in aspects of the procedure that are not under his or her control. In advising about the risks, the doctor may have to explain some difficult statistics, in a manner that is meaningful to the patient. It seems that the doctor may need to advise the patient, if it is the case, that there are other practitioners more skilled in performing the procedure if those greater skills might reduce the incidence of a relevant risk.

The point I emphasise is that, important as the risks of surgery are, they are only one matter for the patient's consideration. Prospects of success, and likely outcomes, are also very important to the patient. There are other matters that the doctor must consider.

I can well understand that from the practitioner's point of view the courts may seem to be elevating advice about risks to an unreasonable level of significance. But, probably betraying my own professional background, I find it difficult to escape from the logic that insists upon the plaintiff being advised of adverse outcomes before undergoing the procedure. The patient has a right to proper advice before submitting to surgery. On the other hand, a point must be reached at which the doctor has done what is reasonable. Identifying that point is not easy in practice.

Let us now assume that the development of condition X, a harmful condition, is a known but remote risk of the procedure. Let us assume that it is an inherent risk. By this I mean it is one that can occur even though the procedure is carried out properly. Assume that condition X is not so remote that the doctor is entitled to disregard it. Assume that B does not give advice about condition X.

Let us assume that the procedure is carried out competently, but condition X materialises. Has B's failure to advise caused the patient to suffer condition X? Often those bare facts would suffice to establish legal liability for condition X. There was a duty to warn about the risk, the warning was not given, the risk ensued. But when the duty is a duty to inform so that a decision can be made, the patient must prove what the patient would have done if warned.[17]

The court will conclude that the failure to warn caused A to suffer from condition X only if A would, on receipt of the information and warning, have acted to avoid or to minimise the risk of injury from condition X.[18]

Let us assume that the court concludes that if B had warned A, A would nevertheless have undergone the procedure when she did undergo it. In that situation the failure to warn has not caused A to suffer from condition X. The lack of a warning is not the cause of the injury, because it was irrelevant to the patient's decision to undergo the procedure that led to her suffering the injury.

Let us assume that the court concludes that having received the warning, the patient would not have undergone the procedure at all. In that situation the failure to warn is the cause of A suffering condition X. But for the failure, A would not have undergone the procedure and would not have suffered condition X.

What if, having received the warning, A would have deferred the procedure while she considered the matter, and while she sought a second opinion. What if A would then have submitted to the procedure, two weeks later? I assume for present purposes that the risk of condition X occurring was exactly the same two weeks later as it was when B carried out the procedure.

In this situation in my view the answer should be that the failure to warn has not caused A to suffer from condition X. A's position is no different from the position of the patient who would have proceeded to submit to the surgery regardless of the warning if given. It can be said that A would not have suffered condition X when she did, had the warning been given. We will never know what would have happened had A had the operation two weeks later. But we do know that if she had done that, she

---

[17] Gaudron J at 268; Kirby J at 239.
[18] Gaudron J at 262.

could not have suffered from condition X, if at all, until two weeks later. Is that a basis to conclude that the failure to warn is the cause of condition X?

In *Chappel v Hart*, some of the reasoning of Gaudron J suggests that in this situation B will be held to have caused A to suffer from condition X. Gaudron J said, referring to what would have happened if Dr Chappel had given Mrs Hart adequate information:

> If he had, Mrs Hart would not *then* have undergone surgery and would not *then* have suffered the injuries which she did or the consequences. Thus, Dr Chappel's "breach" was "still operating", or, "continued to be causally significant when [those injuries were sustained]". (Emphasis added).

That looks very much like the conclusion that if the failure to warn caused the patient to suffer condition X *when* she suffered it, that suffices to establish liability.

But can that conclusion be justified, other than on the further basis that the risk of factor X occurring if the procedure was done two weeks later was less than when it was actually done by B? I would have thought that it is only on this basis that causation can be made out.

Pursuing that thought, can it be said that because the risk was remote and random, and did ensue when B operated on A, that statistically it would not have ensued two weeks later? That is, that the two week deferral means, as a matter of statistics, that condition X would not have ensued if the procedure were deferred for two weeks, or is extremely unlikely to have ensued? I do not know the correct answer, as a matter of statistics. However, viewed prospectively, the chance of X occurring is identical, whether the operation is today or two weeks later. In retrospect, if X did occur when the operation was performed, it can be said that it is unlikely that it would have occurred two weeks later. But I suggest that considerations of policy and justice indicate that in this situation the conclusion should be that B did not cause A to suffer from condition X. As McHugh J argued,[19] a defendant will be held liable for the plaintiff's injury only if the defendant's wrongful act or omission results in an increased risk of injury to the plaintiff and that risk eventuates. If the defendant's conduct does not increase the risk of injury to the plaintiff, the defendant cannot be said to have materially contributed to the injury suffered by the plaintiff. In this situation surely the doctor has not increased the risk of injury. This is what I earlier referred to as a "time and place situation". As McHugh J later pointed out, to hold the defendant liable on this basis is simply to apply the

---

[19] At 244.

"but for" test.[20] On this point, Hayne J agreed with McHugh J. As he pointed out, the evidence was that the risk of Mrs Hart suffering the condition that she did suffer was such a remote risk that it is very unlikely that it would have happened if the operation had been performed on another day. But that is not enough to establish causation.[21]

However, the majority made statements that suggest that in this situation they would have found that the failure to advise A about factor X was the cause of A sustaining the injury. I am not completely confident of this, because the picture is clouded by the fact that the majority accepted that the evidence supported a finding that if Mrs Hart had been warned, she would have undergone the operation later but at the hands of a more skilled surgeon, carrying with it a reduced risk of injury occurring.[22] But there are other observations that suggest that even if the risk was the same at the later date, causation would still be made out, because the risk of the injury materialising was so remote that one could say fairly confidently that if the operation had been done on another day, Mrs Hart would not have suffered the same injury.[23] It is not completely clear to me that this is an independent basis for her decision, but it appears to be. Justice Gummow reasoned that a risk of which there should have been a warning materialised, and that if the surgery had been performed at a different time in all likelihood Mrs Hart would not have suffered the random chance of injury.[24] On that basis, it was the task of Dr Chappel to demonstrate some "quite good reason" for denying recovery. As to the risk of Mrs Hart sustaining an injury at the later date, he again seems to have regarded the risk as one that would have been less, because another and more skilled surgeon would have been retained.[25] But he also said:

> It would, in the circumstances of the case, be unjust to absolve the medical practitioner from legal responsibility for her injuries by allowing decisive weight to hypothetical and problematic considerations of what could have happened to Mrs Hart at the hands of some other practitioner at some unspecified later date and in conditions of great variability.[26]

Justice Kirby also said that as causation was established by showing the breach of duty, and as the risk against which there should have been a

---

20   At 251.
21   At 283-4.
22   Gaudron J at 241; Kirby J at 271.
23   See, for example, Gaudron J at 241-2.
24   At 257.
25   See at 260.
26   At 262.

warning eventuated, there was an onus upon Dr Chappel to displace the inference of causation. He did not do so by proving that she would have been exposed to the same or substantially the same possibility of like injury on another occasion. He said: "On the contrary, the evidence demonstrated that the chances of her receiving such injury in any other operation were minuscule."[27]

It is on the basis of those remarks that I conclude that the majority were prepared to hold that in the situation presently under consideration, B is to be found liable for having caused condition X. On that point, I respectfully disagree. The majority approach leads to the conclusion that the more remote the risk of condition X developing, the less likely it is to have occurred if the procedure were deferred, and the easier it becomes to establish causation in a deferral situation.

What if, on the evidence, A would have deferred the operation, retained a more expert surgeon, and had the procedure done with a significantly lesser degree of risk? In that situation, which was also alluded to by the majority, there is good reason to find that the failure to give the warning caused injury when condition X materialised. The failure has increased the risk.

But a point not addressed in *Chappel v Hart* is the question of the extent to which it is necessary to show that the risk of the condition being suffered would have been less had the procedure been carried out on another occasion or by another doctor. Is it sufficient to say that the risk would be less, without quantifying the diminution in the risk? I suggest that the quantification needs to be done, otherwise how can we say that the diminution in the risk is of any practical significance? The majority in *Chappel v Hart* appear to disagree.

This is a difficult question to resolve. Common sense would tell us that a line must be drawn somewhere. It cannot be that any reduction in risk no matter how minimal will be sufficient to ground a finding of causation. But at what point do we say that a reduction in risk is significant. Is a reduction in risk from 1 in 500 to 1 in 1000 significant? What about a reduction from 1 in 15,000 to 1 in 20,000?

In *Chappel v Hart* only McHugh J alluded to the possibility that not just any reduction in risk would suffice, saying that it must be a "statistically significant lesser risk".[28] The remaining members of the High Court were content that the risk be merely "less", "diminished" or "reduced". While it is clear that the court did not consider such evidence in *Chappel v Hart*, the test suggested by McHugh J raises the issue of whether

---

[27] At 278.
[28] At 249.

it is possible, or appropriate, to resolve this problem by reference to statistical tests designed to evaluate significance on a more or less "objective" basis.

At first sight, the idea of using statistical analysis to give us an objective answer to our question of significance is an attractive one. If such analysis were possible it would solve the difficulty of where the line is to be drawn.

While I do not pretend to be a statistician, my understanding is that in some circumstances there is very little statistical analysis which can be meaningfully carried out in respect of only two pieces of data. Thus, if all we know is that the risk of injury if Doctor A performs the procedure is X and the risk of injury if Doctor B performs the procedure is Y, statistical analysis cannot assist in deciding whether that reduction in risk (from X to Y) is significant let alone important – that is, important relative to what? This means that we must rely upon a subjective analysis by the courts of the relative risks involved. Perhaps this is not such a bad thing. Certainly it avoids submitting the law to what Kirby J described as "the paralysis of statistical abstractions".[29] But that does not mean that we should be content with the approach adopted by the remaining members of the court which did not involve *any* explicit analysis of the reduction in risk at all. In my opinion there must be a real inquiry into whether, in all the circumstances of the case, the reduction in risk is important.

Determining the significance of a reduction in risk of injury is a critical issue and one which may ultimately be determinative in cases like *Chappel v Hart*. As such it is an issue which should in future cases be explicitly addressed. While it would not appear to be possible for courts to engage in any sense in a truly statistical analysis of risk, the level of analysis must surely go beyond a mere finding that there was *some* reduction.

An analysis of the importance of a reduction in risk will in many, if not most, cases be a difficult one and one in which many considerations will need be taken into account. I do not attempt in this paper to canvass all of those considerations. I do, however, mention three in order to demonstrate that such an analysis will not necessarily be a straightforward one.

First, it is necessary to consider absolute as well as relative changes in outcomes. A 50 per cent decrease in the incidence of injury will be far more important if that represents a change from one in 50 cases to one in 100 cases than if it represents a change from one in 500 cases to one in 1000 cases. Secondly, the severity and permanence of injury must be taken into account. The more serious and debilitating the injury the more important will be a small reduction in the probability that the injury will

---

[29]   At 275.

occur. Finally, when assessing the importance of a reduction in risk it is necessary, as indeed the courts have emphasised in the past, to consider the particular concerns and circumstances of the patient involved. Where the risk is loss of eyesight, and the patient is particularly concerned about that or is already blind in one eye, the weight attached to any reduction in risk is likely to be higher.

Conclusion

Chappel v Hart was certainly a difficult test. A close reading of the reasons suggests that it exposes a number of difficult issues in the area of advice about risks. And, I suggest, there are plenty of difficulties lurking in the issue of the duty to advise. As so often happens in the law, *March v Stramare* has bedded down one set of principles, but its application has immediately exposed new issues that will test the courts.

19 Statistical Proof of Causation

ERIC MAGNUSSON[*]

Humans, when watched closely, display their individuality by behaving differently even when the circumstances are exactly the same. One of these behaviours is violent disagreement. The phenomenon is too common to surprise us. We rationalise it by supposing that the natures and nurtures through which the data are filtered can be responsible for contradictory perceptions from identical inputs.

An even stranger behaviour is unquestioning agreement. While most of the world was hunting and gathering, the Greeks were expounding the 256 variations of this curiously powerful format: "If *this*, then *that*; But *this* is true, therefore *that* is also true". Humans declare the argument to be "the Proof of *that*" and subscribe the mystic letters QED. An early user, Euclid, put a set of such arguments into five books, never imagining that his collected theorems would continue as the prescribed texts in the subject for over two thousand years. The behaviour must run very deep.

The strength of the formula and its attendant labels like *proof* and *preuve (Fr)* and *demonstratio (L)* rises from the simple fact that the final clause in the argument cannot be denied without contradicting the earlier ones. A contradiction is something the species strenuously avoids making. "Cognitive dissonance" research surprised us by showing that we protect ourselves from self-contradiction even to the point of disregarding things previously accepted as fact. A world without contradictions comes at the price of damage to its factual base, but it is the world we all prefer.

* Associate Professor in the School of Chemistry, the University College of the Australian Defence Force Academy of the University of New South Wales. I thank Ms Katrin Both, Professor Ian Freckelton, Dr Roger Magnusson, Ms Kylie Patchett and Mrs Rhonda Wheate for advice and assistance with sources.

The word "proof" is strongest when it describes sentences which conform to a logic in which every assertion is either completely true or completely false. Little of the real world fits this requirement, which is why the word can rarely be truly used. We could decide to simplify the world by arbitrarily making true and false the only truth-values allowed, but the world will not comply – the evidence on which to assign these qualities is always only partly certain. Most newspaper reports and almost all of what comes to court require multi-valued logic and are, therefore, ill suited to adjudication by formula. But they are no insuperable problem to courts run by people, creatures constructed to reason with assertions that may be partly true and partly false, or partly known and partly unknown. In such a world probability rules and statistics is its indispensable partner.

That human brains can do statistics is easily demonstrated. By eye, humans can judge the straightness of a line drawn on paper with more precision than the human eye is capable of. The eye is an instrument which uses tiny cells to detect light and this limits the perceived straightness of a dark line on white paper to the straightness of the not-very-straight lines of cells on which the light and dark images happen to fall. But the eye scans along the line and the brain apparently calculates what the line of cells would be if the random displacements of cells from linearity were replaced by their average. This statistical approach makes the eye capable of detecting deviations from straightness more than ten times smaller than the minimum separation of cells in the retina.

Making conscious decisions about masses of data is also natural for the brain. The brain is a device for making connections between neurons, while the mind makes meaning. Somehow the former is the mechanism for the latter. Brains routinely make circuits by the million to store information, preparing us for decisions made later by "weighing up" the effect of the currents flowing through circuits in many different places. In other words, we do "statistics" at this level too.

Although human thinking is statistical, talking about statistical thinking is not. The results of the thinking are evaluated subconsciously and any attempt to inspect the steps taken by the brain is likely to confuse the inspector. The ease with which human beings become confused about statistics is not only raw material for humour, it is a reality to be recognised when statistical science enters a court of law. All the wisdom and all the effort behind statistical evidence is worth nothing if the tribunal cannot comprehend it or, worse still, miscomprehends it. Likewise, statistical analysis of jury decisions is meaningless unless there is independent assessment of the jurors' comprehension of the issues they were deciding. The question of comprehension of statistical statements is a serious one and it will be a thread which runs through the whole of this chapter. In spite of all of this, modern cognitive science is successfully uncovering at least some of the mechanisms that underlie the human thinking process and the results throw light on how people behave when making decisions based on information only partly true or only partly known.

The Profession and Practice of Statistics

Statistical methods allow scientists and engineers to apply common sense to data that, like data of any other kind, are inexact.[1] The errors, which may be random or systematic, cannot be eliminated from measurements and the common sense consists in recognising them, estimating their magnitude, and trying to discover where they come from. When soft data are involved statistical methods are indispensable. Without some way to determine what is constant and what is variable, data obtained from surveys, interviews, human memory and the like would be worthless. This is why social scientists usually know more about statistics than physical scientists.

In this world, the data that come into the adversarial court are soft, error-prone and almost entirely untestable. In addition, the data are introduced through a set of individual and unrepeatable contributions – one man prosecutes, one defends, one expert presents the complex evidence, and one judge presides and rules on issues of law. The jury, when it is present, is the single injection of error reduction into the whole process but, again, the outcome of jury deliberation is vulnerable to a single strong-minded individual. However, even in the jury room, improvement will probably not come until someone "does the statistics".

Statistical reasoning, on the other hand, enters the courtroom often and its impact continues to grow. It is felt in two ways – by the explicit presentation of statistical argument and, more broadly, by taking advantage of the conceptual approach inherent in statistical reasoning. Sir Richard Eggleston's manual is still a rich source of this advantage.[2] As mentioned below, in a statistical setting hypothesis testing is accomplished not by confirming the alternative hypothesis but by rejecting the null hypothesis. The alternative hypothesis can be considered only after it has been demonstrated that the effects of the cause are not the result of chance variation – the differences have to be statistically significant. When events outside the laboratory are viewed through that particular prism, the view

---

1   Scientists frequently subdivide accuracy into two components, precision (repeated measurements all very close together but not necessarily close to the correct value) and accuracy (with their average close to the correct value but not necessarily precise).

2   R Eggleston, *Evidence, Proof and Probability,* 2nd edn, Weidenfeld and Nicholson, London, 1983.

changes and much of the easy inference of life disappears. There ought to be a permanent place for that prism in every court.

One of the truisms of statistical reasoning that has been penetrating the community is that scientific tests sometimes fail. From experience with medical pathology or, maybe, by using do-it-yourself tests from pharmacists, people become familiar with the possibility of "false negatives" and "false positives". The failures need not be symmetrical, the incidence of "false positives" being generally different from that of "false negatives". This recognition, which can be very important indeed in special types of statistical reasoning, is within the grasp of the average juror.

Professional statisticians, at first regarded suspiciously by courts, now occupy a well recognised domain of expertise and their evidence brings with it all the benefits and all the risks of opinion evidence in general. Their contributions as expert witnesses are made almost exclusively in civil cases where the statistical procedures themselves have become major issues in the action. The expert's testimony may be called "statistical methodology evidence" to distinguish it from the much more common "statistical evidence" in which an expert from some other domain provides information for the court in statistical form, usually by use of techniques which have become routine. Although published over ten years ago, *The Evolving Role of Statistical Assessments as Evidence in the Courts,* edited by Fienberg, is still an excellent introduction, combining a fairly detailed analysis of a small number of typical cases with authoritative comment on the whole field including criminal cases.[3]

Statisticians also contribute to the justice system as authorities on existing statistical procedures as well as by developing new methods. Thus, the use of Bayesian statistics has been widely adopted in reporting identification evidence; scientists trained in molecular biology have learned to use the statistical methods appropriate to the forensic science they practise. Statistics is now regarded as an important competency for all forensic scientists but for those working with identification evidence it is indispensable.

An important development in the science and technology sector is the general acceptance of the need for rigorous accreditation of scientists and laboratories that serve the community. This development came rather late to forensic sciences but it has been wholeheartedly adopted worldwide and courts can now find out about the performance of forensic science

---

[3]   SE Fienberg (ed), *The Evolving Role of Statistical Assessments as Evidence in the Courts*, Springer Verlag, New York, 1989.

laboratories and even of individual experts.[4] Making judgments on professional training, experience and ongoing competence is a skill which courts do not usually possess but it is made easier when laboratories and staff submit themselves to the scrutiny currently required for forensic science accreditation in Australia, New Zealand, the United Kingdom and various other countries.[5]

Things Done and Not Done with Statistics

Statistical methodology evidence is often of the kind where different experts favour different methods. In the special circumstances where the data are hard to treat or where the results are closely balanced or where unfamiliar techniques have been used, opinions are apt to vary from one expert to another and the expert evidence falls into the "subjective evaluation" category.[6] The court then hears the contrary opinions of experts giving testimony at a level it cannot ordinarily reach. There is no way for it to know which of the two experts would represent the majority of the profession; possibly neither does. The obverse of this is that highly qualified statisticians in court may find themselves given no more respect than novices. As in other examples of subjective evaluation evidence, the proper solution is by independent corroboration from as many other experts as are necessary for the court to feel confident about the representativeness of the result. New procedures for obtaining opinions from a larger number of practitioners may be required.

The range of problems for which statistical methods are invoked is broad. From the statistician's viewpoint they can be classified by the kind of parameter (variance, regression, etc) relied on to solve the problem and the further distinction made between descriptive statistics (data) and inferential statistics (predictions and likelihoods).[7]

---

[4]   In Australia the accreditation of government forensic science services has reached an advanced stage and is coordinated by the National Institute of Forensic Science.

[5]   Not all laboratories are accredited nor all areas of expertise covered by professional codes of conduct.

[6]   Irrespective of content, scientific evidence can be subdivided into the Qualitative, Quantitative, Comparison-based and Subjective Evaluation categories. An example of the last is psychiatric evidence relating to fitness to plead, depending on multiple factors and not easily reduced to cause-and-effect argument.

[7]   See, for example, DW Barnes, *Statistics as Proof*, Little, Brown, Boston, 1983.

A legal classification is more difficult than a statistical one. Civil suit actions relying on statistical evidence are described in many monographs and collections of which the multi-author volume by DeGroot, Fienberg and Kadane is a good example.[8] No two classify their subject in the same way.

At the head of the list must stand actions, including class actions, charging race and gender discrimination the area of litigation claimed to have generated the greatest demand for witnesses with expertise in statistics in recent years.[9] The first two of five case studies in the committee report edited by Fienberg are in this category and the analysis is of high quality.[10] One feature of the influential *Vuyanich v Republic National Bank* case[11] is selected for mention here. The judge expressed his suspicion that the statistical models presented to him by the two sides were too good; he was dubious about the "precision-like mesh of numbers" in both. That comment was matched by comment from expert statisticians to the effect that the statistical assessments were not really good enough to have taken so much of the judge's time and, particularly, that statistical quality control had not been applied to the evidence. This reinforces the complaint at the beginning of this section and underlines the need for courts to find ways to tell the difference between good and bad expert evidence. The court cannot presume that experts found by litigants will have come from the top of the profession.

The word "Medicine" in the title of this volume requires recognition in this chapter even if it is brief. Probabilistic statements feature strongly in court proceedings involving medicine; one reason being that humans beings are animals with highly developed control systems fitted with "manual override" allowing their psychology to interfere with their physiology. Consequently, they are rarely used as subjects for discovering the laws of nature in the animal kingdom and even less for higher level theories about life; fruit flies and bacteria are much more attractive subjects. The laws of human injury and disease are discovered by epidemiologists working at the observation and generalisation levels of scientific enquiry. Although their discoveries gain value from their work with human subjects, at neither level can genuine cause and effect relationships be established.

---

[8]   MH DeGroot, SE Fienberg & JB Kadane (eds), *Statistics and the Law*, Wiley, New York, 1986.

[9]   In the year 1978 almost 6,000 employment discrimination cases were initiated in the federal district courts of the United States.

[10]   Fienberg, op cit, n3.

[11]   *Vuyanich v Republic National Bank*, 24 FEP Cases 128 (ND Texas 1980), *vac and rem'd*, 723 F 2d 1195 (1984).

Epidemiologists may well discover relationships between variables but they cannot be sure which is the cause and which the effect. Ultimately the question is answered when other discoveries are made and an etiology is accepted. Meanwhile, the public health decisions and lawsuits are too impatient to wait.[12]

Negative epidemiological evidence puts an even bigger burden on the fact-finder's shoulders because the negative evidence cannot disprove the null hypothesis. Fienberg believes that support for epidemiology in this particular negative role is, nonetheless, growing.[13] Well-constructed studies with sufficient statistical power[14] should be taken seriously if they fail to find the health problems posited in the alternative hypothesis. The weaknesses of epidemiological studies listed are those of "lurking variables or synergisms between variables", studies too small to find low level effects, studies too short to find effects with long latencies, and problems with the analysis of studies some of which may be retrospective and some prospective.

Statistical errors are very likely to be made in court by intelligent and careful lawyers, judges, expert witnesses and jurors for the simple reason that statistics is hard. Even if they are not made publicly, people are still prone to make them in their heads. A list would have to include the following:

- Confusing different ways of expressing probabilities. "A chance of one in three" is different from "Odds of one to three". The latter is "a chance of one in four".
- Overlooking the need to quote the "variance" as well as the "central tendency" of a set of data.[15]

---

[12] In a personal communication, a colleague of Sir Ronald Fisher while attached to the University of Adelaide in his retirement tells of the great statistician's reaction to the epidemiological studies which first established the link between smoking and lung cancer. Fisher asked whether susceptibility to lung cancer was inherited by certain people along with their predilections to tobacco smoking. It sounds ludicrous now that it is known how carcinogens damage cell growth control systems, allowing cells ultimately to transform and grow uncontrollably, but it was a theoretically proper hypothesis at the time.

[13] Fienberg, op cit, n3, at p126 et seq.

[14] "Power" is a technical term. It means the ability of a test to reject the null hypothesis – in other words, to provide high levels of confidence that a result is not just due to random fluctuation of a variable.

[15] Average personal income in Ruritania may be a wonderful $50,000 pa, but the high figure may be due to several billionaires living in a highly deprived country, not a high and uniform standard of living. It is hazardous to assume that the variance is small and that individuals are all close to the average.

- Failing to appreciate the impact of sampling error. Whenever a small sample is used to estimate the characteristics of the whole, the probability of error must be stated.
- Over-interpretation of trends, a disease found commonly in futurologists.

But errors in probabilistic or statistical reasoning are not all elementary. There are many ways to classify them, one of which is to distinguish between methodological errors and errors of interpretation or application. Here is a judicial error which straddles the two. Although not dealing in numerical values, the judge is still dealing with probabilities when summing up with the remark *"the evidence is like a rope, unavoidably rather frayed and therefore no stronger than its weakest part. You must decide if it is strong enough to hold the weight of a conviction"* or she may say *"the evidence shines tiny rays of light on the crime scene and one by one they illuminate it better. You must decide if they make it bright enough for you to see the perpetrator!"*[16] Even though some jurors may not see them as anything more than encouragement to think carefully, the two figures of speech imply particular relationships between the items of evidence. The latter comment, borrowed by an Australian judge from Lord Chancellor Cairns in England, implies that the prosecution case becomes stronger the more numerous the items of evidence brought to bear; in other words, that the overall weight of the evidence is an additive function of the individual items. This is true only of items that are independent which was not so in the case in question. Consider a case in which successive witnesses report seeing the intruder to have hairy arms, hairy legs, hairy neck and hairy chest. The case that the hairy suspect must therefore be guilty is not strengthened by the apparent corroboration; characteristics found very commonly together are not independent.[17]

A different kind of error is the heresy of plausible dogma. As statistical information enters our lives, the dogmas come with it. One such is the idea that data which fall outside 95 per cent confidence limits are unworthy of

---

[16] The second quotation, here quoted loosely, was from the South Australian case of *R v Splatt* (see Royal Commission, *Report Concerning the Conviction of Edward Charles Splatt*, South Australian Government Printer, Adelaide, 1984) which made Australian legal history, inciting the government to establish a professional forensic science service which became a model for other Australian states and overseas.

[17] See B Selinger, "Scientific Evaluation", in I Freckelton & H Selby (eds), *Expert Evidence*, 5 volume looseleaf service, Law Book Co, Sydney, 1993-..., 2-523.

scientific notice. If the idea did no more damage than to eliminate a few bright ideas from publication in scientific journals, it may not matter. However, the idea has been imported into other realms and courts are told that data slightly more deviant than the 95 per cent confidence level variety are unacceptable for human consumption of any kind. Usually they are not told, the data being ejected before ever reaching court.

The background is as follows. Data which fluctuate unaccountably, like those for river heights or crime, will usually contain some entries which are extreme. Early in the last century statistical methods were developed to calculate the characteristics of extreme data and determine how frequently extreme events could be expected. Fostered by the great statistician Fisher, the idea grew that a boundary on a chart could help distinguish ordinary chance variation from what was exceptional. The value of the idea came from being able to put the boundary anywhere the statistician thought was appropriate; it was not determined by the mathematics. The result of Fisher's choice, adopted widely because of his influence, is that the 95 per cent boundary has become the obligatory standard for "statistical significance", results falling outside it being regarded as unsuitable for scientific use. Thus data to test a scientific hypothesis that high vitamin intake raises the birth weight of rats will be rejected as "not statistically significant" unless the average birth weight is larger than the 95 per cent limit. Birth weights inside the boundary are, by this usage, within the normal range.

Because the limits are applied so widely, statisticians are apt to use 95 per cent confidence limits in court proceedings as the criterion for accepting data, but this is unwarranted. Hall and Selinger[18] and others[19] have argued strongly that the decision about the significance criterion is a matter for the court, not for the statistician. Just as it is the jury's job to decide the weight of the evidence necessary for it to be "beyond reasonable doubt", so also is it the prerogative of the jury to decide the significance limits for accepting evidence.

Confidence limits, aside from their function as discriminators between normal and abnormal fluctuations in something being examined, may be used directly. Several cases of this are mentioned in DeGroot, Fienberg and

[18] P Hall & B Selinger, "Statistical Significance: Balancing Evidence Against Doubt" (1986) 28 *Aust J Stats* 354.

[19] DW Vick, "Statistical Significance and the Significance of Statistics" (2000) 116 *Law Quart Rev* 575-82. This author notes that the term "statistical significance" is sometimes used in technical discussions in court without their being aware of its technical meaning.

Kadane.[20] One such use is to inform the court of the uncertainty in a statistical result that arises from the fact that it is an estimate based on information from a sample rather than the whole population.

Statistical procedures may sometimes shrink a problem without solving it. Blood alcohol legislation in many jurisdictions refers to devices which measure the alcohol concentration in breath but deliver the result as if it were the alcohol concentration in blood. The conversion is made by use of a factor obtained from measurements of alcohol concentrations in the breath and blood of the same individual, repeating the process on a sample of reasonable size and determining the average. Because of the variance in the distribution of alcohol between a person's blood and the breath, some drivers are disadvantaged by the use of an average. In other words, it takes a higher than average blood alcohol concentration to put some people above the legislated limit for breath and a lower than average level for others. The latter are disadvantaged by the average, the former sometimes protected from the prosecution they would suffer if the blood alcohol concentration were measured directly. One way to handle this problem is for the police to take the enlightened approach of prosecuting only when the breath alcohol result exceeds the legislated limit by a small amount, say one or two standard deviations.

Later in this chapter the need to protect defendants from errors in statistical calculations used in criminal prosecutions is emphasised. Safeguards against error are also necessary in civil proceedings, as some examples indicate. When the steps involved in a statistical procedure are planned we can install a safeguard at each one: (a) choosing the procedure, (b) selecting the sample, (c) calculating the results.

A common procedure in medicine is the controlled clinical trial and, given the financial implications of treatment costs, it is not surprising that trial results should sometimes become evidence in courts. To avoid the placebo effect, a common requirement is that the trial be "blind", subjects being unaware whether they are members of the treatment or the control groups. For various reasons, participants often become aware of the group to which they were assigned and the trial is less blind than was planned. One possible reason is the desire of promoters of, say, pharmaceuticals, to see patients with poor prospects of recovery placed in the control group. A recent examination of the rigour of experimenters in allocating participants to the two groups has shown that very large differences in results occur between "blind" and "not so blind" trials. Odds ratios expressing the

---

[20]   H Solomon, "Confidence Intervals in Legal Settings", in DeGroot, Fienberg & Kadane, op cit, n8.

effectiveness of the treatment were 30 per cent to 40 per cent larger when subjects were able to discover their group.[21]

This section closes with a reference to problems that statistical reasoning cannot solve. Unfortunately, public beliefs that grow from survey data (toxins in the environment or the effects of war service on veterans) that lead ultimately to class actions may bear little relation to the valid conclusions to be drawn from the statistics. Special problems arise when the number of people affected is very small (like cancer in children raised near power lines) or tests not completely reliable. Because many people are unwilling to tolerate risk of any kind, they respond to revelations about risks by demanding that the risk be removed completely. Changing their attitude is hard because the very small (or very large) numbers quoted in the epidemiological reports are so unfamiliar and so easy to exploit.

What Reasoning Is

Reasoning can be a process of moving through a chain of arguments from premises to a conclusion, each step concluding one argument as it provides entry to the next. Human beings can do this on paper or in their heads. The intuitive method allows great speed with little or no conscious oversight of the individual steps. The disadvantage of the speed is that it is accomplished by the use of hard-wired short-cut methods the results of which sometimes conflict with the same person's decision when it is made deliberately. Cognitive scientists term the short cut methods "heuristics" and "biases"[22] and their work is having an effect on how people think about the rules and methods and results of legal proceedings.

For present purposes the most important conclusion of cognitive studies is the finding that human beings, irrespective of training, are "probability blind". Although probabilistic information is being processed and acted on almost all the time, the intuitive responses to it are flawed. People trained in statistics and probability are vulnerable to the same errors as naive subjects and when trying to solve certain types of problems can

---

21   KF Schutz et al, "Empirical Evidence of Bias: Dimensions of Methodological Quality Associated With Estimates of Treatment Effects in Controlled Trials" (1995) 273 *J Am Medical Ass* 408.

22   A Tversky & D Kahneman, "Judgment under Uncertainty: Heuristics and Biases" (1974) 185 *Science* 1124; D Kahneman, P Slovic & A Tversky, *Judgment under Uncertainty: Heuristics and Biases,* Cambridge University Press, Cambridge, 1982.

produce answers that are right only by consciously avoiding the answers that seem right.

Humans appear to cope with the complexity of probabilistic information by simplifying it. Experiments show that if it cannot be simplified, they will discriminate between risks only if the differences are very large. Also, their overall view of risk is biased, so that they habitually take risks to avoid loss but avoid risks to preserve their gains. They try to deal with problems in the way they are presented, avoiding the difficult but sometimes necessary task of "re-framing". Thus positive statements are favoured over the equivalent negatively-framed ones, even though only the latter provide the clue to the right response. They innately break the rules of probability, being quite capable of judging the simultaneous occurrence of two events to be more probable than the same events would be if they occurred separately. Such responses to information usually occur because of the "reasonableness" the subject feels for the linked events or to the plausibility of the overall narrative. This latter feature, the fitting of events into a not-unlikely story, is a powerful influence on the way that the events themselves are judged. The story may be subjective, in the mind of a single person, or it may be suggested to all to manipulate opinion, when it can be very powerful. This type of influence is important in courtroom decision-making and has attracted a considerable amount of recent comment.[23]

In court, these patterns of reasoning can seriously disrupt the result that might reasonably be expected. A particular example is the inability of many people to deal with probabilities below (or above) a certain level. One author suggests that most people will be unable to distinguish between a 99 per cent chance of infection, wealth, injury, etc and a 99.9 per cent chance,[24] a blindness that would seriously interfere with the intended use by jurors of the statistical information given with DNA profiling evidence. Of course, the difficulty is greatly reduced when the statements are put so that the comparison is of a 1 per cent chance and a 0.1 per cent chance. Even so, the same scholar suggests that any probability intuition made by an untrained person has a more than 50 per cent likelihood of being wrong.

Eggleston some time ago commented on the earlier findings of cognitive science,[25] linking them to the alternatives described by Cohen as "Pascalian" and "Baconian" probabilities. Cohen,[26] working from what he

[23]   See, for example, JD Jackson, "Towards a Dialectic Theory of Proof for Legal Procedure" (1991) 154 *J R Statist Soc A* 107.

[24]   M Piatelli-Palmarini, *Inevitable Illusions*, J Wiley, New York, 1994.

[25]   Eggleston, op cit, n2, Chapter 3.

[26]   JL Cohen, *The Probable and the Provable*, Oxford University Press, Oxford, 1977.

thought was actually happening in courtrooms, argued for the intuitive handling (Baconian) of probabilistic material even though it was not necessarily consistent with standard (Pascalian) probability laws. However, the "inference on inference" problem which Cohen used as rationale for disregarding classical probability laws is readily handled by using Bayes theorem.[27] Pending more information about human reasoning under courtroom conditions and under the challenge of statistical information, it would be wise to persist with the standard framework but to work much harder to ensure that the evidence is comprehensible.

The Meaning of Proof

The word "proof" in the title of this chapter was not contributed by its author. "Proof" is a strong word and keeps its place in the legal corner of his consciousness only by a force fit. It is also a seductive word to which we are all vulnerable when we suspect that our arguments may not prevail on their merits alone. Scientists reserve a strong word for strong logical deductions (things you cannot deny without contradicting yourself) because they have learned that most deductions are not strong or logical; they want to be able to flag the difference.

If any justifications for this pedantry were needed, the two words "statistical" and "court" provide it. "Proofs" that are "statistical" must be of the kind where the proposition is believed to be true but not known to be true. The level of belief can be anywhere between the very high and the very low. So, a word is needed for the one fixed point in the scale, certainty, from which all the other points can be located. Secondly, in court, even though the strongest kind of association evidence can never incriminate a person absolutely, it can still exonerate a person absolutely. So, again, a word that only ever means "proved absolutely" would be valuable for preventing the confidence about the one kind of result from contaminating the caution always to be attached to the other.

In spite of all the ink to the contrary, science and the law walk paths that run very close together. Both are searching for truth even though courts have to do it speedily and be content with a qualified result. Science has more leisure but also has to accept that its conclusions are true only "as far as they have been tested". Illusions of certainty often arise, but that

---

[27] CCG Aitken, *Statistics and the Evaluation of Evidence for Forensic Scientists*, John Wiley, New York, 1995.

happens because the qualified nature of the pronouncements has been swamped by the emotion of the verdict.

In deciding how to judge a scientist's claim to have verified an hypothesis, other scientists put the stress on the severity of the tests that the hypothesis has survived. They want to know how well and how comprehensively the tests equipped the scientist to detect false explanations. Karl Popper championed this approach, enshrining the "refutability" of an hypothesis, not its "confirmability", as the key to scientific progress.

The concept of "refutability" provides a good lead for courts to follow. It can be argued that this should be overt. A jury explicitly instructed to protect the person wrongly accused should be all the more ready to convict when each step of the trial process has seen the safeguards applied. The prosecution witnesses will be all the more believable when they have explained why they "were unable to find a test that excluded" the suspect before reporting evidence that incriminated them. A judge who is scrupulous in applying the presumption of innocence rule will satisfy jurors that the trial was fair; they are then freed to bring down a verdict without anxiety about the possible conviction of a person who is not guilty. They do not do so without risk, but they eliminate the anxiety by minimising the risk.

The analogies run even further. Statistical evidence is customarily tested by using the rejection of the null hypothesis as the criterion for considering of the alternative hypothesis – a neat restatement of the presumption of innocence rule. Identification cannot be considered until the court is forced to reject the presumption that the evidence lies within the range of random occurrences.

Jurors' Proof

Nobody knows what juries think proof is. The interplay between knowledge already possessed and knowledge received in the court and the way information is processed en route to a verdict are mysteries. Authorities now seem more ready to authorise research into jury behaviour but, in the meantime, mock jury research sheds some light on the subject. Although quite inadequate in simulating what the jury receives in particular cases, the method is most useful for observing subjects' comprehension levels, biases and attitudes to issues taken one at a time. It can also report on groups large enough to be representative of the community as a whole, it can relate their responses to education levels and demographic factors. It can also vary parameters such as the strength of the evidence and allow investigators to give quantitative estimates of how community members would respond to issues when serving in a jury.

Although not really numerous or comprehensive, mock jury studies have contributed to our understanding of the way in which people deal with probabilities when making decisions. An important early result was the finding that subjects adjust the criminal court standard of proof to the severity of the sentence likely to be delivered. Simon and Mahan found a way of getting their subjects to quantitate the probability of guilt and found that jurors required 0.86 for murder compared with only 0.74 for larceny.[28] Judges, also tested, made the same adjustment, although the standards they required were higher (0.92 down to 0.87). At the standard required for civil suit decisions the numbers would be much lower; it would be interesting to know how much difference there is between jurors' and judges' quantitative assessments and the 50 per cent figure often assumed in legal argument about causation and liability.[29] There are, however, other standards of proof. An example from the United States follows but the argument is probably used very widely, even if it unlegislated. In enforcing the environmental regulatory standard which led to the disappearance of "leaded" petrol from the market, the court said:

> When a statute is precautionary in nature, the evidence difficult to come by, or uncertain, or conflicting because it is on the frontiers of scientific knowledge, the regulations designed to protect the public health, and the decision that of an expert administrator, we will not demand rigorous step-by-step proof of cause and effect ... The Administrator may apply his expertise to draw inferences from suspected, but not completely substantiated, relationships between facts, from trends among facts, from theoretical projections from imperfect data, from probative preliminary data not yet certifiable as "fact", and the like.[30]

With this in mind, the fascinating discussion in Fienberg[31] and its set of relativities of proof may be extended to:

$$1 > p_{crim} > p_{other} > p_{civil} > 0.5 > p_{prot} > 0$$

28 RJ Simon & L Mahan, "Quantifying Burdens of Proof" (1971) 5 *Law and Society Review* 319.
29 See, for example, *Malec v J C Hutton Pty Ltd* (1990) CLR 638.
30 *Ethyl Corporation v Environmental Protection Agency*, 541 F 2d 1 (DC Cir 1976).
31 Fienberg, op cit, n3.

where p_{crim} and p_{civil} are the customary criminal and civil standards of proof, p_{other} the intermediate standard used in deportation proceedings in the United States ("clear, unequivocal, and convincing evidence") and p_{prot} the "public protection" standard referred to in the previous paragraph.

Two early reviews[32] of mock jury research reassure those who fear that statistical evidence might overwhelm jurors and tip the scale far too strongly in favour of the prosecution. In the writer's research,[33] almost a third of the 558 respondents thought that the risk of convicting an innocent person had to be zero and consequently declined to label the accused as guilty even though the identification evidence was quite strong.[34] The proof, for them, had to be absolute. Among the 77 respondents who were university trained, the same fraction insisted on this standard. As pointed out in other reports, these views would be unlikely to prevail in actual jury deliberations, where a unanimous verdict is required and where other jurors might be persuasive. Overall, the willingness to convict was firmly tied to the strength of the identification evidence. Only 8 per cent would convict when the risk was high (20 per cent random match probability), a figure which rose to 69 per cent when the whole group was asked whether they would convict when the random match probability was only 0.5 per cent.

It is evident that jurors become alarmed when the evidence is not quite strong enough for them to be sure beyond reasonable doubt. In the writer's research, respondents were, on the average, unwilling to convict when the odds associated with inclusion were lower than about 10:1. But jurors also become alarmed when the odds are "too large". Odds of the order of 25 billion:1 are beyond common imagination but are frequently quoted in connection with DNA profiling.[35] The reason sometimes given for this

---

[32] WC Thompson, "Are Juries Competent to Evaluate Statistical Evidence?" (1989) 52 *Law Contemp Problems* 9; DH Kaye & JJ Koehler, "Can Jurors Understand Probabilistic Evidence?" (1991) 154 *J R Statist Soc A* 75.

[33] E Magnusson, *Jury Comprehension of Statistical Evidence*, Australian Institute of Criminology Conference, 1994. Respondents in small family groups heard an audio tape simulating the judge's summing up of a criminal trial and then discussed the issues as small juries. Their individual responses were used to test (a) the comprehension of statistical information given and (b) the apparent mental pathway taken through evidence given in a Bayesian format.

[34] Random match probability (using a battery of blood tests) 5 per cent.

[35] The commercial profiling systems "Profiler Plus" (now adopted in Australia for evidence to be used in the national offender database) and "SGM Plus" (used in the United Kingdom for the National DNA Database) both use 10 probes and likelihood ratios in the range "10 billion to one" to "100 trillion to one" would be expected. However, caution is used in the calculations and the results actually reported are usually one or two orders of magnitude smaller. The United Kingdom Forensic Science Service has the policy of uniformly reporting these extremely large odds as "10 billion

reaction is "that such large odds must be impossible because the number 25 billion is larger than the population of the world". The answer is that odds ratios are calculated according to the potential number of persons which the test is capable of distinguishing. Whether or not that number is greater than the population of the United Kingdom, Australia or the world is irrelevant. In the case of the DNA profiling test, the discriminating power is obtained as the product of several factors (one for each "locus") and each of these can be calculated with suitable accuracy from as few as one hundred tissue samples. Increasing the size of the database increases the precision of the result but not its magnitude, so databases of millions of people are not required.

The number of jurors across the world who hear statistical evidence given in connection with DNA profiles is now very large. It is curious how willing appellate courts are to comment on their comprehension of that evidence and their ability to assess it, when neither has ever been measured.

Statistics and DNA Profile Evidence[36]

In its commonest manifestation,[37] DNA evidence is obtained by using chemical "probes" to recognise fragments of DNA in the chromosomes in the nuclei of cells. The evidence, called the profile, consists of a list of fragment sizes.[38] Ten probes are used, one of the current commercial

---

to one" to obviate difficulties due to the lack of scientific evidence to support the independence of loci to this level.

[36]   This section concentrates on DNA profile evidence in criminal courts but, of course, the technology is widely used in other legal settings including paternity disputes, verification of family relationships in immigration applications (United Kingdom) and inheritance claims, disaster victim identification, and missing person identification.

[37]   Other manifestations are the multi-locus probe, Polymerase Chain Reaction method plus promoter to produce protein then identified with a spot test, mitochondrial DNA analysis etc.

[38]   Once separated from the rest of the DNA the sizes of the segments can be measured by electrophoresis. Each probe recognises fragments from one particular location (the "locus") of one particular pair of chromosomes, so, because of the pairing, fragments of two sizes will be found. Characterised by their size, they can be related to the two parents of the individual from whom the tissue originated, the double set of chromosomes in each cell having come originally from the single set contributed by each parent at conception. Numerous loci exist, on different chromosomes, each with inherited segments of varying length and, providing that probes can be found to recognise them, they can all be separated and their size measured in a single operation. The evidence is often presented by a barcode-like diagram of the fragment sizes.

implementations of the technology,[39] to produce a list of the sizes of twenty fragments. The greater the number of probes, the larger and more peculiar the list and the smaller the probability that the profile of another person, selected by chance, should be similar enough to produce a match. With likelihood ratios of many billions to one, the method now provides identification evidence as powerful as was produced with that first achievement of forensic science, fingerprinting. Nevertheless, DNA profiling has not been given the same courtroom status, namely, that of unquestioned individualisation; the statistical evidence is almost always reported in detail.

Most DNA profilers now carry out their statistical calculations on a Bayes' Law framework irrespective of whether they will be allowed to use the name of the 18th century clergyman. The number of trials over which his spectre hovered during the last decade of the twentieth century is the reason he is so well known. However, the Bayesian "subjective" approach was introduced to forensic science well before the advent of DNA profiling after years of extensive discussion in relation to other kinds of evidence.[40] One of its chief virtues is the simple appeal of the argument that the "prior odds" of guilt (deemed to be determined by the court before the DNA evidence is heard) should be increased by a factor to yield the "posterior odds".

The older "frequentist" or "objective" method for presenting identification evidence statistics asks for DNA profiles to be compared and a declaration made about whether they match or not; only then can the random match probability be calculated. It is a "two-stage approach". In practice, declaring a "match" becomes a problem because the behaviour of the DNA fragments during the measurement process is not always uniform. Even though profiles from the same source will have easily recognisable patterns, the actual fragment sizes measured in the laboratory can vary. If too high a significance level is set for a match, then profiles that came from the same source may fail to meet the match criterion and important evidence may have to be discarded. On the other hand, if the significance level is low, it becomes too easy for other fragments of slightly different sizes to qualify so a match provides much weaker evidence.

---

[39] The Perkin-Elmer Corporation's "Profiler Plus" system is licensed to Australian forensic science laboratories and used uniformly by all states for the investigation of crime and for the Commonwealth-wide offender database.

[40] See Aitken, op cit, n27.

By contrast, the Bayesian method asks questions about the DNA profiles obtained from the crime scene sample and the reference sample from the suspect and compares them. The questions are:

- What are the odds that these evidence profiles would be found for samples from the same person?
- What are the odds that they would be found for samples taken from different persons?

The ratio of these two odds values is called the "likelihood ratio". Bayesian reasoning cuts through the knot of unavoidable variation in laboratory results and tells us how much stronger our suspicions ought to be now that we have compared these two profiles and allowed for the two possible hypotheses (same person or different persons). Moreover, without inconsistency, it allows the court to deal explicitly with alibi evidence. If the suspect was in Morocco when the crime was committed in Melbourne, then the posterior odds are zero-to-one because the prior odds are zero-to-one. No matter how large the likelihood ratio, prior odds of zero-to-one must yield posterior odds of zero-to-one.

Mention of an alibi immediately raises the issue of what Thompson and Schumann call the "prosecutor's fallacy"[41] but which is less colourfully named the fallacy of the "transposed conditional". Consider a profile with the rather small random match probability of one in a million. Applying Bayes' Law in the usual situation allows us to conclude that after the evidence of the profile becomes known the odds of guilt are increased by a factor of a million. The fallacy is to conclude, without any knowledge of the prior odds, that the odds of guilt are a million to one. The "defense attorney's fallacy" is to conclude that, since the profile in question was very uncommon, so the odds of guilt must be very low. The latter error is harder to sustain than the prosecutor's fallacy which is very alluring.

The sum of all this is that by about 1995 one of the most valuable applications of science to the investigation of crime had become established across the world and, in parallel, the assumptions used for calculations of match probability had been validated by an unprecedented amount of research[42] and, again, frequentist statistical presentation of the

---

[41]   WC Thompson & EL Schumann, "Interpretation of Statistical Evidence in Criminal Trials: The Prosecutor's Fallacy and the Defense Attorney's Fallacy" (1987) 11 *Law Hum Behav* 167.
[42]   There are numerous matters which can only be resolved by consideration of the statistics of scientific trials of the methodology: whether or not Hardy-Weinberg equilibrium has been reached in a population, band shifting relative to laboratory variation of fragment sizes, possible interdependence of alleles, race variations in the

results had been clearly shown to be inferior to the Bayesian approach. Mysteriously, judges in trial courts and appeals courts continued to accept the first development but many acted as if the latter two had never occurred. They forget, apparently, that Bayes' Law has been used for decades in disputed paternity cases though, of course, those decisions are not usually made by a jury.

The 1997 and 1998 judgments of the English Court of Appeal in *Doheny and Adams*[43] and *Adams (Denis)*[44] contain inconsistencies which should have been eliminated years earlier. The judgments have been analysed by many commentators.

The discussion of *Doheny and Adams* by Evett et al[45] is outstanding. A very important part of it is their rebuttal of the appellate court's view of the goal of DNA profiling. The judges said "... the stage may be reached where a match will be so comprehensive that it will be possible to construct a DNA profile that is unique and which proves the guilt of the defendant without any other evidence." Not so, say Evett et al, the advantage of smaller and yet smaller random match probabilities is in solving special problems; complete individualisation status is not a practical goal for DNA profiling and only remains for fingerprint evidence because its scientific basis was never sought.

Decisions in higher courts have consequences which may persist for a long time. Kaye[46] has given an account of the Arizona Supreme Court's decision in *State v Bible*[47] in which the admissibility of the prosecution's DNA evidence was confirmed but the random match probability information excluded. The court believed, from news accounts and cases in other jurisdictions, that there was "a lack of general acceptance of Cellmark's statistical probability calculations in the relevant scientific community of population geneticists" even though it approved the methods employed by Cellmark[48] to declare a match. In a series of decisions, the

---

frequencies of alleles in populations and in their independence, the desirability of using the "ceiling principle" etc. They lie beyond the scope of this section. Some of them are becoming less important as newer technology is introduced, others as databases become larger.

43 *Doheny and Adams* [1997] 1 Cr App R 369.

44 *Adams (Denis) (No 2)* [1998] 1 Cr App R 377, CA.

45 IW Evett, LA Foreman, G Jackson & JA Lambert, "DNA Profiling: A Discussion of Issues Relating to the Reporting of Very Small Match Probabilities" (2000) *Crim L R* 431.

46 DH Kaye, "Bible Reading: DNA Evidence in Arizona" (1997) 28 *Arizona State Law Journal* 1035.

47 *State v Bible*, 858 P 2d 1152 (Ariz 1993), *cert denied*, 114 S Ct 1578 (1994).

48 Cellmark was the well known United States commercial laboratory carrying out the profiles.

Supreme Court reinforced its *Bible* decision by repeatedly disallowing quantitative probability evidence while seeing no objection in evidence simply stating that "it is most likely that these two samples came from the same source".

Allowing identification evidence to be heard without telling the jury about the risk that the match may not be perfect is hard to justify but the decision is not unique. The idea was dismissed by Hampel J in the Victorian case of *R v Lucas*[49] with the words "I think that there is in this case the danger that consistency could assume the colour of identity, or at least of probability".

The 1996 trial in New South Wales of the serial "back-packer murderer" contained two items of statistical interest.[50] Hunt CJ criticised the term "genetic fingerprinting" as being misleading because DNA evidence does not provide individualisation and the prosecution provided the court with the confidence limits for the random match probability, as deduced from the size of the database. For interest, the expert quoted "one in 188,000" as the middle of the range of probabilities extending from "one in 54,000" to "one in 220,000". The words "coincidence figure" used were unusual but they have the merit of being fairly transparent for jurors who are now faced not by one probability, but by three. However, officers of the New South Wales Forensic Science Service report that it is current practice in the state to meet the requirements of the ruling about confidence limits[51] by mentioning one figure only, the most conservative one.

An especially lengthy challenge to the admissibility of DNA profile evidence was launched by the defence in *R v Karger* in the Supreme Court of South Australia in 2001.[52] Mullighan J conducted a *voire dire* lasting for 14 weeks; his reasons for admitting the evidence occupied 176 pages. Although most of the time was occupied with challenges to the proprietary "Profiler Plus" methodology the statistical evidence was also impugned. The defence's concern was the validity of the databases and the use of a "likelihood ratio" to represent the significance of the alleged profile match. This was an important opportunity for the Australian bench to rule on identification evidence in which the sophistication of the technology is matched by the way it is reported to the court.

The judge's discussion of the technology dominated his report; only about 5 per cent dealt with the statistical matters. The challenges to the

---

[49]   *R v Lucas* (1992) 55 A Crim R 361; [1992] 2 VR 109.
[50]   *R v Milat* (1996) 87 A Crim R 446.
[51]   *R v Pantoja* (1996) 88 A Crim R 554.
[52]   *R v Karger* [2001] SASC 64.

validity of the databases charged inadequate representation of racial/ethnic population sub-groups, the possibility of inter-allele dependence and the inclusion of inapplicable values of the parameter representing the degree of relationship of persons represented in the database. The challenges were disallowed. The use of calculations widely accepted by the profession, the conservative approach of the population geneticist[53] and the Forensic Science Service's policy of reporting a random match probability of one in a billion [the calculated value was one in 90.6 billion, itself the more conservative upper confidence limit] satisfied the judge that the evidence should not be disallowed on grounds of supposed inadequacy of the databases.

The issue of the likelihood ratio was then raised. The defence objections to the way the prosecution planned to report the strength of the evidence were "The use of Bayes' Theorem by the jury is not permitted: the jury cannot make any mathematical estimate of the prior odds" and, consequently, since the likelihood ratio "has no other relevant use" it should be inadmissible. In considering the likelihood ratio challenge the judge referred to the recent United Kingdom appellate decision in *R v Adams*,[54] reiterated in *R v Doheney and Adams*[55] quoting part of the *R v Adams* judgment, to show how the Court of Criminal Appeal saw Bayes' Law. The Court viewed as "an attempt to determine guilt or innocence on the basis of a mathematical formula ... [which] is simply inappropriate to the jury's task." The unfortunate thing is that what was inappropriate in *R v Adams* was not Bayes' Law but the task it was given.[56] The judge rejected the challenge thereby allowing likelihood ratios to be reported but, by default, Bayesian reasoning was excluded. It is ironic that a mathematical (ie correct and logical) way for probabilities to be combined is rejected because it is mathematical (ie inappropriate).

---

53 After analysis of the database the F_{st} relatedness parameter, which is the probability that alleles within a population have a common ancestor, was estimated to be close to 1 per cent but was arbitrarily set at a more conservative 3 per cent. Such a value for F_{st} is equivalent to all individuals in the database being related to the level of second cousins. The likelihood ratio was calculated by using the procedure described in the widely distributed second report of the United States National Research Council. National Research Council, "Report II, The Evaluation of Forensic DNA Evidence" (1999); the procedure appears as Equation 4.10.

54 [1998] 1 Cr App R 377, CA.

55 [1997] 1 Cr App R 369.

56 In this case the DNA profile evidence was incriminating but other evidence supported the defendant's account. A defence witness explained (correctly) how Bayes' Law permitted 20 likelihood ratios for 20 different items of non-scientific evidence to be combined mathematically and used to convert a prior probability of guilt into a posterior probability. It was this proposal that attracted the disapproval of the United Kingdom Court of Criminal Appeal.

With the DNA profile evidence ruled admissible the trial began and the likelihood ratio was reported with the laboratory's standard form of words: "The DNA profile obtained from the sample stains are more than one billion times more likely to match the DNA profile of Mr Karger if he left the stains rather than an unknown, unrelated male". The accused was convicted.

As argued earlier, the very nature of Bayesian reasoning allows it to fit naturally into a narrative of the conceptual steps through the argument put by the prosecution, or an alternative narrative offered by the defence. In cases where scientific-cum-statistical evidence is vital to the case the idea of making the story explicit has two merits. It helps the court manage what would otherwise be confusing detail[57] and it provides the basis for an examination by the court of the validity and reliability issues related to the evidence which need to be settled before the ultimate issue is decided. To do it systematically, some kind of graphic aid[58] would be helpful when jurors are faced with complex and unfamiliar scientific or statistical evidence – displaying the conceptual steps helps the court emphasise the safeguards required at each step before it is safe to make the final decision. For our current purpose we should ignore earlier steps relating to laboratory processes[59] and concentrate on the ones relating to the statistical steps. They are, (a) the choice of the overall statistical procedure, (b) the kinds of alternative hypothesis to be considered, (c) the ethnicity of the database, (d) the representativeness of the database, (e) the relatedness of the individuals in it, (f) the calculation of the statistic and (g) how it will be reported. In the great majority of cases the safeguards are easily put but there are times when the issues are more complex, say when closely related persons are among the suspects, or when some of the suspects are missing.[60] It then becomes especially important for the court to be sure that

---

[57] Investigators almost universally record the complaint from jurors about the difficulty of keeping track of the overall argument during a trial. Some commentators have argued the need to restructure the way in which evidence is marshalled during the adversarial court process; see, for example, Jackson, op cit, n23.

[58] For example, the "inference chart" concept proposed by E Magnusson & BK Selinger, "Forensic Science in Court" (1988) 12 *Crim Law J* 86.

[59] A complete inference chart includes procedural steps (chain of evidence items, sample identification), accreditation steps (qualifications of the scientific expert, accreditation of the laboratory), laboratory investigation steps (choice of procedure, standardisation of reagents, instrument accuracy checks, positive and negative controls), statistical analysis steps and, finally, the steps required in formulating the expert's conclusions for the report.

[60] UE Makov, "A Bayesian Treatment of the 'Missing Suspect' Problem in Forensic Science" (1987) 36 *The Statistician* 251.

each step was properly taken whether or not the evidence is challenged. As statisticians point out, statistical evidence is not fixed by the characteristics of the profile; it also depends on the kind of defence mounted by the defendant.

The Limits of Comprehension

A juror in a criminal trial is required to convert a mass of raw data into a score of exactly guilty or not guilty. The actual mental process is rather like someone finding one of two exits from a maze or, as modern studies of the brain suggest, like a huge crowd simultaneously rushing along myriads of separate and completely unplanned paths through the maze. Which exit they will ultimately find is impossible to know as thousands of seemingly haphazard choices are made at countless junctions. But the tiny benefits of previous choices gradually begin to tell and finally the crowd converges on just one of the two exits. The point is that the process is all the more unpredictable, the more disparate the different kinds of decision required to produce the final result. Worst of all, if the choices have to be made on statistical data, with probabilities rather than just Yes/No decisions required for computing the overall result, the computation might become too hard to make. In such circumstances, jurors do not make no decision, they make the decision on such other grounds as they think fit.

In the author's Canberra jury project, the design of the experiment permitted a certain amount of exposure of the reasoning which respondents used to make their decisions about guilt. One set of results is recounted here. In the audio tape the judge's summing up of the evidence offered minimal comment, the judge purporting to read the scientific expert's conclusions from his report about finding a match and then using blood group data from a database to estimate "the odds that a person drawn by chance from the Australian population would produce the same results from the seven blood group tests as found for the crime scene sample". In the questionnaire, however, a Bayesian framework was used to lead respondents through a set of questions designed to measure comprehension. The results indicated that however it was that "jurors" determined the question of guilt, it was not supported by any high level of understanding of the concepts involved.

When considering evidence indicating odds of 200-to-one against finding the same blood results by chance, 69 per cent of respondents gave a guilty verdict but little over half of these were able to demonstrate a level of understanding considered minimal to making a Bayesian decision.[61] This "minimum level" indicator was a set of correct answers to five early questions in the questionnaire reached, overall, by 41 per cent of respondents. This figure broke down to 18 per cent (2 years of secondary education or less), 37 per cent (3 or more years of secondary education), and 57 per cent (university education) indicating a very strong relationship to education.

Can jurors be brought to the necessary competence with statistical matters by educating them in court? Before hearing the audio tape with the information about the blood tests, half of the respondents in the Canberra project heard a brief exposition of how statistical data can assist courts to determine the weight of identification evidence. No significant difference was found between the results from those who were briefed about statistics and those who were not. If this is any guide, courts have to use jurors as they find them; instruction given during the case may not be effective.

Statistical obfuscation

Although statistical reasoning is unavoidably complex the issue here is the very avoidable complexity with which it is embroidered when it comes to court.

* Odds ratios: Because of the prevalence of betting, odds ratios are well understood and reasoned with by a sizeable part of the population. Probabilities are a different matter.
* Having it both ways: Because of the bias in the expression of probabilities and the risk that jurors will not realise that a high probability of exclusion is equivalent to a low probability of inclusion, it is important to state the data in both ways. Thus, a statement like "there is a 3 per cent chance that a person drawn at random from the population will test positive for the same antibody" should have the opposite statement added at the end – "there is a 97 per cent chance that a person drawn at random ... will not test positive ...".
* Do not elaborate: A frequent source of confusion is the attempt by the teacher (lawyer) to explain in a second sentence what was meant in the first. It should be avoided and the statement made so clear at the outset

---

[61] This minimum level of understanding was taken to be demonstrated by correct answers to the first five questions. The answers were: (1) *No, a person can't be proved Guilty;* (2) *Yes, a person can be Proved Not Guilty; (3) If the odds of guilt were 1-to-1, the risk of convicting the wrong person would be 50%; (4) No, that's not acceptable; (5) Odds get Bigger when blood evidence is included.*

that repetition becomes unnecessary. Spontaneous presentations are unlikely to be safe; lawyers, judges and experts should read from carefully constructed notes.

- Jargon: In statistics, as in every other field of study, a specialised vocabulary helps the practitioner say exactly what he or she means but it makes the subject obscure. It takes real expertise to be accurate and understandable at the same time.

Achievable Goals

The frequently reported death of the jury system is, of course, greatly exaggerated but it is true that its public esteem is shrinking. Arguably, much of that has followed its poor performance in dealing with statistics and probabilities. What follows are suggestions for optimising the performance of courts constituted, be it emphasised, in their present form. The first is rather general.

Comprehensibility does not matter, assessability does

In an age of unparalleled discovery it is no surprise that science and technology should come to court or that the attendant complexity should, at times, threaten the process. Almost without exception moves to change the jury system are urged on the ground that cases in which complex evidence is important it is likely to be misunderstood by lay juries. However, the thing for counsel, judges and juries to do about that is not to try to mop up the water that is swamping them but to learn to swim in it. The challenge is not to try to understand someone else's specialised knowledge but to assess it.

The complexity problem is not unique; decision-makers in government and commerce have also been challenged by the need to act on information they do not understand. They have responded by introducing a process characterised by the word "advice" and in no place is it more needed than when the court is asked to consider statistical or probabilistic evidence. With the proper advice, lay courts and lay juries can equip themselves to take on complex statistical evidence. Instead of role play, trying to comprehend and then adjudicate reasoning in which they are incompetent they should require the expert witnesses from the two sides to provide them with (a) criteria for judging their submissions and (b) evidence that those criteria were met. When the evidence is of a routine kind, the courts could obtain the criteria they want in advance, calling on sources such as national professional organisations or statutory bodies to provide the authority that they do not have of themselves. Where the evidence is especially complex or causes major conflict, those same sources may be required to provide representative professional opinion as to the criteria needed to evaluate it. In this kind of environment, the pressure is on the expert to ensure that their contribution is not so much comprehensible as assessable.

Admissibility versus Strength

Uncertainties about whether a tissue sample from a crime scene was contaminated or not, about whether chemical reagents were properly standardised, about whether control experiments were carried out are issues incommensurate with issues of the weight of the evidence obtained from it. It is beyond the competence of jurors to combine the two kinds of uncertainty to reach a single decision, especially when the evidence is probabilistic. Although questions about the way samples were handled are often considered appropriate for the jury, there are strong reasons why this may be wrong. This argument applies equally strongly to questions about the validity of statistical evidence.

Judges would never hand to the jury a decision about evidence which might have been wrongly obtained or evidence which is hearsay. It would be unthinkable to ask them to combine that probability with the probability implied by the weight of the evidence. In such a case, entirely parallel with the present one, prejudice is avoided by determining issues of admissibility before the jury knows anything about the evidence. It would be a wise course for the courts to accept responsibility for ensuring that the evidence is safe for the jury to hear, and for judges routinely to schedule pre-trial hearings for that purpose whether the admissibility issues are scientific procedures or statistical ones. The jury is then given a clean slate for the difficult job of weighing the evidence. Recent cases in Australia and, indeed, around the world, have seen major challenges to standard DNA testing procedures which were handled by *voire dire* hearings of unprecedented length. The recommendation here is to make the pre-trial hearing standard practice and for judges to dispose of the issue themselves. If criteria for accepting scientific and statistical evidence can be created, then judges should decide whether the evidence is safe for the jury to hear or not. The jury then decides what the evidence is worth.

The attitude of judges to the issue of what the jury should and should not hear is divided but in Australia, under current legislation, almost all would probably withhold claims of faulty laboratory procedures or incorrect statistical methods from the jury. In *R v Humphrey*[62] Bleby J

---

[62] *R v Humphrey* (1999) 103 A Crim R 434.

applied the reasoning of Mullighan J in *R v Jarrett*,[63] the first major Australian challenge to the admissibility of DNA profile evidence by advanced DNA profile methods. He ruled that conflicting expert evidence about databases should go to the jury. The appellate court's attitude in *R v Doheny and Adams*[64] was expressed as "Any issue of expert evidence should be identified and, if possible, resolved before trial."

A further reason for not giving juries two tasks to carry out at the same time is because of the risk that the sheer size of the likelihood ratios obtained by modern DNA profile methods will overwhelm jurors and lead them to assume that questions of the validity of the evidence no longer matter.

Statistical standards are issues on which standard procedures have been developed in connection with the accreditation of laboratories and for which quality assurance criteria are routinely applied. To achieve maximum assurance about its decisions, courts should receive independent advice from organisations at the level of the Australian Academy of Science or, in the United Kingdom, the Royal Society rather than rely on unrepresentative precedents established in individual cases. That consensus is possible between prosecution and defence counsel and scientists was demonstrated by the New York Supreme Court's admissibility hearing and the subsequent ruling in the *Castro* case.[65]

Saying what will help the court

How DNA profile evidence should be given to the jury has occupied the minds of many judges. DNA evidence is now usually extremely strong but the words used to say so can be confusing. Evett et al[66] considered the recommendations of a number of English appellate judgments, not all consistent with one another, and their considered opinion is that the witness tell the jury how to combine the random match probability with the prior odds of guilt, using Bayes' Law, to reach a posterior odds of guilt. Experience in the Canberra mock jury project suggests that jurors need assistance at precisely that level. The example given by Evett et al, modified here by the use of odds ratios rather than probabilities, is:

---

[63] *R v Jarrett* (1994) 73 A Crim R 160.
[64] [1997] 1 Cr App R 369.
[65] *People v Castro*, 144 Misc 2d 956; 545 NYS 2d 985 (NY 1989).
[66] Evett, Foreman, Jackson & Lambert, op cit n45.

If the court considered, based on other evidence, that the odds of the crime stain being left by the defendant were a million to one against, then the effect of the DNA evidence is to change those odds to a thousand to one in favour.

Balding has also argued[67] that the evidence presented to the court should focus on the "directly relevant issue" which is "whether or not the defendant is the source of the crime stain". As he says, it makes more efficient use of the evidence. Evett et al argue that their suggestion does not infringe the jury's prerogative, their statement being merely an illustration of the standard logic for statistical results of this kind. Their basic point is that the extremely small random match probabilities of current DNA profile technology, while not justifying individualisation (statements that "the crime scene sample came from the suspect") should yet be recognised by courts for their strength.

An alternative way of explaining to the court how the evidence of this strength might be used is for counsel to lead jurors through the kind of "minimal level" Bayes pathway explored in the author's Canberra project, doing this before the expert witness is brought on rather than later so as to distance the explanation from the particular evidence the jury will later have to decide about.[68] The responses from that survey showed that the

---

67   DJ Balding, "When Can a DNA Profile be Regarded as Unique?" (1999) 39 *Science and Justice* 257. This important paper shows how a correction can be made to random match statistics to allow for the possibility that a relative of the defendant could have contributed the evidence (brothers and, to a lesser extent, uncles, nephews and cousins, obviously have a higher probability of producing the similar profiles than do other persons in the population).

68   Using language designed to avoid jargon, while still familiarising the court with probability reasoning, the lawyer could say: Suppose you were watching a case on TV where the evidence linking the defendant to the scene of a crime was weak. All the court knew was that the defendant could have been around at the time. Before the jury even knew that there would be DNA evidence one juror muttered to another that it was about fifty-fifty that he was guilty, in other words, odds of one-to-one. Suppose the rest of the jury agreed that the odds were one-to-one. And suppose that, without knowing it, they were right and the odds really were one-to-one because there were only two people who could have committed the crime and the defendant was one of them! Now, if the jury thinks that fifty-fifty odds are good enough for a conviction, what is the chance that they would convict an innocent person? 50 per cent, of course. Would that be good enough for you? Of course not! But now they bring on the DNA evidence and show that the profile taken from the crime scene is very similar to the profile taken from the sample taken from the defendant when he was in custody. The prosecution expert is asked if the profiles come from the same person but he says he does not know. What he does know is that the similarity of these two profiles is estimated to be three million times more likely to be found if the sample at the crime scene came from the defendant than by chance from some other person. Does that effect the odds that the defendant is guilty? The expert says it does and tells the jury, "whatever the odds

proper use of identification evidence by jurors cannot be taken for granted. To obviate the haphazard but binding judgments of courts in relation to evidence as powerful as DNA profiles have now become, not to mention future enhancements of the technology, it would be wise for the matter to be taken up by law reform commissions. As experience so far has shown, over-interpretation of the evidence is possible as well as under-interpretation. Correctives to both must be available.

---

were originally, after measuring how similar the two profiles are, the odds that the crime scene sample came from the defendant are, according to my estimate, three million times higher".

20 Epilogue: Dilemmas in Proof of Causation

IAN FRECKELTON*

Causation is routinely described by English and Australian appellate decisions as a matter of common sense.[1] However, such an analysis in practice is often simplistic and can be unhelpful when the occasion arises for legal advice to be given, for cases to be run in court and for issues of causation to be proved. It broadcasts beguilingly mixed messages to expert witnesses seeking to assist decision-makers to evaluate complex issues such as whether a breach of duty has caused an adverse outcome or is likely to produce such an outcome. It is dependent upon the unarticulated notion that decision-makers are able, unassisted by rules, guidelines or explanations, to reach "the right result" about difficult matters such as connections, influences, aetiologies and causalities by employing some kind of wisdom or intuition. This is curial mysticism at its most problematic.

Within this book the unlikelihood of such a felicitous outcome where the proof offered of causation is by way of statistics is exposed, save if significant steps are taken to assist decision-makers.[2] At a practical level, the common sense test of causation leaves proof of causation by a number

---

* Barrister in full-time private practice in Melbourne, Australia, Professor in the Department of Psychological Medicine, Adjunct Professor in the Law Faculty and an Honorary Associate Professor in the Department of Forensic Medicine at Monash University, Adjunct Professor in the Department of Law and Legal Studies, La Trobe University. The author acknowledges the generous and patient assistance given to him with earlier drafts by Eric Magnusson in relation to his appreciation of scientific matters, and Belinda Bennett, John Devereux, Hugh Selby and Danuta Mendelson in relation to his appreciation of legal matters.

1   See eg *March v E & MH Stramare Pty Ltd* (1991) 171 CLR 506 at 509; *Chappel v Hart* [1998] HCA 55 at [24]; *Fitzgerald v Penn* (1954) 91 CLR 268 at 277-8; *Environment Agency v Empress Car Co (Abertillery) Ltd* [1999] 2 AC 22 at 29.
2   See E Magnusson, "Statistical Proof of Causation", Chapter 19.

of different routes difficult and unpredictable. It fails to address the fact that the application of common sense alone has the potential to generate multiple and variable results, some of them wrong, in a context where consistency and correctness should be legitimate expectations held by parties to litigation.

While proof of causation is fundamental for the resolution of almost all forms of litigation, it is afflicted by many theoretical and practical conundra and is the subject of complex rules involving shifting burdens of proof, and a conceptually problematic combination of objective and subjective tests. Much of such proof derives from the opinions of expert witnesses. Judges and magistrates latterly have expressed considerable concern about unacceptable levels of objectivity and scientific rigour in such evidence.[3] In the recent era, courts have stressed that they particularly value in expert opinions the application of scientific methodology and the expression of comprehensible and objective views on the basis of identified and proven data. Yet in the context of causation, decision-makers are often confronted by problems of evaluation in relation to opinions that are not only complex, conflicting, and conceptually demanding but both partisan and subjectively based.

Causation evidence not only demands high quality inferential reasoning on the part of experts but also a capacity on the part of counsel to subject the opinions of doctors, scientists, accountants and others to effective testing via cross-examination. It offers an important example of the practical application of scientific/medical criteria for proof as against those generally applied in the legal context.

This chapter reviews a selection of contemporary controversies in relation to the proof of causation. It does not purport to provide an exhaustive treatment of the subject but, instead, focuses upon conceptual difficulties and inconsistencies amongst them. It does so against the employment of a threefold division within science in relation to influence and causation, a distinction being drawn amongst "observations", "generalisations" and "explanations".

It is an aim of the chapter to explore the similarities and differences in the scientific/medical and legal views of proof of causation and to tease out some of the contemporary problems experienced in relation to establishment of causation in both civil and criminal litigation. The chapter

---

[3] See in particular *R v Karger* [2001] SASC 64; I Freckelton, P Reddy & H Selby, *Australian Judicial Perspectives on Expert Evidence*, AIJA, Melbourne, 1999; I Freckelton, P Reddy & H Selby, *Australian Magistrates' Perspectives on Expert Evidence: A Comparative Study*, AIJA, Melbourne, 2001.

highlights the connection between the theoretical uncertainties attending the notion of what constitutes causation as a matter of law, thereby building upon a number of other chapters within this selection, as well as the difficulties in interpreting and applying criteria for proof of causation. It argues that the outcome of such problems is an unsatisfactory role for expert witnesses and unhelpful difficulties for fact-finders called upon to evaluate such evidence. It contends that there is a need for clearer tests of causation as a matter of law and for greater synchronicity between scientific/medical criteria for proof of causation and those used in law.

Proof of Causation

Establishment by evidence that an event took place or that inferences can be drawn about matters such as causation is the very essence of the capacity of the prosecution to discharge its burden in criminal litigation and of plaintiffs to discharge their burden in civil litigation. In administrative law matters, the decision-maker needs to reach a level of "reasonable satisfaction" about issues such as causation on the basis of "clear, cogent and exact evidence".[4] The rules of proof which govern the means by which causation can be established, as well as the party which has the burden to prove or disprove causation, are fundamental to the balance within the litigation system. So too is the level of satisfaction that needs to be arrived at by decision-makers in relation to causation. This balance is readily tilted or confused by changes to statutory and court rules, as well as by judicial decisions about evidence, proof and procedure. The balance in both criminal and civil trials has changed in recent decades in a number of countries.

Generally, in the criminal area, proof of facts which need to be established to prove the guilt of the accused, such as the causation of a victim's injuries, must be beyond reasonable doubt. However, even in this regard the distinction between "essential" and "non-essential" facts, "primary" and "secondary" facts, "crucial" and "background" facts, is not easy. Just to articulate the variously termed distinctions draws attention to the diversity of legal approaches to the issue.

In the civil area, proof is on the balance of probabilities. All important elements of a cause of action, such as causation (as distinct from the

---

[4]   *Cuming Smith & Co Ltd v Western Farmers' Co-operative Ltd* [1979] VR 129 at 147; *Anderson v Blashki* [1993] 2 VR 89 at 95-6; *Basser v Medical Board of Victoria* [1981] VR 953 at 969.

quantum of damages), must be established to that level of proof, save where an even higher level is needed, such as where the allegations are tantamount to a criminal charge and carry the potential for serious consequences for the defendant.[5] However, in some situations, proof need not reach so high a level – such as where it relates to a potential future event, including the need for particular treatment measures or, where it is suggested by the defence, that conduct or circumstances other than that for which the defendant is responsible may have contributed to, or may in due course contribute to, the plaintiff's injuries, impairment or loss of capacity to work. Then, statistically relatively unlikely matters can be taken into account. The difficulty is that while the past has already taken place and, in principle at least, is knowable, the future, of its very nature, is a matter of chance, and is a far less certain object of knowledge. To a degree it is always speculative. It is in this context that the evidence of actuaries and epidemiologists can become relevant both in terms of providing circumstantial evidence and in terms of interpreting those facts which might conduce toward an inference of connectedness between suspected causes and outcomes.

The Role of Expert Evidence

Even proof of causation in relation to matters in the past is frequently difficult, though, especially where there have been multiple contributing factors to something that has happened. The light of medical, scientific, accounting and other disciplines often needs to be shone in order to contextualise and clarify the importance of contributing factors and to distinguish between those that might be classified as operative as against those that are "background".[6] In particular, the relativities amongst the factors and the extent to which they can properly be designated as causative are not easily evaluated by fact-finders, frequently needing to be the subject of complex specialised opinions, in respect of which reasonable experts can and do differ. The extent to which matters in the past, but to some degree manifest in consequence now, will affect the future is especially problematic. The line between expert opinion and conjecture in this regard can be grey indeed. This is so even where the evidence upon which such inferences can be drawn is numerical. At one level, such evidence reassures because it looks both certain and precise; at another it is

---

5   See *Briginshaw v Briginshaw* (1938) 60 CLR 336.
6   See eg *Keown v Khan* (1998) 101 A Crim R 503.

prone to be misconstrued and can be misleading because of its assumptions and the methodologies employed en route to the opinions.

The controversies about the contribution of experts to enhance decision-makers' understanding of the potential for nexus arise in part because of the need of the courts for specialised assistance in relation to causation and influence and in part because the assistance is a fragile commodity, prone to go awry, especially in the context of evidence based upon statistical analyses.[7] In certain circumstances, for instance, burdens of proof shift – such as where failure to adhere to a proper standard of care is proved and an injury follows shortly thereafter, as well as where the doctrine of *res ipsa loquitur* applies.[8]

Sometimes, direct evidence can be given which establishes a clear connection between an event and an outcome. Often, though, proof is arrived at via circumstantial evidence and by expert evidence framed in terms of possibility and probability. In toxic tort litigation, and in criminal cases where conduct endangering life is alleged by the prosecution, epidemiological evidence falls into this category.

In criminal charges of sexual assault, evidence from forensic physicians and paediatricians is often prominent in establishing causation. In coronial cases and homicide cases in the criminal domain, evidence from pathologists about cause of death can be important for decision-making. In civil cases involving allegations of medical negligence, evidence from other medical practitioners working in the pertinent area generally carries weight in determining whether there has been tortious malpractice, after which, evidence from accountants and actuaries will address the need to evaluate the adverse financial consequences which may be referable to the negligence. Assertions from plaintiffs that they would not have undergone a procedure, had they been properly advised of risks is more difficult, clearly enough having the potential to be infected by hindsight knowledge and conscious or unconscious self-interest. In psychiatric injury cases, it is reconstructive or projective evidence from psychiatrists and psychologists, postulating the impact which a particular event or events has had or might have upon the mental health of the plaintiff, upon which disagreement is often ventilated before courts.

---

[7]   WC Thompson, "Are Juries Competent to Evaluate Statistical Evidence?" (1989) 52 *Law Contemp Problems* 9; DH Kaye & JJ Koehler, "Can Jurors Understand Probabilistic Evidence?" (1991) 154 *J R Statist Soc A* 75.

[8]   For a useful analysis of the presumptions in the law, see E Ullmann-Margalit, "On Presumption" (1983) LXXX *Journal of Philosophy* 143.

Scientific Views about Causation

Scientific discoveries are made at three levels:

- *Observations:* isolated measurements or records of events. It is important that observations be independently verifiable and that the errors of measurement are properly reported. Facts may sometimes appear to be related, this giving them the potential to mislead. The "observation level" is classified as the lowest kind of scientific discovery but, of course, nothing in science and medicine is possible without observation and inferences based upon it. An example is the reporting and collection in a national database of individual cases of breast cancer including pathologists' and cytologists' reports.

- *Generalisations:* discoveries of connections between observational variables but without any claim that the connections are causal. Experimental generalisations are economical ways of describing in brief compass what otherwise might require volumes of observational data. When they cover important and verified sets of observations in a straightforward way, they are often called "laws of nature". A generalisation might suggest an explanation or a causal nexus but this is not true in general. Correlations may be false, arising from bias, or from experimental error or from too ready an entry into causal inferences, or from faulty methodologies. An example is the discovery that in milk duct breast cancers a highly aggressive character and the absence of oestrogen receptors are strongly correlated with over-production of the HER2 protein.

- *Explanations:* explanatory theories are the real objective of science. Once verified, they show why the laws of nature hold true because they provide fundamental causal connections. A single theory may explain a host of generalisations and unify a wide variety of apparently disparate phenomena in a context-independent way. An example is the discovery that cells of some breast cancers multiply uncontrollably because of the large numbers of the HER2 protein, a molecule which facilitates signalling inside duct cells to initiate cell growth. The more common, less aggressive ductal breast cancers do not grow by this mechanism; as in the case of breast tissue developing at puberty, their cell multiplication is stimulated by the release of oestrogen.

The value of making these distinctions in the forensic context lies in the way they clarify the scientific claims and counter-claims about evidence given during litigation. Most of the disagreement and most of the difficulty in giving proper weight to an item of evidence is related to the differences amongst the assertions at these three levels. Of course, the distinctions can only be applied to the scientific content of items of evidence within the same area of science. Determining the combined weight of items of evidence from different areas of science is another issue altogether and is not generally a scientific question.

In 1966 Hempel[9] usefully argued that two criteria exist for explanation. The first was what he called the criterion of "explanatory relevance": "the explanatory information adduced affords good grounds for believing that the phenomenon to be explained did, or does, indeed occur." That information has two components, one supplied by the scientific theory and the other consisting of auxiliary information. He explained the relationship of providing good grounds as implying or conferring a high probability which is not lowered by the existence of other information. The second criterion to which he had reference was the requirement of testability, made best known by Karl Popper as falsifiability.[10]

Typically within science, therefore, a theory of, for instance, causation is regarded as explanatory if it is possible to carry out an *ex post facto* prediction of the consequence of an act from the theory together with suitable conditions antecedent to the act. The explanatory power of a theory of causation is generally viewed as consisting in its capacity to serve as a basis for the opposite of a prediction, a "retrodiction".

This threefold typology of discovery, as exemplified by Hempel's analysis, is employed within this chapter to classify, where possible, the level of causation theory advanced.

Circumstantial Evidence

An important way in which proof of matters in dispute concerning causation is established in all forms of litigation is via the inferences that can be drawn from circumstantial evidence. Circumstantial evidence is evidence that is suggestive of the existence of a matter needing to be proved in a trial, but does not itself directly bear upon it.[11] Put another way,

---

[9]   CG Hempel, *The Philosophy of Natural Science*, Prentice-Hall, New Jersey, 1966.

[10] K Popper, *The Logic of Scientific Discovery*, Hutchinson, London, 1959; see also T Kuhn, *The Structure of Scientific Revolutions*, 2nd edn, University of Chicago Press, Chicago, 1970. Latterly, see AF Chalmers, *What is This Thing Called Science?*, 3rd edn, University of Queensland Press, 1999.

[11] An earlier term for such evidence was "presumptive evidence": see JH Wigmore, *The Science of Judicial Proof*, Little, Brown & Co, Boston, 1937 at para 6; J Stone & WAN Wells, *Evidence: Its History and Policies*, Butterworths, Sydney, 1991, at p132.

it is "evidence of circumstances surrounding, and related to, a subject of inquiry, from which a court may reason in order to reach conclusions about important facts in dispute", such as the causation of deaths, injuries and losses.[12] Often it is expert evidence about the match of particles, including hairs, fibres and spicules found on the accused to those present at the crime scene. Sometimes it is lay evidence. It is proffered in aid of proof of causation in all areas of the law. However, such causation theories often do not exceed simple "observation level" discoveries and risk the drawing of faulty inferences without the presence of clear information establishing that the factors leading to apparent connectedness are both causal and independent. Such attempts to prove causation are often no better than conjectures based on correlations without causal credentials (generalisation level relationships).

With good reason, circumstantial evidence has prompted anxiety on the part of both judges and commentators. Jeremy Bentham, for instance, called for "rules capable of rendering right decisions secure" to guard against the risks of misestimating such evidence[13] and Burrill in 1868 bewailed the "lamentable mistakes" made by judges acting on circumstantial evidence.[14] However, the dichotomy between "direct" and "circumstantial" evidence is now generally, and for good reason, regarded as lacking theoretical justification,[15] the real issue being the degree of probative value properly attaching to either form of evidence.

Similes seem to have been liberally employed by the courts in an attempt to explain proof by circumstantial evidence. The New Zealand Court of Appeal, for instance, noted that circumstantial evidence has been likened to a rope composed of a series of cords, a sufficient number of which, taken together, may without the others support the burden of proof, some jurors finding it supported by some cords, others by other cords.[16]

In a famous passage Lord Chancellor Cairns in the English House of Lords put the role of circumstantial evidence similarly but employed another analogy:

---

[12]   WAN Wells, *Evidence and Advocacy*, Butterworths, Sydney, 1988, at p218.

[13]   J Bentham, *Rationale of Judicial Evidence* in *The Works of Jeremy Bentham*, Russell and Russell, New York, 1962, Vol VII, pp308-9.

[14]   AM Burrill, *A Treatise on the Nature, Principles and Rules of Circumstantial Evidence*, JS Voorhies, New York, 1856, p207, as to which see Wigmore, op cit, n11, at p795. See also W Wills, *An Essay on the Principles of Circumstantial Evidence*, Butterworths, London, 1902.

[15]   See, for instance, Stone & Wells, op cit, n11.

[16]   See *R v Thomas* [1972] NZLR 34 at 41 per Thomas J.

My Lords, in dealing with circumstantial evidence, we have to consider the weight which is to be given to the united force of all the circumstances put together. You may have a ray of light so feeble that by itself it will do little to elucidate a dark corner. But, on the other hand, you will have a number of rays, each of them insufficient, but all converging and brought to bear on the same point, and when united, producing a body of illumination which will clear away the darkness which you are endeavouring to dispel.[17]

Jurors are entitled to draw an inference of guilt from a combination of facts, none of which viewed alone would support that inference.[18] Those facts may include any number of circumstantial matters. An inference of guilt in a criminal trial, which will have as its basis a series of findings as to causation (such as a blow causing death), can be drawn if it is based upon primary facts which are found beyond reasonable doubt and if it is the only inference which is reasonably open upon the whole body of primary facts.[19] An inference of guilt may properly be drawn, although any particular primary fact, or any collection of primary facts falling short of the whole, would be insufficient to exclude other inferences.

Australia's leading case on the use that can be made of circumstantial evidence is the High Court decision of *Chamberlain v The Queen*[20] in which Gibbs CJ and Mason J (Murphy and Brennan JJ agreeing on the point) held that the process of reasoning in a case featuring circumstantial evidence gives rise to two possibilities of error: first from the chances of error in respect of each fact or consideration forming the steps, and second, from the chance of error in reasoning to the conclusion. However, they held that the various stages in the evaluation process do not have to be disaggregated – findings on questions of primary fact do not have to be made. From a reasoning point of view, this has the potential to be highly problematic, as it risks unrecognised errors residing within the inference-drawing process, such as confusing the "generalisation" and "explanation" levels, or not recognising when facts are dependent.

In Australia, in terms of outcome from reasoning processes, it is clear that jurors who agree in reaching the same ultimate conclusions can

---

[17] *Belhaven and Stenton Perlerage* (1875) 1 App Cas 278 at 279.

[18] *Chamberlain v The Queen No 2* (1984) 153 CLR 521 at 536 per Gibbs CJ and Mason J.

[19] *Chamberlain v The Queen No 2* (1984) 153 CLR 521 at 598 per Brennan J; at 536 per Gibbs CJ and Mason J; see also *Moss v Baines* [1974] WAR 7 at 11.

[20] (1984) 153 CLR 521.

disagree as to what evidence is to be accepted, or as to what inferences should be drawn from evidence which they do accept.[21]

The High Court's decision in *Chamberlain v The Queen*[22] provides a good example of the practical difficulties. The accused mother and father were charged with murder but the body of the allegedly deceased baby was never found. The defence postulated that the cause of the death of the Chamberlain baby was that it had been carried off and killed by a dingo. However, proof of causation of death, namely by infliction of violence on the baby by the accused, remained the burden of the prosecution, only able to be discharged by proof beyond reasonable doubt.

There were no eyewitnesses. The prosecution case was circumstantial and heavily dependent upon scientific evidence. Motive for the parents killing their baby was almost completely absent. The prosecution relied on a number of different groups of evidence: (i) evidence of foetal haemoglobin in the car of the accused and in their camera case; (ii) evidence of likely bleeding if a dingo had seized the baby's head and of the absence of large quantities of blood in the tent in which the deceased had been at the time; and (iii) evidence of the condition of the baby's jumpsuit and singlet and the arrangement of the baby's clothes when they were found.

As it turned out, there were difficulties with the foetal haemoglobin evidence. One of the issues requiring determination by the High Court was whether the fact that the foetal haemoglobin evidence was flawed meant that the jury verdict should be quashed. Chief Justice Gibbs and Mason J drew a distinction between "crucial" (or "primary") facts and "secondary" facts, both of which have the potential to be proved by scientific evidence:

> [T]he jury cannot view a fact as a basis for an inference of guilt unless at the end of the day they are satisfied of the existence of the fact beyond reasonable doubt. When the evidence is circumstantial, the jury, whether in a civil or in criminal case, are required to draw an inference from the circumstances of the case; in a civil case the circumstances must raise a more probable inference in favour of what is alleged, and in a criminal case the circumstances must exclude any reasonable hypothesis consistent with innocence.[23]

---

21   Ibid, at 537-8.
22   (1984) 153 CLR 521; 51 ALR 225.
23   CLR at 536; ALR at 237.

They held that it is not possible for a decision-maker in a criminal case to be satisfied beyond reasonable doubt of an inference drawn from facts about the existence of which he or she is in doubt.

Justice Deane held that it is not the law that a juror is precluded in *all* circumstances from drawing an inference from a primary fact unless it is proved beyond reasonable doubt. However, if a primary fact constitutes an essential element of a crime charged, he held that a juror must be persuaded that that fact has been proved beyond reasonable doubt before properly joining in a verdict of guilty. He found that those bodies of evidence were cumulative:

> The jury was entitled to pay regard to all of them, even if unpersuaded that any or all of them was proved beyond reasonable doubt. Thus a conclusion that the evidence directed to showing the presence of foetal haemoglobin in the car was persuasive only to the extent of balance of probability does not mean that the conclusion and the evidence should be rejected as irrelevant. Even though the evidence, viewed discretely, does no more than establish the presence of foetal haemoglobin on the balance of probabilities, it remains part of the totality of the admissible and relevant evidence in the context of which the ultimate question whether Mrs Chamberlain's guilt was established beyond reasonable doubt fell and falls to be determined.[24]

Causation is frequently determined on the basis of inferences drawn from primary facts. In the criminal domain, where such primary facts are essential to the drawing of the ultimate inferences, decision-makers must be satisfied of them in Australia beyond reasonable doubt, even before they accept expert opinions on the subject. The fact that an alternative interpretation of a primary fact is possible often forms the basis for appellate litigation. This highlights the importance of accurate representation by expert witnesses of a number of matters: the reliability of

---

[24] CLR at 627; ALR at 313. In *Chamberlain v The Queen* the High Court found that although the scientific evidence that blood under the dashboard and in the car of the accused parents was foetal blood and the evidence of a pathologist that he saw on the jumpsuit of the deceased the imprint of a hand in blood were unsafe to form the basis of an inference of guilt, the jury's finding of guilt should not be disturbed because of the existence of other legitimate bases for their decision. In *R v Anderson* [2000] 1 VR 1 at 26 the Victorian Court of Appeal applied the same principle to insist that a jury should have been instructed that they could only accept the opinions expressed by two treating doctors that wounds on the accused had been self-inflicted, to the exclusion of opinions on the same subject expressed by a forensic physician and a forensic pathologist, if satisfied beyond reasonable doubt that the former opinions were correct: see also *R v Sodo* (1975) 61 Cr App R 131 at 134; *R v Van Beelen* (1973) 4 SASR 353.

the "observations" which they have taken into account; the processes by which they have arrived at the inferences that they have drawn; and finally, the actual opinions which they have formed.

Expert Evidence of the Possibility of Causation

An issue that flows from Deane J's analysis, in particular, is the difficult question of the use that can properly be made of expert and other evidence of a low order of probative value, when such evidence contributes to the evaluation of a critical issue such as causation in a criminal or civil case. At one level, there cannot be a simple addition of relatively unlikely or dubious possibilities, resulting in a beyond reasonable doubt or a balance of probabilities determination. Such a process is vulnerable to erroneous inferences on the basis of mere observational data, when in fact there may be alternative explanations or the data may have relationships one to another.

Our legal system has long been mistrustful of "trial by numbers", in good part because it may utterly miscarry. The issue has been controversial and the subject of considerable amounts of heated academic discourse since the late 1960s. A major fillip was given to discussion of the use of statistical proof in the courts by the elementary misuse of statistics in the 1968 Californian decision of *People v Collins*.[25] It prompted Professor Laurence Tribe of Harvard Law School[26] to challenge the overt use of mathematical arguments in courts on grounds of public policy, assuming that the criteria for probability judgments in the courts were in principle mathematical. Shortly afterwards, though, the English philosopher Jonathan Cohen challenged this assumption, arguing in *The Probable and the Provable* in 1977[27] that not all reasoning about probabilities is mathematical (Pascalian) and contending that some judgments of probability can be justified by non-mathematical (Baconian) criteria. This resulted in a substantial debate between Pascalians and Baconians.

---

[25] 68 Cal 2d 319, 438 P 2d 33 (1968).

[26] LH Tribe, "Trial by Mathematics: Precision and Ritual in the Legal Process" (1971) 84 *Harvard Law Review* 1329; see also T Starkie, *A Practical Treatise on the Law of Evidence*, 7th American edition, T & JW Johnson, Philadelphia, 1842, Vol 1, p568: "The Notions of those who have supposed that mere moral probabilities or relations could ever be represented by numbers or space, and thus subjected to arithmetical analysis, cannot but be regarded as visionary and chimerical."

[27] LJ Cohen, *The Probable and the Provable*, Clarendon Press, Oxford, 1977.

Most recently, Rose LJ in the English Court of Appeal in a leading DNA profiling case expressed anxiety about the use of "apparently objective numerical figures" and repudiated the notion that juries should find guilt "by means of a formula, numerical or otherwise", preferring the use of "individual common sense and knowledge of the world".[28] The debate in turn has prompted a series of attempts to make statistical reasoning accessible and applicable to forensic scenarios[29] and the advancement of the argument from some quarters that decision-marking by judges and jurors is, conceptually, a mathematical process.[30]

However, Australian, English and North American courts have exhibited considerable anxiety about the use of statistical evidence, especially in the context of cases where DNA profiling evidence has been proffered by the prosecution,[31] acknowledging the potential for misapprehension by lay decision-makers of the contentions by experts of causation, association and nexus. This has generated particular concern during the past decade in relation to the use to be made of numerically dramatic assertions by DNA scientists of the likelihood of positive matches between crime scene samples and samples taken from other than the suspect. The risks that have been identified are that because of the way in which statistical evidence is presented wrong inferences may be drawn. In addition, because of the "numbers" involved jurors may lose sight of associated issues such as whether or not a "victim" in whom the accused person's semen was found consented to sexual intercourse.[32] In short, there is a risk that jurors will be overwhelmed by the statistics.

Perhaps the greatest danger is that juries will become confused or distracted by some kinds of evidence, lay or expert, which add to the prosecution or the plaintiff's case, but do so only at a low level or only marginally. The issue has been grappled with in the criminal law where persons who have put others at risk of being infected with the HIV virus have been charged with conduct endangering injury or life.[33] If the risk of infection is only one in 200, for instance, but the consequences of such

---

[28]   *Adams v The Queen* [1996] 2 Cr App R 467 at 481.

[29]   See eg P David, "Probability and Proof: Some Basic Concepts" in T Anderson & W Twining, *Analysis of Evidence,* Weidenfeld & Nicholson, London, 1991.

[30]   See eg B Grofman, "Mathematical Models of Juror and Jury Decision-Making" in BD Sales, *The Trial Process*, Plenum Press, New York, 1981.

[31]   See E Magnusson, "Statistical Proof of Causation", Chapter 19.

[32]   See I Freckelton & H Selby, *Expert Evidence: Law, Practice and Procedure*, 2nd edn, Law Book Co, Sydney, 2002.

[33]   See eg *Mutemeri v Cheesman* (1999) 100 A Crim R 397; see also D Groves, "Commentary" (1998) 22 *Criminal Law Journal* 357 at 359; D Lanham, "Danger Down Under" [1999] *Criminal Law Review* 960.

infection are dire, is the conduct, properly analysed, conduct of criminal endangerment? Is the connection between the intercourse and the potential for infection too remote? The question for the court is the likelihood at the time of the intercourse of infection, incorporating for the accused person his or her capacity to foresee such a potential. Epidemiology evidence has been the resort of the prosecution in order to attempt to show sufficiency of nexus between conduct and potential outcome. However, the key to the probative value of such evidence lies in drawing a distinction between evidence at the "generalisation" and "explanation" levels. The evidence may be suggestive of an explanatory theory but epidemiology necessarily seeks correlations and is tightly chained to "generalisation" level relationships.

In the civil context, epidemiology evidence does no more than suggest the potential for a nexus between a teratogen or carcinogen and a birth defect or cancer. It is particularly problematic. As noted previously, the evidence can constitute an assertion about a correlation, but may have very little probative value by reason of its level of generalisation. Viewed in another way, such evidence can relate to the potential for such a nexus at a general level within the population or within a particular population, but fail to factor in circumstances personal to the plaintiff. The difficulty is at its most pronounced where the evidence is adduced only at a general level in terms of enhanced risk of, for instance, contraction of a disease by reason of exposure to a particular substance.

However, the problem can exist also where the statistical association of exposure is personalised to the particular health and lifestyle circumstances of the plaintiff. Judge Weinstein in the United States in the course of the *Agent Orange* litigation defined the issue helpfully:

> While it may be possible to prove, through the use of such proof as ... epidemiological evidence, that such harm – for example cancer – can be "caused" by a particular substance, it may be impossible to pinpoint which particular person's cancer would have occurred naturally and which would not have occurred but for exposure to the substance.[34]

Judge Weinstein is not alone in identifying the potential for misevaluation of epidemiology evidence. Two decades before his decision, Bradford Hill, a renowned epidemiologist, stressed the risk of what might

---

[34]   *In re Agent Orange Product Liability Litigation*, 597 F Supp 740 at 834 (EDNY, 1984).

be called the "association fallacy"[35] – the confusion of association with cause. This is simply another way of acknowledging that there is a risk of confusing "generalisation level" discovery with "explanation level" discovery.

The issue was pointedly raised, too, in the early debates about aetiology of AIDS. It was observed by researchers in the mid-1980s that there was a statistical association between AIDS and the illicit use of nitrate inhalants, leading to suggestions that such inhalants may have caused the depressed immune system in AIDS. Only later was it realised that AIDS was caused by human immunodeficiency virus ("HIV") and that the statistical correlation between AIDS and usage of nitrate inhalants was in no relevant sense causative. It was simply that a considerable percentage of those who contracted HIV and went on to contract AIDS were homosexual and that some of them had used nitrate inhalants.[36] This was a classic example of "generalisation level" analysis being mistaken for "explanation level".[37]

The risks of false imputation of causation have led to considerable concern about the potential for courts, and in particular jurors, to misunderstand the limits of epidemiology evidence.[38] The risks identified by Hill prompted him to develop criteria for the drawing of causal inferences in epidemiology, which have since been applied in many legal contexts:

- *Statistical Association.* There must be some degree of statistical association between a cause and its effect. A strong association (large in magnitude) is more likely to represent causation than a weak association (small in magnitude).
- *Temporality.* A cause must precede its effect. Strength in temporality, such as when a cause immediately precedes its effect, supports an inference of causation.

---

[35] AB Hill, "The Environment and Disease: Association or Causation?" (1965) 58 *Proceedings of the Royal Society of Medicine* 295 at 299.

[36] A point made in another context by P Sherman, "Agent Orange and the Problem of the Indeterminate Plaintiff" (1986) 52 *Brooklyn Law Review* 369 at 384.

[37] Note that parallel to the explanation ultimately found for AIDS causation, there was also an explanation for the valid but misleading generalisation about nitrate inhalants.

[38] See M Dore, "A Commentary on the Use of Epidemiology Evidence in Demonstrating Cause-in-Fact" (1983) 7 *Harvard Environmental Law Review* 429; TA Brennan, "Untangling Causation Issues in Law and Medicine: Hazardous Substance Litigation" (1987) 107 *Annals of Internal Medicine* 741; HM Ginzburg, "Use and Misuse of Epidemiological Data in the Courtroom: Defining the Limits of Inferential and Particularistic Evidence in Mass Tort Litigation" (1986) 12 *American Journal of Law and Medicine* 423.

- *Biological Plausibility and Coherence.* A cause and effect relationship between exposure and disease should be biologically plausible and consistent with other information about the disease or harm.
- *Dose-Response Effect.* Causation is more likely if greater amounts of the putative cause are associated with corresponding increases in the occurrence of the disease or harm.
- *Consistency.* When similar findings are generated by several epidemiological studies involving various investigators, causation tends to be supported.
- *Analogy.* Substantiation of relationships similar to the putative causal relationship increases the likelihood of causation.
- *Experimental Evidence.* Causation is more likely if removing the exposure in a population results in a decrease in the occurrence of disease or harm.
- *Specificity.* When there is but a single putative cause for the disease or harm, causation is supported.[39]

The insight behind these criteria, given that epidemiology was a very young science when they were proposed, genuinely deserves praise. However, they do not displace the need for rigorous, scientific scrutiny of the individual items of epidemiological evidence brought to court. It is notable too that a new sub-science has now been spawned within the epidemiology domain, "meta-analysis" – the analysis of epidemiological analysis to enable the results of epidemiological studies of different types and of different validity to be combined to produce overall conclusions.

The admissibility and probative value of epidemiological evidence has been considered in three illustrative cases: the English medical negligence decisions of *Vadera v Shaw*[40] and *Loveday v Renton*[41] and then at length in the New South Wales Court of Appeal decision of *Seltsam Pty Ltd v McGuiness ("the Seltsam case")*,[42] dealing with allegedly asbestos-caused cancer.

---

[39] Hill, op cit, n35, at 95; see also MM Thompson, "Causal Inference in Epidemiology: Implications for Toxic Tort Litigation" (1992) 71 *North Carolina Law Review* 247.

[40] (1998) 45 BMLR 162.

[41] [1990] 1 Med LR 117.

[42] [2000] NSWCA 347; see also I Freckelton, "Epidemiology Evidence" (2000) 8 *Journal of Law and Medicine* 133.

The English Decisions

In *Loveday v Renton*, the plaintiff sued Dr Renton for damages in the form of permanent brain damage after being treated with pertussis whooping cough vaccine. The question before the court was whether the vaccine had caused or could reasonably have been foreseen to cause brain damage in young children. There were four mechanisms by which the plaintiff in principle could have suffered the brain injury as a result of the vaccine: febrile convulsions, anaphylactic shock, neurotoxic effect and adjuvant effect. The major epidemiology evidence was from the National Childhood Encephalopathy Study which concluded that there was a temporal proximity between the usage of the vaccine and the suffering occasionally of encephalopathy resulting in brain damage. Stuart-Smith LJ held that the four biological mechanisms proposed by the plaintiff were implausible and that the epidemiological evidence did not establish that it was the vaccine which had caused the brain damage. He concluded that the relative risk of 2.5 shown by the studies, a figure which showed that it was two and a half times as likely that a person exposed to the vaccine would contract the illness as one not exposed, was not statistically significant. He took into account that in the revised version of the figures which he employed, there were very few children who contracted the damage. Thus, he concluded that the evidence was not strong enough to enable the plaintiff to establish causation. Put another way, the evidence was at the "observational level", falling well short of the scientific requirements for "explanatory level" relationships.

In *Vadera v Shaw* the plaintiff sued her general practitioner for prescribing and continuing to prescribe her an oral contraceptive pill. The plaintiff began to take "the pill" in October and in November suffered a serious brain stem stroke as a result of a thrombosis in the basilar artery, rendering her almost completely disabled, suffering a condition known as "locked-in syndrome".

The plaintiff was initially prescribed "the pill" when her blood pressure was somewhat raised. High blood pressure was conceded to be a contra-indicator for prescription of "the pill". She also claimed to have informed her doctor that she suffered from migraines, another contra-indicator for the prescription of the oral contraceptive pill. The Court of Appeal found that the trial judge had been entitled to find on the facts that the plaintiff did not suffer from hypertension when she was prescribed "the pill" and to decline to find that the plaintiff had a history of headaches. It also found that the trial judge had been correct in finding on the expert evidence that the causal relationship between "the pill" and strokes had not been established.

It is the final matter, that dealing with the causation issue, which is of most interest in this context.[43] The trial judge concluded that it could *not* be established, applying the discipline of statistics to the available figures, that the association between a person taking the medication and that person suffering a stroke was more than a relationship of chance. It followed (bearing in mind that the burden of proof on this issue rested with the plaintiff) that it could not be established on the balance of probabilities that the plaintiff suffered her stroke by reason of the taking of the medication. He concluded that the studies adduced before him did not establish a statistically significant connection between the medication and strokes. What existed was a set of data established at "generalisation level", but there was no satisfactory justification for equating it with "explanation level" information.

The Court of Appeal upheld the trial judge's decision. Lord Justice Henry for the court held that:

> It is as common sense a conclusion as one could wish to say that if the connection between A and B cannot be shown with confidence to be other than a coincidence, then it cannot be held on the balance of probabilities that A caused B. This is not to allow scientists or statisticians to usurp the judge's function, but rather to permit him to use their skills to discern a connection, or a lack of connection, between two phenomena.[44]

Out of deference to arguments mounted in the case, the court looked at the relevance of the epidemiological evidence, on the assumption that the plaintiff did suffer from pre-existing hypertension. It noted that there was evidence that hypertension implied a 4.6 times increased risk of cerebral thrombosis and, if combined with oral contraception use, a 10.7 times increased risk. The court, however, was influenced by the evidence that oral contraception was but one of a number of risk factors for thrombosis, in fact being a weaker risk factor than a number of others. Moreover, the mechanism of increased risk of arterial thrombosis with oral contraceptives was unclear but was thought to be in the promotion of the thrombosis. The Court of Appeal accepted the argument that since the medication did not increase the risk of hypertension-related stroke when given to a hypertensive patient, it followed that the medication had no more causative effect in relation to a stroke when given to a hypertensive patient than when given to a "normal" patient. This meant that the causal relationship

---

[43] See in this regard R Goldberg, "The Contraceptive Pill, Negligence and Causation: Views on *Vadera v Shaw*" (2000) 8 *Medical Law Review* 316.

[44] *Vadera v Shaw* (1998) 45 BMLR 162, Lexis-Nexis, p13.

between the medication and a stroke is the same as in the ordinary case which, as the court found, on the balance of probabilities could not be shown to exist. In other words, the science employed existed at the level of generalisation, deceptively suggestive of causation.

The *Vadera* decision of the Court of Appeal constituted a sophisticated and careful analysis of the circumstances in which, amongst other things, epidemiology evidence can assist the evaluation of facts proved to a court. It emerged upon such analysis that significant care needed to be taken with the expert evidence – the correlations between hypertension, contraceptive pill use and thrombosis and also between migraines, contraceptive pill use and thrombosis needed to be viewed discerningly. In fact, the combination of factors left contraceptive pill use providing little by way of significant causative nexus in the context of either hypertension or migraines.

Seltsam v McGuinness

The *Seltsam* decision took place against the backdrop of the High Court of Australia having emphasised that the common law test of balance of probabilities is not satisfied by evidence which does no more than establish a possibility of nexus.[45] As Mason J held in *Tubemakers of Australia v Fernandez*:[46] "the plaintiff will fail if all that he can show is that his disability might have been ... caused" by the alleged wrongful conduct. However, expert evidence is not essential in all situations. Findings of causal connection can be made without medical evidence to support them[47] or where the expert evidence does not rise above the opinion that such a connection is possible.[48] The key question is whether "the materials offered justify an inference of probable connection. This is the only principle of law. Whether its requirements are met depends upon the evaluation of the evidence."[49]

The first question determined by the New South Wales Court of Appeal in *Seltsam* was as to the admissibility of "possibility evidence". The primary issue litigated on appeal from the decision of the Dust Diseases Tribunal was whether the kidney cell cancer suffered by the plaintiff had been "caused" by his exposure in the workplace to amounts of crocidolite. The epidemiology evidence on the subject was equivocal.

---

[45] See eg *St George Club Ltd v Hines* (1962) 35 ALJR 106 at 107; *Bonnington Castings Ltd v Wardlaw* [1956] AC 613.
[46] (1976) 50 ALJR 720 at 724.
[47] *Nicolia v Commissioner for Railways (NSW)* (1970) 45 ALJR 465.
[48] *EMI (Australia) Ltd v Bes* [1970] 2 NSWR 238.
[49] *Fernandez v Tubemakers of Australia Ltd* (1975) 2 NSWLR 190 at 197 per Glass JA.

Other facts known to raise the likelihood of contraction of the plaintiff's form of cancer were smoking and obesity. The plaintiff was a moderate smoker and was significantly overweight. Thus, the task faced included how to evaluate what were multiple and potentially connected causes of the plaintiff's cancer.[50]

The key evidence proffered by the plaintiff was epidemiological evidence to the effect that a person exposed to crocidolite was 1.4 times as likely to experience renal cell carcinoma as a person not so exposed.[51] Clear figures of a comparable kind were not available either for smoking or obesity or for the combination of them, still less for the combination of crocidolite exposure, obesity and smoking. A significant difficulty confronted the Tribunal, therefore, in terms of the use which it could properly make of the epidemiological evidence which to a modest degree assisted the plaintiff's case but which, on its own, could not be said to advance it to the point where it proved nexus between exposure and outcome on the balance of probabilities. Framed another way, the question was whether the correlations between the observational variables were in fact causative – was it legitimate to move from the "generalisation level" to the "explanation level" and to determine that a causation relationship existed between crocidolite exposure and the contraction of renal cell carcinoma?

In the leading judgment of the Court of Appeal, Spigelman CJ held that the fact that epidemiology evidence only establishes possibility does not preclude admissibility. The second question determined by the court was as to the use that could legitimately be made of "possibility epidemiology evidence". Chief Justice Spigelman held that when evidence only goes so far as to establish possibility, it must be weighed in the balance with other factors in determining whether or not on the balance of probabilities an

---

50   For a useful analysis of this issue, see D Kaye, "The Limits of the Preponderance of the Evidence Standard: Justifiably Naked Statistical Evidence and Multiple Causation" (1982) 2 *American Bar Foundation Research Journal* 487, also found in W Twining & A Stein (eds), *Evidence and Proof*, Dartmouth, Aldershot, 1992; see also GO Robinson, "Multiple Causation in Tort Law: Reflections on the DES Cases" (1982) 68 *Vanderbilt Law Review* 713. See also AG Celli Jr, "Toward a Risk Contribution Approach to Tortfeasor Identification and Multiple Causation Cases" (1990) 65 *New York University Law Review* 635.

51   Relative ratios between 1.1 and 3 are generally described as "weak" (ARP between 9 per cent and 67 per cent), relative ratios between 3 and 8 are "moderate" (ARP between 67 per cent and 87 per cent); between 8 and 16 as "strong" (ARP between 87 per cent and 94 per cent), and between 16 and 40+ as "extremely strong" (ARP between 94 per cent and 97.5 per cent).

inference of causation in a particular case could or should be drawn.[52] He held that where the whole of the evidence, incorporating the epidemiology evidence does not rise above the level of possibility, either alone or cumulatively, an inference of causation cannot be drawn.[53]

The Chief Justice found that the test for the particular case in respect of causation was whether on the basis of primary facts it was reasonable to draw the inference that the nexus existed on the balance of probabilities.[54] He held that evidence of possibility, including epidemiological studies, should be regarded as circumstantial evidence which has the potential, alone or in combination with other evidence, to establish causation in the particular case. He held that causation, like any other fact, can be established by a process of inference which combines primary facts like "strands in a cable" rather than "links in a chain". In so doing, his Honour was viewing epidemiological evidence in the same way as the New Zealand Court of Appeal, as pointed out above.[55]

He held that in the case before him the "primary" facts consisted in large measure of the epidemiological studies which established that nexus could possibly exist. This, he found, was not necessarily a bar to the plaintiff succeeding as epidemiological studies and expert opinions based on such studies are able to form strands in a cable of a circumstantial case.[56] The question was whether the studies showed the connection between the inhalation of asbestos and renal cell carcinoma to be "sufficiently close" to warrant a reasonable mind to conclude that the possible cause was the actual cause.

In investigating this question, Spigelman CJ held that the issue before the court was whether an increased risk caused or materially contributed to the injury actually suffered. He held that the test of actual persuasion in respect of causation does not require epidemiological studies to reach the level of a relative risk of 2.0 (namely where the incidence of contraction of cancer doubles on exposure by contrast with that applicable without exposure), even when that is the only evidence available to a court. However, he noted that "the closer the ratio approaches 2.0, the greater the significance that can be attached to the studies for the purposes of drawing

---

52 *Seltsam*, at [79].
53 Ibid, at [79].
54 Applying *Layton v Vines* (1952) 85 CLR 352 at 358.
55 See *R v Thomas* [1972] NZLR 34 at 41 per Thomas J.
56 *Seltsam*, at [98].

an inference of causation in an individual case. The 'strands in the cable' must be capable of bearing the weight of the ultimate inference."[57]

Chief Justice Spigelman applied a variant on the Hill criteria, classifying the indicia that he set out as "uncomplicated statements of commonsense propositions" for the interpretation of epidemiological evidence:

- *Strength of the Association*. In general the higher the risk estimate, the less likely the finding is a result of confounding or bias ...

- *Dose Response Effect*. If the risk of the disease rises with increasing exposure, a causal interpretation of the association is more plausible ...

- *Time Sequence*. The exposure or risk factor must precede the disease ...

- *Consistency*. Results from other epidemiological studies of the exposure-disease association should be similar. If similar results are found in different populations using various study designs, the plausibility of a causal interpretation is increased. An alternative explanation of bias or confounding would have to be apply to each of the different studies, a highly implausible explanation.

- *Biological Coherence*. Does the exposure-disease association make biological sense given what is known of the natural history of the disease? Do animal experiments support the association? Do other types of collateral evidence support the association, such as secular trends of the exposure factor in the disease. Unfortunately, for many diseases little is known about their aetiologies, so the informational background by which to judge biological coherence is often limited. Thus, failure of this broad principle does not necessarily weaken the plausibility of a causal interpretation.

The first three principles can be applied to an individual study and used to assist the findings. The last two principles referred to results outside their

---

57   At [137]. See Thompson, op cit, n39, at 251 for a useful analysis of risk ratio, pointing out that it can be calculated as the risk of disease in the exposed group divided by the risk of disease in an unexposed group; or the number of exposed persons developing a disease over time divided by the total number of exposed people, that result being divided by the number of unexposed persons developing disease over time divided by the total number of unexposed people. The attributable risk proportion ("ARP") is the proportion of exposed persons who have contracted the disease for whom the disease in attributable to the exposure. It is calculated as follows: ARP = risk ratio −1 divided by risk ratio.

particular study and relate more to external issues of coherence or consistency. All of the criteria or principles should be viewed as guidelines. Except, perhaps, for time sequence, none is a necessary condition for a causal interpretation.[58]

He held that these criteria could be taken into account in determining whether or not a court should infer, on the balance of probabilities that a particular exposure caused injury in the specific case before the court. However, he noted that while the evidence of epidemiologists with respect to the identification and application of the criteria may be of assistance by force of their reasoning, they did not constitute a scientific opinion which the court was bound to accept. Significantly, too, he found that when assessing expert evidence on causation, the legal concept of causation requires a court to approach the matter in a distinctively different manner from that "which may be appropriate in either philosophy or science, including the science of epidemiology. The commonsense approach to causation at common law is quite different from a scientist's approach to causation.[59] ... An inference of causation for the purposes of the tort of negligence may well be drawn when a scientist, including an epidemiologist, would not draw such an inference."[60] A significant culture clash hereby becomes apparent with a problem existing in terms of the use the law should make of evidence from representatives of other disciplines, but the nature of the culture clash is not so clear. Unfortunately, his Honour did not flesh the question out further. It appears inherent in his analysis though that he was suggesting that the test of at least the civil law may well be lower than that of, for instance, epidemiology, enabling possibility evidence, when added to other forms of evidence, to be sufficient to allow a finding of causation on the balance of probabilities. In terms of proof, this requires very careful usage of terminology both by the law and epidemiology – each may be using words in different ways, opening up significant possibilities of misunderstanding, especially when the ultimate test is formulated in terms of "common sense". However, the curious factor is that at essence, Spigelman CJ for the court was holding that science and the law probably had the same approach to the question at hand. So far as the individual items of epidemiological evidence were concerned, generalisations which might have seemed possible were not justified

---

58   *Seltsam*, at [139].
59   Citing *National Insurance Co of New Zealand Ltd v Espagne* (1961) 105 CLR 569 at 591; *March v E & MH Stramare Pty Ltd* (1991) 171 CLR 506 at 509, 522, 530-1; *Chappel v Hart* (1998) 195 CLR 232 esp at [6]-[7], [23], [62]-[64], [93], [111], [122].
60   *Seltsam*, at [142]-[143].

because the correlations between the variables were too weak. As a matter of science, the evidence did not even reach the level of generalisation and, definitely, in the absence of established causal connections, the "explanation level" had not even been approached. This coincided with the legal reasoning.

A number of aspects of the *Seltsam* decision are at significant variance to the approach adopted in United States cases where even the admissibility of possibility epidemiology evidence has been refused where it falls short of reaching the relative risk ratio mark of 2.0. In the United States an arbitrary, but clear, rule has been developed that the threshold for concluding that an agent is more likely than not the cause of a disease is a relative risk of greater than 2.0. As the Federal Judicial Center *Manual on Scientific Evidence* points out, "When the relative risk reaches 2.0, the agent is responsible for cases equal in number to those from all other background causes. Thus, a relative risk of 2.0 implies a 50 per cent likelihood than an exposed individual's disease was caused by the agent."[61] This has been applied in the context of determining the teratogenicity of a morning sickness medication,[62] the likelihood of asbestos causing colon cancer,[63] the likelihood of swine flu vaccine causing Guillain Barre syndrome,[64] the likelihood of pelvic inflammatory disease having been caused by an intra-uterine device[65] and the impact of Agent Orange upon a variety of diseases suffered by Vietnam Veterans and their offspring,[66] to name just a few examples. The advantage of such a rule is its clarity. The difficulty with an approach which permits epidemiological evidence falling some distance short of 2.0 is that courts will seek refuge in the imprecise language of "possibility" and "common sense" which can result in inexact and impenetrable reasoning.

The New South Wales Court of Appeal has rejected the United States rule and opted to factor epidemiology evidence falling short of the 2.0 relative risk ratio into the mix of factors that can be considered in determining in civil matters whether causation is proved on the balance of probabilities. That this approach is fraught with difficulties is exemplified by the terms on which the Court of Appeal itself divided on the facts, as well as by the criticisms levelled by the majority at the trial judge, in

---

61 Federal Judicial Center, *Manual on Scientific Evidence*, US Government Printing Office, Washington DC, 1994, at p168.

62 *De Luca v Merrell Dow Pharmaceutics Inc*, 911 F 941 at 958-9.

63 *In Re Joint E & S Dists Asbestos Litig*, 758 F Supp 199 at 203 (SDNY 1991).

64 *Manko v United States*, 636 F Supp 1419 at 1434 (WD Mo 1986).

65 *Marder v GD Searle & Co*, 630 F Supp 1087 at 1092 (D Md 1986).

66 *In re >Agent Orange= Prod Liab Litig*, 597 F Supp 740 at 835-7 (EDNY, 1984).

particular that he inadequately evaluated the complex and conflicting epidemiology evidence adduced before him.

The second important question left unresolved by the *Seltsam* decision is the relevance of epidemiological evidence to the particular case, especially where the litigant falls into the category of person with other risk factors for incurring the disease or injury claimed to be attributable to the defendant's negligence. A substantial series of factors personal to the plaintiff may heighten their susceptibility. In turn epidemiology evidence can assist with evaluating the significance of such factors and providing statistical likelihoods of the plaintiff suffering the illness or sustaining the injury, but for the exposure to the agent. The difficulty can be the ambiguities and uncertainties within such categories of information.

The Bradford-Hill criteria and their variant applied by Spigelman CJ furnish a useful set of guidelines against which to measure the probative value of epidemiology evidence about causation. However, only two are necessary for causal inference: temporality and statistical association, although they are not, of course, determinative of causation. The challenge for expert witnesses, advocates and decision-makers is to determine appropriate use of epidemiology evidence that is at a general level, rather than personal to the individual plaintiff's situation, and to evaluate dispassionately associations between exposure and contraction of disease when the hard evidence is ambivalent. The New South Wales Court of Appeal has offered few tools to grapple with this challenge.

The Temporal Dilemma

Important dilemmas exist at the heart of the proof of causation. A number of them lie in the very tests set out by the courts for causation. Decisions have drawn a distinction between establishing causation in different situations. When the issue in dispute is the connection between matters in the past and the present, the test is objective, proceeding on the basis that it is simply a matter of discerning the nexus, using agreed methods and rules, and evaluating whether it constitutes proof of causation. If the plaintiff cannot reach this point on the mathematical probability of more probable than not, more than 50 per cent, they recover nothing. This is the "all or nothing rule". By contrast, though, the law in both England and Australia regards proof of causation between a past event and events in the future, and compensation for them, as resting on subjective considerations. The plaintiff is entitled to receive proportional compensation, commensurate with the probability that they will incur a pecuniary loss. Reconciliation between these approaches is problematic. From the perspective of proof the evidence adduced in support of either issue is generically much the same –

expert evidence that relies inevitably upon a degree of informed speculation. It has to be conceded, though, that particularly difficult challenges are posed for the plaintiffs seeking to persuade decision-makers, be they judges, jurors or magistrates, that mathematical calculations involved in the establishment of percentile chances of loss, rather than a rule of thumb "rough approximation", should be employed to establish future loss.

Troubled as prediction of future loss by reference to statistical likelihood is, a conceptually preferable way of viewing the issue is to dispense with the temporal distinction currently adopted by the law and to acknowledge the subjective, predictive, speculative component in attributing from today's perspective, based upon such "facts" as can be garnered for a court, that one thing caused or will contribute to an outcome. The advantage of constructing the jurisprudential notion of causation in this more flexible way is that it would enable a consistent approach to causation – extending both to past and future matters, and comprehending both determination of what occurred and calculation of damages caused by reason of negligence. However, a consequence of such an approach would be that even calculation of pre-trial loss of earnings would be viewed as non-factual,[67] leading to the abandonment of the "all or nothing rule" in the same way that it is eschewed for future losses. This in turn would place additional pressure on those seeking to assist courts in their calculation of pre-trial losses.

Proving Causation of Injuries

Fundamental to success for plaintiffs in personal injuries litigation is proof that not only has there been a failure to adhere to a proper standard of care by the defendant but that it has been the failure which has caused the plaintiff's injuries. The legal burden of proving causation is a substantial one.[68] In the medical negligence context it has been described as "Herculean".[69] It has also been characterised as "the most formidable

---

[67] Hamer calls such matters "counterfactual": D Hamer, "Proof of Causation and Quantum in an Unpredictable World" (1999) 23 *Melbourne University Law Review* 557.

[68] See the comments of Sopinka J in *Snell v Farrell* [1990] 2 SCR 311 at 320-1.

[69] Russell, "Establishing Medical Negligence – A Herculean Task?" (1998) 3 *Scots Law Times* 17 at 20-2.

obstacle confronting healthcare consumers".[70] Justice Kirby of the Australian High Court has commented of the issue that:

> The reasons include the imprecision of, and uncertainty about, some medical conditions; the progressive nature of others; the complexity of modern medical practice and technology; and the fact that some mistakes, serious enough in themselves, have no untoward results which can properly be attributed to them.[71]

A significant divergence on the issue has opened between the English, United States and Australian courts. The difference has repercussions whose practical significance is often not sufficiently recognised.[72] Its genesis can been seen in the controversial decision of Lord Wilberforce in *McGhee v National Coal Board*[73] which was rejected by the House of Lords in *Wilsher v Essex Area Health Authority*.[74]

In *McGhee* the plaintiff sued the National Coal Board on the basis of dermatitis he had suffered after being required to clean out coal kilns. Although the working conditions of the plaintiff were hot and dirty, the defendant failed to provide proper washing facilities, resulting in McGhee cycling home covered in dirt and grime. The trip home added to his potential for developing the disease. The defendant sought to rely upon this aspect of the plaintiff's behaviour to exculpate itself from all or any of liability for the plaintiff's dermatitis. The House of Lords rejected the defence, holding that a defendant is liable in negligence if its breach of duty has "caused" or "materially contributed to" an injury suffered by a plaintiff, notwithstanding that there may be other factors that have contributed to the plaintiff's injuries. Lord Wilberforce, agreeing in the result with the other members of the House of Lords, advanced an important new interpretation:

> [I]n the absence of proof that the culpable condition had, in the result, no effect, the employers should be liable for an injury, squarely within the risk which they created and that they, not the [plaintiff], should suffer the

---

[70]   R Milstein, "Causation in Medical Negligence – Recent Developments" (1997) 6 *Australian Health Law Bulletin* 21.

[71]   *Chappel v Hart* (1998) 156 ALR 517 at 546.

[72]   This is often the case with matters relating to burden and standard of proof: see A Kiralfy (ed), *The Burden of Proof*, Professional Books Ltd, London, 1987.

[73]   [1972] 3 All ER 1008; for a critical analysis see JG Fleming, "Probabilistic Causation in Tort Law: A Postscript" (1991) 70 *Canadian Bar Review* 136.

[74]   [1988] AC 1074.

consequence of the impossibility, foreseeably inherent in the nature of his injury, of segregating the precise consequence of their default.[75]

So far as the facts of the case were concerned, it is arguable that it fell into the "observational level" of case, the correlation of cause and effect being available to observation, enough to raise suspicion, but not necessarily actually existing. Sufficient data simply were not to hand.

In *Wilsher* Lord Wilberforce's approach fell for review. A premature baby was born suffering from various illnesses including oxygen deficiency. A special baby unit at the hospital was shown to have inserted a catheter twice into the baby's vein, rather than into an artery, with the result that he received too much oxygen. The issue was whether it had been proven by the infant plaintiff that the baby's retinal condition (retrolental fibroplasia) had been caused by the health authority's negligence, the issue being complicated by the fact that his condition had a number of potential aetiologies related to prematurity. The House of Lords overturned the application by the trial judge and by the Court of Appeal of the presumption subsequently applied in the Australian High Court in *Chappel v Hart*. It held that where a plaintiff's injury is attributable to a number of possible causes, one of which is the defendant's negligence, the combination of the breach of the defendant's duty and the plaintiff's injury does not give rise to any presumption that the defendant's negligence is the cause of the plaintiff's injury. The causal link must be proved to the requisite degree. For the infant plaintiff in *Wilsher* this meant that he was unable to discharge his onus of proof to show that it was the defendant's negligence which had caused his retinal condition.[76]

Again, applying the threefold typology, the evidence was equivocal. There was the appearance that there might be a correlation between the

---

[75] *McGhee v National Coal Board* [1972] 3 All ER 1008 at 1013. By contrast, for instance, the position of Lord Salmon (at 1018) was that when it is proved on the balance of probabilities that an employer has been negligent and that the negligence has materially increased the risk of an employee contracting an industrial disease, the employer is liable in damages if the employee contracts the disease notwithstanding that the employer is not responsible for other factors which materially contributed to the contraction of the disease.

[76] A recent development is the decision of the Court of Appeal in *Holtby v Brigham & Cowan (Hull Ltd)* [2000] 3 All ER 421 at 428-9, where the Court of Appeal applied the reasoning in *McGhee* to a case involving serial causation; the plaintiff had been exposed to asbestos by two or more persons. The court affirmed the requirement of *McGhee* that the plaintiff must show that the defendant's conduct materially contributed to the plaintiff's injury. However, it found the defendant liable only to the extent of that injury.

retinal deficiency and the oxygen deprivation but as an isolated datum it never rose above the level of observational potential.

In the United States, a series of cases has reversed the usual burden of proof in cases where difficulty has presented in proving which manufacturer's product was used. The result has been that defendant manufacturers have had to show on the balance of probabilities that the product used was not that of the manufacturer. Where proof is lacking, damages have been apportioned on the basis of the market share of the particular product. The approach was pioneered in a series of cases involving Diethylstilbestrol (DES), an oestrogen hormone,[77] which was discovered to cause vaginal and cervical cancerous growths in daughters between ten and 20 years after their mothers took the drug to prevent miscarriages.[78]

By contrast, while the Australian position on the issue remains somewhat unclear, the position for the moment is that the law is much more advantageous for plaintiffs and assists them when they encounter the logistical problem of proving on the balance of probabilities that it was the departure from due standards by the defendant that was responsible for their injuries.

The Australian law on the subject is best exemplified by the High Court decision in *Chappel v Hart*,[79] in which a series of Australian authorities on the subject from the 1990s were applied.[80] Justice Kirby held that once a plaintiff demonstrates that a breach of duty has occurred which is closely followed by damage, a prima facie causal connection is established and that it is then for the defendant to show that the plaintiff should not recover damages. Generally, such an attempt to gainsay the *prima facie* nexus will be via expert evidence.[81]

Similarly, an important aspect of the decision of Gaudron J in *Chappel v Hart* was that once a physical injury has occurred to a patient, breach of a duty, such as the duty to warn of a risk, is "treated as materially causing or contributing to that injury unless there is 'sufficient reason to the

---

[77]   See *Sindell v Abbott Laboratories*, 607 P 2d 924 (1980); *Hymonowtitz v Eli Lilly*, 541 NYS 2d 941 (CA 1989); see also R Goldberg, *Causation and Risk in the Law of Torts*, Hart Publishing, Oxford, 1999, at p11.

[78]   For the contrary approach, see *Zafft v Eli Lilly & Co*, 676 SW 2d 241 (Mo 1984); *Mulcahy v Eli Lilly & Co*, 386 NW 2d 67 (Iowa 1986).

[79]   (1998) 195 CLR 232.

[80]   *Sutherland Shire Council v Heyman* (1985) 157 CLR 424 at 487 per Brennan J; *Bennett v Minister of Community Welfare* (1992) 176 CLR 408 at 422 per Gaudron J.

[81]   Compare *H v The Royal Alexandra Hospital for Children* [1990] Med LR 297.

contrary'".[82] She regarded inevitability of injury, whether or not the negligence occurred, and randomness of injury, to which the plaintiff consented, as potential examples of "sufficient reason". Justice Gummow, along similar lines, held that in the absence of evidence that a breach of duty had no effect or that the injury that followed would have occurred in spite of the absence of the breach of duty, the breach of duty should be taken to have caused the injury.[83]

Justices Kirby, Gaudron and Gummow therefore appear to contemplate a burden shifting substantively to the defendant to disprove causation of injury, upon the proof on the balance of probabilities of preceding negligence. Justice McHugh, however, did not go so far, only finding that an evidentiary burden shifted to the defendant. He held that although the onus of proving breach of the applicable standard of care, such as to provide appropriate information about risks and side-effects of a procedure, remains with the plaintiff:

> Once the plaintiff proves that the defendant breached a duty to warn of a risk and that the risk eventuated and caused harm to the plaintiff, the plaintiff has made out a prima facie case of causal connection. An evidentiary onus then rests on the defendant to point to other evidence suggesting that no causal connection exists. Examples of such evidence are: evidence which indicates that the plaintiff would not have acted on the warning because of lack of choice or personal inclination; evidence that no alternative course of action would have eliminated or reduced the risk of injury. Once the defendant points to such evidence, the onus lies on the plaintiff to prove that in all the circumstances a causal connection existed between the failure to warn and the injury suffered by the plaintiff.[84]

Thus, from McHugh J's perspective, all that occurs upon the establishment of both breach of a duty and subsequent injury is the transfer of an evidentiary onus, the plaintiff being deemed to have made out a prima facie case for connection. Justice Gummow, subsequently, in *Rosenberg v Percival*[85] specifically adopted McHugh J's analysis in *Chappel v Hart*.

---

[82]   Ibid, citing as authority *Sutherland Shire Council v Heyman* (1985) 157 CLR 424 at 487 per Brennan J; *Bennett v Minister of Community Welfare* (1992) 176 CLR 408 at 422 per Gaudron J.

[83]   *Chappel v Hart*, at [68].

[84]   Ibid, at 527.

[85]   [2001] HCA at [89].

In Mrs Hart's case, in the absence of evidence that the breach of duty to warn properly had no effect on her decision to submit to the Dohlman's Pouch procedure, or that the injury would have occurred even had the warning been given, the breach of duty was found by Gummow J to have caused the injury.[86] Justice Kirby[87] adopted the same approach, as did Gaudron J.

The issue constitutes a vital dynamic in assessing the balance between the parties in personal injuries litigation. As soon as a plaintiff can show a breach of the duty to advise of risks, then under one analysis the burden shifts affirmatively to the defendant to adduce evidence. If no adequate evidence is adduced by the defendant, then the plaintiff succeeds. Alternatively, under the analysis of McHugh J, as now accepted by Gummow J, the evidentiary burden shifts to the defendant but the plaintiff retains the overall burden of proving that the injuries ensuing after the operative procedure are to be attributed to the failure to warn.[88]

The claimed impact of non-provision of information

Different approaches have been adopted internationally to evaluate the protestation by plaintiffs that they would have made a different decision about a medical procedure had they been properly informed of its risks. Again, such evidence has the potential to have a significant impact upon the decision-maker's determination of whether there is a causative relationship between failure to advise of risks and the subsequent adverse outcome sustained by plaintiffs. In some cases though there may be independent evidence that the giving of the warning would have made no difference.[89]

---

86 *Chappel v Hart*, at [68] citing *Bennett v Minister of Community Welfare* (1992) 176 CLR 408 at 420-1.

87 *Chappel v Hart*, at [32]-[34]; *Rosenberg*, at [88].

88 For defendant concern about the impact of the shift in burden, see J Lavery, "*Chappel v Hart*: The High Court's Lost Chance" (1998) 7(3) *Australian Health Law Bulletin* 25 at 29.

89 In the context of Canadian law, the decision of Linden J in *Davidson v Connaught Laboratories* (1980) 14 CCLT 251 is an example. It was held that the warnings from a pharmaceutical company in relation to a rabies vaccine were unsatisfactory but that the role of the doctors in the case showed that even if there had been a proper warning it would have made no difference to the ultimate outcome as the doctors did not discuss neurological side-effects with their patients for fear that they would decline necessary treatment; in other words a proper warning would have been mediated by medical practice and would not have resulted in the patient failing to be exposed to the vaccine.

In Canada and the United States the test is objective, focusing upon what a "reasonable" or "prudent" patient would have done in the circumstances of the plaintiff.[90] What the individual plaintiff says that they would have done is of little relevance. In England, where the test is subjective,[91] the difficulties of evaluating the weight to be given to a plaintiff's assertions from the statement of claim and the witness box have been specifically acknowledged. Justice Hutchison in *Smith v Barking, Havering and Brentwood* recognised too the artificiality of the question posed in the forum of the courtroom:

> Accordingly, it would, in my judgment, be right in the ordinary case to give particular weight to the objective assessment. If everything points to the fact that a reasonable plaintiff, properly informed, would have assented to the operation, the assertion from the witness box, made after the adverse outcome is known, in a wholly artificial situation and in the knowledge that the outcome of the case depends upon that assertion being maintained, does not carry great weight unless there are extraneous or additional factors to substantiate it. By extraneous or additional factors I mean, and I am not doing more than giving examples, religious or some other firmly-held convictions; particular social or domestic considerations justifying a decision not in accordance with what, objectively, seems the right one; assertions in the immediate aftermath of the operation made in a context other than that of a possible claim for damages; in other words, some particular factor which suggests that the plaintiff had grounds for not doing what a reasonable person in her situation might be expected to have done.[92]

The approach in Australia is subjective.[93] The most detailed analysis of the tools by which the standard plaintiff's assertion of causation in a failure to warn case should be accepted by a trier of fact, namely the contention that had the plaintiff been properly warned of the risks of a procedure, they would not have consented to it, is the decision of the High Court in *Rosenberg v Percival*.[94] In that case the plaintiff was a nurse with doctoral qualifications. She submitted to an osteotomy, but without having been

[90]   *Arndt v Smith* [1997] 2 SCR 539; *Reibl v Hughes* [1980] 2 SCR 880 at 898-9; *Canterbury v Spence*, 464 F 2d 772 at 791 (1972).

[91]   *Chatterton v Gerson* [1981] QB 432 at 445.

[92]   (1994) 5 Med LR 285 at 289.

[93]   *Rogers v Whitaker* (1992) 175 CLR 479 at 490; *Chappel v Hart* (1998) 195 CLR 232 at 246 [32], 272 [93]; *Rosenberg v Percival* [2001] HCA 18.

[94]   *Rosenberg v Percival* [2001] HCA 18; see further I Freckelton, "Revisiting the Duty to Warn: the High Court's decision in *Rosenberg v Percival*" (2001) 9 *Journal of Law and Medicine* 5.

warned of a remote chance that temporo-mandibular symptoms, if already existing could be worsened, or even caused, temporarily, by the procedure. Recalled in additional examination-in-chief, and then cross-examined about her assertion, she held firmly to the proposition that had she been properly warned, she would not have agreed to the procedure, instead seeking alleviation of her mal-occlusion by other means.

The trial judge did not accept the evidence of the plaintiff and rejected her as a credible witness. Much of the High Court's decision was devoted to analysis of the circumstances in which it is proper for an appellate court to overturn a trial judge's analysis of credibility, the appellate court lacking the same opportunity as the trial court to observe witnesses and thereby to form impressions of them. The High Court ultimately reinstated the trial judge's rejection of the evidence of the plaintiff. However, in so doing, a number of judgments discussed the circumstances in which this crucial aspect of proof of causation can be satisfied.

The court affirmed its earlier ruling that the test is subjective, and followed the English approach on the subject, finding that the question to be asked is whether the particular plaintiff would have proceeded with the procedure had she or he been warned of material facts about the procedure.[95] However, McHugh and Kirby JJ emphasised that a trier of fact is not bound to accept uncritically protestations by plaintiffs about the hypothetical question of whether they would have behaved differently in respect of the proposed procedure if properly informed about its risks. Justice McHugh held that in a case where there is no direct evidence as to what the plaintiff would have done, an inference could be drawn from the objective facts that the plaintiff would not have undergone the procedure. In what he termed "exceptional cases", he found too that although a plaintiff's testimony may be rejected as lacking credibility, an inference could still be drawn "from the objective facts" that the plaintiff would not have submitted to the procedure: "That inference would ordinarily be based not only on the objective facts but also on the tribunal's assessment of the general character and personality of the patient."[96]

Justice McHugh found that if a plaintiff in a failure to warn case is believed in relation to their protestation that they would not have proceeded if properly warned, they will succeed even though the objective facts may point the other way. However, if the evidence of the plaintiff is rejected, he or she "carries the heavy evidentiary burden of persuading the court to

---

[95] *Watt or Thomas v Thomas* [1947] AC 484 at 488; see also *Paterson v Paterson* (1953) 89 CLR 212 at 224.

[96] *Rosenberg v Percival* [2001] HCA 18 at [25].

make a favourable finding on the causation issue solely by reference to the objective facts and probabilities."[97] He held that the critical fact is whether the patient would have taken action – refusing to have the operation – that would have avoided the harm suffered. But he observed that that fact can only be determined by making an "anterior finding" as to what the patient would have decided to do, if given the relevant warning:

> It is not possible to find what the patient would have done without deciding, expressly or by necessary implication, what decision the patient would have made, if the proper warning had been given. If the court finds that the patient would have decided not to have the operation, it concludes that he or she would not have had the operation. What the patient would have decided and what the patient would have done are hypothetical questions. But one relates to a hypothetical mental state and the other to a hypothetical course of action. The answer concerning the hypothetical mental state provides the answer to the hypothetical course of action. The onus is on the patient to prove that he or she would have decided not to have the operation if given a warning of the risk of harm. That means that the patient must prove what he or she would have decided to do. When the direct testimony of that person on the causation issue has been rejected, it is unlikely, as a matter of fact, that the patient will succeed on that issue unless the objective evidence in favour of the patient is very strong.[98]

Justice Gummow, examining the same question, noted that the credibility of a plaintiff's contention as to what he or she would have done if properly apprised of the risks of a procedure will both be hypothetical and will be "affected, no matter how honest he is, by his own particular experience."[99] Justice Kirby expressed a similar view, finding that courts could be trusted to reject self-interested assertions, lacking in credibility, but acknowledged the "practical problems" of the exercise, and recognised the practicalities of the scenario:

> Allowing that the patient concerned is sufficiently disappointed with the outcome of some healthcare procedure that he or she has ventured upon expensive, time-consuming and stressful litigation to obtain redress, it is

---

[97] Ibid, at [44].

[98] Ibid, at [45].

[99] Citing *Gover v State of South Australia and Perriam* (1985) 39 SASR 543 at 566 per Cox J; see also *Ellis v Wallsend District Hospital* (1989) 17 NSWLR 553 at 559-60, 581.

scarcely conceivable that such a patient would destroy the case by equivocating in evidence over such a matter.[100]

The result of the various judicial analyses in *Rosenberg v Percival* is that the subjective test remains ascendant in Australia, as in England, but that courts will be guided consistently, not so much by what can be expected to be self-serving assertions by plaintiffs that if they had been properly advised they would have behaved differently, but by what medical evidence establishes were the real options for plaintiffs at the time that they underwent the procedure. If expert evidence establishes that a particular plaintiff had little option but to submit to the procedure, the chain of causation flowing from the negligent non-disclosure is likely to be regarded as broken. The uncertain scenarios will be where plaintiffs maintain that even at a risk to themselves they would have delayed the procedure or, perhaps, sought to have it performed by another professional who may have run a lower risk of the complication of which they were not advised by reason of the other professional's skill and competence. Much will depend on the decision-maker's assessment of whether such a delay or a procedure undertaken by different hands would have made any difference to the outcome for the patient and therefore whether the adverse sequelae in fact experienced were attributable to the negligent non-disclosure.

Evaluation of the Causation of Psychiatric Injuries

One of the most difficult issues faced by plaintiffs in psychiatric injury cases lies in proving that a single tortious act caused or at least materially contributed to the current state of a plaintiff's psychiatric condition. Frequently, plaintiffs in sexual assault claims, for instance, have been reared in circumstances of familial dysfunction. They may have been the victims of childhood sexual or physical abuse. In their teenage years they may have exhibited signs of a conduct disorder, incorporating self-harming behaviours, such as self-mutilation, substance abuse, and precocious sexual activity, or impaired learning performance and difficulties with authorities, such as law enforcement personnel. Whether or not their allegation is that they were sexually assaulted during their childhood or adult years, attribution of causation from a trigger to their adult psychiatric and psychological condition becomes extremely problematic, to the point often of bordering on the arbitrary and the capricious.

---

[100] *Rosenberg v Percival* [2001] HCA 18 at [155].

Again, the threefold typology can offer conceptual assistance. The mere existence of a wrongful behaviour by a defendant and a subsequent psychiatric condition does not take matters beyond the "observational level". From a scientific perspective, more is necessary. Unfortunately, the research necessary to establish the connections at the generalisation level has not yet been performed.[101]

Additional aspects of difficulty which regularly present to fact-finders are when a plaintiff maintains that he or she was sexually or physically assaulted over an extensive period of time but is only able to pinpoint a modest number of specific incidents with sufficient particularity for them to be properly alleged in a statement of claim. Another common problem is where incidents comparable to those the subject of the litigation occurred prior to or subsequent to those alleged in the litigation. The question arises of the extent to which, therefore, there is a pre-existing condition, prodromal condition or a subsequent condition which complicates assessment of the extent to which the tortious incident is responsible for the plaintiff's condition as now identifiable.

A plaintiff is entitled to be compensated for the injury caused to them by a tortious act. The "talem qualem rule" provides that a defendant is liable to compensate a plaintiff even though the defendant's wrongful conduct has caused harm of an extent which they could not have foreseen. So long as the defendant could reasonably have foreseen that his or her conduct would be likely to cause some damage to a victim, the defendant is liable to compensate the victim, taking the victim as they are at the time of the tortious action inflicting injury.[102]

Where the action of a tortfeasor renders symptomatic a latent or degenerative condition that was previously asymptomatic, or aggravates a previously symptomatic condition, the tortfeasor will be held liable for that condition, but the fact that the condition was present and would in due course have become symptomatic must be taken into account. Thus, in *Wilson v Peisly*[103] Barwick CJ held that:

---

[101] See the aspiration of the courts in the "child sexual abuse accommodation syndrome" cases for a clear correlation between childhood sexual abuse and later behavioural "symptoms": *R v B* [1987] 1 NZLR 362 at 368; *R v Accused* [1989] 1 NZLR 714; *Ingles v The Queen*, unreported, Tasmanian Court of Criminal Appeal, 4 May 1993; *R v C* (1993) 60 SASR 467; *J v The Queen* (1994) 75 A Crim R 522; *F v The Queen* (1995) 83 A Crim R 502.

[102] See *Tame v Morgan* [2000] NSWCA 121; *Beavis v Apthorpe* (1962) 80 WN (NSW) 852 at 857; *Bourhill v Young* [1943] AC 92.

[103] (1975) 7 ALR 571 at 575.

The trauma of the accident for which the appellant was responsible no doubt made a present reality of that which was ever a real possibility. Thus, whilst the appellant must pay for bringing out that condition, what he must pay must, in my opinion, justly reflect the fact that that condition was not merely latent in the respondent but that events, not of an unusual or unlikely kind, could and might in the ordinary course of life have evoked that condition had not the appellant's negligence intervened.

It is thus necessary in Australia to assess the damages in respect of the bringing on of a latent disorder by considering its onset following the accident compared with its hypothetical onset had the accident not occurred, applying the principles set down by Deane, Gaudron and McHugh JJ in *Malec v JC Hutton Pty Ltd*[104] and discounting the award of damages to take account of the probability of onset in any event[105] (see below).

Where the plaintiff suffered from a pre-existing anxiety, depressive or other psychiatric condition, the pecuniary entitlement of the successful plaintiff is calculated by reference to the extent to which the tortious act exacerbated their previous condition. If the plaintiff's life circumstances simply rendered them vulnerable to a particularly adverse response to the tortious act, that is unfortunate for the tortfeasor – the tortfeasor must take his or her victims as they come, sometimes unusually resilient, sometimes with an egg-shell psyche. However, such an articulation of conventional legal principle can be beguiling. At the practical level of proof, the assessment of the distinction between pre-existing vulnerability and pre-existing illness can be a fine one. It is at its most difficult, as indicated above, where it is contended by the defendant that the plaintiff was previously prodromal or would have developed their subsequent condition, regardless of the commission of the tort by the tortfeasor.

A typical case involving complexity of causes occurred in the Victorian criminal injuries compensation case of *Martin v Crimes Compensation Tribunal*.[106] The applicant for compensation had lived for some time in an abusive relationship with a man who was an amphetamine addict, subject to worsening paranoias and to considerable lability of mood. He had threatened a murder-suicide on a number of occasions. One night he returned to the home from which he had been excluded by his de facto wife, was heavily intoxicated, mostly by amphetamines, and was hallucinatory and delusional. He insisted on staying with his children for

---

[104] (1990) 169 CLR 638 at 642-3.
[105] See eg *Thompson v Evanoss* [2000] ACTSC 73.
[106] (1995) 8 VAR 39; (1997) 91 A Crim R 301.

the night. When his de facto wife arose in the morning, after only a very short period of sleep, she found him acting eerily and surrounded by weapons with their children within arms' reach. She panicked and ran for help, fearing all the while that he would plunge one of the weapons into her back. As it turned out, he neither did her nor their children any physical harm. It was for the trauma arising from this incident for which she applied for compensation. But he had been violent toward his wife on many occasions previously and some months later than the incident the subject of the application again persuaded her that he had turned over a new leaf. He returned temporarily to cohabit with the applicant before becoming violent again and being excluded from the family home once more. A particularly difficult issue of proof arose in the context of evaluating the extent to which the applicant's psychiatric symptoms were attributable to one incident which, while it had particularly frightening and memorable characteristics, was just one in a substantial sequence of acts of violence perpetrated against the plaintiff. The difficulty would have been even more pronounced had the plaintiff been assaulted by a number of persons other than the defendant. It is not rare for people to become involved in serial violent relationships. This is not a far-fetched scenario.

Much devolved in *Martin v Crimes Compensation Tribunal*, and devolves in other cases, to the ability of the experts called for the applicant/plaintiff to identify the significance in terms of the victim's mental health history of the incident the subject of the litigation. The task can be an artificial one, but decision-makers are obliged to have regard to the actual case before them, namely the impact of the particular incident, only after that assessment evaluating where the incident ranks, within the context of other potential contributions to the victim's current mental health. On occasions, this can involve evaluating whether a particular incident caused a condition such as post-traumatic stress disorder and even whether a plaintiff can legitimately be diagnosed as having more than one post-traumatic stress disorder at the one time, arising from more than one traumatic incident occurring at different times in their presence.

Proof of Psychiatric Injury

A practical response within the litigation context has been a propensity for psychiatric injury claims during the past decade to assert a post-traumatic stress disorder ("PTSD"), rather than a depression, an anxiety disorder or an adjustment disorder, to have been caused by the tort of the tortfeasor. The forensic advantage of a PTSD diagnosis is that it postulates as one of its prerequisites that the psychiatric condition of the victim has been caused by the event (or tort) which is the subject of the re-experiencing phenomena. Thus, in short, if the person has a PTSD which is referable to a tortious event, it can readily be claimed that the condition has been caused by the event. This presumptive nexus, inherent within the indicia of PTSD, makes it the single most attractive psychiatric disorder within DSM-IV-TR and ICD-10 from the perspective of plaintiffs.

However, something of a backlash may be seen to what has been described as the litigation epidemic of PTSD during the 1990s. Controversies rage about the extent to which diagnosis of PTSD has been excessive and of poor quality, with suggestions from a number of eminent quarters that PTSD too often is nomogenic.[107] It has been argued in many cases and by a number of academic writers and clinicians that the diagnosis is unreliable by reason of its heavy reliance upon self-report of symptomatology by plaintiffs.

What can be discerned in PTSD cases in a number of countries is an escalating insistence by the courts that the criteria for the disorder, as defined by DSM-IV-TR and ICD-10, be rigorously proved.[108] Without such proof, nexus between the tort and the subsequent symptomatology becomes problematic from a scientific point of view, using the threefold typology, and also from a legal point of view. This has resulted in an escalation in the incidence of informed and probing cross-examination of plaintiffs and the expert witnesses commissioned on their behalf with a focus upon whether the self-report of symptoms by plaintiffs is accurate and has been accepted uncritically by forensic assessors, be they psychiatrists or psychologists.

Given the importance of PTSD as a means of proving both psychiatric injury and causation of adverse mental health symptomatology, it is inevitable that the demands for scientific rigour in diagnosing the condition will continue to grow both in the clinical and forensic domains. It is likely that greater scrutiny will be given to clinical assessments unsupported by psychometric and other testing in recognition that in such circumstances

---

[107] See eg AA Stone, "Post-Traumatic Stress Disorder and the Law: Critical Review of the New Frontier" (1993) 21(1) *Bulletin of the American Academy of Psychiatry and Law* 23; AC McFarlane, "Post-Traumatic Stress Disorder" in I Freckelton & H Selby (eds), *Expert Evidence*, 5 vol looseleaf service & CD Rom, Law Book Co, Sydney, 1993-...; LA Neal, "The Pitfalls of Making a Categorical Diagnosis of Post-Traumatic Stress Disorder in Personal Injury Litigation" (1994) 34 *Medicine, Science and the Law* 117; J Ellard, "The Epidemic of Post-Traumatic Stress Disorder: A Passing Phase" (1997) 166 *Medical Journal of Australia* 84.

[108] For a fuller analysis of this issue see I Freckelton, "Trauma Evidence" in I Freckelton & H Selby (eds), *Expert Evidence*, 5 vol looseleaf service & CD Rom, Law Book Co, Sydney, 1993-...; I Freckelton, *Criminal Injuries Compensation: Law, Practice and Policy*, Law Book Co, Sydney, 2001, Chapter 13.

the nexus required within the criteria for the disorder will not have been established adequately. The stakes for defendants will provide the incentive for consistent and demanding scrutiny in the witness box of the soundness of expert diagnoses of PTSD.

Discounting of Damages for Injury where Injury Likely to Have Ensued Anyway

A particularly difficult issue of proof relates to the calculation of damages where the injury attributed by the plaintiff in civil litigation may have ensued through other causes, not the fault of the defendant, had the defendant not been tortiously responsible for the injury being sustained.

For Australia, the key decision is that of the High Court in *Malec v JC Hutton*[109] where the defendant employed the plaintiff as a labourer in a meat works between 1972 and 1980. In 1977 the plaintiff was diagnosed as suffering from brucellosis, a disease acquired from animals. A possible sequela of brucellosis is the development of a depressive illness; another is the development of an organic condition which results in a degenerative condition in the spine. The trial judge found that since at least 1982 the plaintiff had suffered from symptoms in his cervical and lumbar spine but was not satisfied that the condition was a consequence of the brucellosis. In other words, the connection between the exposure and the injury was weak, existing at "experimental level" but unable to satisfy the requirements of the "generalisation level".

He concluded that a neurotic illness which was diagnosed in 1979 was precipitated by the brucellosis but found that it was at least as probable as not that the neurotic condition from which the plaintiff suffered at the time of trial was unrelated to the brucellosis. What is involved in this context is therefore a conditional scenario where the existence of the neurosis could have been related to the physical illness but could also have had another aetiology. From a scientific perspective, unless the evidence clearly demands rejection of the null hypothesis ("the neurotic illness would have developed even in the absence of the exposure"), the alternative hypothesis cannot be considered. In this case, the null hypothesis could not be rejected.

This set of findings about causation led to an important analysis by the High Court of Australia. The court identified the kinds of proof necessary for the recovery of damages for injuries existing by the time of the trial. It

---

[109]   (1990) 169 CLR 638 at 642-3.

held that since the plaintiff proved that, at the date of the trial, as the result of the defendant's negligence, he suffered from a psychiatric condition which rendered him unemployable, subject to an allowance for the ordinary vicissitudes of life, the plaintiff was prima facie entitled to be compensated for the near certainty that, as the result of the defendant's negligence, he would suffer from his psychiatric condition and be unemployable for the rest of his life. This meant that Mr Malec, who was 49 at the time of trial, had to be compensated for his loss of earning capacity.

The majority of the court held that the "all or nothing" approach to damages for past and present events applied in the context of evaluation of eligibility for future damages. This meant that if a court determines on the balance of probabilities that an injury occurred and was attributable at least to the level of a 51 per cent probability, that is treated as certain, while if it concludes on the balance of probabilities that something may not have occurred, namely not being satisfied to the 50 per cent level, it is concluded as certain that it has not occurred. In this instance the plaintiff could show on the balance of probabilities that he did contract brucellosis as a result of the defendant's negligence. This then was treated as a certainty. The plaintiff further established on the balance of probabilities that he had contracted a psychiatric illness which was a medical sequela of brucellosis, and that the psychiatric condition had rendered him unemployable. Thus, the High Court was prepared to treat these two past events and a future prediction of unemployability stemming from them as a certainty, and to assess his damages accordingly.

By contrast, it found that the plaintiff was unable to show on the balance of probabilities that his painful cervical and lumbar spine were attributable to brucellosis. This meant under the "all or nothing" rule that he should not receive any compensation for it.

These were past and present events. The employer argued that, on the balance of probabilities it was likely that the plaintiff's back condition would have rendered him unemployable at the age of 44 even if he had not contracted brucellosis. It contended that there was a chance that as a result of the spinal condition and consequent unemployability, the plaintiff would have developed a psychiatric condition similar to that which was accepted by the court to have occurred as a result of brucellosis. This meant, according to the employer, that damages for the pain and suffering occasioned by the psychiatric condition which he developed as a result of brucellosis should be awarded only for the period 1979-1982, and that no award should be made for care and attention provided by his wife because the plaintiff had a similar psychiatric condition consequent upon a condition for which the employer should not be held responsible and which would have necessitated similar attention and care.

The High Court of Australia rejected the employer's arguments on the basis that the employer was inviting the court to take account of hypothetical events the proof of which is unattainable. It accepted that questions as to the future or hypothetical effect of a physical injury or degeneration are not commonly susceptible of scientific demonstration or proof. It found that it was proper to have resort to the probabilities of such events occurring, accepting that the probabilities may be very high or very low. Thus, courts must assess the degree of probability that an event would have occurred, or might occur. On that basis they should adjust their award of damages to reflect that degree of probability. These hypothetical or future events can be established as possibilities. When so established, it found that a court can take them into account when assessing damages, but only in terms of adjusting (either by an increase or a decrease) the amount of damages which would otherwise have been awarded.

For the plaintiff, this meant that he was entitled to be compensated for the near certainty that he had contracted a psychiatric condition as a result of which he would thenceforth be unemployable. The court accepted that there was a chance that the plaintiff's back condition, for which the defendant was not responsible, would have rendered him unemployable. It was appropriate for his damages for his future loss of earning capacity to be reduced on this basis. There was also a chance that although his back condition would have made him unemployable, he would have gone through life without suffering a neurotic condition of the kind with which he presented. It found that in determining the chance that unemployability as the result of the back condition would have precipitated a similar neurotic condition brought into play two factors:

- the degree of probability that he would have become unemployable in any event as the result of his back condition; and
- the degree of probability that the unemployability as a result of the back condition would have caused a neurotic condition.

The court found that it was appropriate to multiply these two possibilities. If, for example, there was a 75 per cent probability of his becoming unemployable by reason of his back condition even if he had not contracted brucellosis and a 75 per cent chance that that unemployability would have caused a similar neurotic condition, there was only a 56.25 per cent chance (75 per cent x 75 per cent) that, if he had not contracted brucellosis, he would have developed a similar condition.[110]

---

[110] Ibid.

In short, therefore, it found that the plaintiff was entitled to be compensated for pain and suffering on the basis that his neurotic condition was the direct result of the defendant's negligence. However, it accepted that the damages should be reduced to take account of the chance that factors unconnected with the defendant's negligence might have brought about the onset of a similar condition. This analysis also entailed that the plaintiff was entitled to be compensated for the care and attention provided by his wife, an amount to be reduced to take account of the chance that factors unconnected with the defendant's negligence would have necessitated similar care and attention.

Thus, in the wake of *Malec v JC Hutton* two different tests exist for determination of causation. The test in relation to the nexus between matters in the past, such as a negligent act or omission, and the current condition of a plaintiff must be proved on the balance of probabilities, whereupon it transmogrifies into a certainty in the "all or nothing" approach for calculating damages. This is in spite of the fact that it is common for there to be multiple logistical difficulties lying in the way of the plaintiff proving the nexus or the degree of nexus between his or her current health condition and a previous negligent act or omission. By contrast, even remote percentile chances are taken into account when the focus is turned toward the future. This means differing problems for the marshalling and presentation of expert evidence and a potentially highly confusing situation for decision-makers, especially jurors, who at the one time are instructed to entertain sophisticated estimates of chance by statisticians and epidemiologists and at another are told that if proof falls even marginally short of 50 per cent causation is not established and recovery is not permitted.

Res Ipsa Loquitur

In some limited circumstances the law has accepted that strict proof is not required that an accident was caused by a breach of a duty of care and that the defendant was the person responsible. In Australia a plaintiff can rely on the notion that the circumstances speak for themselves, that *res ipsa loquitur,* provided that the trier of fact is persuaded that:

- there is an "absence of explanation" of the occurrence that caused the injury;
- the occurrence was of such a kind that it does not ordinarily occur without negligence; and

- the instrument or agency that caused the injury was under the control of the defendant.[111]

Prima facie the conduct of the defendant must have been of a kind that does not ordinarily happen without negligence and it must be clear that it was the defendant who was responsible.[112] The principal function of the doctrine of *res ipsa loquitur* is to absolve the plaintiff of the need to prove matters which are clear without proof and where the facts may not be within the plaintiff's knowledge or easy means of proof. It functions as a presumption of negligence,[113] described by Field[114] as "almost impossible to define, since it is merely the operation of a natural principle which ensures that when one party produces a cogent case which *prima facie* points the finger of blame at the other, then that other party would be well advised to adduce evidence which dispels the presumption of culpability thereby created."[115]

In the early case of *Byrne v Boadle*[116] Pollock CB spoke of the doctrine in terms of a "presumption".[117] It appears that the predominant view in

---

[111] *Schellenberg v Tunnel Holdings Pty Ltd* [2000] HCA 18 at [25]. In *Mummery v Irvings Pty Ltd* (1956) 96 CLR 99 at 116 Dixon CJ, Webb, Fullagar and Taylor JJ emphasised that the requirement that the accident "must be such as in the ordinary course of things does not happen if those who have the management use proper care is of vital importance and fully explains why in such circumstances *res ipsa loquitur.*"

[112] Thus for instance in the leading Scottish authority on the subject, *Devine v Colvilles Ltd* (1969) SLT 154 a workman who had leapt from a platform as a result of a nearby violent explosion, it was found that it was self-evident that an explosion of such violence that causes fear of imminent danger to workers does not occur in the ordinary course of things in a steel works if those who have responsibility for management use proper care.

[113] Although technically to describe it as a presumption is not helpful, a better approach being to describe it as an inference of negligence or even as a subset of circumstantial evidence: see JW Strong, *McCormick on Evidence*, West Publishing Co, St Paul, 1992; WL Prosser, *Handbook of the Law of Torts*, 4th edn, West Publishing Co, St Paul, 1971.

[114] D Field, *The Law of Evidence of Scotland*, W Green & Son, Edinburgh, 1988, at p83.

[115] See also WL Morrison, "The Quantum of Proof in Relation to Motions for Non-Suit and Verdicts by Direction" in HH Glass (ed), *Seminars on Evidence,* Law Book Co, Sydney, 1970.

[116] (1863) 2 H & C 722; 159 ER 299.

[117] Two years later in *Scott v London and St Katherine Docks Co* (1865) 3 H & C 596 at 601; 159 ER 665 at 667 Erle CJ enunciated the basis of the *res ipsa loquitur* doctrine in terms that have subsequently been consistently applied in Australia, New Zealand and England: "There must be reasonable evidence of negligence. But where the thing is shown to be under the management of the defendant or his servants, and the accident is such as in the ordinary course of things does not happen if those who have the management use proper care, it affords reasonable evidence, in the absence of explanation by the defendants, that the accident arose from want of care." See later

Australia[118] and New Zealand,[119] as well as formerly in Canada,[120] although not in England,[121] is that the doctrine raises no more than a permissive presumption, entitling an inference about a fact in issue from circumstantial evidence. This means that the burden of proving the case remains with the plaintiff[122] – if an accident is wholly unexplained and there are two hypotheses about its cause, one consistent with the negligence of the defendant, the other inconsistent with it, the doctrine will not apply, meaning that the plaintiff will not have discharged the burden of proof.[123] The contrast with the situation applying to the inferences that should be drawn after a breach of duty is proved and an injury follows under the approach of Kirby and Gaudron JJ is apparent and not easily reconciled.

While many difficult issues continue to envelop the circumstances in which technically a *res ipsa loquitur* allegation of tortious impropriety can be made out,[124] expert evidence adduced on the part of the defendant can go a significant way to proving that the maxim should not apply. Such evidence can raise the serious possibility that causation other than tortious conduct by the defendant could have been responsible for the accident which caused injury to the plaintiff. Such evidence will often be counter-intuitive in the sense of raising for consideration possibilities of causation of an accident which would not otherwise readily occur in the mind of the trier of fact. When such matters become apparent, proof depends on "observational level" information – an apparent nexus is illusory because other factors may have been responsible for the outcome.

Moore v R Fox & Sons [1965] 1 QB 596 at 611; *Schellenberg v Tunnel Holdings Pty Ltd* [2000] HCA 18 at [21ff].

[118] See eg *Nominal Defendant v Halbauer* (1967) 117 CLR 448; *GIO v Fredrichberg* (1968) 118 CLR 403.

[119] *Hawke's Bay Motor v Russell* [1972] NZLR 542.

[120] *Temple v Terrace Co* (1966) 57 DLR (2d) 631. More recently, however, the Supreme Court of Canada has repudiated the doctrine in *Fontaine v British Columbia (Official Administrator)* [1998] 1 SCR 424; see further M McInnes, "The Death of *Res Ipsa Loquitur* in Canada" (1998) 114 *Law Quarterly Review* 547.

[121] *Moore v Fox* [1956] 1 QB 596; but see *Lloyde v West Midlands Gas* [1971] 1 WLR 749 at 755; see further PS Atiyah, "*Res Ipsa Loquitur* in England and Australia" (1972) 35 *Modern Law Review* 337.

[122] *Anchor Products Ltd v Hedges* (1966) 115 CLR 493 at 500 per Windeyer J; *Schellenberg v Tunnel Holdings Pty Ltd* [2000] HCA 18 at [72] per Gaudron J.

[123] *Schellenberg v Tunnel Holdings Pty Ltd* [2000] HCA 18 at [98] per Kirby J.

[124] For instance, there is ongoing uncertainty in Australia about whether the maxim is applicable to medical negligence cases: see eg *Elliott v Bickerstaff* [1999] NSWCA 453.

Proving Causation of Injuries and Offending at the Sentencing Hearing

A difficult and important question at the sentencing stage of criminal proceedings relates to proof of causation, and impact, of offending, an issue that has the potential both to improve and to worsen the situation of the accused person. It arises frequently in the context of the offender attempting to point to indirect factors as explaining, albeit not justifying, his or her offending and the prosecution seeking to ensure that the sentencer has an appreciation not just of the bare facts of the offending but the full context of the criminal behaviour, including its impact upon the victim. This will involve the sentencing judge or magistrate taking into account the physical and psychological effects of the crime upon the victim and also factoring into consideration a range of mitigatory facts asserted to detract from the offender's culpability.

Generally, it is the prosecution that seeks to adduce victim impact information in order to apprise the sentencer of the context in which the sentencing exercise is taking place. Often the victim impact statement will highlight sequelae of the crime which demonstrate in an eloquent way how adversely the offence has impacted upon the primary victim and even upon secondary victims, such as the surviving relatives of a homicide victim. Such information has the potential to worsen the disposition imposed by the sentencer.

Because of its ramifications for the disposition, there is an incentive for the accused to dispute the assertions of the victim. Generally the victim impact statement will simply be the expression of sentiment and (subjective) experience by the victim. This is not to downplay its legitimacy, simply to reflect that it is the articulation of the experience of pain and distress by the victim, often its tone depending upon the stage of resolution or accommodation which the victim has reached psychologically to the consequences of what has been done to them by the offender. On occasions, too, the victim impact information is bolstered by evaluation of the victim's condition by expert assessment – frequently by the victim's treaters, sometimes by forensic assessors.

A further consideration also intrudes from time to time upon the information placed before the court at the time of sentencing. In a number of Australian jurisdictions, in particular in New South Wales, Victoria and South Australia, substantial awards of compensation have been made by courts against offenders.[125] It is in the interests of the victim of the crime to

---

[125] See I Freckelton, *Criminal Injuries Compensation: Law, Practice and Policy*, LBC, Sydney, 2001.

have such information placed before courts in order to maximise the award of compensation. Tactically the best time for this information to go before a court is at the time of sentencing – at this stage the defendant is likely to be at his or her most conciliatory, seeking to minimise their sentence.

It can be advantageous for the offender to be seen not to oppose an application for compensation by a victim. It tends to suggest insight into the consequences of the offending and a preparedness to take responsibility for the ramifications of the crime – in short, it suggests a diminished likelihood of recidivism, thereby raising the possibility of a sentence that is not too oriented toward retribution, punishment and individual deterrence. In South Australia, the sentencing legislation even obliges the sentencer to take into account the compensation order for the sentencing disposition to be imposed on the offender.[126] It is likely that unofficially this occurs in other jurisdictions also.[127]

Although it is advantageous for the victim to make an application for compensation against an offender, where the offender has means, and although there can be forensic opportunities for the offender in being seen to acquiesce in such an order, this does not mean that the information thereby placed before a court will always be accurate. In fact, there are considerable reasons why the provision of such information may be exaggerated or embellished – either deliberately or inadvertently. In such circumstances, there can be good reason for the offender to contest the assertions of psychological and somatic harm and to dispute the aetiology of the victim's current condition, contending that the victim suffered a pre-existing condition or that other factors have influenced the seriousness of their current symptomatology.

It is standard sentencing law that, broadly speaking, an offender takes his or her victim as they are.[128] In Australia, it appears reasonably clear that if the victim of criminal violence has suffered particularly adverse consequences, that can constitute an aggravating feature for the purposes of sentencing.[129] However, where the commission of an offence produces an outcome which is totally unforeseen and was unforeseeable by a reasonable person, then the outcome is not regarded as relevant for sentencing purposes, save as evidencing the infliction of some degree of harm to the victim.[130] By contrast, if the victim has been particularly resilient or stoic

---

126 *Criminal Law (Sentencing) Act* 1988 (SA), s53.
127 Arguably, s50 of the *Sentencing Act* 1991 (Vic) enables this to be done to some extent.
128 See eg *R v Webb* [1971] VR 147 at 150-1.
129 See eg *R v Mallinder* (1986) 23 A Crim R 179 at 184-5.
130 See *Agius* (2000) 115 A Crim R 387 at 389, 401; *Feldman v Samuels* [1956] SASR 55 at 57; *Mayne* (1987) 137 LSJS 100 at 101; *Boyd v The Queen* [1975] VR 168 at 172.

and has suffered less than might have been expected by way of negative sequelae, this does not constitute a mitigating factor.[131] However, if an offender was in a position to appreciate the particular vulnerability of the victim, such as that they would be vocationally, educationally or psychologically harmed by the crime, this constitutes an aggravating matter for the purposes of sentencing.

The other side of the coin is that offenders frequently wish to inform the sentencer of personal circumstances, such as abuse previously visited upon them, impaired educational opportunities, dependence upon alcohol or drugs, and a range of life's vicissitudes which might be regarded as detracting from their moral turpitude in having offended. Such information is routinely provided from the bar table but, where it is important, and really has the likelihood of bearing upon the sentence to be imposed, it is unsatisfactory for courts to be dependent upon assertions made from the bar table. Such assertions need to be the subject of evidence and proof in the usual way.

The question that rose for the Australian High Court in *Olbrich v The Queen*[132] was as to whether different standards of proof apply to information proffered by the prosecution to the detriment of the offender, on the one hand, and evidence proffered by the offender to his or her advantage, on the other. It held that there are different standards, the court applying an earlier Victorian Court of Appeal decision on the subject.[133] It determined that where information placed before the sentencing court is deleterious for the offender, it must be proved beyond reasonable doubt. However, where the information is advantageous for the offender, it need only be proved on the balance of probabilities. This has important tactical and practical consequences. It means that while it is strategically incumbent or advantageous for the victim to set before the court their circumstances at the time of sentencing, such matters, need only be proved to the civil standard. However, where information placed before the court is adverse for the accused, it needs to be proved by the prosecution to the criminal standard. An example of such material is evidence that tends to establish a particularly adverse impact of the crime upon the victim, perhaps even in circumstances that were reasonably within the foresight of the offender. Thus, putting such material before the sentencing court, and proving it beyond reasonable doubt is advantageous for the prosecution. Viewed another way, the offender is best positioned to contest such

---

See also *Teremoana* (1990) 49 A Crim R 207 at 208; *Royall* (1991) 172 CLR 378 at 398-9; 412, 451. Compare *Inkson* (1996) 88 A Crim R 334.

[131] See eg *Wiidkey, Boogna and Charles* (1994) 76 A Crim R 302 at 318.

[132] [1999] HCA 54; (1999) 108 A Crim R 464.

[133] *R v Storey* [1998] 1 VR 359.

material at the time of sentencing; if a compensation application is made at the time of the sentencing hearing or shortly afterwards the victim will need to prove the impact only on the balance of probabilities.

The ruling of the High Court stops short of the practice in England where upon a plea of guilty and there being a conflict on the facts, a sentencing judge is regarded as having three options: (1) to empanel a jury to determine the issue; (2) to decide the issue him or herself on the basis of evidence; (3) to hear submissions on the issue but if there are substantial conflicts on the issue, so far as possible to accept the position advanced on behalf of the accused.[134]

The tenor of both the Australian and the English approaches is to facilitate the offender placing before the court information which has the potential to put into context how it was that they came on this occasion to break the criminal law, thereby causing harm or injury to the victim. What would otherwise be a heavy burden in the criminal process for the offender to prove such matters is eased where there are conflicts between the prosecution and the offender, and in Australia where the offender seeks to establish facts that are put as mitigatory. By contrast, where information is sought to be advanced that would aggravate the situation of the offender, the prosecution is put to a high level of proof, thereby in principle enabling the offender to contest such matters effectively. However, the realities of the criminal trial leave the prosecution in a strong position where it is contended that the offending has caused serious sequelae for the victim. First, there is a major disincentive for the offender to be seen to dispute such matters, for fear of being perceived as lacking in empathy and insight for the victim's plight, such a perception on the part of the sentencer making a heavier sentence for the offender more likely. Secondly, the entitlement of the offender to have the victim medically examined to ascertain the reliability and objectivity of the victim impact information placed before the sentencing court by the prosecution is dubious. This means that although the evidentiary rules about burden and standard of proof are relatively benign so far as the offender is concerned, the realities for the offender in relation to disputing the extent and causation of the victim's post-crime injuries are otherwise.

---

[134] *Newton v The Queen* (1982) 77 Cr App R 13; see also *R v Gandy* [1990] Crim LR 346. See Z Cowen & PB Carter, *Essays on the law of Evidence*, Greenwood Press, Westport, 1955, at p242ff about the earlier confusion in relation to standard of proof applied by the English courts in a variety of contexts.

Conclusion

It is apparent that many items of evidence suspected of belonging to a causal relationship in fact reach no higher level than "observations" or "generalisations". It is important for the accuracy of the fact-finding process that these levels not be confused with the "explanation level" where science and medicine would say with confidence that one fact has been a cause or the cause of another. This requires a sophisticated understanding by triers of fact about distinctions and subtleties in areas of endeavour outside the law. Such an understanding can be acquired by effective and sophisticated communication within the body of forensic reports and via oral evidence in the courtroom. However, all too often expert evidence, especially of a numerate form, has fallen short of such standards and has had the potential to lead to misunderstanding and mis-estimation by lay persons such as judges, magistrates and jurors. Not only this; it has fuelled the mistrust and anxiety about expert evidence harboured by both appellate and trial judges.

Proof of causation lies at the very heart of the resolution of most civil and criminal litigation. The identity of the party carrying the burden of proof and the standard of proof needing to be discharged by a litigant establish the ground rules for how the litigation contest is fought and resolved. One of the difficulties that has pervaded the various legal tests applicable to the means by which causation can be proved and disproved is the uncertain formulations enunciated by the law about what actually constitutes causation, as well as the resort in desperation to idealised notions of intuition and common knowledge. Where recourse is had by the courts to such vague formulations as common sense, in rejecting options such as the "but for test", it leaves the role of proof – especially by expert evidence – problematic and uncertain. This is especially so where such evidence is far from determinative but simply forms part of a body of information which is indicative of connectnedness between what is said to be a wrongful act and an adverse outcome.

In Australia, by contrast with most parts of the United States, it is now the law that possibility expert evidence in the civil context, such as epidemiology evidence of a low order, is admissible. However, how decision-makers will actually integrate such evidence into the task of determining whether a teratogen or carcinogen claim is established is much less clear.[135]

---

[135] In relation to matters where potentially confusing statistics are a feature of the evidence, one option is the increased use of court-appointed experts. For a case example of this device, see R Coulam & SE Fienberg, "The Use of Court-Appointed

In the context of evaluating the extent in the civil trial to which the tortfeasor's tortious behaviour has resulted in the current physical and psychological condition of the plaintiff, rather than merely contributing to a condition affected by pre-existing or subsequently caused injuries, or that was latent or prodromal at the time of the commission of the tort, again expert evidence plays a major role. However, the extent to which psychiatrists and psychologists *ex post facto* can accurately arrive at such opinions is open to significant doubt, the task being inherently a forensic, and an arbitrary one, not a role customarily encountered in the clinical context where the focus is upon remediation rather than attribution of contribution to different incidents and events.

When it falls to the defendant to contest the nexus between a tortious act and a subsequent injury, the burden again falls heavily upon expert evidence. In Australia, once a tortious act is established, a presumption appears to exist that an injury manifesting in its aftermath is attributable to the tort. Whether the presumption is substantive or evidentiary is unclear but what can be said is that if the defendant must disprove causation, this is not an easy task in personal injuries litigation or in the context of a medical negligence trial. It is clear that limited weight will henceforth be given to plaintiffs' assertions in "failure to warn cases" that had they been properly warned they would not have submitted to the procedure or would have made different arrangements for the procedure to be undertaken. More weight will be placed upon what options from a medical point of view actually were open to them.

The provision of such informed opinions by specialist witnesses requires dispassionate, evidence-based expert opinion. Generally the theories underlying such evidence will need to be falsifiable, to have been ventilated for peer assessment in appropriate professional literature, to be subject to controlled tests and to be accepted by a reasonable percentage of professionals practising in the area.[136] This is so in the United States federal jurisdictions as a threshold admissibility criterion and as a factor assisting evaluation of the probative value of such evidence in other countries. Evidence complying with such demands is consistent with the

---

Statistical Experts: A Case Study" in MH De Groot, SE Fienberg & JB Kadane (eds), *Statistics and the Law*, John Wiley & Sons, New York, 1986.

[136] See *Daubert v Merrell Dow Pharmaceuticals*, 125 L Ed (2d) 469; 113 S Ct 2786 (1993); *Kumho Tire Co Ltd v Carmichael*, United States Supreme Court, 23 March 1999; see also *R v Johnston* (1992) 69 CCC 395 at 415; *R v Meleragni* (1992) 73 CCC (3d) 348 at 352; *R v Calder*, unreported, High Court of New Zealand, 12 April 1995; *R v Brown*, unreported, High Court of New Zealand, 19 September 1997.

movement toward evidence-based clinical practice in medicine[137] and with rigorous scientific standards generally in respect of causation.

In determining the adequacy of causation evidence about the relationship between the current or future condition or capacity of a plaintiff and an earlier breach of duty by a defendant, the law has created a distinction between the kinds of proof required. As to the future, probabilities falling even well short of likelihood are contemplated. At a practical level, the complexities in such an exercise are significant indeed. For the past, expert evidence must simply be addressed to whether it is more likely than not that the breach of duty caused the current condition. To this extent, at least, the task for the decision-maker, while conceptually difficult to justify, is somewhat more straightforward. The difficulty is that, while it is comforting to think of the past as knowable and definite, frequently in practice exigencies of available evidence render the situation otherwise. The best that a combination of pertinent expert and lay evidence can do is to satisfy a decision-maker to a degree that a correlation that is causative exists. Thus the need for a consistency between the criteria for determining correlations between past and the future, on the one hand, and past/present and the future, on the other. However, it must be conceded that were such an approach to be adopted the pressure would be placed even more squarely upon decision-makers to be enabled to assimilate and effectively deal with the kinds of complex statistical evidence that is presented to them in *Malec v JS Hutton* scenarios.

Similarly, there can be a gap between the technical rules of proof and the reality. An example exists in the sentencing phase of criminal trials. The considerable strategic disincentive and logistical impediments to the offender effectively contesting an assertion by the prosecution about the aetiology and extent of the victim's allegedly criminally caused injuries render it highly problematic for the offender to dispute the contentions of the prosecution. This is the more serious because the expert evidence from the prosecution/victim will tend to be from treaters of the victim and may well be advanced in the anticipation of second-phase litigation relating to entitlement to criminal injuries compensation. If such evidence is to be reliable, much will depend upon individual experts' commitment to objectivity and fair-mindedness of assessment.

Proof of causation therefore is dominated by considerations of likelihood and chance, as well as being dependent upon experts' capacity

---

[137] See WA Silverman, *Where's the Evidence? Controversies in Medicine*, Oxford University Press, Oxford, 1998; S Hamer & G Collinson, *Achieving Evidence-Based Practice*, B Tindall, Edinburgh, 1999; DF Friedland, *Evidence-Based Medicine: A Framework for Clinical Practice*, Appleton & Lange, Stamford, 1998.

to make such notions accessible. As already described, legal tests for causation and its proof remain in a considerable degree of flux and by reason of their ambiguity are difficult of practical exegesis and application. The day-to-day pressure is placed upon expert witnesses and report-writers to address these complex issues and mathematically expressed potentials to produce a forensic outcome. In principle, the hallmarks of expert evidence that will constructively inform decision-makers are scientific rigour, the extent to which it is based upon data and evidence of fact, and the degree to which its reasoning processes are both transparent and falsifiable. However, for as long as the law seeks refuge in unscientific notions such as common sense and intuitive assessment of causation, and for as long as it arbitrarily imposes different tests for matters that are conceptually indistinguishable, proof of causation by expert and lay evidence alike will remain the unsatisfactory handmaiden of such phenomena as the aura of persuasiveness of an individual witness on a given court day. This is a recipe for inconsistency and error in decision-making.

Table of Cases

Board of Management of Royal Perth Hospital v Frost (WA FC, Malcolm CJ, Rowland & Wallwork JJ, 26 February 1997, unreported, BC9700642)

Bonnington Castings Ltd v Wardlaw [1956] AC 613

Bourhill v Young [1943] AC 92

Bourke v MacNeil [2000] NSWCA 144 (NSW CA, 14 June 2000, unreported, BC200003177)

Boyd v The Queen [1975] VR 168

Breen v Williams (1996) 186 CLR 71

Bridge Printery Pty Ltd v Mestre [1999] NSWCA 342 (NSW CA, 5 October 1999, unreported, BC9906401)

Bridgewater v Leahy (1998) 194 CLR 457

Briginshaw v Briginshaw (1938) 60 CLR 336

Brisbane South Regional Health Authority v Taylor (1996) 186 CLR 541

Burnie Port Authority v General Jones Pty Ltd (1994) 179 CLR 520

Bush v Commonwealth 78 Ky 268 (1880)

Byrne v Australian Airlines Ltd (1995) 185 CLR 410

Byrne v Boadle (1863) 2 H & C 722; 159 ER 299

Caltex Oil (Australia) Pty Ltd v The Dredge "Willemstad" (1976) 136 CLR 529

Campbell v The Queen (1981) WAR 286

Candlewood Navigation Corporation Ltd v Mitsui OSK Lines Ltd [1986] AC 1

Canterbury v Spence, 464 F 2d 772 (1972)

Caparo Industries Plc v Dickman [1990] 2 AC 605

Carter v United States, 252 F 2d 608, 617 (DC Cir 1957)

Cartledge v E Jopling & Sons Ltd [1963] AC 758

CES v Superclinics (Australia) Pty Ltd (1995) 38 NSWLR 47

Chamberlain v The Queen No 2 (1984) 153 CLR 521

Chaplin v Hicks [1911] 2 KB 786

Chapman v Hearse (1961) 106 CLR 112

Chappel v Hart (1998) 195 CLR 232

Chatterton v Gerson [1981] QB 432

Chief Commissioner of Police v Hallenstein [1996] 2 VR 1

Clay v A J Crump & Sons Ltd [1964] 1 QB 533

Cole v Whitfield (1988) 165 CLR 360

Commercial Bank of Australia Ltd v Amadio (1983) 151 CLR 447

Commissioner for Transport v Adamcik (1961) 106 CLR 292

Commissioner of Police v Hallenstein [1996] 2 VR 1

Commonwealth ex rel Ivory Weston v John Weston, 193 A 2d 782 (1963)

Commonwealth v Amann Aviation Pty Ltd (1991) 174 CLR 64

Commonwealth v Craig, 783 SW 2d 387 Ky (1990)

Commonwealth v McLean (1996) 41 NSWLR 389

Commonwealth v Zamarripa, 379 Pa Super 20, 549 A 2d 980 (Pa Super Ct 1988)

Compassion in Dying v Washington, 79 F 3d 790 (9th Cir 1996)

Cook v Lewis [1951] 1 SCR 830

Council of the Municipality of Waverley v Bloom (1999) Aust Torts Reps 81-517

Cowan v Kitson Insulations Ltd [1992] PIQR Q19

Craig v East Coast Bays City Council [1986] 1 NZLR 99

R v Cato (1976) 62 Cr App R 41

R v Cheshire (1991) 93 Cr App R 251

R v Cook (1979) 2 A Crim R 151

R v Coroner for Inner North London, ex parte Diesa Koto (1993) 157 JP 857

R v Cox (1992) 12 BMLR 38

R v Doheny and Adams [1997] 1 Cr App R 369

R v Evans and Gardiner (No 2) [1976] VR 523

R v Faber [1976] 2 SCR 9

R v Gandy [1990] Crim LR 346

R v Hallett [1969] SASR 141

R v Halliday (1889) 61 LT 701

R v HM Coroner for Birmingham, ex parte Secretary of State for the Home
    Department (1990) 155 JP 107

R v HM Coroner for Coventry, ex parte Chief Constable of Staffordshire (2000)
    164 JP 665

R v HM Coroner for East Berkshire, ex parte Buckley (1992) 157 JP 425

R v HM Coroner for Exeter & East Devon; ex parte Palmer (unreported, Court of
    Appeal, 10 December 1997)

R v HM Coroner for North Humberside and Scunthorpe; ex parte Jamieson [1995]
    QB 1

R v HM Coroner for Northamptonshire, ex parte Tomkinson [1996] COD 191

R v HM Coroner for Solihull; ex parte Nutt [1993] COD 449

R v HM Coroner for South Yorkshire, ex parte Stringer (1993) 158 JP 453

R v HM Coroner for Swansea and Gower, ex parte Chief Constable of Wales (199)
    164 JP 191

R v HM Coroner for Western District of east Sussex; ex parte Homberg (1994)
    158 JP 357

R v HM Coroner for Wiltshire, ex parte Clegg (1997) 161 JP 521

R v Holland (1841) 2 Mood and R 351

R v Humphrey (1999) 103 A Crim R 434

R v Inkson (1996) 88 A Crim R 334

R v Jakac [1961] VR 362

R v Jarrett (1994) 73 A Crim R 160

R v Jemielita (1996) 81 A Crim R 409

R v Johnston (1992) 69 CCC 395

R v Jordan (1956) 40 Cr App R 152

R v Karger [2001] SASC 64

R v Kinash [1982] Qd R 648

R v Lucas (1992) 55 A Crim R 361; [1992] 2 VR 109

R v Mackie (1973) 57 Cr App R 453

R v Malcherek [1981] 2 All ER 422

R v Mallinder (1986) 23 A Crim R 179

R v Marjoram, The Times, 3 December 1999

R v McKechnie (1992) 94 Cr App R 51

R v Meleragni (1992) 73 CCC (3d) 348

R v Michael (1840) 9 C and P 356

R v Milat (1996) 87 A Crim R 446

Scott v Echegaray (1991) Aust Torts Reps 81-120

Scott v London and St Katherine Docks Co (1865) 3 H & C 596

Scott v Shepherd (1773) 2 Wm Bl 892; 3 Wils 403; [1558-1774] All ER 295

Secretary to the Department of Natural Resources and Energy v Harper (2000) 1 VR 133

Secretary, Department of Health & Community Services (NT) v JWB and SMB (Marion's case) (1992) 175 CLR 218

Secretary, Department of Health and Community Services v Gurvich [1995] 2 VR 69

Sellars v Adelaide Petroleum NL (1994) 179 CLR 332

Seltsam Pty Ltd v McGuiness (2000) Aust Torts Reps 81-547; [2000] NSWCA [2000] NSWCA 29

Shoeys Pty Ltd v Allan (1991) Aust Torts Reps 81-104

Sindell v Abbott Laboratories, 607 P 2d 924 (1980)

Sinka v Mayne Nickless Ltd [1964] VR 524

Sirinjui Biagwei v R (1962) 36 ALR 9; (1962) 1967-68 PNGLR 209

Sleiman v Franklin Food Stores Pty Ltd (1989) Aust Torts Reps 80-266

Sloane v McDonald & Sutherland (WA FC, 14 November 1997, unreported, BC9706153)

Smith v Barking, Havering and Brentwood (1994) 5 Med LR 285

Smith v Jenkins (1970) 119 CLR 397

Smith v R [1959] 2 QB 35

Smith v State of Louisiana, Dept of Health and Hospitals, 676 So 2d 543 (1996)

Sneesby v The Lancashire and Yorkshire Rly Co [1875] 1 QB 42

Snell v Farrell [1990] 2 SCR 311

South Pacific Manufacturing Co Ltd v New Zealand Security Consultants & Investigations Ltd [1992] 2 NZLR 282

Spencer v General Electric Co, 688 F Supp 1072 (ED Va 1988)

Spring v Guardian Assurance Plc [1995] 2 AC 296

St George Club Ltd v Hines (1962) 35 ALJR 106

Stapley v Gypsum Mines Ltd [1953] AC 663

State of Montana v Howery, 204 Mont 417, 664 P 2d 1287 (1983)

State v Allewalt, 308 Md 89, 517 A 2d 741 (1986)

State v Angelina 80 SE 141 (1913)

State v Bible, 858 P 2d 1152 (Ariz 1993), cert denied, 114 S Ct 1578 (1994)

State v Hall, 330 NC 808, 412 SE 2d 883 (1992)

State v Marks, 231 Kan 645, 647 P 2d 1292 (1982)

State v McCoy, 400 NW 2d 807 (Minn App 1987)

State v Petrich, 101 Wash 2d 566, 683 P 2d 173 (1984)

State v Saldana, 324 NW 2d 227 (Minn 1982)

State v Scates 50 NC 409 (1858)

State v Wilkerson, 295 NC 559, 247 SE 2d 905 (1978)

Steinhauser v Hertz Corp, 421 F 2d 1169 (2d Cir 1970)

Stephenson v State 179 NE 633 (1933)

Sturch v Wilmott (Qld SC, Thomas J, 13 April 1995, unreported, BC9505737)

Sturch v Wilmott [1997] 2 Qd R 310

Willis v The Commonwealth (1946) 73 CLR 105

Willson v Minister of Defence [1991] 1 All ER 638

Wilsher v Essex Area Health Authority [1988] AC 1974; 2 WLR 557

Wilson v Horne (1999) 8 Tas R 363

Wilson v Peisley (1975) 7 ALR 571, 50 ALJR 207

Wilton v Farnworth (1948) 76 CLR 646

Woods v Lowns (NSW SC, Badgery-Parker J, 9 February 1995, unreported, BC9504451)

Zafft v Eli Lilly & Co, 676 SW 2d 241 (Mo 1984)

Bibliography

Aagard, TS, "Identifying and Valuing the Injury in Lost Chance Cases" (1998) 96 *Michigan L Rev* 1335

Abel, RL, "A Critique of Torts" (1990) 37 *UCLA L Rev* 785

Active Voluntary Euthanasia – A Timely Reappraisal, University of Tasmania Law School Occasional Paper (1991)

Ad Hoc Committee of the Harvard Medical School, "A Definition of Irreversible Coma" (1968) 205(6) *Journal of the American Medical Association* 85

Adams, JA, & Knudson, S, "Genital Findings in Adolescent Girls Referred for Suspected Sexual Abuse" (1996) 15 *Arch Pediatr Adolesc Med* 850

Adeney, E, "The Challenge of Medical Uncertainty: Factual Causation in Anglo-Australian Toxic Tort Litigation" (1993) 19 *Mon U Law Rev* 23

Aitken, CCG, *Statistics and the evaluation of evidence for forensic scientists*, John Wiley, New York (1995)

Alcorn, G, "Marshall Law", *The Age* (Melbourne), 24 May 1995

American Academy of Paediatrics, "Guidelines for the Evaluation of Sexual Abuse of Children: Subject Review" (1999) 103(1) *Paediatrics* 186

American Medical Association, *Guides to Permanent Impairment*, 4th edn, AMA, Chicago (1993)

American Psychiatric Association, *Diagnostic and Statistical Manual of Mental Disorders – DSM-IVTR*, American Psychiatric Association, Washington, DC (2000)

Amunden, DW, & Ferngren, GB, "Evolution of the Physician/Patient Relationship: Antiquity Through Renaissance" in EE Shelp (ed), *The Clinical Encounter*, D Reidel Pub Co, Dordrecht (1983)

Andenaes, J, *The General Part of the Criminal Law of Norway*, Fred B Rothman, South Hackensack NJ (1965)

Angell, M, "Evaluating the Health Risks of Breast Implants: The Interplay of Medical Science, the Law, and Public Opinion" (1996) 334 *New Eng J Med* 1513

Annas, GJ, "The promised end-constitutional aspects of physician-assisted suicide" (1996) 335 *New England Journal of Medicine* 683

Annot, "Admissibility, at Criminal Prosecution, of Expert Testimony on Rape Trauma Syndrome," 42 ALR 4th 879 (1985)

Anon, "Police Review 1975" in T Williamson, "Police Investigations – Separating the False and Genuine" (1996) 36(2) *Med Sci Law* 135

Appelbaum, PS, & Gutheil, TG, *Clinical Handbook of Psychiatry and the Law*, 2nd edn, Williams & Wilkins, Baltimore (1991)

Aranda, S, & O'Connor, M, "Euthanasia, nursing and care of the dying; rethinking Kuhse and Singer" (1995) 3 *Australian Nurses Journal* 18

Aristotle (trans W D Ross), *Nichomachean Ethics,* Clarendon Press, Oxford, Book V, 2

Ashby, M, "Of Life and Death: the Canadian and Australian Senates on palliative care and euthanasia" (1997) 5 *JLM* 40

Ashby, M, "The fallacies of death causation in palliative care" (1997) 166 *Medical Journal of Australia* 176

Ashby, M, "Palliative care, death causation, public policy and the law" (1998) 6 *Progress in Palliative Care* 69

Ashby, M, & Stoffell, B, "Artificial hydration and alimentation at the end of life: a reply to Craig" (1995) 21 *Journal of Medical Ethics* 135

Ashby, M, & Stoffell, B, "Therapeutic ratio and defined phases: proposal of an ethical framework for palliative care" (1991) 302 *British Medical Journal* 1322

Ashby, M, & Wakefield, M, "Attitudes to some aspects of death and dying, living wills and substituted health care decision-making in South Australia: a public opinion survey for a parliamentary select committee" (1993) 7 *Palliative Medicine* 273

Atiyah, PS, "*Res Ipsa Loquitur* in England and Australia" (1972) 35 *Modern Law Review* 337

Atiyah, PS, *Accidents, Compensation and the Law*, 1st edn, Weidenfeld & Nicolson, London (1970)

Australian Association for Hospice and Palliative Care Inc (AAHPC), "Voluntary Euthanasia – Position Statement", 27 October 1995, The Association, Perth (1995)

Australian Law Reform Commission, *Human Tissue Transplants*, Report No 7, AGPS, Canberra (1977)

Bacon, W, "Experts on Trial", *The Sydney Morning Herald* (5 July 2000) 1 and (6 July 2000) 11

Baden, M, *Unnatural Death: Confession of a Medical Examiner*, Sphere Books, London (1989)

Balding, DJ, "When can a DNA profile be regarded as unique?" (1999) 39 *Science and Justice* 257

Barnes, B, "Belief Action and Determinism: the Causal Explanation of Scientific Change" in B Barnes, *Scientific Knowledge and Sociological Theory*, Routledge and Kegan Paul, London (1974)

Barnes, B, *The Elements of Social Theory*, UCL Press, London (1995)

Barnes, DW, *Statistics as proof*, Little, Brown, Boston (1983)

Barr, JS, et al, "Evaluation of End Results in Treatment of Ruptured Lumbar Disc" (1967) 125 *Surgery, Gynaecology and Obstetrics* 250

Beck, U, *Reflexive Modernization: Politics, Tradition and Aesthetics in the Modern Social Order*, Polity, Cambridge (1994)

Beh, PLS, "Rape in Hong Kong: an Overview of Current Knowledge" (1998) 5 *J Clin For Med* 124

Bellamy, R, Ruwende, C, Corrah, T, McAdam, KPWJ, Whittle, C, & Hill, AVS, "Variations in the NRAMP1 Gene and Susceptibility to Tuberculosis an West Africans" (1998) 338 *N Eng J Med* 640

Bentham, J, *Rationale of Judicial Evidence* in *The Works of Jeremy Bentham*, Vol VII, Russell and Russell, New York (1962)

Berger, A "Encyclopedic Dictionary of Roman Law" in (1953) 43(2) *Transactions of the American Philosophical Society*, Philadelphia

Berger, M, "Eliminating General Causation: Notes Toward a New Theory of Justice and Toxic Torts" (1997) 97 *Columbia Law Review* 2117

Biddle, J, *Lumbar Disc Pathology*, Medical Report Council Special Report No 1, HMSO, London (1930)

Billings, J, & Block, S, "Slow euthanasia" (1996) 12 *Journal of Palliative Care* 21

Blackwood, J, "Humpty Dumpty Was Pushed Off the Wall ..." (1996) 15 *Univ of Tasmania LR* 306

Bloor, D, *Knowledge and Social Imagery*, 2nd edn, University of Chicago Press, Chicago (1991)

Borkowski, A, *Textbook on Roman Law*, Blackstone Press, London (1994)

Bowyer, L, & Dalton, ME, "Female Victims of Rape and their Genital Injuries" (1997) 104 *Br J Obstet Gynaecol* 617

Brennan, TA, "Untangling Causation Issues in Law and Medicine: Hazardous Substance Litigation" (1987) 107 *Annals of Internal Medicine* 741

Burghardt, E, *Colposcopy Cervical Pathology*, Teorg Thieme Verlag, Stuttgart (1984)

Burrill, AM, *A Treatise on the Nature, Principles and Rules of Circumstantial Evidence*, JS Voorhies, New York (1856)

Bursten, B, *Beyond Psychiatric Expertise*, Thomas, Springfield, IL (1984)

Bursztajn, HJ, Harding, HP, Gutheil, TG, & Brodsky, A, "Beyond Cognition: the Role of Disordered Affective States in Impairing Competence to Consent to Treatment" (1991) 19 *Bulletin of the American Academy of Psychiatry and Law* 383

Caffey, J, "The Parent-Infant Traumatic Stress Syndrome" (1972) 114 *Am J Radiology* 218

Caffey, J, "Pediatric X-Ray Diagnosis," in *Yearbook*, Medical Publishers, Chicago, 7th edn (1978)

Callinan, I, *The Coroner's Conscience*, Central Queensland University Press, Rockhampton (1999)

Campbell, B, "Uncertainty as Symbolic Action in Disputes among Experts" (1985) 15 *Social Studies of Science* 429

Canadian Pain Society: "Use of opioid analgesics for the treatment of chronic noncancer pain in a consensus statement and guidelines from the Canadian Pain Society" <www.pulsus.com/Pain/03_04/opio_ed.htm>

Cane, P, "Corrective Justice and Correlativity in Private Law" (1996) 16 *Ox Jo LS* 471

Cane, P, *Atiyah's Accidents, Compensation and the Law*, 6th edn, Butterworths, London (1999)

Carter, R, "Give a drug a bad name," (1996) *New Scientist*, 6 April, 14

Cartwright, PS, & the Sexual Assault Study Group, "Factors that Correlate with Injury Sustained by Survivors of Sexual Assault" (1987) 70 *Obstet Gynecol* 144

Cass, A, Gleich, P, & Smith, C, "Male Genital Injuries from External Trauma" (1985) 57 *Br J Urol* 467

Casswell, DG, "Rejecting Criminal Liability for Life-Shortening Palliative Care" (1990) 6 *Journal of Contemporary Health Law and Policy* 127

Ceci, SJ, & Hembrooke, H (eds), *Expert Witnesses in Child Abuse Cases*, Washington, DC, American Psychological Association (1998)

Celli, AG Jr, "Toward a Risk Contribution Approach to Tortfeasor Identification and Multiple Causation Cases" (1990) 65 *New York University Law Review* 635

Chalmers, AF, *What is This Thing Called Science?*, 3rd edn, University of Queensland Press (1999)

Cohen, A, "Unreliability of Expert Testimony on Typical Characteristics of Sexual Abuse Victims" (1980) 74 *Georgetown L J* 429

Cohen, JL, *The Probable and the Provable*, Oxford/Clarendon Press, Oxford (1977)

Cooke, R, "Remoteness of Damages and Judicial Discretion" [1978] *Cam LJ* 501

Cooper, C, & Dennison, E, "Do Silicone Breast Implants Cause Connective Tissue Disease?" (1998) 316 *Brit Med J* 403

Cooper-Stephenson, K, *Personal Injury Damages in Canada*, 2nd edn, Carswell, Scarborough, Ont (1996)

Coote, B, "Chance and the Burden of Proof in Contract and Tort" (1988) 62 *ALJ* 761

Cordner, S, "Deciding the Cause of Death after Necropsy" (1993) 341 *Lancet* 1458

Cordner, S, Linehan, B, El Nageh, M, Wells, D, & McKelvie, H *Ethical Practice in Laboratory Medicine and Forensic Pathology*, WHO Regional Publications, Eastern Mediterranean Series, WHO Regional Office for the Eastern Mediterranean, Alexandria, Egypt (1999)

Corner, J, "More openness needed in palliative care" (1997) 315 *British Medical Journal* 1242

Corns, C, "Withdrawal of life-support: some criminal prosecution aspects" in I Freckelton & K Petersen (eds), *Controversies in Health Law*, Federation Press, Sydney (1999)

Coulam, R, & Fienberg, SE, "The Use of Court-Appointed Statistical Experts: A Case Study" in MH De Groot, SE Fienberg & JB Kadane (eds), *Statistics and the Law*, John Wiley & Sons, New York (1986)

Cowen, Z, & Carter, PB, *Essays on the law of Evidence*, Greenwood Press, Westport (1955)

Craig, G, "On withholding nutrition and hydration in the terminally ill: has palliative medicine gone too far?" (1994) 20 *Journal of Medical Ethics* 139

Crowe, S, "Forensic Neuropsychology" in I Freckelton & H Selby (eds), *Expert Evidence*, Law Book Co, Sydney (1993)

Culler, JD, *On Deconstruction*, Cornell University Press, Ithaca, New York (1982)

Dans, AL, Dans, LF, Guyatt, GH, & Richard, S, "Users' Guides to the Medical Literature XIV: How to Decide on the Applicability of Clinical Trial Results to Your Patient" (1998) 279 *J Am Med Assoc* 545

David, P, "Probability and Proof: Some Basic Concepts" in T Anderson & W Twining, *Analysis of Evidence,* Weidenfeld & Nicholson, London (1991)

de Furia, JW Jr, in "Testamentary Gifts Resulting from Meretricious Relationships: Undue Influence or Natural Beneficence?" (1989) 64 *Notre Dame L Rev* 200

DeGroot, MH, Fienberg, SE, & Kadane, JB (eds), *Statistics and the Law*, Wiley, New York (1986)

Devereux, J, "Competence to Make Decisions" in I Freckelton & K Petersen (eds), *Controversies in Health Law*, Federation Press, Sydney (1999)

Devlin, P, *Easing the Passing: The Trial of Dr John Bodkin Adams*, The Bodley Head, London (1985)

Dewees, D, & Trebilcock, M, "The Efficacy of the Tort System and its Alternatives: A Review of Empirical Evidence" (1992) 30 *Osg Hall LJ* 57

Dietz, P, "The Mentally Disordered Offender: Patterns in the Relationship between Mental Disorder and Crime" (1992) 15 *Psych Clin North America* 539

Dore, M, "A Commentary on the Use of Epidemiology Evidence in Demonstrating Cause-in-Fact" (1983) 7 *Harvard Environmental Law Review* 429

Dorries, C, *Coroner's Courts: A Guide to Law and Practice*, John Wiley & Sons, Chichester (1999)

Drukteninis, AM, "Overlapping Somatoform Syndromes in Personal Injury Litigation," presented at the annual meeting on 30 March 2000 of the American College of Forensic Psychiatry in Newport Beach, CA

Dworkin, R, *Life's Dominion: an argument about abortion, euthanasia, and individual freedom*, Knopf, New York (1993)

Easlea, B, *Witch-hunting, Magic and the New Philosophy: An Introduction to the Debates of the Scientific Revolution 1450-1750*, Harvester Press, Brighton (1980)

Edgarth, K, Von Krogh, G, & Ormistad, K, "Adolescent girls investigated for sexual abuse: history, physical findings and legal outcome" (1999) 104 *Forensic Sci Int* 1-15

Edmond, G, "Science in Court: Negotiating the Meaning of a 'Scientific' Experiment during a Murder Trial and Some Limits to Legal Deconstruction for the Public Understanding of Law and Science" (1998) 20 *Sydney Law Review* 361

Edmond, G, "Deflating *Daubert*: *Kumho Tire Co v Carmichael* and the inevitability of *general* acceptance *(Frye)*" (2000) 23 *University of New South Wales Law Journal* 31

Edmond, G, "Judicial Representations of Scientific Evidence" (2000) 63 *Modern Law Review* 216

Edmond, G, & Mercer, D, "Scientific Literacy and the Jury: Reconsidering Jury Competence" (1997) 6 *Public Understanding of Science* 329

Edmond, G, & Mercer, D, "What Judges Should Know about Falsification" (1997) 5 *Expert Evidence* 29

Edmond, G, & Mercer, D, "Trashing 'Junk' Science" (1998) *Stanford Technology Law Review* <http://stanford.edu/STLR/Articles/Index. htm>

Edmond, G, & Mercer, D, "Juggling Science: From Polemic to Pastiche" (1999) 13 *Social Epistemology* 215

Edmond, G, & Mercer, D, "Litigation Life: Law-science Knowledge Construction in (Bendectin) Mass Toxic Tort Litigation" (2000) 30 *Social Studies of Science* 265

Edwards, A, & Heenan, M, "Rape Trials in Victoria: Gender, Socio-cultural Factors and Justice" (1994) 27 *ANZ J Criminol* 213

Eggleston, R, *Evidence, Proof and Probability,* 2nd edn, Weidenfeld and Nicholson, London (1983)

Ellard, J, "The Epidemic of Post-Traumatic Stress Disorder: A Passing Phase" (1997) 166 *Medical Journal of Australia* 84

Emans, J, Woods, E, Allred, E, & Grace, E, "Hymenal Findings in Adolescent Women, Impact of Tampon Use and Consensual Sexual Activity" (1994) 125 *J Paediatrics* 153

Engel, GL, "The Clinical Application of the Biopsychosocial Model" (1980) 137 *Am J Psych* 535

Engelhardt, HT, "Relevant Causes: Their Designation in Medicine and Law" in S Spicker, J Healey & H Engelhardt (eds), *The Law Medicine Relation: A Philosophical Exploration*, D Reidel Publishing Company, Dordrecht (1981)

England, I, "Informed Consent – The Double-faced Doctrine" in NJ Mullany & AM Linden (eds), *Torts Tomorrow: A Tribute to John Fleming*, LBC Information Services, Sydney (1998)

Epstein, RA, "Symposium on Causation in the Law of Torts: Causation – in Context: an Afterword" (1987) 63 *Chi-Kent L Rev* 653

Evans-Jones, R, & MacCormack, G, "Obligations" in E Metzger (ed), *A Companion to Justinian's Institutes*, Cornell University Press, Ithaca, New York (1998)

Evett, IW, Foreman, LA, Jackson, G, & Lambert, JA, "DNA Profiling: A discussion of issues relating to the reporting of very small match probabilities" (2000) *Crim L R* 431

Evidence Based Medicine Working Group, "Evidence Based Medicine: A New Approach to the Teaching and Practice of Medicine" (1992) 268 *J Am Med Assoc* 2420

Expert Working Group of the European Association for Palliative Care, "Morphine in cancer pain: modes of administration" (1996) 312 *British Medical Journal* 823

Fairweather, DS, & Campbell, AJ, "Diagnostic Accuracy: The Effects of Multiple Aetiology and the Degradation of Information in Old Age" (1991) 25 *J Royal College Physicians of London* 105

Farrell, PJ, "The XYY Syndrome in Criminal Law: An Introduction" (1969) 44 *St John's L Rev* 217

Faunce, T, & McSherry, B, "Chinese whispers: judicial narratives and the regulation of clinical medicine" (1997) 4 *JLM* 326

Federal Judicial Center, *Manual on Scientific Evidence*, US Government Printing Office, Washington DC (1994)

Feinstein, AS, & Horwitz, RI, "Double Standards, Scientific Methods, and Epidemiological Research" (1982) 307 *N Eng J Med* 1611

Field, D, *The Law of Evidence of Scotland*, W Green & Son, Edinburgh (1988)

Fienberg, SE (ed), *The Evolving Role of Statistical Assessments as Evidence in the Courts*, Springer Verlag, New York (1989)

Final Report of the Review of Professional Indemnity Arrangements for Health Care Professionals (Chair: Fiona Tito), *Compensation and Professional Indemnity in Health Care* (1995)

Finkel, M, "Technical Conduct of the Child Sexual Abuse Medical Examination" (1998) 22(6) *Child Abuse & Neglect* 555

Finkelhor, D, & Wolak, J, "Non Sexual Assaults to the Genitals in the Youth Population" (1995) 274 *JAMA* 1692

Fish, S, *Doing What Comes Naturally: Change, Rhetoric and the Practice of Theory in Literary and Legal Studies*, Duke University Press, Durham (1989)

Fleming, JG, "Probabilistic Causation in Tort Law: A Postscript" (1991) 70 *Canadian Bar Review* 136

Fleming, JG, "Preventive Damages" in NJ Mullany, *Torts in the Nineties*, LBC Information Services, Sydney (1997)

Fleming, JG, *The Law of Torts*, 9th edn, LBC Information Services, Sydney (1998)

Foster, K, & Huber, P, *Judging Science: Scientific Knowledge and the Federal Courts*, MIT Press, Cambridge (1998)

Frank, A, "Low Back Pain: Regular Review" (1993) 306 *British Medical Journal* 901

Freckelton, I, "Expert Proof in the Coroner's Jurisdiction", in H Selby (ed), *The Aftermath of Death*, Federation Press, Sydney (1992)

Freckelton, I, "Trauma Evidence" in I Freckelton & H Selby (eds), *Expert Evidence*, 5 vol looseleaf service & CD Rom, Law Book Co, Sydney (1993-...)

Freckelton, I, "Contemporary Comment: When Plight Makes Right – The Forensic Abuse Syndrome" (1994) 18 *Criminal Law Journal* 29

Freckelton, I, "Malpractice Actions Against Health Care Professionals" in I Freckelton & K Petersen (eds), *Controversies in Health Law*, Federation Press, Sydney (1999)

Freckelton, I, "Epidemiology Evidence" (2000) 8 *Journal of Law and Medicine* 133

Freckelton, I, "Revisiting the Duty to Warn: the High Court's decision in *Rosenberg v Percival*" (2001) 9 *Journal of Law and Medicine* 5

Freckelton, I, *Criminal Injuries Compensation: Law, Practice and Policy*, Law Book Co, Sydney (2001)

Freckelton, I, *The Trial of the Expert*, Oxford University Press, Melbourne (2002 – forthcoming)

Freckelton, I, & Petersen, K (eds), *Controversies in Health Law*, Federation Press, Sydney (1999)

Freckelton, I, & Ranson, D (eds), *Coronial Law and Medicine*, Oxford University Press, Melbourne (2002 – forthcoming)

Freckelton, I, Reddy, P, & Selby, H, *Australian Judicial Perspectives on Expert Evidence*, AIJA, Melbourne (1999)

Freckelton, I, Reddy, P, & Selby, H, *Australian Magistrates' Perspectives on Expert Evidence: A Comparative Study*, AIJA, Melbourne (2001)

Freckelton, I, & Selby, H, I Freckelton & H Selby (eds), *Expert Evidence*, 5 vol looseleaf service & CD Rom, Law Book Co, Sydney (1993-...)

Freckelton, I, & Selby, H, *Expert Evidence: Law, Practice and Procedure*, 2nd edn, Law Book Co, Sydney (2002)

Friedland, DF, *Evidence-Based Medicine: A Framework for Clinical Practice*, Appleton & Lange, Stamford (1998)

Frolik, LA, "The Biological Roots of the Undue Influence Doctrine: What's Love Got To Do With It?" (1996) 57 *U Pitt L Rev* 841

Fuchs, S, & Ward, S, "What is Deconstruction, and Where and When Does it Take Place? Making Facts in Science, Building Cases in Law" (1994) 59 *American Sociological Review* 481

Galen (trans J Reedy), "On Cancer and Related Diseases" (1975) 10 *Clio Medica* 229

Geiryn, T, *Cultural Boundaries of Science: Credibility on the Line*, Chicago University Press, Chicago (1998)

Gerber, H, "Lipovac v Black: was Dr Black Negligent?" (1999) 170 *Med J Aust* 550

Gilbert, J, & Kirkham, S, "Double effect, double bind or double speak" (1999) 13 *Palliative Medicine* 365

Gilbert, N, & Mulkay, M, *Opening Pandora's Box: A Sociological Analysis of Scientist's Discourse*, Cambridge University Press, Cambridge (1984)

Ginzburg, HM, "Use and Misuse of Epidemiological Data in the Courtroom: Defining the Limits of Inferential and Particularistic Evidence in Mass Tort Litigation" (1986) 12 *American Journal of Law and Medicine* 423

Glasgow, G, & Casey, ME, "The Problem of Monetary Compensation for Post-traumatic Epilepsy" [1968] *NZLJ* 9 and 56

Goldberg, DP, *The Detection of Psychiatric Illness, by Questionnaire*, Oxford University Press, London (1972)

Goldberg, R, *Causation and Risk in the Law of Torts*, Hart Publishing, Oxford (1999)

Goldberg, R, "The Contraceptive Pill, Negligence and Causation: Views on *Vadera v Shaw*" (2000) 8 *Medical Law Review* 316

Goodyear-Smith, F, & Laidlaw, T, "Can Tampon Use Cause Hymen Changes in Girls Who have not had Sexual Intercourse? A Review of the Literature" (1998) 94 *For Sci Int* 147

Gourevitch, D "The Paths of Knowledge", in MD Grmek, *Western Medical Thought from Antiquity to the Middle Ages*, Harvard University Press, Cambridge, Massachusetts (1998)

Graziotti, P, & Goucke, R, "The use of oral opioids in patients with chronic non-malignant pain" (1997) 167 *Medical Journal of Australia* 30

Green, M, *Bendectin and Birth Defects*, University of Pennsylvania Press, Philadelphia (1996)

Grofman, B, "Mathematical Models of Juror and Jury Decision-Making" in BD Sales, *The Trial Process*, Plenum Press, New York (1981)

Grove, WM, & Barden, RC, "Protecting the Integrity of the Legal System: The Admissibility of Testimony from Mental Health Experts Under *Daubert/Kumho* Analyses" (1999) 5 *Psychology, Public Policy and Law* 224

Groves, D, "Commentary" (1998) 22 *Criminal Law Journal* 357

Grubb, A, "Commentary: Attempted Murder of Terminally Ill Patient; R v Cox" (1993) 1 *Med Law Rev* 232

Gutheil, TG, & Sutherland, PK, "Forensic Assessment, Witness Credibility and the Search for Truth through Expert Testimony in the Courtroom" (1999) 27 *J Psychiatry & Law* 289

Guze, SB, *Criminality and Psychiatric Disorders*, Oxford University Press, New York (1976)

Hadler, NM, *Medical Management of the Regional Musculoskeletal Disorders*, Grune & Stratton, Orlando, Florida (1984)

Hafner, H, & Boker, W, *Crimes of Violence by Mentally Abnormal Offenders*, Cambridge University Press, Cambridge (1982)

Hale, M, 1 *Pleas of the Crown*, London, E & R Nutt 1736 (1680)

Hall, P, & Selinger, B, "Statistical significance: Balancing evidence against doubt" (1986) 28 *Aust J Stats* 354

Hallenstein, H, "Coronership – the Practical Application of Law, Medicine, Science and Specialty Knowledge", paper presented to Australian Institute of Criminology Conference, Surfers Paradise, Institute of Criminology (1993)

Halper, T, "Time, Law and Responsibility: Additional Thoughts on Causality" in S Spicker, J Healey & H Engelhardt (eds), *The Law Medicine Relation: A Philosophical Exploration*, D Reidel Publishing Company, Dordrecht (1981)

Hamer, D, "'Chance would be a Fine Thing': Proof of Causation and Quantum in an Unpredictable World" (1999) 23 *MULR* 557

Hamer, D, "Proof of Causation and Quantum in an Unpredictable World" (1999) 23 *Melbourne University Law Review* 557

Hamer, S, & Collinson, G, *Achieving Evidence-Based Practice*, B Tindall, Edinburgh (1999)

Hardy, DW, "Multiple Personality: Failure to Diagnose and the Potential for Malpractice Liability" (1988) 18 *Psychology Annals* 543

Harrison, ARW, "Aristotle's *Nichomachean Ethics*, Book V, and the Law of Athens" (1957) 77 *Journal of Hellenic Studies* 42

Harrison, J, & Moller, J, "Learning from Experience – Toward Prevention", in H Selby (ed), *The Inquest Handbook*, Federation Press, Sydney (1997)

Hart, HLA, & Honoré, AM, *Causation in the Law*, 1st edn, Oxford University Press, Oxford (1959)

Hart, HLA, & Honoré, T, *Causation in the Law*, 2nd edn, Oxford/Clarendon Press, Oxford (1985)

Haugen, P, "Pain Relief for the Dying: The Unwelcome Intervention of the Criminal Law" (1997) 23 *William Mitchell Law Review* 325

Hazlick, R, & Goodin, J, "Mind Your Manners Part III Individual Scenario Results and Discussion of the National Association of Medical Examiners Manner of Death Questionnaire, 1995" (1997) 18(3) *American Journal of Forensic Medicine and Pathology* 228

Hemingway, H, & Marmot, M, "Evidence Based Cardiology: Psychosocial Factors in the Aetiology and Prognosis of Coronary Heart Disease: Systemic Review of Prospective Cohort Studies" (1999) 318 *Brit Med J* 1460

Hempel, CG, *The Philosophy of Natural Science*, Prentice-Hall, New Jersey (1966)

Heuston, RFV, & Buckley, RA, *Salmond and Heuston on the Law of Torts*, 21st edn, Sweet & Maxwell, London (1996)

Heydon, JD, & Byrne, DR, *Cross on Evidence*, Australian looseleaf edition, Butterworths, Sydney

Hilgartner, S, "The Dominant View of Popularisation: Conceptual Problems, Political Uses" (1990) 20 *Social Studies of Science* 519

Hill, AB, "The Environment and Disease: Association or Causation?" (1965) 58 *Proceedings of the Royal Society of Medicine* 295

Hill, P, & Shirley, D, *A Good Death. Taking More Control at the End of Your Life Choice in Dying*, The National Council for the Right to Die, Addison Wesley, New York (1992)

Hill, RB, & Anderson, RE, *The Autopsy – Medical Practice and Public Policy*, Butterworth, Boston (1988)

Hill, T, "A Lost Chance for Compensation in the Tort of Negligence by the House of Lords" (1991) 54 *MLR* 511

Hippocrates, "The Nature of Man" in (trans J Chadwick & WN Mann), *The Medical Works of Hippocrates*, Springfield, Ill, Charles C Thomas (1950)

Hippocrates, "The Sacred Disease", GER Lloyd (ed), (trans J Chadwick & WN Mann), in *Hippocratic Writings*, Penguin Classics, Harmondsworth (1983)

Hippocratic Corpus, *The Sacred Disease* IX (18)

Hobbs, C, Wynne, J, & Thomas, A, "Colposcopic Genital Findings in Prepubertal Girls Assessed for Sexual Abuse" (1995) 76 *Archives of Disease in Childhood* 465

Hodgins, S (ed), *Mental Disorder and Crime*, Sage, Newbury Park, CA (1993)

Hodgson, D, "Probability: The Logic of the Law – A Response" (1995) 15 *OJLS* 51

Hodgson, DH, "The Scales of Justice: Probability and Proof in Legal Fact-finding" (1995) 69 *ALJ* 731

Hodson, JD, "Annotation, Medical Malpractice: 'Loss Of Chance' Causality" 54 ALR 4th 10 (1987, as supplemented to September 2000)

Hoffman, D, "Doctoring the Evidence" (1990) 15 *Leg Serv Bull* 76

Hoffmann, L, *Common Sense and Causing Loss*, Lecture to the Chancery Bar Association, 15 June 1999

Holder, J, & Elworthy, S, "The BSE Crisis" in H Reece (ed), *Law and Science: Current Legal Issues*, vol 1, Oxford University Press, Oxford (1998)

Holdsworth, W, *A History of English Law*, 4th edn, Vol II (1936)

Holdsworth, W, *A History of English Law*, 5th edn, Vol III, Methuen, London (1942)

Holdsworth, W, *A History of English Law*, Vol 1, 7th edn, Methuen & Co, London (1964)

Holmes, LB, "Teratogen Update, 'Bendectin'" (1983) 27 *Teratology* 277

Holmes, W, & Slap, G, "Sexual Abuse of Boys: Definition, Prevalence, Correlates, Sequelae and Management" (1998) 280(21) *JAMA* 1855

Honoré, T, *Ulpian*, Oxford University Press, Oxford (1982)

Honoré, T, "Necessary and Sufficient Conditions in Tort Law" in DG Owen (ed), *Philosophical Foundations of Tort Law*, Oxford (1995)

Honoré, T, "The Morality of Tort Law – Questions and Answers" in DG Owen (ed), *Philosophical Foundations of Tort Law*, Clarendon Press, Oxford (1995)

Honoré, T, "Causation and Disclosure of Medical Risks" (1998) 114 *LQR* 52

Honoré, T, "Medical Non-Disclosure, Causation and Risk: *Chappel v Hart*" (1999) 7 TLJ 1

Honoré, T, *Responsibility and Fault*, Hart Publishing, Oxford (1999)

House of Lords, *Report of Select Committee on Medical Ethics*, HMSO, London (1994)

Howard, C, *Australian Criminal Law*, Law Book Co, Melbourne, Sydney (1965)

Huber, P, *Galileo's Revenge: Keeping Junk Science out of the Courtroom*, Basic Books, New York (1991)

Hult, L, "The Munkfors Investigation" (1954) *Acta Orthop Scand* (Supp 16) 1

Human Rights and Equal Opportunity Commission, *Human Rights and Mental Illness. Report of the National Inquiry into the Human Rights of People with Mental Illness*, Australian Government Publishing Service, Canberra (1993)

Hunnisett, RF, *The Medieval Coroner*, Cambridge University Press, Cambridge (1961)

Hunt, R, "Palliative care: the rhetoric-reality gap" in H Kuhse (ed), *Willing to Listen, Wanting to Die*, Penguin, Melbourne (1994)

Hunt, R, "Taking responsibility for affecting the time of death" (1999) 13 *Palliative Medicine* 439

Hurley, AW, "Prospects of Recovery in Negligence and under Statute for Creutzfeld[t]-Jakob Disease resulting from Human Pituitary Gland Derived Hormone" (1996) 4 *TLJ* 60

Hyams, AL, "Expert Psychiatric Evidence in Sexual Misconduct Cases Before State Medical Boards" (1992) 17 *Am J Law & Medicine* 171

Irwin, A, & Wynne, B (eds), *Misunderstanding Science: the Public Reconstruction of Science and Technology*, Cambridge University Press, Cambridge (1995)

Jackson, JD, "Towards a dialectic theory of proof for legal procedure" (1991) 154 *J R Statist Soc A* 107

Janowsky, EC, Kupper, LL, & Hulka, BS, "Meta-analyses of the Relation Between Silicone Breast Implants and the Risk of Connective Tissue Diseases" (2000) 342 *N Eng J Med* 781

Jansen, N, "The Idea of a Lost Chance" (1999) 19(2) *Oxford Journal of Legal Studies* 271

Jasanoff, S, "Contested Boundaries in Policy-Relevant Science"(1987) 17 *Social Studies of Science* 195

Jasanoff, S, *Science at the Bar: Law, Science and Technology in America*, Harvard University Press, Cambridge (1995)

Jasanoff, S, "Expert Games in Silicon Gel Breast Implant Litigation" in M Freeman & H Reece (eds), *Science in Court*, Dartmouth, Aldershot (1998)

Johnson, J, "Coroners, Corruption and the Politics of Death: Forensic Pathology in the United States" in M Clark & C Crawford, *Legal Medicine in History*, Cambridge University Press, Cambridge (1994)

Johnstone, G, "An Avenue for Death and Injury Prevention", in H Selby (ed), *The Aftermath of Death*, Federation Press, Sydney (1992)

Johnstone, G, "Coroners' Inquiries and Recommendations" in H Selby (ed), *The Inquest Handbook*, Federation Press, Sydney (1998)

Jones, DS, *Speaking for the Dead*, Ashgate, Dartmouth (2000)

Jones, E, & Wessely, S, "Case of Chronic Fatigue Syndrome after Crimean War and Indian Mutiny" (1999) 319 *Brit Med J* 1645

Jorm, AF, & Henderson, AS, *Dementia in Australia*, Department of Health and Family Services, Australian Government Publishing Service, Canberra (1998)

Jouanna, J, "The Birth of Western Medical Art" in MD Grmek, *Western Medical Thought from Antiquity to the Middle Ages*, Harvard University Press, Cambridge, Massachusetts (1998)

Justinian, *Digest*, translation edited by Alan Watson, vol 1, University of Pennsylvania Press, Philadelphia (1985)

Kahneman, D, Slovic, P, & Tversky, A, *Judgment under Uncertainty: Heuristics and Biases*, Cambridge University Press, Cambridge (1982)

Katz, AM, "Evolving Concepts of Heart Failure: Cooling Furnace, Malfunctioning Pump, Enlarging Muscle" (1997) 3 *Journal of Cardiac Failure* 319

Kaye, D, "The Limits of the Preponderance of the Evidence Standard: Justifiably Naked Statistical Evidence and Multiple Causation" (1982) 2 *American Bar Foundation Research Journal* 487

Kaye, DH, "Bible Reading: DNA Evidence in Arizona" (1997) 28 *Arizona State Law Journal* 1035

Kaye, DH, & Koehler, JJ, "Can Jurors Understand Probabilistic Evidence?" (1991) 154 *J R Statist Soc A* 75

Kempe, CH, Silverman, FN, Steele, BF, Droegemueller, W, & Silver, HJ, "The Battered Child Syndrome" (1962) 181 *J Am Med Assn* 17

Kennedy, D, "Freedom and Constraint in Adjudication: a Critical Phenomenology" (1986) 36 *Journal of Legal Education* 518

Ketal, R, "Affect, Mood, Emotion and Feeling: Semantic Considerations" (1975) 132 *Am J Psychiatry* 1215

Keyserlingk, E, "Assisted suicide, causality and the Supreme Court of Canada" (1994) 39 *McGill L J* 708

King, JH, Jr, "Causation, Valuation, and Chance in Personal Injury Torts Involving Pre-Existing Conditions and Future Consequences" (1981) 90 *Yale LJ* 1353

Kiralfy, A (ed), *The Burden of Proof*, Professional Books Ltd, London (1987)

Kortmann, JS, "*Ab alio ictu(s)*: Misconceptions about Julian's View on Causation" (1999) 20 *Legal History* 95

Kuhn, T, *The Structure of Scientific Revolutions*, 2nd edn, University of Chicago Press, Chicago (1970)

Kuhn, T, "Concepts of Cause in the Development of Physics" in T Kuhn, *The Essential Tension*, Chicago University Press, Chicago (1977)

Kuhse, H, et al, "End of life decisions in Australian medical practice" (1997) 166 *Medical Journal of Australia* 191

Langlois, N, & Gresham, G, "The Ageing of Bruises: A Review and Study of the Colour Changes With Time" (1991) 50 *Forensic Science International* 227

Lanham, D, "Euthanasia, Painkilling, Murder and Manslaughter" (1994) 1 *J of Law and Medicine* 146

Lanham, D, "Danger Down Under" [1999] *Criminal Law Review* 960

Laor, N, & Agassi, J, *Diagnosis: Philosophical and Medical Perspectives*, Kluwer Academic Publishers, Dordrecht/Boston (1990)

Lavery, J, "*Chappel v Hart:* The High Court's Lost Chance" (1998) 7(3) *Australian Health Law Bulletin* 25

Lavery, JV, & Singer, P, "The 'Supremes' decide on assisted suicide: what should a doctor do?" (1997) 157 *Canadian Medical Association Journal* 405

Law Commission of New Zealand, *Coroners*, Report No 62, Law Commission, Wellington (2000)

Law Commission, *Report on Personal Injury Litigation – Assessment of Damages* (Law Com No 56, 1973)

Law Commission, *Structured Settlements and Interim and Provisional Damages* (Law Com No 224, 1994)

Law Reform Committee of Victoria, *Legal Liability of Health Service Providers* (1997)

Lee, RW, *The Elements of Roman Law*, 4th edn, Sweet & Maxwell, London (1956)

Lenahan, L, Ernst, A, & Johnson, B, "Colposcopy in Evaluation of the Adult Sexual Assault Victim" (1998) 16 *Am J Emerg Med* 183

Levine, MA, "Readers' Guide for Causation: Was a Comparison Group for Those at Risk Clearly Identified?" (Jan-Feb 1992) 116 *Am Coll Phys Journal Club* A-12

Levine, M, & Pyke, J, *Levine on Coroners' Courts*, Sweet & Maxwell, London (1999)

Levine, M, Walter, S, Lee, H, Haines, T, Holbrook, A, & Moyer, V, "Users' Guides to the Medical Literature IV: How to Use an Article about Harm" (1994) 271 *J Am Med Assoc* 1615

Liebs, D, "Ulpiani Regulae – Zwei Pseudepigrapha" in *Romanitas-Christianitas. Untersuchungen zur Geschichte und Literatur der römischen Kaiserzeit* (1982)

Loeser, JD, & Egan Kelly, J, *Managing the Chronic Pain Patient*, Raven Press, New York (1989)

Lunney, M, "What Price a Chance?" (1995) 15 *Leg Studs* 1

Luntz, H, "Mrs Whitaker's Gothic Cathedral" (1996) 4 *TLJ* 195

Lynch, M, & Jasanoff, S (eds), "Contested Identities: Science, Law and Forensic Practice" (1998) 28 *Social Studies of Science* 675

MacLaine, GDH, MacArthur, EB, & Heathcote, CR, "A Comparison of Death Certificates and Autopsies in the Australian Capital Territory" (1992) 156 *Medical Journal of Australia* 462

Magnusson, E, *Jury Comprehension of Statistical Evidence*, Australian Institute of Criminology Conference (1994)

Magnusson, E, & Selinger, BK, "Forensic science in court" (1988) 12 *Crim Law J* 86

Magnusson, R, "The Future of the Euthanasia Debate in Australia" (1996) 20 *Melbourne University Law Review* 1108

Makov, UR, "A Bayesian treatment of the 'missing suspect' problem in forensic science" (1987) 36 *The Statistician* 251

Martin, S, "Studies in the New Causality", *The New Yorker*, 26 October 1998

Masel, G, "Damages in Tort for Loss of Chance" (1995) 3 *TLJ* 43

Mason, A, "The Recovery and Calculation of Economic Loss" in NJ Mullany, *Torts in the Nineties*, LBC Information Services, Sydney (1997)

Mason, J, & McCall Smith, RA, *Law and Medical Ethics*, 4th edn, Butterworths, London (1994)

Massaro, TM, "Experts, Psychology, Credibility and Rape: The Rape Trauma Syndrome Issue and its Implications for Expert Psychological Testimony" (1985) 69 *Minn L Rev* 495

Masson, JM, "Freud and the Seduction Theory" (February 1984) *Atlantic*, p33

Matthews, P, "Involuntary Manslaughter: A View from the Coroner's Court" (1996) 60 *Criminal Law Journal* 189

Mawson, D, "Specific defences to a criminal charge: assessment for court" in R Bluglass & P Bowden (eds), *Principles and Practice of Forensic Psychiatry*, Churchill Livingstone, Edinburgh (1990)

McCann, D, "The Range of Findings Open to the Coroner" in H Selby (ed), *The Aftermath of Death*, Federation Press, Sydney (1992)

McCann, J, "Use of the Colposcope in Childhood Sexual Abuse Examinations" (1990) 37(4) *Pediatric Clinics of North America* 863

McCann, J, Reay, D, Siebert, J, Stephens, B, & Wirtz, S, "Postmortem Perianal Findings in Children" (1996) 17(4) *Am J Forensic Med Pathol* 289

McCann, J, Simon, M, & Voris, J, et al, "Perianal Findings in Prepubertal Children Selected for Nonabuse: A Descriptive Study" (1989) 13 *Child Abuse Negl* 179

McCord, D, "The Admissibility of Expert Testimony Regarding Rape Trauma Syndrome in Rape Prosecutions" (1985) 26 *Bost Coll L Rev* 1143

McCord, D, "Syndromes Profiles and Other Mental Exotica: A New Approach to the Admissibility of Nontraditional Psychological Evidence in Criminal Cases" (1987) 66 *Oregon L Review* 19

McCormick, CT, *Handbook on the Law of Damages*, West, St Paul, Minn (1935)

McFarlane, AC, "Post-Traumatic Stress Disorder" in I Freckelton & H Selby (eds), *Expert Evidence*, 5 vol looseleaf service & CD Rom, Law Book Co, Sydney (1993-...)

McGee, R, "Does Stress Cause Cancer?" (1999) 319 *Brit Med J* 1015

McHugh, P, "Psychiatric Misadventures" (Autumn 1992) *American Scholar* 497

McHugh, PR, "How Psychiatry Lost its Way" Commentary (December 1999)

McInnes, M, "Failure to Warn in Medical Negligence – A Cautionary Note from Canada" (1998) 6 *TLJ* 135

McInnes, M, "The Death of *Res Ipsa Loquitur* in Canada" (1998) 114 *Law Quarterly Review* 547

McKelvie, PA,, & Rode, J, "Autopsy Rate and a Clinicopathological Audit in an Australian Metropolitan Hospital – Cause for Concern?" (1992) 156 *Medical Journal of Australia* 456

McKeown, T, *The Modern Rise of Population*, Edward Arnold, London (1976)

McLachlin, BM, "Negligence Law – Proving the Connection" in NJ Mullany & AM Linden (eds), *Torts Tomorrow: A Tribute to John Fleming*, LBC Information Services, Sydney (1998)

McLaughlin, JA, "Proximate Cause" (1925) 39 *Harvard Law Review* 149

McMahon, MJ, "Annotation, Medical Malpractice: Measure and Elements of Damages in Actions Based on Loss of Chance" 81 ALR 4th 485 (1990)

Meisel, A, *The Right to Die*, Wiley, New York (1989)

Memmler, RL, Cohen, BJ, & Wood, DL, *The Human Body in Health and Disease*, JB Lippincott Co, New York (1992)

Mendelson, D, "Medico-Legal Aspects of the 'Right to Die' Legislation in Australia" (1993) 19 *MULR* 112

Mendelson, D, "Quill, Glucksberg and palliative care – does alleviation of pain necessarily hasten death?" (1997) 5 *Journal of Law and Medicine* 110

Mendelson, D, "The Breach of the Medical Duty to Warn and Causation: Chappel v Hart and the Necessity to Reconsider Some Aspects of Rogers v Whitaker" (1998) 5 *Journal of Law and Medicine* 312

Mendelson, D, *The Interfaces of Medicine and Law: The History of the Liability for Negligently Caused Psychiatric Injury (Nervous Shock)*, Dartmouth, Ashgate (1998)

Mendelson, D, *Torts*, 2nd edn, Butterworths, Sydney (2000)

Mesthene, E, "The Role of Technology in Society" in A Teich (ed), *Technology and Man's Future*, 2nd edn, St Martin's Press, New York (1977)

Metzger, E (ed), *A Companion to Justinian's Institutes*, Cornell University Press, Ithaca, New York (1998)

Miller, C, "Coal Dust, Causation and Common Sense" (2000) 63 *Modern Law Review* 763

Milstein, R, "Causation in Medical Negligence – Recent Developments" (1997) 6 *Australian Health Law Bulletin* 21

Mixter, WJ, & Barr, JS, "Rupture of the Intervertebral Disc with Involvement of the Spinal Canal" (1934) 211 *New England Journal of Medicine* 210

Molloy, A, et al, "Role of opioids in chronic non-cancer pain" (1997) 167 *Medical Journal of Australia* 9

Monahan, J, "Mental Disorder and Violent Behaviour/Perceptions and Evidence" (1992) *American Psychologist* 47

Monahan, J, & Steadman, HJ, "Crime and Mental Disorder: An Epidemiological Approach" in M Tonry & N Morris (eds), *Crime and Justice; An Annual Review of Research*, No 4, University of Chicago Press, Chicago (1983)

Moran, D, "Child Sexual Abuse – Genital Findings in Prepubertal Girls" (1989) 160 *Am J Obstet Gynaecol* 328

Moran, D, "Child Sexual Abuse: Relationship between Sexual Acts and Genital Findings" (1989) 13 *Child Abuse and Neglect* 211

Moran, D, & Laufer, M, "Limitations of the Medical Evaluation for Child Sexual Abuse" (1999) 44(12) *J Reprod Med* 993

Moran, M, "Seriously Mentally Ill Do Have Higher Rates of Violence, Torrey Reports" (19 November 1993) *Psychiatric News* 5

Morrison, WL, "The Quantum of Proof in Relation to Motions for Non-Suit and Verdicts by Direction" in HH Glass (ed), *Seminars on Evidence,* Law Book Co, Sydney (1970)

Moshinsky, N, "Loss of Chance of Successful Treatment: Naxakis v Western General Hospital Considered" (2000) 8 *Journal of Law and Medicine* 216

Mount, B, "Morphine drips, terminal sedation, and slow euthanasia: definitions and facts, not anecdotes" (1996) 12 *Journal of Palliative Care* 31

Mullany, NJ, "Fear for the Future: Liability for Infliction of Psychiatric Disorder" in NJ Mullany (ed), *Torts in the Nineties,* Law Book Co, Sydney (1997)

Mullens, A, *Timely Death. Considering Our Last Rights,* Alfred A Knopf, Toronto (1996)

Muram, D, "Anal and Perianal Abnormalities Seen in Prepubertal Victims of Abuse" (1989) 161 *Am J Obstet Gynecol* 278

Muram, D, Arheart, K, & Jennings, S, "Diagnostic Accuracy of Colposcopic Photographs in Child Sexual Abuse Evaluations" (1999) 12 *J Pediatr Adolesc Gynecol* 58

National Committee of Inquiry into Compensation and Rehabilitation in Australia (Chair: Sir Owen Woodhouse), *Report* (1974)

National Health and Medical Research Council, *A Guide to the Development, Implementation and Evaluation of Clinical Practice Guidelines,* NHMRC, Ausinfo, Canberra (1999)

National Research Council, "Report II, The evaluation of Forensic DNA Evidence" (1999)

Neal, LA, "The Pitfalls of Making a Categorical Diagnosis of Post-Traumatic Stress Disorder in Personal Injury Litigation" (1994) 34 *Medicine, Science and the Law* 117

Nemetz, PM, Ludwig, J, & Kurland, LT, "Assessing the Autopsy" (1987) 128 *American Journal of Pathology* 362

New South Wales Law Reform Commission, *Contribution Between Persons Liable for the Same Damages* (1999)

Nicholas, B, *An Introduction to Roman Law,* Oxford University Press, Oxford (1962)

Nordby, J, "Can We Believe What We See, If We See What We Believe? Expert Disagreement" (1992) 37(4) *Journal of Forensic Sciences* 1115

Nörr, D, "Causam Mortis Praebere" in N MacCormick & P Birks (eds), *The Legal Mind: Essays for Tony Honoré,* Clarendon Press, Oxford (1986)

Norris, JG, *The Coroners Act 1958: A General Review,* Law Printer, Melbourne (1981)

Nutton, V, "Healers in the Medical Market Place: Towards a Social History of Graeco-Roman Medicine" in A Wear (ed), *Medicine in Society,* Cambridge University Press, Cambridge (1992)

Nutton, V, "Medicine in the Greek World, 800-50 BC" in LI Conrad, M Neve, V Nutton, R Porter & A Wear, *The Western Medical Tradition 800 BC to AD 1800,* Cambridge University Press, Cambridge (1995)

Otlowski, M, *Voluntary Euthanasia and the Common Law,* Oxford University Press, Oxford (1997)

Palmer, H, "Dr Adams' Trial for Murder" [1957] *Crim LR* 365

Palmer, V, "A General Theory of the Inner Structure of Strict Liability: Common Law, Civil Law, and Comparative Law" (1988) 62 *Tul L Rev* 1303

Parliament of the Commonwealth of Australia, *Senate Legal and Constitutional Legislation Committee, Consideration of Legislation Referred to the Committee. Euthanasia Laws Bill 1996*, Canberra (1997)

Parsons, T, *The Sick Role: The Social System*, The Free Press, Glencoe, Illinois (1951)

Peck, C, "Negligence and Liability Without Fault in Tort Law" (1971) 46 *Washington L Rev* 225

Perrochet, L, Smith, SL, & Collelo, U, "Lost Chance Recovery and the Folly of Expanding Medical Malpractice Liability" (1992) 27 *Tort & Ins LJ* 615

Perry, SR, "Protected Interests and Undertakings in the Law of Negligence" (1992) 42 *Uni of Toronto LJ* 247

Piatelli-Palmarini, M, *Inevitable Illusions*, J Wiley, New York (1994)

Pijneneborg, L, et al, "Nationwide study of decisions concerning the end of life in general practice in the Netherlands" (1994) 309 *British Medical Journal* 1209

Pilowsky, I, & Spence, N, *Manual for the Illness Behaviour Questionnaire*, University of Adelaide (1981)

Pirsig, RM, *Zen and the Art of Motor Cycle Maintenance: An Inquiry into Values*, W Morrow, New York (1983)

Pokorny, S, Murphy, J, & Preminger, M, "Circumferential Hymen Elasticity: A Marker of Physiological Maturity" (1998) 43 *J Reprod Med* 943

Pokorny, S, Pokorny, W, & Kramer, W, "Acute Genital Injury in the Prepubertal Girl" (1992) 166 *Am J Obstet Gynecol* 1461

Popper, K, *The Logic of Scientific Discovery*, Hutchinson, London (1959)

Popper, K, *Unended Quest*, Fontana-Collins, Glasgow (1976)

Porter, J, & Jack, H, "Addiction rare in patients treated with narcotics" (1980) 302 *New England Journal of Medicine* 123

Porter, R, *The Greatest Benefit to Mankind: A Medical History of Humanity From Antiquity to the Present*, Harper Collins, London (1997)

President's Commission for the Study of Ethical Problems in Medicine and Biomedical and Behavioural Research, *Deciding to Forego Life-Sustaining Treatment* 82 (1983)

Prior, J, Hill, J, & Packham, D, "Penile Injuries with Particular Reference to Injury to the Erectile Tissue" (1981) 53 *Br J Urol* 42

Proctor, R, *Cancer Wars: How Politics Shapes What We Know and Don't Know About Cancer*, Basic Books, New York (1995)

Prosser, EL, *Handbook of the Law of Torts*, 4th edn, West Publishing Co, St Paul (1971)

Quill, T, "The rule of double effect – a critique of its role in end-of-life decision-making" (1997) 337 *New England Journal of Medicine* 1768

Rabin, R, "A Sociolegal History of the Tobacco Tort Litigation" (1992) 44 *Stanford Law Review* 853

Rambow, B, Adkinson, C, Frost, TH, & Peterson, GF, "Female Sexual Assault: Medical and Legal Implications" (1992) 21(6) *Annals of Emergency Medicine* 727

Rappeport, JR (ed), *The Clinical Evaluation of the Dangerousness of the Mentally Ill*, Thomas, Springfield, IL (1967)

Reece, H, "Losses of Chances in the Law" (1996) 59 *MLR* 188

Reece, H, "*Pedro Juan Cubillo v Commonwealth of Australia*: Right Result, Wrong Method" in H Reece (ed), *Law and Science: Current Legal Issues*, vol 1, Oxford University Press, Oxford (1998)

Reichenbach, H, *The Rise of Scientific Philosophy*, University of California Press, Berkeley (1951)

Reidenberg, M, "Barriers to controlling pain in patients with cancer" (1996) 347 *Lancet* 1278

Rein, JE, "Ethics and the Questionably Competent Client: What the Model Rules Say and Don't Say" (1998) 9 *Stanford Law & Policy Rev* 241

Report Concerning the Conviction of Edward Charles Splatt, South Australian Government Printer, Adelaide (1984)

Report of the Committee on Death Certification and Coroners, 22 September 1971, Cmnd 4810

Report of the Inquiry into Child Abuse in Cleveland 1987, HMSO (1988)

Restak, R, *The Brain Has a Mind of Its Own*, Crown, New York (1991)

Restak, R, "Violence and the Brain" (November-December 1992) *Sciences* 4

Restak, RM, "See No Evil/The Neurological Defense Would Blame Violence on the Damaged Brain" (July-August 1992) *Sciences* 16

Rier, D, "The Versatile Caveat Section of an Epidemiological Paper: Managing Public and Private Risk" (1999) 21 *Science Communication* 3

Robertson, G, *The Justice Game*, Random House, London (1998)

Robinson, GO, "Multiple Causation in Tort Law: Reflections on the DES Cases" (1982) 68 *Vanderbilt Law Review* 713

Roche, PQ, *The Criminal Mind/A Study of Communication Between the Criminal Law and Psychiatry*, Greenwood Press, Westport CT (1958)

Roe, RJ, "Expert Testimony in Child Sexual Abuse Cases" (1985) 40 *U Miami L Rev* 97

Root, I, "Head Injuries from Short Distance Falls" (1992) 13(1) *Am J Forensic Med Pathol* 85

Rosenberg, CE, & Golden, J, *Framing Disease: Studies in Cultural History*, Rutgers University Press, New Jersey (1992)

Ross, SE, "Memes as Infectious Agents in Psychosomatic Illness" (1999) 131 *Ann Intern Med* 867

Rudavsky, S, "Separating Spheres: Legal Ideology v Paternity Testing in Divorce Cases" (1999) 12 *Science in Context* 123

Russell, "Establishing Medical Negligence – A Herculean Task?" (1998) 3 *Scots Law Times* 17

Russell, B, *History of Western Philosophy*, 2nd edn, Routledge, London , New York (1961)

Sackett, DL, Strauss, SE, Richardson, WS, Rosenberg, W, & Haynes, RB, *Evidence-based Medicine. How to Practice and Teach EBM*, 2nd edn, Churchill Livingstone, London (2000)

Salmond, JW, *The law of torts: a treatise on the English law of liability for civil injuries*, 6th edn, Sweet & Maxwell, London (1924)

Samuels, G, "Medical Truth and Legal Proof: Changing Expectations of the Expert Witness" (1998) 168 *Med J Aust* 84

Sanders, J, "The Bendectin Litigation: A Case Study in Life Cycles of Mass Torts" (1992) 43 *Hastings Law Journal* 301

Sanders, J, *Bendectin on Trial: A Study of Mass Tort Litigation*, University of Michigan Press (1998)

Sandler, G, "The Importance of the History in the Medical Clinic and the Costs of Unnecessary Tests" (1980) 100 *Am Heart J* 928

Schmorl, G, & Junghanns, H, *The Human Spine In Health And Disease*, Grune & Stratton, New York (1971)

Schneiderman, B, "A Winnipeg Inquest: a case of natural death or physician assisted suicide?" (1996) 24 *Manitoba Law Journal* 365

Schöber, P, "The Lumbar Vertebral Column and Backache" (1937) 84 *Munchener Medizinische Wochenschrift*, Munich 336

Schuck, P, *Agent Orange on Trial: Mass Toxic Disasters in the Courts*, Harvard University Press, Cambridge (1986)

Schutz, KF, et al, "Empirical evidence of bias: Dimensions of methodological quality associated with estimates of treatment effects in controlled trials" (1995) 273 *J Am Medical Ass* 408

Scott, W, "Causation in Medico-Legal Practice: A Doctor's Approach to the 'Lost Opportunity' Cases" (1992) 55 *MLR* 521

Selinger, B, "Scientific Evaluation", in I Freckelton & H Selby (eds), *Expert Evidence*, 5 volume looseleaf service, Law Book Co, Sydney (1993-....)

Senate of Canada, *Of Life and Death: Report of Special Senate Committee on Euthanasia and Assisted Suicide* (Ottawa, 1995)

Shackley, S, & Wynne, B, "Representing Uncertainty in Global Climate Change Science and Policy: Boundary-ordering Devices and Authority" (1996) 21 *Science, Technology and Human Values* 275

Sherman, P, "Agent Orange and the Problem of the Indeterminate Plaintiff" (1986) 52 *Brooklyn Law Review* 369

Shuman, DW, "The Diagnostic and Statistical Manual of Mental Disorders in the Courts" (1989) 17 *Bull Amer Acad Psych & Law* 25

Silverman, WA, *Where's the Evidence? Controversies in Medicine*, Oxford University Press, Oxford (1998)

Sim, J, & Ward, T, "The Magistrate of the Poor? Coroners and Deaths in Custody in Nineteenth Century England" in M Clark & C Crawford, *Legal Medicine in History*, Cambridge University Press, Cambridge (1994)

Simon, GE, Daniell, W, Stockbridge, H, Claypoole, K & Rosenstock, L, "Immunologic, Psychological, and Neuropsychological Factors in Multiple Chemical Sensitivity: A Controlled Study" (1993) 119 *Ann Intern Med* 97

Simon, RJ, & Mahan, L, "Quantifying burdens of proof" (1971) 5 *Law and Society Review* 319

Singer, C, & Underwood, EA, *A Short History of Medicine*, 2nd edn, Clarendon Press, Oxford (1962)

Singer, P, *Rethinking Life and Death*, Text, Melbourne (1994)

Skegg, P, "Drugs hastening death" in *Law, Ethics and Medicine: Studies in Medical Law*, Clarendon Press, Oxford (1984)

Skegg, P, *Law, Ethics and Medicine*, Clarendon Press, Oxford (1984)

Skegg, P, "Pain-killing drugs and the law of homicide" (1995) 4 *Otago Bioethics Report* 8

Skene, L, *Law and Medical Practice*, Butterworths, Sydney (1998)

Slaughter, L, Brown, CRV, Crowley, MN & Peck, R, "Patterns of Genital Injury in Female Sexual Assault Victims" (1997) 176 *Am J Obstet Gynecol* 609

Sloane, W, (AP news release), "Russian Cannibal Convicted in Killings," 15 October 1992

Smith, D, "Measurement of Joint Movement: An Overview" (1982) 8(3) *Clinics in Rheumatic Diseases* 523

Smith, D, Letourneau, E, Saunders, B, Kilpatrick, D, & Resnick, H, "Delay in Disclosure of Childhood Rape: Results from a National Survey" (2000) 24(2) *Child Abuse & Neglect* 273

Smith, R, & Wynne, B (eds), *Expert Evidence: Interpreting Science in the Law*, Routledge, London (1989)

Solomon, H, "Confidence Intervals in Legal Settings", in DeGroot, Fienberg & Kadane (eds), *Statistics and the Law*, Wiley, New York (1986)

Somerville, M, "Euthanasia by confusion" (1997) 20 *NSWLJ* 550

Spence, DP, *Narrative Truth and Historical Truth/Meaning and Interpretation in Psychoanalysis*, Norton, New York (1982)

Spitzer, RL, First, MB, Williams, JBW, Kendler, K, Pincus, HA, & Tucker, G, "Now Is the Time to Retire the Term 'Organic Mental Disorders'" (1992) 149 *Amer J Psychiatry* 240

Stanley, F, "Litigation versus Science: What's Driving Decision Making in Medicine?", 2nd Eleanor Shaw Lecture, 29 August 1995, Melbourne

Stapleton, J, "Duty of Care Factors: A Selection from the Judicial Menus" in P Cane and J Stapleton (eds), *The Law of Obligations: Essays in Celebration of John Fleming*, Clarendon Press, Oxford (1998)

Stapleton, J, "The Gist of Negligence" (1988) 104 *LQR* 389

Stapleton, J, "The Gist of Negligence, Part II: the Relationship between 'Damage' and Causation" (1988) 104 *LQR* 389

Stapleton, J, "In Restraint of Tort" in P Birks (ed), *The Frontiers of Liability*, Oxford University Press, Oxford, New York (1994)

Stapleton, J, "Duty of Care: Peripheral Parties and Alternative Opportunities for Deterrence" (1995) 111 *LQR* 301

Stapleton, J, "The Normal Expectancies Measure in Tort Damages" (1997) 113 *LQR* 257

Stapleton, J, "Perspectives on Causation" in J Horder (ed), *Oxford Essays in Jurisprudence*, 4th series, Oxford University Press, Oxford (2000)

Stapleton, J, "Legal Cause: Cause-in-Fact and the Scope of Liability for Consequences" (2001) 54 *Vanderbilt LJ* 942

Stapleton, J, "Unpacking 'Causation'" in P Cane & J Gardner (eds), *Relating to Responsibility*, Hart Publishing, Oxford (2001)

Starkie, T, *A Practical Treatise on the Law of Evidence*, 7th American edition, T & JW Johnson, Philadelphia, Vol 1 (1842)

Stauch, M, "Causation, Risk, and Loss of Chance in Medical Negligence" (1997) 17 *OJLS* 205

Stein, P, "The Development of the Notion of *Naturalis Ratio*" in A Watson (ed), *Daube Noster,* Scottish Academic Press, Edinburgh (1974)

Stein, P, "The Development of Law in Classical and Early Medieval Europe: Interpretation and Legal Reasoning in Roman Law" (1995) 70 *Chi-Kent L Rev* 1539

Stewart, G, "Chemokine Genes – Beating the Odds" (1998) 4 *Nature Medicine* 275

Stewart, I, *Does God Play Dice? The Mathematics of Chaos*, Penguin, London (1990)

Stjernsward, J, & Teoh, N, "The cancer pain relief programme of the World Health Organisation" (1989) 4 *Palliative Medicine* 1

Stoffel, B, & Ashby, MA, "On Natural Death and Palliative care" in L Shotton (ed), *Health Care Law and Ethics*, Social Science Press, Katoomba (1997)

Stone, AA, "Post-Traumatic Stress Disorder and the Law: Critical Review of the New Frontier" (1993) 21(1) *Bulletin of the American Academy of Psychiatry and Law* 23

Stone, J, & Wells, WAN, *Evidence: Its History and Policies*, Butterworths, Sydney (1991)

Strong, JW, *McCormick on Evidence*, West Publishing Co, St Paul (1992)

Summit, RC, "The Child Sexual Abuse Accommodation Syndrome" (1983) 7 *Child Abuse & Neglect* 177

Sutton, T, "The Deodand and Responsibility for Death" (1997) 18 *Legal History* 44

Teixeira, W, "Hymenal Colposcopic Examination in Sexual Offences" (1981) 2 *Am J Forensic Med Pathology* 209

Thatt, ER, Wagh, M, & Kulkarni, NI, "Identical Unusual Subtotal Amputation in Children: a Report of Four Cases" (1993) 46(6) *Br J Plast Surg* 535

Thomas, PJ, *Introduction to Roman Law*, Kluwer Law and Taxation Publishers, Deventer, Netherlands (1986)

Thomas, R, Ridley, C, McGibbon, D, & Black, M, "Anogenital Lichen Sclerosis in Women" (1996) 89 *J R Soc Med* 694

Thompson, MM, "Causal Inference in Epidemiology: Implications for Toxic Tort Litigation" (1992) 71 *North Carolina Law Review* 247

Thompson, WC, & Schumann, EL, "Interpretation of Statistical Evidence in Criminal Trials: The Prosecutor's Fallacy and the Defense Attorney's Fallacy" (1987) 11 *Law Hum Behav* 167

Thompson, WC, "Are Juries Competent to Evaluate Statistical Evidence?" (1989) 52 *Law Contemp Problems* 9

Tintinalli, JE, & Hoelzer, M, "Clinical Findings and Legal Resolution in Sexual Assault" (1985) 14 *Annals of Emergency Medicine* 447

Trebilcock, MJ, Dewees, DN, & Duff, DG, "The Medical Malpractice Explosion: An Empirical Assessment of Trends, Determinants and Impacts" (1990) 17 *MULR* 539

Tribe, LH, "Trial by Mathematics: Precision and Ritual in the Legal Process" (1971) 84 *Harvard Law Review* 1329

Trout, KS, "How to Read Clinical Journals IV: To Determine Aetiology or Causation" (1981) 124 *Canad Med Assos J* 985

Tversky, A, & Kahneman, D, "Judgment under Uncertainty: Heuristics and Biases" (1974) 185 *Science* 1124

Twining, W, & Stein, A (eds), *Evidence and Proof*, Dartmouth, Aldershot (1992)

Twycross, R, *Pain relief in advanced cancer*, Churchill Livingstone, London (1994)

Twycross, R, et al, "A survey of pain in patients with advanced cancer" (1996) 12 *Journal of Pain and Symptom Management* 273

Ullmann-Margalit, E, "On Presumption" (1983) LXXX *Journal of Philosophy* 143

Underhill, R, & Dewhurst, J, "The Doctor Cannot Always Tell – Medical Examination of the Intact Hymen" (Feb 1978) 18 *Lancet* 375

Vahasarja, V, Hellstrom, P, Serlo, W, & Kontturi, M, "Treatment of Penile Incarceration by the String Method: Two Case Reports" (1993) 149 *J Urol* 372

Valway, SE, Sanchez, MPC, Shinnick, TF, Orme, I, Agerton, T, Hoy, D, Scott Jones, J, Westmoreland, H, & Onorato, IM, "An Outbreak Involving Extensive Transmission of a Virulent Strain of Mycobacterium Tuberculosis" (1998) 338 *N Eng J Med* 633

Van der Maas, J, et al, "Euthanasia and other medical decisions concerning the end of life" (1991) 338 *Lancet* 669

Van der Maas, P, et al, *Euthanasia and Other Medical Decisions Concerning the End of Life*, Elsevier, Amsterdam (1992)

Van der Maas, P, et al, "Euthanasia, physician-assisted suicide, and other medical practices involving the end of life in the Netherlands, 1990-1995" (1996) 335 *New England Journal of Medicine* 1699

Vegetti, M, "Between the Knowledge and Practice: Hellenistic Medicine" in MD Grmek, *Western Medical Thought from Antiquity to the Middle Ages*, Harvard University Press, Cambridge, Massachusetts (1998)

Vick, DW, "Statistical Significance and the Significance of Statistics" (2000) 116 *Law Quart Rev* 575

Vickers, RH, *The Powers and Duties of Police Officers and Coroners*, TH Flood & Co, London (1889)

Waddams, SM, *Law of Damages*, 2nd edn, Canada Law Book, Toronto (1991)

Waddams, SM, "The Principles of Compensation" in P Finn (ed), *Essays on Damages*, Law Book Co, Sydney (1992)

Waddams, SM, "Damages: Assessment of Uncertainties" (1998) 13 *JCL* 55

Waddams, SM, "Causation, Physicians and Disclosure of Risks" (1999) 7 *Tort L Rev* 5

Waddell, GA, "A New Clinical Model for the Treatment of Low Back Pain" (1987) 12 *Spine* 632

Waddell, G, Feder, G, McIntosh, A, Lewis, L, & Hutchinson, A, *Low Back Pain Evidence Review*, London Royal College of General Practitioners (1996)

Wagner, W, "Trans-science in Toxic Torts" (1986) 96 *Yale Law Journal* 428

Wagner, W, "The Science Charade in Toxic Risk Regulation" (1995) 95 *Columbia Law Review* 1613

Wakefield, M, Beilby, J, & Ashby, M, "General practitioners and palliative care" (1993) 7 *Palliative Medicine* 117

Walker, DM, *Oxford Companion to Law*, Oxford University Press, Oxford (1980)

Walker, L, *The Battered Woman Syndrome*, Springer, New York (1984)

Walker, L, & Monahan, J, "Scientific Authority: The Breast Implant Litigation and Beyond" (2000) 86 *Virginia Law Review* 801

Waller, K, *Coronial Law and Practice in New South Wales*, 3rd edn, Butterworths, Sydney (1994)

Ward, T, "Law's Truth, Lay Truth and Medical Science: Three Case Studies" in H Reece (ed), *Law and Science: Current Legal Issues*, vol 1, Oxford University Press, Oxford (1998)

Watson, A, *The Law of Obligations in the Later Roman Republic*, Clarendon Press, Oxford (1965)

Weiler, PC, *Medical Malpractice on Trial*, Harvard Univ Press, Cambridge, Mass (1991)

Weiler, PC, et al, *A Measure of Malpractice*, Harvard Univ Press, Cambridge, Mass (1993)

Weinberg, A, "Science and Trans-science" (1972) 10 *Minerva* 209

Weinrib, EJ, "The Special Morality of Tort Law" (1989) 34 *McGill Law Rev* 403

Weinrib, EJ, "The Gains and Losses of Corrective Justice" (1994) 44 *Duke LJ* 277

Weir, R, *Abating Treatment with Critically Ill Patients. Ethical and Legal Limits to the Prolongation of Life*, Oxford University Press, New York (1989)

Weir, T, "The staggering march of negligence" in P Cane and J Stapleton (eds), *The Law of Obligations: Essays in Celebration of John Fleming*, Clarendon Press, Oxford (1998)

Welborn, A, *Adult Sexual Assault*, Monash University, Victoria (2000)

Wells, D, "Genital Trauma in Young Boys" (1996) 3 *J Clin For Med* 129

Wells, D, & Young, S, "Circumstances and Findings in Women Alleging Rape", Proceedings, International Conference on Emergency Medicine, Sydney (1996)

Wells, D, El-Nageh, M, Linehan, B, Cordner, S, & McKelvie, H, *Ethical Practice in Laboratory & Medicine & Forensic Pathology*, WHO Regional Publications, Eastern Mediterranean Series, Egypt (1999)

Wells, D, Ogden, E, & Young, S, "Child Abuse" in I Freckelton and H Selby (eds), *Expert Evidence in Criminal Law*, Law Book Company, Sydney (1999)

Wells, WAN, *Evidence and Advocacy*, Butterworths, Sydney (1988)

WHO, International Classification of Impairments, Disabilities and Handicaps, WHO, Geneva (1980)

Wigmore, JH, *The Science of Judicial Proof*, Little, Brown & Co, Boston (1937)

Williams, G, *Textbook of Criminal Law*, 2nd edn, Stevens, London (1983)

Williams, R, *Key Words: a Vocabulary of Culture and Society*, rev edn, Oxford University Press, New York (1985)

Wills, W, *An Essay on the Principles of Circumstantial Evidence*, Butterworths, London (1902)

Wolfstone, LL, & Wolfstone, TJ, "Recovery of Damages for Loss of a Chance", *Personal Injury Annual 1978*

Wood, O, & Certoma, GL, *Succession: Commentary and Materials*, Law Book Co, Sydney (1990)

Wood, P, & Bevan, T, "Child Sexual Abuse Enquiries and Unrecognised Vulval Licen Sclerosus et Atrophicus" (1999) 319 *BMJ* 899

Woodling, B, & Heger, A, "The Use of the Colposcope in the Diagnosis of Sexual Abuse in the Paediatric Age Group" (1986) 10 *Child Abuse & Neglect* 11

Wright, R, "Causation in Tort Law" (1985) 73 *Cal L Rev* 1735

Wright, R, "Causation, Responsibility, Risk. Probability, Naked Statistics, and Proof: Pruning the Bramble Bush by Clarifying the Concepts" (1988) 73 *Iowa Law Review* 1001

Wright, RW, "Substantive Corrective Justice" (1992) 77 *Iowa Law Rev* 625

Wright, RW, "Right, Justice and Tort Law" in DG Owen (ed), *Philosophical Foundations of Tort Law*, Clarendon Press, Oxford (1995)

Wynne, B, *Rationality and Ritual: The Windscale Inquiry and Nuclear Decisions in Britain*, British Society of the History of Science, Chalfont St Giles (1982)

Yeo, S, "An Australian Evaluation of Causation in Fright Cases" (1943) *J of Criminal Law* 390

Young, S, Wells, D, & Ogden, E, "Lichen Sclerosis, Genital trauma and child sexual abuse" (1993) 22(5) *Australian Family Physician* 729

Zech, DF, et al, "Validation of World Health Organization Guidelines for cancer pain relief: a 10-year prospective study" (1995) 63 *Pain* 65

Zenz, M, & Willweber-Strumpf, A, "Opiophobia and cancer pain in Europe" (1993) 341 *Lancet* 1075

Zimmerman, R, *The Law of Obligations*, Clarendon Press, Oxford (1996)

Index